LEWIS MUMFORD

A Life

Other books by Donald L. Miller

The New American Radicalism
The Lewis Mumford Reader (editor)
The Kingdom of Coal (with Richard E. Sharpless)

LEWIS MUMFORD
A Life

Donald L. Miller

Weidenfeld & Nicolson
New York

Published by Weidenfeld & Nicolson, New York
A Division of Wheatland Corporation
841 Broadway
New York, New York 10003-4793

Published in Canada by General Publishing Company, Ltd.

Library of Congress Cataloging-in-Publication Data

Miller, Donald L., 1944–
Lewis Mumford, a life / Donald L. Miller
p.   cm.
Includes index.
ISBN 1-55584-244-5
1. Mumford, Lewis, 1895–   . 2. Social reformers—United States—
Biography. 3. City planners—United States—Biography.
4. Architects—United States—Biography. I. Title.
CT275.M734M55 1989
973.9'092'4—dc19
[B]
89-5248
CIP

Manufactured in the United States of America

This book is printed on acid-free paper

Designed by Irving Perkins Associates

First Edition

1   3   5   7   9   10   8   6   4   2

To Rose

Acknowledgments

I began this book in the summer of 1977 after meeting Lewis Mumford for the first time at his home in Leedsville, New York, and it could not have been written without his generous cooperation and the unfailing assistance of his wife Sophia. I am also indebted to Alison Mumford Morss, who helped me to piece together the story of her father's life and was supportive throughout my long struggle to capture in words this elusive, many-sided man.

Several friends gave me encouragement and shrewd advice: Vincent DiMattio, Donald Meyerson, David Johnson, Richard Sharpless, Jacob E. Cooke, Robert Leitman, Fred Provencher, Edwin Clausen, Terry Summons, and the late Peter Lowry, who accompanied me on my first visit to Leedsville and who was ever on my mind as I worked on the book.

My most important source for materials on Mumford's life was the Lewis Mumford Collection at the Van Pelt Library of the University of Pennsylvania. I owe a special debt of gratitude to the staff of the Department of Special Collections, particularly Neda M. Westlake (retired), Daniel Traister, Kathleen Reed, Nancy Shawcross, and Ellen Flack. They made my many months at Van Pelt a pleasurable experience and were of enormous assistance to me throughout my research. I would also like to thank the able research librarians of Lafayette College, particularly Richard Everett and Ronald Robbins, for helping me in the early stages of my work.

I was able to begin this book in earnest with the help of a fellowship from the National Endowment for the Humanities, which allowed me to visit and conduct research in the European cities

Mumford favored in his early writing and travels. I was also assisted by several grants from Lafayette College's Committee for Advanced Study and Research. Sir F. Anthony Gray of Christ Church College made it possible for me to spend part of a year at Oxford University completing the final draft of this book, and made my stay at Oxford one of the great experiences of my life.

My thanks to Sherman Paul, Eric Josephson, and Rick Kott for allowing me to examine Mumford materials in their possession; and especially to Dr. Henry A. Murray, one of the outstanding minds of this century, who gave me unrestricted access to his voluminous correspondence with Mumford, and spent many hours with me at his home in Cambridge, Massachusetts, talking about his close friendship with Mumford. Sadie Wurster Super, the daughter of Catherine Bauer, shared with me her impressions of her mother's relationship with Mumford and allowed me to quote from her mother's letters to him.

Of the many other people I interviewed for this book I would like to thank particularly Martin Filler, Malcolm Cowley, Wolf Von Eckardt, Charles Ascher, Martin Meyerson, Ian McHarg, Aline MacMahon Stein, Edward Spingarn, Robert Spiller, Perry Norton, and Eric Josephson.

I am indebted to libraries holding manuscript materials by Mumford and his circle: the American Academy of Arts and Letters; Bentley Historical Library, University of Michigan; Butler Library, Columbia University; Smith College Library; Yale University Library; Stanford University Library; Houghton Library, Harvard University; The Library of Congress; Cornell University Libraries; Newberry Library; University of Arkansas Library; University of Oregon Library; National Library of Scotland, Edinburgh; University Archives, University of Strathclyde, Glasgow, Scotland; Minnesota Historical Society; Archives of American Art, Dartmouth College Library; the New York Public Library; Frieberger Library, Case Western Reserve University; George Arents Research Library, Syracuse University; Brown University Library; Mid-Hertfordshire Division Library, Welwyn Garden City, England; Christ Church Archives, Christ Church College, Oxford.

Elmer S. Newman's excellent bibliography of Mumford's writings up to 1970 was an invaluable source. Jane Morley is presently preparing for publication a complete bibliography of Mumford's work, which will include a guide to archives containing Mumford materials, and has also compiled an annotated bibliography of writings on Mumford. I am indebted to her for sharing with me her bibliographical information.

I wish to thank those who read parts of or the entire draft of this book and offered advice: Martin Filler, David Johnson, Leo Marx, Alan Trachtenberg, Sam Bass Warner, John Thomas, Margaret Lynn, Helena Franklin, Sara Bershtel, Michael Zuckerman, Jean Morgan, Marsha Siefert, Thomas Hughes, James Hoopes, Charles Molesworth, Kenneth Stunkel, and, finally, Gina Maccoby, my literary agent, who was always there with good advice and warm encouragement. She is responsible for guiding this book into the competent hands of William Strachan of Weidenfeld & Nicolson, who demonstrated to me that editing can be a creative art.

I owe a special debt of gratitude to Hilda Cooper of Lafayette College, who expertly typed this book in its many incarnations and offered invaluable editorial assistance. She helped me to see this project through from beginning to end.

Contents

xi

PREFACE

Call Me Jonah!

Life is better than utopia.

—LEWIS MUMFORD

In December 1972, Lewis Mumford was presented with the National Medal for Literature for the excellence of his contribution to the world of letters. In a sense he was being honored for being an anachronism—one of America's last surviving men of letters. The author of some thirty books and over a thousand essays and reviews, he had supported himself entirely by his pen, producing a body of work almost unequaled in this century for its range and richness. His first book, *The Story of Utopias*, appeared in 1922, so this was his Golden Jubilee, his fiftieth year as a writer of books. "In a world of words Mumford is a master builder," his friend Mark Van Doren described his unique genius. "He builds cities, societies, civilizations, cultures—truly builds them, with the most durable stuff available to man: ideas. He has shown lesser builders where they went wrong, and then he has shown them how they may return to rightness. All this in books both massive and brilliant, both comprehensive and acute." That December Lewis Mumford was seventy-seven years old, and he still had important work ahead of him.[1]

The day before he was to receive his award at the headquarters of the Ford Foundation in New York City, Mumford came to Manhattan from Leedsville, the upstate hamlet where he had been living for the past thirty-six years with his family, in a simple wooden farmhouse two miles or so from Amenia, an old iron-making center not much larger than Emerson's Concord. Here, in a tiny study off his book-lined living room—a monk's cell, really—he had done most of his best work; for while he loved the variety and velocity of the city, country living suited him better. In slow-moving Leedsville he lived a life in line with his temperament, writing in the mornings and walking, sketching, and gardening in the afternoons.

The day he learned he was to receive the National Medal for Literature he had gone straight to his desk to prepare his acceptance speech, and he was still working on it the morning of the awards ceremony. It was especially important to him that this address strike the right note; he was being honored by his fellow writers on the National Book Committee, only the eighth author to receive this award. For some reason, however, he was unable to complete any of the several versions of the speech he planned to give. It was not until he sat on stage on the afternoon of the presentation listening to Dr. René Dubos's tribute to him as a utopian, a dreamer of large dreams, that he decided to give an impromptu talk he had been composing in his mind for some time, a review of his life in terms of the Book of Jonah.

As he stepped forward to accept his bronze medal he was slightly nervous, although he gave no hint of it. He seemed relaxed and perfectly composed. He was a balding, solidly set man, with flashing brown eyes, a closely trimmed mustache, and a handsome, strong-featured face. Square-shouldered and erect, he looked, he had often been told, like a retired British army officer. As he began speaking—deliberately, in a rich, full voice—he gripped the upper corners of the rostrum with his powerful hands.

After thanking Dubos for his "eulogy," he proposed to give a different picture of himself than his friend had presented: he was neither a utopian nor even an optimist, he declared with emphasis, turning with a smile to Dubos. While the promise of our age had been his insistent theme, he had never sought after the perfect society, the perfect personality. Even in the exuberance of youth, he realized that "life is better than utopia."

Nor, for that matter, did he care to be considered a prophet of doom because of his thundering attacks on the misuses of science, technology, and concentrated political power. He had issued his share of warnings about the direction the world had been taking since the years of Hitler and Hiroshima, but he would die a happy man, he claimed, if these words could be carved on his tombstone: "This man was an absolute fool. None of the disastrous things that he reluctantly predicted ever came to pass!" And he would continue to risk being a "fool" because he had certain moral responsibilities as a writer. His remarks that afternoon centered on that reluctant role he had marked out for himself.

Lately, he said, he had developed a strong fellow feeling for the biblical Jonah, "one of the minor prophets, not to be mentioned in the same breath as Amos or Isaiah." Jonah, however, figured in his personal life "not as a character to imitate, but as an admonitory figure, exposing my failings, taking me down when I am too elated by some minor success, jeering at my most acute forecasts."

His "private" Jonah was not the Jonah of popular lore, that irritating fellow who keeps telling people what they don't want to hear, warning them that if they fail to change their ways they will be doomed. Mumford confessed that there was something of himself in this "mythical" Jonah, but the Jonah he most identified with was the Jonah of Father Mapple's stirring sermon in Melville's *Moby Dick*, the prophet who hears the voice of the Lord, and, in panic, runs away from it. This Jonah does not want to deliver God's angry message to the city of Ninevah—"If you go on this way you will be destroyed"—and he almost welcomes being buried in the belly of the whale for three days and three nights.

It is this betrayal of Jonah's mission as a prophet that Father Mapple denounces, in what Mumford considered one of the most morally consequential passages in all of literature: "It teaches something we must all learn if and when Truth calls us. For what is the lesson of science? What is the lesson of religion? Whenever Truth commands us, we must obey it and utter it aloud whether our friends and neighbors and countrymen like it or not."

Although Mumford did not say this himself, few modern writers had lived closer to that injunction than he had. A solitary thinker, he had made his writing his life; but whenever the occasion had called for it, he had turned from his study to passionate engagement in public life, "a man of principle," in Emerson's words, ". . . immovable in the waves of the crowd." He had spoken out strongly against the appeasement of Hitler in the 1930s, against the use and further development of the atomic bomb in the 1940s, against Senator

Joseph McCarthy in the 1950s, and, lately, against American military involvement in Vietnam. In every case he had paid a heavy personal cost for his moral activism—temporary disfavor as a writer and a despondency that made it difficult for him to go on with his work.

But Mumford wanted to share with his audience that evening a lesson in the Book of Jonah that Melville had passed over. It came out, he said, in Jonah's complaint to God after God had rescued him from the belly of the whale and spared the people of Ninevah after they covered themselves with sackcloth and repented. "Jonah actually feels let down by God because God didn't carry out his threat" to destroy Ninevah. "In effect, God made a fool of Jonah by acting more mercifully than Jonah thought he would; and the people of Ninevah had made a double fool of him by tearfully repenting for their sins, from the King down." Jonah's great error "was to imagine he knew in advance how badly both the people of Ninevah and God would behave."

In the final passage of the Book of Jonah "it is plain that God had no more confidence than had Jonah that the people of Ninevah would permanently change their ways; but he was touched by at least their public remorse over their violence and villainy. That was something: so perhaps in the future the garbage would be collected more regularly and officials would blush when they took a bribe or broke a law. That was all God seems to have expected from this proud city of six score thousand people." Mumford need not have spelled out his moral. "Woe to the prophet who confuses his own voice with the voice of the Lord and who thinks he knows in advance what God has up his sleeve!

"Now you know why I have told you this story," he concluded, a smile breaking across his face. "In a sense it is the story of my life," and explains as well, he added, what he expected of life, "because I am much closer to the mythic Jonah in all his ways, not least his temptations, than I am to any utopian dreamer. If anything, I am an anti-utopian who knows that a blessing repeated too often may become a curse, and that a curse faced bravely may become a blessing. . . .

"That is the sort of man who is talking to you tonight: neither a pessimist nor an optimist, still less a utopian or a futurologist. And now, at the end, I want . . . to record the depth of my gratitude, . . .

to those nameless voices coming from the distance and the deep, when I was entombed in the belly of the whale. Their response to my words has given me the faith to struggle out of that darkness and rise up into the sunlit air again. In the name of Jonah, the biblical Jonah, Melville's Jonah, my private . . . Jonah, and above all God's Jonah, I thank you."[2]

This is the first biography of Lewis Mumford, whom Malcolm Cowley has called "the last of the great humanists."[3] It is based on ten years of research and on a close working relationship with Lewis Mumford and his wife, Sophia. My principal source of information was Mumford's enormous collection of original manuscripts, private papers, and correspondence at the University of Pennsylvania's Van Pelt Library. Most of this archive is now available to qualified researchers, but I was given permission by Mumford to examine the restricted portion of the collection. The Mumfords also made available to me their private family papers, which are currently at their home in Leedsville, New York. These letters, notes, and journals deal with deeply personal matters, and they throw light on Mumford's interior life and his development as a writer and man.

Though Lewis and Sophia Mumford have allowed me unrestricted use of these materials, and talked freely and frankly with me about their lives, this is not an official biography. I was not commissioned or even encouraged to write it; in fact, for several years Lewis Mumford tried his best to discourage me from doing so. He wanted to be the first to tell the story of his life, and he had as well the subject's understandable distrust of his prospective biographer. Old age and failing health, however, kept him from completing his full autobiography, and, in time, he and I developed a relationship grounded in mutual trust and respect. It was at this point that he made available to me his most personal papers and correspondence; and, as well as he was able to—for he is an intensely private person—he let me into his life.

Sketches from Life, the book Mumford published as his autobiography in 1982, takes the story of his life only up to the mid-1930s. Though it is a captivating retelling of his formative years, it gives but a glimpse of his personal life, nor does Mumford discuss in any detail his writing—that aspect of his life that best defines him. This biography tries to depict the complete man, his works as well as his days, as he struggles to move the world, and his own life, in the direction of his desires.

As a very old man, Lewis Mumford remarked to me in conversation that his profoundest ideas and ideals might prove significant in view of the manner in which the past century diverged from rather than fulfilled them. But he had no reason to complain, he added with a teasing smile. He had taken up the challenge that Emerson had thrown out to the young American scholars of his day, and he rested his hopes for his long-term reputation on this: "If a single man plant himself indomitably on his instincts, and there abide, the huge world will come round to him. . . . A nation of men will for the first time exist."[4]

Chronology

1895   Born October 19 in Flushing, New York.

1909   Enters Stuyvesant High School to prepare to become an engineer.

1912   Decides to become a writer; enrolls in City College of New York.

1915   Discovers writings of Patrick Geddes, his master; becomes a student of the city and surveys New York region on foot; begins program of self-development to free himself of his "invalidism."

1918   Joins U.S. Navy.

1919   Mustered out of the navy; joins staff of *The Dial* and meets Sophia Wittenberg, his future wife.

1920   Moves to London to become editor of the *Sociological Review*; returns to New York and writes for *The Freeman*.

1921   Marries Sophia Wittenberg.

1922   Publishes *The Story of Utopias* while living in Greenwich Village; moves to Brooklyn Heights.

1923   Cofounder of the Regional Planning Association of America (RPAA); helps RPAA plan Sunnyside Gardens, Queens.

1924   Publishes *Sticks and Stones*, his first book on architecture.

1925   Son Geddes born on July 5; lectures in Geneva and visits Patrick Geddes in Edinburgh; moves to Sunnyside Gardens, Queens.

1926   First summer in Amenia, New York; publishes *The Golden Day*; helps found *The American Caravan*.

1927   After visit to Chicago writes essays rediscovering the Chicago School of Architecture.

1928   Helps RPAA plan Radburn, in Fair Lawn, New Jersey.

1929   Publishes *Herman Melville*; begins part-time visiting professorship at Dartmouth College.

1931   Publishes *The Brown Decades;* joins *The New Yorker* staff—writes "The Sky Line" and, later, "The Art Galleries" columns.

1932   Begins research in Europe for Renewal of Life series.

1934   Publishes *Technics and Civilization;* appointed to New York City Board of Higher Education.

1935   Daughter Alison born on April 28.

1936   Moves to Amenia, New York.

1938   Publishes *The Culture of Cities;* prepares planning reports for city of Honolulu and for the Pacific Northwest Regional Planning Commission; writes screenplay for *The City;* intense involvement in battle against American neutrality.

1939   Publishes *Men Must Act.*

1940   Publishes *Faith for Living;* joins Committee to Defend America by Aiding the Allies.

1941   Ends friendship with Frank Lloyd Wright and others over issue of American neutrality.

1942   Moves to California to join faculty of Stanford University—helps design new humanities program.

1944   Resigns from Stanford and returns to Amenia; publishes *The Condition of Man;* son Geddes killed in combat in Italy on September 13.

1945   Moves to Hanover, New Hampshire, to be near close friends.

1946   Visits England to advise on postwar urban planning; publishes *Values for Survival.*

1947   Publishes *Green Memories,* a biography of his son; begins campaign against further use and development of the atomic bomb.

1948   Moves back to New York City for four years; battle with Robert Moses over Stuyvesant Town.

1951   Beginning of ten-year association with University of Pennsylvania as a visiting professor; publishes *The Conduct of Life,* final volume of Renewal of Life series.

1952   Publishes *Art and Technics.*

1956   Publishes *The Transformations of Man.*

1957   Research trip to Europe for his history of the city; begins visiting professorship at MIT.

1958   Leads campaign against Robert Moses's plan to build roadway through Washington Square.

1961   Publishes *The City in History*—wins National Book Award; visiting professor at University of California, Berkeley.

1962   Returns to Amenia to work on autobiography and write a two-volume history of technology and human development.

1963   Stops writing "The Sky Line" column.

1964   Drafts city plan for Oxford, England; awarded the Presidential Medal of Freedom.

1965   Protests U.S. involvement in Vietnam.

1967   Testifies before U.S. Senate subcommittee on urban renewal; publishes *The Myth of the Machine: I. Technics and Human Development.*

1968   Supports Eugene McCarthy's bid for presidential nomination; publishes *The Urban Prospect.*

1970   Publishes *The Myth of the Machine: II. The Pentagon of Power.*

1972   Awarded the National Medal for Literature; publishes *Interpretations and Forecasts.*

1975   Made honorary Knight Commander of the British Empire; publishes *Findings and Keepings.*

1976   To Paris to accept Prix Mondial del Duca for lifetime contributions to letters.

1978   Begins uncompleted history of human evolution, his final literary project.

1979   Publishes *My Works and Days;* breaks with his publisher, Harcourt Brace Jovanovich.

1982   Publishes autobiography, *Sketches from Life*—nominated for American Book Award.

1986   Awarded the National Medal of Arts.

In many lives it is the beginnings that are most significant: the first steps, though seemingly effaced, leave their imprint on everything else that follows.

—LEWIS MUMFORD

When I reveal most I hide most.

—THOMAS MERTON

LEWIS MUMFORD

A Life

I

A Solitary Tree

*Solitary trees, if they grow at all, grow strong; and a boy
deprived of his father's care often develops, if he escapes the
perils of youth, an independence and a vigour of thought
which may restore in after life the heavy loss of early days.*

—WINSTON S. CHURCHILL

He grew up on the island of Manhattan, a place that shaped his life
and his work. "I was a child of the city," he opens his luminous
autobiography, *Sketches from Life*. "New York exerted a greater and
more constant influence on me than did my family."[1] The New York
of Lewis Mumford's boyhood—the New York of Teddy Roosevelt,
J. P. Morgan, Harry Houdini, and the Great White Way—had a
population of nearly three and a half million, half of whom were
foreign-born. Already in 1900 six of its buildings were over three
hundred feet tall, a skyward advance made possible by the elevator
and the new steel-frame construction. In its drive and diversity
alone, there was no place quite like it in all of the world.

As a boy Mumford was introduced to nearly every part of Manhattan on leisurely weekend walks with his German grandfather.
And by the time he was twenty years old he was systematically
exploring the city on foot, making notes on its neighborhood life,
studying its buildings, bridges, and street plans, and taking specimens for an amateur geological survey of Manhattan. On these
solitary afternoon rambles he would occasionally stop here and

there to do a quick pencil sketch of a street scene or a rooftop water tower, or of the city's spacious harbor, crowded with steam ferries and tugs, and with freighters and superliners from every part of the globe.

On a clear summer day in 1916, the year he turned twenty-one, we might have found this lanky young man, dressed in khaki, with a knapsack on his back, perched on a ledge on the Palisades painting a watercolor of the Hudson. By this time he had decided to drop out of college and take all of Manhattan as his university. This was his city and he was driven by a desire to know it completely, in the way that Aristotle, the originator of city studies, had known his native Athens. "My present interest in life," he declared in one of his early notebook entries, "is the exploration and documentation of cities." He was as interested "in the mechanism of man's cultural ascent," as evidenced in the evolution of cities, "as Darwin was in the mechanism of his biological descent."[2] In studying the city he would be studying civilization itself; vast and various New York was, for him, no less than the human condition.

This was the morning moment of Mumford's maturation, and the beginning of his career as a writer on architecture, the city, and civilization. The road to this point in his life, however, had been strewn with obstacles. For most of his life, few people, even his own children, knew how much he had to overcome. Like Joyce, Ibsen, and Samuel Johnson, he rose from small, narrow-focused people.

In 1982, at the age of eighty-seven, Lewis Mumford published his autobiography, as honest and passionate a book as he ever wrote. In it he revealed something known previously only to himself, his wife and daughter, and a few others—that he was the illegitimate son of Lewis Charles Mack, a Jewish businessman from Somerville, New Jersey. His mother (born Elvina Conradina Baron), a German Protestant from an immigrant family of servants, waiters, and clerks, had had a brief affair with this young man while she was the housekeeper in the home of his uncle, the man she really loved, and who Lewis Mumford, as a child, secretly suspected was his father. Difficult as this may be to believe, Mumford had never asked his mother about the circumstances of his birth while he lived with her, although he certainly knew that he was illegitimate. When, at the age of forty-seven, he finally drew forth his mother's secret from her—at his wife Sophia's insistence—he shared it with his son Geddes, who was about to enter military service, but kept it from his daughter Alison for another twenty-five years, despite her desperate desire to know about her paternal grandfather. She would have to wait until after his death, when his autobiography was published, to learn what he could not reveal to her now, he told her, never explaining why this had to be kept a secret. Only when Alison learned the truth in her early twenties from another member of the family and confronted her father, did he decide to publish his autobiography in his lifetime. Although this resolutely self-enclosed man had kept others from entering this part of his past, he did so, as we shall see, at an enormous emotional cost to his family and to himself.[3]

Sketches from Life gives a glimpse of another side of Lewis Mumford that he had suppressed in earlier accounts of his life. Those who knew him well were aware that his family had been poor, that his mother had been barely able to support herself and her only child. Only a few people outside his immediate family, however, knew what he disclosed in a chapter titled "Faded Family Album." The opening word of that chapter gives its theme and meaning: "dissipation." That word, he explains, "[calls up] the kind of life that was lived in my mother's family circle."[4]

Elvina Mumford belonged to a family that had been in the service of some of the wealthiest households in New York City, and they shared some of the vices of those they worked for. They lived considerably beyond their incomes, and spent their free days in a never-ending round of card games, idle gossip, and afternoon pilgrimages to the racetrack or the stockbroker's office. By the time Mumford was in high school his mother had squandered what little savings she had on long-shot bets, and had slipped into a life of extreme poverty and invalidism. Although she used to tell Lewis that she lived entirely for him, she actually had very little time for him. As a child he loved books, but she never thought to join a public library, and only rarely did she read to him. She was proud that he turned out to be a straight-A student in grammar school, but the only times she bothered to visit his school were to pull him from his classes early in the day to take him with her to the horse races. In a passage Mumford deleted from the published version of his autobiography, probably because it would have given too grim a picture of his mother's self-absorption, he recalls the "desolate" late afternoons he spent standing alone on the street outside their West Side apartment, at the age of eleven, waiting for her to return from the racetrack.[5]

Elvina Mumford was actually a kindly, caring woman; her greatest flaw was her docility. She slipped too easily into her family's social routine. This would instill in Lewis Mumford a somewhat cynical disdain for family life, which he would shed only when he married and had a family of his own. Her docility also aroused in him a powerful contrary urge to be his own self, to have his own center. As a young man he formed himself in rebellion against his mother and her world.[6]

When Mumford went on to study at New York's City College he came under the powerful influence of the work of Ralph Waldo Emerson. Later in his life, as the commencement speaker at his daughter's graduation from Radcliffe, he spoke of what he found eternally significant in Emerson. "Nothing is sacred but the integrity of your own mind." That, for Mumford, was the kernel of Emerson's central doctrine, the idea of self-reliance. "Your main need," he counseled the graduates, "is to have a firm inner center, based on your own identity and your own work: an affirmative self-respect that no institution, no outward circumstance . . . can violate. Your own Yes and No."[7] As a very young man Lewis Mumford formed that sense of identity by psychologically distancing himself from his own family, by taking on a sense of Emersonian separateness, even before he read the sage of Concord. Encountering Emerson as an undergraduate reaffirmed in his mind the path he had already taken toward his self-development.

In his mature writing Mumford would recommend that social engagement be "counter-balanced by seasons of withdrawal and solitude." This is what recharges our capacity for self-direction; and without that capacity for self-direction "we shall become the victims of [an acquisitive] culture that is steadily expanding its power and productivity in every dimension, while it allows the very core of our life to become hollow and dismally empty."[8] Hollow and dismally empty. In *Sketches from Life* Mumford uses almost these very words to describe the family life he coolly withdrew from as a young boy.

Emerson would touch him in other equally significant ways.

While he would later claim that it was his background of poverty that made him content to live for many years on a meager income, as a struggling writer, it was Emerson's admonition to live a life of "handsome bareness and simplicity" that helped him turn what could have been a shameful disadvantage into an instructive lesson.[9] All his life he hewed closely to this idea of Emersonian simplicity, even at the peak of his influence and earning power.

Self-understanding, self-control, self-direction, and self-transcendence: mankind's hope, Mumford would argue in all his writings, lies in an increase in these, not in an increase in power or wealth. Looking at his beginnings it is easy to understand why this became his refrain.

So from a very early age Lewis Mumford was driven by an overpowering sense of purpose. He knew what he wanted to be, and he became that kind of man. We can almost say that he willed himself into being. He also dared to remain himself while the world around him changed, holding steadfast to the values and principles he preached in his first published writings. When we see him in *Sketches from Life*, against the background of his culturally impoverished, spendthrift family, it seems almost miraculous that he emerged as the man who wrote the book we read, one of the commanding thinkers of the twentieth century, a writer who put forward his views with an air of priestly certainty.

Lewis Charles Mumford was born on the morning of October 19, 1895, in a small cottage at 10 Amity Street in Flushing, Queens. He was delivered by his mother's physician, who rushed out from Manhattan on the Long Island train just before the birth. Lewis Mumford would never see his father, Lewis Mack, nor would he ever lay eyes on the man whose name he carried, John Mumford, an Englishman his mother had married twelve years before his birth when she was only eighteen years old. That brief, storm-swept marriage had been annulled, and John Mumford had disappeared; in a sense Elvina was twice "widowed" before she bore her only child at the age of thirty.

She was then a pleasant-looking, bosomy woman with flowing chestnut hair and sparkling eyes. She had a lively sense of humor but she carried a deep sadness inside of her. She had had an appalling, almost Dickensian childhood, and in the final months of her pregnancy, which she spent with her mother and stepfather in a cottage they rented so that she could carry and deliver her child in secret, she was disconsolate, almost suicidal. She knew that her baby would never have a father, and she feared that she would never have another chance to marry. She also wondered how she would manage to support herself and her child on the miserably small allowance the Mack family had set aside for them. Most of all, she felt helpless and terribly alone, for while she was strongly attached to her mother she held her accountable for much that had gone against her in her life. When Elvina would be too preoccupied as a mother to give *her* son the attention he needed, she would be carrying on a family pattern of parental self-absorption she herself had been victimized by.

Elvina's mother's side of the family, the Hewels, had emigrated to America from Hanover, Germany, in the 1850s, and most of the family had settled in New York City. Her mother, Anna Maria Louise Hewel, married a ship's steward named Baron, and had four children by him, three daughters and a son, until he left her just before the son was born. Elvina's mother, who did not remarry until Elvina had left the household, supported herself and her children by keeping boarders in an old house she rented on East Tenth Street, a redbrick building Lewis Mumford would sometimes pass on his early walks through the old Bouwerie section of Manhattan.

The family was always poor, and Elvina's mother was an ungiving woman—vain, self-centered, and coldly indifferent to her children. Their responsibility, she made clear to them, was to help to make her life a little easier, for although she was poor she had many beautiful dresses and loved to go to parties and balls. In the household of Anna Maria Hewel "the young were sacrificed to the old."[10]

At the age of ten or eleven Elvina was pulled out of school to work full-time for her hard-driving mother; at fifteen she was apprenticed at a pastry shop, where she slept in an attic dormitory with other female workers. The following year she was sent to Philadelphia to help her aunt Elvina, who kept boarders in her house. Elvina Ebeling was a kindly woman with an aristocratic bearing and rigid morals. She taught her niece correct manners and trained her to be a skilled housekeeper and an excellent cook.

Elvina enjoyed her stay in Philadelphia, away from a household so grim that one of her sisters had filed a police complaint against her mother for cruelty, but she was forced to leave when she became attracted to one of the boarders, James Schleicher, a handsome young Belgian-born engineer who was a friend of Elvina Ebeling's husband. One evening when they were alone together in the living room, James Schleicher pulled her toward him and kissed her. The next day, when she innocently disclosed to her aunt what had happened, her aunt told her that she had committed a grave breach of household ethics and would have to leave at once. Elvina was puzzled by her aunt's angry reaction. Only later did she learn that her aunt was also fond of James Schleicher; and, in fact, a little while later, after her husband died, she married him. (Elvina was to have her own form of Victorian vindication. When James Schleicher's wife died and he recovered from his grief, he wrote to Elvina, who was now in middle age, to tell her that he had been in love with her since the moment he had set eyes on her. He began sending her poetry, and she visited him occasionally. But it was too late to bring these two thwarted lives together.)

About the same time that Elvina was expelled from her aunt's household she suffered two other setbacks. First, she began to be bothered by painful toothaches and begged her mother to send her to a dentist. When her mother learned that it would be cheaper to have her daughter's upper teeth removed than to have them repaired, she insisted that this be done, a terrible blow for a young girl who was proud of her looks. Elvina never forgave her mother, although she kept her anger inside.

A little while later she began to have severe abdominal attacks. Her doctor told her she had bleeding ulcers and put her on a strict diet, which only intensified her feelings of hopelessness. She felt she had no one to comfort her, or to fall back on for support. At this early age she began to experience prolonged periods of depression and started her slow slide into chronic invalidism.[11]

Her life brightened somewhat when at eighteen she became attracted to John Mumford, a man more than twice her age who rented a room in her mother's boardinghouse. When he asked her to marry him she was probably not in love with him, but she saw marriage as her only chance for another kind of life. Six months or so after they were wed, however, Jack Mumford got into some sort of trouble with his employer over his bookkeeping accounts and fled to

Canada by himself. After he became established there he sent for Elvina, but she was pressured by her family to remain in New York. A short time later her family arranged an annulment, on the grounds that the marriage had never been consummated. Elvina kept John Mumford's name, however, and with it the status in those days of a married woman. So "his is the family name that I bear," Lewis Mumford remarked later, "without a single drop of his blood running in my veins."[12] Jack Mumford's only legacy to him was a complete set of Dickens's works, in a cheap Collier edition, which his mother passed on to him when he was a child, claiming it was a gift from a close friend of hers. It is inscribed "From Jack to Elvie."

The only love of Elvina Mumford's life was Jacob Mack (J.W., as he was referred to in Elvina's family), a well-to-do New York lawyer she went to work for as a housekeeper in her early twenties. He was a lifelong bachelor who had emigrated from Frankfurt am Main, a handsome, strong-bodied man who had dark features and a somewhat severe, overrefined manner. Although he was quite a bit older than Elvina, she fell in love with him as soon as she joined his household. "I have found him at last," she wrote in her autograph album just after meeting him. "My dream is fulfilled."[13]

Jacob Mack never made a direct advance on her, but she made it clear to him that she loved him, and for a time he treated her as if he wanted her to be his lover. He put her in charge of his household, with two housemaids under her direction, took her for sleigh rides in Central Park and to dinner at the Claremont Inn on Riverside Drive, brought her expensive gifts from his trips to Europe, and copied out verses and quotations in five languages in her autograph album. On one occasion he had her accompany him as his companion on a vacation in the Poconos, although they stayed in separate rooms, and nothing happened between them. Elvina was so attracted to him, she later said, that "failing marriage," she would happily have allowed him to seduce her. After a time, however, she began to suspect that he didn't try to make love to her because he was impotent.[14]

As it turned out, it was Jacob Mack's nephew who took the initiative with Elvina. When Lewis Mack came to New York City for dinner and the theater, he would often spend the night in the home of his favorite uncle. There he and Elvina had a brief passionate affair, and in mid-January 1895 she became pregnant. She thought she knew the exact night that it happened. She felt a surge of pleasure throughout her entire body, unlike anything she had ever experienced. "They tell me now," she later confided to her son's wife, "it was what they call an orgasm." To her it was the miracle of conception.[15]

When both families found out that Elvina was pregnant there was considerable consternation, although no one suggested an abortion. Without clearing it with her family, Lewis Mack did offer to marry Elvina, but she had the courage and good sense to say no, realizing that he was acting out of honor rather than love for her, though he did claim to care for her deeply. She also felt guilty that she had yielded to a man five years younger than she. Besides, she was still in love with his uncle, and would dream of marrying him for at least another ten years. In any event, both families agreed that a marriage was simply out of the question. It was a matter of both religion and status. He was from a well-placed Jewish family who had made a fortune in manufacturing and finance. She was a poor Protestant girl from a family who waited on the wealthy.

When Elvina went to Flushing with her parents for her confinement, Lewis Mack would take a train out to visit her on his lunch hour. But as the birth approached his family persuaded him to stop seeing her, fearing that he might become attached to his child and agree to marry Elvina after all. His family arranged a meager settlement for Elvina, some $600 a year, and Elvina never saw Lewis Mack again. He died in his early thirties, and for a long time after his death Elvina carried his obituary notice in her purse. When Lewis Mumford, in his forties, first looked at a picture of Lewis Mack his mother had kept hidden with her personal items, he saw no physical resemblance between himself and his father. "I . . . find it as hard to acknowledge him as my biological progenitor as if I had been the product of an artificial insemination from an anonymous donor."[16]

After Elvina had her baby she still hoped in her heart to return to Jacob Mack's household and perhaps win him eventually as her husband, but her hopes were crushed when Jacob Mack told her that she could return only if she agreed to put her child in an orphanage. This she refused to do, although it would have made her life comfortable and put her near the man she loved. Jacob Mack, however, did not walk out of her life immediately; for a time he served as a kind of substitute father for her son.

For reasons perhaps even she didn't fully understand, Elvina chose not to tell her son who his father was; and her family, a group of people who liked to gossip, never let a word leak on this matter around him. But, ultimately, she was able to maintain her silence because her son never pressed her for an explanation. He sensed, he explained later, that this was a "forbidden" subject, never to be discussed.[17] There is more to it than this, however. He must have assumed, from an early age, that Jacob Mack was his father. All the evidence he had available to him would have led him to this conclusion. Jacob Mack visited the Mumford household almost every Saturday afternoon until Lewis was five or six years old; and every Christmas he sent Lewis a bundle of handsomely made toys. Elvina also reminded her son that he must do well in school so as not to disappoint Mr. Mack, who regularly inspected his report cards. About this time she told Lewis that Mr. Mack was one of his legal guardians, and she made no effort to hide her love for him: his photograph hung prominently over her desk, alongside an oil painting he had done. It was as if Elvina wanted her son to believe that Jacob Mack was his father.

If he had any doubts about his parentage they were probably answered in his own mind one day when he was six years old. He had been arguing with a friend in the backyard, and when he rushed into the house flushed with anger, his mother asked him what was the matter. "I'll never play with that dirty Jew again," he blurted out. "Never use those words again," Elvina warned him sharply. "Your father was a Jew."[18] Not long after this Elvina removed from her autograph album and diaries all references to Jack Mumford and Lewis Mack, but not to Jacob Mack.

"As the years passed, the barrier between my mother and me on this subject became more formidable," Mumford recalls. "The lock that might have opened easily in my earlier years became rusted." He saw no need to force a "showdown" with his mother, he later confided to a friend, because he simply assumed that he was illegitimate and part-Jewish, and had no great interest in knowing for certain who his father was. His father, he reasoned, had had nothing to do with him, or with what he had become; so why should he show concern about him at the risk of troubling his mother? Nor was he ashamed of being illegitimate. As a college student he would joke with one of his closest friends about having Jewish blood and being "a little bastard."[19]

Much later in his life he learned from his mother that she had continued to keep her secret from him after he was married and had a family of his own because she feared that if he and Sophia found out what had happened they might think less of her or even "cast her off." But when she finally told Lewis her secret in 1942, he and Sophia embraced her warmly and assured her of their love. "Don't worry, mother, I am in good company," Lewis said with a smile. "Leonardo da Vinci and Erasmus were also illegitimate." She was relieved he took it so well, but she later confessed that she had no idea who Erasmus was.[20]

Lewis Mumford's first clear memories are of a four-story brownstone on West Sixty-fifth Street that his mother rented in a never-successful effort to make a living as a boardinghouse keeper. Here his conscious life began at the age of three. He remembers lying in bed in the morning in what was originally the music room, a tiny, airless space between the narrow front and back parlors. The rooms, he recounts his first memories of that dreary brownstone, were crowded with heavy walnut furniture, and the dark walls, covered with oil paintings, framed lithographs and engravings, gave the downstairs a shut-in, imprisoning feeling. The heavy drapes closed off the sunlight, and even on the brightest morning he was barely able, on awakening, to tell whether it was daylight yet. As he began to peel off his bedcovers, he could hear his Uncle Charley, a lifelong bachelor who boarded with them, rattling around upstairs; and in the kitchen his mother was making breakfast. He could smell the rolls in the oven and fresh coffee brewing in the pot. In the back parlor his grandmother, who shared this room with her second husband, Charles Graessel, was standing before a large walnut wardrobe, looking into a mirror as she adjusted her black bonnet on her once-beautiful face. Lewis Mumford's next memory of her has her in her sickbed, a few months later, an enfeebled old woman, too weak, even, to cry out for help. "You must be quiet when playing, Lewlie," are the first words he remembers hearing from his grandfather, "granmer is very sick."[21] A little while later she died of Bright's disease.

Lewis had a confined, uneventful childhood. He was a shy, frail, and somewhat solemn boy, never robustly healthy, eager for games but never very good at them; and from a very early age he had a deep fear of death. Although he loved to hear the nursery rhyme about Cock Robin, he always insisted on skipping the page in his book that had a picture of Cock Robin's funeral; until he was seven or eight he never went to bed without an adult beside him. About the time he started to go to bed alone, he stopped having a dream he had been having since infancy: "the sense of existing in the midst of space, with infinity pressing in upon me from every direction." He especially dreaded the enormous pressure of that "emptiness." This, of course, is what Freud called the oceanic dream, a recollection of life in the womb surrounded by amniotic fluid. "I shall never forget this dream," Mumford remarked many years later.[22] Yet what is noteworthy is not the dream itself but his amazingly clear memory of it—and of so many of the other events from his earliest childhood. Like so many bright and lonely children, he was remarkably observant, blessed with a painter's eye for detail. He combined this with an absolutely tenacious memory.

Although he was something of a mother's boy, he was left alone for long stretches of the day. As a young boy he had few playmates, as his family changed residences eight times in his first twelve years; and as a teacher's pet he was often unpopular with the other boys. Until he was well into grammar school, his only steady playmate was his cousin Edwin Niedermeyer, whose family boarded with Elvina and her stepfather for a time. They would occasionally ride their bicycles together or play tag or red rover with other kids from the neighborhood, but Lewis would spend most of his out-of-school time indoors, playing with his toy soldiers or drawing pictures of castles and horses, the beginning of a lifelong interest in sketching and painting. His world was the world of his mother's family—an adult's world—and from an early age he struggled to break free from it. Out of that fiercely fought inner rebellion permanent character traits were formed. Lewis Mumford might have been, as he says, "a Son of Manhattan," but he was also the only child of Elvina Baron Mumford, who had a far greater influence on him than he was ever willing to admit.

In his early childhood his mother was a bright-spirited, pleasant-looking woman who still had suitors calling on her. She wore dresses that accentuated her fashionably full figure, and wore her flowing brown hair coiled attractively in braids. She was sweet-natured and easy to please, and she had a lovely voice. When she worked around the house she would sing her favorite tunes from *Madame Butterfly*. At the dinner hour she would call her boarders to the table with a deep-throated whistle.

Elvina was an excellent cook, passing on that talent to her son, but she never quite learned to manage a boardinghouse. She treated her boarders, her "paying guests," she called them, regally, serving them cuisine well beyond what they paid for and often allowing them to let their rent payments lapse.[23] Elvina had absolutely no regard for money, the result perhaps of her long stay in the expansive household of Jacob Mack, and also had a wild streak of impracticality. Even when she was nearly broke she went to vaudeville shows and racetracks at least once a week, and shopped at only the best stores, buying her son's clothing, including his first tuxedo, at Altman's, where she had a charge account. In the spring and summer she vacationed at Atlantic City, Lake George, or fashionable Saratoga Springs; in the winter months there were card parties and kaffee klatsches nearly every day at the home of one or another of her sisters or cousins; and once a month there was a formal evening, with the men dressed in tails and the women in their finest dresses. Her son remembers meeting, with some wonderment and jealousy, her escort at one of these evenings, "a debonair, vacant minded dandy" noticeably younger than she.[24]

Much later in her life, when her daughter-in-law asked Elvina what she most regretted about her youth, she thought a moment, gave a quick sigh, and replied: "I never danced enough; I would have liked to have danced more."[25]

As a mother Elvina Mumford was a puzzling combination of devoted concern and unthinking detachment. On the one hand, she "spoiled me," her son claims. "I was the center of her life."[26] "I have lived so entirely for you . . . ," she wrote him around his twenty-fifth birthday, "that there is little else in life for me that is worth while!" Like Mary, mother of Jesus, she had been put on this earth, she used to tell her family in her old age, to deliver a great child.[27] She was so proud of him and, later, of what he eventually became, that she left strict instructions in her will that only these words were to be placed on her tombstone.

ELVINA
1865–1950
MOTHER OF LEWIS MUMFORD

Mumford fondly recounts this episode in *Sketches from Life,* but there is another way of reading his mother's final injunction. Just after her death he himself suspected what he dared not admit in his autobiography—that feeling guilty about the way she had ignored him in his childhood, tragically repeating her own mother's mistake, even to the point of not taking him to a dentist until his teeth were chronically decayed and some of them had to be pulled, Elvina feared that he might fail to visit her when she was gone. "Perhaps the only active religion in her life," he wrote shortly after her burial, "was the religion of the family gods, served by frequent visits . . . to the cemetery."[28] So her instructions in marking her grave might have been her own form of insurance against any neglect on her son's part.

Elvina probably never thought of herself as a negligent parent for, compared with her sisters, she was a model of smothering parental devotion. She only, if ever, became fully aware of her weaknesses as a parent late in her life, when as a grandmother there was a touch of jealousy and guilt in her attitude toward the way her son's wife devoted herself to her children. Elvina often complained to Lewis that Sophia was spoiling the children, that she was "a slave to parental duty," undoubtedly thinking that if her daughter-in-law was right to indulge her children as she did, she herself had been wrong in the way she had brought up her son.[29]

Instead of entering more into her son's life, Elvina had dragged him into hers, bringing him along with her to the racetrack, to the stockbroker's office, to her string of favorite department stores and Japanese auction houses, and to interminable Sunday visits with their New York relatives. Of these excursions, Lewis did enjoy their trips together to the horse races at Belmont Park or Sheepshead Bay, when they would ride out to the track on an open-air trolley car, passing through a landscape of rolling meadows and well-kept truck gardens, with the south wind bringing the scent of fresh-cut grass and ocean spray. The horses and the jockeys, dressed in their bright-colored silks, were exciting to watch, and after the races he and his mother would go to a local hotel for a heaping feast of soft-shelled crabs. He eagerly looked forward to these afternoons, but he hated the long shopping trips and the drawn-out hours at the broker's office, where his mother and her sisters would sit on a stiff bench and watch the big board, hoping for the stroke of luck that would change their fortunes.

Most of all, he loathed the Sunday visits with his aunts and uncles. His mother, her sisters and cousins, and their spouses would play poker all afternoon and late into the evening, leaving the children alone and bored, and sometimes a little frightened when the arguments at the card table became loud and ugly. On many a Sunday evening in winter Lewis would be put to bed among the pile of overcoats on his aunt's king-sized bed. Even as an old man he could still recall, with sharp poignancy, being shaken awake by his mother at one or two in the morning, dressed hastily, and taken out into the icy evening air.[30]

As a child Lewis was often sick, usually from some form of respiratory problem (he also had an overactive heart). He probably used these illnesses as a way of getting attention, the foundation of a mild hypochondria he would suffer from most of his life, but he rarely got the results he hoped for. Even when he was absent from school with some illness, his mother generally went about her business as usual. Later, when he was in college, a doctor told him that he had a tubercular lesion on his lung. For a time he kept this from his mother for fear that he would alarm her, but when she was called in by the doctor for a consultation she took the news in stride, and did not seem unduly concerned about him during his extended period of invalidism. By this time she was an invalid herself, and her own problems consumed her attention.

In *Sketches from Life*, Mumford tries to minimize the hurt his mother's detachment caused him, reverting to what had become for him a common practice of explaining a liability as a hidden asset (the familiar formula of the writer who reconstructs his life as a lesson and an education for others). "On the whole [my mother's] aloofness was fortunate for me. We were close enough together as it was; and had she been more attentive, more overly solicitous, I might never have been able to sunder the bond between us."[31] This is not entirely convincing. Although he felt close to his mother throughout his life, he was never able to completely forgive her for her self-absorption. While he lived with his mother, however, he buried these feelings, which is not surprising. "The deprived child," as one writer has observed, "cherishes the little attention his parents do give him; he cannot risk losing it."[32]

It was not until Mumford began his autobiography in 1952, two years after his mother's death, that he became fully aware of how much he had resented her behavior as a mother. Nonetheless, in the account of his mother he did eventually publish in his autobiography, he transposed his long-buried hurt and anger into several moving recollections of moments in their lives when they were together alone. He treasured most of all the time, in 1907, they rented a small cottage in Atlantic City for the spring and summer. In the mornings his mother would spend hours poring over the daily racing form, but after she placed her bets with her bookie he had her completely to himself for the rest of the day. They would bake pies and cakes, and take long walks on the boardwalk. In the evenings they would lie in bed under the covers reading Dumas or Sir Walter Scott.[33]

But for him there were too few moments like these. Elvina was never the mother he wanted her to be, and it is not unfair to say that, later in his own life, he was not the father he thought he should have been, because of his own form of self-absorption—his complete commitment to his writing. "When I analyze . . . my mother's preoccupation with her adult world, to my exclusion," he writes in the account of his mother's life he never published because he thought it too critical of her, "I am conscious of many similar sins of my own."[34]

Elvina's attention to her son's needs lapsed even further as he neared adolescence. Her stepfather, Charles Graessel, who continued to live with her after her mother's death, had been a headwaiter at Delmonico's, where he made a decent salary. When he died in 1906, several years after his retirement, he left Elvina and Lewis a modest inheritance of about $3,500. Instead of setting aside this money and spending it prudently, Elvina gambled it away at the racetrack. She sank into extreme poverty, and when Lewis was twelve years old they settled into a run-down apartment house at 100 West Ninety-fourth Street, where they lived together for the next twelve years. In high school Lewis was undernourished and ill-clothed; he could not even afford to buy a new shirt once a year. His mother aged rapidly, her face became changed with suffering, and suitors stopped calling on her. Disappointed in life, and without hope for a brighter future, Elvina lapsed into a long period of invalidism, which further fueled her self-absorption. Her son was left to raise himself.

At the age of twenty Lewis Mumford observed in his notes that his mother's greatest gift to him was to leave him alone so that he could find his own feet. "When men of mark write autobiographies in their sentimental old age they unfailingly attribute their greatness to the fond care and preoccupation of their mothers. If I ever find myself in the same boat I shall not hesitate to attribute what small ability I possess to my mother's fond carelessness. . . . By doing nothing for me she accordingly did a great deal."[35] By this time he was already his own person. He had learned to be self-sufficient, and in his hours alone he had developed the habits that would serve him well as a writer. While there is some truth to his claim that his mother helped him to become self-reliant by not interfering in his life, because of her mother's intrusion into her life, family circumstances—and Elvina's self-absorption—made it utterly necessary.

Mumford had formed himself up to this point, in fact, in direct opposition to his mother and her New York relatives, a family he once sarcastically described to a friend as "a breed of gamblers, wastrels, cheap sports, adulterers on an almost professional level." Even as a child he had a strong sense of alienation from his family. "You simply didn't belong to the rest of your family," his boyhood chum Jerry Lachenbruch confided to him later in their lives. "And that is why we jested about your birth," speculating that it was perhaps his Jewish blood that set him apart from them. "Neither you nor I could understand how you could have sprung from the family that outwardly surrounded you."[36]

A self-contained, unassertive boy, Lewis Mumford rejected the world of his mother's family by withdrawing from it. And because his mother sheltered him at home and took him with her almost everywhere she went, his withdrawal and rebellion was almost entirely psychological. He built a mental wall between his family's world and his own fast-developing inner world. They might have him around them while they gambled and gossiped, but they could never enter into, or become a part of, his fiercely protected interior world: that was always and entirely his own province.

This helps to explain the kind of man he became. Although he got along well with his friends in high school and college, they saw him as somehow different from them. He was always something of an outsider; and to some of his closest friends he seemed too severely controlled. There would be only a few people, all of them women he loved, to whom he would ever let down his defenses and reveal the passionate man behind that iron reserve. "Perhaps one of the reasons why you found my reserve so hard to penetrate," he wrote to his daughter much later in his life, trying to explain why he had not shared with her the "secret" of his paternity, "lies outside the province of the 'secret,' in the fact that I disliked so many members of my mother's family . . . : so my aloofness, my self-sufficiency, became engrained."[37]

Given his background of poverty and parental neglect, it is not surprising that he was drawn to Horatio Alger stories at the age of eight or nine. The young heroes of these books, which he read with vivid empathy, were invariably poor; they were hard-driving from an early age; and they were sometimes orphaned, or at least obliged to support a family. They came from hopeless circumstances, but they were never without hope; and they had absolutely no self-pity. Undaunted, they strove on, looking for that straight channel to success. They knew that with luck and pluck they could be just about anything they set out to be. And if they had an identity crisis, as Mumford later remarked, "the young idiots never recognized it."[38]

So from a remarkably early age Lewis Mumford was determined not to live in the weather of his mother's spirit. His mother had fallen into a pattern of drift and dissipation. He would seize hold of his life, set clear goals and schedules for himself, keep orderly records, save what money he had, and live a settled, concentrated life, whether it be as a lawyer, poet, artist, reform politician, or electrical engineer, the various careers he thought of entering at one time or another in early adolescence, convinced, as he was, that one had to start early if one wanted to be a great man.

His family's problems and poverty produced in him not despair, then, but a tremendous fixity of purpose that was the key to his eventual success as a writer. In his teens he put up "study schedules" on his bedroom wall—books he should read, places he should visit, essays and plays he hoped to write. For a time he became so absorbed in his studies—in his self-directed program of self-development, not in his actual schoolwork—that his friends found it hard to get him to leave the house for the Saturday walks in the countryside they knew he enjoyed. All his life he continued to be a deeply disciplined, almost compulsively orderly person, with an eye always on his own future. Early in his maturity he fell into a habit he followed most of his life with religious regularity. Every New Year's Day he would sit down at his desk and compose a full review of the previous year of his life, concluding each account with freshly fashioned goals for the coming year. He combined this with a related habit of making schedules for himself: when he should be finished writing this book or essay; when he should start another project; and where he hoped to be as a writer, and as a human being, at the conclusion of this year or this decade. He was quite clearly a driven man, but he was usually driven along a course he had carefully charted for himself.

Although Mumford was baptized an Episcopalian he was not brought up in a formal faith and never attended church regularly. Nonetheless he acquired strong ethical standards early on in his life, and the values he prized most were those most conspicuously absent from his mother's life: self-restraint and self-discipline. His constant aim, as evidenced by his earliest notes, was to live what he called "the good life," a life of material simplicity and balanced self-development. At an early age he began to see life itself as a moral struggle, forming a personal philosophy that would forever guide him. Later, when he read Thorstein Veblen, the sardonic satirist of conspicuous consumption, he was fully prepared for him; and he himself went on to become one of this century's severest critics of what E. H. Tawney has called "the acquisitive society."

Yet though he became almost the opposite of his mother, he remained like her in revealing ways. In her early thirties, before she slipped into extreme invalidism, Elvina Mumford might have been a cheerful woman, but underneath her sunny exterior was a deep melancholia. One of her son's most vivid memories is of her sitting alone at the piano in the music room of her sister Teresa's apartment "playing . . . softly, picking out a melody she had learned in her youth, wistful, as if recalling a vanished promise."[39] At regular intervals in his own life he would be brought low by similar bouts of depression, so extreme, at times, that he would be pulled into prolonged periods of blackening despair. He and Elvina also had "a horrid common capacity to anticipate the future too anxiously, and even, on the whole, to have our worst fears justified," he confessed to a friend just after his mother's funeral.[40] It is in the young Lewis Mumford that we find the temperamental sources of the admonitory social prophet, who, with Ruskin, would "see thunder on the horizon as well as dawn."

By cutting himself off from his family surroundings Lewis Mumford achieved, at an early age, his own emancipation. What he would call his renewal and "awakening" would begin when he first fell in love at the age of sixteen.[41]

But what explains his youthful self-confidence, his inner certainty that he was to succeed in some important way? It is the confidence that often comes to self-made persons in their willful struggle to remake themselves; several small successes sometimes give the feeling that anything is possible. But Mumford had his own theory. At the age of sixty-eight, after reading Ernest Jones's biography of Freud in preparation for writing his own autobiography, he made this revealing note: "A man who has been the indisputable favorite of his mother," he paraphrases Freud's idea, "keeps for life the feeling of conqueror, that confidence of success that often induces real success. I can say the same. . . . Also, like Freud, I was breast fed."[42]

The fact is, however, he had had two "mothers," who by loving him and accepting him for what he was, gave him a strong feeling of emotional security. For the first ten years of his conscious life, Nellie Ahearn, his Irish nurse and constant companion, was actually more of a mother to him than Elvina Mumford.

Nellie, or Nana, as she was called by everyone in Elvina's household, became Lewis's nurse when he was one year old, and stayed on as their cook and housekeeper until Elvina could no longer afford to pay her. Even after she left their service to become a private maid to the owner of The Dakota, however, she kept a generous watch over both Lewis and Elvina, visiting them regularly, bringing them bags filled with birthday and Christmas presents, and offering novenas for their physical health and spiritual salvation. At a time when Elvina was too ill with stomach ulcers to keep up her household,

Nellie would drop by regularly and spend her vacation day cleaning the apartment, her only reward a glass of whiskey and a quick conversation over coffee with the boy she doted over.

Nellie was "black Irish," with raven hair, oval eyes, a large nose, and a receding chin that pulled down the corners of her mouth into a permanently sorrowful expression. She had a deeply expressive face and a village woman's unquestioning Catholicism. At the age of sixteen she had been sent to America as a servant girl by her widowed mother to raise money for her struggling family back in Ireland, and she entered the service of Elvina Mumford after working for a prosperous New York family. She lived alone in New York for the rest of her life; her only true friends, she once told Lewis, were Jesus and her beloved St. Anthony. She never forgave her mother for "exiling" her to America, and though she prayed for her and dutifully mailed money to the Old Country every month, not once did she return to her seaside village of Youghal, not even for a brief visit. Some of that stubborn pride she passed on, by example, to Lewis Mumford.

What Mumford learned as a boy of the rites and rituals of religious faith he picked up from this serene and gentle woman. Standing by her in the kitchen as she sliced potatoes and onions, he heard wonderful stories of saints and martyrs. Nellie made him promise never to swear—it was a sin, she told him, and besides, "gentlemen never do it"—and she taught him proper manners. A tolerant woman, she was, as he would become, unyielding in matters of right and wrong.[43]

Though she never tried to convert him, she secretly hoped, no doubt, that he would eventually find the true faith. But just to make sure of his salvation she took him regularly to the church of the Paulist Fathers on Columbus Avenue and Fifty-ninth Street to anoint him with holy water and light a votive candle for him. Surely on one of these occasions she baptized him, for her favorite priest had told her that it was permissible for a layperson to baptize an innocent heathen.[44]

She gave herself completely to his care and thoroughly spoiled him, affectionately calling him "Your Royal Highness." It was she, not his mother, who picked him up at school on rainy days, where she would be waiting for him inside the door with a black umbrella under her arm and a reassuring smile on her face; and she took him to parades on Fifth Avenue, for walks in Central Park, and for occasional visits to her Irish neighborhood in the West Forties, where he encountered a poverty far worse than any he would ever know. Nellie would "discuss life" with him—she was his only true confidante—and she helped him with his homework as best she could, for she was barely literate. When he was a child she sang him to sleep with soft Irish ballads, and on stormy nights, with the lightning flashing through the windows, this simple woman, whose heart had never left her village on the Irish Sea, would sit on the edge of Lewis's bed, cross herself, and say with a sigh: "God pity the poor sailors on a night like this!"

All his life Lewis loved to tell stories of Nana's "Irishisms," as he called them, such as her hardheaded, commonsense advice to him: "never be backward in putting yourself forward," advice he took to heart permanently, though he declares in his autobiography it was "largely lost" on him.[45]

Although there was an understandable tension between her and Elvina, Nellie remained in the household out of love for Lewis. She walked out several times in anger, but always returned because she could not bear to be away from him. Later she became almost as devoted to Lewis's children as she was to him, and on her death she left them each $300, her entire worldly savings. But it was Lewis she was most proud of. She remained a second mother to him until her quiet death in a nursing home in 1940, just days after one of his regular visits with her.

He attended the funeral mass for her, with his mother, in a sadly run-down church on West Forty-second Street. Even though Nellie had never succeeded in winning him to Catholicism, at that moment, in that church, he realized one other thing she had indelibly instilled in him: an appreciation for the power and mystery of religious ceremony and ritual. "Even if one did not share the Church's ultimate assurances of heavenly salvation and resurrection," he later described Nellie's funeral mass, "it bestowed a cosmic dignity on these last moments that no secular rite has yet rivaled. I am not sure that translating the Mass into an intelligible national language, still less with jazz music to accompany it, has made it more efficacious."[46]

2

A New York Boyhood

"Little old New York's good enough for us"—that's what they sing.

—O. HENRY

As a boy Lewis Mumford's ties to his grandfather were almost as strong as they were to Nellie Ahearn. Charles Graessel was actually his mother's stepfather, but their relations "were as solid as blood could have made them." And it was he who introduced Lewis to turn-of-the-century New York.[1]

Charles Graessel, the son of a Black Forest miller, arrived in America in the 1860s after traveling about Europe as an apprentice waiter. Until his last days he spoke English with a heavy accent, and he remained a German through and through, although he had none of the Teutonic severity of some of Lewis Mumford's other German relatives, and had no illusions about German superiority, preferring French food to German and the "Marseillaise" to "Die Wacht am Rheim."

He was a kindly, genial man who loved to play teasing little tricks on Lewis, and he brought him cakes, truffles, and masks from the lustrous costume balls at Delmonico's. Thick-set and square-shouldered, he had an erect, formal bearing, a large head, arching eyebrows, and bushy sideburns that reached all the way to his chin. Proud and polished, with the impeccable manners of those who wait on the wealthy, he wore handsomely tailored Prince Albert waistcoats, even in the afternoons, and had his black boots, which he would polish to a glare, specially made for him by an old bootmaker on Canal Street. His cigars he ordered handmade from Keyser and Klug. He didn't have an extensive wardrobe, but everything in his closet was of the finest quality. Later in his own life, his grandson would follow his example. Even as an impoverished young writer Mumford bought well-made suits of English woolens, preferring to buy one or two of these every couple of years to purchasing a new suit of cheaper make and fabric once or twice a year. And he took his grandfather's motto—"enough is plenty"—as his own, although he never followed that old gentleman's habit, in his retirement, of "inaugurating" each day, precisely at ten-forty-five, with a tall Manhattan cocktail.[2]

Almost every day from the time Lewis was four years old, he would accompany his grandfather on leisurely walks around Central Park or down fashionable Riverside Drive, the eastern and western boundaries of his childhood. As they walked his grandfather would recite to him the names of the residents of the fabulous stone mansions along Riverside Drive or Fifth Avenue, if they happened to range that far. He had waited on them all, he would boast, the Astors, the Vanderbilts, the Depews and the Schwabs, and he knew their habits and ways. On bright afternoons he would sit with Lewis on a bench just off the carriage drive in Central Park and watch the parade of broughams, hansom cabs, and tallyhos pulled by big chestnut geldings with blocked tails. "Look, there goes Russell Sage," he would point excitedly. "The man's a miser. He watches every penny; but the Old Lady is very nice."[3]

On weekends he and his grandfather would walk all around Manhattan, visiting his grandfather's friends and former cronies, or just "taking the air." Occasionally they would head all the way over to Brooklyn, crossing the Brooklyn Bridge, to visit relatives and go to an afternoon band concert in Prospect Park. At the end of the day they would walk home up Broadway, which was then lined by elms and called the "Bullivard" by West Siders. On rainy afternoons they would spend hours at the Metropolitan Museum of Art or the American Museum of Natural History, Lewis's introduction to these vast and wonderful places. "This is your city and you should learn to know it," his grandfather would tell him. And as they walked about, he would stop now and then, look intently at his gold pocket watch, and then at Lewis, who, if he could correctly guess the time, would be rewarded with a candy or a shiny penny. These walks exerted a lasting influence on Mumford. When, a number of years later, he began to explore New York on his own, "reading the buildings as if they were so many pages of a book, I was but continuing in solitude," he recalls, "these early rambles."4

His ideal city would always be the kind he imagined New York to have been in his boyhood, or perhaps we should say his own little section of New York, the almost solidly middle-class Upper West Side, where, above Sixty-fifth Street, there were still vegetable markets that brought the touch and smell of the countryside to the city, and German beer gardens where he would go with his grandfather on Saturdays to hear the oom-pah bands and eat sausages smothered with spicy mustard. The New York of his childhood, as he would remember it later in his life with increasing nostalgia, was a city of safe and friendly neighborhoods within easy walking distance of green parks and waterfront views; a city where grocers sent a boy around early in the morning to collect orders, and where there were white-walled dairy shops that sold nothing but milk, eggs, butter, and cheese; a city that had trolleys, trains, and ferries and, after 1905, double-decker buses that took everybody, cheaply and in some comfort, to amusement parks and museums, dance halls and vaudeville theaters, and, yes, even to the cemetery, a trip that was always, for young Mumford, a much anticipated diversion "on account of the journey itself if not its somber destination."5

Once a month, often with a group of uncles and aunts, he and his mother would go to Woodlawn Cemetery to visit the grave of his maternal grandmother. "My elders would comment on how well or ill the hired florist was keeping the grave bed in order, on what sort of inscription was to be put on the tombstone when my grandfather died, or on how—dear me!—the cemetery was filling up so fast."6 After leaving the cemetery the family would stop at a German roadhouse for beer and sandwiches, with glasses of sarsaparilla or ginger ale for the children.

As a boy Mumford also loved to go to the vaudeville houses, to the great parades on Fifth Avenue, and to the outdoor music festivals that were so popular in turn-of-the-century New York, the beginning of his lifelong interest in theater and spectacle, and the seed of his idea of the city as a vast stage for the drama of life. One of his

most vivid early memories is of being held in his Nana's arms as they
stood in a crowd on Broadway, near the Seventh Regiment Armory,
watching the soldiers in their red and blue capes marching off to the
Spanish-American War. That impression became forever linked in
his mind with the Admiral Dewey parade on Fifth Avenue several
years later. The soldiers and sailors marched smartly under a vast
plaster arch to the tunes of blaring military bands, while the fleet of
victorious battleships drifted at anchor in the harbor. On occasions
like these—and he would never forget as well the magnificent song
and light festival he saw on the lower lake of Central Park—the city
became a communal theater, and its residents became actors and
participants, as well as spectators, in the urban drama.

About the time that Mumford reached adolescence he began to
frequent Manhattan's vaudeville houses with a small group of neighborhood boys. This was the golden age of vaudeville, and he saw
Vesta Tilley, "the swagger" Anna Lloyd, and the queen of musical
comedy, Eva Tanguay. "It's all been done before," Eva would sing
teasingly, "but not the way I do it."7

For a 15-cent ticket you could then see a single vaudeville program
that included acts from all over the world. There might be a troupe
of Arab gymnasts, an Italian acrobatic team, a London comedian, a
Spanish escape artist, a French chanteuse, some American clog
dancers, and a whistling soloist from Norway. The palatial, richly
decorated vaudeville theater, packed with excited spectators from
every age group, walk of life and part of the globe, was itself the
theatrical counterpart of the modern metropolis. When one of their
favorite singers came on stage the audience would become a spontaneous chorus, and the entire hall would rock to the singing, piano
music, and rhythmic clapping and foot stomping. The entire show
ran continuously, one breathtaking act after the other, and its tempo
mirrored the rapid pace of big city life. "Wasn't it great," Mumford
and his friends would comment to one another as they walked up
Broadway after the show, humming one of the stage tunes—Anna
Lloyd's "There Was I, Waiting at the Church," or the great Tony
Pastor's "Down in a Coal Mine"—and mimicking the self-assured
movements of the magicians and jugglers. These turn-of-the-
century vaudeville performers helped to give Mumford, an awkward adolescent, "a sense of style." Even the best of them had a
dignity, poise, and assurance that he hoped to have someday. In his

old age, his eyes would light up with excitement when he talked about these endless afternoons at the old Colonial Theater on Broadway and Sixty-second Street.[8]

The middle-class New York that Mumford so richly recalls in *Sketches from Life* largely disappeared after World War I, replaced by an even faster paced city of tall, impersonal office towers, built right on top of one another. Mumford never cared for these changes. In the 1950s, when he was the architecture critic for *The New Yorker*, he would occasionally leave the magazine's offices in the afternoon and head uptown to his old neighborhood, even though it had "disappeared," and he now felt like a stranger there; the geography of his youth had been changed irrevocably. "New Yorkers over fifty," as he once said, "are all Rip Van Winkles."[9]

As much as Mumford loved the city, however, he was equally drawn, at an early age, to the countryside. As a boy he liked to read accounts of country living in English novels, and when he turned nineteen he would take long walks through the hills and along the back roads of nearby Westchester County on weekend afternoons. As a young boy, from the time he was eight years old to when he was thirteen, he would spend part of the summer on a farm near Bethel, Vermont, owned by a widowed friend of his family, Josephine French. So pleasing were his first memories of country life that he originally began his autobiography not with a sketch of tumultuous turn-of-the-century Manhattan, but with a chapter on his summers in Vermont, a chapter he wrote from the converted farmhouse in Leedsville where he spent the most intensely productive years of his life as a writer.

Mrs. French's farm rested on a stony slope of the White River valley, just across from a marble quarry linked to Bethel by a primitive switchback railroad. It was a world such as Henry David Thoreau had known, rustic but not wilderness, with farms and fields and streams and woods, close to small towns and local industries; and it was a world Mumford would reverence in his book on the art and life of Thoreau's time, *The Golden Day*. Mumford was too indrawn and bookish to explore this environment alone, but his cousin Herbert did teach him how to handle a 22-caliber repeating rifle, and how to hunt woodchucks and squirrels. On this farm he gained his first glimpse of a simpler, more deeply satisfying life than he found in the world of his New York relatives. And here, at age eleven, he fell for a brown-haired local girl named Bertha, to whom he wrote a "hot, impassioned" letter that she never returned.[10]

"The charm of those Vermont summers," he writes in *Sketches from Life*, "has stayed with me, undiminished for more than seventy years. In fantasy it is always a sunlit world, innocent, [and] fragrant."[11] The farm was not a prosperous one, but it was well-maintained, and Mrs. French, a woman of stout character and independent ways (she smoked and would often wear white duck trousers), treated Lewis with special care.

When he wasn't reading, hunting, fishing, or walking around the farm, Lewis would spend hours lying in a hammock, suspended between two maples in front of the house, listening to the rustling of the leaves above him. Initially it was this—the seclusion and quiet of country living—more than its closeness to nature, that drew him, a world ideal for a young daydreamer, and, later, for a writer and thinker. This, he must have thought as a boy of nine, was what sound family living ought to be like, with plenty of food served fresh, plenty of room to roam around in, and plenty of time to spend in idle thought, with everything presided over by a caring person like Mrs. French, "the embodiment of bosomy, motherly qualities, still a little strict about manners, but always kindly."[12]

But the impressions that lingered strongest and longest with him were not those of Mrs. French, but of her brother, Sam Day, who had died just before Lewis started visiting the farm. It had been his farm and his spirit still stalked the grounds. Day was a farmer, an outdoorsman, and something of a village intellectual as well, who was held in heroic regard by his neighbors for his knowledge of the classics and for his experiments with horticulture and new farm and household technology (he was the first in his neighborhood to install an indoor flush toilet—a turd machine, he called it). He had a library of some three hundred books that Lewis Mumford hungrily explored on his summer afternoons, taking particular pleasure in John Ruskin's *Modern Painters*. (This was Mumford's first contact with books of real quality.) Day also had a tiny writing room, just about the size of the study Mumford would make for himself in his Leedsville home. It might be stretching it to say that Sam Day was a kind of mythical father figure for Mumford, but when Mumford was older, and better able to appraise the meaning of these summers, he saw Day, and Mrs. French, as proof that people could still be rooted in their region and be part of a larger universe.[13]

While vacationing in Vermont in the late summer of 1906 Lewis received word from New York that his grandfather had died. When he put aside the telegram and went to his room he remembered his grandfather's last words to him, spoken from his sickbed earlier that summer. "Remember, Lewlie, all the things your mother used to blame me for, she'll blame on you when I am gone. . . . Be good to her and take care of her."[14]

After the death of his grandfather Lewis became closer in spirit to two of his uncles, at an age when young people tend to identify with models outside the home that provide a wider horizon. They possessed qualities he too hoped to possess; their example urged him to achievement.

With his mother, and then on his own, he would visit his great-uncle Louis Siebrecht and his great-aunt Dora, his grandmother's sister, at their modest home on Cumberland Street in Brooklyn, between De Kalb and Nostrand avenues. Here he found a style of life bracingly different from that of his own home; here learning was prized, and the highest standards of personal conduct were expected.

Like Lewis's grandfather, Louis Siebrecht had apprenticed as a waiter in Europe, leaving his native Hanover for Copenhagen, and eventually settling for a time in the broad-boulevarded Paris of Napoleon III. There he learned to speak French fluently and acquired a taste for the novels of George Sand. In New York, where he met and married Dora Hewel, he became steward at the Harmonie Club, an exclusive Jewish men's club. In a thinly fictionalized account of his New York childhood that Mumford later wrote for *The New Yorker*, he merged his Uncle Louis and his grandfather into one figure, his earliest ideal of correct gentlemanly conduct.[15] Ponderously slow-moving and courtly in the extreme, with white hair and a perfectly trimmed mustache and goatee, Louis Siebrecht wore jackets to meals, even on the hottest days, and insisted that all other males at the table do the same: if they didn't he wouldn't sit down to eat. At family dinners at his house, Lewis would find himself adopting his uncle's severely formal table manners, and he would be careful never to speak except when spoken to. That, he knew, was the rule of the household for children.

Uncle Louis read widely and encouraged his favorite nephew to read; he also supported his plans, at age nineteen, to go on for a Ph.D. in philosophy. He thought philosophy an honorable occupation, and was disappointed when Lewis didn't follow through with his plans. Although he was an unusually frugal man—he was known to sift the ashes of his furnace for some salvageable nuggets of anthracite—he took great pride in owning fine things. His nephew admired his concern for the "quality, durability, [and] functional fitness" of everything he purchased for long-term use, and perhaps this influenced, in a subtle way, his own later opinions of architectural excellence.[16]

But it was Uncle Louis's exacting standard of personal rectitude that Lewis most admired. At an early age he heard from his mother a story about his uncle that forever influenced his feelings about him. During the depression of 1893 his uncle's employers at the Harmonie Club called him in and informed him that the wages of all club employees would have to be cut, but that the ownership would make an exception in his case because of his rare abilities. Uncle Louis, however, stiffly insisted that his salary be reduced in the same proportion as the men under him. That gesture later fixed him in his nephew's mind as an example of the highest kind of person.

Lewis came to see his uncle James Schleicher as much the same kind of man. This was the same James Schleicher who, years earlier, as a boarder in the household of Lewis's great-aunt Elvina, had kissed Lewis's mother when she was only sixteen. He was now married to Aunt Elvina, and as a teenager Lewis became quite close to both of them, visiting them now and then at their redbrick house near Logan Square in Philadelphia. Schleicher was an engineer who had made a modest success for himself as a businessman, but he was an engineer, as Lewis remembers him, with the soul of a poet. He had been well-trained in the classics: he read Latin and Greek, and enjoyed the fables of La Fontaine. And it was he and his wife who gave Lewis his first copy of the works of Shakespeare. They both hoped he would become a writer, but one who would not, as his uncle warned him, "cater to the approbation of [the] masses & majorities." From his Uncle James, Lewis got an early sense of the "aristocratic ideal" that would surface occasionally in his later writing, the view that public life should be the province, as his uncle once told him, "of [a] right-thinking and knowing minority."[17]

Such strong role models were doubly important to Mumford as a young boy, for he found almost no human inspiration in his early education. Elementary school, for him, was a tedious grind. His first teachers in the succession of West Side public schools he attended were men and women who had grown gray in the New York educational system; almost all were kindly and caring, but entirely without imagination. Drill and discipline were their pedagogical imperatives. Every lesson was preceded by an order: "Attention! Desks down! Hands on desk, place!" Sitting ramrod straight at his confining wooden desk, scrubbed and neatly dressed, with his hands behind his back (the correct posture when not reading or writing), Mumford remembers feeling like a prisoner sentenced for a crime he had not committed.[18]

Like most creative people, he had little liking for such rote, but he submitted without complaint to this routine, never misbehaving and receiving almost straight A's, even though no subject greatly absorbed him. Pampered by his teachers and driven by an inner unwillingness to be second-best at anything he tried, he skipped three grammar school grades and graduated in 1909, the valedictorian of his class. Small and frail, with piercing brown eyes and a thin, piping voice that had not yet broken, he dutifully memorized and delivered a short speech written by his teachers. "Mumford," his favorite teacher told him just before the graduation exercises, "you can do anything you have a mind to do."[19]

At this point in his life Lewis dreamed of becoming an electrical engineer, and he was drawn to New York's Stuyvesant High School, which had a reputation for preparing students for careers in the sciences and engineering. Mumford was brought up in the great age of American invention, and his earliest heroes were Edison, Marconi, and the Wright brothers, innovators who were constantly in the news. At the same time, his reading interests turned from Horatio Alger to H. G. Wells, whose utopias envisioned a caste organization of samurai, benevolent technicians who would use science's godlike powers for social improvement. Along with almost everyone else, Mumford expected much of the new century. Science and democracy seemed about to usher in a permanent period of world peace and universal prosperity; and technology, in all its wondrous applications, from the airplane to the automobile, had given man newfound freedom and mastery. In every sense of the word, Lewis Mumford was a child of the new century. Though the new breakthroughs in physics were still in the future, he vividly remembers his high school physics teacher holding up a pencil before the class and saying: "If we knew how to unlock the energies in this carbon, a few pencils would be enough to run the subways of New York."[20]

By the age of thirteen Mumford had made his first awkward imitation of a biplane modeled after the one that Orville and Wilbur Wright had assembled in a workshop on the sand dunes of Kill Devil Hills, but his consuming interest was radio, which was then called wireless telegraphy. With the help of an instrument maker his family doctor introduced him to, he built a crude wireless transmitter from catalogue designs, and he and a school chum tried to send messages back and forth from their apartments a block or so apart. It did not matter to them that they had not mastered Morse code. The excitement was in the effort to build an apparatus that could, by some miraculous process they struggled to understand, send messages through space. For these enthusiastic experimenters "the medium was the message," the struggle its own reward.[21]

As a student at Stuyvesant, Mumford became an avid reader of popular technical magazines, and at the age of fifteen he had an article accepted by *Modern Electrics* on new breakthroughs in radio receivers. It was eight lines long, and for his efforts he received his first royalty check, for 25 cents. This early interest in technology was sustained by his introduction at Stuyvesant to basic technical arts: wood and metal turning, casting, forging, pattern making, and carpentry. He liked to work with machines and to watch how well-made machines worked. This fascination with technology carried over into his entire life. When he became a writer and traveled about in this country and Europe, he rarely passed up an opportunity to tour a factory, power plant, or technical museum. He also liked to talk shop with architects and engineers, and to inspect their projects with them while they were still in the construction stage.[22]

This interest in technology led him in another, not unrelated direction. In his Stuyvesant classes, when his mind would drift from the subject at hand, he would dream of constructing imaginary machines such as the kind he had read about in the fantasies of H. G. Wells. And there is not all that much difference between constructing imaginary machines and constructing imaginary societies. Mumford's first published article was about building electrical receivers; his first published book was about building utopia.

For young Lewis Mumford, however, Stuyvesant offered more than an absorbing technical education; it opened to him a different side of city life. The school was located on the Lower East Side, the heart of New York's immigrant quarter, the home of Tammany Hall, Tom Starkey's saloon, and the painted prostitutes of Forsyth Street. This was a world apart from Mumford's largely middle- and lower-middle-class West Side neighborhood, where most of his schoolmates were second-generation Irish or German, and where almost everyone spoke "plain Manhattanese." At Stuyvesant he encountered the fast-talking, streetwise sons of Jewish greenhorns from Poland, Russia, and Rumania, boys whose brash, aggressive spirit made him feel "like a sick goldfinch among a flock of greedy sparrows." They were quick to grab their food in the school lunch line, fast with the right answers in the classroom, and could play circles around most of the other boys in basketball and other playground games. Mumford found them just "a little overwhelming."[23]

He was thin and pale, and very much a "gentleman," and these tougher kids often picked on him. His initials were L.C., for Lewis Charles, so they began calling him Elsie. By the end of his freshman year, however, he had become friends with a number of these boys, who came to respect the way he threw himself into sports and physical games. He was so intent at proving himself physically that he would run in races with other boys with his head flung back and mouth wide open, in imitation of the track stars whose photographs he studied in the newspaper, not realizing that "their tilted heads and open mouths showed that the race was over."[24]

After school Mumford would sometimes spend his carfare on candy and walk home with some other West Side boys. Their route took them diagonally across Manhattan; usually they walked up Broadway, but sometimes they would cut through the exposed railroad yards of the New York Central and across Central Park. The city was then undergoing a tremendous physical change. The completion, in 1902, of Daniel H. Burnham's Flatiron Building on

Fifth Avenue at Broadway, the world's first freestanding skyscraper, announced this new era in the city's history. In the following ten to fifteen years, a citywide subway system was built; four major bridges over the East River were completed; automobiles and bright green double-decker buses began to crowd the streets; and work went forward on the new Grand Central Terminal at Forty-second Street opposite Park Avenue, and on the New York Public Library at Fifth Avenue and Forty-second Street, enormous construction sites Mumford would pass by on his way home from Stuyvesant.

New York was fast becoming a city of tall towers, but Mumford's memory of that earlier New York remained forever fixed on the "openness of the midtown district then, its low buildings and the vast unbuilt spaces on Park Avenue," which had a wide grassy strip down the middle that served as a pedestrian promenade.[25] The cross streets he walked on his way home from high school were lined with unbroken rows of two- and three-story brick or brownstone residences, with high front stoops; and on the street corners, raggedly dressed newsboys hawked their papers, filling the afternoon air with their piercing cries of "Extra! Extra! Read all about it!"

When he entered high school Mumford's political views were thoroughly conservative, a conservatism, however, that matched his native temperament more than his knowledge of public affairs, for he knew and cared very little about politics. Stuyvesant did a lot to change him. Many of his teachers were young men who had graduated from progressive schools like Cornell and the University of Wisconsin, and they exposed their students to socialism and to the struggles between capital and labor. Some of them even admitted to being socialists, and although Mumford remained resistant to socialism his teachers' thoughtful criticisms of capitalism started him thinking about issues of social justice, and for a time, in his sophomore year, he aspired to be a politician, a reformer like Teddy Roosevelt and the progressive governor of New Jersey, Woodrow Wilson.

Almost all of Mumford's teachers at Stuyvesant were excited about their subjects, and they excited in him a passionate interest in learning for the sheer enjoyment of it. For the first time in his young life, he actually looked forward to going to school, and, on his own, he began to read voraciously. Quite the best of these challenging young teachers, in his view, was Thomas Bates, his freshman

English instructor, a solemn, intense young man with freckles and flaming red hair. Bates took a strong personal interest in Mumford, and after hearing Lewis read one of his compositions, he prophesied a career for him in literature, as a novelist or playwright, and began to guide him in that direction, telling him, at one point, that he had "the gift of genius."[26] He encouraged Mumford and several of his classmates to write, produce, and act in a school play, often staying after school to discuss their project with them. And it was Thomas Bates who introduced Mumford to George Bernard Shaw, who became one of the inspirations of his adolescence.

Mumford would grow to regret the hold that Shaw had on him as a young man, feeling that Shaw's level-eyed rationalism and coolly controlled sexuality had a damaging influence on his early sexual and marital life, and that he had caused him, for a time, to undervalue the passional drives that are behind most so-called rational actions.[27] But for a time Mumford fell completely under the spell of Shaw, reading almost all of his plays (his favorite was *Man and Superman*) and trying to write like him. He was attracted by Shaw's cerebral cleverness and devastating wit, but, most of all, by his disdain for conventional morality and family life, indeed of most Victorian attitudes about correct behavior between men and women. This was the Shaw who dismissed sexual pleasure as childish, and who regarded the family as a hindrance to a young man's creativity, the detached observer who, writing to H. G. Wells on the occasion of his wife's death, urged him to go and witness her cremation, for he had found his own wife's cremation a most fascinating spectacle.[28] Shaw's clever satires on love and family life, where the young male protagonist, often a promising writer, struggles to escape the smothering influence of a woman, be it his mother or a sweetheart, further darkened Mumford's estimation of family life, feelings he retained until he was married and had children of his own.

Through Mumford's early interest in Shaw and the theater, he became the most active member in Stuyvesant High School's tiny dramatic society, and his amateur productions helped to pull him into the school's social life. He met new friends; he became interested in tennis and was named captain of the school's tennis team in his senior year; he helped to edit the *Caliper*, the school's monthly paper; and he even became a cheerleader at the basketball games, and covered the football games as a sports reporter for the *Caliper.* By his sophomore year he was also writing poetry and short stories on his own, and doing pencil sketches and watercolors in his spare time, for he found that he had some ability as an artist. As he became more absorbed in school and school-related activities, however, his grades dropped. He simply did not have enough time for his new interests and for schoolwork as well; and he also discovered that he had little aptitude for mathematics, flunking a basic course in algebra. In fact, he did well consistently in only one subject— English—and his grades would not have gotten him into a respectable college today. He had made progress as a writer, however, even if he was not yet sure what kind of writer he wanted to be, and by the time he was ready to graduate from Stuyvesant he was sure of one thing: he did not want to be an engineer.[29]

Mumford's earliest essays and verses give no hint whatsoever of his later literary talents. They collapse under the weight of his self-consciousness and do not even possess the virtue of brevity. The only attribute of a writer he possessed early on in his life was a hungering desire to become one.

He also had the constant encouragement of Thomas Bates and some of his other English teachers. They were tough-minded but encouraging critics who continued to show an interest in his progress after he left Stuyvesant. The person who had the strongest influence on Mumford's decision to pursue a career in literature, however, was a young girl he fell in love with at the age of fifteen, Beryl Morse, or Ted, as her friends called her. In trying to please her in his letters by being clever, witty, and worldly, he found himself "caring for words and seeking to use them more effectively." She was his first great love, and she played such an important part in his life that he devotes an entire chapter of his autobiography to her. In an unpublished section of this chapter he describes his meeting her as the beginning of his "awakening."[30]

Beryl Morse first entered Mumford's life when they were both ten years old. She was part of a small group of boys and girls who played games—tag, cops and robbers, and jumping and running contests—on the dirt footpaths of Central Park, and she was, even then, beautiful and gracefully athletic, a child actress who played Wendy in a popular Broadway production of *Peter Pan*. She was always ringed by admiring boys who, behind her back, called her Beer Bottles because she had such shapely legs. Mumford fell for her from the first time he set eyes on her, but was too timid to approach her. She became part of his adolescent fantasies, however, and he had a secret and strong desire to make love to her, even though he had absolutely no idea yet how a man and a woman did so.[31]

He ran into Beryl again when they were fifteen years old. She was tossing a ball with another girl near the old grass tennis courts in Central Park, at Ninety-sixth Street, where Mumford practiced his game nearly every summer afternoon with a gang of tennis regulars. She had become by then, he says, "one of those ruthless beauties who are never at ease until they put five or six men simultaneously in a state of torture." She was tall and shapely, and had flowing brown hair, full lips, and large gray-green eyes. She was still something of a tomboy, but she had poise and "lady-like grace"; and she was more daring than any girl Mumford had ever encountered, entering tango contests for prize money and being the first girl in her high school to wear a one-piece bathing suit at a public beach. Not long after they met she became a popular model for magazine illustrators and artists, and her picture appeared on the cover of a number of national magazines.[32]

When Mumford finally raised the courage to approach her, he found that she had a serious side that belied her striking good looks and her carefree manner. And here, he must have sensed immediately, was his chance, his only chance as an ungainly boy with a bad acne problem and ill-fitting clothing, to get closer to her. Shortly after they met they began talking about writing, literature, art and the theater, and soon became close friends. She liked to sketch and paint, she confided to him, and she composed poems and essays, several of which were published and won prizes in *St. Nicholas*, a somewhat sophisticated young people's magazine. To his surprise, Mumford discovered that her reading was well in advance of his. At a time when he was still making his way through Dickens and Cooper, she had moved on to Balzac and Dostoyevsky. She also had a command of Latin and spoke with impeccable diction, even though she came from a broken home as impoverished as his own. Like him, she lived with her mother in a cramped, run-down apartment they could barely afford.

Beryl had not yet learned to play tennis, but she came to the Central Park courts anyway, to meet her friends and to lounge on the grassy bank behind the courts and talk with her new "pal," Lew, as he was known to his friends. When they couldn't meet at the courts they wrote deeply earnest letters to each other, and more often than not they wrote even though they had seen each other earlier in the day. He was, she told him that summer, her "dearest friend," and he read more into that innocent declaration than she probably intended. He knew he was in love with her, even though he was too unsure of himself to ever tell her so; and that summer he was certain that she loved him. 33

The year he met Beryl Morse, he writes in his autobiography, was "one of the most intense, the most emotionally absorbed, the most rewarding years of my life, though streaked with painful jealousy and adolescent despair." 34 Beryl lived on Morningside Heights, and every afternoon he would walk her part of the way home from the courts. He even began going to church that summer because of her. She thought that church was a lovely place to spend part of a Sunday morning, and he sheepishly went along with her to services, just for the extra chance to be near her. Beryl aroused all of his awakening sexual instincts, but he didn't once try to kiss her, and she was too coy to make the first move. Theirs, he told her, was what writers called a platonic friendship (with the help of a *Century Dictionary* he became first acquainted with Plato). That is how things stood until the end of the summer, when Beryl returned from a vacation with the news that she had fallen in love with another boy, a little older and surely more emotionally mature than her "Lew." 35

He tried to cover his disappointment with sarcasm; she tried to comfort him with assurances that he would always be her truest friend. And they remained close for the next five years or so, during which time she had a succession of boyfriends and admirers. Although he didn't care for the peripheral role she had assigned him in her life, as her "comrade" and intellectual confidant, meeting with her regularly to talk about books and ideas, and clinging to him occasionally to get her bearings when her life became too compli-cated, he grudgingly filled that role. He had no choice if he wanted to stay close to her. All along, however, he secretly hoped, and for a time managed to convince himself, that she would someday become his lover, and perhaps even his wife. For the next five or six years she remained the focus of all his desires and dreams.

When he entered the Evening Division of New York's City College in the fall after graduating from Stuyvesant High School, he and Beryl would meet once a week at her apartment to talk over the new books and ideas he began taking an interest in. Before going there Lewis would put ice on his cheeks to make them red, hoping to distract attention from his unsightly acne, and he would then squeeze his neck, where his acne was most pronounced, into a high, tight collar. He usually arrived at Beryl's at seven-thirty and always left exactly at ten o'clock, nervously checking his pocket watch every five minutes or so in the hour before ten.

And what would he do, alone in a room with that "voluptuously cold creature," his whole body alert with expectation? While she lounged on the couch, her long hair thrown back over a pillow, he would pace back and forth in front of her, repeating a class lecture he had heard earlier that week or reading one of his stories to her. Sometimes she would look at him teasingly, pat the sofa cushion next to her, and he would sit down beside her and they would read together. "A hundred times I would be seized with an impulse to kiss her, . . . to embrace her, to throw her down on the [couch] and ruffle her hair and clothes," he described these evenings to a later lover who helped break down his self-censuring behavior with women, "and every time, with a constancy that would have pleased the saints in heaven, or rather made them envious, I turned the temptation aside." There he would be, every week, "wanting everything and daring nothing."[36]

Although he rarely felt good about himself afterwards, he always looked forward to these evenings with Beryl. When she would write to tell him that she had to break an appointment with him for the sake of what she used to call a more "hectic" evening, he would become morose and sullenly jealous. Several times after she canceled one of their evenings together, or he learned about one or another of her new suitors, he told her that he never wanted to see her again. He always came back, however, usually after receiving a note from her telling him how much she admired and respected him, and needed to have him as a friend. He hated the way she seemed to control his life (he gave up sketching temporarily that summer and

decided he would never be an artist when she told him that he had
no talent in that direction), but remained her friend in the hope of
eventually capturing her by an appeal to her maturer instincts.[37] He
was so intent in his quest that, later in their friendship, he would get
up at five in the morning to play tennis with her on the courts near
her apartment where she practiced every morning before going to
work as a model.

He never really had a chance of winning her. For one thing, she
was emotionally and sexually more mature than he was. (What he
needed to do, she told him at one point, is "to get to know a nice
chorus girl or two *intimately*.")[38] For another, they were temperamental opposites. She was extroverted and adventurous, a constant
challenge to his cautious, superserious ways, and during the time
they were close he became even more solemn and indrawn, sometimes to the point of being downright lugubrious. He also became,
to Beryl's annoyance, her insistent superego, a role he would play
with a number of other women in his future. He warned her that she
was wasting her talents by giving so much time to her "frivolous"
social life; this was making her shallow and superficial and "a little
hard."[39] While it would be wrong to make too much of this, he
surely saw parallels between Beryl's endless pursuit of her "hectic"
life and his own mother's near-total absorption in card playing,
visiting, and the horse races, diversions that pulled both of the
women he loved further away from him. In a pattern that resembled
his mother's, Beryl seemed to him to be ready to be friends with
anyone who would rescue her for a few hours from her poverty-
constricted home life.

When he related to Beryl in this priggish way—as a censoring
conscience—she would sharply remind him that they "were still
kids" and had plenty of time to get serious about things. For now,
she wanted to be popular, to "go everywhere and see everything
[and] . . . to have one fellow crazy over me after another . . . ," she
wrote him when he became jealous about one of her boyfriends.
"My grandmother may have been expected to choose the fellow she
liked best when *she* was sixteen, but I don't think it's exactly required
by law for me to do so now." Mumford, as one of his high school
teachers told him, talked and acted, at times, like a "disillusioned
man of sixty."[40]

But Beryl did help to change him, however slowly. She taught him how to act around girls and to have more confidence in himself around other people. His Shavian heroes were rude and often downright inconsiderate, but she browbeat him into opening doors for her and offering her his hand when she stepped down from a streetcar. She even tried to teach him to dance, but after holding her in his arms for a few minutes "I boorishly begged off in the middle of the lesson," he recalls, "[because] my penis [was] roused to a point of . . . exotic delight that almost became pain." She even helped him to improve his grammar and diction. "So in the sunlight of her smile," he writes in a verse about his love for her at age nineteen, "I budded into a flower; Unconscious of her influence, And prideful of my power."[41]

When Beryl became engaged, in 1916, to a young businessman who voted Republican and subscribed to the *Saturday Evening Post*, Mumford was devastated. At first he blamed himself; he was always talking with her about marriage in general, and what Shaw thought about marriage, but he had not had the courage to step forward and ask her to marry him. This, he tried to convince himself, was because he was afraid she might have accepted, and then demanded that he give up writing and settle into a steady job and a family routine. He had lost her because of his timidity; and now he tried to console himself with the delusion (the product of his reading) that he actually felt relieved that he had avoided "the trap" of marriage, escaping a woman who, like a character in a Shaw play, wanted to entrap and dominate her "prey." "None but the brave deserve to escape the fair," he closes a little Shavian skit he put together after learning of Beryl's engagement.[42]

Surely he must have known that she was not prepared to marry him, and that she didn't love him in the way that he loved her. He simply couldn't face the truth. Actually he *had* already informed her that he wanted to marry her "eventually." When he said this to her one summer evening on the street in front of her Morningside Heights apartment, she asked him to go around the corner and pick up a box of ice cream. When he returned they went up on the tin and gravel roof of her building, and there, eating ice cream from a white paper carton, she told him that they would always be the best of friends. He knew instantly what that meant, and as he left her apartment that evening and headed home to West Ninety-fourth Street he had a vague premonition that this might be, symbolically, their final parting.[43]

He wrote Beryl several friendly letters after she married and moved to suburban Philadelphia, but she wrote back that her husband would not permit her to carry on a correspondence with another man. Unsatisfied as a housewife in a place she called "The City of Brotherly Bores," Beryl divorced her husband after they had two children and ran off with the motion picture director Gregory La Cava. She hesitated to marry him, however, before she had introduced him to Mumford. At this time Mumford was married, and when he and Sophia met Beryl and her new fiancé they all went to see one of La Cava's pictures that was playing in New York, a comedy so crushingly dull that Mumford remembers fearing for their marriage "on that ground alone." But he crossed his fingers and gave Beryl his "blessing" anyway.44

That marriage did not work either, and the next time Mumford saw Beryl was in 1931 when she was living in New York with her mother. He ran into her at an art exhibition, and she invited him to her mother's apartment on Central Park West for part of a morning to talk about what had happened to both of them since they last met. They had a delightful few hours together. Mumford found her, at age thirty-six, as beautiful as at nineteen. He also thought that he was mature enough now to be her lover. As it happened, however, he had just begun an affair with an attractive single woman he had met at the offices of his publisher, Harcourt Brace. Meeting Beryl now, moreover, he had the feeling that life had caught up with them too late. Still, as he left her apartment that morning, after kissing her in parting, the first time he had ever done so, he had a fantasy of having three women simultaneously as lovers. In the following weeks he phoned Beryl several times to ask her to meet him, but each time he was told by the maid that she was out, and she made no effort after this to get in touch with him. He later claimed that he felt relieved, as he had much earlier in his life, by Beryl's apparent rejection of him. This time he wasn't deluding himself: tempted as he was, he knew "such a triple tension could not be maintained without undue suffering through any single lifetime."45

When he next met Beryl, toward the end of the 1930s, she was remarried and living in Hollywood. She and her new husband were Marxists active in left-wing causes. She had, after years of psychoanalysis, found some purpose in her life, although her politics struck Mumford as naïve and doctrinaire. This time, as they had lunch together at the Chatham, he was not tempted by her. He had just gone through a marriage-threatening crisis, and Beryl was no longer the striking beauty he had fallen in love with.

Four years later he saw her in San Diego, where he was giving a lecture to a group of teachers. When it was over several people approached the podium to talk with him. As they drifted away he noticed a heavyset elderly woman, with a round red face, standing a few yards from him. "Lew," she said as she moved hesitatingly toward him, "don't you know me? It's me, Ted!" At that moment he realized that she had become the very image of her mother. His Beryl was gone, and his embarrassingly long silence told her that, too. They never met again.[46]

He never got over her, however. Even into his fifties he would talk about her around the house so often that both his wife and daughter would tease him about it. And it remained extremely important for him to believe that he had played an equally strong part in her life.

In *Sketches from Life* he recounts an incident that gives the reader the impression that he had. At a party he attended in the late 1930s he met a psychiatrist who had analyzed Beryl. This doctor had had too much to drink, and when he was introduced to Mumford he said loudly: "Not Lewis Mumford! . . . I know you! You're the Lewis who used to keep popping into one of my patient's dreams. Mrs. La Cava; you knew her once, yes? You meant a lot to her." But not as much, he secretly suspected, as she had meant to him. He would go to his grave, he remarked toward the end of his life, wishing that he could have an opportunity to go back in time and spend an afternoon with the ravishing girl he had known at age nineteen. He would tell her how strongly he had felt about her, and he would want to know exactly how she had felt about him.[47]

3

A Jovian Father

[Geddes's] work and his philosophy have sprung out of the
fullness of his life, as Hermes the traveler; as Apollo the
thinker; as Ares, the husband and father; as Hercules, the
cleanser of the slums of Edinburgh, and now, at the summit
of his life, as Jove, the wise parent of spirit-children scattered about the world in New York, Bombay, Calcutta,
Indore, Jerusalem, Edinburgh, Montpellier, London, and
where not.

—LEWIS MUMFORD

When Lewis Mumford graduated from Stuyvesant High School his
course was clear: he would be a writer. Columbia University's new
Pulitzer School of Journalism had just opened its doors, and he was
drawn to its innovative curriculum. With some professional training
he might be able to succeed as an independent writer, or perhaps
eventually as a playwright. The problem, however, was that he had
neither the money nor the grades to enter Columbia. He was convinced, nonetheless, that if he could somehow raise the tuition he
would be admitted on the basis of his promise as a writer. At this
point, without consulting Lewis, his mother wrote to Jacob Mack,
asking him to pay for her son's education. His family was honor-
bound, she told him, to help this eager boy who carried their blood.
But Jacob Mack flatly refused, saying that the city of New York had
a perfectly fine tuition-free college for all who qualified.[1]

For some reason, Mumford had not thought to apply to City College in his senior year at Stuyvesant, so now he decided to try to make it for a time as a newspaperman, saving enough money to pay for a year of college, and then trusting to luck and savings from summer jobs to get him through three more years of school. Newspaper work would also give him the worldly experience he felt he needed if his writing was to improve, for by this time he realized that most of what he knew about life he knew from books.

Mumford tried for a time to land a job on the *Morning Telegraph*, whose city editor, Shep Friedman, was a friend of the family. Mumford was only seventeen at the time, but he was eager and doggedly persistent. He would stop by the *Telegraph*'s office regularly, late in the afternoon, just before Friedman "had started the heavy business or the heavy drinking of the day." Occasionally Friedman would ask him to join him for a few beers at the corner bar, and although Friedman wouldn't recommend Mumford to anyone at the *Telegraph*, he did give him several notes of introduction, scribbled hastily on scraps of paper, to city editors at other newspapers. After six frustrating months Mumford finally adjusted his ambitions and went to work on the *Evening Telegram* as a copy boy, with the expectation of rising rapidly to cub reporter. All the while he took courses at the Evening Division of City College of New York, where he had enrolled in September 1912.[2]

At the *Telegram* Mumford was assigned the early-morning shift, reporting for work at 4 a.m. He would rise before three, make his own breakfast, and take the Sixth Avenue El to Herald Square, while reading a few pages of Plato or William James as his train sped through the sleeping city.

The *Telegram* was still presided over by James Gordon Bennett, Jr., the son of the founder and editor of the New York *Herald*. Now a man well past his prime, Bennett, who had originated the "exclusive" news story and had sent the Stanley expedition to Africa to find the explorer David Livingstone, would show up only occasionally at his office. When he did, however, everything was in waiting for him. An ice chest in the city room was filled every day just in case he would stop in and demand ice for his champagne; and in his private office, now more a shrine than an active working place, his beautiful alpaca coat hung on a hook—"waiting." The Old Boy's spirit haunted the place: no one would dare refer to Teddy Roosevelt, Bennett's hated enemy, by name; around the office he was referred to simply as "The Third Termer."

At first Mumford found it exhilarating just being in the clamorous surroundings of a busy metropolitan newspaper office. He would begin his day by fetching beer, coffee, and egg sandwiches for the rewrite men; then he would set out the copy in the stale air of the city room. Sometimes he would do a little rewriting himself, if one of the rewrite men arrived too late or too hung over; and occasionally he would be sent out to cover a late-breaking story in the neighborhood. "But a sewer explosion or a burning mattress was about all that came my way, and my pride suffered as my boredom grew." So he quit the job after two months, never again to seek "Life" in a newspaper office.3

The Evening Session at City College was an altogether different experience, and it changed his life profoundly. The September following his high school graduation, while still searching for newspaper work, Mumford had come across an announcement in the newspaper that the Evening Session of City College was about to begin its fall semester, and he enrolled at once, after passing the entrance exam. Attending classes at night would not interfere with any work he might find, and there was no required curriculum, so he could choose the subjects he was most interested in—English literature, politics, psychology, and philosophy. "With that," he recalls, "began my first great awakening to a whole world I had never explored, hardly even suspected. . . . This superworld of the mind, I promptly discovered, was what I had been waiting for all my days."4

The recently established Evening Session enrolled only about five hundred students, all of them male and most of them part-timers. Admission was by competitive examination, and the number of applicants far exceeded the number accepted. The Evening School had the intimacy and intellectual esprit of an exceptional small college, but it was a small college set in one of the world's most stimulating urban environments.

The new City College campus was built in the early 1900s on a magnificent site—a high, rocky bluff on Hamilton Heights looking out over the borough of Manhattan, with its new skyscrapers reaching for the clouds. (The old main campus was at Lexington Avenue and Twenty-third Street.) This was to be, in the words of its president, J. H. Finley, "the Acropolis of the City, its sacred enclosure . . . , like the crowned hill of ancient Athens."⁵ In line with this lofty conception, graduating students took the ephebic oath at commencement, pledging like the ephebi, the newly enrolled citizens of ancient Athens, to serve their city to their utmost ability.

The tiny campus—comprising only four city blocks—even today gives the appearance of being much larger, with the five main buildings laid out to form a handsomely symmetrical quadrangle, in the style of Oxford University. The main buildings are late English Gothic, constructed of a rough gray Manhattan schist, quarried from a nearby subway excavation, and are trimmed with a brilliant white terra-cotta. "The architecture," Mumford recalls, "had a powerful effect when one climbed the hill past the Hebrew Orphan Asylum through the deepening October twilight and saw the college buildings, in their dark stone masses and white terra-cotta quoins and moldings, rising like a collection of crystals above the formless rocks of the hill."⁶

The students in the Evening Session weren't ordinary undergraduates. They were mostly mature men with a questing, aggressive approach to learning and they spoiled Mumford for any other kind of student. This, to his mind, was the best kind of education, with students learning as much from their peers as they did from their professors. One of the night students, an employee at the Metropolitan Museum, stimulated Mumford's interest in Emerson; another, Irwin Granich, a tough Chrystie Street radical who later wrote a proletarian classic, *Jews Without Money*, under the name Michael Gold, gave him his first exposure to Marxism and the workers' movement. Although Mumford never adopted the creed he would occasionally stamp envelopes with Gold at the Second Avenue headquarters of the Industrial Workers of the World.⁷

Many of the students were men of considerable experience in the world. One was a maritime lawyer; another a South American consul. There were also businessmen, engineers, doctors, lawyers, and newspapermen. "There is something amoeboid about the ordinary undergraduate," Mumford would observe years later, "but we night students had a shape and a backbone and a definite point of view. Our discussions were battles, and though we often lived to change sides, there was nothing tentative or hesitating in our espousals; we did not suffer from the academic disease of evasive 'open-mindedness.'"[8]

After the conclusion of Evening Session classes, groups of students would crowd around their professors and fire questions at them; and sometimes Mumford and a band of his fellow students would be invited to an instructor's home nearby to continue a heated classroom argument. At the close of the evening they'd all march down Riverside Drive, locked in intense discussion about Spinoza and Kant, Berkeley and Plato. On Saturday and Sunday afternoons Mumford and a group of students who shared similar literary interests would cross the Hudson River on the 125th Street ferry and take long walks along the almost unspoiled Palisades, following footpaths and dirt roads for some fifteen or twenty miles through hamlets and small towns, "arguing fiercely, cracking jokes, singing lustily, full of animal spirits."[9] Sometimes they'd even plan their walks on topographical maps.

Several of these weekend hikers became Mumford's first lasting friends; the one he became closest to was Jerome Lachenbruch, an aspiring writer seven years his senior. He and Mumford shared a number of common interests and a common German background, and on Saturdays they would frequent the German theaters in Yorkville. "He impressed me," Lachenbruch recalls Mumford in his student days, "as a shy, searching lad . . . , a young man looking for a friend."[10] Mumford found in Lachenbruch not only a good friend but a much-needed older brother. He urged Mumford to pursue a career in writing; and he read almost everything Mumford wrote in these years, dispensing criticism of sometimes penetrating quality.[11]

At City College a new universe opened up to Mumford, the world of Plato, Aristotle, Descartes, and William James; and he could not get enough of it. For a good part of the next two years he spent almost every weekday evening in the massive Main Building of the college, either in class or in the intimate oak-paneled library, and he became greatly influenced by three professors in particular: Earle Fenton Palmer in English literature, J. Salwyn Shapiro in politics, and John Pickett Turner in philosophy. Palmer introduced him to English poetry; Turner to Plato and William James; and Shapiro, a devoted student of the Progressive historian James Harvey Robinson, turned him to the study of politics, sociology, and social history. All three men, in their own way, impressed upon him an educational fundamental he would never forget: that "knowledge," as he wrote in his notebook at the time, "does not consist in knowing the things you know: it consists in knowing the things you don't know."[12]

Like all memorable teachers, these men left a profoundly personal imprint. They stirred Mumford as much by their physical presence as by what they had to say in their lectures. It was their human side that Mumford would remember long after the pages of his class notebooks had faded to a dusty yellow. "I and mine do not convince by arguments," an older Mumford liked to quote Whitman, in recalling his student days. "We convince by our presence."[13]

These were professors who cared passionately about ideas, and who carried that passion into the classroom. Mumford remembers Palmer, a tiny bespectacled man, taking his class through Pancoast's anthology of English poetry, as he danced around the podium. But it was John Pickett Turner, a bulky, handsome man with deep-set eyes and an intent manner, who impressed him the most. A philosophic pragmatist, Turner took William James's view that all ideas are rooted in experience and transformed it into a gimmick to enliven his classes, drawing the case histories in his psychology class from his own personal and sexual experience. It was Turner who made Mumford want to be a philosopher; and since Turner was a pragmatist, a disciple of William James and John Dewey, Mumford, too, took that philosophy as his own for a time.[14]

Relations between students and professors at the Evening Session were unusually close. In imitation of the monastic practice, professors referred to students as Brother rather than Mister, and Mumford developed warm friendships with several of his professors and kept in touch with them long after he left City College, particularly with Shapiro and Turner. When Mumford met Shapiro in the early 1950s, for what was to be the last time, that aged professor—his total devotion to the lives of his students undiminished—launched into a two-hour critique of Mumford's recently published book, *The Conduct of Life*.

Mumford encountered a number of other excellent professors after he left the Evening Session and enrolled as a day student, but the teacher who touched him most directly was one he would not meet face-to-face for almost a decade. In Patrick Geddes, the Scot-

tish botanist, sociologist, and town planner, young Mumford found
his master.

The day Mumford came upon the work of Geddes in the biology
department's library at City College his life was changed. From this
point on Patrick Geddes became the single most important personal
influence on Mumford's development, "a Jovian father," as Mumford once described him, "stern and practically omniscient."[15]

Geddes had begun his professional career as a biologist, a student
of Thomas Henry Huxley, Darwin's "Bulldog," but his flashing
mind and astonishing range of interests carried him into the fields of
sociology, urban planning, religion, census analysis, anthropology,
economics, paleontology, and Eastern culture. Like Socrates,
Geddes was primarily an oral teacher, an incessant talker, barely
audible sometimes, his rapid-fire soliloquies muffled by his thick
red beard and mustache. And he was hopelessly disorganized, leaving behind hundreds of unfinished projects and tasks. Ideas flew off
him like sparks from a fireball. Many of his most original ideas were
picked up and carried further by others, for Geddes had neither the
patience nor the discipline to fully develop them. "I am like the
cuckoo bird that lays her eggs in other birds' nests," he once told
Mumford, and then flys off, giving them the credit for hatching
them. "The main thing is that the egg should develop—not that the
cuckoo's ego should be gratified."[16]

What we know of Geddes's ideas is largely contained in a series of
rapidly written books, pamphlets, and planning reports, most of
them dictated to his secretary and stenographer. Geddes never
wrote the opus that would bring together his life's work, but many
of those he reached ranked him one of the outstanding minds of his
age.

Like so many other remarkable Victorians, Geddes learned as
much from the world around him as from the books he read. His
interest in biology, in living plants and animals, had been awakened
by walks with his father in the scenic countryside of his native
Perthshire, leisurely rambles not unlike Mumford's Sunday strolls
through upper Manhattan with his German grandfather. Geddes
carried this delight in the outdoors, and this emphasis upon field
experience, into all his studies of the biological and social world.

He began his formal scientific training under Huxley at the Royal School of Mines in South Kensington. Later he worked under Lacaze-Duthiers in Paris and Haeckel in Jena; and for a time, in Sir John Burdon-Sanderson's London laboratories, where he met Charles Darwin, whose excitement about the natural world made an unforgettable impression upon him.

As a young man Geddes established himself as one of the most promising botanists in Great Britain, but his biological career was cut short at age twenty-five by a mysterious eye ailment incurred while doing field research in Mexico. Unable to use the microscope for extended periods of time, he became increasingly absorbed in social and economic questions. While he never left botany completely, Geddes spent most of his time in the years between 1888 and the outbreak of World War I in a tenement district of his adopted city of Edinburgh, where he launched a campaign of slum improvements that opened the way for his second career as a town planner and sociologist. The books and pamphlets he authored in these Edinburgh years outlined an approach to city studies and town revitalization that had an enormous influence on Mumford.[17]

A pioneer of environmental studies, of town and regional planning, and, above all, of ecological thinking, Geddes was the first English-speaking sociologist to draw attention to the formative role of the city in the process of cultural evolution. His books and reports on urban development, based upon experience in surveying and planning over fifty cities in Scotland, Palestine, India, and Pakistan, fired Mumford's interest in urban studies and taught him a new way of looking at cities, an approach based upon direct observation and a biologist's sensitivity to organic relationships.

A disciple of the French empirical sociologist Frédéric Le Play, whose work he discovered while studying biology at the Sorbonne, Geddes developed an observational sociology that studied communities as an outgrowth of the organic interaction between place (*lieu*), work (*travail*), and family (*famille*). A legitimate sociology, Geddes maintained, had to draw its theory from firsthand observation of human communities, just as Darwin, the speculative biologist, had founded his great explanatory idea upon exhaustive field study in the natural world.

Geddes never began a planning project without first spending at least a week wandering on foot through a city, letting it "speak" to him, absorbing as much as he could of its history and habits from its buildings, terrain, and people. The major problem of modern planning, in his view, was its ignorance of everyday life in cities. Urban planning, as he used to point out, "cannot be done in the office with ruler and parallels."[18]

Whenever possible, Geddes also viewed the city from a nearby high point—a mountain or a hill—to take it in "synoptically," as an interrelated whole, as Aristotle had viewed ancient Attica from the cliffs of the Acropolis. Aristotle knew, Geddes was fond of saying, that "large views in the abstract . . . depend upon large views in the concrete."[19] Long before Jan Smuts coined the term, Geddes practiced what we now call holism, arguing that no living organism could be understood except in terms of the total environment in which it functioned. This is one of the most important ideas he passed on to Lewis Mumford, who became, in time, America's leading proponent of holistic thinking.

Geddes was also sensitive to the connection between city and country, insisting that the problems of the city could be successfully attacked only on a regional basis. He saw the entire city region as a complex, interconnected ecosystem that one had to understand before suggesting alternatives that might upset its delicate natural balance. Such an approach demanded familiarity with every aspect of the metropolitan region. From his Outlook Tower Observatory and study center, atop Edinburgh's Castle Hill, with its spectacular view of the old city and the gray Lothian hills that blended into the horizon, Geddes undertook a systematic survey of the Edinburgh region, examining its environmental characteristics as well as its history and cultural heritage. To Geddes, the survey method—detailed firsthand diagnosis of the region's natural and human resources—was the foundation of any regional or urban planning effort.[20]

The survey, Geddes insisted, would also allow the investigator to see things in the enlarged perspective of history, for the key to its success was its historical, developmental approach, its search for the origins of present regional customs, ideas, and institutions. Unlike a number of American sociologists who adopted the survey method, Geddes, the evolutionist, refused to confine the regional survey to the spatial society of the present. In his city surveys he started with the present and moved backwards through time, examining the imprint of the past on current city forms and institutions. The survey's combination of historical perspective, specialized field research, and integrative, "ecological" analysis would, he believed, produce realistic plans for regional revitalization. "This type of evolutionary inquiry," he once observed, "is but common sense."[21]

After reading *The Evolution of Sex* by Geddes and J. Arthur Thomson, Mumford wrote to the Outlook Tower requesting pamphlets and materials that he remembers receiving "with an elation equal only to that upon the publication of my own first book."[22] In late 1915 he wrote to Edinburgh again, inquiring about the possibility of studying at the Tower after the war.

Geddes's Outlook Tower was an idea as much as a building. Its physical design embodied the complete Geddesian philosophy, which Mumford quickly became acquainted with through the literature he began receiving from Edinburgh. An imposing stone structure of crenellated roofs and medieval turrets, it still stands today on Castle Hill at the top of the Royal Mile, peering out to the lovely crescents and squares of the city's Georgian quarter.[23]

Before Geddes purchased it, the Tower had belonged to an optician, who added a turret in which he installed a camera obscura—a rotating mirror that projects images through a lens onto a round white table in the darkened room below. With this ingenious instrument (still in use, although now as a tourist attraction), the viewer can see Edinburgh and its surrounding region flashed on the table as a continuous series of brightly colored images. Geddes hoped these sharply focused images—the colors made more vivid by the pitch-black surroundings—would sensitize the viewer to the beauty of the most commonplace aspects of the cityscape. In the bowels of this enlarged camera box, one could view the city's buildings and neighborhoods with the eye of the artist.

Geddes used the entire tower as an instrument of visual reeducation. The camera integrated experience into harmonious wholes, while from the open-air balcony, just below the camera room, there was a panoramic view of the entire city region. Standing on this windswept roof, looking out to the Salisbury Crags, an excited

Geddes would lecture visitors on the rich evidences of their physical and social heritage which lay before their eyes "if only they knew how to look."[24]

In escorting visitors through his tower, Geddes preferred to start at the top, rushing them up the winding back stairs at breakneck speed. The exertion of the quick climb would make the blood circulate more rapidly, preparing mind and body for the exhilarating thrill of the views from the top. After the visual experiences of the balcony and the camera obscura, Geddes would lead guests through a curtained doorway into a tiny room, furnished with a single chair. This bare-walled cell provided an opportunity for meditation, so that the observer could digest what he had seen and prepare for the "in look" experiences that were to come. The cell was a symbol as well of the idea that only by understanding himself can man hope to understand his environment.

After pausing in the meditation room, the visitor descended the Tower's five stories, proceeding through a series of rooms laid out as an index museum to the world. On the top floor was the Edinburgh Gallery; below were floors devoted, respectively, to Scotland, Great Britain and the English-speaking nations, Europe, and the Oriental civilizations. Each room contained elaborate visual materials and displays: paintings, prints, photographs, colorful historical charts tracing the development of modern history, botanical globes, relief maps designed by the eminent geographers Elisée Reclus and A. J. Herbertson, and a host of other graphic displays and Geddesian paraphernalia, including a vast relief map of his famous "valley section," a model for studying former civilizations and replanning modern ones. This topographical model summed up the geographic components of a region and its typical occupations, and was one of Geddes's favorite teaching tools.[25]

The entire Tower was a living exemplification of the regional survey method and of the process of integrative thinking. But for Geddes it was much more than this. It served as a laboratory for social action—the world's first sociological laboratory—where he continually reordered exhibits as well as ideas, trying out new combinations that might reveal new possibilities for civic reform. Adjoining the Edinburgh room was a civic business room, where the main practical work of the Tower was concentrated. From here Geddes directed the renewal of historic Edinburgh, the beginning project of a lifelong effort to influence the replanning of cities world-wide. And from here he organized masques and festivals, participatory rituals aimed at helping people to rediscover and relive the history of the city.[26]

In 1915 Mumford desperately wanted to be part of Geddes's Outlook Tower efforts. His letters to the Tower were answered by Frank Mears, Geddes's son-in-law and architectural assistant. Geddes was then in India on a city planning expedition, Mumford learned, and in his absence the Tower was an all-but-deserted place. So Mumford had to be content to learn all he could of Geddes's ideas through studying the books and pamphlets he began receiving by mail from Mears. But in 1917 a letter of Mumford's did finally reach Geddes in India, the beginning of a correspondence that would last until Geddes's death in 1932. In these first letters Mumford addressed Geddes as Professor; it was not long, however, before he began calling him Master.

Patrick Geddes's city studies stirred one of the great interests of Mumford's life, and influenced his entire approach to the study of cities and regions. But initially it was not Geddes the city planner and sociologist that Mumford was most strongly drawn to; it was Geddes the educator and activist, who called for the development of the total person, of all our capacities for reason and calculation, passion and poetry, mental work and full-bodied living. Geddes's writing—and his personal example—helped Mumford chart a new direction for his life.

When Mumford first read Geddes in the fall of 1914 he was at a critical juncture in his emotional development, passing through what we might call a crisis of late adolescence. This was a time of anxious questioning and self-doubt, and of his first focused rebellion against the governing values of his upbringing. In its initial stages his youthful alienation took the form of a revolt against conventional education, a rebellion that led him to question, and then revise, his entire approach to life and learning.

The "crisis" came to a head with his decision, on the advice of Professor Turner, to transfer into the Day Session of City College in the fall of 1914, in order to prepare for graduate work in philosophy. No sooner had Mumford begun the semester than he began to question his decision to study for a Ph.D. His principal complaint concerned the kind of education he was receiving.

Mumford was forced to enter the Day Session as a freshman, since he hadn't taken his courses in the proper sequence as an evening student, and, in addition, he was required to take subjects he found tiresome, including Latin, which he had flunked in the Evening Session, or subjects that he had little aptitude for, like mathematics and chemistry. Turner had convinced him to take such a curriculum in order to toughen and discipline his mind for advanced work in philosophy, but the experience had exactly the opposite effect. It nearly killed his interest in getting a college degree.

The prevailing method of instruction in the Day Session was the lecture system, which Mumford found uninspiring compared to the bracing give-and-take of his Evening Session classes. To make matters worse, his second confrontation with Latin was a disaster, and he dropped the course early in the semester. He also found most of his fellow students callow and tractable compared to his mature brothers in the night session. They were perfectly content, as Mumford wrote later, to "fill out the form: sign the dotted line: report promptly: [and] . . . not live with a thought lest the thought keep you from turning over memorizable papers and acquiring insignificant marks."[27] To Mumford's mind, already spoiled by richer fare, this was too meager and monotonous a diet. If this was learning he wanted no part of it.

Mumford rebelled against the Day Session education by withdrawing from it.[28] He had already had several of his short pieces published, so he considered himself a writer first and a degree-seeking student second. By the end of the semester he was cutting his classes with increasing frequency, giving his time instead to writing plays and stories. Even the library no longer excited him. He would wander aimlessly through the stacks, indifferent toward the books and journals that had once excited him. "By the time December, 1914 had come around," he writes in 1915, "both my body and mind seemed to have decided to go on a strike: my body because it had not been cared for and exercised enough, my mind because it had been cared for and exercised altogether too much."[29] He desperately wanted to quit school, but he couldn't raise the nerve to do it. Finally illness forced the issue.

Feeling exhausted and feverish, he consulted a City College doctor, who detected an active spot on his lung, which he diagnosed as the first signs of tuberculosis. He advised Mumford to suspend his education at once and to live for a time at a reduced pace. The diagnosis frightened Mumford, but the therapy, he would later insist, saved his life—not that he was in any immediate danger of dying. (His ailment, he suspected later in life, after consulting several specialists, was actually an overactive thyroid that sometimes presents symptoms similar to tuberculosis.) "Had I remained in college," he observes in his notes at the time, "I would have followed the advice Turner gave me and become more hopelessly academic than ever."[30]

This temporary release from formal education, along with the influence of Geddes, led Mumford to reexamine his entire approach to life and learning. A one-act play he began at the time, "The Invalids," captures his gathering dissatisfaction with what he now saw as a sheltered, excessively bookish existence.

This undisguisedly autobiographical play is set in the living room of a brownstone on New York's Upper West Side, and its main character, Regius Storm, is a thin, stoop-shouldered youth of nineteen or twenty, "slack and flabbily developed," a student with vague dreams of becoming a writer. An only child, he lives with his mother, his aunt, and an aged, sickly uncle. The uncle is physically an invalid; but Regius, it turns out, is the play's real invalid, a superficially healthy young man suffering from a crippling ailment of another kind. "A product of his mother's tender care, his aunt's devotion, his nurse's solicitude, his teacher's coddling," he has been cut off from any "vital contact with the world." Regius's problem, as he admits in a moment of self-diagnosis, is that he has "been too brought up."

But Regius sees his problem as more than a narrowly constricted upbringing. He is emotionally backward because he has been exposed to "the most vicious institution of present-day civilization: our so-called educational system." The "barrenly intellectualized training" he has received in school "has ingrained in him the habit of living at second hand; with the result that though he has apparently a vast knowledge about art, industry, science, love, friendship . . . he has never had the least direct acquaintance with any of these. He is emotionally starved . . . while intellectually he is prodigious."[31]

Through Regius, Mumford expresses his rising rebellion against his schooling and upbringing. His mother had hardly been a smothering figure, but neither had she opened him up to the world beyond her tiny circle of friends and family. This he came to resent. But, interestingly, most of Regius's anger is directed not toward his mother but toward himself. He is disgusted with himself for succumbing to this insulating existence. There is some evidence of self-hatred in this play, but there are signs of health as well. The mere fact that Mumford wrote the play is an indication that he was on the way to overcoming his invalidism. He had identified one of the root problems of his life, and the notes he took in this period are filled with resolutions to do something about it. He must cease to live at second hand, he reminds himself over and over again.

This is the real importance of Patrick Geddes's influence. Geddes provided exactly what was lacking in Mumford's educational routine. The benchmark of Geddes's philosophy was the Athenian ideal of balance—reason and imagination must be equally developed, with thought and action interlinked. *Vivendo discimus* (By living we learn) was his motto. Education—real education—was not something one got from a book or in a lecture hall. Rather, it was life itself, an ongoing process of growth comprising all of man's activities.

Inspired by Geddes's example, Mumford decided to postpone indefinitely his plans to go for a degree in philosophy. Before he went any further with his education he would have to learn more about life itself. And the place to begin was in his own city of New York.

At age twenty Mumford began to use the city itself as his university, exploring its buildings, neighborhoods, museums, libraries, and art galleries. "The city . . . ," he would write years later, "is the point of maximum concentration for the power and culture of a community. . . . Here is where the issues of civilization are focused."[32] Here is where this wide-eyed son of Manhattan went for his first real education.

4

A Man in the Making

*Potentially creative men . . . build the personal fundament
of their work during a self-decreed moratorium, during
which they often starve themselves socially, [and] erotically
. . . in order to let the grosser needs die out, and make way
for the growth of the inner garden.*

—ERIK H. ERIKSON

In Patrick Geddes's work Mumford found a philosophy of release, release from the smothering habit of living "at second hand." Whereas in the past he had led a shuttered, bookish existence, he was now determined "to be fully alive, alive in every pore, at every moment, in every dimension."[1]

In early 1915, after leaving City College, Mumford began following a strenuous program of self-development to free himself of his "invalidism." He took greater care of his body, exercising in the morning and walking for several hours in the afternoon; he learned new disciplines and skills that enabled him to better understand his region, chief among them geography and geology; he sharpened his visual awareness, his eye for architecture and the landscape, through painting and sketching. And he wrote essay after essay, all of them unpublished, on his awakening plans for civic reform. In the years between 1915 and 1919, when he finally gained recognition as a writer, Mumford made himself into an all-around student of the city, able to understand almost every phase of its development.

These were the seed years of his life. Ideas he would spend a lifetime refining and elaborating first came to him in this period of
intense self-study and self-absorption. In these years Lewis Mumford remade himself into a new person—healthier, more confident,
and more alive than he had been at any time before.

But this four-year period of inner toughening and preparation
took its toll. Mumford's new therapeutic routine, along with his
writing, left him no time for a full-time paying job. (Nor was he
fully certain that he had the physical stamina for sustained work of
any kind.) So he held on to his meager inheritance, which paid for
his living expenses, by not going out to the theater, or on dates, or on
"sprees" of any kind; and this increased his diffidence in his relations
with women, bringing on a period of acute emotional repression. [2]

It was all worth it, however—or so he claimed years later in his
autobiography. [3] But the mature writer and the mature man were
slow in the making; it would be ten years before he shed almost
completely his habits of invalidism. Yet every year after 1915 was an
advance over the one previous, as he struggled to change his outlook,
his habits, his very physical appearance.

After Mumford dropped out of City College, his doctors warned
him not to overexert himself, and not to treat colds and infections too
casually if he hoped to live to the age of forty. Mumford took this
advice seriously—perhaps too seriously. His notebook entries of
this period show a vigilant, almost neurotic concern with matters of
bodily health. He reports every minor affliction, fulsomely detailing
the symptoms, including the sometimes severe melancholia that
accompanied these minor illnesses. He continued to be plagued by
colds and sore throats, usually at periods when his work was going
poorly or his emotional life was in upheaval, and these minor maladies would set him back for weeks, sometimes months, periods
during which he did little or no work. But the difference after 1915
was that he decided to try to do something about it—to build up his
physical constitution and his physical resistance.

He was aided in his recovery by the commonsense advice of his
mother's physician, Dr. Snyder, who treated him after he left City
College. Instead of sending him to a sanitarium, then a common

therapy for tubercular patients, he simply urged Mumford to live at a slower pace and to report for regular physical checkups. This wise doctor, who knew Mumford's mother and some of the circumstances of his upbringing, also recommended psychoanalytic counseling, surely suspecting that Mumford's physical symptoms—his weak respiratory system and his rapid, erratic heart—might have a psychological origin. For reasons Mumford fails to explain in his autobiography, he didn't take that advice (instead he read several books on Freudian psychology). But, on Dr. Snyder's recommendation, he did go to Ogunquit, Maine, that summer, where he could be near a young psychiatrist who shared Snyder's Park Avenue office. There is no record that Mumford ever consulted with this young doctor, but, no matter. The time away from home was itself therapeutic. The month he spent by the seashore sunbathing, exercising, and reading Plato and Whitman "shook me free of my cramped, dingy past," he recalls, perhaps too nostalgically, "and irradiated the rest of my life."4

Still, as Mumford himself admits in his own account of his early development, he continued to suffer from a "hypochondriac concern about 'keeping fit,' " which he claims he did not throw off until his middle years.5 The evidence suggests that he never really stopped being overanxious about his health (a bad habit that is perhaps one of the secrets of his longevity). From this point on, he would face every day of his life as if it were his last, giving to every hour an exaggerated significance. That early advice—that he might not live long if he didn't take extremely good care of himself—also helps to explain his continuing concern that his files be kept up to date and in perfect order. As he told a close friend late in his life, one must always have one's "travelling bag ready, like a pregnant mother who expects to go to a hospital."6

In the years between 1915 and 1919, Mumford followed a fairly regular routine. In the morning he would read or write in his room and exercise for an hour or so. Then he would take a long hot bath, eat a hearty lunch, and take a leisurely afternoon walk through the city, when the weather permitted. On rainy days he would spend afternoons in a museum or a library, or just stay at home and sketch or paint. On his frequent visits to the Metropolitan Museum of Art, one particular figure worked a spell on him, a statue of a Greek athlete, bearded, graceful, and muscular, using a strigil to wipe the cleansing oil from his body. Mumford wanted to look like him, although he didn't care for the beard.

As much as he loved New York's museums, however, it was the Central Library at Fifth Avenue and Forty-second Street that became his favorite urban place. The museums were but his "visits"; this was his "home." Thomas Hastings's massive neoclassic building, which occupied the site of the old Croton reservoir, had just been completed in 1911, and when Mumford began studying there he found it a spacious place of "soul-filling silence." Paging through Emerson's *Journals* in the Main Reading Room, with the afternoon sun streaming through the big arched windows, he had the sense that he was in a building "lifted above the rush, the congestion, the pressures of the teeming city outside."[7]

Even the classical motifs did not bother him then, as they would later, in his first book on architecture. After an hour or so of reading, he would lean back in his chair and pick out one of the figures on the ceiling to study. He composed a poem to one of these ceiling figures, a nude woman, who for months afterwards drifted in and out of his erotic fantasies.

When he wasn't in the library or a museum Mumford was walking the streets of the city. The walking, which he saw as a sheerly educational experience, served another purpose as well. It was therapy for his anxiety, a welcome release from the confines of his home. In these troubled years of late adolescence, walking probably did for Mumford what it had done for his favorite novelist, Charles Dickens. As a young man Dickens formed the habit of walking the streets of London, usually late at night, trying to "still his beating mind." Young Samuel Johnson, too, would take long solitary walks, expecting that this physical exertion "might still the demons that haunted him." Like Johnson and Dickens, city men of limitless curiosity, Mumford learned much of the "bustling, bourgeoning" places his walks carried him through.[8]

Once Mumford embarked on his new physical schedule he began to put on weight and acquire more musculature.[9] "My chest," we find him boasting in the summer of 1915, "is well developed! my belly hard, and my flanks smooth and strong."[10] The thin, slackly developed Regius Storm was now a well-set, straight-shouldered young man, five feet ten inches in height and weighing a sturdy 170 pounds.

Mumford had a severe acne problem that continued to trouble him for several years, but once he began to build up his body, his face didn't cause him as much concern, and to his great relief, the acne gradually moved from his face to his back. (It would finally disappear when he married and had sex for the first time.) In a note he took down late in life, Mumford tried to recall the way he looked in these years just before he reached the full flush of maturity. With Byronic collar and a crew cut that turned to a wavy pompadour, he remembers appearing almost " 'poetic' in an older romantic fashion." But these "soft lines," he adds, are "deceiving: underneath, a well-articulated armature of iron has been forming."[11]

Photographs of him at age nineteen, and his own self-portraits in pencil, bear this out. The set of his chin, jutting out confidently, marks this inner growth, indicating a more determined attitude. His piercing eyes give him an alert, confident look. Women, mostly a little older than he, began to make polite advances. He was still unsure of himself around women, covering this up with a self-protective aloofness, no doubt to avoid the possibility of rejection; but he felt a strong sexual urge that was making him a little less timid around several of his new female friends, although these friendships remained platonic, probably because he didn't take the first step.

These were far more troubled times than he admits in his autobiography, times of agonizing personal difficulties, made worse by his failure to break into the publishing world. But working alone, with no pressing outside obligations, he formed habits critical to his development as a writer.

At this moment in his life Mumford came under the spell of the ancient Greeks. Professors Turner and Palmer had incited in him an interest in the Plato of the *Republic* "who," as Mumford would write in his first book, "pictured a community living a sane, continent, athletic, clear-eyed life; a community that would be always, so to say, within bounds."[12] The Plato who beckoned to him in late adolescence is the Plato of the *Dialogues*, whose intimate acquaintance with his city gave him insight no amount of reading could have instilled.

But though Mumford read Plato and Aristotle avidly in 1916, it was the work of another freelance Scottish scholar and educator, Thomas Davidson, one of the founders of England's Aristotelian society, who introduced him to the Greek way of life, with its emphasis upon balance and proportion as essential for the full development of the person. One particular passage in Davidson's work illuminates what Mumford found most compelling.

"The men who fought at Marathon, Salamis, and Plataea were puritans, trained in a hard school to fear the gods, to respect the laws, their neighbors, and themselves, to reverence the wisdom of experience, to despise comfort and vice, and to do honest work. They were not enfeebled by esthetic culture, paralyzed by abstract thinking, or hardened by professional training. They were educated to be men, friends, and citizens, not to be mere thinkers, critics, soldiers, or money makers."[13]

From Davidson Mumford graduated to Sir Alfred Zimmern's *The Greek Commonwealth*, which he lists in his notes of 1915 as one of the several books that was altering his philosophy of life. *The Greek Commonwealth* is a magnificent introduction to the politics and thought of ancient Athens and, incidentally, one of the first books Mumford encountered that emphasized the importance of geography and climate—of the air, the sea, and the soil—on human habits and institutions. Reading Zimmern's account of the ancient Greeks, Mumford was overcome by the feeling that he had been "born out his due time. Athens during the early sixth century B.C. would have been more to my liking than New York in the twentieth after Christ," he writes in 1915. "It is true this would have cut me off from Socrates, who lived in the disappointing period that followed. But then I might have been Socrates."[14]

One further important figure who came into Mumford's life about this time was the writer Samuel Butler. In 1914, in imitation of Butler, whose *Notebooks* he was reading at the time, Mumford began to take down random notes on an almost daily basis, among the first indications of his intellectual and literary self-awareness. The notes would help him to catch his ideas "on the wing," his impressions of books and buildings, friends and lovers, and of himself and his own development.[15] His first notes are mostly self-conscious reflections on books he happened to be reading, but they quickly build in astuteness as Mumford, in imitation of Plato and Aristotle, takes in more of the world around him.

A surprising number of these earliest notes reveal ideas and themes Mumford would spend the rest of his life trying to develop and substantiate. They show, for example, an early environmental awareness that would mark all his mature work, and there is also sensitivity to the importance of placing limits on physical growth (an outgrowth, perhaps, of his reading of Geddes and the Greeks) and of the need to distribute the fruits of economic growth more equitably. "All matter and energy is a gift. No one has created it, no one has earned it, no one 'deserves' it, and therefore no individual or institution should be allowed to appropriate it selfishly. Man's economic function is simply to wrap Nature's gift in convenient parcels for wider distribution. . . ."[16]

Mumford continued this practice of note-taking throughout his lifetime, entitling his most intensely personal notes "Personalia." The latter form a continuous inner record of his emotional and sexual development and are written in a confessional manner, often at the lowest points and in the darkest crises of his life. They tell a great deal about his marriage, about his relations with women other than his wife, Sophia, and about his own problems and weaknesses.

After 1915 Mumford also began writing annual accounts of his principal activities of the previous year, but it is the random notes that form the grist for his books and articles. From this point on, wherever he went he took a notepad and pencil with him; and at home he kept these pads near his favorite reading and working places. Later, he had some of his jackets specially tailored so that he could conveniently slide his four-by-six-inch pads into a side pocket.[17]

In the spring and early summer of 1915, Mumford threw himself into Butler's work, the *Notebooks, Evolution, Old and New,* and *The Way of All Flesh.* Butler, a former New Zealand sheepherder, was, like Patrick Geddes, a many-sided man: a novelist, classicist, painter, satirist, journalist, composer, and one of the finest science writers of his time. He had a deep interest in biology; and in his essays he stressed the importance of man's interdependence with all living things. Give-and-take, not dog-eat-dog, is the "rule of life" for Butler, Mumford writes in his early notes.[18]

In Mumford's regular visits to the American Museum of Natural History on Central Park West, just a short walk from his mother's apartment on West Ninety-fourth Street, he found the ecological ideas of Butler, Darwin, and Geddes vividly brought to life. The museum was at that time beginning to establish itself as one of the world's first ecologically organized museums. Its curators were breaking free from the so-called trophy collection approach of other museums of natural history, where stuffed animals and bleached bones were showcased in random fashion. They were, instead, exhibiting wild creatures in case displays and whole galleries that set them in their natural environment, in association with other related species. In these lifelike displays, habitat groups replaced single mounted figures, and the natural scenery was re-created by the breathtakingly realistic murals of Charles Robert Knight.

For Mumford, however, the highlight of the Natural History Museum was its Hall of Evolution, where the curators had assembled a spectacular presentation of the entire course of evolution, from the lowest forms of life to man. Here also were displays illustrating the laws of natural science and heredity uncovered by Charles Darwin, Gregor Mendel, August Weismann, and their contemporaries. The museum was much more than a fascinating collection of bones and specimens; it was an education in biological, ecological thinking. It perfectly complemented Mumford's reading of Butler, giving him a sense of nature as an interdependent whole.[19]

Excited by his new discoveries in biology, Mumford moved further into Butler's work. In *Evolution, Old and New* Butler mapped out a neo-Lamarckian theory of evolution that gave the human mind a shaping role in the advance of the species. Butler stressed the idea of purposefulness, a purposefulness found in the organism itself, not in a Divine Creator. Variations in a species occurred largely as the result of changes in the environment and in the varying needs arising from these changes. Natural selection was not, contrary to Darwin, the cause of the variations.

It was Butler the amateur biologist, not Butler the author of *Erewhon*, the savage satirist of machine culture, who excited Mumford's interest. A philosophic vitalist and a follower of Henri Bergson, Butler replaced the Malthusian picture of life as an ungiving struggle for domination and survival with the picture of "creative evolution," where a mysterious life force inside human beings forever invents new forms of life and drives us to clearer understanding and greater self-consciousness, an idea Shaw explained as the law of life in *Man and Superman*. This is what linked Mumford to Butler, Shaw, Bergson, and, a few years later, to Alfred North Whitehead.[20] And this, of course, is what had first drawn him to the writings of Patrick Geddes.

At the risk of digression, it is important at this point to briefly survey Geddes's ideas on evolution, since they joined with those of Butler to exert a powerful and continuing influence on Mumford's thought. To the very end of his life Mumford remained intensely interested in biology, and in evolution in particular. The final project of his life, which he began at age eighty-five, was a wide-ranging study of human evolution inspired by the neo-Lamarckian thinking of Samuel Butler and Patrick Geddes. That ambitious uncompleted work brought his life full-circle.

Geddes pioneered a sociology grounded in his subtle understanding of the life process—"bio-sociology," as he called it. A neo-Lamarckian (or vitalist), he attributed to the organism an active, purposeful role that more mechanistic interpretations of evolution denied. While some nineteenth-century biologists described life almost solely in terms of nature's impact upon the organism, Geddes stressed the organism's capacity to strike back at the environment in an effort to overcome the forces threatening it. While Geddes deeply admired Darwin, he was never comfortable with natural selection as an encompassing explanation of plant and animal evolution. Cooperation and willful purpose were, he believed, as important in evolutionary development as tooth and claw competition and blind chance.

As a young biologist Geddes had been particularly intent on refuting August Weismann's germ plasm theory, which maintained that all organisms contain within their cells a special hereditary substance that cannot be formed anew or influenced by the environment. This theory seemed to leave man a passive creature in the evolutionary process, helpless to direct his own destiny. In *The Evolution of Sex*, Mumford's initial introduction to Geddes, Geddes and J. Arthur Thomson argued that organisms acquire new characteristics in two ways: the first, through "some property inherent in the fertilized cell"; the other, contrary to Weismann, through environmental influences. It would be a veritable physiological miracle, they insisted, "for the reproductive protoplasm to lead a charmed life away from external disturbance."[21]

Geddes found Lamarck's theory of the inheritance of acquired characteristics through environmental adaptation a more convincing evolutionary hypothesis than Weismann's. In *Zoological Philosophy,* Lamarck pointed out that organisms make efforts of their own to transform themselves as well as their environment. This capacity of the organism to overcome the conditioning process, a trait Geddes called insurgency, reached its apex in man. This ability to willfully modify our personalities and our environment was, Geddes said, our most magnificent endowment. Along with George Bernard Shaw and Samuel Butler, Geddes found in this Lamarckian notion a comforting alternative to some of the more uncompromisingly mechanistic interpretations of Darwinism. Later, Mumford would turn Geddes's idea of insurgency into an argument for human control of technology, insisting that while the machine has long dominated us, we have within ourselves the capacity to regain control of our lives and our futures. This was the idea upon which he would build his final books on technology and culture.

Geddes impressed Mumford as one of the few non-Marxists of his time to ground his work in the dialectical method, for his biological training had given him a keen appreciation for life as an ongoing interplay between organism and environment. The ancient questions of free will versus determinism and of nature versus nurture were not, for Geddes, simple matters of either/or. Man, in his view, was simultaneously free and determined. Environment sometimes dominated the organism, as the mechanists argued, but at unexpected moments the organism moved out, and by cunning, energy, and skill, mastered the environment, making life a never-ending process of dialectical interaction.[22] "Holland," as Mumford would later observe, "made the Dutch; but the Dutch, with their dikes and windmills and their land reclamation, also made Holland."[23]

The Butler of the *Notebooks* was an equally heroic figure to Mumford, almost a role model. He had a muscular, no-nonsense prose style, and he carried through his arguments with driving logic. Nor was there another writer who gave himself more completely to his work. "The only living works," Butler writes in the *Notebooks,* "are those which have drained much of the author's own life into them."

Butler, moreover, was a relentlessly challenging thinker whose ideas ran up against the commonplaces of Victorian thought and practice. "Lord, I do not believe, help Thou mine unbelief."[24]

Young Mumford, in the advanced stages of rebellion against middle-class convention, found an elder soulmate in Samuel Butler. Here is Butler on The Seven Deadly Sins: "Want of money, bad health, bad temper, chastity, family ties, knowing that you know things, and believing the Christian religion." On marriage—and ideology: "It is not nice to be wedded to anything—even to a theory." On God: "He might begin the Day of Judgement, but he would probably find himself in the dock before it was over." And on the family: "I believe more unhappiness comes from this source than from any other—I mean from the attempt to prolong family connection unduly, and to make people hang together artificially who would never naturally do so."[25] As he read the *Notebooks* Mumford must have thought that Butler was speaking directly to him.

The *Notebooks* are the work of a thinker who refused to ride in harness with anyone, who, like Thoreau and Emerson, trusted most of all his own intuition. Butler was the kind of fiercely independent thinker Mumford dreamed of becoming, and during the summer of 1915 Mumford spent weeks on an article on Butler, which was rejected by two magazines.

Another of his new heroes was Leonardo da Vinci, the subject of a play he completed in 1917, "The Gorgon's Head." Here Leonardo is the herald of a new era in art and science, a period of creative synthesis. "To know a thing by its parts is Science"; Leonardo tells his companion Nicolette, in Mumford's play, "to feel it as a whole is Art. The first is the method of death, of my dissecting table; the second is the way of life, of my canvases." It is a "folly," he adds, to think that science and art conflict. "The body without a skeleton cannot live; but neither can a skeleton without organs. Life is a compromise between flesh and skeleton, between the vital and the mechanical, between innovation and tradition."[26] This theme—the vital versus the mechanical—strikes the opening note of the rest of Mumford's intellectual life. He would spend a lifetime attempting to find a common ground where "the subjective and the objective, the artistic and the scientific . . . could meet and exchange their gifts."[27]

Mumford's Leonardo is a young man much like himself, aflame

with new ideas, in search of new relationships. Years later he would
describe himself in this period as a young man "vehement, almost
choking with ideas, trying on new thoughts as [one] might try on
costumes, one day a pragmatist, next a Spinozist, now an anarchist,
now a socialist, now a Ruskinian Tory, now a Shavian, now a
Platonist, now a disciple of Samuel Butler, a Whitmanite, a Geddesian, or a Tolstoian."[28] No one creed contained all the new ideas he
took on; no one figure, not even Geddes or Leonardo, fully embodied all the ideals he was reaching for. But as he extended his interests, his inner confusion and rebellion grew apace.

This exposure to Leonardo and Butler, to Geddes and the Greeks,
fortified Mumford's discontent with conventional education, but the
break with formal education was more difficult to make than he indicates in his autobiography. He wasn't yet certain what he wanted
to do with his life, and he thought that he had better get a degree just
in case he decided on a career, such as philosophy, that required
college training.

So in September 1915 he reentered the Day Session of City
College, suntanned and healthy and ready for serious study. But the
grinding routine of college—lectures, note-taking, exams—wore
him down within a month. He again did poorly in Latin, a subject
required for graduation; once more his class attendance in all his
subjects dropped off; and, as before, he found it difficult to fit in
with the students, most of whom struck him as lacking "strong
desires, high hopes, passionate indignation."[29]

It was at this point that he read in succession Patrick Geddes's *City
Development* and *Cities in Evolution*, books that gave shape to his
youthful hopes and aspirations, and put him on the road to his
proper vocation. Civilization, Geddes wrote in *Cities in Evolution*, is
a product "not of the individual, but of the city."[30] These words
worked an inner revolution in Mumford, who read the book in one
concentrated stretch after importing it from England. "My present
interest in life," he scribbled excitedly in his notebook, "is the
exploration and documentation of cities. I am as much interested in
the mechanism of man's cultural ascent as Darwin was in the mechanism of his biological descent."[31] He did not yet, he realized, possess the skill or seasoning to write anything of telling consequence.
But he prepared himself for the next fifteen years to write just such

books. His masterworks on the city, *The Culture of Cities* (1938) and *The City in History* (1961), are the finest examples in the English language of Geddes's holistic approach to the study of human communities. They are the kinds of books Geddes set out numerous times to write, but never disciplined himself to carry through—richly imaginative accounts of the progress of urban civilization, histories packed with a thousand lessons for architects and urban planners. Mumford would take his method from his old Scots teacher and outdo him in the end, erecting on the foundation of the great historic cities a design for the city of tomorrow.

Mumford could not have been more perfectly prepared for a book than he was for Geddes's *Cities in Evolution*. What most impressed him, as we have seen, was Geddes's emphasis upon outdoor field research and social surveying, a useful approach, Geddes thought, for all citizens, not just professionals. In *Cities in Evolution*, Geddes explained how to "read" a city, using its geography, architecture, and urban plan, and how to understand it better through the study of its history. Explore the city on your own; and when you begin to understand its problems and possibilities, take action with others to make it a better place. These are the most important civic lessons young Mumford learned from Geddes.

Thus, though Mumford's disillusionment with formal education was not quite as extreme as that of his character Regius Storm, his return to college reinforced his conviction that if he was to mature, both as a person and as a writer, he would have to reach further for his education. Formal learning, as Geddes noted, substituted knowledge about life for direct acquaintance with it.

So in early 1916, Mumford decided to quit college again and give most of his time to his writing and his city studies. Over the next several years he took some occasional courses at New York University, Columbia University, the New School for Social Research, and in 1917 back at the Evening Session of City College, but only in those subjects that fit the new curriculum he began to shape for himself, courses that would train him to be a student of the city. Although he eventually accumulated enough credits to graduate, he never took a degree, and he saw no need for it. He wanted to be a writer, not a professor, a writer whose master theme was the city itself. Under the spell of Geddes, he began to study the city like a biologist at work in nature, looking for links and interrelationships, placing buildings and neighborhoods, roadways and bridges, within the wider ecological context of the city and its surrounding region. His daily walks through New York took on a new purpose, as he struggled to translate what he learned on his urban surveys into a plan for a reconstituted city, the New York of his youthful dreams.

5

Son of Mannahatta

This is the city and I am one of the citizens,
Whatever interests the rest interests me,
politics, wars, markets, newspapers, schools,
The mayor and councils, banks, tariffs,
steamships, factories, stocks, stores,
real estate and personal estate.

—WALT WHITMAN

In the first months of 1916, Mumford walked all over Manhattan—
East Side, West Side, north and south. Usually he walked alone, a
solitary witness to one of New York's most spectacular periods of
physical growth.

His first surveys were of New York's East Side, up as far as Sixty-
third Street, the densely packed area of tenements and factories that
rimmed the East River. He started in the Lower East Side, a place he
grew to know well from his frequent visits to the Chrystie Street flat
of his friend Irwin Granich (Michael Gold). This was the area
Whitman described as the "region of Jews, jewelry, and secondhand clothing."[1] In Mumford's youth it was the world's largest
Jewish ghetto, and there was no place quite like it in all of New
York.

As Mumford threaded his way down Chrystie Street toward
Granich's apartment, he would pass through a "tenement canyon
hung with fire-escapes, bed clothing, and faces. . . . Always these

faces at the tenement windows. The street never failed them. It was an immense excitement. It never slept. It roared like a sea. It exploded like fireworks."[2]

In New York's Jewish quarter he encountered foul-smelling, clotted tenements he would later compare to those of Juvenal's Rome, but here also he got his first real taste of the lively street life and village-like sociability he would always consider the blood and soul of urban living. Here was "an abundant, vigorous associative life." One found it in the tenements, in the streets, in the synagogues, in the basements of the trade union centers. The East Siders were brought into the streets by the cries of the peddlers, and were kept there by conversation and the whole raucous spectacle around them. "In any plan for establishing a Jewish garden city," Mumford remarks in the careful notes he began to take of his urban excursions, "this habit of life should be provided for: the model should be a Greek agora," with a temple at one end and "an adjacent refreshment place, and many protected stalls, and much elbow room for gesticulation." And, he adds, there should be a number of ethnic eating clubs like Strunsky's on "Yiddish Fifth Avenue," where he and Gold would sit and drink tea late into the evening, arguing about anarchism and literature, Trotsky and Kropotkin, with the local "intellectual aristocracy."[3]

All of Mumford's architectural and urban writing is grounded in these early firsthand surveys of his native New York. And many of these walks, of course, were journeys of rediscovery, as he passed through neighborhoods he had been introduced to by his grandfather. Now, as he explored the city on his own, he would stop occasionally to do a pencil drawing of a tenement or a skyscraper or one of New York's arching bridges. Later in the day, back in his tiny bedroom on West Ninety-fourth Street, he would paint small watercolors of New York's street scenes and cityscapes. These luminous watercolors, with their wealth of brilliant blues, reds, and yellows, were inspired by his first encounter with Monet's work in Boston in 1916, one of the great aesthetic awakenings of his youth.

Mumford's early artwork trained his eye for urban observation and gave him a heightened awareness of buildings, not as isolated structures but as part of the entire living environment of the city. A good building, he would say later, must not stand out—it must fit in. His painting and sketching also helped him to develop "a double vision which sees with both eyes, the scientific eye of actuality and the illuminated eye of imagination and dream."4

Mumford brought to his architecture criticism the visual sensitivity of the artist. Yet his early interest in architecture was as "a home for man"; it was the housing problem that first drew him. "All along the East Side," he writes after returning from one of his city surveys, "there was not a block after leaving Madison Avenue that was not dingy, grimy, . . . dull, [and] hopeless."5 The absence of space, sunlight, and fresh air—"the sense of all the human qualities that were missing—taught me, by contrast," he observed in retrospect, "what to demand in every work of humane architecture."6

Mumford realized that crowding sometimes had its unexpected social benefits; that it encouraged, for example, the spirited street life of the Jewish, Slavic, and Italian neighborhoods. But he was convinced that this kind of spontaneous meeting and mingling could occur in a city without the horrible conditions he saw in the worst sections of New York. Aristotle's Athens seemed proof of that.

But it was not just the poor who lived in such constricting surroundings. The fashionable rich of Park and Fifth avenues "allow themselves to be herded in lofty tenements," superslums, Mumford calls them in his notes, "whose sole outlook is upon the walls or courtyard of—another lofty tenement."7 Even the brownstone areas of upper New York, with their low-set buildings, Mumford found dingy, confining, uninspiring. "In health [they produced] slackness and malaise; in thought, debility and cynicism; in social affairs, a preoccupation with the trivial forms of energy dissipation, as in motoring, bridge, poker, . . . billiard playing, and the like."8 These are the perceptions of a young urban observer who had his own family life very much on his mind. What, after all, does architecture have to do with "dissipations" like poker and bridge?

It was around this time that Mumford began referring to himself as a "Geddesian Eutopian."9 Temperamentally, however, he was, like his Scottish master, a deep-dyed conservative who saw the city's spectacular growth, what Walt Whitman called its "pull-down-and-build-all-over-again spirit," destroying buildings and neighborhoods of irreplaceable character, and uprooting people in the interest of financial gain. Well over a century earlier a young Whitman, another solitary walker of the city's streets, had complained about the "rabid, feverish, itching for change" that had infected New

Yorkers of his time. In 1842 a woman with a loaded pistol guarded the graves of her husband and family in a burial ground at Delancey Street against real-estate speculators. Whitman, drawn to her cause, noted that a mob rioted to save the graveyard. But "the divinity of trade" won out; the burial ground was dug up by the Hudson Fire Insurance Company and sold for house lots. And the company, Whitman reported, "actually set people to work with spades and pick axes to dig down and pitch out the decayed relics of bodies buried there . . . as loafers pitch pennies upon the dock."[10] At the age of twenty-one Mumford identified this reckless drive for profit and physical expansion as the great disease of twentieth-century New York.

In the spring and summer of 1916, Mumford extended his surveys to the outer boroughs of the city—to the Bronx, Brooklyn, and Queens, places that were then in the throes of a furious physical expansion. Queens held a particular fascination for him. He would take the ferry to North Beach, and then either walk or take trolleys all across middle and southern Queens. The boat ride up the murky East River gave him a magnificent view of the upper length of New York City—first the wharves, storage yards, factories, and breweries, then miles of four- and five-story redbrick tenements that crowded the shoreline. Riding smartly over the churning harbor waters on these "turtle-like creatures" he felt close to the sea and the sky and "the wide sweep of the city itself." The boats were "worth running," he later observed, "if only to give sustenance to poets and lovers"—and to lonely young people like himself.[11]

From the excursion decks of the ferries, his own versions of Patrick Geddes's Outlook Tower, he had an open view of the great spreading city, and was better able to appreciate the extent of the physical expansion it was then undergoing. He also saw the "scarifying" effects of industrial growth. From the Forty-second Street Ferry, which he would take north to Fort Lee or as far down as Hoboken, New Jersey, he looked out on an ugly unbroken area of factories and refineries, and grimy mud flats crowded with scows and barges.[12]

But it was New York's suburban movement that he was most interested in in his first surveys of the city, for it seemed to hold the promise of a new kind of metropolitan pattern. On the rim of the city, the process of growth and speculation had not yet worked its full damage—not yet.

Many of the sections of northern and middle Queens he regularly walked through were still semirural, with truck farms, wooded hills, and wide stretches of swampland. The entire area, however, was on the verge of a great change. The northern and middle sections of Queens had been laid out in streets and home lots; and transit lines had already been put in and were waiting for the anticipated invasion of prospective homeowners. An access bridge, in fact, had just been completed in 1909, the Queensboro span, connecting with Fifty-ninth Street in Manhattan; and one year later a tunnel had been driven under the river—the Pennsylvania Railroad Long Island Tunnel. In that year the population of Queens was just over a quarter of a million. In the following two decades it would almost quadruple.

Mumford was a keen-eyed observer of the first stages of this vast resettlement process, and he foresaw the consequences of what was to come. All of Queens, he feared, was about to succumb to the "disease of growth" that had already destroyed much of the Bronx, Brooklyn, Hoboken, and almost "every submetropolitan region." Mumford, however, still had no answer to the question he kept putting to himself in his notes, the central question of all his later work on the city: "How can we burke this development, get control of it, set it on healthier, better considered foundations?"[13]

These metropolitan excursions were the beginning, then, not only of Mumford's fascination with the city, but of his disillusionment with it as well. Overbloated cities like New York, with their "bleak streets, their mean dwellings, and their reeking atmosphere do violence to the name of civilization," he declared in one of his first unpublished essays on city development.[14] But what were they to be replaced with? At the conclusion of the summer of 1916, after acquiring a closer understanding of his native city through work on a survey of its leading industry, Mumford came up with some answers.

In June 1916, Mumford got a summer job as an investigator for the dress and waist industry's Joint Arbitration Board. The purpose of the investigation was to determine if both the union and the employers had kept to the terms of earlier labor agreements made between the industry and the recently formed International Ladies' Garment Workers' Union (ILGWU).

The garment industry was then centered in the heart of Manhattan, between Sixth and Ninth avenues from Thirtieth to Forty-second street. Almost every loft building in this impossibly congested area was honeycombed with shops, most of them employing no more than thirty workers. The streets were lined all day with trucks loading and unloading material and garments. Between them darted "push boys," recklessly maneuvering swaying racks of clothing. The whole district was alive with noise—the shrieking horns of the trucks, the shouts of the loft bosses and buyers, and the whirring of the sewing machines, which could be heard on the street below through the open windows that lined the workrooms. A young man could not have chosen a better place to learn the ins and outs of a big-city industry.

Mumford's work took him on foot through the entire loft section of Manhattan and into the workrooms and bookkeeping offices. He set up investigative appointments in the four hundred shops that were surveyed, delivered messages at union headquarters, gave printing orders, and visited shops throughout the district, distributing and collecting name and occupation slips. It was exhausting work, and in late July, at the end of six weeks, he resigned, even though the investigation had only another week to run. He was simply too run-down, he told his employer, to complete his work. [15]

As part of his duties as investigator Mumford was expected to make a record of his impressions and contribute suggestions for reform of the industry. He titled the hastily assembled 6,000-word report he prepared that August, "The Geographic Distribution of the Garment Industry," an audacious, if ill-digested plan to save the industry through a joint labor-management policy of regional decentralization. Instead of continuing to operate almost solely in the central district of Manhattan, an area of high rents, taxes, and wages, Mumford recommended that the industry set itself up on a regional basis, with all the local centers completely unionized. This would put sweatshop competitors out of business and bring about a better distribution of urban population. The report, however amateurish, is one of the first indications of Mumford's interest in regionalism as a solution to the problems of the overcrowded city. [16]

Later that year, influenced by Patrick Geddes's *City Development*,

Mumford tried to turn the report into a book-length study of the entire New York metropolitan region.[17] To write such a book, he felt he would have to learn more about the natural physical forces that had helped to shape New York. So in the fall of 1916 he began an independent program of study in geography and geology. The following January he joined the American Geographical Society and spent his winter afternoons in their reading rooms, where he discovered the writings of a group of French geographers who had a lasting influence on his thinking about cities and regions. In *Le Régionalisme*, Charles Brun, the leading French regionalist, called for the creation of geographic regions as the basis for French administrative, judicial, economic, and cultural life. Brun, Vidal de la Blanche (*Les Régions Françaises*), and a number of other French regionalists Mumford eagerly included in his new reading program, convinced him that any successful strategy of decentralization would have to be based upon geographic regions, "non-political groupings with respect to soil, climate, vegetation, animal life, industry and historic tradition."[18]

To get a firmer hold on these fields, Mumford enrolled in a night course in geography at Columbia in early 1917; and in the fall semester he took a course in geology in the Evening Session of City College. Every Sunday morning he did amateur geological fieldwork around New York City, and with the help of his geology professor he made topographic sketches of Manhattan, and began combing the city for geological keys to its development. He took extensive notes of these geological reconnaissances, which he typed up and filed in his thickening collection of urban observations. All of his city studies bear the mark of this early interest in the shaping role of geography and geology on human communities.[19]

All around him Mumford detected signs of a growing movement toward regionalism. Industries were escaping the great metropolitan centers; little communities were appearing within the mass cities; and New York and New Jersey were showing interest in a regional Port Development Commission whose jurisdiction would cut across political boundaries. It was his hope that these developments would burgeon into a movement to divide the entire country into regional units of political administration. Throughout 1917 and 1918 he worked steadily on his book and a number of related essays on the theme of regionalism, trying to adapt the ideas of the French regionalists to American circumstances. None of this work was published, nor did it deserve to be, but it formed the basis for later, more sharply developed writings that would establish Mumford as America's leading advocate of regional decentralization.

In May 1917, Mumford interrupted work on his book to take a temporary job that a friend, John Tucker, offered him in the cement-testing laboratory of the Bureau of Standards in Pittsburgh. He needed the money; besides, he had set down Pittsburgh on his "plan-chart" as a place he ought to visit after reading Paul Kellogg's path-breaking *Pittsburgh Survey*. Pennsylvania's steel city struck him as America's best example of what Geddes called the new "urban hell" industrialism had created.

John Tucker, an angular, red-haired science buff several years Mumford's senior, had been trained as a civil engineer at Stevens Institute in Hoboken. He and Mumford had met on the tennis courts of Central Park, where they both became friends with Beryl Morse. Mumford has described Tucker, his first close friend, as "precisely dogmatic, coldly enamored of mathematics and the physical sciences."[20] In some ways, however, Tucker was like his younger friend—a bit cynical and aloof, and something of an outsider. And although he had no interest in social reform schemes and would often ridicule Mumford's developing passion for regional renewal, Tucker showed an almost brotherly concern for Mumford's welfare.

When Mumford arrived in Pittsburgh he took a tiny room in the same lodging house where Tucker was staying on North Craig Street, at the foot of Squirrel Hill. Every morning the two would walk to work together over the Bloomfield Viaduct to Arsenal Park in Lawrenceville, where the Bureau of Standards was then located. Mumford's job was mixing cement and making batches of briquettes, which were dried and tested for their breaking point to see if they met government standards. He stayed on the job for only a little over two months, but the Pittsburgh experience left an indelible impression. For one thing, it was the first time he had taken a position away from home; after arriving in the city in May he boasted in his diary notes that he had taken "a greater leap than I had ever before made."[21] Then there was Pittsburgh itself, a city that held the same fascination for him that Manchester held for Friedrich Engels almost a century before.

Mumford didn't get to see as much of the city as he had hoped to—he was too busy in the evenings and on weekends typing his book, and continuing his reading program at Carnegie Library. But when he could, he surveyed Pittsburgh as he had New York, dutifully recording his observations, which he returned to twenty years later when he wrote the powerful chapter on Coketown in *The Culture of Cities*.[22]

Mumford never had a chance to penetrate the social life of the community, to talk with the workers and their families. This explains his notebook observation (no more than an intuition, he admits) that in many of the workers' neighborhoods there was little family or communal life, a misconception shared by numerous other middle-class observers. (One Saturday evening at a lodge hall or in the home of a Slavic steelworker's family might have changed Mumford's thinking on this.) So it was only the physical landscape that he surveyed, a cardinal characteristic of his later urban writing, which usually gives a more visual than a visceral feeling for the city. Most of his survey notes have the strengths and limitations of finely detailed scene painting.

In mid-July, Mumford quit his job and returned to New York. He didn't like his work at the laboratory, and he and Tucker were beginning to get on each other's nerves. He also wanted to free himself to finish his book on New York City.

Later that summer he sent an unfinished version of his manuscript to two publishers, who wrote back that they weren't interested. He then tried to get Appleton's, which had published a series on American cities, to consider a proposal for what he called a sociological "Tale of Four Cities": Boston, Philadelphia, Pittsburgh, and New York. "At twenty-two," he admitted later, "this was a preposterous undertaking, and I shudder to think what a mess I might have made of the job before I acknowledged my inadequate preparation."[23] But there must have been something of interest in his précis, for W. W. Appleton himself invited Mumford to his office to discuss it, although he told him in advance that he would not be able to publish such a book.

The proposal that Mumford sent Appleton is a fascinating document, an almost complete foreshadowing of Mumford's mature writing on the city. It contains the guiding canons of his later research into urban forms and origins, and shows how far his independent research had taken him toward a sensitive, many-layered understanding of the entire process of urban development. That he wrote it at age twenty-two, and at a time when there was very little scholarly literature on the city, is all the more remarkable.

Mumford proposed a book different from anything that had yet been written on the American city. The civic renascence in America, which had been going forward since the Chicago Exposition in 1893, had created a growing body of literature about cities—civic surveys, city histories, and city guidebooks—that reported city problems from every conceivable angle, focusing on rents and taxes, budgets and charters, education and housing. But Mumford found one aspect "strangely neglected." No one had yet attempted "to describe concretely the problem of cities in relation to their environments," and to the environments of the regions of which they were a part (what Mumford called ecological history). Nor had there yet appeared an "evolutionary" account of urban development, describing those features of a city's history and heritage most directly responsible for its current "achievements and defects."

Mumford suggested to Appleton a series of books on the city written from this perspective, boldly asking for the chance to write the lead volume, which would treat the four cities he claimed to know firsthand—New York, Philadelphia, Pittsburgh, and Boston, where he occasionally visited his friend Irwin Granich, then a student at Harvard. In dealing with the historic evolution of these cities, Mumford, in imitation of Geddes, proposed to include a staggering range of topics, among them geography, industry, transportation, immigration, parks and open spaces, architecture, neighborhood life, government, city planning, health and sanitary conditions, housing, and "the institutions for social betterment." But his approach, he tried to assure Appleton, would not be thinly encyclopedic. All of his research would be governed by one criterion: "that historic growth should be examined on the basis of present day conditions, and that the weight given to any particular growth should be a function of its importance in the contemporary scheme."[24] To improve our cities, we would need to have a clear understanding of the soundest features of older cities, as well as of the mistakes of past urban planners. It was Mumford's passionate interest in the cities of the future that inspired his interest in the cities of the past.

By the time he wrote this proposal, Mumford had discovered a new type of city that would influence every proposal for urban reform he advanced over the next half century. In *Garden Cities of Tomorrow,* published in 1898, Ebenezer Howard, the British urban visionary, outlined a plan to stop the unbounded growth of the industrial city and restore it to human scale by relocating its excess population in new medium-sized cities situated in the outlying countryside. These regional cities would be ringed by greenbelts of farm- and parkland placed so as to prevent urban sprawl. Land would be communally owned, and the towns and their surrounding region planned as an interlocking whole. In these attractively sited regional centers, people would have the best of both country and city living—a neighborly feeling of community, social variety, fresh air, and plenty of green space to garden, play in, and even farm. "Town and country will be married," Howard preached, "and out of this joyous union will spring a new hope, a new life, a new civilization."25

Howard advanced his garden city strategy as an effort to save the city, not to escape it, as some of his critics have charged. He was an urbanite by birth, residence, and temperament, a Londoner who delighted in the variety and sociability of metropolitan life. Yet he saw the London of the 1890s as a city on the slide—crowded, filthy, and crime-ridden, a place hostile to life itself. The chief source of this decline, he argued, was the tidal movement of people from the countryside into the city. London, in his estimation, had become too large and socially fragmented to function as a real human community. When in 1916 Mumford read Howard on London, he felt he was reading about his native New York.

Howard did more than dream of the garden city; he built two of them just north of London—Letchworth and Welwyn Garden City. In doing so, he set in motion a new town movement that has been responsible for the creation of several score of British garden cities. Howard's larger aim, however, remained unrealized. He hoped that these first two planned communities would give impetus to a peaceful movement to democratic socialism. Few of Howard's followers appreciated the radical intent of his urban proposal, yet this is exactly what drew young Mumford, now something of a socialist, to it.

Howard's garden city idea appealed to another, seemingly contradictory side of Mumford—his fear of proletarian revolution. Howard's was an ingenious strategy for achieving socialism without the blood and chaos of class upheaval. Enlightened social planning would bring about the cooperative community many radicals believed could be achieved only through violent revolution. Unlike so many visionaries, Howard, moreover, had actually built a working model of his new world, demonstrating its feasibility to a skeptical public. "The utopia which had seemed so lofty and unattainable," Mumford observed in his first essay on the garden city, "came down to earth."[26] In Howard, Mumford thus found a cautious insurgency appropriate to his sober temperament and to his Platonic ideals of balance, order, and good form.

Mumford was strongly drawn to Howard's suggestion of a marriage of country and city. On Sunday afternoons he loved to walk in the countryside just north and west of New York City, and he wanted to save areas like this around America's growing cities for recreation and farming. In his mature writings he would describe his ideal community as one that combined the dynamism and diversity of the city with the enduring values of the village—order, neighborhood stability, and community closeness. While he was an urban man to the core, he would spend over half of his life in an old wooden farmhouse in the hamlet of Leedsville, in Dutchess County, New York, a hundred miles and a world away from the city in which he grew up and made his career. Out of this deep-layered understanding of the best features of these two opposite worlds—the village and the city—Mumford wove his vision of the good life.

Mumford did not get to see Howard's garden cities until much later in his life, but the American city of his youth which came closest to what he thought a garden city ought to look like was Boston, which he first visited in 1915. Boston was then still an old-fashioned walking city; and Beacon Hill, where Mumford's friend Irwin Granich had a room at No. 10 Joy Street, had some of the most gracious urban squares and neighborhoods anywhere. It was a city in touch with its provincial past, a city of soaring church spires,

crooked streets, and solidly built redbrick neighborhoods. And it
had not yet succumbed to skyscraper mania, as had New York.

On the outskirts of Boston was a ring of small communities, more
like country towns than dormitory suburbs, which were connected
to Boston by a train and trolley system. These small communities
were separated from one another by agricultural greenbelts maintained independently by farmers and market gardeners, and were
further protected by Frederick Law Olmsted's "emerald necklace," a
green strip of parkland and pathways extending outwards from the
center of the city. Boston needed only a little further "remodeling,"
Mumford believed, to become a genuine regional city, in which the
satellite towns would maintain a life "of their own while participat-
ing in all the diversified activities of a large city—and without
paying the price in population, environmental degradation, or suburban sprawl."[27]

About the time Mumford discovered Ebenezer Howard he
encountered also the writings of George Russell, the Irish poet,
economist, painter, and propagandist, who with William Butler
Yeats had helped to launch the Irish literary renaissance. Russell, as
much as anyone else, influenced Mumford's developing interest in
regional and rural life; after reading *Co-operation and Nationality*
(1912) Mumford signed up for a course in agricultural economics at
Columbia University.

At an early age Russell had given up a promising career as a painter
and, swayed by his friend Yeats, turned to poetry and, soon thereafter, politics, becoming an organizer for Sir Horace Plunkett's Irish
Agricultural Organization Society, bicycling through the Emerald
Isle spreading its message of agricultural cooperation. A bear of a
man—huge, bearded, and red-faced—Æ, as he was called, was an
enormously popular poet and a legendary conversationalist. But
these were not the qualities that attracted Mumford to him.
Although they struck up a friendly correspondence, he and Mumford met only once—at a New York reception for Russell in the
1920s—so Mumford never got to experience an important side of Æ's
appeal, and he never really cared for Russell's poetry. It was the
Russell of *Co-operation and Nationality*, the philosopher of the Irish
cooperative movement and one of the founders of the Irish rural
revival, who joined company with Geddes, Howard, and the French
geographers to transform Mumford into a passionate regionalist.

To this tally of influences must be added one other: Walt Whitman, whom Mumford described in 1917 as "the soundest personality I have yet encountered in the pages of a book."[28] Whitman, like Russell, dealt equally in his writing with the material and the spiritual.

> *I am the poet of the body*
> *And, I am the poet of the soul.*[29]

But it was Whitman's songs of the city that made the strongest impression on young Mumford. "Of Mannahatta a son," Whitman had walked through every part of the city and had mixed with "the million-headed throng on the streets," but for all his delight in crowds and lively street life, Whitman, like young Mumford, was often a lonely observer of urban life. "Saw many I loved in the street or ferry boat or public assembly yet never told them a word."[30]

Nourished by these influences, Mumford started to pull his life into shape. "From this year on," he confidently wrote in 1917, "I am no more a 'literat' [Whitman's word]: I am a literat equipt [sic] with the tools of science and at work in the service of regionalism: and this is something quite different."[31] And with Whitman, he realized that the new world he was working for could not be brought into being by legislative programs and economic adjustments alone. There would have to be a revolutionary transformation of values and ideals. "The change for which we must work," he observed in an unpublished essay, "is not merely one of monetary distribution. . . . It must be a change in habits of thinking, habits of acting, in the whole . . . conduct of life. . . . We have not merely to redistribute cash, we must refix values. Nothing short of new ideas of heaven and hell—those orientation marks—will be satisfactory."[32] He had seen visions of hell in Pittsburgh and on New York's Lower East Side; and heaven—well, he knew there could never be a perfect world, but Ebenezer Howard had certainly given him a glimpse of a better one.

By the end of 1917, Mumford had found a clearer direction for his life. He would not be a city planner or an architect. His task, he decided, would be "to enlarge the vision" of those who did the actual planning and building.[33] Such a career would allow him to utilize his developing aptitudes in literature, architecture, philosophy, art, and the biological sciences. He could be a specialist without ever ceasing to be a generalist, applying his varied talents and interests, as Geddes had, to the study and improvement of cities. Mumford, at the time, might have been familiar with Samuel Butler's advice on choosing a career; and, if he was, it undoubtedly gave him some much-needed bolstering. "Woe to the specialist who is not a pretty fair generalist, and to the generalist who is not also a bit of a specialist."[34]

For the first time in his life Mumford felt he possessed the one thing he believed every truly self-directed person ought to have—"a calling to which his genius leads him."[35] In "The Brownstone Front," a play he began in 1917 and returned to at several points in his life, we have a clear indication of his new sense of purpose. The play's central character is a young urban reformer, of illegitimate birth, who styles himself as the poet and prophet of an urban renaissance that he sees just on the horizon.[36] But even before he wrote this play, Mumford had been captivated by the city's potential as a theater for heroic reform efforts.

On his own, then, Lewis Mumford turned his youthful invalidism into a period of preparation. By 1918 he was well on the way to transforming his private alienation into specific personal and public aspirations. He now possessed the one thing that is absent from the lives of most alienated youths—a vision of a better world, and the confidence that he would play a part in bringing that world to fulfillment.

This is what we have come to call a sense of identity, and it is perhaps best described by William James in a letter to his wife. "A man's character is discernible in the mental or moral attitude in which, when it came upon him, he felt himself most deeply and intensely active and alive. At such moments there is a voice inside which speaks and says: 'This is the real me!' "[37]

"If you have a philosophy, and if you believe in that philosophy with all the God-given fire of your soul; and if you find that that philosophy conflicts with Life, then with all the God-given fire of your soul try to change life: don't try to change your philosophy."[38] Mumford wrote these fervent lines in 1915; he was soon patterning his actions to this resolve.

When Mumford returned to these shaping years in his auto-biography, one experience, he claims, stood out over all others, a vision that came to him as he crossed the Brooklyn Bridge on a windswept March afternoon. Peering out at the Manhattan skyline through the bridge's lacy steel cables, he experienced a sudden heightened awareness of the promise of his own life, and of the life of the great city spread out in front of him. "Here was my city, immense, overpowering, flooded with energy and light . . . chal-lenging me, beckoning me, demanding something of me that it would take more than a lifetime to give, but raising all my energies by its own vivid promise to a higher pitch. In that sudden revelation of power and beauty all the confusions of adolescence dropped from me, and I trod the narrow, resilient boards of the footway with a new confidence that came not from my isolated self alone but from the collective energies I had confronted and risen to."39

With Whitman, he had "reason to be the proudest son alive"—for he was the son of the "City of the World."

> *Proud and passionate city—mettlesome, mad, extravagant*
> *city!*40

6

A Grub Street
Apprenticeship

*They were big strong days—our young days, days of prepa-
ration: the gathering of the forces.*

—WALT WHITMAN

"Many people came to New York in order to write. But I was born
here, and I can scarcely remember the time when writing, writing
in the Grub Street sense, to earn porridge and pickles, was not part
of my young life."[1] Lewis Mumford wrote these words in 1938,
peering back over the first quarter century of his up-and-down
career as a New York writer, years during which he worked constantly under the lash of necessity. By then he was finally making
enough money from his books to give almost full time to them, and
less time to writing articles and reviews for magazines like *The New
Yorker.* He had established himself as an independent, self-supporting man of letters, one of the only surviving authors in American life
who earned his entire livelihood as a freelance scholar.[2]

The road to that point had been strewn with obstacles. The
earliest years of his literary apprenticeship, between 1914 and 1917,
were the most difficult of all. In this formative period, when he
couldn't get a single thing published or produced—not a play,
poem, short story, nor review—only his tremendous self-discipline,
his steel-hard inner resolve, and his willingness to live a materially

restricted life kept him going. They are the same qualities that kept him at his work—through good times and bad—over the course of a lifetime in literature.

Mumford wrote his first published essay, as we have seen, when he was only fifteen, and the acceptance of that short article for *Modern Electrics* gave him more excitement than the publication of any of his books.

When his interest in radio diminished he had turned to movies, writing scripts for photoplays in 1913 with Beryl Morse. That year he also began to write short articles, poetry, and epigrams that he submitted to *Life*, *Smart Set*, and *Puck*. Shortly thereafter he began a novel, which he never completed, called *The New Emile*, after H. G. Wells's *The New Machiavelli*. And, of course, he wrote a number of one-act plays. But he wasn't proud of any of this work; even from the early perspective of 1916 he saw it as stiff and stilted, and most of it he consigned to the wastebasket.

But as he slowly slipped out of his invalidism, his writing grew more assured and less self-consciously Shavian. He ceased to try to imitate Shaw, Wells, or Butler and began to shape a style uniquely his own. What helped to spur him on was the feeling that at least *someone* thought enough of his work to publish it. In 1914, at the age of eighteen, he had two of his essays printed in Mitchell Kennerley's *The Forum*, a spirited monthly of the arts, and earlier that same year he finished as a runner-up in a contest sponsored by *Metropolitan Magazine* for an answer to George Bernard Shaw's "The Case for Equality." Lincoln Steffens won the $500 first prize, but Mumford was paid $87.50 for his contribution, which was published. This "false dawn" confirmed his decision to be a writer, although he still wasn't sure whether he wanted to be an essayist, playwright, novelist, or sociologist.[3]

For the next four years he gave himself completely to his writing, despite his failure to get his work published, for he possessed that quixotic combination of self-assurance and blindness that so often results in eventual success. In these years Mumford acquired the regular, disciplined habits of a serious writer. He tried to write at least a thousand words a day, whether he felt like it or not. But as the rejection slips came down on him like a succession of hard punches he sometimes found it impossible to stick to his routine, "wondering whether the next blow might not lead to my being carried out of the ring."4 More than not, however, he met his daily quota of words.

"What impressed me and all our other young friends who . . . visited his home," Jerry Lachenbruch wrote of Mumford during these years of literary apprenticeship, "was Lewis's . . . stick-to-it-ive-ness, his fanatical persistence in any work he undertook." On a narrow wall beside his bed was a large chart, a meticulously detailed study plan, of the books he proposed to read and the essays and plays he planned to write in the coming weeks and months. "This persistence and his interests were such that he would not go on a [weekend] walk with [his friends] unless he had finished his week's stint."5 Years later, reviewing Lachenbruch's account, Mumford strenuously denied that he was quite *that* disciplined; he liked to think of himself as being better balanced, less scrupulously studious, but the evidence supports Lachenbruch.

At this early age his writing was already his life, but as disciplined and self-confident as he was, he still needed support and encouragement. He received this from several sources. In his autobiography Mumford recalls an encounter that had a great effect on his development as a writer. In 1915 he decided that he wanted to become a philosopher; not just an academic philosopher, but a philosopher directly familiar with the ways of everyday life in the manner of William James. What better way to acquire such experience, he reasoned at the time, than through newspaper work, and with that in mind he went to see Talcott Williams, dean of the Columbia University School of Journalism. He told Williams, who listened patiently to his story, that he was prepared to invest the remainder of his trust fund, over $4,000, to get an education in journalism and philosophy. Williams, however, told him to hold on to his money as long as he could, although he said that Columbia would be happy to admit him. "It's your margin of freedom, while you have it, you need never be driven to do work that goes against your conscience or offers you no inner reward. . . . Spend that capital, if you have to spend it at all, like a miser. . . . Remember: *it's your freedom.*"6

Mumford immediately recognized this as sound advice and took it to heart. He dropped the idea of going to journalism school, and with it the notion of going into newspaper work, for he had no intention, after his experience on the *Evening Telegram*, of trying again to make it as a reporter without any previous training. The money he saved supported him for the next six to eight years, when he was finally able to make some money on his writing. More importantly, it kept him in the kind of work he most wanted to do.

Williams gave him some of the best advice he ever got, but Mitchell Kennerley gave him something even more important— confidence in himself as a professional writer. Kennerley was the audacious young publisher of some of the best young writers of that day, including D. H. Lawrence, Edna St. Vincent Millay, Walter Lippmann, Max Eastman, and Van Wyck Brooks, and he was the only publisher to show any interest in Mumford's earliest work, seeing in it a promise others did not. Even after he sent back Mumford's third contribution to *The Forum* he kept in touch with him, and wrote to Walter Lippmann recommending him for a position on *The New Republic*. (On learning that Mumford had already sent *The New Republic* an article that they had turned down, Kennerley advised him as to what might have been the problem. "I'm afraid your article had an opinion in it. It's a journal of opinion, you know, and they don't like to publish other people's.")[7]

When Mumford's literary fortunes hit bottom in the fall of 1916, Kennerley took him on as a reader for his firm, where Mumford soon learned the courtly, sharp-witted Kennerley could be a most exasperating man to work for. Kennerley had a reputation for his slipshod, sometimes shady business practices, and Mumford fell victim to one of Kennerley's unfortunate habits—that of hiring young readers for an indefinite period at a salary to be determined later and then "forgetting" to pay them.

Mumford spent a month in Kennerley's "employ," resigning in frustration when Kennerley ignored his several requests for pay and more regular work. Mumford left Kennerley that December bitterly disappointed, but though the two men never saw each other again he had no regrets or ill feelings about the experience. Kennerley's "belief in me outweighed a ton of rejection slips."[8] For a brief moment he had been on the inside with an office of his own, meeting famous editors and authors, making judgments on manuscripts, correcting copy. Even though he knew his position was shaky, it was a reassuring experience.

The Kennerley episode redoubled Mumford's determination to make it in the New York literary world, and early in 1917 he decided to devote more of his time to writing plays. As a playwright he might have a better chance of making some money or of gaining a name for himself more quickly than as a writer about cities and regions.

There were a number of spirited "Little Theater" groups that were gaining attention in New York, and that winter of 1917–18 he worked steadily on "The Brownstone Front," hoping that one of the best of them, the Washington Square Players, which had expressed some interest in his Leonardo play, might produce it.

Mumford continued to think highly of the rough first act of "The Brownstone Front," but it suffers from the same defects that marred his other plays: the ideas overwhelm the plot and the dialogue, badly slowing down the action of the play. In truth, none of his plays, then or later, possessed sufficient dramatic drive. The clever but stiffly-written plays he wrote before 1920 are the work of a young man who had not yet tasted life deeply enough to write psychologically mature drama. Yeats, the brilliant friend of his beloved Æ, not Shaw, would have served him better as a literary master.

Though Mumford had many mentors in these years—Shaw, Geddes, Emerson, and others—in the end it was his flesh and blood friends and fellow writers who sustained him in his decision to remain a writer in the face of one crushing disappointment after another.

The person whom Mumford credits with giving him the most help as a struggling writer was Edward Wickes, an editor of *The Writer's Monthly*, a cheaply produced sheet that conducted correspondence courses and provided information to aspiring writers on the state of the publishing market. Mumford met Wickes, a fast-talking literary hustler then in his mid-thirties, in one of his City College classes, and together they edited the Evening Session's section of the college's 1914 yearbook. Wickes looked like the stock villain of a silent movie. He had a pale yellow complexion, long, sleek black hair, stooping shoulders, and he liked to dress entirely in black. When he grinned, a gold tooth shone in the front of his mouth.

Wickes had come up the hard way, learning to write on his own, teaching himself grammar, composition, and rhetoric from a series of standard texts. Although his writing was clumsy in the extreme, and in conversation he seemed barely literate, he was successful, in a way, making around $8,ooo a year, mostly ghostwriting autobiographies for movie queens.

Wickes was a hack writer, but he was on the inside, on Grub Street, where Mumford enviously wanted to be, and for a year or so Mumford found it exciting to be in his company. He regularly went to Wickes's Union Square office for advice about his own writing, and about how to get it into print, for on the latter, at least, Wickes professed to be something of an expert. Mumford soon learned, however, that he wouldn't get very far with this man guiding him.

When one of Mumford's photoplays, "The Bells," was accepted by the Edison Company, he took the contract to Wickes to ask him to look it over before he signed it. Wickes read it closely and then handed it back to Mumford with a quizzical smile, and said: "Hell, yes: I guess it's all right. It's the first time I ever [sic] seen one of them damn things. You know I ain't ever had a script of mine taken, though I think I'm on a hot trail now."

Still, Mumford credits Wickes with teaching him a lesson he sorely needed at the time: that talent itself wasn't enough for success in "the writing game," as Wickes liked to call it. The writer needed patience and tenacity, and Wickes, despite his mediocre abilities, had a kind of "Grant-like doggedness" that reinforced Mumford's obstinate determination to succeed. Wickes also served as a valuable early critic of Mumford's short stories, which, after meeting him, he began to send to a number of literary magazines.[9]

By the time Mumford was twenty he had become friends with a circle of writers and would-be writers, most of whom he had met in the Evening Session of City College. This group included Lachenbruch, Herbert Feis, Henry Hazlett, and a number of others who shared his passion for writing, literature, and social thought. The most talented member of this society of apprentice scribblers and Sunday hikers was Irwin Granich (Michael Gold). Occasionally Mumford would meet Granich, Feis, and his other City College pals downtown at MacSorley's saloon, one of Granich's favorite hangouts, where, munching onions and crackers and gulping cold ale from pewter mugs, they'd argue earnestly about politics and poetry. Granich had recently joined the radical labor union, the Industrial Workers of the World, and not all of the members of the group cared for his political views, or for his way of expressing them. (When the mood was right Granich would shoot out of his seat and begin singing the Wobbly song, "Hallelujah! I'm a Bum," in his rich baritone voice.) But he was, in Mumford's eyes, brilliantly engaging and passionately alive. He was, moreover, the first among them to get into print (in 1915, Max Eastman published one of his poems in *The Masses*). For that, at least, they all admired him.[10]

On many of their afternoons and evenings together the group would gather first at one of Mumford's favorite places, the Forty-second Street Library, to study together, every one of them secretly anticipating the day when their first book would appear in the great library's card catalogue. From the library they'd head downtown to Greenwich Village, either walking or riding on the uncovered top of a Fifth Avenue bus, to Strunsky's on Second Avenue, or to Polly's on Fourth, between MacDougal Street and Sixth Avenue, a popular gathering place for Village artists and revolutionaries. There they were served inexpensive drinks and meals by Hoppolyte Havel, Paula Holladay's infamous anarchist cook-waiter. Havel, a menacing-looking man with a full-flowing mustache that spread like wide wings from his face, edited *Blast*, one of the first radical magazines to publish Granich's work. Jailed several times in this country and abroad for his revolutionary politics, he showed open contempt for every member of the capitalist class. As he rudely shoved plates of steaming food in front of customers he suspected of being capitalists he'd often sneer loudly, "Bourgeois pigs!"[11]

Upstairs, on the second floor of Polly's, was the equally famous Liberal Club, the Village meeting place of Emma Goldman, John Reed, Lincoln Steffens, Theodore Dreiser, Eugene O'Neill, and Randolph Bourne. From their table in crowded, smoke-filled Polly's, in front of one of the restaurant's big open fireplaces, Mumford and his impressionable little band of literary achievers occasionally caught a glimpse of one of these legends of the Left sitting at another table, or talking with Polly in the kitchen, or hurrying upstairs to the Liberal Club to attend a poetry reading, a Cubist art exhibit, or one of the club's notorious Friday-night wine-and-talk parties.

This was the heyday of Village bohemianism, when the Village was "the Left Bank of the United States," and it was through Granich that Mumford first experienced this fervent atmosphere of radicalism, feminism, and lively experimentation in social living.[12]

At first Mumford must have felt a little pale and inferior around Granich, who was tough, ghetto-smart, and proud of his proletarian roots. He was born in the tenement and the tenement, he used to say, was in his blood. Granich had quit school at an early age to earn a living working for the Adams Express Company. In 1916 he went to Harvard as a special student, but quit after several months to give full time to his writing. In the years between his conversion to radicalism in 1914, after attending a labor rally in Union Square, and 1921, when he became an editor of *The Liberator*, the successor to *The Masses*, Granich traveled all over America and championed a host of leftist causes. He also wrote one-act plays for the Province-town Players, and after rehearsals with the Players in New York, at a converted stable on MacDougal Street, he'd go drinking with Eugene O'Neill and some of their anarchist friends at the Hell Hole, a bawdy neighborhood barroom, where O'Neill, whiskey glass in hand, would recite "The Hound of Heaven."[13]

Although Granich and Mumford both loved Whitman, tempera-mentally they could not have been further apart, and Granich later confessed to having a hard time figuring out this lean, lonely "big-nosed goy."[14] But he took a quick liking to Mumford, admiring his determination to succeed as a writer and his enthusiasm for new ideas and thinking. He also came to trust Mumford as a friend; when Granich fled to Mexico to escape the draft in 1918 he left Mumford to handle his mail and manuscripts, and asked him to send him some money he had left behind.

For a time the two friends shared a common social dream—that of a cooperative community of free and equal men—or at least Mum-ford thought they did. When Mumford first met him Granich was an anarchist and a committed decentralist, strongly drawn, with Mumford, to the ideas of Peter Kropotkin, the Russian anarchist. It was Granich who introduced Mumford to the anarchist Ferrer Soci-ety in Harlem, where in 1917 Mumford gave his first public lecture, on Kropotkin and the philosophy of regionalism. But while Mum-ford was moving toward a new appreciation of regional decentraliza-tion, Granich was moving in the opposite direction, toward revolutionary centralism. Following the Bolshevik Revolution, Granich (now Michael Gold) began to preach for an immediate revolution in this country to plant a dictatorship of the proletariat. Mumford, temperamentally more conservative and far less angry about things, preferred the peaceful, gradualist approach of Geddes and Howard, and he distrusted Granich's mystical idealization of the proletariat.

Mumford had not read Marx closely, but he had heard socialist speakers giving their version of the doctrine on street corners on his way to City College, and later, with Granich, in the socialist clubs and restaurants of the Village. What Mumford heard and what he read did not impress him. His desire for a more humane economic system emerged from Plato, Ruskin, Morris, Tolstoy, and Kropotkin, not from Marx or Engels.

Shortly before America's entrance into World War I, Mumford joined the alumni chapter of the Intercollegiate Socialist Society and attended their meetings in the back room of a Village restaurant. Granich also attended these meetings, and afterwards they'd go for long walks through the crooked Village streets, ending the day with a late supper at Polly's or Three Steps Down. At one of these meetings Mumford gave a brief address outlining his arguments with Marxism, after which he was roundly denounced by everyone in the room as a reactionary. By this time Granich was fed up with Mumford's politics, and he told him that in so many words. Granich's stridency offended Mumford, who wanted somehow to remain friends with him despite their political differences. But Granich seemed unwilling to let that happen. He wanted to convert Mumford, and when he failed he drew away from him. After he left for Mexico, and Mumford went off to navy service, they rarely saw each other and corresponded only occasionally.[15]

When they ran into each other again in New York in the early 1920s—their first meeting since 1918—Gold was a different person. Not satisfied to be "of" the proletariat, he wanted to look like a proletarian as well. He wore dirty shirts and a black Stetson and smoked cheap Italian cigars; and he had a habit of spitting on the floor, whether he was in a barroom, his office, or the home of a rich supporter of radical causes. "I am not a mystic any more," Mumford remembers Gold telling him. "I am a Communist now. . . . It's damned rot to wait for people to move by themselves; they have to be forced into it by a minority that knows what's what and that sees what's to be done. You intellectuals will all be swept off the fence sooner or later; you don't get anywhere with all your 'thinking' and 'dreaming' and emotionalizing. Unless you can put your ideas over, they're not worth a row of pins."16

So they parted, each ironically thinking the other was a hopeless idealist. Later, Mumford would blame Gold for their separation: he "had nothing but contempt for me as a bourgeois liberal."17 But that was not entirely true. Their intermittent correspondence shows that Gold continued to have great respect for Mumford. Until the end of his life he clung to the hope that the friend of his youth would eventually embrace Marxism, and he never stopped trying to convert him. "You are still in the Shelley stage . . . ," he wrote to him in 1954, "planning Utopian cities with Sir Patrick [Geddes] and hoping you can persuade Winston Churchill . . . and the like into building them. . . . You could [be the] John Strachey [of American communism]—You have the equipment. Come on in, the water is fine." It was a familiar plea—"the same old lecture," Gold himself admitted—but he always seemed convinced that *this* time it would work.18

Mumford, by the same token, continued to hope that Gold would see the error of his ways and drop his almost religious allegiance to Russian Communism. "There was always something vehement, defiant, deeply human in Gold," Mumford told Daniel Aaron in 1959, "that made his conversion to communism and his acceptance of its regimentation of mind deeply foreign to his character."19 It was those independent, robustly human qualities that prevented Mumford from cutting himself off completely from Gold. When *Jews Without Money* was published he wrote Gold an affectionate letter praising the book; Gold wrote back, thanking him warmly. Politics had divided them irrevocably; both were the type of men who seal and break friendships over ideas. But despite their differences Mumford felt an almost brotherly kinship with Gold, or rather with Irwin Granich, his friend from his City College days.

In 1917, Mumford and Gold took opposite sides on another large issue, the Great War. Mumford supported Woodrow Wilson's declaration of war against Germany in April 1917, but Gold thundered against it. One evening less than a year later Gold slipped quietly out of an El Paso hotel and waded across the Rio Grande River into Mexico to avoid being drafted, or possibly prosecuted for antiwar activities with John Reed, Max Eastman, Art Young, Floyd Dell, and his other radical associates. In 1917, while Gold agonized over this question of whether to stay in the country or leave, Mumford wrestled with another decision—whether or not to enlist in the armed services.

In Pittsburgh, while working in Tucker's cement-testing lab, he decided to wait it out, convinced that he wasn't in sound enough health to pass the physical examination for the draft. Besides, he was in no real hurry to get into the fight, for he suspected by then that nothing good would come out of it.

When war erupted in Europe in August 1914, Mumford was an eighteen-year-old student at City College. Like most Americans, he was shocked that such a thing could happen in an era of upward progress and advancing democracy. He tried to preserve his neutrality, taking turns cursing the militaristic ambitions of the Germans and the imperialistic designs of the French and British, but his heart eventually went out to the Allies, whose cause he came to support despite his German ancestry and his Uncle James's vehement tirades against the British, a race of "barbarians" whom he blamed for "degrading" the classics by calling Titus Livius "Livy" and Marcus Tullius Cicero "Tully."[20] Mumford rejected out of hand the bombastic pro-German propaganda his uncle pushed on him; but along with a good many other patriots, he believed, at least in part, the French and English reports detailing the atrocities of the marauding "Hun" armies in Belgium and northern France. He even wrote a play in this spirit, "The Great Captain."

Still, he took a rather aloof attitude toward the war, claiming that he didn't feel "personally involved."[21] His principal fear at the time was that the war would finish his career, although he was not even sure what that would be. But while he had utterly no desire to join the struggle, neither was he a pacifist. He believed that there were causes worth fighting for; he was simply unsure if this was one of them.

In the 1916 presidential election Mumford rallied to Wilson, bound to him by his solemn promise to keep America out of the war. Six months later the United States was in the fire, and Mumford was still standing with Wilson, backing the American war effort with enthusiasm. His opinions at the time were in perfect sympathy with the editors of *The New Republic*, who, with John Dewey as their lead spokesman, assailed pacifism as an indefensible position and urged that the United States pursue the fight with resolve, using its moral force to fashion a fair peace and a postwar order of international cooperation.

By the summer of 1917, however, Mumford had shifted his position. Wilson was now urging "force without stint or limit" as the formula for victory, and his administration was moving to crush all domestic opposition to its war program.[22] In June 1917, Wilson signed the Espionage Act and the government moved immediately to deny mailing privileges to socialist publications. Thus began what John Reed called a reign of "judicial tyranny"; by the end of the war almost every leading Socialist Party official had been indicted for antiwar activities.[23] This "violent inquisition of pacifists" and "hysterical suppression of free discussion" made Wilson's "morally stirring original pronouncements" seem pretty hollow, Mumford wrote to Gold that summer. Still, he could not turn against his President or his country—he was too much of a patriot, he told Gold.[24]

Mumford hoped that his poor health would keep him out of the war. But if drafted, "I shall go submissively, a good citizen," he wrote in his notes in 1917, "in the mood of Socrates quaffing the poison cup."[25]

As it turned out, when he was offered the poison cup he didn't take it. His draft board called him for a medical examination in February 1918, and to his complete surprise and horror he was declared fit for military service. He immediately requested another examination, and when the doctors at Roosevelt Hospital pronounced him fit for class I duty he realized that he had no choice but to go. But he had no intention of serving in the trenches if he could help it. Following the advice and example of Herbert Feis and Jerry Lachenbruch, he enlisted in the navy for training as a radio operator before his number turned up for induction into the "man-hungry army."[26] The navy recruiting officer told him that if he signed up for the duration of the war he would be sent to radio school at Harvard after a brief training period at Newport. This would give him a chance to survey the Boston region, something he had put on his calendar to do in 1918 anyway.

At six o'clock on the morning of April 5, Lewis Mumford was sworn into the navy. Late that same afternoon he sailed out of New York harbor on the night steamer for Newport, known colloquially to sailors as the "arsehole of the Universe." The slow-moving Fall River liner reached Newport at two o'clock in the morning, and the drowsy recruits, some of them miserably seasick, were immediately put through processing: signed in, medically examined, and assigned hammocks. Then they marched off to a breakfast of bananas and beans, which they ate standing up. After eating they staggered back to their tents for a few hours of sleep, to be awakened by sharp bugle blasts to their first full day of navy basic training.

From the start Mumford was "in the navy but not of it." His mind remained elsewhere, and this is probably what enabled him to endure basic training. Navy life was doubly difficult for him, for he was not vigorously healthy, nor was he ready for the drill and discipline of basic training, although this is probably just what he needed at the time to toughen him up and to break him from his restricted invalid's routine. The navy did help to strengthen him physically, but he found the whole routine of basic training repugnant.[27]

Yet he survived; and he did so surprisingly well because navy life gave him as much personal freedom as he could hope for under wartime conditions: he even had time to do some studying and writing. Years later he would boast of carrying a copy of Emerson's essays in his middy blouse, reading it on the chow line or while resting between drills.

His new friendship with David Liebovitz, an aspirant novelist from New York City, also helped to lighten the burden of navy life. He and Mumford were quartered in the same barracks, and they became friends while working together on the coal pile. The boredom, Liebovitz recalls, drew them into conversation, and they quickly learned that they shared many interests, particularly literature and ideas.[28] Liebovitz loved the theater, had read Ibsen and Strindberg, and he, too, had been recently disappointed in love. Sitting on a bench by their bunks after drill, he and Mumford would recite Rilke to each other and plot their literary careers.

Liebovitz was a keen judge of character, and he knew that it was more than the war and his reluctance to serve that was behind his friend's stony detachment and self-absorption. In a memoir he wrote of their friendship in 1964, four years before his death, he incisively describes the Mumford he knew in 1918, and the man he would eventually become. Mumford was "a little shut up in himself," Liebovitz observes, probably because "he had been forced to depend on his own resources since his crucial early years." Later, he "would make a virtue of this, and prefer to stand alone testing his rigor and independence. . . . A certain aloofness to guard his independence—and, more pointedly, independence of judgment—would always be characteristic of him." To his friends, "he might have once seemed humorless, but his was only apparent: he was slow to give out in the beginning in any casual way, which may be accounted for [by] a residual shyness from his childhood. But there was much about him that I did not know, and some things that I would never know. He was not the sort of whom one asked questions."²⁹ That was as fine an assessment of one side of Mumford's character as anyone would make.

It was not that Mumford was unfriendly. Though he kept to himself most of the time, he mixed well with the other men, some of whom must have thought him a strange bird, this lanky, indrawn New Yorker who walked with a spring in his step and who was extremely fastidious about his appearance. Even then, Liebovitz must have guessed that while they might become warm friends, he would never be able to get on intimate terms with such a guardedly self-protective soul; few of Mumford's friends were able to do that.

Before he entered the navy Mumford had been advised by Jerry Lachenbruch to try at all costs to avoid military service. "The chance of your going under is too great," he warned him, concerned about his fragile health. But if he *was* drafted, he further advised him, "try to be discharged."³⁰ Mumford ignored that last piece of advice, but he was successful in avoiding military combat. This was not easy, for part of his training was in Morse code, which he mastered quickly, and there was a desperate shortage of radiomen in the Atlantic fleet. Some of his barracks mates were being sent into the Atlantic to complete the remainder of their training, but Mumford managed to get out of this by coming down with a case of the measles on the very morning he was to be shipped out. A Roman Catholic chaplain helped him to get assigned to the new radio school at Harvard, and when he left Newport he felt that he had escaped a term in hell. When he arrived in Cambridge and spent his first night at Winthrop House, "I knew that I had arrived in heaven."[31]

The Radio Training School at Cambridge was badly overcrowded, and to house the growing number of recruits, the navy was beginning to build wooden barracks on the Harvard Commons. While the huts were being constructed recruits were permitted to live off-campus in nearby student boardinghouses. Shortly after arriving in Cambridge, Mumford took a room in a spacious white house at 33 Kirkland Street, had his typewriter sent from New York by railway express, and plunged into his urban research and writing, which he had ample time for in the late afternoons and evenings.

In his free hours, when he was not studying and writing, he explored Boston and the towns around it in much the same manner he had his native New York, on foot, equipped with notepad, sketch pad, a box of watercolors, and navy topographic maps. On these leisurely afternoon rambles he acquired his first appreciation for the architecture of Henry Hobson Richardson, whose greatest Boston work was Trinity Church on Copley Square. As it turns out, he didn't have to go very far to find the work of this then underrated American genius, for his morning classes were in the Law Library of Austin Hall, one of Richardson's several masonry masterpieces. A number of years later Mumford revived the reputation of this "colossal man," who created the beginning of a new American architecture.[32]

The man who helped to introduce Boston's architecture to him was a fellow Kirkland Street boarder named William Bigelow, formerly an architect with the original firm of McKim, White and Bigelow. When Mumford met him he was a curious, somewhat eccentric old man, still pert and spirited and ready for good conversation, and he and Mumford would have long talks in the summer evenings about architecture. Although Mumford was still too untrained in architecture to ask Bigelow the right questions, Bigelow was the first person to inspire him to write about architecture.

So in Cambridge, "a sailor's paradise," Mumford had abundant opportunities to follow his interests.[33] He even tried to make some money writing, entering a contest on housing ideas sponsored by the *Journal of the American Institute of Architects*. Confident of his chances of winning the first prize of $1,000, he worked on his essay steadily from July into October, first at 33 Kirkland Street and then, when he was called back to quarters at Harvard, in a tiny room he rented just to write in at 40 Kirkland Street. He didn't win, but his essay foreshadows some of his better writing on housing, particularly in its suggestions for functionally designed cluster housing.

The influenza epidemic in the fall, which killed tens of millions of people worldwide, delayed Mumford's graduation from radio school. During the epidemic the navy officers at Cambridge called a quarantine and canceled classes for several weeks. Mumford didn't graduate with a second-class radio electrician's rating until the end of November, and by that time, to his great relief, the war was over. Early in December he was shipped to Pelham Bay, and in February 1919 he was discharged. A "triumph," he called it.[34]

At the time Mumford considered his navy experience as little more than a bothersome interruption of his career, but the navy had given him some freedom to continue his work. He had acquired as well the firsthand knowledge of navy life he needed later to write a biography of Herman Melville, for the navy he served in was still much the same as that Melville described in *White Jacket*.[35] Even Newport had not been all that horrendous an experience. He hated the base and the hard discipline, the shrill incessant bark of his chief petty officer, but he had used his few hours of leave time to take mind-soothing strolls through the narrow streets of the old seaport or out along the cliffs by Narragansett Bay, where the titans of iron and finance had built their sprawling summer palaces.

The navy had helped to mature him somewhat, and to toughen him physically, but he was too self-possessed and set on his course to be greatly affected by his service experience. And the navy, for that matter, was not much of a maritime "experience"; the only time he had set foot on a boat was when he pulled stroke oar on a whaling boat on Narragansett Bay.

A "vision" he had at Newport, on a weekend leave, similar to the one he had experienced earlier on the Brooklyn Bridge, reaffirmed his confidence in himself and his future. After spending a few quiet hours in Peter Harrison's old Redwood Library, a refined colonial building in the Palladio style, he walked back to his quarters by way of a bridge that joined the mainland to the island. As he was halfway across the span he paused to watch the afternoon sun drop in the sky, and he was suddenly overcome with what he describes as an "exalted sense of my whole future life spreading out before me. Perhaps this is what religious people have meant when they speak of communing with God. To me the experience said that the world had meaning: and life itself even at its worst was more wonderful than anyone had been able to say in words. . . . In that breathless moment past and future, my past and the world's past, my future and the world's future, came together. . . ."[36]

With this inner feeling that he was absolutely designated for success, but with hardly enough money in his possession to cover his board and lodging at home, Lewis Mumford, age twenty-four, returned to Manhattan to take one more crack at Grub Street. He knew that his chances of earning a decent living from his writing were slim, but he was prepared to make any sacrifices that might be necessary. He also had greater confidence in his work now; just before he entered the navy several of his pieces were accepted for publication, ending a four-year period of editorial rejection and acute personal frustration. *The Scientific Monthly* agreed to publish an article of his on New York museums; *The Public*, a small political journal, took his essay on the Russian situation; and a theater company in Baltimore tentatively accepted "The Invalids," although they never produced it. The editors of *The Public* also asked him to do occasional book reviews.

Mumford was still not certain what kind of writer he would seek to become; his immediate concern was to land a job, any job in which he could write for a living. There were still lots of little magazines in New York in 1919, and he heard from Jerry Lachenbruch that one of them, *The Dial*, which he had begun to read in the navy, was giving young writers books to review. Early in March he went to the Village offices of *The Dial* at 112 West Thirteenth Street and was hired immediately by Robert Morss Lovett, *The Dial*'s editor-in-chief. After only two reviews Lovett asked him if he would consider joining the staff as an associate editor.

Before he was formally offered the job Mumford was taken to the office of *The Dial's* owner, Martyn Johnson, for an interview. After discussing Mumford's qualifications Johnson reviewed the history of *The Dial* and outlined its editorial policy. He told him that the magazine was not in sound financial shape, and that another young writer, Geroid Robinson, was also being considered for the position. Then, as Lovett recalls, "with the aplomb of the captain of a sinking ship who thinks that one or two more victims will make no difference," Johnson hired both Mumford and Robinson as assistant editors, at what was for Mumford the "fabulous" salary of $25 per week.37

The Dial, which took the name of Emerson's old organ of transcendentalism, was founded in Chicago in 1880 as a fortnightly review of literature, and under the editorship of its founder, Francis F. Browne, it gained a reputation as a regional literary voice of excellence. Not long after Browne's death in 1913, the magazine was taken over by Johnson, a midwestern journalist sympathetic to leftist causes, and turned into a journal of politics and social reconstruction. To help carry through this transition Johnson hired Harold Stearns, a Harvard graduate, later the editor of *Civilization in the United States*, the mordant postwar manifesto of America's disillusioned intellectuals. In June 1918, Johnson moved the magazine to New York, bringing with him from the Midwest Clarence Britten, an English professor at the University of Wisconsin, and a little later Robert Morss Lovett, of the University of Chicago. Randolph Bourne became a regular contributor; and John Dewey, Thorstein Veblen, and Helen Marot, a feminist and labor writer, were made contributing editors. Scofield Thayer, a rich young Harvard graduate, recently returned from Magdalen College, Oxford, where he had studied the classics and philosophy, became the magazine's chief financial backer. Although Thayer preferred that *The Dial* devote itself mainly to literary concerns, for the first year he left editorial direction to Johnson, who wanted to model *The Dial* after the London *Athenaeum*, a political and literary journal of considerable reputation.38

Under Johnson, *The Dial* dedicated itself to preparing for the reconstruction movement that the editors expected to follow immediately after the war. For radicals of all stripes it was a time of high hopes, and Mumford eagerly made himself a part of *The Dial's* plans for a new America. "This is the happiest time of my life," he remembers saying to himself more than once in these first exciting months on "The Reconstruction *Dial*," as Johnson liked to call it.[39]

Before the war Michael Gold had introduced Mumford to life in Greenwich Village, but he had "only gotten close enough to smell what was cooking and to feel my mouth watering." Now on *The Dial*, with its handsome offices in the heart of the Village, he was part of this spirited fraternity of dissenters, strolling around Washington Square or having lunch at the Lafayette with writers and radicals he had once enviously admired from afar. His new friends—Geroid Robinson, Clarence Britten, and Helen Marot—did not seem to care a lick for money, clothes, or fast cars; their world was that of art, ideas, and reform.[40]

On the staff of *The Dial* Mumford had an opportunity to get on closer terms with one of his new intellectual heroes, the economist and sociologist Thorstein Veblen, who occasionally showed up for editorial meetings, sitting through them Buddha-like, a bored look on his lean ashen face, his cold eyes peering straight ahead.

Mumford had met Veblen before joining *The Dial*'s staff. Just after leaving the navy he took a course from Veblen at the New School for Social Research, the recent creation of Charles Beard and James Harvey Robinson. Mumford found Veblen an unimpressive classroom teacher. He spoke in a hushed monotone, almost a whisper, leaning lazily on the podium, his shabby jacket and baggy pants draped over his gaunt frame. Even when he could be heard it was difficult to follow his torturously complex arguments and circumlocutions. But Mumford admired his ruthless powers of analysis and devoured his ideas, and for a time on *The Dial* Veblen took him under his wing.[41]

Before he encountered Veblen as a teacher, Mumford had read with enthusiasm all of his books, finding him much like Geddes in his refusal "to recognize the no-trespass signs that smaller minds erected around their chosen fields of specialization."[42] Veblen was at once a linguist, sociologist, ethnologist, anthropologist, historian, philosopher, folklorist, and economist. He also impressed Mumford as a writer scrupulously concerned with every detail of his craft. Working on *The Dial*, he spent endless hours preparing his copy for print, and he didn't believe that the editors should fool with it. If they did, and they happened to make a mistake—God help them, for he had a ferocious temper.

Mumford had read *The Theory of the Leisure Class* while studying at City College, and this book initially attracted him to Veblen. No wonder; Veblen's bitterly ironic indictment of conspicuous consumption and display were exactly the theories that this somewhat down-at-the-heels young writer needed to feel superior to those with more expensive tastes and habits. Mumford also found Veblen's economic thinking, with its grounding in American history and culture, a bracing alternative to the theories of Marx and Engels.

In 1919, Veblen was enjoying his greatest vogue, for his economic ideas were in line with the planning proposals for postwar America being endorsed by John Dewey and a number of other influential non-Marxist reformers. Veblen believed the nation's industrial plant was capable of producing virtually limitless abundance, yet the ancient dream of universal plenitude was being "sabotaged" by the capitalist businessman, who often curtailed production in the interest of higher profits. In *The Engineers and the Price System* he laid down a plan for a bloodless revolution by engineers and technicians—those, he believed, who actually performed the essential work in industry. Since these groups were indispensable to the productive process, they could, through the threat of a general strike, bring down capitalism with little violence or disruption of the going technology. Once in control, they would move to replace absentee ownership with a "soviet" of economic experts whose supreme concern would be the full release of industrial production.

Mumford was in sympathy with Veblen's withering criticisms of the price system and the wasteful practices of the kept classes. He, too, believed in the importance of comprehensive economic planning conducted by public planning boards and of management-sharing in the factory. But he had absolutely no faith in Veblen's scheme for an engineer's revolt. The whole idea seemed elitist and authoritarian, and just a little fantastic. Still, this solemn, unmannered Norwegian always remained a heroic figure for Mumford, and for a brief moment in 1919 he and Veblen both looked forward to a reconstructed America.[43]

Nineteen nineteen. Mumford couldn't have chosen a more historically decisive year to walk into the New York literary and political world. Nineteen Hundred and Nineteen, the name of William Butler Yeats's evocative poem, and the year John Dos Passos chose as the title of the second volume of his American trilogy, *U.S.A.* In that year America, the world in fact, approached a crucial crossroads. "We may well be within measurable distance of universal collapse and anarchy throughout Europe and Asia," a worried Winston Churchill wrote Prime Minister David Lloyd George, fearing the consequences of the collapse of the old order.[44] But others, Mumford included, viewed things differently. For an exhilarating moment a whole new world seemed immediately possible. That year everyone was watching events in Russia, where less than a year before the Bolsheviks had stormed to power. That upheaval seemed to have started something no one could stop. Even Mumford backed the Bolshevik Revolution in his *Dial* editorials and reviews, convinced that it would set loose long-needed changes worldwide.

But "all too soon the bright dreams faded out."[45] In the immediate aftermath of the Seattle general strike in early 1919 radicals were attacked all over the country by vigilante groups, many of them marching under large American flags. Mumford was given a frightening firsthand view of this fanatical patriotism when, that summer, his colleagues Helen Marot and Martyn Johnson were called before the Lusk Committee of Congress and cross-examined in secret for the alleged revolutionary activities of their magazine. Just weeks later, Attorney General A. Mitchell Palmer, "The Fighting Quaker," whose Washington home had been bombed in April by a demented anarchist, launched the first of his illegal raids on the headquarters of radical organizations, beginning a campaign of chilling resolve against suspected Reds. This came directly on the heels of the announcement of the Treaty of Versailles, a document that Mumford and *The Dial* denounced as a violation of the spirit of Wilson's pleas for a fair and lasting peace.

Earlier Mumford had sided with John Dewey in his debate with Randolph Bourne over American participation in the war, but now he recanted. Bourne had been correct about the war and its impact on the soul and spirit of the nation. "The war animus . . . was one of the most important psychological by-products of the war," Mumford wrote in April 1919, "and to those who accept the liberal points of view it appears at long last the most dangerous."[46] Mumford still opposed pacifism, as did Veblen, but now they both turned against Wilson. He had betrayed them, or so they thought at the time.

The "Age of Confidence" was over. The Age of Normalcy began officially with the election the following November of Warren G. Harding. Mumford was not as disillusioned as some of his radical friends, who impulsively threw over their former commitments and rejected their former lives in the movement, yet he could not help being affected by the growing mood of spiritual disenchantment. "Perhaps we are at the beginning of a new Dark Age," he remembers agreeing with one of his friends at the time.[47]

The Dial was one of the casualties of 1919. Its troubles began in December 1918 when Scofield Thayer withdrew from the publishing corporation, incensed over the editor's support of the Bolshevik Revolution. He continued to give money to the magazine throughout 1919, but not enough to save it. All that year Martyn Johnson worked frantically to keep *The Dial* alive; he even tried unsuccessfully to make a quick killing in the stock market to raise money for his fiercely anticapitalist journal. Finally, in November, he announced to his staff his decision to sell *The Dial* to, of all people, Thayer and his cousin, Dr. James Sibley Watson, a well-heeled Harvard man with literary ambitions who was then studying for his M.D. at New York University Medical School.[48]

Thayer immediately moved to convert *The Dial* into a literary magazine. Under him it became, in Malcolm Cowley's estimation, "the best magazine of the arts that we have had in this country," publishing distinguished fiction, poetry, and essays, as well as reproductions of paintings and sculpture.[49] Mumford, Robinson, Lovett, Marot, Stearns, Dewey, and Veblen were let go; only Clarence Britten and his young assistant, Sophia Wittenberg, remained to help carry through the transition. Thayer, who had never cared for the sociological emphasis of "The Reconstruction *Dial*," gave Mumford and Robinson only two weeks' notice. Johnson, fighting back tears, told them in early November that he would pay them for an additional two weeks out of his own pocket. That afternoon Mumford and Robinson walked for hours through the streets of the Village and down to the waterfront "wondering about what our next step would be . . . what openings we might find and what plans we might make together."[50] Mumford refused, however, to see this as a crushing personal setback. "I start life anew," he wrote Michael Gold that October, "with twenty dollars in capital, together with a motto: 'my right wing is broken, my left is in retreat, the situation is excellent—I shall proceed to attack.' "[51]

For the next eight years he tried repeatedly to land a position as an editor on one of New York's magazines of politics or the arts, but to no avail. In these years he supported himself and his family, including his mother, to whom he gave $50 a month in support, almost entirely on the pittances he received for his essays and reviews in magazines like the *Menorah Journal*, *The Freeman*, and *The New Republic*, where Robert Morss Lovett welcomed his work. Not until 1942, when he took a faculty position at Stanford University, was he again to have a regular job with a regular salary.

This journalistic writing on a wide range of topics and concerns stretched him too thin at times, and prevented him from doing the kind of sustained research that went into his work from the mid-1930s on, when he finally began to make enough money on his books to support his family comfortably, and to set aside a good part of the year for uninterrupted study and writing. More than once in the decade following his departure from *The Dial* some of his closest friends, including Robinson, urged him to restrict his field, but he had to take on assignments editors were interested in or else give up writing for something else. Besides, this kind of work saved him from what he referred to as the disease of overspecialization.

By 1920, Mumford knew in his bones that he was a writer, that he had passed through his apprenticeship. Nonetheless, he had no job and no money, and no solid prospects of work in sight. He was also laboring under emotional and sexual problems, carryovers from his period of invalidism. After ten months of hardening in the navy, he was still an overcautious person, and oversolicitous of his health—never keeping late hours, never greatly exerting himself physically. And he remained nervously unsure of himself around women.

That year several things occurred which, while they did not immediately solve his deeper problems, changed the course of his life. First, he fell deeply in love with Sophia Wittenberg, whom he met in the offices of *The Dial*. And while he was trying to win her, he received two exciting offers of professional collaboration, one from Patrick Geddes and the other from Geddes's coworker, Victor Branford. In terms of both his emotional state and his literary career, 1920 "turned out to be," in his own words, "among the most fateful [years] of my whole life."[52]

7

Sophiology

If I ever set my mind to sociology as ardently as I have applied it to Sophiology . . . my reputation will be made within a year.

—LEWIS MUMFORD, LETTER TO
SOPHIA WITTENBERG, JUNE 7, 1920

After learning that he would lose his position at *The Dial*, Mumford had sent two letters in a desperate attempt to save his literary career. One was to Patrick Geddes, then in India on a city planning expedition; the other was to Geddes's co-worker, Victor Branford, who was in London establishing the new headquarters of the Sociological Society, the organization he and Geddes had launched before the war to propagate their social ideas.

Adrift, with no job prospects in sight, Mumford asked Geddes if he might "sit at his feet for a while," and perhaps assist him in several of his sundry projects. This would be an ideal way of rounding out his literary apprenticeship, and would also give him some much-needed time to try to land a more permanent position in New York. Being associated with Geddes also might open new avenues of opportunity for him. "To be a spoke in [Geddes's] wheel might be a short way of traveling far."[1]

While waiting for Geddes's reply he had rushed a similar note to Branford, with whom he had been corresponding since agreeing to review one of Branford's books for *The Dial*. "What are the prospects for a literary man in London or Manchester?"[2]

Branford replied first, inviting him to come to London as editor of the *Sociological Review*, the revived journal of the Sociological Society. Branford could pay Mumford only £75 for his first year's work, which would not even cover his basic expenses, but he suggested that Mumford might find additional work once he became acquainted with the London literary scene. He also invited Mumford to live rent-free in a room at Le Play House, the new Pimlico headquarters of the society.[3]

Branford's offer arrived just after Mumford was turned down for a position on *The Freeman*, a new journal of opinion, where his friend Geroid Robinson had landed an editorial job. He was feeling increasingly anxious about his immediate career prospects, and this was at least a straw to grab hold of. So in early January he cabled Branford accepting his offer, figuring he would be able to supplement his income by doing occasional short pieces for *The Freeman*, where he could count on Robinson to intercede for him.[4]

Just as he was laying plans to leave for England in early spring, Geddes wrote asking him to join him in Jerusalem, where he had a commission from the Zionist Federation to help replan the city and to suggest a design for a new university. After completing their work in Palestine he and Geddes would go directly to Bombay, where Geddes held a chair of sociology and civics. There they would collaborate on several books outlining Geddes's sociology. Geddes offered Mumford £200 to help cover his expenses.

To Mumford, this looked like the opportunity of a lifetime, and he wrote Geddes at once accepting his terms. "I only await word from Professor Geddes to make preparations for departure," he notified Branford of his change of plans. But several weeks later he received word from Geddes that their rendezvous in Jerusalem would have to be postponed. Geddes's appointment in Palestine was stalled by political complications. Geddes advised him, in the meantime, to take Branford's offer and to wait in London for further word from him.[5]

So Mumford again adjusted his plans, making arrangements to leave for London in April, with the expectation of joining Geddes in Jerusalem sometime later in the year. He was understandably anxious about this next step in his career, but he had only one real regret about leaving New York—and her name was Sophia Wittenberg.

Sophia was the dark-haired secretary who had an office next to his at *The Dial.* He had been seeing her regularly the past several months, and in the course of the following year she took complete possession of him. Sophia has been "the most profound influence in my life—and she has shaken and twisted me to the very foundations," he confessed in one of his Personalia notes, which give a richly revealing account of their tense, on-again, off-again relationship.[6]

Even before he joined the staff of *The Dial,* Mumford had spotted Sophia on several occasions walking in the Village near the Rand School on East Fifteenth Street, where she did volunteer work for the Socialist Party. With her sandals, her long flowing skirt, and purposeful walk, she reminded him of "the Nike of Samothrace but better! for her head, now kindly restored by nature, had a kind of Greco-Oriental cast, with a straight nose, an almost Greek chin, and flashing dark-brown eyes."[7] In the brilliant sunlight her coal-black hair took on the color of copper. From the first time he set eyes on her he felt she was exactly the kind of woman—graceful, confident, and smartly poised—that he wanted to fall in love with and marry.

When they first got to know each other as officemates at *The Dial* he and Sophia had a painfully difficult time establishing a close relationship, for Sophia wasn't physically attracted to him. She was also a little withdrawn and unsure of herself around the writers and editors at *The Dial.* They seemed so bright and confident, while she was only twenty years old and had not attended college.[8] But Sophia was a stunningly beautiful woman, and she seems to have impressed everyone who came into contact with her in these years. It was not just her great beauty: she was a captivating combination of sensitivity and subdued passion. Her outward manner was serene and relaxed; she appeared sometimes to be almost unaware of her splendid good looks. She put men at ease with her pleasing, quietly gracious ways. They could think of her as both an understanding confidante and a lover. Not surprisingly, she had a number of writers and artists chasing her while she worked in the Village.

Around *The Dial* offices Sophia was, for the first year or so, reserved and nervously shy. But underneath her calm exterior was fire and passion. More than once she got into hotly contested office arguments with the publisher, Scofield Thayer, only to calm down a little later over lunch with him at a quiet Village restaurant around the corner from *The Dial* building. "Stormy and defiant, capable of hatred as well as love," she would conjure up "magnificent storms" and then "sweep the sky blue with a gale of laughter or a clear spot of shameless sunlight," her husband later wrote of her.9 Where he was detached and reserved, she wore her moods on her expressive face. In many ways they were opposites, and that made her all the more appealing to him.

Still awkward around women, Mumford approached Sophia warily, asking her at first to have lunch with him and some other *Dial* staffers. Then he invited her to dinner, where, alone, they had their first real chance to get on closer terms. He was at first stung by her apparent aloofness and unresponsiveness, but this was perhaps as much his fault as hers. His stiff, diffident manner probably gave Sophia the impression that he wasn't all that interested in her. Later, when he informed her otherwise, telling her he wanted no one but her as his "mate," she politely told him that she didn't want to tie herself to one man or to think about marriage just now. She was too young, she said; besides, she had just found an exciting career. Her father was a socialist, and as a high school student she had marched in socialist and suffrage parades in Manhattan. At *The Dial* she was working for causes she truly believed in, and she didn't want to give this up.10

But she soon came to like the pleasant young writer who doggedly pursued her, and she began to see more of him in the fall of 1919, just as he was about to lose his job at *The Dial*. They would take long walks along Ocean Parkway, near her Brooklyn home, or out along the Palisades; and she began inviting him to her home for dinner or for evening visits. Mumford eagerly accepted these invitations, even though he realized that his relationship with Sophia was beginning to resemble his relationship with Beryl Morse. Sophia, like Beryl, wanted him for a friend, not a lover.

The more he learned about Sophia the more he was convinced that she was exactly the kind of woman he wanted to settle down with eventually. There was perhaps a double attraction here: the

Wittenbergs were a close, old-world family who had a sense of togetherness that was missing from his own.

Sophia's parents were emigrée Russian Jews who had arrived in this country recently married and virtually penniless in the early 1890s, at the beginning of the great Jewish exodus to America. But William (Volodya in Russia) was not fleeing religious persecution; he had no intention of jeopardizing his marriage to the attractive Elizabeth (Elisaveta Mironovna Plesetskaya) by serving a long term in the czar's army.

In a brief account Sophia wrote in 1952 of her parents' lives, which she placed in the family records, she describes the story of their coming to America as a "truly heroic saga," and it was.

William was born on March 20, 1869, in Kritsky, a small non-Jewish village where he lived until he was seven or eight, at which time the family moved to Sirotina, a Jewish village of eighty houses with one small street of non-Jews. A quiet, dreamy boy, William was sent at the age of sixteen to live with his maternal grandfather, a man of considerable wealth and standing in St. Petersburg's Jewish community. His parents undoubtedly thought that this would give him a good start in the world.

In St. Petersburg he worked for a while for his uncle, who was a fur trader, before finding work of his own in a tailor's shop. Two years later, at the age of twenty-one, he met Elizabeth in her home village in southern Russia, and shortly thereafter they were married. William was handsome, a member of a good family, and came from The Big City. To Elizabeth he was "a good catch."

But William was facing a long military term, and under a new edict Jewish wives were not permitted to follow their husbands outside the Pale. So the couple decided to emigrate to America, even though they had no money and knew no one in that far-off place. It was necessary, they learned, to have a sponsor in order to be admitted to the United States, but the only person they could locate who had preceded them to America was the brother of the town cobbler. They wrote to him, and he sent them the requisite letter.

After scraping together enough money to bribe some men to provide them with false passports and guide them to Germany, they boarded a covered wagon and were driven to the border. A week or so later they were in ship's steerage, headed for America.

They were met in New York by their sponsor, a ragged, uncouth man, angry because he had to miss a day's work to come to claim them. He took them to his home, a filthy subbasement with little light or fresh air. They could stay there the night, he muttered sourly, but in the morning they had to be on their own. "So this is the Golden America," William said to himself as he prepared for bed.

They had arrived with only $50 and they came during the depression of 1893, when work was almost impossible to find. After taking various odd jobs, William wound up in the needle trades, the largest industry in the city and the beachhead into the economy for so many Jews. Working sixteen hours a day, he eventually earned enough money to buy his own sewing machine. In those days it was customary for each man to own his machine and to look for work with it strapped to his back.[11]

In time William became the owner of a small garment factory. He was a skilled, tireless worker, but he had no business sense. He cared more for his workers than for what they produced. Even as an owner, and a manager, he remained a dedicated socialist; and he never employed children, though Italian women would come to him with their children of six or seven years, begging him to hire them.[12]

He struggled to make it in business, but success eluded him. Later, as an old man, he would sit in the home of Sophia and Lewis and reminisce about his first years as an immigrant in New York. It was his day-to-day contacts with the workers, most of them peasants from Russia, Poland, and Italy, that "Father William," as Sophia and Lewis called him, remembered most fondly, an indication of the kind of man he was. The "old days" William really liked to talk about, however, were of his boyhood in his village in White Russia, where in the spring he would lie on the banks of the Kritsky River and watch the boatmen float their logs to market; and where in the winter he would ice-skate with the bones of a cow tied to his shoes.[13]

It was William Wittenberg's deep love of nature that tightened the bond between him and his son-in-law later. In Mumford's autobiography he figures as one of the truly memorable characters. "When he was in his nineties," Mumford—by now an old man and a villager himself—writes of Father William, "he would still sit for hours at a time at the end of the bush-lined allee—where our home acres then opened, gazing into the clouds and imagining for himself a better world than the one he had found."[14] These words proved prophetic. When Mumford himself reached his nineties and was no longer able to write, he fell into the same habit. No longer able to move the world in the direction of his dreams, he reached back for solace to the brighter world he had known as a young man in New York at the start of his career.

Elizabeth, too, had lived in a small town, but she was a different kind of person than her husband. Where William was dreamy, gentle-mannered, and deferential, she was high-strung, strong-willed, and forceful. She had energies and ambitions that he would never possess. Sophia was a much softer woman than her mother, but she inherited her energy and persistence.

As a young girl in Russia, Elizabeth had worked as a seamstress in the home of a wealthy gentile family, and she took on many of their habits and mannerisms, along with an urgent desire to raise herself in the world. She possessed an extraordinary singing voice, and she dreamed of becoming a successful concert singer. That dream did not fade easily or gracefully. In an effort to introduce a little culture into their simple lower-middle-class home, Elizabeth purchased a piano; and in years to come the family would sing together Gilbert and Sullivan operettas, most of which they knew by heart. Yet despite what Mumford describes as her "fierce mothering instincts," she remained, at least in his mind, a bit too self-absorbed, too self-admiring. "Some deep residue of bitterness, of vain sacrifice and unfulfilled life, remained; remained and deepened, I fear, during her final years." There was always a certain tension in their relationship, and as Mumford himself cautions in his autobiography, this description of Elizabeth is a description of a woman he came to know later. "What I saw and felt immediately in this Flatbush house was a warm, close-knit family, which, if ruffled by temperamental conflicts, was sustained by kindness and deep loyalties."15

The Wittenbergs were not practicing Jews, but they observed many of the habits of their faith and of their native land. In their modest Brooklyn home Mumford sat down to simple dinners of traditional Russian dishes and to conversations enlivened by bright Yiddish humor. At the time Mumford first met Sophia this old-country feeling of family unity impressed him more perhaps than he would dare to admit, for, influenced by George Bernard Shaw, he was in revolt against middle-class family conventions—or at least he thought he was.

Sophia's mother was not happy to see her daughter dating a Gentile, "and a poor one at that." (Neither she nor Sophia knew of Lewis's Jewish father.) But as long as Sophia was not too serious about him she tolerated the relationship, and she and William made Lewis feel comfortable in their home.

Mumford had fallen totally in love with Sophia by the time he received Branford's first offer to come to England, but they continued to be, in her eyes, simply close friends, "pals," as she used to say, not knowing that this painfully reminded him of the way Beryl had treated him. Mumford made several desperate efforts that winter to bring her closer to him, but she remained unresponsive, and he grew more frustrated and irritable. He had trouble writing, and he even found it difficult to read with concentration. She blasted to sand his disciplined work habits.

How could he win her? That was the great "reforming" task he set for himself in the months before he left for London. But while he couldn't seem to change Sophia she began to change him.[16]

Around women he had been the perfect Shavian—aloof and self-possessed. This thin armor of indifference protected his all-too-fragile ego, hiding his inner uncertainty. Sophia broke through it. He started to open up around her; he was less stiff and formal. And for the first time in his life he found himself telling a woman exactly how he felt about her. Yet at every turn Sophia rejected him. This is what hurt most: Sophia had unhelmed his extraordinary composure, and he was getting no response out of her.

When in December, after a late Manhattan dinner, he first told her that he loved her, she replied levelly: "How does one recognize the condition?" For an instant, he felt relieved to be "free again." (Here is that inner desire to escape women that comes through in his early one-act plays.) But then he was overcome with a commingled feeling of depression and humiliation. What a "howling ass" he had made of himself.[17]

But he recovered enough of his confidence to continue to try to conquer her, convinced, despite everything she told him, that they would someday be husband and wife. He wanted beyond all hope and dreaming to be a noted writer; now he wanted Sophia as much as that.

Before leaving for London he tried to get some sort of commitment from her. He first asked her to join him later in London; he would try to find her a job. When she wavered he tried to get her to agree that they had a future together, but she wouldn't budge.

He was allowing his overwhelming attraction to her to override every objection he had previously had to marriage: his precarious financial state, his dedication to his career as a writer, his commitment to support his mother and his Nana. He had assured his mother before he became serious about Sophia that he had no intention of marrying for many years; marriage would take too much of his time from his work. "I am already married to my work," he wrote Elvina in 1918, "and until I establish a position in society for *that* mistress I can harbor no thought of any other." But then, as he told her in this same letter: "I am not acquainted with a single feminine soul I would under any circumstances get wedded to."[18] Now he was, and this changed everything.

But how could he marry someone who gave no hint that she wanted to marry him? By the time he was ready to leave for England their sexual relationship hadn't gone beyond some innocent kissing and touching. Sophia still claimed to feel no passion for him; and that's how things stood when he boarded the old White Star liner, the *Adriatic*, in early April, bound for England. When he first opened his cabin door he found a big steamer basket from Sophia, a gesture that gave him hope that she cared for him in some small way.[19]

Before he sailed for London, Mumford was advised on dealing with the English by Walter Fuller, the managing editor of *The Freeman*. Fuller, a former Manchester man, told him to repeat to himself every night before retiring: "The English don't mean to be rude; the English don't mean to be rude."[20] But at first this was hardly a problem. On board the *Adriatic* Mumford met the writer John Cowper Powys, a cordial, good-humored man who gave him sound advice about making it as a writer in London. And Mumford's host, Victor Branford, turned out to be the soul of Victorian hospitality. Mumford took to him instantly, and indeed the whole country seemed to give off an air of welcoming cordiality. He felt good to be there.

Le Play House itself was a disappointment. It looked to Mumford like a New York brownstone freshly done over with a coat of dark stucco. It stood—one among hundreds like it—on a long gray

Victorian street that rimmed Belgravia. Most of the buildings in this
area had once housed workers from nearby factories, and their
exteriors were scarred a sooty black from accumulations of coal dust.
It was an altogether dreary section of London, made worse, Mumford soon discovered, by the absence of any decent restaurants,
teahouses, or shops.

Inside, the place gave off a pungent odor of coal fires, a smell
Mumford would never get used to. His tiny room on the upper floor,
a former servant's quarters, was sparsely furnished, but "it was
bright and cheerful . . . , and there was a glass of flowers—five
narcissus and a tulip!—with a note on the mantel shelf." The young
woman who had extended this courtesy was Branford's secretary,
Dorothy Cecilia Loch. Her note informed him that Branford was at
his home in the countryside, and that he should go there "right off."
He would be expected.[21]

Branford, who had made a handsome sum in finance and investments, lived like a country squire with his family in an old brick
farmhouse on the edge of a moor in the New Forest of Hampshire.
As Mumford stepped down from the train at New Milton station,
there waiting for him, like some scene out of Chaucer, were Branford's governess and the children, sitting in a donkey cart. Halfway
to Branford's farm the ancient donkey stopped and refused to move,
so all walked the rest of the way down the lovely hedge-lined road.

As he approached the house Mumford spotted his host, a courtly,
slender man with a lean face and a pointed Elizabethan beard,
waiting for him in the garden. After showing his young guest to his
room Branford pointed out the primitive privy arrangements. "Perhaps you will do as I do," he said with a smile. "We have no
neighbors for half a mile, and the gorse is thick and beautiful."[22]

Branford was a considerate but not suffocatingly hospitable host.
He gave Mumford lots of time to himself to walk the wild acres
around the farm and to rest and read in his room. In this, he was, as
Mumford would soon find out, the very opposite of Patrick Geddes,
who demanded complete attention to his needs, and who would not
allow anyone to break into his endless monologues.

Branford was quiet-mannered and gracious, and a bit withdrawn.
When challenged and tested he could be as stubbornly obstinate as
his Scots collaborator, but around those, like Mumford, who were
sympathetic to his ideas, he had the patience of a beloved grand-

father. He even took a personal interest, which Geddes would never show, in Mumford's background, asking him the day after they met to recount his experiences as a student of the city and an apprentice writer. Mumford would later describe him as one of the greatest teachers he ever encountered. "If you have been my intellectual parent," Mumford wrote Geddes in 1922, "[Branford] has been my nurse."[23]

As a thinker Branford never gained the recognition Mumford always insisted he deserved. Even today he is usually classified in people's minds with Patrick Geddes and, as a result, is not given enough credit for his original insights. But part of the problem was Branford himself: he was too loyal and self-effacing a disciple. Invariably he would begin his many books and pamphlets on social issues, ranging from war to ancient religion, with tiresomely detailed summaries of the entire Geddesian system, only to get down to his own ideas toward the close of the argument. By that time the reader was convinced it was P.G. speaking through his loyal V.B. Even Mumford's later descriptions of Branford's "original ideas" seem forced, almost as if he is straining to convince his readers that he is not so much in debt to Geddes by showing his equal debt to another extraordinary teacher.

Branford's first book of consequence was *Interpretations and Forecasts*, which was published in the United States just before World War I. (Mumford later borrowed the title for an anthology of his own writings on culture and technology.) But the work that most influenced Mumford as a young man was *Science and Sanctity*, a book that brings together Branford's ideas on science and art, religion and social life. Branford's interpretation of the role of religion as the binding element in all human communities is a theme Mumford would return to much later in his career, when it would form the crux of several of his most important books.

Mumford had considerable trouble with Branford's prose. It was, in its own way, almost as dense as Geddes's, but where Geddes was too cryptic, Branford was windy and irritatingly florid. But Mumford found in this very defect, this extravagant emotionality, a hint of Branford's strength as a thinker. Branford "brought to science and social observation not merely a good eye and an analytical judgement; he brought the whole man, with his capacity for feeling and emotion."[24]

By occupation, Branford was a successful accountant and an investor, but he always considered himself first and foremost a sociologist. He and Geddes had founded the Sociological Society in 1904 in order to make sociology, in the manner of Le Play, a "true observational science, dealing not with abstractions, such as Conflict, Cooperation, the Herd Instinct, the Common Will, but the actual processes and functions of definite regional societies."[25] The aim of the civic survey was to further such firsthand study of cultures and communities.

Mumford learned a great deal from Branford's books and from listening to his public lectures, but he learned even more from him in their more private conversations. He especially loved to walk with him in busy London or in the surrounding countryside, where Branford was more relaxed, down-to-earth, and interesting as a man. Mumford credits him with enriching his developing architectural education by pointing out the hidden significance of seemingly ordinary buildings and patches of landscape. He found that Branford had Ruskin's genius for bringing to life stones and mortar, rolling fields and rugged farmhouses. Walking with him was one of the greatest pleasures of his first stay in England.

Beneath Branford's seemingly imperturbable demeanor there was a "wild Elizabethan need for passionate adventure and romance." Striding London's crowded pavements with him, Mumford was shocked when Branford, on passing a young woman with a shapely figure, would spin all the way around to admire her. This was the man who almost ten years later, at the age of sixty-six, a year before he died, won a prize in figure skating in Switzerland with an attractive young woman as his partner.[26]

When Branford was in London on business he would stay overnight at Le Play House in a room barely larger than a closet. There, at the end of a tiring day in the city, he would sometimes invite Mumford to visit his room for a late-night talk. Entering the cramped cell Mumford would find Branford lying on his hard cot, motionless, his eyes shut. He would begin talking in this same position, but then as they warmed to an issue of some interest to Branford, he would suddenly spring to his feet and begin pacing the room, leaving a white trail of cigarette smoke behind him. Wide-eyed and wonderfully alive, he would argue a point for hours.

This was the Victor Branford Mumford most admired, a man

whose whole being would "take fire with an idea."[27] When they met for the first time, however, Branford was reserved and restrained. He spent their first weekend together at his country cottage going over the history of the Sociological Society and presenting his plans for its revival. The society, he explained to his new American co-worker, had gotten off to a promising start, but after five years it had begun to decline as he, and then Geddes, began to spend increasing amounts of time away from London. Finally, the war completely disrupted its activities. Now he was determined to revive it; the time was exactly right, he told Mumford, his eyes bright with excitement, for change was in the air.

Branford was operating in the same spirit that had moved Mumford and his associates on *The Dial*. The war, he believed, had set in motion a great avalanche of change. It was unstoppable, but it could be deflected in a certain direction. That he was determined to do, with Mumford's help.

Although Mumford's experiences on *The Dial* had left him temporarily with a less sanguine view of postwar opportunities, he was impressed by one of Branford's strategic ideas, which was close to an idea he himself had been trying to develop for the past several years. This was the concept of the party of the Third Alternative.

Branford had first laid out the idea in a pamphlet, "The Drift of Revolution," in which he analyzed the historic aims and accomplishments of what he called the party of order and the party of revolution. "He showed," as Mumford described his argument, "how one tended to beget the other: hence an oscillation of ferocious dictatorships, and a deadlock in the fulfillment of all that was positive in their programs." Branford suggested a new composition of forces called the party of the Third Alternative. It would differ from the other two parties in that its emphasis would not be upon abstract slogans and shibboleths, but upon "concrete, realizable aims: reforestation, better houses, more adequately designed towns, coöperative agriculture, socialized credit, regenerated schools."[28]

In Mumford's first book, *The Story of Utopias*, he would expand this idea into a social program for his own country, but this is to anticipate. While he was at Le Play House he was not of much use to Branford's plans for a reconstituted Britain. For one thing, he felt no great allegiance to England; for another, he simply didn't know much about the country, its problems, or its potential. But there was a deeper reason, of course—his preoccupation with Sophia. He would spend most of his evenings alone in his room, dreaming not of a new world but of that "aloofly beautiful girl" he had left behind in New York.[29]

In the next several months, despite the fact that Sophia wrote him regularly, things between them grew worse. This was the onset of what Mumford would describe one year later, with lovesick melodrama, as "the most distressing period I had ever passed through in my life."[30]

In early June, Mumford received a letter from Sophia that convinced him that he was in danger of losing her. Sophia confessed to him that she had recently had a "passionate encounter" with a dashing Italian sculptor named Ruotolo. He was handsome, talented, and, to make matters worse, a political radical—an anarchist—which made him even more appealing to Sophia. After meeting her at an outdoor concert he had tried repeatedly to seduce her, telling her he was wildly in love with her and wanted to marry her. Although she rejected his sexual advances, she admitted to Lewis that he had stirred her. She found it exciting to be around him.

This aggressive Italian was the first man, apparently, to unlock the eroticism in Sophia. It would not be long, Lewis feared, before he "conquered" her.[31]

Sophia continued to see Ruotolo that summer. The relationship helped to open her up emotionally and enhanced her self-assurance. Her job on *The Dial* and the new friends she was meeting in the Village also raised her self-confidence. She began to acquire a different set of aspirations; and marriage, for the time being, wasn't one of them. In her letters to Lewis, she made this clear.

In the predictable fashion of the rejected lover, Mumford began to review the history of his relationship with Sophia to see if he could discover where *he* had gone wrong. It didn't take him long to reach a conclusion. As with Beryl, he hadn't been aggressive enough.

Actually, both he and Sophia were extremely inexperienced in sexual matters; both were virgins and neither had dated extensively. Mumford had never even seen a woman's naked body. The first time he did—a year later when Sophia showed herself to him—he was astonished to discover that the vulva was set vertically, not horizontally.[32]

Sophia was almost as naïve. Whereas Mumford at least had read a number of textbooks on sexual practices, she hadn't even come that far. Sophia apparently didn't know what a penis was, and she had no idea at the time they first met how a woman became impregnated. During the war, at a dance at the Rand School, she had been asked to dance by an older black man who had held her so tightly that she feared for weeks that she might be pregnant.[33]

But now she was changing, and that sent him into a jealous spin. He found it almost impossible to work at his writing or to concentrate on the affairs of the Sociological Society. He knew he had to win her back, and fast.

His first strategy, which he executed clumsily, was to tell her "with double barrelled frankness" how he felt about her sexually. If the Italian "Bull" had aroused her, she should know that he could, too. "My outward impeccability," he wrote Sophia, "is simply a reflex of the sheltered and solitary life I've so long been leading, and though this had made deep channels of habit which in a sense 'protect' me, I simply wouldn't give tuppence for the sort of chastity and purity this signifies." He wasn't a prig, he insisted—he had all the erotic drives of a young man his age; and now he was ready to "act in terms of [his] deepest desires."[34]

But while Sophia began to lead a more carefree life in New York he continued to live like a celibate priest at Le Play House. He dated no one. The only woman he saw was Branford's secretary, Dorothy Cecilia Loch, a thin, primly attractive woman who dressed, even in summer, in heavy tweeds and shirtwaists. Their relationship remained entirely platonic. She was "one of the few girls," he confessed to her a year after leaving England, "who had not adopted me as a brother, and about the only one toward whom I genuinely feel the way I imagine a brother ought to feel."[35]

They talked often and openly about a hundred things, but mostly about Sophia. But even this everlastingly understanding woman was unable to ease his emotional pain, jealousy, and frustration.

That troubled summer he had only one brief period of well-being, a fortnight he spent with Alexander Farquharson, Branford's young Scottish assistant, preparing and giving a course on postwar reform at High Wycombe, in the Chilterns. In his notes and recollections of this experience we have a vivid record of his early attraction to village living, and of his ascendant tendency to associate the city—the hectic, rapid-paced metropolis—with his own personal problems.

"For the first time in three quarters of a year," he wrote Jerry Lachenbruch from High Wycombe, "I have a sense of well being and intellectual assurance. I think that a great city like New York or London is positively the worst place on earth in which to work through a mental crisis; there are times when the city itself lies like a dull load on one's chest. . . ."[36]

The High Wycombe of that time was all that London was not. The town was set in a narrow valley, close to a wide stretch of perfectly tended fields and farmland, and the town center was itself a tiny English village that still wore the tracings of its late-medieval heritage. There were winding streets, sturdy cottages, and on a high mound, an old and handsome parish church.

Although it had become in the last century a busy industrial town, known for making the popular Windsor chair, High Wycombe had managed to retain many of the traditions of the handicrafts. In his tour with Farquharson through the memory-laden hills around the town, thick with beech forests that ringed country houses and storybook villages, he witnessed chair legs being turned by craftsmen on an ancient lathe.

Here, amidst thriving village industries such as Kropotkin and William Morris had evoked in their works on labor and living, he glimpsed with his own eyes the possibilities of a regionalized civilization built around industries that did not savage man or nature. The garden towns he would later press for in his work for a regionalized America were updates and transplantations to American soil of the kind of "balanced" living he observed in these country communities of the Wycombe valley.

After delivering his lectures at a special summer school in High Wycombe Mumford returned to Le Play House. "The fact that London is by all odds a much more genial city to live in than New York," he wrote Sophia the next day, "doesn't prevent it from being a damned, plagued, unhealthy, depressing hole. The result of this journey will be to make my analysis of Metropolitanism more savage and relentless. A civilization that produces London is capable of making No Man's land anywhere."[37]

Later in his life Mumford grew to love London, but on his first visit his reaction to the city was at best mixed. An observant young man from a family of servants, housekeepers, and waiters, he was acutely sensitive to the class prejudice and snobbery he encountered everywhere. He had read Shaw's *Pygmalion*, and now he saw for himself how the English listened to and secretly catalogued those they met, "mentally 'placing' them, either respectfully or condescendingly," upper class or lower class.[38]

Mumford was introduced to upper-crust London society by Victor Branford, who moved with effortless ease in the company of bluebloods and the peerage. So did Miss Loch, who came from a long line of high-ranking foreign service people, but who had lived in Edinburgh as a young girl and loved to poke fun at the social snobbery of the southern English, as she called them. She helped this lonely, ungraceful Yankee adjust to London society life, advising him what to wear for dinner or for tea, and what to talk about, or not talk about in certain circles. She even brought him to recognize the "utter inescapability" of tea at four o'clock, a custom he adopted for many years after he returned to New York. But despite this well-intentioned tutoring, Mumford could never quite feel at home in the company of high-society Britishers. The letters he sent home are filled with angry blasts at the suffocating snobbery of the English "leisure class," and he began to call Miss Loch Delilah, because in trying to get him to conform to British ways, she behaved like a modern Delilah, "shearing the rough locks of her young American Samson."[39]

Mumford's loathing of the British social system was aggravated by his firsthand observation of the terrible poverty of London. While London contained some of the most commodious urban areas he had ever seen, Mumford found much of the city horribly depressing in appearance.

Mumford's occasional walks through the dingy Victorian London of Charles Dickens's novels reinforced his conviction that cities like this must soon give way to the kind of communities Ebenezer Howard was building in the surrounding countryside. For some reason, however, Mumford never got a chance to go out to Letchworth, Howard's first garden city, or to Welwyn Garden City, then under construction.

By August, Mumford was anxious to return to New York. He was homesick and lovesick, and he began to feel he was wasting his time. That entire summer he had written only a few short pieces for *The Freeman*, and he had spent barely three or four working days attending to the affairs of the *Sociological Review*.[40]

Mumford also began having trouble working with Branford. It became clear to him that Branford was determined to make the society not a professional sociological society in the best sense of that term—lively, experimental, open to fresh and challenging ideas—but a society dedicated to the spread of his and Geddes's version of sociological truth. Branford had no use for ideas that differed markedly from his own. The weakness of the society, Mumford complained to Geddes in a letter to India, "has been the weakness of the Aristotelian school after Aristotle: the work of the founder has been so comprehensive and magnificent and inspiring that it has in appearance left nothing for the scholars to do except to go over and annotate and dilute the master's work."[41]

Mumford was willing to learn from Branford, but he did not want to become Branford's or Geddes's "office boy."[42] This isn't what he bargained for when he first agreed to come to London, and Branford's rather patronizing attitude toward him made him all the more impatient to return to New York. "I have discovered the weaknesses of England and the strength of America," he wrote a friend back home, "whilst before I had a very keen sense of the weaknesses of America and the strength of England. I no longer despair quite as freely about my own country . . . and I see much more clearly what must be done to preserve the valuable part of the American heritage."[43] That summer he had been reading Van Wyck Brooks's essays on the promise of American culture in *The Freeman*, and they solidified his emotional alliance to his country. He wanted most of all to write about American themes, American issues. Despite its many problems America, he was beginning to see, was still more "ready, responsive, and in some degree [more] malleable, more open to favorable human pressures and plans" than England or the rest of Europe.[44]

He also had his career to consider. If he was to advance as a writer he would have "to stick to literature, pure literature, and shun anything that looks like a sufficient and lucrative job," he wrote Sophia about his decision to leave Le Play House. "I hate like the devil to go back to the parsimonious habit of life that I cultivated in the days of my early apprenticeship, but short of doing this I don't see any way of escaping a mechanical routine as editor, literary hack, or what not that will stunt my development during a period in which I am still capable of growing."[45] So when Branford informed

Mumford that he couldn't afford to offer him the kind of salary that would make it possible for him to stay for an extended period in London, Mumford was secretly relieved.

In August, just as Mumford was making plans for his trip back to New York, he received an invitation from Geddes to join him in Bombay for a year as his assistant. There is much important civic work to do, Geddes pleaded with him, and "you can help me [with] my manifold unfinished Mss." Geddes offered to take care of his passage to India and to pay him a small salary. Come at once and "we must try not to overwork each other!"[46]

For a week or so Mumford considered taking the offer, and, in fact, he was so close to accepting Geddes's invitation that he went to the steamship booking agent to inquire about the cost of passage and sailing schedules. But after standing around for half an hour or so "without evoking even a quiver of attention from a seemingly idle clerk, I suddenly decided that my die was cast. Heaven had spoken! *I would not go to India.*"[47]

It wasn't fate that decided the issue; it was Sophia Wittenberg. Sophia begged him to leave her out of this decision, but how could he? "It's all very well to think of India as being the great chance of my life," he wrote her, "but I'm not so sure that going back to America may also be the chance of my life. At just this moment, I feel . . . that you mean ever so much more to me than India does."[48]

When Mumford boarded ship for New York in mid-October he had only one thought in mind—to convince Sophia to marry him.

8

New York Again

A person who has never had sexual experience is as unfit for marriage as a person who has never handled money is unfit for a big inheritance.

—LEWIS MUMFORD, LETTER TO
PATRICK GEDDES, JANUARY 15, 1922

When the S.S. *Adriatic* cleared the long bent arm of Sandy Hook and steamed into New York harbor, Lewis Mumford, standing on the ship's prow, felt a surge of excitement run through his body. Here again was New York as he had seen it countless times before from the decks of the rust-red five-cent ferries.

As the huffing, soot-faced tugs pushed the stately liner into its Hudson River slip, he spotted Sophia waiting for him in the crowd at the pier, waving a handkerchief. When he bounded down the ramp she greeted him with a kiss, and she seemed to be in bright spirits, but by the time they picked up his baggage and sat down to lunch they were quarreling. She would not be able to see him the following evening, she told him. She had promised Ruotolo weeks before that she would go to the opera with him. He also learned that there was more than one rival.

He and Sophia had planned to spend a week together in the country as soon as he got back from London, and he had eagerly looked forward to this, convinced that the time spent alone together would help to close the abyss between them. Now she called this off, explaining that she was going through a great change. She had been meeting more men in the last few months, and she liked the attention she was getting. She found herself drawn to the fast, carefree life of her new friends at *The Dial,* and she was "sick and tired of people who had consciences or social principles or that sort of thing." Last year she had "looked forward to a home and babies and helping her husband in his career." Now she wanted "something different."[1]

Sophia was seeing two other men that fall: Ruotolo and Scofield Thayer, her new boss at *The Dial.* By November, Mumford had reason to worry more about Thayer as a rival than "the Italian."

Slender and pale, with classical features and luminous black eyes, Thayer was everything Mumford was not—rich, polished, witty, and widely traveled. He had had the finest education that his father's considerable millions could buy, and at Harvard he had been a favorite student of George Santayana. Later he became a friend of Sigmund Freud, the man he called "The Great Magician" after undergoing analysis with him in Vienna in 1921.[2]

Alyse Gregory, who was later managing editor of *The Dial* and Thayer's lover, describes Thayer in her memoirs as part monk and part millionaire aesthete. He dressed simply, unconcerned to be seen in the same jacket and tie he had worn since his college days. And when he was writing he went at his work with the concentrated fidelity of a medieval scribe, closing himself off from nearly everything around him. But he also loved to entertain artists and writers, either in a special dining room he set aside for that purpose on the top floor of the old brownstone that housed The Dial Publishing Company, or at his apartment on Washington Square, which was hardly a monk's cell. The walls of this sumptuously furnished top-floor flat were covered with priceless drawings and paintings, and Thayer's bookshelves bulged with rare first editions and folios of prints. Thayer also had an eccentric Japanese man-servant, Gregory recalls, "a subscriber to *The Nation,* who, to salve his outraged pride, would sometimes enter the room backwards."[3]

Sophia and Thayer never had a sexual relationship, but they greatly enjoyed each other's company. They would often dine together or go to the theater or spend autumn Saturdays on Thayer's sailing yacht on Long Island Sound. Sophia was captivated by him and by the kind of sparkling people he gathered around him at *The*

Dial. He introduced her to a new style of living, and she loved the round of literary parties, theatergoings, and art openings.

She also respected Thayer as an editor, though he could be autocratically imperious, firing out orders to his staff in his high, shrill voice. At the first sound of that siren-like bark they would snap to attention "as if Tiberius himself had set foot on the stairs."[4] But they all knew he wanted to put out the finest literary magazine in the country, so they tolerated his occasional bullying.

Under his and James Sibley Watson's direction, *The Dial* published a remarkable array of writers, the up-and-coming as well as the solidly established—among them, Ezra Pound, Marianne Moore, William Butler Yeats, Wallace Stevens, Carl Sandburg, Henry Miller, D. H. Lawrence, e. e. cummings, Edmund Wilson, Joseph Conrad, James Joyce, T. S. Eliot, and John Dos Passos. *The Dial* was also handsomely illustrated, perhaps the best-looking magazine ever published in this country. Watson, too, was an art collector, and he and Thayer filled their magazine with reproductions of the work of Auguste Renoir, Pablo Picasso, Georges Braque, Marc Chagall, Henri Matisse, Georgia O'Keeffe, and others. Behind the entire effort, overseeing every detail, was the insistent Thayer, who possessed "an inflexible morality against 'the' nearly good."[5]*

Thayer administered much of his wealth as a literary trust to sponsor young writers and artists. As an editor he was ever on the lookout for new writing talent. Mumford knew this and submitted a number of pieces to *The Dial*, but the editors considered them too sociological for their magazine, which published almost nothing on politics, architecture, or the social sciences. This made Sophia's attraction to Thayer doubly difficult for Mumford to accept, and he kept insisting to her that he was "a man of letters," not a "sociologist," as Thayer condescendingly referred to him. Under the influence of Thayer, Sophia, he feared, was beginning to look on him as far too somber and serious.[6]

By December, Mumford felt he had lost Sophia for good. That month he told her that he didn't want to see her any longer, even

---

* Sophia Wittenberg resigned from *The Dial* in 1925, the year Alyse Gregory left the magazine to return to England with her husband, Llewelyn Powys. Ellen Thayer, Scofield Thayer's cousin, took over her job. Marianne Moore took over the position of acting editor in 1925; shortly thereafter Thayer quit *The Dial* to devote more of his time to writing. *The Dial* ceased publication in July 1929.

casually. It was too painful to be around her, hovering "like a remote but monstrous superego," the same role he had played with Beryl Morse. So he withdrew with an ultimatum: if she changed her mind about him and wanted him to be her lover, and not just her "comrade," she would have to look him up and propose to him. But this, of course, expressed his hurt more than his intentions.[7]

That winter he felt lonelier in New York than he had ever felt in his gloomiest hours in London. His health deteriorated (his recurring hypochondria), and again he found it almost impossible to write. In this state he began reading some of the more popular American and British Freudians, and searching his own past for the reasons for his repeated failures as a lover. He began to suspect that a "parental fixation" was behind his problems with both Sophia and Beryl. This mother fixation had kept him "in a more or less infantile state of adjustment," making demands upon women he dated for treatment similar to that which he expected from his mother. He was forever trying to change the women he cared for, instead of trying to change himself.[8]

There was probably some truth to this, but, as usual, when he was overburdened with personal problems he tended to blame himself. If both Beryl and Sophia had spurned him it must have been for something that *he* had done wrong.

For a time he thought of returning to England or of joining Geddes in India, but he wasn't ready to give up on Sophia. By late January he was seeing her again and trying to talk her into marriage. "Another week of restlessness and fitful work," he complained in his notes. "I don't know how much longer this sort of thing can go on; . . . my health is being undermined and my work is going to the dogs."[9]

Then, barely a month later, Sophia began to show greater interest in him, just after she stopped dating Scofield Thayer. She told him she was falling in love with him, was "thinking" of marrying him, and that spring they decided to make an "experiment at marriage." He wanted a wedding right away, but Sophia protested that she had seen too many couples whose marriages had failed. So they agreed to live together for at least six months. If this worked out well they would probably get married.[10]

Neither he nor Sophia had any moral qualms about the arrangement they were entering into. They truly were, as Mumford recalls, a baffling "combination of sophistication and innocence, intellectually liberated in matters of sex, but with almost no actual experience with sex."[11] Though Sophia thought of herself as a liberated Greenwich Village woman, she was shocked when he suggested that she get some advice about contraceptives. To a friend, Mumford claimed to be surprised by this, but it is interesting that he asked *Sophia* to inquire about the matter.[12] He was apparently too shy and embarrassed to take care of it himself.

They decided to set up a household in the fall; and that summer they slept together for the first time, both of them virgins. The place they chose for their first tryst could not have been more idyllic—a spacious estate in the hill country of southern New Hampshire, within sight of historic Mt. Monadnock. Mumford, on the recommendation of his new friend, Paul Rosenfeld, *The Dial's* music critic, had been invited to take over Padraic Colum's position, teaching literature at a small summer school near Peterboro, on the estate of Arthur and Joanne Johnson. "The school is endowed by a Renaissance princess," Mumford wrote Dorothy Cecilia Loch from Peterboro, "a very charming and fashionable young woman, whose father acquired the renaissance flair in, I believe . . . paper boxes." This "Lady of the Manor" had established her summer school to give her two young children "stimulating companions during the vacant days of summer."[13]

It was a cushy job, despite the meager pay, with plenty of time for writing and loafing. Each morning Mumford and the other three instructors taught literature, with the aid of games and dramatizations, to a group of children, most of them from the village. The teachers lived in a white frame cottage at the bottom of a hill, reached by a path through deep woods; and they gathered for dinner with the Johnsons and their guests at the mansion, in a large timbered hall where they were waited on by a stuffy English butler named Jones. There were tennis courts, a swimming pool, terraces and gardens, an open-air gymnasium, and a spring-fed lake situated directly in front of the instructors' cottage. Mumford would spend his afternoons writing or sunning himself on the shores of the lake with the other teachers, for their formal duties ended at noon.

For the first time in over a year he began to feel relaxed and emotionally at ease. The only thing that was missing was Sophia. From the moment he arrived at the school he had been scheming to bring her up to New Hampshire for a visit. Sophia was agreeable to this, but he wondered if Mrs. Johnson might think it scandalous to have a young unmarried couple sharing the same cottage. He finally got around this by shading the truth, asking Mrs. Johnson if his new "wife" might join him for a week as a guest of the school. She cordially agreed to this, but just to be safe he advised Sophia to go out and buy a cheap wedding ring. She got a ring at a Woolworth store, and made one more, in this case an unfortunate precautionary preparation. On the day before she left for Peterboro she had herself fitted by a gynecologist with the wishbone pessary, then a popular contraceptive device worn in the vagina. "Neither of us," Mumford recalls, "had enough experience or imagination to realize how blighting that cold surgical rupture of the hymen would be next day to our first tantalizing essay at full-blown lovemaking."[14]

"Full-blown," he emphasizes, because they had already had their first taste of lovemaking. This occurred on a warm May afternoon at Sophia's home in Flatbush, in an unoccupied room in the back of the house. There she stripped off her clothes to let him look at her body. Although he embraced her it didn't occur to him to take off his clothes, even after she gave him a tantalizing lead. "I feel free when I am naked," she said as she stood unselfconsciously in front of him. "I am proud of my body and I like to show it off." But he was too shy and inexperienced to follow this up.[15]

This innocently hopeful start had a disastrous second act. On her first day at Peterboro, Sophia nearly drowned in the lake; Mumford, unable to pull her to shore, almost went under himself. Luckily the school's athletics instructor happened to be walking by the lake, and seeing them floundering in the deep water, jumped in and saved Sophia, while Lewis, freed from her panic-stricken grasp, swam beside them to shore.

That night, and for the remainder of Sophia's stay in Peterboro, they were unable to complete sexual intercourse despite, or perhaps because of, Sophia's surgical deflowering. They parted at the end of the week feeling run-down and miserably frustrated.[16]

On returning to New York, Sophia announced to their Greenwich Village friends that they were married, displaying her ring as proof. But despite Sophia's new pride in their relationship, Mumford was inwardly convinced that their week at Peterboro had reinforced her doubts about a permanent relationship. And her letters to him indicate that she was indeed wavering. "I *am* uncertain. I never will be otherwise until I find something satisfying to do, or until I resign myself to being a female whose sole aim in life is to attract and charm. The one seems out of my reach, the other unattractive. I'm between the devil and the deep blue sea, now, which is one reason why I can't be as sure of myself as you are. You have your work, and you figure that I won't interfere with it. . . . You have your work cut out for you! And I?"

But Sophia *was* ready to give their "marriage" an honest try. "I can't escape the feeling that we're going to emerge triumphantly," she wrote him.[17]

In his autobiography Mumford reports all this faithfully. What he fails to add is that *he* began to have serious doubts about marriage just at the time Sophia suggested that they live together. Although this bout of uncertainty lasted only a few months, it provides an interesting insight into Mumford's character and personality and foreshadows serious difficulties in their relationship.

His problem, he told Sophia, was that he found it impossible to forget her frigid treatment of him on his return from London, and her turn to him only after she ceased to be interested in Thayer. Her past behavior made him fear that she would want other men after they were married.[18]

His insecurity surfaced in a number of other ways, all of them indicating that he was reluctant to marry a woman who would try to be the controlling force in the marriage. Sophia, he believed, had "an advantage" on him. She knew that he loved her, but he was still unsure that she loved him. "You seem to like me in waves but it's damned uncomfortable shivering in the wind when the tide is out."[19]

He was also worried that he was about to pass up a "great intellectual adventure," a year with Geddes in far-off locations, "for the sake of a romance that may prove in the end to be neither great nor adventurous."[20] And he feared as well that it was primarily the lure of sex that was pulling him into marriage. Living alone over the past several years, with few social contacts, had intensified his sexual frustration, making it impossible for him to achieve any kind of personal equilibrium. He worried most of all, however, about the impact that marriage would have on his writing career, for he might have to take a full-time job to support his family if Sophia quit her job to have a baby. Marriage, he had read in Shaw's plays, was especially dangerous to the artist of great purpose; it could turn him into a mere breadwinner.

But in surrendering his freedom and taking this risk, he would be living, in compensation, a fuller emotional life, and this would surely overflow into his work, filling a deficiency Jerry Lachenbruch, for one, had detected in his writing. Jerry had been warning him for some time that his sexual and emotional backwardness might dangerously affect his writing; and just as he was preparing to move into an apartment with Sophia, Lachenbruch approached him again with the same advice. This came in the form of an astute appraisal he made of Mumford's novel *Scantling*, which Lewis had sent him to read. The letters Lachenbruch wrote him that summer located a real failing in Mumford's previous work, a flaw he would work hard to correct. Concerning his literary style, Mumford never received shrewder advice.

"Perhaps the worst defect in the book as a novel is the general feeling of detachment in which it seems to have been written. Though you may have expended a lot of personal emotion, anger, love, etc. in the writing, they didn't get over." Lachenbruch found his writing too coolly observational. This reflected what he thought was Mumford's basic "attitude toward life"—not an attitude that he consciously tried to convey, but one that his "temperament" unconsciously dictated. Lachenbruch admitted that he suffered from the same "handicap." "We are both critical and spectatorial. We share the emotions of our fellows but are far from sharing their experiences."[21] These words must have carried special significance to a young man who had determined years before to cease living at "second hand."

Mumford also received some sound advice from Lachenbruch about another potential threat to his personal development and to his future with Sophia—his close, guilt-edged relationship with his mother. In one of his letters Lachenbruch made a veiled reference to Mumford's strong attachment to his mother. Stung by this, Mumford explained, perhaps a little too defensively, that while his "lack of success" with Beryl might have been due to "the oedipus complex," he no longer had such a fixation. His recent experiences in the world—in Pittsburgh, in the navy, in London—had "served in good part to break this down."[22] But he was not being entirely forthright, for as we have seen, he himself secretly suspected that a "parental fixation" might have been responsible for his failure to win Beryl and his initial problems with Sophia. And his Personalia notes show him laboring under fears that Lachenbruch's diagnosis was essentially correct.[23]

He probably should have sought psychiatric help at this juncture, he admitted to a friend some years later.[24] Instead he became his own analyst, painstakingly reviewing his past life for the poisoned sources of what he diagnosed as a severe neurosis. Though his mother had not devoted herself to him "with quite the same zeal as a parent of my generation might have," he confided to a friend years later, in a letter that touches to the heart of his problem with Elvina, "I was, in another sense, the center of her life and probably the main cause of her not getting married again; and this naturally brought about far too close a tie."[25]

So one of the great worries Mumford had as he approached marriage in 1921 was that his mother might consider his union with Sophia a betrayal of her, for she was an invalid and depended on him for attention and financial support. That was the burden of guilt he carried, and it would bother him a great deal into the first years of his marriage.

Later in his life he would learn from his mother that he had overreacted. She never considered his marriage a threat to her, she made it clear to him; and she never interfered in his relations with Sophia, before or after their marriage.[26] All the evidence suggests that he found it more difficult to break with her than she did with him, and that he probably wanted her, as a sign of her love, to be more upset about his marriage than she was.

Mumford had another "mother" to be concerned about as he approached his trial marriage with Sophia—Nellie Ahearn, his beloved Nana. Nellie had been living with Elvina for the past four years, but the two women had never gotten along well; the only thing that had kept Nellie in the household was her parental attachment to Lewis, "so my leaving home," Mumford explained to Dorothy Loch that September, "has faced us with the necessity of finding another home for her—as both mother's place and mine, with Sophia in it, would be impossible under present conditions." In this letter Mumford describes the breaking up of his old home as "a terrible blow to Nana, who had expected to live with me to the end of our days, and had not really counted upon my marriage." And later, when he found a place for her at the Catholic Home for the Aged on West Fifteenth Street, he confessed to feeling "hardhearted and disloyal."[27]

But, as with his worries about Elvina, this is more indicative of his own state of mind—and of his own insecurities—than of the facts of the situation. Nellie, it turns out, reacted remarkably well to his marriage. With Lewis gone, she had no desire to remain in Elvina's household. Nor did she ever ask or want to live with Lewis and Sophia, as Lewis intimates in these letters to Dorothy Loch. Her simple wish was that he always be happy in whatever he did.

The real obstacle Lewis and Sophia faced as they made final preparations to begin their "trial marriage" was Sophia's mother. Elizabeth Wittenberg angrily insisted that she didn't want her daughter living with any man out of marriage; and she certainly didn't want her marrying a Gentile. The day Sophia broke the news to her about her plans to live with Lewis, Elizabeth had a fainting spell, and when she recovered she went into hysterics. "I wish I had followed my father's advice and lied to her about it," Sophia wrote Lewis that evening.[28]

At this point Lewis told Sophia that he suspected he was part-Jewish, and Sophia made this known immediately to everyone in her family. About this time Elvina Mumford, on her own, without her son's or Sophia's knowledge, went to Brooklyn to meet with Mrs. Wittenberg. She thought it only honorable that she tell Mrs. Wittenberg that her prospective son-in-law had been born out of wedlock, and that his father was Jewish, secretly hoping, no doubt, that this would break down her objections to the marriage. (Sophia and Lewis didn't find out about this meeting of their mothers for some twenty years after they were married.)

Still, Elizabeth refused to give her blessing to a common-law marriage, even though her husband had no objections. "I'll never be able to feel the same respect for you and Lewis, whenever I think of what you've done," she told her daughter.[29] Sophia's brother Philip, a young lawyer, added weight to their mother's objections, advising his sister that the living arrangement she was entering into was as binding legally as a real marriage, and just as difficult to get out of.

This was enough to convince Sophia, who finally consented to a legal marriage.

So one morning in late September, just after they had moved into the apartment Sophia had found for them on West Fourth Street, they went to Brooklyn Borough Hall and were married by a coldly officious city clerk.

Their four-room apartment on 142 West Fourth Street was on the top floor of a run-down, cockroach-infested tenement, with a foul-smelling public hall that caused Elvina to break down and cry on her first visit. "To think that I've lived to see my own son sink to this," she sobbed on entering their apartment.[30] The plumbing arrangements were ancient and in bad repair; there was no icebox; and the old tin bathtub was dingy and badly dented. To make matters worse, there was a horse stable next door, still in use, which emitted such a foul odor that they had to use the room that faced it as a storeroom and occasional guest room. The apartment was also expensive for them—$60 a month. But there was a severe housing shortage in New York in the years after the war, and they counted themselves lucky just to have such a place. It was, after all, ideally located—in Greenwich Village, exactly where they both wanted to be.[31]

The marriage got off to an unpromising start. When they moved in Lewis informed Sophia, to her amazement, that he preferred that they sleep in separate beds for health reasons—he still had the tubercular's fear of colds and infections. He would take the study; she could have the adjoining bedroom. This set a pattern for the rest of their lives together.

At first, he did most of the cooking and food shopping, and some of the cleaning as well. He had more experience in these household matters and more free time, for Sophia continued to hold a full-time job. This arrangement, which he initially agreed to, soon caused problems. He grew increasingly jealous of her freedom and her carefree relations with the literary crowd at The Dial, for he still feared that she was in love with Scofield Thayer. He also found these routine household chores taking up too much of his time.

Arguments invariably arose when Sophia would call around five o'clock to say that she would be joining an author or editor for dinner after work. Not long into the marriage Mumford decided he wasn't going to succumb so tractably to this "wifely" role. One evening he met Sophia at the door of their flat with a towel over his arm and an apron around his middle. Throwing down the towel and pulling off the apron, he declared that from now on they would go out for dinner. He would no longer be "a kitchen slave." They both had a good laugh over this, and for the next several years, until Sophia became pregnant, they usually went out to dinner.[32]

The most painfully persistent difficulties they encountered in marriage were sexual. For the first year, at least, he was an anxious, unsatisfactory lover, in part due to inexperience—his as well as Sophia's. He had what he called "the hair-trigger sensitiveness of virginity," whereas Sophia was slow to be aroused.[33] He was speedily learning, he confided to Patrick Geddes that winter, that "a person who has never had sexual experience is as unfit for marriage as a person who has never handled money is unfit for a big inheritance."[34]

They did, however, have many good moments together in the first flush of marriage. "Often we awoke in the morning relaxed and amorous," Mumford writes of their early sexual relations, "for musical comedy's 'But in the Morning, No,' had not yet been added to public advice for too-eager lovers."[35] But Sophia had only to cancel a luncheon date or arrive home late in the evening to arouse his jealousy. He would never raise his voice—a trait she found exasperating—but by ignoring her he raised the tension level higher, perhaps, than an angry exchange would have.

Many of these arguments were about Scofield Thayer, but Mumford also worried about the recurring dreams and fantasies Sophia confessed to having. She dreamed of other men, other possible lovers; and she dreamed as well of being trapped and of struggling to get free. His dreams were "anxiety dreams" that pictured her leaving him; hers were predominantly "wish dreams" that began with arguments and ended with her leaving him for another man. "If I don't capture Sophia," he wrote in his notes, "someone else will."[36]

Despite his outwardly reserved manner he was a man of strong sexual passions, and now he feared that, apart from jeopardizing his marriage, these jealousies and sexual strains were beginning to imperil his will to work and his emotional balance.

The source of his difficulties with Sophia, he convinced himself, was that she really didn't want to be married to him, that he wasn't "her kind of man."37 But Sophia's feelings were more complex than that. She had decided to marry him, not because she was over-whelmingly in love with him, but because she thought that he was the kind of clear-purposed man she wanted to spend her life with.38 Yet though, at first, she was less certain of her love than he was, she desperately wanted the marriage to last. What she objected to was his insistence that they both remain sexually loyal and that she not go out with other men. She confided to him early in the marriage that she might like to explore sex with someone else before she "settled down for good," and that, at the very least, she wanted to continue to see other men socially, including Thayer. But this was more freedom than he was willing to allow her. "I'd never experi-mented," she confided to a friend a number of years later, "and I hated to feel that he was going to be the beginning and the end of an aspect of life I had just awakened to."39 A high-spirited woman, she refused to capitulate completely or easily. But when she returned from her innocent evenings out with friends, she suffered the conse-quences of her more open idea of marriage—the anxious question-ing, the cold stares, the smoldering anger and jealousy.

He wasn't willing to give Sophia her own life, and that's what she feared most. In a letter just before their marriage she had made this clear to him: "I don't want to be submerged in the personality of one who has a definite sphere. . . . You have your medium, you've started on your road, and I'm still fumbling for my path. I haven't found it yet. And I'm envious." She enjoyed the social scene, she told him, but this was just a passing thing. "The way you are going is the way I *want* to go, though I find it hard at first."40

Marriage intensified this dilemma for Sophia, for Lewis wouldn't give her the freedom to work it out herself. He kept trying to "conquer her," words that recur repeatedly in his diary notes. This had more than a sexual side; he wanted to win her completely to his lifestyle and his philosophy of life. He would never be a "social" person like Thayer, he realized. He disliked small talk and he didn't mix well with large crowds of people at New York parties. But that was the way he was, and he wasn't about to change—even for Sophia.41

After several years of stubborn resistance, "I finally admitted myself vanquished," Sophia later confided to a friend. "I let my own natural timidity and slackness drift me back to his channel and that alone . . . I accepted his point of view so completely that I made it my own, and ceased to grow."[42]

Sophia's early capitulation to his ways, however, led to unforetold difficulties later in the marriage, when Lewis eventually swung around to the position Sophia had originally taken on the marriage and became romantically involved with a succession of women. These relationships deeply hurt Sophia and caused her to resent even more the role she had reluctantly drifted into earlier in the marriage, when, as she once told him, she was not strong enough to counter his desire, or willing to hurt him.[43]

These problems would take them many years and several near marriage-breaking crises to resolve, but in the first years of their marriage what kept him and Sophia together is more significant than what drove them apart. They were two young people who were, despite everything else, irreversibly in love, and "somehow," as Lewis remarked later, "by a combination of patience and ardor, we finally came through."[44]

9

Beyond Utopia

Civics as an art has to do, not with imagining an impossible [utopia] where all is well, but with making the most and best of each and every place, and especially of the city in which we live.

—PATRICK GEDDES

If the first years of their marriage were often stressful and stormy, Lewis and Sophia Mumford at least had the compensation of living in Greenwich Village when it was one of the most stimulating urban environments anywhere. In the early twenties, the Village was still a backwater, a miraculously preserved piece of provincial New York that had somehow managed to escape the city's rigid grid design and the swarm of traffic that these long straight streets invited. In the first decades of the century, "the Village," in the words of one writer, "became a haven from the City; it protected those who lived there against the horrors and the nervous efficiency of urban life."[1] But that isn't how Mumford saw it. To him, it *was* the city, urban life the way it was meant to be lived.

It was in Greenwich Village, New York's old Ninth Ward, not in any smartly planned garden community, that Mumford learned "what a city could and should be."[2] Greenwich Village "is a little like Chelsea or Bloomsbury," he explained in a letter to Delilah Loch, who had never been to America; "artists, writers, rich folk, paupers, and Italian factory workers are intermingled within a fairly small area, all of which has an atmosphere quite different from any other section of New York."³ In the Village almost everything he and Sophia needed for a stimulating life in the city was within easy walking distance. It was an old yet lively urban place; and on afternoon walks through its medieval-like maze of streets he sometimes felt that he might bump into Herman Melville or Edgar Allan Poe.

Most of Lewis's and Sophia's friends lived within a few blocks of their apartment on West Fourth Street, and it was only a short walk to the offices of *The Freeman*, on Thirteenth Street, where Mumford would stop by regularly to see his new friend and New York sponsor, Van Wyck Brooks, the magazine's noted literary editor. Their luncheons together at Polly's, where in summer they would eat in the open under a canopy at a long boardinghouse-style table, were the beginnings of a lifelong literary friendship.

What he and Sophia couldn't find in the Village they could usually find uptown, only a short bus or subway ride away. Occasionally they'd walk home from Carnegie Hall or a Broadway show, stopping on the way for coffee and hotcakes and a late-night conversation with friends at a white-tiled Child's. And on weekends they continued to take hikes along the Palisades or into the Westchester hills.

Yet as stimulating as he found Village life in the early 1920s, Mumford spent most of his days alone in his bedroom-study reading on an ever-widening range of subjects, and writing book reviews and short pieces for several New York magazines, chief among them *The Freeman*. He had become connected with this spirited new weekly in the spring of 1920, just before he sailed for London, when his friend Walter Fuller introduced him to Van Wyck Brooks and asked Brooks to consider him as a reviewer and occasional contributor. At the time Brooks, almost ten years Mumford's senior, was this country's leading literary critic. He had just agreed to come east from Carmel, California, where he had recently completed *The Ordeal of Mark Twain*, to take over the literary department of *The Freeman*.⁴

After a hasty luncheon meeting Brooks began sending Mumford work, and when Mumford returned from London in the fall Brooks took him under his wing. Brooks, Fuller, and Geroid Robinson tried to get their editor, Albert Jay Nock, to hire Mumford as a staff member, but Nock, like the editors of *The Dial*, considered Mumford's work too "sociological" and disliked the "academic long-windedness" of his style.[5] Nor could Mumford land any other editorial positions he applied for in these years. He had to settle instead for the unsteady life of the freelancer, taking what came his way, work that provided him with little more than a bare financial minimum.

The Freeman was the first magazine after *The Dial* to open its pages to Mumford's work on a regular basis, and he drew encouragement from this, despite his recurring run-ins with the irascible Nock. Nock and Francis Neilson, a rich Englishman who had been at one time or another a professional actor, playwright, novelist, librettist, manager of Covent Garden Opera, and Liberal member of Parliament, had founded *The Freeman* to promote the economic gospel of Henry George, the American land reformer, whose single tax they embraced as a panacea for all social ills. Both men were also stridently antistatist, promoting a vaguely fashioned form of philosophical anarchism modeled on the ideas of the German political theorist Franz Oppenheimer, who envisioned a world free of the exploiting state, where laborers would enjoy the privilege of "Freemen's Citizenship." All this was to be achieved, in Nock and Neilson's view, without a violent revolution. Indeed their weekly rarely addressed issues of practical politics. Theirs was a program without a politics of transition. But *The Freeman* continued to proclaim itself a radical magazine, despite the fact that it was backed by the fortunes of two of America's legendary capitalist families, the Swifts and the Morrises of Chicago's meat-packing industry, through Neilson's marriage to Helen Swift Morris, the daughter of Gustavus Swift and the widow of Edward Morris, whose father had been one of the first packers in Chicago.

Mrs. Neilson thought that a magazine would be an interesting project to occupy her husband's idle hours, but Neilson quickly tired of the routine day-to-day affairs of publishing, leaving these tasks to Nock, who soon became the moving spirit at *The Freeman*. While Neilson golfed and fished all over the world, *The Freeman* became Nock's magazine.[6]

Nock was a secretive, deliberately mysterious figure who hid his past even from those closest to him, though he had a background almost as colorfully varied as Neilson's. At one time or another he had been an ordained Episcopalian pastor, professional baseball player, muckraking editor for *The American Magazine*, assistant to Brand Whitlock, the Progressive mayor of Toledo, and unofficial emissary for Secretary of State William Jennings Bryan. His obsessive concern for privacy was the subject of a number of humorous stories at *The Freeman*. No one apparently knew where he lived, and staffers claimed that if you encountered Nock going out the door at the end of the day and asked him which way he was heading, he'd invariably reply, "The other way."[7]

On economic issues Nock claimed to be a radical; in almost all other things he was rigidly conservative. Cranky, willful, and decidedly old-fashioned, he joined his friend H. L. Mencken in heaping scorn on the excesses of American mass culture and on the Sunday School optimism of reformers and "settlement sharks" like Jane Addams. Nor did he have an ounce of tolerance for experimentation in the arts. John Hall Wheelock recalls that he stopped submitting his work to *The Freeman* after Nock altered one of his poems so that each foot was a regular iamb.[8]

Under Nock *The Freeman* became one of the best written reviews in the country, the equal in many categories of *The Dial*. Though Nock was full of crotchets and had his crazy pet theories, he had the good sense to allow his staff almost complete freedom to express their own views, so long as they did it well and with good taste. His editorial motto was "Do what you like."[9]

Brooks was given virtually free rein in his department, and he attracted to *The Freeman* some of the finest literary talent in this country, England, and Ireland. At first he turned to older, more established friends for contributions—to Thorstein Veblen, Charles Beard, Carl Sandburg, Lincoln Steffens, Bertrand Russell, and Conrad Aiken. But it was the up-and-coming writers he was most intent on publishing and promoting—authors like Malcolm Cowley, John Dos Passos, Harold Stearns, and Matthew Josephson—for he was convinced that they had in them the promise of "A New America."

Brooks spent only two working days a week at *The Freeman*, commuting to the city by train from the seaside village of Westport, Connecticut, where he and his wife Eleanor had a cottage on a hill, close to their friend Paul Rosenfeld. Brooks did most of his writing there; when he was in the city he was preoccupied with editorial duties. As one of his assistants at *The Freeman* said later, it seemed as if "all the young writers in New York tramped up and down the steps to his office all day long."[10] On entering *The Freeman* offices, they would be piloted by one of the secretaries to Brooks's book-lined office, where Brooks dispensed his literary patronage like a quietly efficient ward boss, matching the reviewer to the book.

Even before Mumford met Brooks he had been influenced by his literary ideas. To young writers like Mumford, Brooks was the commanding figure of modern American literature, the "little colo-nel," as Rosenfeld called him.[11] For Mumford, Brooks was "the image of the true man of letters," a writer who had dedicated himself completely to the literary life; and he was powerfully drawn to Brooks's plea for a new American literature no longer subservient to Europe or any other culture.[12] In the writing of Henry James, Mark Twain, and Walt Whitman, the Whitman who had edited a paper called *The Freeman* in Brooklyn in the 1840s, Brooks found the beginnings of an authentically American culture.

When he was in London, Mumford had followed Brooks's essays in *The Freeman*, and that beckoning voice had helped summon him home to his own country to take up the tasks Brooks had set for the coming generation of American writers. For Brooks, the mission of literature was preeminently social, even utopian—to help bring about what he called "The Beloved Community." In direct opposi-tion to The New Criticism, Brooks argued that "form" in literature was secondary to purpose, that the subject and the content dictated the form or style. This was the literary equivalent of Louis Sullivan's architectural dictum—form follows function—and Mumford found it a most exciting idea. "We have had too much talk in this country about the technique of writing," Brooks declared in a *Free-man* essay that Mumford eagerly read in London. What is needed is a redefinition of the responsibility of the writer. "Who but he can project images of a beautiful, desirable and possible social order?" Let the writer begin by fashioning "in American terms" an image of the hero as artist, Brooks echoed Emerson.[13]

In his later work on the American literary past, Mumford would return to these themes and concerns Brooks had helped to plant in his mind; he and Brooks would become coworkers in the task of reclaiming America's literary heritage. Their first common project, however, was not a work of creative affirmation, but a solemnly pessimistic appraisal of "Civilization in the United States."

This collaborative effort was the brainchild of Harold Stearns, a young cast-about writer who had a brief term as an editor on *The Dial* before Mumford joined the staff. After graduating from Harvard in 1913, Stearns had gravitated to the Village, becoming something of a fixture, almost part of the furniture, at Polly's, the Liberal Club, or the Boni Brothers Washington Square Book Shop, next door to the club. He possessed that reckless youthful spirit that Village writers like John Reed celebrated in their poetry. At Harvard he had led a heated student discussion on modern science, insisting that the law of gravity was a mere concept. To prove this, he stepped out on the sill of a third-floor window and walked calmly out into the night, breaking his leg and losing his point. In the Village he became something of a literary bum, rarely changing clothes, shaving only once a week, and always managing to look very preoccupied and very superior. He made a bare living writing for a number of New York magazines and papers, including *The Freeman*, where Brooks, who recognized his potential, was receptive to his work.

Stearns came up with the idea of compiling a full-scale attack on American culture late one evening while he and a group of friends were sitting around drinking bootleg liquor and complaining about the Eighteenth Amendment. What kind of country, they wondered, would even think of outlawing booze? In January 1921 he approached Mumford, Brooks, and Clarence Britten about his proposed project, and several weeks later he called together a larger group to discuss the idea in the dingy basement of his run-down house on Barrow Street.

At first the group thought of putting out an American equivalent of Denis Diderot's Encyclopedia, but they quickly realized that this would be an impossibly ambitious undertaking. So they went back to Stearns's original idea of an all-out assault on the mediocrities and moral pretensions of contemporary American life. They met every other Sunday at Stearns's place, planning their book and talking about a hundred other things over jugs of Marsala purchased from a local Italian bootlegger.

"That winter," Mumford recalls, "furnished the best sustained conversation I can recall over any period in America."[14] The group included such princes of the art as Clarence Britten, Paul Rosenfeld, Joel Spingarn, Van Wyck Brooks, and the long-bearded Irishman, Ernest Boyd. The volume that finally emerged from their meetings was a capacious collection of articles on the American scene, most of them uncompromisingly critical, for the aim of the book was to stir people up. Stearns wrote about "The Intellectual in America," Ring Lardner about sports, H. L. Mencken contributed an essay on "the incurable cowardice and venality of American politics," Brooks took as his topic "The Literary Life," Elsie Clews Parsons wrote on "Sex in America," Katherine Anthony diagnosed the ills of "The American Family," and Mumford offered a scathing analysis of metropolitan civilization. The book, Malcolm Cowley later observed, was "like an inquest over a man everyone disliked."[15]

Although it later became popular sport to ridicule *Civilization in the United States*, in 1922 it was something of a literary sensation, at least in New York. Stearns added to the legend that came to surround the book by leaving for Paris after delivering the manuscript to his publisher. By doing this, he hoped to prove that at least *he* practiced what he preached. Stearns stayed in Europe for thirteen years, resuming his life as a literary vagabond, too poor at times to buy his own clothes or to rent a cheap room. "Broke, bitter . . . and alone . . . without a friend or a woman to keep me," he picked up occasional cash by writing horse-race columns for the Paris edition of the *Chicago Tribune*. He appears in Ernest Hemingway's novel of The Lost Generation, *The Sun Also Rises*, as Harvey Stone, hunched over a table at his favorite bar, The Select, a pile of dirty saucers in front of him. Knowing tourists were heard to say on seeing him at The Select, drunk and asleep, with his head on the table: "There lies civilization in the United States."[16]

Most of the other contributors to *Civilization in the United States*, however, held out more hope for their country. We "loved our country," Mumford emphasized years later, whatever reservations we had about it.[17]

While working with the Stearns group and writing for *The Freeman* Mumford began to lead a different weekly routine—more active and varied and less self-consciously solitary. He was getting to be known around New York for his columns in *The Freeman* and for his membership in the Stearns group; and he began to go out more—to dinner parties, the theater, and literary luncheons. He even learned to dance, largely to please Sophia. But he didn't find this new life to his taste. He wanted a way of living that was "more intense and purposeful," and he yearned for a great project that would test and stretch him.[18] Before, he used to complain that he had too few friends; now in New York he had so many friends and acquaintances that his main problem was to occasionally avoid their company so that he could have time to himself.

But it was not just the social distractions that began to bother him; it was the kind of work he was doing. His essays and reviews were being accepted by some of the top New York magazines, yet he didn't see journalism as his real work. If he had to write essays and reviews to support himself, at least he ought to be at work on a big book. This was the advice he received from well-placed friends like Brooks, Spingarn, and Geroid Robinson. He knew they were right. But "the difficulty," he confessed to himself, "is to begin: the damned difficulty is to begin."[19]

His problem was that he had so many ideas for a book that he had trouble focusing on any one. At this difficult time in his life three friends—an old friend and two new ones—helped him to start a project.

In 1921, Jerry Lachenbruch, now living in Germany picking up literary leads for American films, wrote him a long letter analyzing his potential as a writer and advising him on his future path. Mumford later described this as one of the most important letters he ever received. Mumford had told Lachenbruch that he wanted to write novels dealing with "great ideas" and had sent him some samples of his most recent fiction. As before, Lachenbruch was not impressed: "The moment you sit down to write [about people's lives] you forget the people and think only of their abstract qualities. That makes you [primarily] a sociologist." There was another problem with his fiction: his characters were merely "illustration[s]" of his own pet ideas; they did not have a life of their own.

But if he was not a novelist, neither was he merely a sociologist, for he had a playfully imaginative mind and great descriptive powers as a writer. Why not, therefore, write a book or several books, Lachenbruch advised him, dealing with both the imaginary *and* the real world, with the world both as it is and as it ought to be? This would center and reconcile Mumford's twin interests—literature and sociology. "I am suggesting a tremendous job . . . I am asking you to write an encyclopedia of 'Should Be' for future generations to strive towards."²⁰ This advice helped to drive Mumford's work in a new direction. If he abandoned his hopes for being an imaginative writer it was not by abandoning his imagination but by applying it to areas other than fiction: in the case of his first book, to "the domain of 'Should Be.' "²¹

At about the time Mumford received Lachenbruch's letter, Van Wyck Brooks was urging him to write exactly this sort of book, and so was Geroid Robinson. His essays diagnosing the ills of modern life would do little good, Robinson told him, unless he offered "solutions to the muddles they disclose." And this demanded more than an article. "It deserves a fat book."²² This, and Brooks's steady encouragement, cinched it. That December Mumford decided to begin a book on the "foundations of the New Jerusalem." His aim would be to get his readers to think not of Utopia, no-place, but of Eutopia, the best place possible. *Beyond Utopia* was his first choice for a title, and although he didn't stick to it this was the underlying theme of the book. It "will begin with Plato," he told a friend, "and end with Lewis Mumford."²³

Mumford had been thinking of writing a book on this theme since the publication of *Civilization in the United States*. That book had delivered the "*coup de grâce* to all that was false and shoddy" in American life, but Mumford thought Stearns and other disaffected writers were wrong to leave their country. With Brooks, Mumford considered it the writer's responsibility to remain at home in order "to plant the seed of a different culture."²⁴

That autumn, when the Stearns group broke up, Mumford, Brooks, and Walter Fuller had begun laying plans to issue a subscription series of short paperback books, one a month, covering the whole range of topics Stearns's review had included, from sex and sports to music and philosophy. Only their series would strike a more confident, forward-looking note. Fuller, a student of Roman history, suggested that they call these books "Scipian Pamphlets" to contrast the audacious frontal attacks of Scipio Africanus with the retreating tactics of Fabius and of Britain's modern-day Fabians. In this spirit, the contributing writers would be encouraged to move beyond criticism to an exploration of the possibilities of a new America. Mumford, who agreed to edit the series, saw it as an effort to rekindle the spirit of cultural experimentation and political insurgency that had blazed brightly in the Village before the war.²⁵

The Scipian Pamphlets were never published; none of the three men who dreamed up the idea had the time, experience, or money to carry off such an ambitious publishing venture. But this wasn't the end of the idea. In their own separate ways Mumford and Brooks took up the challenge they had set for themselves—to prepare for an American cultural renaissance. "If we are not able to launch the series . . . ," Mumford wrote Delilah Loch in 1922, "I shall work the theme up anyway and write a little book aimed at the younger generation," who, since the war, had lost interest in reform or revolution. Russia had ceased to be "a beacon," and there were no other movements of hope and change to look to for inspiration. At just this moment "[we need] to throw a rainbow into the sky," Mumford told Brooks.[26]

In January 1922, Mumford approached the publisher Horace Liveright with an idea for a book "not of the actual deeds of men but of their underlying ambitions and wishes."[27] The following month Liveright invited him to his office to talk about his project and offered him a contract and an advance of $300. The two men sealed the deal with a handshake, and in March, after only a month or so of intensive reading, Mumford began his book, completing it—a book of some three hundred pages—in early June. The following month he made corrections of the final proof and left with Sophia for a vacation in Europe.

This was perhaps the low point of their marriage. That spring they had come close to breaking up. While he had been hard at work on *The Story of Utopias*, writing on a makeshift desk in their tenement apartment on West Fourth Street, Sophia was immersed in her work at *The Dial*, still fascinated by Thayer and the writers he drew to his magazine. "They were artists," Mumford recalls the hurt and jealousy he felt in those years; "I was only a sociologist. They were gay, irresponsible, dashing: I was sometimes morose, depressed, . . . constantly jealous, not perhaps without cause."[28] *The Story of Utopias* was written under the most dreadfully unfavorable circumstances, yet the mere writing of it helped Mumford to keep his balance.

He and Sophia sailed out of New York harbor on the S.S. *Adriatic* in July. Sophia had long been dreaming of a trip to Europe, while he was eager to introduce her to his English friends and to show her around London and the English countryside. Down deep, however, they both looked on the trip as therapy for their ailing relationship.

As it turned out the "cure" worked, and the healing process begun that summer in Austria and England continued, not without occasional reversals, into early 1925, when Mumford gained a surer sense of career direction and settled down to write an ambitious study of the progress and decline of American culture.

The moment they boarded ship that July they both felt an immediate sense of relief—Lewis especially, since he blamed most of their marital problems on Sophia's association with the writers and editors at The Dial. Now he had her all to himself, and the time they would spend together would do their marriage a world of good, he thought. For Sophia it was exhilarating just getting away. A sheltered Brooklyn girl, she was on her first trip abroad, her first trip anywhere far from home. She was in top spirits throughout the entire ten-day cruise to France, sunning herself on the ship's deck, making new friends, and even getting a little tipsy now and then from too many after-dinner ports or Benedictines. "The gossips are speculating eagerly . . . as to whether or not we are truly married," Mumford wrote his mother from his cabin at sea; "we seem to enjoy each other's company too much to be regularly and properly joined, unless we were on our honeymoon."29

But just when he found himself falling more deeply in love with Sophia, he met another woman who swept him off his feet. Dorothy Swaine Thomas was a young American graduate student in sociology on her way to England, by way of Paris, to study at the London School of Economics. Sophia discovered her on deck one afternoon reading Lewis's chapter on "The City" in Harold Stearns's Civilization in the United States. She introduced her to Lewis and they all got along famously. By the end of the trip, Lewis and Sophia had adopted Dorothy as their marital confidante, letting her in on many of their bedroom secrets. They were both desperate to talk with someone about their problems, and Dorothy seemed so bright, sympathetic, and interested in offering advice. But she turned out to be interested, most of all, in Lewis Mumford.

In "The Little Testament of Bernard Martin," an autobiographical prose-poem Mumford wrote in 1928, Dorothy appears as Bertha, a tall, imposing Nordic woman with large limbs and "a trunk that rises like a figurehead into defiant breasts and prowlike chin."³⁰ Actually, she was slender and frail, a lovely girl of twenty-two, with tousled blonde hair, blue eyes, and sensuous lips. She had a quick mind and a wide-open, forthright manner, and Lewis found himself immensely attracted to her. She was the first woman to tempt him to infidelity. On deck they practiced their French together from exercise books, and both of them, he recalls, broke "into self-conscious giggles when I read her the sentence: 'Show the gentleman what you have.' "³¹

Sophia realized what was going on, but made no effort to step in. Lewis suspected that Sophia was encouraging him to have an affair with Dorothy so that she could gain some freedom for herself, but she simply thought that a little flirting wouldn't hurt their marriage. She was confident that her cautious, passionately jealous husband wouldn't get involved with another woman. But he was more tempted by Dorothy than Sophia suspected.

The day after they arrived in Cherbourg they took the train to Paris, with Dorothy joining them. To their disappointment, they found Paris depressingly drab. The Great War had killed off a good part of an entire generation of young men, and their surviving relatives still walked the streets dressed in mourning.

They were both lonely in Paris. Aside from Dorothy, they knew no one in the city, except Harold Stearns, with whom they spent a day; nor was their French good enough to allow them to feel comfortable in restaurants and shops. After several weeks of idle sight-seeing, they boarded a train for the Austrian Tyrol. They were to meet a group of Lewis's English friends there for a hiking and mountain-climbing excursion. After a draining day and night trip they arrived at Mayrhofen in the Zillertal and climbed the six miles to the spot where their British friends had set up camp. They both found it liberating to be away from the noise and crowds of the city; but camping in the icy outdoors, high in the rugged Alps, was not for them. So they took a room at a cozy pine-walled Hütte, which looked out over a swift-running glacial stream.

He and Sophia, regular weekend walkers, arrived eager to do some hiking and climbing, but not, it turns out, the kind of hiking and climbing their seasoned British companions had in mind. Their guide and group leader, Mabel Barker, a big-limbed, robust woman, reputed to be one of the finest Cumberland mountain climbers of her day, had a strenuous program mapped out for them. Their first day out they climbed far up beyond the tree line, over razor-edged boulders and across narrow, treacherously icy footpaths, to a spot 10,000 feet above sea level, where they stopped to explore a spectacular ice cave. By the time they got there, however, Lewis and Sophia had had enough. They decided to make their way back alone the following day to the warm comfort of the Gasthütte.

A few days later they headed to Innsbruck, a lustrous city of bridges and arcaded streets encircled by a shimmering wall of Alpine peaks and emerald lakes. They spent a relaxing several days there exploring the city, a showcase of Austrian imperial architecture. Then they returned by train to Paris, refreshed and in good spirits, to prepare for the trip to London, where they planned to spend several months.

Coming back to London was for Lewis like "coming home." Their first few nights in the city he and Sophia stayed at Le Play House, deserted in the holiday month of August except for Mrs. Long, the devoted Scots housekeeper, who gave them a hardy, homey welcome. They stayed in Alexander Farquharson's room, and when he returned they moved to a seedy room on Doughty Street, before finally locating in a comfortable rooming house in Upper Bedford Place. Most of their time, however, they spent in an apartment Dorothy Thomas had found for herself in Mecklenburgh Square. Dorothy, whose days were occupied at the London School of Economics, gave them a key, and they had the run of her place.[32]

Dorothy made friends quickly in London, and she soon brought Lewis and Sophia into her growing social circle. Lewis, in turn, introduced her and Sophia to Delilah Loch, and they both took to her immediately. For the first time in their married lives Lewis and Sophia began to share common friends, and they also found themselves enjoying each other's company more. In London, Lewis began to feel his competence more strongly. He knew this vast and baffling city of contrasts, the city of Dickens and Victoria, of cockneys and courtiers, and he took pride in showing it to Sophia.

Away from New York and Scofield Thayer's *Dial* crowd, Lewis also grew more self-assured around Sophia; he began to notice a change in Sophia, too. She was more animated and amorous, more strongly drawn to him sexually. Perhaps it was her jealousy of Dorothy, but whatever the reason, their sexual relations improved.

He began to feel that he was on the road to "conquering her"; "I've [finally] acquired a little skill in the art of Love," he proudly declared in his notes.33

He enjoyed London more this time than he had in the summer of 1920, when he had spent most of his evenings alone in his spare cell at Le Play House, homesick and desperately worried about his relations with Sophia. Still, bothered by a kind of nervous uncertainty, he was not completely happy. His symptoms were familiar, and he well knew the source of the problem: he was without a large project to give himself to. Despite his love for Sophia, work remained his commanding passion.

Every morning he would trudge to the British Museum to do some random reading, hoping that some new project would form itself in his mind. But nothing came. He would later regret that he didn't get to see more of the city or at least have tried to look up Shaw or Wells, two of the heroes of his youth. But the time he was spending with Sophia was repairing his marriage.34

Their most unforgettable experience in England that fall was the walking tour they took through the Cotswold Hills. They set out in early October from Oxford, where they attended a sociological conference with the Victor Branfords. They had been warned about the heavy autumn rains, so they prepared for the worst, stuffing their knapsacks with plenty of extra clothing. But luck walked with them. On the morning of their departure the clouds broke and they hiked across ancient meadows under a brilliant blue sky.

Mumford had formed a number of his ideas about historic cities before this, but what he saw on this October trek verified his commitment to a pattern of community design he found splendidly preserved in these golden-stone villages just east of the Severn River.

Once a flourishing wool center, the Cotswold Hills shelter some of the most handsome villages in Europe. It is an area laced by small clear rivers that thread through picture-book countryside, tied by twisting roads to village market centers. Walking these hills and curving country roads, Lewis and Sophia felt as though they had been transported back several centuries to the time when this lovely area of old England had reached the pitch of its development.

They spent their first night at Burford, the gateway to the Cotswolds, an almost unspoiled medieval town west of Oxford. The following day they walked through Whitney and Minster Lovell on their way to Bybury, England's "most beautiful village," in the opinion of William Morris. After spending the night in the gabled cottage of one of the villagers, they set out the next morning for Cirencester, an old Roman town crammed with historic interest, and wound up one evening in the sooty industrial city of Stroud, where they stayed in a run-down Temperance Hotel. The next day they walked on to Chipping Campden before returning to London.

This area of England would leave much the same imprint on Mumford as it had on William Morris. In the Cotswolds, Mumford found communities built to nature's contours and scaled to human needs, living examples of the kind of organic planning he had favored since first reading Patrick Geddes. Later, in his classic works on the city—*The Culture of Cities* and *The City in History*—he would write of the many lessons these venerable old cities supplied contemporary urban designers. But it was not the physical form of these villages that Mumford was most interested in; he was primarily drawn to the kind of life they had fostered, to the kind of men that had built them. Mumford was convinced the builders of England's Bybury and Chipping Campden had a profounder understanding of the fundamental needs of life than any of our modern capitalist town builders. For them, the economic motive had not been all-engrossing; they constructed their communities with other considerations in mind. How might we revive that earlier spirit and give it an expressly modern form? That was the question Mumford would take up in his work following his return from England, beginning with *Sticks and Stones*, his second book. He had given thought to this question before ever setting foot in the Cotswolds, but these splendid stone villages worked their subtle influence, bringing him closer to the tasks to which he would give most of the middle part of his life.

Before leaving England in November, Lewis and Sophia spent a relaxing weekend with the Branfords, who had moved from Hampshire to Hastings, to a cottage close by the sea. Branford had given up hope of bringing Mumford back to the *Sociological Review*, but he urged him again to help Geddes get his sociological ideas into a readable volume. Mumford resisted, however, insisting that he would rather write a biography of Geddes than immerse himself in a collaborative effort, and the two men left it at that.

The Branfords again were perfect hosts, leaving Lewis and

Sophia plenty of time to themselves to explore the East Sussex countryside. On finishing breakfast, Sybella would rise and announce: "The village is to the right, the sea to the left. We lunch at one-thirty and shall see you then."[35] Later in the day they'd all get together for tea and dinner. Lewis felt more at ease in Branford's company than he had in 1920, and he left Hastings feeling closer to him than he had ever felt before.

Their stay in Europe had done him and Sophia a world of good. They hadn't, of course, resolved all their problems, but they felt that their marriage was on far firmer footing.

And so was Lewis's career, as they learned when they returned to New York in the fall. *The Story of Utopias* had just been published and was receiving the kind of reviews that turn an author's head. Perceptive critics recognized that this was no mere description of other writers' utopias; it was a book about the shattering impact of World War I on the mind and moral outlook of an entire generation, the generation of its author.[36]

The Story of Utopias is a young man's book, filled with energy and fresh thinking. It is not a tightly disciplined book, as Mumford stuffed into it nearly every idea he had found compelling in his education; and in many places in the book a platitude is put forward with as much fanfare as an original idea. Nonetheless, *The Story of Utopias* is perhaps the single most important book for understanding Lewis Mumford's career and achievement. "Lewis was one of the few men," Van Wyck Brooks once said, "who have not *ideas* but *an idea*, and he was to spend his life working this out."[37]

In *The Story of Utopias* Mumford first addressed that dominating idea and theme—the rise of the machine and the mechanistic outlook in the Western world. Here also he developed a closely related theme that runs through all his later work—the idea of the creative artist as prophet and revolutionary. In this vividly written book Mumford presented a program for a new kind of American radical movement, inspired and led not by insurgent politicians or aroused proletarians but by "creators and originators" in the mold of Emerson, Whitman, and Thoreau. A young idealist with a powerful sense of personal destiny, Mumford wanted to give this movement shape, impetus, and direction. "To the artist," Whitman said, "has been given the command to go forth into all the world and preach the gospel of beauty. The perfect man is the perfect artist."[38] In this spirit Lewis Mumford began his wide-ranging career as a writer and self-proclaimed revolutionary.

Although *The Story of Utopias* is not directly about World War I, the central global event of Mumford's early life, the war's impact on Mumford's generation is one of its central concerns. World War I had not greatly disrupted Mumford's personal life or touched him as directly as it had Hemingway, Dos Passos, and other young writers who had seen it up close. Still, the war and what occurred immediately after it—the punitive Treaty of Versailles, the Allied invasion of revolutionary Russia, the Red Scare, and the collapse of the American socialist movement—profoundly influenced him and became the central theme of his earliest published work. It was no wonder that the young prefer "to live for the moment," concerned primarily with their own personal freedom and enjoyment, he explained in one of his early *Freeman* editorials. The recent past had been a nightmare for them, and the future "seemed unlikely to be much better than the present."[39]

What "our generation" suffers from, he argued in another *Freeman* essay, is "the loss of to-morrow. . . . Civilization is the magic instrument by which men live in a world of time that has three dimensions—the past, the present, and the future. . . . The drama of the present tends to move in a given direction only when it receives the double impact of the past and the future; and if the past is too frightful for remembrance or the future too cloudy for anticipation, the present ceases to move in any particular direction and teeters fitfully about from point to point."

This was the crux of the modern problem. His generation was living in a present "divorced from a past and a future." If the best younger writers were to fulfill their potential they would need two things: a cultural tradition to identify with, and a vision of a brighter tomorrow to lure them forward.[40]

This argument is essential for understanding Mumford's outlook on life, then and later. His entire career can be seen as a connected effort to provide the living tradition and the vision of renewal he called for in the pages of *The Freeman*.

At about this time Mumford came across a dictum of Taine's that addressed the modern problem and suggested a possible solution.

"Beneath every literature there is a philosophy. Beneath every work of art an idea of nature and of life. . . . Whoever plants the one, plants the other. . . . Place in all the minds of any age a grand idea of nature and of life, so that they feel and produce it with their whole heart and strength, and you will see them seized with the craving to express it, invent forms of art and groups of figures."[41] To contribute such "a new philosophic idea" seemed to Mumford more important in the aftermath of the war than to engage in battles against this or that social evil.[42]

The Story of Utopias is about the collapse of modern political ideology. The war and the political repression that followed convinced Mumford of the inadequacy of both liberalism and socialism, which had as their common moral foundation a faith in irreversible human improvement through the advance of science, technology, and social planning. There was a need for a new social philosophy alert to the destructive capacity of modern technology and appreciative of the limitations of social planning as an instrument of human improvement.

Although a hopeful book, one that aimed to give his generation a new vision to live by, *The Story of Utopias* is persistently anti-utopian in argument and emphasis, as Mumford found most of the classic utopias he investigated hopelessly weak and inadequate. It was the modern utopian tradition, beginning with Bacon's Atlantis and extending through the technological dreamworld of Edward Bellamy, that he found most wanting. These machine-age utopias were too rigidly planned and too reliant upon technology to bring about the good life. Fearing revolutionary violence and disruptive class action, utopian writers had so ordered life in their fictional futures as to remove all possibilities for genuine individuality or real personal change; the one rule they would not tolerate is " 'live and let live.' "[43]

Most modern utopian writers also presented the problem of reconstructing society as a simple matter of economic and social reorganization—a fatal error they shared with liberalism and socialism—the principal "partial utopias" of the past century. It was these partial utopias that drew most of Mumford's fire.

Both liberalism and socialism, he insisted, looked to technology, social engineering, and mass production to bring about a new age of universal abundance and human cooperation. Starting on the assumption that modern industrial civilization possessed all the resources and technology essential to establish a just society, they demanded merely a change in power and political control—an expansion and redistribution of the comforts and conveniences of the bourgeoisie. They both saw economic growth as the *sine qua non* of human progress; they merely differed on the question of how to distribute the fruits of such expansion. It was this very ideal of ever-increasing material growth, the modern idea of "progress," that Mumford assailed, calling instead for a human ethic committed to the ancient Greek ideals of measure, balance, and economic suffi-ciency, not to the achievement of limitless economic abundance.

Moreover, like Plato and Emerson, Mumford held strongly to the notion that the good life involves more than a reordering of eco-nomic and political institutions. While essential, this would have to be preceded by a transformation of the mechanistic mode of life—the psychological submission to the machine process and the power state—that had created a new personality type—bureaucratic man—in capitalist *and* socialist societies. Mumford called for a complete transformation of the consciousness of industrial man, the creation of a "new humanism," an organic mode of thinking and acting that recognizes "the inner and the outer, the subjective and the objective, the world known to personal intuition and that described by science [as] a single experience." While some radicals expected such a value change to occur after the revolution, for Mumford, this value change *was* the revolution.44

The place to begin this process of cultural change, Mumford declared, was not with the nation, an artificial creation of statesmen and politicians, but with the geographic region, an area possessing a common climate, natural environment, and culture. He urged his fellow reconstructionists to begin by thinking small. Avoid sweep-ing national crusades for change and start immediately in your own region and locale to lay the basis for the renewal of life, he advised, just as Geddes had done in Edinburgh.

Mumford saw Patrick Geddes's civic survey method—a detailed, firsthand diagnosis of a region's natural and human resources—as the starting point and foundation for all regional reconstruction efforts. The outstanding feature of Geddes's sociological method, in his view, was its union of "concreteness and synthesis." The solid foundation of "localized" knowledge that would emerge from the survey was precisely what he found absent from most radical and utopian schemes, "paper programs for the reconstruction of a paper world."45 But in synthesizing the work of a number of regional investigators from a variety of fields and professions, the survey avoided as well the narrow compartmentalization of knowledge and the restricted vision that characterized specialist studies. Geddes had pioneered a sociology that combined theory and action, detailed field research and daring synthesis. In his own way, he had outdone Marx.

More than Geddes, however, Mumford emphasized the role of the creative artist in the process of social transformation. Attracted to both sociology and literature, he described a role for the insurgent intellectual that perfectly embodied his twin interests. A systematic sociology, Geddes had taught him, must be linked to a vision of the good life; and in *The Story of Utopias* Mumford declared it the responsibility of the artists to suggest this. They would be responsible for the first, the most important step in any general reform— the reconstruction of our inner world—by suggesting images of a more balanced, spiritually satisfying life. These could then be woven into the plans of the regional surveyors, whose job it would be to recommend social programs for each of the various regions of the country.46

Unlike the Utopians he wrote about, Mumford was not driven by the dream of social perfection. The world would never be swept clean of evil and injustice, so rather than trying to imagine an impossible "no-place" where all was well the modern reformer should concentrate on the practical task of building Eutopia, the best place possible.

Mumford possessed no natural instincts or abilities for politics, nor did he consider political change important at the moment. "Our most important task at the present moment is to build castles in the air."47

This, in itself, shows his enormous faith in the transforming power of ideas. Throughout his life he continued to consider intellectual forces, not machines, economic classes, or political factions, as the catalytic agents of human change. From this view, the writer, the man of letters, truly mattered. It was his mission to improve the world, not by storming the barricades, but by suggesting a better idea.

This was no argument for delay, however. The process of value renewal must begin at once, he argued in his work of the early 1920s, and it must begin first in America, a nation of unlimited promise. He and other young writers and artists would prepare the soil for this New World *risorgimento*. For this they would need a cultural tradition with which to align themselves. It was time for American intellectuals to stop looking to Europe for guidance and to take a fresh look at their own culture, for they would find there a vigor and creative promise that had not been sufficiently appreciated. In association with Van Wyck Brooks, Waldo Frank, Paul Rosenfeld, Constance Rourke, and other "scouts and prospectors," Mumford would dedicate himself over the next ten years to uncovering what he called America's buried cultural past. This was his first contribution to the creation of the new humanist synthesis he called for in the closing pages of *The Story of Utopias*.

Mumford's first book on American culture was devoted to architecture, which he considered the most important of the social arts. *Sticks and Stones*, published in 1924, brought together the essays on American architecture and civilization he had published that year in *The Freeman*. Just before beginning work on these essays, he helped to found the Regional Planning Association of America, a group of young architects and planners who were preparing to build American variations of Ebenezer Howard's garden cities. Most students of Mumford's work have treated separately his three principal concerns of these years: architecture criticism, regional planning, and American cultural history, but these are interlinked aspects of a program of cultural renewal that established him in the 1920s as a virtually independent moral force on the American Left.

Architecture as a Home for Man

Our architecture reflects us, as truly as a mirror.

—LOUIS SULLIVAN

Lewis Mumford's earliest city surveys awakened his interest in architecture, and before he was twenty-five years old he was exploring the architecture and landscape of the northeastern seaboard as closely as he was the streets and structures of his native Manhattan, learning to use buildings as "documents" in much the same way that an archaeologist does.[1] The outpouring of these walking surveys was a fresh body of criticism and observation that, as early as 1924, with the appearance of *Sticks and Stones: A Study of American Architecture and Civilization*, established him as this country's most promising young architecture critic. "I believe in your genius," Frank Lloyd Wright wrote him early in his career, "and see great things ahead of you."[2]

Mumford's rapid emergence as a preeminent critic was hastened by the absence of strong competition in the field. In the early 1920s architecture was not a popular theme; even architects themselves took little interest in anything but the stylistic history of their practice. The only noteworthy architecture critic America had produced, Montgomery Schuyler, had died in 1914, leaving the field to a scattering of academics and a few older hands like Claude Bragdon, Herbert Croly, and Irving Pond.[3]

Architects, even more so than novelists, were acutely sensitive to criticism of their work, fearing a hostile review might jeopardize their reputation or even their livelihood. Mumford's predecessor as architecture critic for *The New Yorker,* George Sheppard Chappell, was challenged with a lawsuit and forced to apologize for his harsh criticism of a Fifth Avenue building. The threat of such expensive lawsuits caused most professional journals to avoid honest assessments of buildings. So architects became used to flattery and appreciation. Like physicians they had a tight code of professional etiquette, and as long as their buildings did not fall down, their work was largely immune from searching critical investigation.[4]

Mumford refused to be bound by this prevailing code. He brought to architectural appreciation a rigorously critical attitude and a set of consistent standards that continue to guide many of his successors. More than this, his criticism had a strong, almost old-fashioned moral point of view. He never let architects and urban planners forget that their work had moral as well as aesthetic consequences. They had a responsibility to help create what he called "the good life" for all citizens, not just for a privileged few. When Mumford took over *The New Yorker's* "Sky Line" column in 1931 he was not afraid to take on some of New York's biggest developers and best-placed architects, and his highly provocative criticism sometimes made his editor, Harold Ross, a little nervous. But his knowledge of literary law, learned from two brothers-in-law who, as attorneys, had specialized in this legal area, did reassure Ross somewhat, and Mumford was given a free hand to say what he pleased.

Years before he met Ross, Mumford was fortunate to have found an influential friend and sponsor who was in sympathy with his ideas on architecture—Charles Harris Whitaker, the editor of the prestigious *Journal of the American Institute of Architects.* During World War I Whitaker turned that journal's emphasis from polite, sumptuously illustrated appreciations of the historic monuments of the Old World to an enthusiastic assessment of the new movements in housing and architecture that were sweeping Europe—to German and French modernism and to Ebenezer Howard's new town movement. He published essays on the relation of housing to the community, the training and professional status of the architect, and

the social responsibilities of architecture, making his journal a rally-
ing point for the best young minds in American architecture and
urban planning—men like Clarence Stein, Benton MacKaye, Frederick Lee Ackerman, and Henry Wright, all of whom would
eventually join Mumford in the Regional Planning Association of
America.

These wartime essays helped to give Mumford an education in
community architecture, and after leaving the navy in 1919 he had
one of his articles on urban design published in Whitaker's journal.
The appearance of this short piece, "cribbed," he later admitted,
from Geddes and Branford, marked the beginning of his career as a
critic of architecture.[5] Mumford and Whitaker soon became close
friends, and by 1923 Mumford was writing regularly for Whitaker's
journal and doing occasional essays on architecture for *The Freeman*
and *The New Republic*.

This was not yet first-rank criticism, for this eager apprentice was
learning his trade while he practiced it, without, incidentally, the
guiding assistance of a master. But it was criticism distinguished by
an unwavering point of view—a conviction that architecture should
serve the people who use it.

Mumford never considered architecture as solely, or even primarily, an art form. Unlike painting or poetry, architecture must be
shaped to useful human purposes. Its first responsibility is a social
one—to elevate the quality of everyday living. While this might
sound like common sense today, in the 1920s it struck many readers
of Mumford's essays as a new and challenging idea.

Mumford's first architectural essays caught the attention of Alvin
Johnson, director of the New School for Social Research, and in
1923 he invited Mumford to give a course there on the history of
architecture. The six months Mumford spent reading for his lectures unified and focused what he feared were his still too amature-
teurish assessments. Though the course had to be canceled when
only six auditors showed up the first evening, that winter Mumford
tried to recoup the failure by turning his lectures into magazine
articles.

The following autumn Johnson renewed his offer. This time the
course was sufficiently enrolled, thanks to the promotional efforts of

a circulation librarian at the New York Public Library who took a mothering interest in Mumford's career, convincing a number of her co-workers to sign up for the class. This was probably the first course offered at an American university on the whole range of American architectural development. The course lectures and the articles Mumford had written earlier for magazine publication formed the first draft of *Sticks and Stones*.

Mumford had originally planned to write a full history of architecture in America, but the criticism he received on the first few chapters from *The New Republic*'s Herbert Croly made him realize that "this attempt [was] a little premature."[6] *Sticks and Stones* is not a comprehensive survey of American architecture, but it is the first broad cut into new territory, a book of bold originality. Though Mumford would later confess to being a little embarrassed about the book, which he felt was too hastily written and wistfully romantic, it endures as a small masterpiece of American architecture criticism.

It is a book, as Mumford would write of Melville's youthful novel *Typee*, that "belongs to the morning of the imagination." Where *Typee* is a book "to make one go visiting tropical islands," *Sticks and Stones* inspires the reader to go out and experience the architecture Mumford magnificently brings to life. "The book of architecture that does not take the reader to the building," Mumford wrote in a 1926 layman's guide to architecture, "is not worth consulting."[7]

In *Sticks and Stones* Mumford developed an approach to architecture he never deviated from. "Architecture, properly understood, is civilization itself"; and "what is civilization? It is the humanization of man in society." These allied observations by, respectively, W. R. Lethaby and Matthew Arnold, sum up Mumford's view of architecture. *Sticks and Stones*, as its subtitle denotes, is a study not just of architecture but of "architecture and civilization."

From John Ruskin, Mumford learned that every stone has a tongue and every tongue tells a story, that buildings are so many records of a community's life and spirit. "Each generation writes its biography in the buildings it creates."[8] Beginning with *Sticks and Stones*, with its evocative opening chapter on the medieval influence on Puritan town building, Mumford taught historians to look beyond the written record to the shape and style of buildings and cities for clues to the underlying spirit of a community's life. But whereas Ruskin confined himself to the great landmarks and masterpieces of architecture, Mumford reached out to consider as well simple, commonplace structures—houses, barns, factories, bridges, post offices, even street-corner luncheonettes—as reflections of a people's purposes and aspirations. "One must first learn what is common to all musical composition before one begins to play Chopin and Beethoven," he described the method of his own architectural education. "We all live in houses, buy in stores, do work in factories, or offices, or schools, or barns, and dwell in the midst of open landscapes or in cities. Let us appreciate what is good and bad, interesting or dull, in our immediate environment; and if we do this keenly we shall heighten our feeling for the great epics and dramas and symphonies in stone, when we finally come to them."9

On another point Mumford broke decisively with Ruskin. A building, to Ruskin, was one thing; architecture another. A building became architecture only when it rose above the mundane requirements of function and structure and acquired beauty and elegance and, more than not, monumentality. Mumford assailed this as a false theory, insisting that good architecture is simply good building, the art of creating "form" in civilization by giving to every house, factory, and neighborhood the imprint of excellence and order. He was one of the first critics to break down the false distinction between architecture and building, and to open our eyes to the beauty and worth of vernacular forms, or what is often called architecture without architects.

Mumford's earliest architecture criticism is distinguished by another important trait—a profound respect for the past. Repeatedly, he uses the best historic architecture as a standard by which to judge the stylistic miscalculations of his own time. Yet he warns modern architects not to ransack the past for their styles and standards. Excellent architecture is organically part of the culture of its time, a symbol of its prevailing values and interests. So while we might be captivated, like Henry Adams, by the grandeur of Mont-Saint-Michel, a precise expression of the early medieval mind and spirit, we can never hope to reproduce it.10

Mumford was referring here to the derivative historic styles of early-twentieth-century New York skyscrapers, some of them neo-classic, others neo-Gothic, fanciful styles that have come back into vogue today, in our retreat from the geometric simplicity of the International Style. "The severe athletic lines of the Brooklyn

Bridge are many times finer," he believed, "than the birthday cake Gothic of the Woolworth building; one shows a plain honest face, the other a weak mask." Cass Gilbert and the architects of the eclectic style failed to see that there could be no such thing as a "modern" Gothic style. Their skyscrapers were "born old."[11]

This was no injunction, however, to abjure history. The architect needed a clear understanding of the past precisely so that he would not reproduce styles that no longer struck the right note.

Mumford was one of the first critics in this century to campaign for a distinctly modern style in the arts. The machine had produced new physical materials and technics, and he urged architects and artists to bring these into their work, following in the tradition of the nineteenth-century master builders whose reputations he helped to revive—Henry Hobson Richardson, Louis Sullivan, and the Roeblings, John A. and his son Washington, whose Brooklyn Bridge, a poem of granite and steel, Mumford hailed as a Chartres Cathedral of the epoch of steam and steel. These artists had accepted the best new ideas and materials of the industrial age, turned them into aesthetic ends, and produced native works of genius and permanency. Young artists, Mumford advised, would do well to work in that spirit, creating their own uniquely modern forms.

Yet Mumford never permitted his enthusiasm for modern style to violate his sensitivity for architecture as a social art. His undeviating attention to basic human needs led him to criticize that characteristically American architectural form—the skyscraper—marking him from the beginning as a maverick in his profession.

Visually, there is perhaps nothing in the world to match New York's spectacular skyline. "The New York Harbor is loveliest at night perhaps," the English poet Rupert Brooke observed in 1913. "On the Staten Island ferryboat you slip out from darkness right under the immense skyscrapers. As they recede they form into a mass together, heaping up one behind another, fire-lined and majestic sentinel over the black gold-streaked waters."[12] Mumford had come upon this same scene many times in his youth, returning from afternoons on the tennis courts of Staten Island. But the city was even then in a stage of furious upward expansion. The Manhattan of Mumford's childhood, a city of thickly crowded buildings rarely exceeding six stories, had become the world's first vertical city by the time he published his first architectural essays. Mumford had seen these colossal columns of stone and steel, one higher than the next, proceed like an advancing army up the avenues, from the tip of the island into the heart of the new midtown, forming, by the early 1920s, one continuous skyline, which appeared like a great cloud-enshrouded wall from Brooklyn Heights, where he and Sophia took an apartment in 1922. Hailed by many as symbols of the new century of American power and expansion, these "cathedrals of commerce," as their promoters called them, were for Mumford dark foreshadowings of the decline of metropolitan civilization. By the mid-1920s, New York, in his eyes, had become "the center of a furious decay, which [is] called growth, enterprise, and greatness."[13]

Mumford was not immune to the skyscraper's physical allure. From the prow of the Staten Island ferry, the "great towers of the tip of Manhattan" looked to him like "fairy stalactites on an opened grotto." But that, he warned in one of his first architecture essays, was not the best vantage point to appreciate their true impact upon the city. Seen from the streets of Manhattan, which were being turned into sunless, windswept corridors of stone and steel, they were not nearly so visually satisfying. This was an architecture not for office workers and pedestrians, but for "angels and aviators!"[14]

The first skyscrapers had fit reasonably well into New York's existing built environment. They stood out, yet did not cut off natural light or prevent views of the cityscape. Then came a period of surging upward growth.

By the 1920s, the architects of New York and their wealthy commercial clients were caught up in an almost compulsive effort to build higher and higher buildings; and to build many more of them. As a boy Mumford had seen the 600-foot Singer Building and the 792-foot-tall Woolworth Building far overshadow Daniel Burnham's triangular-shaped Flatiron Building at Broadway and Fifth Avenue, whose twenty-one stories had made it the marvel of turn-of-the-century New York. In the late 1920s taller buildings went up, like the seventy-seven-story Chrysler shaft, with its gleaming silver spire bedecked with stylized eagles. The construction of the Empire State Building in the early 1930s completed this stage of frantic skyward expansion.

Most New Yorkers enthusiastically welcomed the skyscrapers. For many people the skyscraper represented progress itself, the unstoppable economic growth of the nation and the city. New York had become the city center of the most powerful economic empire in the world, and the skyscraper boldly announced that fact. The skyscrapers, as one writer declared, are "the Mountains of Manhattan . . . the Accepted Badge of its cityhood."[15]

But for Mumford the skyscraper was a principal cause and symbol for everything that had gone wrong with Walt Whitman's "Mannahatta": its overgrowth, its congestion, its noise, its dizzying pace, its almost suicidal vitality, its never-ending pursuit of the dollar. "The heavy, low musical roar, hardly ever intermitted," which, to Whitman, had characterized the New York of the 1860s, had increased by the 1930s to a nerve-straining din, as the automobile added to the noise and congestion of the downtown streets.[16] The spectacular growth that everyone was celebrating in the decade of Republican prosperity was ruining the city Mumford loved. Many decades before the issue was even seriously raised, he was insisting that excessive skyscraper development was injurious to the quality of life in New York City.

Mumford, however, did not oppose the skyscraper in all its forms, as some of his critics have charged. He accepted it as an unavoidable fact of modern urban life, and as a critic he assessed its strengths and weaknesses as a building style. His early essays might be overly critical of the showy historicism of the newest skyscrapers in Manhattan, but in the deliberately modern tall buildings of Chicago architects like John Wellborn Root and Louis Sullivan, sturdy structures that matter-of-factly expressed the functions of their expanding city of railyards, foundries, steel and iron, he found the beginnings of a distinguished American architecture.

Modern skyscraper architecture was born in that turbulent center of prairie commerce and industry. We know that today, but in the 1920s Chicago's architecture had to be rediscovered, and in this effort Mumford led the way. Writing in the magazine *Architecture*, he reintroduced his countrymen to an architecture of power and simplicity that had already inspired such European advocates of modernism as his friends Erich Mendelsohn and Walter Curt Behrendt.

In 1927, when Mumford first visited Chicago, Fiske Kimball, the most respected architecture historian of the old school, was still dismissing the work of the Chicago architects as "barbarous." While Mumford had never agreed with that stuffy verdict, until then the names of these Chicago pioneers, with the exception of Sullivan and Wright, "were almost unknown to me," he later admitted, "and their buildings had scarcely cast a shadow on my consciousness."[17] Touring the Loop with the architect Barry Byrne, who had begun his career as an office boy of Frank Lloyd Wright, Mumford had his first look at the staggering achievements of the Chicago renascence of the 1880s and 1890s: Dankmar Adler and Louis Sullivan's Auditorium Hotel and Theatre, John Wellborn Root's Monadnock Building, and Sullivan's Schlesinger and Mayer Department Store. Later that week he went to suburban Riverside and Oak Park to see several of Frank Lloyd Wright's prairie houses. And when he returned to New York he went to work immediately on the series of articles that were the first full assessment of what are now universally acknowledged classics of modern architecture.[18]

These essays, like all of Mumford's early writings on architecture, have one ruling purpose—to identify and encourage a style for the approaching age. Mumford was excited by design developments in engineering, from sleek, streamlined automobiles and airplanes to modern American kitchen equipment and bathroom fixtures. They struck him as evidence that engineering could occasionally rise to the level of art. He was encouraged, too, that artists, chiefly in Europe, were taking inspiration from these developments. Brancusi and Duchamp-Villon in sculpture, Braque and Duchamp in painting, and Stieglitz and Strand in photography were putting us in touch with "a world in which machinery exists not only to perform useful services but to be, as far as possible, enjoyed."[19]

Mumford found the most hopeful signs of a new modernism in the arts in architecture and city design—the "master arts," in his view—and his early writing focused on American developments in these fields. In the work of Henry Hobson Richardson, John Wellborn Root, Louis Sullivan, and, above all, Frank Lloyd Wright he found the promise not just of a new architecture but of a new organic civilization.

In *The Brown Decades: A Study of the Arts in America, 1865–1895*, published in 1931, Mumford gave his most complete appraisal of the Chicago builders and his most concise expression of what modern architecture should be. In *Sticks and Stones* Mumford had treated

Richardson, however respectfully, as a purely Romantic architect seeking to work out a modern symbolic variation of the Romanesque. In *The Brown Decades* he took a closer look at Richardson's work after 1880—when Richardson attacked new building forms like the railroad station, warehouse, and office building—and pronounced him the "originating genius" of modern architecture.[20]

Mumford was also drawn to Richardson's domestic architecture, which he had seen on his tramps up and down the northeastern seaboard before he had written a word on architecture. He found Richardson's shingled cottages, with their long steep roofs, wide windows, and ample bays, superb examples of regional architecture, of a building style in harmony with the land and the climate.[21] If a regionalist movement emerged in America, Mumford hoped that its architects would take inspiration from Richardson's staggering achievement.

Richardson was a master of stone. Though he died just before the transition was made from masonry to steel-frame construction, his contemporaries Sullivan and Root, working in the powerful tradition he had established, carried on the revolution in architecture he had begun. Drawn to Chicago by the opportunity created by the Great Fire of 1871, they set out to develop a distinctly American architecture. In the sixteen-story Monadnock Building, still working in masonry with an internal iron frame, John Wellborn Root expressed the new vision. This was the building that most impressed Mumford when he surveyed Chicago's architecture for the first time: a "straight up-and-down" structure of severe simplicity, wholly without ornament, its rigidity of line broken only by its gently projecting window bays, which allowed more sunlight and space in the rooms.

Before he visited Chicago for the first time, Mumford had come under the influence of German modernism through his reading of *Die Form*, and he assessed most American buildings in the late 1920s by the antihistoricist standards of Walter Gropius and the *Deutscher Werkbund*. By these standards, the Monadnock Building succeeded brilliantly. An uncompromising "brick box," it unabashedly announced the purpose for which it was erected—it was a business building; the architect who built it *"meant business."* For their inspiration New York's architects went to "crumbled civilizations; confident Chicago was its own inspiration."

Working with a newer medium—steel—Louis Sullivan achieved in the best of his buildings a similar synthesis of form and function. In the steel skyscraper the outside wall functioned as a kind of thin curtain or, perhaps more aptly, as skin on the frame, not as a supporting device. A light but strong steel frame did the work of the walls. This freed architects to reach the sky. Led by Sullivan, the father of the modern skyscraper, they did just that.

A skyscraper, Sullivan said, should be "a proud and soaring thing," and he gave it a spiritual as well as a functional service to perform: it was to be a symbol of the power and energy of a confident democracy. Sullivan accentuated the vertical lines of his office towers, and in an effort to give them some "personality" he embellished many of them with lacy ornamentation—carved, stylized designs of trees, flowers, and bushes.

On first seeing Sullivan's Chicago work, Mumford felt both of these design ideas were a mistake. Sullivan's ornamentation seemed to defy his own dictum that form should closely follow function. Mumford believed it wrong, furthermore, to invest skyscrapers with moral meaning, when "in actuality, height in skyscrapers means either a desire for centralized administration, a desire to increase ground rents, a desire for advertisement, or all three of these together—and none of these functions determines a 'proud and soaring thing.'"

But Mumford would not deny Sullivan his greatness. Sullivan, he believed, was the first architect in America to come to know himself with any fullness in relation to his soil, period, and civilization, and Mumford pronounced him "the Whitman of American architecture." But he saw Sullivan as the living link between two even "greater masters," Henry Hobson Richardson and Frank Lloyd Wright, the young draftsman who entered Sullivan's offices in Chicago in 1889. When Wright reached his full stature, modern architecture, Mumford declared after seeing his first prairie houses, was truly born.

But before Wright could do his best work, American architecture went into a period of decline. This, at least, is how Mumford saw things in the strong-opinioned history of American architecture he pieced together in the 1920s, a viewpoint that is much disputed today, yet one he held to throughout his life. Instead of taking further the work of Richardson, Root, and Sullivan, "the architects of America, having scaled the heights too quickly, paused for a dizzy moment and then fell—fell into the easy mechanical duplication of other modes of architecture, frigidly predicted by the Chicago Exposition of 1893 . . . turning out a rapid succession of Roman temples and baths, Florentine villas and French palaces and Gothic churches and universities."[22]

So as a young man Mumford stood with the modernists in their battle against Victorian imitation, yet he could not agree with most of the ideas of the unchallenged leader of this new impulse in the arts, Le Corbusier, born Charles-Edouard Jeanneret, the son of an artisan family from a French-speaking village of watchmakers north of Geneva. In 1920, in the opening issue of their polemical journal *L'Esprit nouveau*, Le Corbusier and his young painter associate, Amédée Ozenfant, proclaimed a new epoch in architecture and the arts. The machine, they predicted, would become the basis of a social order of harmony, simple beauty, and good form.

Two years before the publication of Le Corbusier's *Vers une architecture*, with its call for a new style based upon the machine, Mumford was arguing independently for much the same thing in his essay "Machinery and the Modern Style." Yet these two young artistic insurgents, Le Corbusier and Lewis Mumford, would become implacable adversaries.

Mumford and Le Corbusier were actually alike in many ways. Both were largely self-trained; and as young men both had read Morris and Ruskin with enthusiasm, lamenting the destruction by industrialization of the communal village, with its honored tradition of handicraft. (Le Corbusier had personally witnessed the erosion of this world in his own village of La Chaux-de-Fonds.) But unlike Ruskin and Morris, these two moderns refused to turn back to the Middle Ages for an ideal of order, integration, and sound workmanship. That world, they agreed, was forever lost. The machine was inevitable; nothing could stop it.

On yet another point they were in early agreement: architecture must press the fight for the good life, a belief that led both of them, early in their careers, to campaign for soundly designed, affordable workers' housing. For both men architecture and social planning were inseparably interlinked, although, as we shall see, they came to favor dramatically different kinds of community planning. As a young man Le Corbusier urged architects to address themselves to the everyday needs of domesticity. Many of his first designs were for simply constructed houses, like the Dom-Ino house, which was divided into standardized compartments, each of which could be manufactured cheaply by mass production and assembled quickly on the site. Mumford, in the 1920s and 1930s, was equally enthralled by the possibility of mass-produced housing.

The architecture of Le Corbusier's Dom-Ino houses is bare and undistinguished, but "Corbu" argued (as Mumford would later argue in defense of the functionally designed houses and apartments of his friends Clarence Stein and Henry Wright) that by grouping these individual units in a well-designed layout the architect could create an image of handsome orderliness, each unit contributing to the beauty of the whole. In developing these parallel ideas, moreover, Mumford and Le Corbusier were influenced by the same example—the houses of Hampstead Garden Suburb designed by the garden city architects Barry Parker and Raymond Unwin. With Parker and Unwin, they searched for a plan appropriate for cooperative living. Le Corbusier even designed a low-density garden suburb for La Chaux-de-Fonds, so unlike his chillingly formal Voisin Plan for Paris. Architecture, for him, was more than the art of fashioning good buildings. It led naturally to the design of the total human-created environment.[23] So although their ideas on urban planning were to diverge dramatically, both Le Corbusier and Mumford were driven throughout their lives to shape the city of the future. Neither built the city of his dreams, but there are no more influential figures in twentieth-century urban planning.

It is not difficult to see why Mumford was drawn so strongly as a young man to the ideas of Le Corbusier and the German Bauhaus architects. The modernists were in rebellion against the cumbersome clutter and fake historicism of Victorian architecture, and they rejected as well the stuffy bourgeois culture that had produced it. The modernists stood against everything Mumford disliked about the culture and architecture he had grown up in.

No one can truly appreciate the appeal of modernism, Mumford would write of his own upbringing, who has not lived in a closed and cluttered Victorian brownstone, with its living room packed with the weekend collectings of a lifetime—china vases, Japanese figurines, cheap statues of crocodiles, elephants and dancing nymphs, and often, as in Elvina Mumford's sitting room, lamps and lampshades "as frilly and pink-bosomy as Lillian Russell." This cluttering was made claustrophobic in the Mumford home by the window coverings of floor-length drapes and lace curtains that closed the rooms to sunlight and fresh air. For Mumford and many other children of the Gilded Age bourgeoisie who had grown up in these "chambers of aesthetic horror," modernism performed a useful task of purification, opening the way for a fresh start in architecture and the other arts.[24] Yet Mumford could never accept the full doctrine of modernism. He found the pure white flat-roofed houses of Le Corbusier hauntingly devoid of the human touch. They were truly, as Le Corbusier intended them to be, machines to live in.

Influenced by Patrick Geddes's organicism, Mumford refused to associate functionalism with the machine. Nor did he consider the machine the perfect symbol of the new age, as Le Corbusier did. The machine was undeniably an expression of our so-called industrial society, but only one part of it. Man might be a toolmaker, but he was also a dreamer and a seeker after ideals. True functionalism, in this view, had to be related to the entire range of humankind's needs and purposes, the physical and biological as well as the spiritual and transcendent, our needs for community and privacy, for health and nurture, for comfort, sunshine, and space in our work and leisure. Sometimes mere boxes would do; other times they wouldn't. There were even occasions when expression and symbolism should take precedence over strictly functional requirements, as they had in the medieval cathedrals.[25]

Behind all of Mumford's early ideas on design is a plea for what he called an organic architecture, a harmonious reconciliation of function and feeling. In the architecture of Frank Lloyd Wright he found such a synthesis.

Mumford was the first American critic to fully appreciate Wright's organic architecture and to write about it with insight and imagination. Mumford believed that Wright had strongly influenced the work of Adolf Loos, Erich Mendelsohn, Peter Behrens, and other European modernists, and that his architecture was fully as "modern" as theirs. But Philip Johnson, who with his fellow critic and historian Henry-Russell Hitchcock, would organize the famous International Show at New York's Museum of Modern Art in 1932, introducing Americans to the work of the European modernists, could not agree. "Wright was a great pioneer but he is a romantic and has nothing more to do with architecture today," Johnson wrote Mumford in 1931, just at the time when Wright was about to enter the period of his greatest achievement as an architect.[26]

"It has been said that Lewis [Mumford] discovered me," Wright reflected later, referring to Mumford's support of him when many thought he was finished as an architect. "If he did I am proud of his company."[27] Mumford considered Wright America's greatest living architect; and Wright considered Mumford (whom he affectionately called "lieber Llewis," adding an "l" to his name, no doubt, to place him in the same august company as himself) as "the most valuable critic our country has—a mind of Emersonian quality—with true creative power."[28]

Mumford first met Wright in 1927 when Wright invited him to lunch at his favorite New York hotel, the Plaza. In *Sticks and Stones* Mumford had praised Wright's low-lying prairie houses for their close attention to human needs and to the characteristics of the terrain and the climate; and that book had greatly impressed Wright, who wrote Mumford an admiring letter after reading it. This was the start of an affectionate but somewhat guarded friendship.

Mumford didn't know quite what to expect when he first sat down to lunch with the man he considered the "Fujiyama of Architecture . . . at once a lofty mountain and a national shrine."[29] He knew of Wright's legendary ego; his incessant, sometimes pathetic attempts to dominate everyone around him. "Being so sure of my ground and my star so early in life," Wright once remarked to Mumford, "I was soon forced to choose between honest arrogance and a hypocritical humility. . . . Well, the world knows I chose honest arrogance."[30] But as Mumford approached the Plaza that afternoon in 1927 he half-expected to confront a broken man, bent and burdened by a thousand personal problems. Wright was near bankruptcy, he had all but ceased to build, and he had just passed through a succession of lavishly publicized personal crises. Yet the first impression Wright made on Mumford was that of a man of total inner confidence. He was friendly and easygoing, his face "unseamed, his air assured, indeed jaunty." He admitted that he was

financially broke; he had come to New York, he told Mumford, to
sell his valuable collection of Japanese prints to forestall his credi-
tors. And he was disarmingly forthright about his other personal
difficulties.[31]

The two men were barely a half hour into their conversation
before Wright began to spill out the details of his marital problems.
They had begun as far back as 1909 when he left his wife Catherine
and his six children, and his lucrative Oak Park architectural practice, and fled to Europe with Mamah Borthwick Cheney, the wife of
a former client. With Catherine unwilling to release him from the
marriage, Wright had returned to America in 1911 and built a home
for Mrs. Cheney and himself in the Wisconsin countryside where he
had spent part of his childhood on his grandfather's farm. He named
it Taliesin, which in Welsh means "shining brow," and it was a
virtually self-contained shelter from the world—a residence, studio,
and farm, with its own water and power supply, a stone house
beautifully blended into its site in the side of a hill looking out over a
picturesque valley.[32]

In 1914 one of Wright's house servants went mad and set fire to
Taliesin, murdering Mrs. Cheney and her two daughters with an
axe as they fled from the burning house. Wright set out immediately
to rebuild Taliesin, but he had no passion for the effort. In 1916 he
escaped to Japan, where he had a commission to build the Imperial
Hotel in Tokyo, and when he returned to the United States six years
later with the sculptor Miriam Noel, with whom he had been living
in Tokyo, his work had fallen out of popular favor.

Catherine finally agreed to a divorce and Wright married Miriam
in 1923, on a bridge at Taliesin, but they separated one year later. He
then met and fell in love with his final mate, Olgivanna Milanoff,
daughter of the Chief Justice of Montenegro and a follower of the
philosopher Gurdjieff. He brought her to the valley of his grandfather, but Taliesin was again badly damaged by fire, although this
time no one was hurt. Undaunted, Wright mortgaged everything
that remained in order to begin rebuilding it and to raise money for
his expected alimony payments to Miriam. Their failure to reach a
settlement set in motion a final series of public embarrassments. In
1926, Miriam, insanely jealous of the younger Olgivanna, who had
just had Wright's child, had a warrant issued for her husband's arrest
for adultery. Wright went into hiding in Minneapolis with

Olgivanna, but was located by police one month later, charged with criminal adultery and violation of the Mann Act (transporting a woman across state lines for immoral purposes), and jailed briefly.

A short time later Miriam agreed to a divorce and dropped all criminal charges, and after the one-year waiting period required by state law Wright and Olgivanna were married. Meanwhile, Wright's friends bailed him out of debt and helped him to hold on to Taliesin, where he returned with Olgivanna to reestablish his architectural career.

Wright came through these tragedies a strengthened man, and Mumford's recollection of their first meeting at the Plaza bears this out. "His ego," Mumford recalls, "was so heavily armored that even the bursting shell of such disastrous events did not penetrate his vital organs. He lived from first to last like a god: one who acts but is not acted upon."33

Mumford gives a clue here to the reason he and Wright never became closer friends. Wright and Mumford got together frequently in New York in the 1930s, and Wright invited Mumford to Taliesin several times for a visit; in the early 1930s he even asked Mumford to take up residence at Taliesin to help him run the school for architects he had established there. But Wright, like Patrick Geddes before him, found it difficult to accept Mumford's resolve to remain a totally independent writer; and he was annoyed by Mumford's unwillingness to drop his own work on a moment's notice to visit him, when *Wright* happened to be free, at Taliesin East, or at Taliesin West, the magnificent home, studio, and school he built in the Arizona desert in the 1930s. How could America's most brilliant critic of architecture refuse an invitation "to come [to Arizona] to this capitol [sic] of the modern world of Architecture[?]," Wright wrote Mumford at one point.34 But, for Mumford, to have gone to Taliesin would have been an act of discipleship, and as much as he liked and admired Wright he did not want to be beholden to him in any way.

Even in the little time he and Mumford spent together, Wright showed signs of the domineering arrogance that had destroyed so many of his closest personal relationships. One steaming summer day, as they sat in a New York bar, he criticized Mumford for insisting on having his Irish whiskey on ice rather than in plain water, as he preferred it; and another time he reproached Mumford for not walking with his toes pointed outward in the military manner he favored. In their conversations and letters Wright, moreover, demanded an almost worshipful acceptance of his own political and artistic views. Any murmur of dissent, any criticism, no matter how constructively cast, he considered high heresy. So in his relations with Wright Mumford learned to keep his distance, if for no other reasons than to retain his admiration for him. He had acted the same way with Patrick Geddes.

Mumford found in Wright qualities he prized in himself. Wright, too, was a self-made, self-reliant artist. He had virtually forced himself on the world. He had no formal training as an architect. He made his way, like Mumford, on the strength of his directed passion and his outsized ability; and he, too, had that bottomless reservoir of inner confidence that comes, as Freud tells us, from being the favorite of one's mother. In his more understated way Mumford was as self-confident and as sensitive to criticism as Wright, and that made it easier for him to accept Wright's imperial manner.

But it was with Wright's architecture that Mumford found himself in closest sympathy. A building, Wright declared early in his career, should not have a design imposed upon it. It should grow organically out of the natural surroundings in which it is built; and it should be built to the requirements of comfortable living, not to the specifications of a favored historic style. Above all, Wright, with Louis Sullivan, wanted to produce an architecture expressive of his "own country and his own people."[35] And that, as much as anything, is what drew Mumford to his work. He saw Wright as an ally in his effort to encourage an American cultural renascence.

For most of the first part of his career, Wright concentrated on domestic architecture, building houses for well-heeled businessmen in Oak Park and other suburbs of Chicago. These sprawling houses of stone, wood, and glass, as flat as the prairie itself, made Oak Park "a pilgrimage spot, the Ile-de-France of modern architecture," in Henry-Russell Hitchcock's words.[36] Wright broke decisively with the elaborate historical styles of his day, building earthbound, unpretentious houses of simple materials. Wherever he could, he did away with walls as dividers and introduced glass, grouping windows in long continuous banks, opening the house to light and air. Frederick Law Olmsted and Ebenezer Howard brought the garden into the city; Wright brought it into the home itself, filling his houses with living plants and flowers. The living rooms, dining rooms, and dens of his houses tended to flow into one another, creating one great space around "the hearth," the cavernous fireplaces he favored.

Mumford found in Wright's early architecture two qualities he prized in good building: "a sense of place and a rich feeling for materials."37 Wright preferred to use regional materials—stone, brick, and wood from the surrounding locale; and he dramatically accentuated these natural materials, leaving beams exposed and woods unfinished. Refusing to fix on any one design, he experimented with a rich range of regional forms.

This bothered modernists like Henry-Russell Hitchcock and Philip Johnson, who favored a single inclusive style, the International Style. Although they acknowledged that Wright's work showed the promise of this new style, Hitchcock and Johnson were disturbed by the very quality Mumford believed contributed most to Wright's architectural achievement—his never-ending aesthetic experimentalism.38

With Wright, Mumford favored not one all-encompassing style but a variety of styles suited to the peculiarities of the region, the site, and the diverse needs of those who would use the building. This is why neither he nor Mumford could accept the International Style uncritically. In Wright's architecture Mumford saw what he valued in life itself—balance, variety, and an insurgent spontaneity.

Wright showed in his early work the synthesis of form and function Mumford had called for in some of his first essays on architecture—retaining Cubism's respect for function and regular geometric forms, and Art Nouveau's exuberant expressiveness. But Wright had done much more than that. The most important union he had brought about, in Mumford's view, was that between man, nature, and the machine. Wright's architecture was the expression not of Le Corbusier's machine age, but an approaching organic age when architecture would be tailored to changing human purposes and regional realities.

Mumford never made an extensive on-site study of Wright's entire work, but he made sure to look for Wright's buildings wherever he traveled. It was not until 1953, however, that he attempted his fullest appraisal of Wright's architectural achievement. By that time their friendship had all but ended, a casualty of the war of opinion over

American intervention in the fight against Hitler. Wright was an isolationist; Mumford a passionate interventionist. And although Wright was ready to continue the friendship in the face of these irreconcilable political differences, sending the Mumfords annual Christmas messages, Mumford was not. After the war Wright made one more attempt at reconciliation, sending Mumford a catalogue of one of the international exhibitions of his work, inscribed: "In spite of all, your old F. Ll. W." On reading this, Mumford recalls that he turned to his wife Sophia and said: "I've just written a book in which I've said that without a great upsurgence of love, we will not be able to save the world from even greater orgies of extermination and destruction. If I haven't enough love left in me to answer Wright in the same fashion as this greeting, I'd better throw that book out the window." So he wrote back, repeating these words. In reply, Wright sent a signed Japanese print. Neither of them referred to their breach after this.39

But they never really reestablished the friendship. It would have been difficult to do so, for Wright was the builder and Mumford the critic, and Wright could not abide criticism of his work. When Mumford published his two-article appraisal of Wright's career in *The New Yorker* in 1953, tempering his enthusiasm with some tough criticism, Wright blew up.40

He read Mumford's first article in an airplane and became so incensed about it that he wrote him a letter at once, mailing it when he landed. He referred to Mumford in the third person and ended the letter by calling him a "mere scribbler," and, worse, an "ignoramus."41

Mumford wrote back immediately, telling Wright that he "respected his greatness too much to belittle it by sweetening my critical appreciation with undiluted praise." He had written about him in "the same unsparing manner" in which he had written in *Green Memories* about his own son who was killed in World War II, "out of admiration and love." He signed this letter, as Wright signed his own letters, "With all respect and admiration, as from one Master to another."42

Wright did not reply to that explanation, but neither did he comment on Mumford's second article, which must have been even more unacceptable to him than the first. Their last chance to repair the friendship came in 1956 when Wright invited Mumford to take

Robert Moses's place at a Chicago dinner keynoted by Wright. Mumford had decided, reluctantly, to accept Wright's offer, but on reading the invitation more closely he realized that the dinner was to promote Wright's design for a skyscraper "A Mile High." He would have no part in a proposal that he thought caricatured Wright's, and his own, conception of organic architecture.

"Don't be a dear old Mule," Wright wrote him two years after this. Come to visit Taliesin West and we'll "plan a few days going over auld lang syne."[43] He even offered to pay Lewis and Sophia's travel expenses, and to provide them with a Chrysler and a driver to tour the Arizona desert. But Mumford claimed he was too busy to break free. "I understand a man's absorption in his work to the exclusion of any honor he may bestow on an old friend by his presence," Wright wrote him plaintively in the last letter of their relationship. "But this absenteeism . . . ," he guessed correctly, "has other causes into which I will do well not to 'dig' . . .

"Salute! dear . . . 'lieber Llewis'—[and] look out for the ingrowing of a special talent amounting to genius."[44]

A year later Mumford was scheduled to give a public lecture to the architecture students at the University of Pennsylvania, where he was a visiting professor on and off throughout the 1950s. Up to the last minute he couldn't decide on a topic. Then, on the morning of the scheduled address he learned of Wright's death. As he approached the School of Design he saw that the American flag hanging near the entrance was at half-mast with black streamers suspended below it. He realized at that moment that there was only one possible subject for his lecture—Frank Lloyd Wright's life and work.

We have no record of this lecture; Mumford delivered it extemporaneously. In it, he tried to do justice to Wright's greatness as well as to his faults and flaws as a builder and as a man. Wright, for all his accomplishments, had fallen short of his promise, and his most fiercely demanding critic found it hard to forgive him for that. Wright had broken the one architectural canon Mumford held sacrosanct: that architecture is primarily a social art. But Mumford did not save this criticism for this dramatic post-mortem retrospective. He had advanced it again and again, in ever sharper language, while Wright still lived and built, and this, in fact, was the central charge of his 1953 *New Yorker* articles.

For all his dazzling gifts Wright, Mumford wrote in that brilliant appraisal, is an "Isolato," the word Melville applied to Ishmael in *Moby Dick*. Each of his buildings stands in sheer isolation—a monument to his own towering greatness. In the end, the client he sought most of all to satisfy was himself.[45] From Wright's perspective, the architect must do more than design the building; he had to invent new methods of construction, design new types of furniture, pick out rugs, chinaware, pictures, and sculpture.[46] Many of his buildings were efforts at complete works of art, every detail, even, on occasion, the clients' wardrobe, was to be determined by the architect, an attitude that linked him, in Mumford's mind, with Le Corbusier.

Wright's houses were individual solutions to what was essentially a community problem—the problem of good housing for all Americans. Mumford considered the freestanding suburban house something of an anachronism. Most Americans simply could not afford it. A socially responsible architecture had to be a community architecture. But Wright, who believed that "each [American has an] inalienable right to live his life in his own house in his own way,"[47] was transfixed by the dream of the freestanding house in a natural setting. In the end, Wright had avoided what Mumford considered the preeminent problem of architecture—the task of translating its great individual accomplishments into community designs to serve the housing needs of all Americans.

The distinguishing mark of all of Mumford's architectural criticism is this emphasis upon the entire human complex into which a building is set. A building, for him, is not a freestanding, self-contained structure to be appraised on its aesthetic merits alone. It is but an element in a larger urban design. Gardens, parks, streets, and courtyards should all be treated as integral parts of the building, he argued, and not introduced as mere afterthoughts. It is not individual buildings that make cities attractive and livable, but the grouping together of buildings to make streets and neighborhoods. More than anyone in his time, Mumford is responsible for introducing a sense of the environment into architectural consciousness.

At the very beginning of his career Mumford saw American architecture beset by one overriding problem: our best buildings were not complemented by intelligent community design. The result: isolated masterworks in the midst of spreading physical disorder. America would never have a distinguished architecture, as opposed to distinguished individual works of architecture, until our advances in design were incorporated in communal projects that restored a sense of orderly beauty and human scale to the city.[48] Inspired architecture demanded inspired city planning. It was this conviction that drew Mumford to the young architects, planners, and environmentalists who formed the Regional Planning Association of America (RPAA) in New York City in 1923, the year that he began work on *Sticks and Stones*.

But the way Mumford stated the problem in *Sticks and Stones*, the future of architecture did not rest with either the architects or the planners. Since society was the principal source of architectural form, any real improvement in the frame of civilization hinged on a transformation that was essentially valuative and psychological. Architecture, in other words, could be no better or worse than the society that produced it. In the end, *Sticks and Stones* is more than a history of American architecture; it is an argument for a new moral order.

Architecture or Revolution
Revolution can be avoided.

This was Le Corbusier's call to action, but for Mumford, great architecture was impossible *without* a revolution—a radical reorientation of our social values. In Ebenezer Howard's garden cities he found the first promise of this new orientation. All of his writings on architecture and cities, beginning with his work for the Regional Planning Association of America, are an effort to carry forward the spirit and aim of Howard's garden city movement.

I I

New Towns for America

Many are the things that man
Seeing must understand.
Not seeing, how shall he know
What lies in the hand
Of time to come?

—SOPHOCLES

The Regional Planning Association of America was founded by a group of planners and architects who had worked for the federal government during World War I building housing communities for defense workers based on the most advanced thinking on urban design. Among its leaders were three of the outstanding figures in twentieth-century American planning: Clarence Stein, Henry Wright, and Benton MacKaye. Mumford, who met Stein and MacKaye through Charles Harris Whitaker, was appointed the organization's secretary in 1923, and within a year he became the RPAA's leading spokesman and theoretician. Working with a young but seasoned group of planners and builders, he had his first opportunity to carry into practice the ideas of Patrick Geddes and Ebenezer Howard. This turned out to be an immensely exciting time for him. His work for the RPAA brought into focus his nascent ideas about regionalism, city planning, and conservation policy; and in these years he made himself into an urban thinker of the first rank.[1]*

Clarence Stein was the RPAA's chief talent recruiter and its principal administrative officer. He was most responsible for setting organizational policy and for running the day-to-day affairs of the RPAA; and for a time he was Mumford's closest friend in the organization, and the one most sympathetic to his ideas on urban planning.

A rare blend of "artist and organizer," Stein was born into comfortable circumstances, his father having made a fortune as head of the National Casket Company.[2] After an education at the Columbia School of Architecture and Ecole des Beaux-Arts in Paris, he joined the New York firm of Bertram G. Goodhue, eventually becoming its chief designer.

While serving in the Army Corps of Engineers during the war, Stein became excited by the government's emergency housing initiative for war workers, and he became closely associated with Henry Wright and others involved in the program. This launched him on a lifelong career as a leader in housing and community planning.[3]

Stein's physical appearance disguised his considerable talents for leadership. He was thin, pale, and scholarly-looking, and all through his life he was plagued by psychosomatic disabilities. Perhaps to compensate for his frail appearance, he smoked thick black cigars, talking out of the side of his mouth as he chewed on the end of his cigar. Stein had a personality ideally suited to his role as head of a loosely structured organization of dreamers and builders. For one thing, he was a crack administrator; he kept things together and focused the group's energies on a precisely defined reform agenda. He could be steel-willed and decisive, but he was never inflexible or dogmatic. A modest man, withdrawn but congenial, his special talents were his sound judgment and his experimental tempera-

* Other prominent members of the RPAA were Charles Harris Whitaker; Frederick Bigger, a Pittsburgh planner; Robert D. Kohn, Stein's architectural associate; Frederick Lee Ackerman, an architect and disciple of Thorstein Veblen; Edith Elmer Wood, an influential crusader for public housing; Henry Klaber, the architect; Robert Bruère, editor of *The Survey Graphic*; Alexander M. Bing, a wealthy, semiretired real-estate magnate interested in community housing for workers; and, later, Catherine Bauer, a housing specialist.

ment, his eye for talent and his hospitality to new ideas. Mumford liked him immensely and learned to appreciate as well his political skills. Stein, who was thirteen years older than Mumford, was a visionary, but he had a keener sense of political realities than Mumford or anyone else in the RPAA. As a New York State housing official, he linked the group to the reformist administration of Governor Al Smith, giving the RPAA its first real opportunity to influence community and statewide projects.

In 1923, Governor Smith appointed Stein chairman of a committee he had just formed to deal with the state's acute postwar housing shortage. Up to this time the state's housing movement, under the leadership of Laurence Veiller, had confined itself almost solely to upgrading existing housing stock through code controls and zoning; there had been no government effort to actually build new housing. As chairman of the Commission of Housing and Regional Planning (CHRP) from 1923 to 1926, Stein pushed for a bold program of public assistance for low-income housing, using as supporting evidence a survey by Mumford of various forms of government housing aid in Europe. Although Stein was not able to carry through his ambitious agenda of reforms, he helped to lead New York State and the nation into a new era of government responsibility in the housing area.[4]

Working with Stein as a researcher on a number of state-sponsored projects, Mumford gained what amounted to a postgraduate education in public housing. In the process he developed strong lifelong friendships with Stein and his wife, Aline Mac-Mahon, the radiant Broadway actress. However, the person he became closest to, and felt most comfortable with, on the RPAA was Henry Wright, a brilliant architect and landscape planner who had done most of his early work in the St. Louis suburbs. Mumford enjoyed working with Wright because Wright was, above all, an idea man, with a spacious and creative mind. He and Mumford were neighbors for a time at Sunnyside Gardens, Queens, the RPAA's first experimental community, and they would often sit for hours around a table in Wright's kitchen spinning plans for the new towns of their dreams.

Wright's favorite game was chess, and he claimed that his chess skills made him a better planner, always thinking ahead, always open to new alternatives. There were never any final answers for

Henry Wright; his life was given over to the search for fresh approaches to every planning problem he uncovered. "If I had my way," he once remarked to Stein, "over the gate of every university I would carve a great question mark."[5]

But these very strengths sometimes made Wright a difficult man to work with. His independence, varied interests, and explosive temper needed a settling influence. Stein provided this. His firm persistence and determination to see things through kept Wright in line when his nervous curiosity threatened to take him off in a hundred different directions. Temperamentally and professionally, they were ideally matched: Stein, the architect and steady administrator, and Wright, the audaciously creative site planner.

The RPAA was never a tightly knit organization with a universally agreed-upon plan for regional change; it was more like an informal association of friends. "In our most intimate days," Mumford recalls, "we could sign each other's memoranda without undue boggling or haggling, and at deliberations we almost never took formal votes."[6] Throughout its existence the RPAA remained a small organization, with a membership that rarely exceeded twenty-five. The most active members could fit quite comfortably in the living room of Clarence Stein's elegant New York apartment overlooking Central Park. In the early years of the organization the group gathered there for policy discussions as often as two or three times a week.

In ideas and outlook the RPAA was a broadly diverse group, but its inner core—Stein, Wright, MacKaye, and Mumford—agreed upon a basic strategy for regional resettlement, and these four men charted the organization's ideological direction. Under their leadership, the RPAA achieved an influence vastly out of proportion to its size. It was the first organization in America to critically assess the new order created by modern industry and mass transportation, which Mumford called metropolitanism. But the RPAA took criticism to its next level, developing a program for redirecting the country's urban settlement, a plan filled with ideas that still remain fresh and relevant.

The members of the Regional Planning Association not only questioned the dominant trend of urbanization—toward building larger and larger cities; they questioned as well the prevailing trends in city planning. Most city planning schemes at the time encouraged congestion through the creation of roads and transit technology that brought people to the core of the city to work and shop, and then returned them to their suburban settlements. Even some of the more intelligent plans for regional development, such as the plan the Russell Sage Foundation sponsored for New York and its environs, the most wide-reaching scheme for urban planning proposed in the 1920s, assumed that intensive urbanization was inevitable and recommended an expanded transit system to handle it.

The RPAA, however, insisted that the trend toward ever-larger urban concentrations was not destiny. Mumford, drawing on the ideas of Patrick Geddes and Peter Kropotkin, the Russian anarchist, was most instrumental in shaping the organization's thinking on this point. Whereas the old coal and steam economy had concentrated population and industry along railroad lines and their termini in the big ports and junctions, the automobile, telephone, radio, and long-distance electric power networks promised to bring about a new age of industrial and residential decentralization. With the introduction of the electric power grid, power for industry could now be made available over a wide area, making it unnecessary for industry to locate close to the pithead, port, or valley bottom. Meanwhile, the automobile and expanding highway system was decentralizing transportation, making entire new areas economically accessible, and allowing a wider dispersal of population and business. These breakthroughs, Mumford pointed out, were restoring the "center of gravity" to small rural-based factories and cottage-type industries run by skilled workers and technicians, just as Kropotkin had predicted in his book *Fields, Factories and Workshops* (1899).[7]

Both Clarence Stein and Henry Wright had their own strongly held ideas about urban design, but Mumford pushed them to propose a more ambitious plan for regional settlement than they envisioned before they met him. This plan drew heavily on the ideas of Ebenezer Howard, but Mumford refashioned Howard's garden city plan into an urban resettlement program shaped to American circumstances. And this program flowed directly from a sociological theory of the city that owed more to his Scottish master than to Ebenezer Howard, a far less creative thinker than Geddes.

Most of Mumford's formative ideas about the city grew out of a theme he developed from his earliest exposure to Geddes—not

Geddes the planner or the biologist, but Geddes the dramatist, who in 1911 had written and staged a "Masque of Learning," which was performed under his direction in Edinburgh and London.[8] The city, for Geddes and Mumford, was above all a stage, or physical setting, for the complex drama of living. In the city, with its sprawling cast of characters and pulsating energy, the drama of human life reached its highest pitch. A city's physical setting—its architecture and urban plan—could either frustrate this drama or intensify it. This was Mumford's real complaint with the skyscraper—it discouraged social interaction by sealing people off from one another in air-conditioned towers of glass, concrete, and steel. In order to stimulate effective human drama, cities had to be cut to human measure, designed to encourage the greatest possible number of meetings, encounters, and challenges.[9]

Mumford was one of the first modern writers on the city to question the still widely held notion that physical expansion and higher land prices are unmistakable signs of urban progress. The real losers in New York's current growth mania, he argued in a prophetic 1926 essay, "The Intolerable City," are the citizens themselves, for prosperity often collided directly with culture. Ironically, as the city grew in size and wealth it became less able to afford the things that make urban life truly interesting and enriching. Higher rents made it virtually impossible for parks, museums, civic centers, art galleries, and other less profitable or nonprofitable cultural concerns to compete with lavishly financed commercial projects for urban space.[10]

Mumford was equally concerned with the ecological impact of urban expansion. His first essays for the RPAA contain the kernel of what is perhaps the first environmental argument against the metropolis in urban literature. Comparing the city to a living biological organism, Mumford argued that when it grew too large it disrupted its symbiotic relationship with its surrounding territory, destroying the ecological balance that originally prevailed between city and country in the first stages of urbanization. Growth overtaxed local resources, and in order to continue to grow the city had to reach out further and further for water, fuel, food, building materials, and sewage disposal areas. At this point its relationship with its region became a parasitic one, and a cycle of ecological imbalance began. The metropolis, in fact, usually merged into its contiguous communities, consuming precious farmlands and forests, and creating a continuous belt of settlement—a megalopolis, an ecological disaster area. The only alternative to megalopolis, Mumford kept emphasizing in early RPAA meetings, is to fight the forces of congestion at their source by building new cities in the countryside to draw off population and industry from the bloated metropolis.[11]

Mumford joined Howard in arguing for new cities with populations of between 20,000 and 30,000, with an additional 2,000 or so people living in the greenbelt area. He refused, however, to be dogmatic about this; in some cases, as in the crowded northeastern industrial corridor, he was willing to accept new cities of up to 300,000 people. The important thing was not to set an arbitrary ideal size for new settlements, but to establish the fact of limits. What mattered most to Mumford was that cities have a socially defined size, form, and boundary.[12]

But Mumford envisioned the process of decentralization going much further than this. Our new regional cities, he repeatedly reminded Stein and Wright, must be divided into cellular units, with each cell, or neighborhood, strictly limited in size and density. When a city reached a point where it could no longer perform its essential social functions readily, when it ceased, in other words, to be a city of workable neighborhoods, it should divide as a cell divides, and form another city. This growth by fission would prevent cancerous urban sprawl. Mumford saw a long-established American precedent for such controlled urban expansion in the Puritan towns of New England, many of which were founded when older towns filled up and could no longer effectively perform their civic and religious functions.[13]

Both Mumford and Howard have been accused by their critics of arguing for a green suburb in the name of a city, of defining "wholesome housing in terms only of suburban physical qualities and small town social qualities."[14] While there is an undeniable touch of rural nostalgia in their proposals, a yearning for the clean comforts and simple living of the country town, such criticism is unfair to both of them. They envisioned the garden city as a real urban settlement, compact and clearly bounded, not as a country town or dormitory suburb. Mumford, in fact, saw the garden city, with its broad industrial base and provisions for housing all income groups, as a healthy alternative to the income-segregated, culturally homogeneous suburbs that were beginning to ring many American cities in the 1920s. This is why he preferred the term "regional city" to "garden city," for garden city connoted to many people a leafy suburban enclave, not the kind of lively and diverse small city he favored.

But could a garden city be a "lively" place? Mumford's friend, *The New Yorker* writer E. B. White, doubted that it could. The very things that Mumford liked most of all about New York—its theater life, music, art, mind-stretching diversity—were, in White's opinion, "the by-products of congestion. . . . Were I to allow a benevolent government to transplant me and my possessions to Hightstown, New Jersey," he once remarked, "I would fully expect to catch, in the still country air, some distant sounds of a metropolitan falling off, caused by my having quit the place."[15] And as for congestion, many New Yorkers didn't mind it at all. The art critic Henry McBride spoke for others as well when he said, "I have . . . to confess shamefacedly . . . I like life enormously as it is . . . lived in New York. . . . The congestion that so disturbs Mr. Mumford seems . . . much to the taste of average New Yorkers. They particularly like to go where they think *everybody* is going and if a percentage of them get killed in the effort to see Mr. Babe Ruth play baseball, why it is apt to be considered a more than usually successful afternoon. As for the looks of the place, that suits me too. Of course it is anarchic. . . . But it has a wild and curious beauty."[16]

The regional city, Mumford realized, would have to provide more than jobs for its residents if it was to draw and retain vital people. It would need theaters, opera houses, libraries, bookstores, museums, and sports teams. No small city of 30,000 could hope to provide the kind of cultural opportunities that a big city could. He proposed, therefore, a regional constellation of cities interconnected by a rapid transit system, with a common regional government for its overall activities. A cluster of such cities grouped around a larger regional center could give the residents of the urban network all the benefits of a metropolis of one million without the headaches of congestion. Each city could perhaps have its own cultural specialization, be it an opera house or great library, and there would be provisions for distributing the region's cultural and human resources—books, art works, orchestras, dance groups, medical care, education. Mumford saw America's interlibrary loan system as a model of the kind of cultural interchange he had in mind.[17]

But what would become of the older metropolitan centers? A new town program would give cities like New York an opportunity to rebuild themselves on a more open pattern by siphoning off excess population and driving down land values inflated by congestion, Mumford argued with the doubting Thomases in the RPAA, who felt his program was far too visionary. In Mumford's scheme, the suburbs would trade some of their excessive green space for social space—places for spontaneous meeting and civic association— while older cities would do exactly the opposite, introducing more sunlight, air, private gardens, squares, and pedestrian malls. And larger cities, he suggested, might have their own form of greenbelt, a ribbon of green running through the neighborhoods, forming a continuous web of garden and park. In the 1950s, while teaching at the University of Pennsylvania and advising on city planning matters, Mumford suggested that Philadelphia convert its narrow back alleys into green malls, which would widen at places into generously shaded plazas, rimmed by shops and cafes. For Mumford, "the building up of older cities, the breaking up of congested centers and the establishment of new centers" were to be "parts of one process, which aims to rehabilitate the region."[18]

Mumford had no illusions about the costs and difficulties of such a massive resettlement process. Business groups with a direct stake in congestion, and city officials fearful of bankruptcy, would fiercely resist the program. To make even the initial steps possible, heavy federal and state subsidies for new towns and old would be necessary.[19] Unlike Howard, who relied on private philanthropy, Mumford was convinced that only a sympathetic government could carry through a new town effort of such magnitude. On this point, Stein and Wright agreed with him completely.

The three men further agreed that the planning profession itself would have to be brought around to their ideas about regional renewal if their new town program was to have any chance of long-term success. So in 1927, when the noted urban planner John Nolen invited Mumford to address the nineteenth anniversary conference on city planning in Washington, D.C., Mumford eagerly accepted the invitation.

Mumford challenged the planners to jettison the idea that city planning "is merely a way of providing the physical means for the continuous expansion and congestion of our cities," and to use their influence and expertise to build, "region by region," a "humanized" environment, "with countryside and city developed together for the purpose of promoting and enhancing the good life."[20] But as the historian of planning, Mel Scott, has said, this impassioned plea "perhaps found favor with most [planners] in much the same way that a fine sermon pleases a congregation rutted in its worldly ways." Most professional urban planners worked within the context of existing municipal institutions, and considered visionary thinking as a "luxury, and bold schemes for the reorganization of urban areas as futile." Even those planners sympathetic to Mumford's ideas were afraid of moving too far ahead of public opinion or of challenging vested interests within the business and political communities. To propose plans for the extension of the city was far safer, and in the end more profitable for them as professional planners, than to fashion plans for radically new cities.[21] It would be another ten years before some of the RPAA's more advanced ideas gained favor with younger members of the planning profession.

While still working within the Smith administration for housing reforms, Stein, Mumford, Wright, and their RPAA colleagues decided to pursue bolder initiatives in the private sector. Their method, like Howard's, was to persuade public-spirited investors to support a limited dividend housing corporation that would test the garden city idea on a small scale. The RPAA, however, had greater faith in public planning than Howard, hoping that the success of such privately financed pilot programs would lure government into the housing field to extend them and to incorporate them into a sweeping program of new town development.

In 1923, after returning from a study tour of the British new towns, Clarence Stein persuaded his friend Alexander M. Bing, a wealthy New York real-estate developer, to back the building of an American garden city. The following year the RPAA formed the City Housing Corporation, a limited dividend company with a ceiling on profits, and began plans to build a garden community of some 25,000 people on a square mile plot on the edge of New York City. Unable to raise sufficient funds for this project, the leaders of

RPAA decided to try their ideas on a smaller scale, with a more cautious investment in Queens. They purchased an undeveloped waste site from the Pennsylvania Railroad, close to Manhattan's business center, and in 1924 began constructing a community— Sunnyside Gardens—for workers and the lower middle class.

These were good years economically for the city and nation, and Sunnyside's houses and apartments filled up almost as soon as they were built. By 1928 the project was completed and the City Housing Corporation had realized a profit. Sunnyside Gardens was by no means a complete garden city, but the knowledge and experience the RPAA gained there were soon put to use building a larger community, Radburn, in Fair Lawn, New Jersey, also with City Housing Corporation money.

At Sunnyside Gardens, Stein and Wright wanted to avoid the standard gridiron or checkerboard street design, and to cluster houses instead in an encircling pattern around interior parks or courtyards, with no through streets piercing the living areas. The land at Sunnyside, however, had already been laid out in city blocks and the borough engineer would not allow any changes in the existing plan.

Forced to work within the strictures of New York's standard grid layout, Wright and Stein built a community fashioned to the requirements of everyday family living. They laid out tight groups of narrow houses and apartment buildings, many of them fronting inward toward common greens, which were designed "for restful gatherings or for quiet play."[22] Stein and Wright were convinced that row houses of no more than three stories were the ideal design for privacy and economy. The freestanding custom-made house, they agreed with Mumford, was simply too expensive for most Americans, and was tremendously wasteful of ground space. It crowded the land, allowing little privacy or garden space, a tightly built group of them creating a kind of suburban slum.

The houses Wright and Stein built at Sunnyside were small, but the tight living quarters were offset by the plenitude of greenery and garden in the attractive public courtyards, with their trim lawns, bright flower beds, and spreading poplars. The houses were only two rooms deep, but they were oriented by Wright for maximum sunlight and summer breezes. Behind the houses were private service roads that connected to the public streets, and these wider streets ran like so many moats around the perimeters of the partially enclosed blocks, giving the community clear outer boundaries.

Sunnyside's village-like atmosphere made it particularly attractive to Lewis and Sophia Mumford, who moved there in 1925 from Brooklyn and made it their home for the next eleven years. When the community was completed and the trees were full and the flowers in bloom, Lewis would take leisurely afternoon walks through its winding network of interior gardens. And at Sunnyside he took up gardening, which became one of the delights of his life.

For a time Sunnyside looked as if it might become a community of intellectuals and artists. Wright and several other RPAA members moved there, holding spirited meetings, which often turned into spontaneous parties, in Wright's tiny basement. Other young New York writers about to become parents joined them at Sunnyside, causing some people to refer to it as "the Maternity ward of Greenwich Village."[23] But the artists never outnumbered the families of lower-middle-class, nonprofessional workers—mechanics, office workers, tradesmen. They made Sunnyside a real community, with lots of interaction and group activity, and with an active homeowners' association. In no community that Mumford ever resided did he have a fuller sense of the possibilities of neighborhood life in a city.

Early in 1928, just after finishing work on Sunnyside Gardens, the City Housing Corporation bought a large piece of undeveloped farmland in Fair Lawn, New Jersey, sixteen miles from New York City, and began building another experimental community, this one intended for 25,000 residents. Radburn was never completed—it became a victim of the Great Depression, which bankrupted the City Housing Corporation—but the two large neighborhoods, or "superblocks," which were completed, and which by 1931 housed 1,000 people, demonstrated a new form of town building commonly referred to by planning experts as the "Radburn Idea."[24]

At Radburn, with no grid arrangement to constrict them, the RPAA planners constructed a community that incorporated some of the most important housing innovations of this century, a good number of them suggested by Mumford. "Radburn," as he enthusiastically described it, "[is] the first major departure in city planning since Venice."[25]

Radburn was to be a special kind of garden community—a town planned for the automobile age. In 1908, Henry Ford had introduced the mass-produced Model-T Ford, inaugurating a new age in automobile consumerism; by 1923, Detroit was producing 23 million cars a year. For good or ill, the motorcar was a force of the future, and the RPAA planners were alert to this fact.

Mumford, who never drove a car in his life, would become one of this country's fiercest critics of what he called the religion of the automobile, but in the 1920s neither he nor any other member of the Regional Planning Association was unalterably anti-automobile. They saw the automobile as an important part of a balanced transportation system that included the maintenance and improvement of America's extensive railroad and trolley network. It was not the automobile itself, but its injurious impact on the city that they were most concerned about. They saw the automobile as a powerful promoter of urban congestion, noise, and pollution. The city's grid design, which made all streets equally inviting to traffic, compounded the harm caused by the automobile, particularly in the residential neighborhoods.

Most urban planners in the 1920s were not interested in changing these conditions. City planning was, even then, automobile-centered, concerned with adjusting the old street systems to the new demands of the gasoline-powered engine, leaving the pedestrian and the resident to fend for themselves. Radburn was America's first community planned expressly for pedestrians, a town "safe for motor-age living."[26]

At Radburn the neighborhoods are free from the invasion of the automobile. As an alternative to the grid pattern, Stein and Wright built two campus-like superblocks—neighborhood units sealed off from motor traffic, with many of the houses and other buildings facing inward, away from the streets, toward a small park or garden. Within the superblocks are attractively landscaped interior parks flanked by narrow walkways that thread through the entire community and lead to shopping areas, schools, and playgrounds. They give Radburn something of the look and feel of a secluded English village.

The superblock is merely one of a number of planning innovations at Radburn. There is, for example, a strict separation of pedestrian from vehicular traffic, a system of underpasses and overpasses such as Frederick Law Olmsted and Calvert Vaux provided for in Central Park, an idea Mumford pressed very hard for when the RPAA began planning Radburn. These allow vehicular and pedestrian traffic, through traffic and transverse traffic, to function simultaneously. When a footpath crosses a road, a bridge or underpass separates them, making the community safer for children, who can walk to schools or playfields several blocks from their homes without ever crossing an intersection (the bridge was later taken down). At Radburn the automobile is not an intrusive force. The houses are turned inward, as at Sunnyside, with the main living and sleeping rooms facing the interior gardens. The kitchens face small access or service roads, where the residents park their cars and deliverymen bring their goods. As for industry, Stein and Wright proposed to locate it in a separate industrial zone screened off from the residential areas by a curtain of greenery; but this became a moot point, as Radburn was never able to draw industry; nor was there enough land available for purchase to create a protective greenbelt.

Radburn—the Highwayless Town—produced in the fertile mind of Benton MacKaye a related idea for a new kind of transportation artery. In Radburn's separation of pedestrian and automobile, roads and houses, MacKaye saw a model for highway development beyond the limits of the city. In a 1931 essay, "Townless Highways for the Motorist," he and Mumford urged the building of a system of limited-access four-lane highways, with all the abutting land owned by public authorities and strictly zoned against private development. Only well-spaced gas stations and restaurants would be permitted along these highways.[27] While highway engineers and planners like Robert Moses have often built the kinds of roadways MacKaye and Mumford suggested, their most important advice has usually been ignored—that the highway stay clear of the city. Had Radburn been completed as a full-scale garden city, Mumford envisioned the construction of a townless highway connecting it with the access arteries leading into New York City. There, on the rim of the city, would be vast underground parking lots where commuters could leave their cars and take trains or buses into Manhattan.[28]

Although Mumford welcomed the automobile and other new breakthroughs in technology, his great ideals, the ideals of William

Morris and John Ruskin, remained those of the fourteenth century—form and unity. The garden city he envisioned, and which he saw only partially realized at Radburn, was a kind of reconstituted medieval village, a city, certainly, in its size and supply of social variety, but one that preserved in its neighborhoods and in its architecture the social cohesion, unity of form, and human scale that he saw as the quintessence of medieval town life.

The key to Radburn's success as a planned community, in Mumford's view, was not its architecture, which he considered mediocre, but its provision of civic nuclei, in the form of shopping areas, schools, and parks, to draw the population together, and outer boundaries—greenbelts or roadways—to give them a sense of belonging together; its provision, in other words, for the form and unity that the city had sacrificed to unbounded expansion. Stein and Wright had drawn on the best new planning techniques to slow down the city, curb its outward expansion, and create in the neighborhood "a stage upon which the drama of social life may be enacted."[29]

While this kind of neighborhood planning can be carried out best in thinly settled areas outside the city, where the entire site can be laid out, Mumford believed that a variation of the neighborhood unit would work in older, built-up cities like New York. By blocking off some streets to vehicular traffic and relocating schools, branch libraries, small health clinics, shops, movie theaters, and parks within the new superblocks, city planners can relieve the urban transit system of much of its burdensome load, and provide safe environments for raising children, he argued in his urban essays of the 1920s and thereafter.[30]

Mumford saw the garden city as more than an alternative to the overgrown metropolis. The garden city movement was to be one of the first social challenges to the dominant growth ideology of the West, and would, he hoped, open the way to a new age of urban and rural resettlement, of limits to growth, and ecological balance. The changes Mumford argued for were not just changes in living places, but changes in living habits. Without such a complete reorientation of values, these planned communities, he argued in 1927, could not survive in a culture dominated by the twin drives for profit and physical expansion.[31]

This was the direction Mumford wanted the Regional Planning Association to take. Stein and Wright "have just made an interesting discovery," Mumford wrote Patrick Geddes just after work at Sunnyside Gardens had begun. "They are quite confident of being able to plan a beautiful shell: they are completely at sea as to what sort of *community* to provide for." Mumford told Geddes that he had quoted them Victor Branford's idea that the town planner needed the assistance of the poet; they had agreed, he said, and had given him that role within their organization. At planning meetings at Stein's apartment, he introduced them to the regionalist movement in Europe—in Provence, Catalonia, and Ireland—and suggested that regionalism be made the cultural objective of their movement.[32]

Mumford's regionalism is, at bottom, a plea for the preservation of local literature, language, and ways of life, for those shared experiences that tie people together more than any social system or ideology. He saw the spread of a standardized metropolitan culture destroying America's varied regional life, ironing out all cultural differences based upon locale and place. His early reading of Geddes and Kropotkin certainly influenced him in this direction, but so did the writings of Emerson and Hawthorne, the Hawthorne who had once said that New England was as big a piece of earth as could claim his allegiance.

Mumford also saw regionalism as a way of cutting back the power of the nation-state, an idea he borrowed from Harold J. Laski's *Authority in the Modern State*, which he read just after World War I. Under Laski's plan, the nation-state would continue to exist, but most of its powers would be divided among local and regional groups—towns, cities, labor unions, universities, and producer and consumer cooperatives. The state would be merely one association among many, its primary purpose "to preserve justice and liberty among its constituent cities, regions, associations, corporations."[33] In some of Mumford's stronger pleas for regionalism, he sounded as if he was arguing for the resurrection of the medieval economy of free cities, with their powerful guilds and semiautonomous corporate bodies.

In lobbying within the RPAA for this more radical form of regional decentralization, Mumford had a strong ally in Benton MacKaye. A tall, lean, sharp-eyed New Englander, "an Uncle Sam without the whiskers," MacKaye lived in the tiny village of Shirley

Center, Massachusetts, where he had spent most of his youth after his family moved there from Manhattan when he was a boy of nine.³⁴ From his father, the Victorian actor and playwright Steele MacKaye, he inherited the family gift for racy wit and colorful storytelling. But for all his homespun charm and easygoing sociability, MacKaye was an intensely private person, living alone after 1920 at Shirley Center in a ramshackle cottage crammed with musty books and faded family portraits.

Mumford and MacKaye met just before the formation of the RPAA, and they remained close comrades in spirit and temperament. Though they saw each other infrequently, mostly at RPAA gatherings, they corresponded regularly until MacKaye's death in 1975 at the age of ninety-six. Early in their friendship Mumford found in MacKaye the kind of balance he aspired to in his own life. MacKaye was a hard-muscled outdoorsman who was also familiar with the ways of the city; a Harvard-trained intellectual with an appetite for the real world; an outgoing, affable man who preferred, however, to live a solitary life of Thoreauvian self-reliance in a village only twenty miles from Concord and on the same railroad line.³⁵ He remained for Mumford a living link with the older America of Emerson and Audubon. "Since I came too late to know Thoreau," Mumford wrote MacKaye on his ninety-second birthday, "I am glad that I at least had the good fortune to be your contemporary."³⁶

At Harvard, MacKaye had studied under two pioneer environmentalists, Nathaniel S. Shaler and William Morris Davis, receiving his master's degree in forestry in 1905. He then joined the United States Forest Service during the administration of Theodore Roosevelt, serving under Gifford Pinchot. He remained in the Forest Service until 1916, spending most of his time outdoors, reclaiming and improving public woodlands. During the war he worked in the Department of Labor under the single taxer Louis Post on a scheme to settle groups of returning veterans on the land. Nothing came of this, but in Washington he met Stuart Chase, a fellow hiker and rural explorer, and later Charles Harris Whitaker, who drew him into his growing circle of young architects and planners. After the war and the death of his wife in 1921, MacKaye, a shattered man, returned to Shirley Center, where he went into a virtual retreat until the 1930s, living off a small pension, too absorbed in his work and his ideas to take a full-time position. His consuming ambition was to develop a program for saving America's landscape. His first project was an idea for an Appalachian Trail.

During a visit to Whitaker's farm at Mt. Olive, New Jersey, near Netcong, MacKaye explained to Whitaker, in excited tones, his idea of a regional recreational trail stretching all the way from Maine to Georgia. Whitaker liked the idea immediately and introduced MacKaye to Clarence Stein, who was in the area designing a cow barn for the Hudson Guild Farm. Stein felt MacKaye's scheme would give the garden city concept a much-needed regional perspective, and bring together the conservation movement and community planning. He and Whitaker then persuaded MacKaye to spend the next few days at Whitaker's New Jersey home writing an article on the trail for the *Journal of the American Institute of Architects.*

MacKaye feared that Americans were losing touch with the open countryside and the raw wilderness. As a relief from the anxious routine of the city, he urged the creation of a walking trail on the crest line of the still primeval Appalachian Mountains, a wilderness recreation area within a day's ride for half of the population of the country. The trail would be the backbone of a system of wild reservations and parks, linked together by feeder trails, and would be built by local voluntary groups. MacKaye had a simple faith in the therapeutic value of the wilderness, even for those afflicted with mental illness. "They needed acres not medicine." Once in touch with the "health-giving powers" of nature, weekend campers and hikers might even decide to move there permanently, setting in motion a geographic redistribution of the population. The trail could then be transformed into a larger project in community living, with urban refugees raising food cooperatively and forming their own farm camps. This settlement idea never materialized, but MacKaye's scheme incited local groups to lay out and mark a trail, section by section, over the next thirty years. The Appalachian Trail remains one of America's great natural treasures.[37]

MacKaye's Appalachian Trail proposal incorporated most of the key concerns of the RPAA members—conservation, population redistribution, landscape improvement, and regional planning. Occasionally the members of the RPAA would gather together with their wives for weekend seminars at the Hudson Guild Farm in Netcong, New Jersey, and at one of these meetings the group decided to expand MacKaye's idea of an Appalachian Trail into a full

program of regional planning. In this effort Mumford and Mac-
Kaye, it was decided, should take the lead.

MacKaye began work on a book called *The New Exploration*, which
outlined his ideas on regional planning. MacKaye's ungainly prose
style made it difficult for him to interest a publisher, but Mumford
managed to persuade Alfred Harcourt to publish it, on the proviso
that he act as editor. This gave Mumford his first opportunity to visit
MacKaye on his home acres, and MacKaye's historic hamlet left a
memorable impression on Mumford. When he collaborated on the
classic film *The City*, which was first shown at the New York's World
Fair of 1939, he brought the camera crews to Shirley Center to shoot
the scenes on the colonial village.

The years between 1924 and 1928, when Mumford and MacKaye
worked together on MacKaye's book and a number of RPAA-related
projects, were the strongest of their friendship. Although Mumford
found it impossible to shape *The New Exploration* into a tight-focused
essay, he considered it a seminal study in regional planning and
vigorously promoted the book, not only out of loyalty to MacKaye,
but also because he believed it perfectly identified the social aims of
the Regional Planning Association. It is "a book," he would claim
later, "that deserves a place on the shelf that holds Henry David
Thoreau's *Walden* and George Perkins Marsh's *Man and Nature*."[38]

The Regional Planning Association itself never had the resources
to conduct the ambitious regional surveys and plans MacKaye and
Mumford recommended to it, but in 1926, Clarence Stein's Committee on Housing and Regional Planning published a state planning report that embodied many of Mumford's regionalist ideas.
Henry Wright was its principal author, but in drafting the report he
drew extensively on the advice and ideas of Mumford and MacKaye,
who conducted specialized studies for the committee. Although
their report fell short of being a complete plan for New York State, it
is a masterly survey of the historic forces—physical, economic, and
social—that have shaped New York State's past and an evaluation of
the new forces that were altering its present mold. More than a mere
survey, it is a plan for the decongestion of the greater New York area
and for the upbuilding and resettlement of the more thinly popu-
lated areas of the state. The aim of this report, Wright emphasized,
in a statement that probably marked it for the political graveyard,
should be to improve the conditions of life "rather than to promote

opportunities for profit."[39] Considered together with the special 1925 edition of *The Survey Graphic* on regionalism in America, which Mumford edited and wrote several articles for, Wright's plan shows how accurately the leading minds in the RPAA foresaw the problems of metropolitan growth that led to the kinds of urban and regional problems we have yet to solve.[40]

The period during which Mumford worked with MacKaye, Wright, and Stein in planning Radburn, preparing the New York State report, and editing the regional issue of *The Survey Graphic* was one of the busiest and most fulfilling times of his life. He was given a unique opportunity to influence the direction of a movement committed to the kind of future he had envisioned as a very young man, under the spell of Patrick Geddes, and in 1925 he wrote to Geddes, informing him that America was finally moving "towards all the things you've stood for."[41] A great regional transformation seemed close at hand, but he wondered what role he would play in it. This is the question of a proper career he had been struggling with since his return from Le Play House in 1920. In resolving this dilemma and setting for himself a clear personal direction, Lewis Mumford opened the way to the most creative period of his young life.

Libra

*The ideal personality for the opening age is a balanced
personality, not the specialist but the whole man.*

—LEWIS MUMFORD

By late 1924, as Mumford entered the period of his most active
involvement in the Regional Planning Association, he was still
unsure what role he should play in encouraging the great social
changes he anticipated. *Sticks and Stones* had gained him a reputation
as a promising critic of architecture, but his interest in that subject
was far from all-absorbing. He was "a little bored with architecture," he told Sophia after completing *Sticks and Stones*, and was
eager "to have a try at other things."[1]

He still wanted most of all to be a creative writer—a novelist or
playwright—but all he had to show for his labors were an unfinished novel and a pile of unproduced plays. One stage production
success probably would have confirmed his dedication to the theater, but that never came. He felt he had talent and seasoning enough
to be a "mediocre playwright or novelist but not to be one of first
rank—and I disdain the easy second or third place," he confessed to
a friend.[2]

There was always criticism, which most of his friends considered
his real forte. Yet he felt that this kind of work didn't test him
sufficiently; he labored among "the Sophists of journalism" mostly
for the money.[3] Reviewing books and writing critical essays also

gave him some control over his time, always his most closely guarded possession, as he took on only enough work to leave at least one-third of the year for uninterrupted stretches of concentrated study and writing. But even with two well-received books behind him, he remained anxious and nervously dissatisfied. He wanted to absorb himself in larger projects than he had tackled so far, and he felt that he wouldn't be able to do this until he acquired a surer sense of what kind of writing his natural gifts best suited him for, and in what areas he was likely to have the greatest impact.

Throughout this period between 1920 and 1924, when his vocational crisis reached its most acute stage, he was never completely healthy, despite his robust physical appearance. The thin, stoop-shouldered Regius of "The Invalids" had matured into a splendidly handsome young man, lank and firm-muscled, with wavy dark hair, sculptured features, a rakish mustache, and a supremely confident manner. Striding the pavements of New York wearing a flowing riding cape he had picked up in London, he was a young man people noticed. He and the darkly beautiful Sophia made a striking pair. "I thought of Lewis and Sophy Mumford," Van Wyck Brooks recalled their days together in the early 1920s, "as a new Adam and Eve, with whom the human race might well have started, for one could scarcely have imagined a handsomer pair. I always felt as if they had just stepped out of Utopia and were looking for some of their countrymen."[4] But in these same years Mumford continued to slip into periods of near-paralytic exhaustion and depression, usually following a strenuous bout of work or an emotional setback. And he remained anxiously apprehensive about his health, unwilling to take on projects or commitments that might draw too excessively on his shallow reservoir of strength and stamina.

"I do not like your periodic break-downs and half break-downs," Jerry Lachenbruch wrote him from Vienna in 1924. Lachenbruch was undergoing psychoanalysis, and he thought his friend ought to do the same. "Persons who are thoroughly adjusted to their environment and to their life partners do not have nervous attacks. . . . I know that your marriage has released a lot in you; it has matured you considerably, given freedom to a lot of pent-up-ness. But I wish you [would] . . . find out what it is that is keeping you from going on steadily." Lachenbruch's analyst had been recommended to him by Freud himself, and he felt the therapy was accomplishing wonders for him. "I wish that you could undergo this treatment, for I am sure that no only son ever lived who has not been handicapped in life." But Mumford continued to seek his own cure, relying on his Personalia notes as a form of self-analysis and therapy.[5]

He and Sophia were getting along better in 1924 than they had in the first trying years of their marriage. But several unresolved problems remained, sexual and otherwise, that prevented him from achieving the complete peace of mind he felt he needed to take on the big literary project that had recently come into his mind—a book on American culture centered on the age of Whitman, Emerson, and Melville.

During this period his total earnings from his writing averaged barely $15 a week, part of which went to support his invalid mother. He had spent his modest inheritance, and without Sophia's salary at *The Dial* (she was now assistant editor), they wouldn't have been able to pay the rent on their Brooklyn apartment. Throughout these tough times Sophia gave him unquestioning support. She never interfered with his regular work schedule, and when he was writing she protected his privacy, politely keeping away both friends and relatives, even Lewis's mother. Nor did she pressure him about their financial condition. She was used to being poor and didn't mind it at all, she assured him.

He and Sophia cut expenses in every way imaginable, furnishing their apartment with hand-me-down items from relatives, walking rather than taking taxis or buses, and leading a severely limited social life. On weekends they would visit friends and relatives in the city or go hiking in the country; on weekday evenings they usually stayed close to home. Most evenings they had dinner at Joe's, a lively, old-fashioned eating house a short walk from their apartment. In the winter they usually returned to their apartment after dinner, but in the summer their flat was unbearably hot, and noisy to boot, for the city was making massive repairs on the Fulton El, which ran behind their rear window. So Lewis and Sophia would stay out late on Montague Street Plaza, which looked out over the harbor. There they could see the Manhattan skyline and smell the salt air.

This restricted routine was more in line with Lewis's idea of sound living than Sophia's, but she made the necessary adjustments. If this is how they had to live in order for her husband to achieve "greatness" as a writer—and she never doubted that he was "headed for greatness"—she would do it, and without complaint.[6]

Sophia managed their finances and learned to be incredibly resourceful. She took an extra job in the mornings as an apprentice teacher at the Walden School and worked afternoons at *The Dial*. She also made most of her clothing, and she came up with some ingenious ways to keep down their food budget. Each morning she soured that day's bottle of milk, after they had taken the cream off for their coffee, and hung up the curds in the evening to drip, so that the following morning they would have cottage cheese instead of butter for their toast.

The hardships seemed to draw Lewis and Sophia closer together, as did Sophia's slow surrender to his conception of marriage. By 1923 she had given up the idea of experimenting with other men and was thinking of quitting her job at *The Dial* to have a baby. While Lewis was still a little uneasy about having children, fearing that he might have to find a full-time job to support Sophia and a child and unsure about what kind of father he would be, never having had a real father himself, her new attitude toward their marriage put him at ease. He became less jealous and sullenly contentious. "Part of [our] difficulty," he confided to Jerry Lachenbruch "was due to the fact that Sophia had been, as it were, intellectually seduced by . . . [*The Dial*'s Scofield Thayer]; and capturing her mind and her interests was perhaps the hardest task in conquering her; and curiously enough, marriage calls for and *means* such a conquest: there is no leaving one's mate alone, for to leave her alone is to leave her literally unmated."[7]

Living in the city, Mumford thought, made it doubly difficult for him to win Sophia completely. In his later accounts of his life he makes much of his strong ties to New York, and to big cities in general, but the private record he preserved of these years does not completely square with this. From the time he fell in love with Sophia he saw New York City itself as a threat to their relationship, for Sophia was drawn to the free and easy social life of *The Dial* writers and editors, which he found tedious and empty. Parties and literary teas distracted him from his work and pulled Sophia further away from him—from his world, his way of life. Nor had he ever felt completely healthy or spiritually at ease in big cities, he confided to Delilah Loch, whom he wrote to regularly about his relationship with Sophia.

All this deepened his intellectual commitment to regionalism and to rural living. "Sophie likes my kind of world well enough," he wrote Delilah, "but . . . my kind of world does not exist; and the present reality is a metropolitan civilization which baulks our natural, creative impulses at every turn and sends them into the various channels of dissipation which are associated with luxury, display, conspicuous expenditure, and sexual adventure." The city, it is clear from this, was associated in his mind with the sour memories he had of the free-and-easy lifestyle of his New York relatives, which had left his mother little time for him. Now he undoubtedly feared the same thing was happening with Sophia.

"Unless we can in some small measure create *my* kind of world, Sophie will disdain the shabby compromise of living with me in the metropolitan world," he told Delilah, "and . . . will endeavor to extract from metropolitan existence all that it offers—which means the end of our marriage." The issue in their marriage, as he saw it, was "Regionalism versus Metropolitanism." He and Sophia were never completely "at one till we are in the open country together."[8]

But if they could not live in a real regional city, perhaps they could spend at least part of the year in the countryside. After their first trip to Europe together even Sophia was drawn to this idea, and she and Lewis got their first real taste of country living the following February, when Charles and Gene Whitaker went off for a three-month vacation to Europe and offered them their farmhouse in Mt. Olive, New Jersey, rent-free. Cockneys to the core, they were a little nervous about living alone in the country, but their only proprietary duties, the Whitakers assured them, would be to stoke the coal furnace and feed a dozen or so ragged hens. They accepted the offer after Sophia negotiated a leave of absence from *The Dial*.

The Twelve Opossums Farm was on a low sloping hill facing a picturesque valley. The nearest neighbors were a half mile away, and to buy groceries Lewis had to walk some six miles to the village of Bartley. For the first time in their marriage Sophia began to cook and clean; she even did some experimental baking. She didn't care to be so isolated, but she enjoyed almost everything else about country life. And to her and Lewis's great joy, they found that country living drew them closer together.

When they returned to Brooklyn from Mt. Olive they began looking for another apartment. "A group of rowdies" had rented the flat directly below theirs, and "the hellish pounding of a mechanical piano, worked by a song-loving Spanish cigar-maker with a surly temper and the air of a murderer" became too much to endure.[9] That September they found a place nearby, on the port side of Brooklyn Heights, in an antebellum brownstone at 135 Hicks Street. Their new apartment was even smaller than their previous one—one and a half rooms—but it had a fireplace and a lovely rear garden that looked out on a sandstone Gothic church.

Bounded by the East River, Fulton Street, Atlantic Avenue, and Court Street, the Heights was (and still is) a splendid little neighborhood of Victorian houses resting on a rugged promontory above the river, and almost cut off from the rest of Brooklyn. Toward the end of the century it had been a bedroom community of the well-heeled merchants of lower Manhattan, whose trading ships were docked nearby. When the opening of the IRT subway broke the seclusion of the Heights, causing many of the wealthier families to flee, their spacious homes were partitioned into apartments and studios, and artists and writers began to pour in, many of them escaping Greenwich Village. The area was quiet and clean, yet close to the heart of Manhattan, reached by an easy walk across the Brooklyn Bridge. And the view from Columbia Heights, the street that rimmed the sandy bluff, was one of the most breathtaking in all of the world. One looked out across the harbor, lined with wharves and warehouses, to the New York skyline; in the distance, when the morning haze lifted, you could see the Statue of Liberty and spot an occasional ocean liner as it prepared to make the sweeping turn around the tip of Manhattan to head upriver to its midtown berth. This was the locale of *The Harbor*, an Ernest Poole novel that had moved Mumford as a younger man; and here at 110 Columbia Avenue, Washington Roebling, the crippled engineer, had directed the completion of his great East River span. In the same year Lewis and Sophia moved to the Heights, unknown to them at the time, Hart Crane moved into Roebling's old house, into the very room where the bedridden Roebling had watched the construction of the bridge through a telescope, after being striken with caisson disease. The twenty-four-year-old Crane had come to New York from Cleveland to write a poem to "the most beautiful bridge in the world."[10]

The Brooklyn Bridge connected Lewis and Sophia Mumford to Manhattan—still the center of their working lives—but in tree-shaded Brooklyn Heights they found escape from Manhattan's maddening pace. Here they found a near-perfect mix of urbanity and community, gracious green places and spirited street life—restaurants, shops, and open-air markets. Shortly after they moved into their Hicks Street apartment, Sophia became pregnant, and the next several years were among the best of their lives. "Suddenly everything began to go right."[11] They were not only living in better surroundings; Lewis's career took off. After completing *Sticks and Stones* in the spring of 1924, work began to pile "in upon me thick and fast," he wrote Jerry Lachenbruch. "Editors who used to treat me with cold disdain now ask me to review or write for them."[12]

One editor who had made an unexpectedly abrupt turnabout was his old *Freeman* nemesis, Albert Jay Nock. Nock had, at first, objected to Mumford's use of "sociological neologisms" borrowed from Geddes, Branford, and Veblen, but Van Wyck Brooks, the literary editor, liked Mumford's work and kept him on as a regular contributor. The elegantly crafted essays on American architecture Mumford began submitting to *The Freeman* in late 1923 (which formed the early chapters of *Sticks and Stones*) changed Nock's mind about Mumford as a writer. At one point Nock wrote his young contributor a note praising his work and suggesting that he stop by his office sometime soon to "talk about writing in general." At this surprisingly congenial meeting Nock asked Mumford whether he remembered the suggestion he had once made to him about writing a history of civilization in the United States. "You have genius, Mr. Mumford," Nock told him in an almost fatherly way, "and very great literary ability. I should like to see you do such a book, and if you have a mind to, we can perhaps find some way to subsidize you."[13]

Mumford considered accepting Nock's offer, but in February 1924 *The Freeman* suddenly announced it was suspending publication. Unlike Mumford's experience following the collapse of *The Dial*, this time other journals were eager to publish his work. And this time, when Patrick Geddes once again came forward with an offer of collaboration, he was not even tempted to take it.

* * *

In this American disciple, forty years his junior, Geddes thought he had found his Boswell. Mumford would write the synthesis of all knowledge Geddes had long dreamed of undertaking, in imitation of Auguste Comte and Herbert Spencer. For a time, while studying at Le Play House, Mumford had considered giving himself to this effort, but it became clear to him that Geddes wanted a secretary, not a collaborator, someone who could slavishly work at transforming a lifetime of scattered discoveries into a single volume.[14]

But Mumford still planned to write a biography of Geddes, a task he felt temperamentally better suited for than collaboration, and while he was actively considering this project, and resisting Geddes's pleas for closer cooperation, the master decided to come to the United States to finally meet his American disciple and to renew acquaintances with some old associates.

Geddes made plans to arrive in early May 1923 and to stay through most of the summer. He hoped to line up enough lectures to help pay his expenses, and he left Mumford in charge of making the arrangements. To ensure that his young disciple would give him his undeviating attention that summer, he sent him $200 to allow Mumford to free himself from writing the book reviews and magazine essays that were then paying his bills.

" 'HE' came last week," Mumford notified Delilah Loch that May. "I speak of Him in capital letters; for now that I have seen a little of him I am more convinced than ever that he is one of the Olympians. Of course *that* is the difficulty. Jove never walked among the sons of men without the sons of men getting the worst of it. . . . He is a terrible and determined old man, and now that he is ready to set down his philosophy, he wants to make use of me to the full."[15]

Miss Loch had warned Lewis about what to expect, offering sisterly advice on how to handle this endlessly demanding, old man, now a sixty-nine-year-old widower fresh from a series of exhausting planning projects in India and Palestine. "Geddes must be accepted as a good Catholic accepts grief, with an open heart and no reserves, *if* he is to benefit those whom his presence scourges. . . . Don't forget he is an old man and lonely, and the very-most-vicious-cave-barbarian when sad, angered, or thwarted."[16] Ms. Loch was not exaggerating; Geddes's son Alasdair once remarked that "no human being could live as well as work with P.G. and survive."[17]

Mumford had tried, in advance of Geddes's arrival, to arrange a lecture tour for him, despite Victor Branford's warning to Geddes that he lacked the mediocrity to be a successful lecturer in the United States; but Mumford didn't have enough lead time to line up a tour appealing to Geddes. He arranged, therefore, to have Geddes give a short course of lectures at the New School for Social Research, with a few trips to other places to see friends and colleagues. Mumford did not accompany Geddes on these trips, and in fact, Geddes paid embarrassingly little attention to Mumford that entire summer. Whatever thin chance they had for collaboration the old Scotsman killed by his near-total self-absorption.

At first Geddes found Mumford a bit too reserved and tightly controlled, but he quickly took a liking to him; and he had long been impressed by his mind and his vivid writing style. Yet no matter how great their mutual respect for each other, or how tight their intellectual bond, the two men were unable to develop a genuine relationship. It was the age difference, certainly, and it was ego—they both were proud, fiercely independent spirits. But in the end it was Geddes's almost callous self-centeredness that prevented them from becoming closer; that and his Olympian self-confidence. Young Mumford was brilliant and self-confident, but not as arrogantly so as his old master.

In the presence of this imperious, incessantly active man, the reserved, well-mannered disciple never had a chance. The day after his arrival on the S.S. *Adriatic* Geddes exposed what was perhaps his real intention in coming to America. Seizing Mumford by the shoulders and staring intently at him, with tears flooding his eyes, the old man declared that Mumford was the image of his dead son Alasdair, who had been killed in France in the war. "You must be another son to me," he told an incredulous Mumford, who had heard enough about Alasdair to know he looked nothing like him, "and we will get on with our work together." The directness of that desperate appeal embarrassed Mumford, and this encounter, unfortunately, caused him to suppress some of the great affection he felt toward Geddes. He certainly did not want to encourage Geddes to see him as a son.

In the following weeks Geddes treated Mumford more like an acolyte than an associate, dominating his time, ordering him around like a grammar school pupil, and even subjecting him to a blackboard grilling in the elements of his complicated graphs and diagrams, or thinking machines, as he called them. Mumford had arranged through Alvin Johnson, the director of the New School, to have Geddes stay for a few days at the college's faculty hostel on West Twenty-fourth Street until he could find a more permanent place, but once settled there Geddes refused to move. He not only stayed all summer, but he also took possession of the New School's entire academic building on Twenty-third Street, filling the rooms with his charts, diagrams, and papers, which he had shipped over in advance.

Mumford reorganized his entire summer schedule to fit his master's needs. Geddes would rise at four or five in the morning, reserving these early hours for uninterrupted thought. Mumford would then meet him at the New School after breakfast, attend his lectures, dutifully taking notes, escort him around the city, drop him off at his rooms late in the afternoon, and rush off to meet Sophia for dinner, too exhausted by this nonstop "Ancient" for good conversation.

Mumford even found it impossible to collect materials for his biography. He assaulted Geddes with questions about his life and accomplishments, but the impatient master was not in the least interested in reviewing his career. "Time for that later," he would say. By "later" Mumford knew he meant after he was in his grave.[18]

But they did have a few memorable moments together. In his letters Mumford had been sharing with Geddes his excitement about the new regional planning group Clarence Stein and Henry Wright had founded, and about the RPAA's interest in P.G.'s work. "You can count at least two dozen architects and planners in New York who are ready to sit at your feet and absorb all you can give them," he had written Geddes just before his arrival.[19] That summer he took Geddes to an RPAA gathering at the Hudson Guild Farm, and Geddes, sitting cross-legged under an oak tree, like a wrinkled Hindu guru, told the group tales about his town planning projects in India.

Geddes got along especially well with Benton MacKaye and agreed to stay at the farm with him for two days after the conference ended. When it was time for Geddes to leave MacKaye walked the six miles with him to the railroad station, a walk interrupted again and again by Geddes's quick sprints into the roadside fields to collect botanical specimens. When they got within sight of the train station they had to run the last hundred feet or so for Geddes to catch his train.

This was the Geddes Mumford loved most—spirited, unpredictable, and magnificently alive, the man who four years later, at the age of seventy-three, took a second wife many years younger than he, hinting to Mumford that he was looking for something more than mere care and companionship. Geddes, as Mumford learned, could be absolutely delightful. He had a quick Rabelaisian wit, and on occasion, a naughtily unprofessorial manner. After reviewing the plans for a monstrously large building in Manhattan, capped by a great dome, he remarked to Mumford that "it looked as if the Devil had farted into Saint Paul's and raised the dome three hundred feet into the air."[20]

The old teacher was never at a loss for words or shy about offering advice. He even butted into Mumford's marital relations. The independent Sophia still retained her maiden name in 1923 and wore no wedding ring. Geddes could accept the retention of her original name, but "how does one know she is a married woman?" he bluntly asked Lewis when he met Sophia. "Oh! there's the ring." At this point a blushing Sophia hid her ringless hand behind her back. The next day the young couple asked Mumford's uncle, a jeweler at Tiffany's, to make them both wedding rings. Geddes approved of Lewis's ring when he saw it because, he said, it would warn away single women who might test his fidelity.[21]

Mumford desperately wanted to meet Geddes on equal ground as a friend, confidant, and colleague, but Geddes would not let him be any of these things. There was another problem, however. Mumford still considered Geddes one of the gods: "My respect for you is so great," he wrote Geddes that summer, in a desperate effort to unravel the reasons for their inability to get along better, "that it reduces my mental reactions in your presence to those I used to feel in the presence of my teacher when I was twelve years old—that is, complete paralysis!"[22]

Mumford wrote this frank, somewhat plaintive letter after a typical Geddesian oversight. He and Sophie had invited Geddes to spend a Sunday afternoon with them at their tiny Brooklyn apartment. It was to be the master's first visit to their home, but he somehow forgot the engagement and never even phoned to apologize.

The next day, instead of meeting Geddes at the New School, Mumford stayed home and wrote a long letter to him complaining that he had the "feeling that we have yet to *meet*. . . . You came over with a somewhat over-idealized portrait of me in your mind as a vigorous young apprentice who might work at the same bench with you for a while. . . . You are naturally disappointed to find me bound up with literary vocations, and to find that by natural bent and by training I am of the tribe of Euripides and Aristophanes rather than of Pythagoras and Aristotle. . . . Faced with an actual me, you have naturally tried to make me over into the idealized portrait, whose aims and interests and actions were more congruent with your own; and, instinctively, I find myself resisting these frontal attacks. . . ."

This was not quite as tough-minded a letter as Mumford seemed to think it was, for it failed to mention the real source of their recent personal difficulties—Geddes's ruthless self-absorption. And Mumford concluded with a plea that Geddes merely set down a "more regular plan of work and intercourse," as if this—Geddes's irregularity—was the heart of the problem. "Please command me," he ended the letter.[23] Geddes thus found it easy to give a generous, apologetic reply, emphasizing his interest in Mumford's development as a fully independent thinker.

When the two men met again they had a splendid day together, but then Geddes fell back into his old habits—lecturing at, rather than conversing with Mumford, making impossible demands on his time, alternately pleading with or ordering him to help him put his ideas into a book that would reach a wide audience.

One day close to Geddes's departure he demanded that his disciple spend the morning alone in a classroom of the New School putting on the blackboard all the graphs and charts Geddes had taught him. Hurt and humiliated, Mumford nonetheless went through with the exercise, feeling more alienated from Geddes than he ever had in his life. But the capping insult came on the final evening of Geddes's stay, when he left Mumford behind at the New School to pack his disheveled heaps of clothing, notes, diagrams, and charts while he rushed off to dine with Lillian Wald and the Lewisohn sisters. This was a task Mumford likened to "putting the contents of Vesuvius back into the crater after an eruption."[24]

When Geddes returned from dinner Mumford loaded his bags

into a waiting taxi, but did not accompany him to the pier; he was too hurt and angry to carry out that courtesy. As the two men hastily shook hands on the pavement in front of the New School they both perhaps realized that they would never close the gap between them that Geddes's American visit had widened.

Mumford saw Geddes one last time in Edinburgh in the late summer of 1925 on his return from a lectureship in Geneva. The old master, his health weakened by an intestinal infection suffered in Bombay the year before, was living temporarily in his Outlook Tower, trying to decide what to do with his bales of old manuscripts and notes, and he invited Mumford to join him there in the hope, perhaps, that he could finally collar him into bringing order to these materials. But Mumford would not take the bait, and the five days he spent there turned out to be a concentrated version of Geddes's New York visit: "engagements broken," Mumford wrote in his notes from Edinburgh, "time wasted on trivial idiots, and in the interim an unceasing volume of anecdotes, suggestions, and diagrammatic soliloquy."[25]

Mumford had arrived in Edinburgh with memories of their New York encounter, anxiously anticipating the worst, but his first day there was unexpectedly fulfilling. The moment he walked out of the tunnel at Waverly Station into the summer sunshine he fell in love with Edinburgh, Robert Louis Stevenson's ruggedly beautiful "city of masonry and living rock."[26] The "Athens of the North," as Geddes liked to call it, its historic medieval quarter was perched majestically, like the Acropolis, upon a spectacular glaciated ridge. Here, on one of the highest points of Castle Hill, Geddes had established his Outlook Tower study center. The day Mumford arrived in Edinburgh he and Geddes climbed to the top of the Tower, and from the circular open-air balcony Mumford looked out across a wide green park to Robert Craig's New Town, a gracefully planned quarter of formal gardens, boulevards, and linked circles of Georgian townhouses. Just below the Tower, off the High Street, was James Court, with its tall stone tenements, the place where Geddes had begun his earliest urban restoration efforts. Indeed, from Geddes's Tower Mumford could take in the entire Royal Mile, a historic sequence of steeply sloping streets stretching from Edinburgh Castle, just a stone's throw from the Tower, to Holyrood Palace, the home of the Stuart dynasty. One of the noblest streets in Europe, it has buildings that are a living record of Scotland's history, but when Geddes had moved to a rented flat in James Court with his new bride in 1889, this stately old area of Edinburgh was a scandalously neglected slum. Young Patrick Geddes had set about to change that, and now as he stood with Mumford on the Outlook Tower balcony, he began telling him how he had done it.

Scrubbing, painting, whitewashing, and repairing, he and his wife had transformed No. 6 James Court into a model of tenement reclamation. They then persuaded their neighbors to clean up their own quarters and medieval closes. Clad in an old nightshirt, the diminutive Geddes, "the Professor" as his new neighbors called him, directed many of these efforts himself, sweeping out the cluttered closes, building window boxes, painting mural decorations on the tenement halls, and gardening leftover open spaces. A master fund-raiser, Geddes had also provided entrepreneurial direction, raising money for the purchase of old buildings and entire blocks of flats for the purpose of renovating them and renting them to workers, or to students and faculty from neighboring Edinburgh University.

Mumford had already read Geddes's books on city planning, but what he saw in Edinburgh made all of Geddes's ideas about cities come alive for him. An earlier-day preservationist, Geddes had tried to save as much of the architectural heritage of Old Town as he possibly could. But where there was insufficient light and air within the historic closes, he had urged that individual buildings be torn down. "Conservative surgery," as he called it—preserving what was valuable in the existing physical and human setting while boldly introducing desirable innovation—was Geddes's contribution to modern urban rebuilding, an idea Mumford carried on in his own work. In Edinburgh and in all the cities he planned, Geddes recommended the removal of only enough urban tissue to allow for the continued growth of the "organism," an approach to city planning radically different from the then-fashionable and more grandiose rebuilding schemes of Baron von Haussmann and Daniel Burnham, planners of modern Paris and Chicago.

Geddes distrusted political centralization and metropolitan bureaucracies, preferring to leave the major part of the urban redevelopment process to the people of the various neighborhoods. Calling for the "Resorption of Government into the body of the community," Geddes proposed to "let cities, towns, villages, groups, associations, work out their own regional salvation."[27]

When Mumford arrived in Edinburgh he was eager to see all of Geddes's old projects, and he wanted to see them with Geddes himself. After they viewed Edinburgh from the Tower, Geddes took Mumford through the cobbled streets of Old Town, showing him the many improvements that he had made or initiated. Geddes had left his imprint all over Old Town. Even the beggars knew of his work, as Mumford learned when a ragged street urchin grabbed him by the hand and pointed to a bust of Socrates Geddes had placed over an entrance to a building and blurted: " 'Luv, that's the Professor.' "[28]

That evening Mumford slept in a makeshift cot in the Outlook Tower library, surrounded by bookcases and boxes of musty notes, alone, as in his adolescent dream, with the master himself.

But the next day and in the days that followed his guide to the city was not Geddes, but his goddaughter and assistant, Mabel Barker, the robust mountain climber he had met several years earlier in the Tyrol. Geddes was completely absorbed in his newest project, the founding of a residential college in the south of France. Mumford would meet him briefly for breakfast, and at the end of the day for a short whiskey before retiring, but P.G. had little time for him in between.

In the moments they did spend together alone, Geddes pressed Mumford with urgent pleas for collaboration, his voice plaintive, a mist forming over his eyes. Shortly after Mumford arrived Geddes escorted him through the ruins of his great stone Tower, now a half-empty reminder of the many projects he had initiated before the war. Geddes showed him the mountains of unorganized manuscripts and notes that contained his thoughts of three decades. "Ay de mi!" he sighed, throwing up his arms in despair. "How am I to get these graphs and notes in order? A lifetime's accumulation, never really sorted out. I need your help, Mumford. . . . Bring your wife and bairn over next winter, when I am settled again in Montpellier. I need you, and while you're working with me, you can get your Doctorat Etranger at the University—an excellent place—and become a professor yourself. Writing is a poor trade. We professors have it easier and live longer. All you need is to present a creditable thesis in French."[29]

But Mumford had prepared himself to resist Geddes's offers. If he had any doubts about this matter they were put to rest one afternoon near his departure when he and Geddes were viewing Edinburgh from the balcony of the Tower. Geddes would not let Mumford see the city in his own way; he had to see it through Geddes's eyes, as Geddes held him roughly by the shoulders and demanded that he pick out of the panorama exactly what he was seeing.

As Geddes walked to Waverly Station with Mumford in their final hour together, he continued to run on with suggestions for combined projects and plans, insisting again that Mumford become a professor, perhaps eventually a college president, or an American ambassador like James Russell Lowell—everything, in sum, but what Mumford himself had set out to be. When Mumford took his seat on the train—after persuading Geddes not to stay to see him off—he took out his notebook and jotted down a final assessment of his insistent master. "He is perfectly loveable in his human moments; in fact he is enchanting; a portrait of him at thirty . . . showing a black-bearded rather chubby man with red cheeks, almost choked me with emotion. Here is a man I might have worked with and merged myself with. But . . . what am I to do with the pathetic tyrant . . . who preaches activity and demands quiescence or at least acquiescence. . . . I have still to have an hour's conversation with him."

And yet he loved and respected Geddes and still considered him "the most prodigious thinker in the modern world. If I have perhaps seen him for the last time . . . I shall retain of him, not the memory of the stern, sorrow-laden old man, interminably talking . . . ; no, I shall retain the memory of the older comrade I found too late."[30]

The thought that he would never get any closer to Geddes left him with a sense of sorrow that was soon offset by a feeling of release. He was about to turn thirty and his apprenticeship was over. He had needed only this final meeting with his master to realize how independent he had become.

Mumford might have felt free, but that persistent "Old Bull of the Herd" would not relent. In Geddes's letters to Mumford he continued to besiege him with ever more desperate pleas for cooperation, claiming that he wanted no "ordinary assistant, but just the sort of free utilisation of my stuff as you describe."[31] Geddes had by then taken up winter residence at his new Collège des Ecossais, on an arid hillside near Montpellier, looking out over the moors toward the Mediterranean. Geddes wanted Mumford to bring Sophia and young Geddes to live there while Mumford helped him finish his sociological synthesis.

Geddes's "collège" was a makeshift institution, with no formal curriculum or degree-granting power. There were a couple of run-down stone buildings, a handful of students—most of them foreigners living there while studying at the University of Montpellier—and, of course, the master himself, who would give impromptu lectures to anyone who cared to listen while strolling along the paths of the college's terrace gardens, which he laid out in the form of his graphs and thinking machines. When not absorbed in their own academic work, the student residents would help Geddes with his never-ending building projects. Some of P.G.'s friends helped him with the administration of the college, but most of his family and his closest friends were adamantly opposed to this expensive project, which ate up a good part of his second wife's fortune.

Geddes, still the dreamer into his middle seventies, hoped that students would come from all over the world to study at his hilltop residential college, and that their countries would eventually contribute residence halls, or colleges, but nothing came of this. In his final years Geddes, the scientist and sociologist, became an overbearing and querulous master builder, and this frustrated Mumford, who, in his letters, tried to draw him back to his writing. Mumford was at least relieved that Geddes had completed his two-volume treatise on biology with J. Arthur Thomson, *Life: Outline of General Biology*, which was published in June 1931. "I thank heaven for Thomson's persistence in keeping you on your biological cooperation," he wrote P.G. that year. "Looking back over the past, I . . . wish . . . that I had been five years older when we met in 1923: I was then too unstable and too full of unsolved problems of my own, with still too shaky intellectual foundations, to be of any real help to you then: in order to keep from being completely absorbed . . . I had to stand too far away and I can see now the loss to both of us. . . . It is too late for practical collaboration now: our habits of work are too different, and a good secretary would be of more advantage to you than I could at my most sympathetic best."[32]

In the winter of 1932, Geddes traveled to London to accept the knighthood he had declined twenty years earlier, and he stayed on for the investiture despite his doctor's warnings that London's harsh winter climate could be perilous to his health. In March he returned to Montpellier, a gravely sick man. He tried to resume his former activities, but after three weeks he was bedridden. His condition worsened rapidly, and he died on the evening of April 17, before the doctor could arrive from Montpellier. Mumford learned of his death in the New York newspapers, just as he was about to leave on a European tour that would have taken him to Montpellier for a weeklong visit with P.G.

His friends and students, Mumford learned by letter, gathered for a final farewell on the hillside of the college, in the gardens Geddes had hacked out of stone and irrigated with water hauled by donkey carts. The students sang his favorite folk ballads, and there were words of praise and celebration. Then his body was carried down the hill between the rows of Mediterranean flowers and shrubs and taken to a crematorium in Marseilles. "As his uncoffined corpse was placed on the furnace fire, his beard and hair instantly flared alight and for an evanescent moment his whole outworn body became pure flame."[33]

Almost thirty years later Mumford wondered "what Old Geddes would say to me, if we could meet after these many years." What still lived most vividly in Mumford's mind was "the animation, the fire, the fierceness and intensity . . . the bristle of the beard-tips, the wing-like look of the parted hair, the almost frightening bulge of the brow"—all the attributes of a man who once said he regarded thoughts as orgasms.[34]

That was it. That was what he owed most to Geddes, the teacher who had taught him how to live a life.

Mumford would never write Geddes's biography, though Geddes had named him in his final will as the one to undertake that task. While he would always believe that he was the person best equipped to do so, Mumford felt that in order to give a full and fair assessment of Geddes he would have to point out his weaknesses as a person and a thinker, and that would have been distasteful to him; and might, he feared, have been interpreted as a betrayal of the man to whom he owed so much.35 But there was another factor at work here. In criticizing the master, does not the disciple sometimes diminish himself by comparison?

Mumford continued to draw on Geddes's ideas and example, but it was always on his own terms and for his own purposes. "It is only the spiritual Judas," he once said of his relations with Geddes, "who remains completely loyal to the word and form of the master's statement. Thus treason to the teacher is really loyalty to life, and to every part of his teaching that adequately expresses life."36

He had fought Geddes, he had evaded him, because he had his own work to do, his own life to live. In the end this was perhaps the greatest gift Geddes had passed on to him—the courage to break free from the man he admired like a father.

Patrick Geddes gave his American disciple one other great gift: the self-confidence to become a generalist. From afar, he, more than anyone else, helped Mumford through the career crisis he faced in the early 1920s, when Mumford found himself working hard and well, but without a clear sense of direction.

By the spring of 1924 the tension between him and Sophia had eased enough for them to decide to have a child. Still, for Lewis, there remained the Emersonian problem of a proper vocation. He would be a writer, certainly, but what kind of writer? "What," he continued to ask himself, "is my real work?"37

"What *am* I? A journalist? a novelist? a literary critic? an art critic? a scholar? a sociologist? ... MUST I TAKE A DEFINITIVE LINE?"38 His private notes of these years indicate that he didn't care to specialize in any one thing. His interests had become too broad-ranging; his curiosity too capacious. "Had I taken to sociology professionally I should have devoted myself to the morphology and physiology of cities," to their origins and their evolution, to their architecture and their social life, he wrote a fellow regionalist, "and I have not lost my old interest."39 Yet he found himself equally drawn to literature—to creative writing as well as to literary studies. To be a truly successful writer, would he have to choose between literature and what he called sociology?

By 1925 he had become convinced, mostly by the example of

Geddes's many-sided life, that he did not, in fact, have to take on any one profession. He would instead assume his master's coat of many colors, becoming a generalist, "one who is more interested in putting the fragments together in an ordered and significant pattern than in minutely investigating the separate parts."[40]

This career decision was in near-perfect alignment with one of his greatest natural talents—an amazing facility for synthesis. Although he says that it was not until he took a Rorschach test in 1947 that he became fully aware of his ability, "amounting to genius," for bringing together widely diverse material into a unified pattern, he had been told this much earlier in his life by a fortuneteller whom his mother had hired to put together his horoscope. "You are born under the astrological sign of Libra, symbolized by the Balance. . . . Libra people have a fine sense of harmony and proportion. They are natural arbitrators," and possess a gift for synthesis. "They make excellent judges, bankers, diplomats, architects and engineers. They often succeed in artistic careers."[41]

In this gradual and complicated process of career formulation, 1925, then, was the decisive year for Mumford. In 1925, moreover, Lewis Mumford, at age thirty, settled upon the great theme of his entire career as a generalist—"to describe what has happened to the Western European mind since the breakdown of the medieval synthesis, and to trace out the effects of this in America."[42] In the Middle Ages he discovered in his reading of John Ruskin, William Morris, and Henry Adams, he found an ideal balance between man's emotional and rational sides, his spiritual and material concerns—a balance he felt had disappeared, for the most part, in the one-sided age of science and rationalism that followed.

He called the book he began fashioning in his mind in the summer of 1925, while lecturing in Geneva, Switzerland, *The Golden Day*. The Golden Day he evoked, however, was not Europe in the age of walled towns and soaring cathedrals but America in the period of Whitman, Emerson, and Melville. In the work of these writers he found a living link between the Middle Ages and the immediate concerns of his own time. Van Wyck Brooks had been directing him toward a reappraisal of these native geniuses, but it was his short stay in the Old World that gave him a new perspective on the culture of his own country. In three boldly original books, written one after the other—*The Golden Day*, *Herman Melville* (1929), and *The Brown*

Decades (1931)—he located in the work of the literary greats of mid-nineteenth-century America a rich native tradition in the arts. He hoped that this would serve as a creative source and inspiration for the regional movement he was simultaneously encouraging in his work for the Regional Planning Association of America.

What "[we need] is a vision to live by," he wrote Delilah Loch, restating the theme of his very first book, *The Story of Utopias*. In that book he had called for a new image of the good life, but had not been able to describe it with any fullness. Now he thought he could, drawing on the work of the writers of the Golden Day.[43]

13

Golden Days

I claim that in literature, I have judged and felt every thing from an American point of view which is no local standard, for America to me, includes humanity and is the universal.

—WALT WHITMAN

The summons to Geneva had come from Alfred Zimmern, author of *The Greek Commonwealth*, one of the crowning books of Mumford's early education. Lewis had not yet met this distant "hero" of his, or even corresponded with him, so the letter of invitation "had the effect of coming from heaven," he excitedly wrote Patrick Geddes just after receiving it. [1] In this case, however, there turned out to be a familiar intervening angel.

Zimmern, a fellow of New College, Oxford, had become friends with Van Wyck Brooks in London before the war, and when he began searching for lecturers for his newly formed summer school for international students in Geneva, he wrote to Brooks, who recommended his younger friend. Zimmern needed no coaxing; he had been greatly impressed by *The Story of Utopias*, which he had reviewed several years earlier, and he wrote to Mumford immediately, offering him a handsome fee to deliver a course of lectures that August on "The Development of American Culture."

This opportunity came at a near-perfect time in Mumford's life. For one thing, he badly needed the money: Sophia had recently left her job at *The Dial* and was expecting a baby in July. More importantly, these Geneva lectures would point his still unsettled career in a new and richly promising direction.

Since completing *Sticks and Stones*, Mumford had been giving thought to writing a companion volume on American literature, a book that would strike a more positive note than Harold Stearns's *Civilization in the United States*. The more "[I become] acquainted with the provincial America," he wrote Joel Spingarn in 1923, "the more it seems to me that there were at least the fertilized seeds of a new cultural growth in that early environment; and that most of our misfortunes resulted from the blight of the Civil War."[2] He would devote his Geneva lectures, he now decided, to this theme, expanding them later into a full-scale study of the American literary imagination.

This was the kind of all-engrossing literary project he had been anxious to get at for some time, a project that matched his endowment of ability and ambition. Writing the book, with Zimmern's fee to help underwrite his living expenses, would release him for a time from the treadmill of journalism. Like another sometime journalist before him—Samuel Johnson—he continued to find this work ill-suited to his pure aspirations and creative bent, even though, as with Dr. Johnson, some of his best books would grow from his published essays.

The previous winter Mumford had taken on a heavy load of projects—editing, writing, part-time teaching and lecturing, mostly on architecture and regional planning. "You were the person I used to envy because you had time to think," Henry Wright teased him at a regional planning meeting that spring. "And now you are as bad as the rest of us." But that was all behind him, he emphatically told Wright. For the next year he was going to cut loose from most of these responsibilities and return to "literature."[3]

Actually, he had already made a start in this direction before receiving Zimmern's invitation to Geneva. After editing the Regional Planning Association's *Survey Graphic* issue, he had cleared his calendar for two full weeks and gone back to the play he had begun eight years before—"The Brownstone Front." In its original form the play had spanned the entire nineteenth century, but in revising it Mumford focused the action on the Civil War period, and changed the title to "Asters and Goldenrod: an American Idyll."

He rewrote the play in nine furious days, and on completing it he thought he had a strong piece of theater and began at once to look for a producer. This time he had a warmly encouraging patron, Aline MacMahon, the young Broadway actress who was engaged to Clarence Stein. He had met her at a dinner party in Stein's family home, and later that evening he revealed to her that he had always secretly wanted to be a playwright. The following day he received a note from her which simply said: "Write a play for me!"

"The play is more beautiful than my dreams," she wrote him after reading the script of "Asters and Goldenrod." But the two critical scenes, she regretted to tell him, lacked dramatic drive and impact; they were "shaped in words, not in action."[4] Although bitterly disappointed, Mumford was forced to agree that this was indeed a fatal flaw in his play, and he decided to put it aside for at least a year or so.

The hours he had spent on it weren't a total loss, however. The writing, coming after a solid year of labor on architecture and planning, opened him up, releasing creative energies that would flow into *The Golden Day*, a book built on a similar theme and structured in much the same way as "Asters and Goldenrod." And while working on "Asters and Goldenrod" he began to map out other literary projects. He thought of writing a novel and of doing some more plays, one of them an epic drama on the building of the Brooklyn Bridge. But when he received Zimmern's offer he put all these projects on hold and began to pull together in his mind the book that he hoped would establish him, finally, as a "literary man," and not just a writer on cities and architecture. He would be thirty in October—the age Plato had designated for maturity and parent-hood—and "it's time," he vowed to himself, "that I tackled man's work." All this, he reminded himself in his diary notes, would require steel-hard discipline in his daily life, "more solitude and fewer contacts."[5] But first there was Geneva; and the new baby.

Almost immediately after he and Sophia decided to have a baby their sex life improved, as they were able to come together more spontaneously, without the cumbersome, passion-killing routine of contraceptives. Sophia had trouble conceiving at first, but when she discovered that she was pregnant, they both panicked momentarily. With Sophia, it was the anxiety of a woman about to give birth for the first time; Lewis was worried most about a possible interruption to his career. But when Sophia delivered a son they named Geddes on July 5, 1925, at Brooklyn Hospital, his mood changed almost immediately.

He had been so indifferent about the imminent birth that after rushing Sophia to the hospital that morning, getting her there just in the nick of time, he had not even bothered to wait around for the baby's arrival. He left Sophia in her hospital room, her contractions only several minutes apart, and calmly walked to his mother's home nearby for a heaping breakfast. "It was not until a little later, when I beheld the crumpled, beet-faced, quite ugly little creature that I became aware of the change that had taken place, not just in my status, but far more profoundly in my feeling about life."[6] Fatherhood moved him in a way he had not anticipated.

Their first weeks of parenthood were tense and stressful. They had had no experience with children (neither of them had ever changed a diaper), and Geddes was not an easy baby to handle. He was several weeks premature and the birth had been difficult. Like his namesake, Geddes came "into the world tumultuously and unexpectedly," Lewis wrote Delilah Loch.[7] For the first several days after his birth he seemed to want to return to the womb, refusing to take his mother's milk or to open his eyes for more than a few seconds at a time. After he was put into an incubator and fed through a tube he improved rapidly, only to later develop an allergy to milk albumen which he didn't overcome for three years. To make matters worse, not long after Sophia brought Geddes home from the hospital she came down with a bad case of jaundice, which made her too weak to launder his diapers. "Her plight would have been pitiable—there were no diaper services or public washing machines in those days—had not the wife of our janitor, out of the goodness of her heart, taken on this job for the next few weeks," Lewis recalled later.[8] It never appears to have occurred to Lewis that *he* might have taken on this emergency domestic duty, nor, apparently, did Sophia expect him to. He was hard at work on his Geneva lectures, and she didn't want to cut into his concentration, feeling perhaps a little guilty about pushing him to have a child, as her later letters to him in Switzerland indicate.

One of these letters is particularly revealing on the entire matter of her attitude toward parenthood and the obstacles it threatened to put in the way of her husband's career. She writes that while Geddes is generally "well-mannered," he "does cry on occasion. And I'm praying your room [in the new apartment she had just found for them in Sunnyside Gardens, Queens] will prove properly insulated so's [sic] you won't curse my maternal desires. But I'll take the child out in his carriage and walk him about all morning if he interferes with your work."⁹ While she would never do exactly that, the sentiment was honest—and she proved true to it. For the next several years Sophia did everything in her power to make sure that little Geddes never disturbed his father while he worked. Lewis's writing came first: he insisted on this, and she agreed to it.

On occasion he carried this attitude to inconsiderate extremes. When, for example, they moved into their cramped Sunnyside apartment he converted two small bedrooms into one so that he could have an ample workplace and private bedroom. Sophia uncomplainingly agreed to sleep in the living room; and whenever Lewis had company in the evening she slept with a screen in front of her bed, for as a nursing mother she needed her sleep.

Before leaving for Geneva, Lewis had arranged for Sophia and the baby to stay with her parents in Brooklyn until he returned. Their parting wasn't an easy one, as Sophia felt a little helpless, while he was burdened with guilt about leaving her and Geddes so soon after the birth. But it is revealing of his remarkable powers of self-absorption that once he boarded the *Aquitania* his anxieties about Sophia and the baby disappeared. The seas were silken smooth the entire journey, allowing him to work serenely on his lectures; and away from Sophia, he found himself falling more deeply in love with her.

In Geneva he began to feel physically stronger and healthier than he had in years. The old city itself helped to revive his strength and spirits. On idle afternoons he would wander through its courts and alleys and steep narrow streets, or sit on the embankment above the Ile de Rousseau and watch the white swans preen themselves while he read Sophia's letters, packed with news of the progress of their son.

Lewis found Geneva a little too smug and stuffy—John Calvin's spirit still brooded over this great Protestant city—but his days there were stimulating beyond his expectations. He would usually begin the day with a light breakfast and a swim in the clear, cold waters of Lake Geneva; later, after a stretch of writing, he'd have drinks and a leisurely lunch with the Zimmerns and their friends and guests at the Hotel Russia. In the evening he gave his lectures in English to an audience of some eighty students from all over the world. The following morning they were repeated in French by Jean de Menasce, a lean, classically handsome young man who also acted as Lewis's interpreter in the question-and-answer sessions that followed.

Later, mostly through correspondence, a bond developed between him and Jean de Menasce, and after de Menasce's death Lewis would describe him as "perhaps the most luminous and beautiful spirit" he had ever known. From Geneva, de Menasce went on to become a world authority on Persian religion, gaining a chair at the Sorbonne. After the Second World War the Mumfords would visit him on their occasional trips to Paris. By then he was Father de Menasce, a Dominican monk, living a contemplative life in a convent at Neuilly. "With Father de Menasce," Mumford would write in his memoirs, "I felt as I was later to feel about Pope John XXIII: given two Pope John's I could become a Catholic; three might even turn me into a Christian."[10]

In Geneva, Mumford met someone else who would become an energizing force in his life, Josephine Strongin, who was then a sixteen-year-old American auditor at Zimmern's school. Of Russian-Jewish origin, she was frail and pixie-like, with smooth white skin and gleaming black hair. "Jo" loved music, but poetry was her passion. Mumford found her poetry, which she first read to him one afternoon while sitting on a bench in the Promenade des Bastions, powerful and original, and the following year he convinced his fellow editors of *The American Caravan*, a yearbook of the arts, to accept some of her sonnets for publication.

Jo Strongin had an untamed spirit that would lure her in and out of several unfortunate love affairs, one of them the very next winter with the French novelist Céline. When Lewis met her, however, he was not drawn to her sexually, although she found him devastatingly attractive. Though some ten years later they almost became lovers, in the years immediately following Geneva he acted more in the role of teacher and "uncle" to her.[11]

Mumford spent most of his social hours in Geneva with the Zimmerns, Alfred and his bright-spirited French wife, Lucie. And it was the combative Lucie who urged Mumford to shake up his

European audience with some unconventional thinking. That, as it turns out, is exactly what he had already decided to do in his first lecture. In his courteous but emphatic manner, Mumford told the students that many of the qualities which Europeans regarded as characteristically American had their origin in the Old World: the worship of money and material things; the utilitarians' blind faith in the curative powers of technology; even the restless pioneering spirit, which he characterized as "the Romantic movement in action." A vulgar America was not corrupting Europe; if anything it was Europe that had originally corrupted America. [12]

We can only guess that he delivered this challenge a little too stiffly, for he was not yet a relaxed and poised public speaker. But it went over well with the audience, and so did the other lectures, with perhaps one exception. Just as he was approaching the podium to begin his second lecture he realized that he had left his notes back in his pension. He did all right at first, but midway through his talk his mind went completely blank, and he stood frozen and silent for an agonizingly embarrassing minute or so, before he was able to pull himself together and go on. The next day when he went to Zimmern to apologize, Zimmern advised him to leave his notes behind whenever he lectured; it would make him a better teacher.

"My lectures have occasionally been jumbled but they have had meat in them," he wrote Sophia proudly from Geneva, "and in some ways have taken the haughty and condescending foreigner off his feet." [13] What probably most impressed his audience was his passionate defense of the literature of his own country. In these lectures, and in his spirited afternoon discussions with the Zimmerns and their friends in the crowded cafes of Geneva, Mumford found himself rising to the defense of his country, arguing a point of view that ran directly opposite to that of most American expatriate writers of the 1920s. They were attracted to Europe, to the Old World, because it had become for them the New World, all that America had once stood for—the promise of a fresh start. In London, Paris, and Berlin, in the work of insurgent experimenters like Joyce, Picasso, and Le Corbusier, a new age seemed to be in the making. By comparison, the America of the Red Scare and the Harding scandals was crude, corrupt, and tiresomely conventional in its politics, morality, and entire outlook on the arts.

This, of course, was also the European view of America. "Your country lacks a distinguished culture because it lacks a distinguished past," Mumford kept hearing from the Europeans he encountered in Geneva. "You Americans have no history, no secure tradition in arts and letters to fall back on." But America had had its great writers and artists, Mumford kept insisting; it had only to recover and reclaim them. "And we are beginning to do just that," he reminded de Menasce, Zimmern, and others in Geneva, pointing to the work of Van Wyck Brooks, Waldo Frank, Paul Rosenfeld, Randolph Bourne, and other fellow spirits who had first called for a "rediscovery" of the American past in the pages of the short-lived *Seven Arts*.[14]

As a struggling young writer in New York, a vicarious participant in the Village ferment of those prewar years, Mumford had felt, with the editors of *Seven Arts*, that he was living in the opening days of an American renascence. But the clearest, strongest call he had heard for a new America came from a more distant place and time, from the world of Walt Whitman as it had unfolded for him in *The Leaves of Grass*, one of the forming books of his youth. This was the Whitman who had called for American artists to unite in a "close phalanx, ardent, radical and progressive" for the purpose of creating a "grand and true" native art.[15] In Geneva, Mumford was better able to see his own work, beginning with *Sticks and Stones*, as part of this ongoing effort to inspire a cultural flowering that would begin in the arts and pass into every area of life.

Mumford left Geneva for Edinburgh, for what turned out to be his final meeting with Patrick Geddes, and stopped off in London to see his friend Dorothy Cecilia Loch, who immediately noticed a change in him. "You seem more mature; you look stronger and more confident," she told him, looking directly into his eyes. "I feel it, too," he replied. He was no longer "afraid of shopkeepers," nor did his pulse race out of control when he was introduced to a young woman.[16]

It was on board the *Aquitania* on his return to New York that he definitely decided to write the book that had been forming in his mind since receiving Zimmern's offer. It would be his most ambitious project up to now, and he was eager to get on with it.

On his return to New York, he and Sophia moved from Brooklyn Heights to their new apartment in Sunnyside Gardens, Queens. Around them were fields and goat pastures and a lone surviving farmhouse. This surrounding land, however, had been subdivided into blocks and unpaved streets, and even in the fall, when the ground was carpeted with bright sunflowers, it was a dreary environment. Nearby was a dilapidated railroad yard and some industrial ash heaps, and out toward Newtown Creek there was a foul-smelling chemical factory.

Gradually, however, Sunnyside itself took on a more pleasing look as the residents—most of them first-time homeowners—developed pride in their community. Gardens and rows of trees were planted, and the grassy courts behind the homes came to be handsomely landscaped. When Geddes was old enough, his parents could walk him to his nursery school by taking the hedge-lined footpaths across Sunnyside's courts. It was a safe and convenient environment for children, and Geddes, after all, was the principal reason they had moved there.

Whatever its other limitations, they never felt alone or isolated at Sunnyside. Two of Sophia's sisters' families moved there, as did several of Lewis's colleagues in the Regional Planning Association, including Charles Ascher and his wife Helen, with whom they sometimes vacationed on Cape Cod. Their two closest friends at Sunnyside, however, were Avrahm Yarmolinsky, the scholar who headed the Slavonic Language Department at the New York Public Library, and his wife Babette Deutsch, the poet. Because of Lewis's monkish work routine (up early and to bed by 10 p.m.) and the demands of a new baby, they did little other socializing. Lewis usually cooked breakfast and dinner, and Sophia did almost everything else. By the end of the day they were too tired to go out or to entertain.

The first year at Sunnyside they lived in a cooperative apartment on Gosman Avenue, but in the spring of 1927 they moved to a tiny five-room row house, built on a grassy terrace, with a row of poplars in front. The house was a little cramped, even for a family of three, but Lewis had a compact, brightly painted study, easy to keep shipshape, and in the cellar he made a workshop, where he did occasional carpentering. And while the encircling blight of Long Island City might occasionally depress them, they had only to remind themselves that they were less than twenty minutes by subway from the heart of Manhattan. On a clear day they could glimpse the gleaming silver tip of the new Chrysler Building, and it was to the city that they were drawn for almost everything but their immediate domestic needs.

In their first months at Sunnyside, Lewis threw himself into the writing of his new book, which he completed in an astonishingly short time. He did some background reading and outlining in the fall and early winter, and by the late spring he had a solid first draft. That summer he put the finishing touches on the book while living with Sophia and Geddes in a rented cottage in Leedsville, the picturesque Dutchess County hamlet they would be drawn back to summer after summer until they finally settled there in 1936, in an old farmhouse hard by the Leedsville Road, near the winding Webutuck River.

They were invited up to Leedsville—two hours from New York City by train, and three miles from Amenia—by Joel Spingarn. Spingarn had a parklike estate there, Troutbeck, named after the famous pond in the English Lake District, and he liked to invite his literary friends to spend their summers in the string of cottages he owned nearby. When Lewis first met him Spingarn was a senior editor at Harcourt, Brace and Company, a firm he had helped to found in 1919. He had been a professor of comparative literature at Columbia University, known widely for his early work of genius, *Literary Criticism in the Renaissance*, which he wrote when he was only twenty-four, and for the challenging essays on aesthetics he published as *The New Criticism* in 1911. The year that book appeared, however, he was fired from Columbia for coming to the defense of his friend and colleague Henry Thurston Peck, who was dismissed by President Nicholas Murray Butler for his involvement in a messy legal battle.

Spingarn easily could have found another academic position, but the circumstances of his dismissal—he was supported in his battle against Butler, waged on grounds of academic freedom, by barely a handful of his colleagues—turned him forever against university life. A scholar-activist in the style of Theodore Roosevelt, whom he considered one of the greatest Americans, Spingarn became convinced by his experience at Columbia that academic life didn't produce the kind of men he prized most—moral and manly and capable of meeting the full demands of modern life, a view Mumford shared with him. [17] When he left Columbia, Spingarn put into

verse his thoughts on the matter in "Héloïse (A Modern Scholar to a
Medieval Nun)":

> *O passionate Héloïse*
> *I too have lived under the ban,*
> *With seven hundred professors,*
> *And not a single man.*[18]

Following his dismissal from Columbia, Spingarn returned to
Troutbeck, and there, until his death in 1939, he lived the life of the
country gentleman—gardening, improving his land, reading the
classics, and writing poetry and criticism. He bought the local
newspaper and improved its quality and circulation, and threw
himself into a host of community improvement projects, without
losing his absorbing interest in national affairs.[19]

Although Spingarn and Mumford were separated by twenty
years in age and were worlds apart in their views on politics and
literature, they were slowly drawn into friendship after first meeting
in Harold Stearns's grubby Varick Street basement. Occasionally
Mumford would drop in on Spingarn at his offices at Harcourt,
Brace to exchange ideas or to seek advice about his career; and
Spingarn invited him up to Troutbeck several times for the "sympo-
siums" he liked to convene in the beamed-ceiling library of his
twenty-eight-room mansion.[20]

Mumford would never enjoy a more perfect string of months than
those he spent in "The Domain of Troutbeck" that summer of 1926
with Sophia and Geddes. "We have escaped into Paradise!" he wrote
Spingarn after settling into The Maples, a spacious cottage in a tree-
sheltered spot off the Leedsville Road.[21] The pastoral village and the
invigorating country living, which included daily swims in Troutbeck Lake and afternoon walks over the low country hills, helped
him to bring to life the Concord of Emerson and Walden Pond of
Thoreau. Mumford truly had the feeling that he was living in his
book as he wrote it.

That summer convinced Lewis and Sophia that they must move
to the country as soon as they could afford to. They seemed to get
along better when they were outside the city, and Lewis found that
his writing came more easily when he was away from Whitman's
"nettlesome, mad, extravagant city." He not only got more work

done; he was more relaxed when he was away from his desk. Like most writers, when he worked well he breathed more easily. Joel Spingarn was amazed at how Mumford could completely detach himself from his work once he finished his bout of writing in the morning; even in their wide-ranging afternoon conversations in Spingarn's great garden, set by a lovely brook, Mumford rarely mentioned his work.[22]

On occasional afternoons Spingarn would show up in front of The Maples with his long, luxurious limousine and take the whole Mumford family for a drive through the surrounding countryside to nearby historic relics like the old iron furnaces that made this sheltered valley an early center of iron production. These afternoon excursions introduced Lewis to the Amenia scene and strongly increased his interest in local history.

He never worked so well. Almost every day that summer he would rise at the break of daylight, give three or four hours to his writing, and then put on his shorts and run a mile or so to Troutbeck Lake for a swim and a quiet period of thinking. If the sun was in the sky and the wind was blowing high and cool he'd linger for an hour or so, stretched out on his back on the lake's old wooden diving platform. Then he would join Sophia back at The Maples for lunch, which they often ate picnic-style on the front lawn. Afterwards, they would walk the grounds of Troutbeck, an estate of some eight hundred acres, approximately the size of Central Park, the first ample green space Lewis had explored as a child. It was a simple life and he would never be truly happy leading any other kind.

Spingarn owned most of Leedsville, and Troutbeck, his estate, was on the eastern edge of the village, reached by an arching stone bridge. The house had casement windows and the kind of heavy slate roof that William Morris loved, and it was set in a protected spot, in a hollow under a hill. The large front lawn—"not a lawn," Sinclair Lewis once described it, but "a grass grown cathedral"— sloped down toward a spring-fed trout brook, which dropped into the slow-flowing Webutuck.[23] The mansion was fronted by a row of towering sycamores and surrounded by exotic shrubs, greenhouses, sunken gardens, terraces, and rivulets; and everywhere trellises supported Spingarn's two hundred varieties of clematis.

Out back were tennis courts, and beyond them the sloping meadow led to Oblong Mountain, the limestone ridge that formed the western boundary of Troutbeck. Not far away, set between Oblong Mountain and a line of white birches and cedars, was Troutbeck Lake, where in the summer the Spingarns (Amy, Joel, and their four children) and their guests, along with the children from the village, would spend afternoons swimming and sunning themselves on its sloping banks. The whole estate—a circuit of some three and a half miles—was a vast private park over which the Spingarns' friends and frequent guests could wander at will.

Joel and Amy Spingarn, who struck some people as a bit too stiff and formal, were generous hosts; and for the next dozen years Lewis and Sophia would spend many pleasant afternoons and evenings at Troutbeck, enjoying tennis, lawn picnics, luncheons, dinners, and even nighttime hayrides on the rutted country roads. But that first summer at Leedsville was the summit of their lives there. "The Golden Day," Mumford later wrote Jo Strongin, "was written in the way Diderot said all good books should be written," with unhurried leisure, "as if one were talking to a woman, and trying both to instruct her and please her."[24] When he finished the book he knew it was good and he felt full of accomplishment.

In *The Golden Day* Mumford describes the settlement of America as the concluding moment of one process, the breakdown of the medieval synthesis and the start of another, the new age of timekeeping, science, Protestantism, and capitalism. When the Europeans settled in America they brought with them the seeds of this new culture, with its preoccupation with practical utility, material advancement, and the conquest of nature. In the soil of the New World these ideas took root, producing over time the characteristic American, with his commitment to individual freedom, hard work, invention, science, and money-making. From the beginning, the besetting problem of the American writer was how to survive and create in this one-sided utilitarian society. Most American writers were in one way or another "curbed and crippled" by this culture of the quick buck and the easy answer.[25]

In developing his argument Mumford drew freely on the work of Van Wyck Brooks, yet *The Golden Day* differs in an important way from Brooks's earlier biographies of Mark Twain and Henry James, which bemoan America's failure to produce a literature of world stature. Whereas Brooks found only failure and incompletely developed genius in his country's cultural past, Mumford found two periods of achievement and integration: one distinguished by its handsome accomplishments in the arts of architecture and community design; the other in the art of producing sound and balanced human beings. In these two periods America came as close as it had yet come to producing the cultural synthesis that Mumford considered the signal achievement of the age of the cathedrals.

Before the westward migrations of the footloose pioneer there was a brief period of order and settled development. In the "provincial period," in the hamlets and towns of the northeastern seaboard, "the Middle Ages at their best lingered" for a time. The Puritan village—with its communal traditions, balanced economy of farmers, craftsmen and traders, and consensual dedication to common spiritual ends—was the outstanding example of the medieval tradition in America. For Mumford, these New England towns were earlier-day versions of the garden cities he hoped to build in America, well-planned communities that had placed limits on their physical growth, and that had divided their land according to social need and function, not profit.[26]

These were ideas Mumford had first sketched out in *Sticks and Stones*, but in *The Golden Day* he showed that this felicitous village culture was not confined to seventeenth-century New England. Similar communities were planted on the Atlantic seaboard and up the region's river valleys well into the nineteenth century. By 1850 these communities had established a well-rounded industrial and agricultural life and had created a thriving regional culture. In the age of the young Herman Melville, American culture had its "Golden Day." The five commanding figures of this New World renaissance—Emerson, Thoreau, Whitman, Hawthorne, and Melville—represented a new kind of American personality, combining intellectual insight with emotional openness; each possessed what Mumford called complete vision, the quality he most admired in the thought of the Middle Ages. And while they drew upon the wider cultural inheritance of Europe, they did not return to the past for their model of culture. They welcomed the new forces of exploration, science, steam power, and democracy, absorbing them into their work to create a fresh outlook and orientation.

This was the New Man Emerson had celebrated, and of all the

writers of the Golden Day Emerson had the largest continuing influence on Mumford's life. Emerson is clearly a figure such as young Mumford wanted to be—a moral reformer concerned primarily with values, not with the details of political or economic readjustment; a prophet and preacher, not a planner or politician. Like Emerson, Mumford would speak out against the injustices of his day, but he never joined any political movements or sects. This isolated him and made him less effective in the short term, but it allowed him to keep his integrity intact and his ideas remarkably consistent throughout a lifelong struggle for a reconstructed world.

On completing *The Golden Day* Mumford realized that he had, in fact, written two books: one a boldly positive assessment of the power and potential of American culture; the other an assessment of its gravest defects. In the book the Civil War stands out as the great dividing point in American development. In the years following the war, America's promising regional civilization was steadily undermined, as manufacturing, finance, and culture were drawn to the growing metropolitan centers. This deterioration of local life was accompanied by a devastation of the natural environment by the pioneer, lumberman, miner, and industrialist.

All this had a blighting impact on the American imagination. The post–Civil War novelists and philosophers, with certain brilliant exceptions, either acquiesced to the age, accepting the new industrial values and practices, or retreated, with Henry Adams and George Santayana, to an earlier, more spiritually centered culture, as an orderly alternative to the turmoil of their time. Even generous-spirited critics of capitalism, like Edward Bellamy, Henry George, and William Dean Howells, "could envisage only a bourgeois order of society in which every one would have the comforts and conveniences of the middle classes."[27]

These were America's "Brown Decades," the somber autumnal days after the stormy summer of the Civil War had "shook the blossoms and blasted the promise of spring." Society took on a new physical appearance—darker, dingier, drabber, "adapting its colouration to the visible smut of early industrialization."[28]

Almost as soon as *The Golden Day* was published Mumford began to have second thoughts about his chapters on Gilded Age America, feeling that he had not given due weight to the creative forces in that period. His visit to Chicago in 1927 opened his eyes to some of the outstanding achievements of that age—as did his reading of the work of Emily Dickinson and the philosopher Charles Sanders Peirce, and his first exposure to the paintings of Albert Pinkham Ryder and Thomas Eakins. Two years later, when he was invited to give the Guernsey Center Moore Lectures at Dartmouth College, he made his formal amends with the age. While the Golden Day had been our most creative period in literature, the succeeding three decades, he now argued, had seen an equally impressive flowering in the arts, particularly in architecture, landscape design, and painting. These lectures became the basis of *The Brown Decades*, his last book-length study of American culture. Published five years after *The Golden Day*, this slim, sparkling book is very much a part of that earlier one and must be considered as such. Beyond their many common themes, both books are works of creative rediscovery.

In the achievements of a number of Gilded Age artists, writers, and builders, Mumford found a "Buried Renaissance." Some of those whose contributions he reevaluated, like Frederick Law Olmsted, Louis Sullivan, the Roeblings, and the environmentalist George Perkins Marsh, though well known in their day, had been largely neglected since then. Mumford's book led the way toward a reappreciation of their work, reopening entire new areas of America's cultural inheritance for future scholars.

Mumford felt a close spiritual kinship with the writers and builders of *The Brown Decades*. They, too, had faced the aftermath of a great war that had undermined an age of cultural promise and reform. Working in a similar postwar environment of overheated financial speculation, public corruption, and spiritual disillusionment, they had pushed on with their work, humanizing the landscape and creating an expressive modern art and architecture. Mumford summoned his contemporaries to take inspiration from these earlier "makers and finders" and carry forward the work they had begun so well.[29]

The signs, Mumford believed, already pointed to a revival of regionalism. In the writings of midwesterners like Sherwood Anderson, Willa Cather, and Carl Sandburg, and southerners like Howard Odum, John Crowe Ransom, and John Gould Fletcher, and in the architecture of Frank Lloyd Wright and the community planning efforts of the RPAA, there was a renewed interest in region and place. And the economic basis of this emerging regional culture was the technological revolution that had produced the automobile and long-distance electrical power transmission. These developments, as Mumford pointed out in his essays on behalf of the RPAA, spelled the end of the old centralized economy of coal and steam, and the beginnings of a regional dispersal of industry and population. Mumford's interpretation of American development thus led directly to an argument for the regional city, which was, in his mind, an update and extension to the entire continent of that rooted, well-balanced life America had known in its Golden Day.

Mumford's is clearly an idealized account of America's coming of age. But for literary prophets like him and Van Wyck Brooks, the past had no "objective reality."[30] It was the responsibility of each generation to recover and reshape history to its own purposes, to rewrite it on behalf of a better future. It is no coincidence, then, that the creative artists who were to head Mumford's regional movement were also the formative figures in his histories of American development. In their lives and in their work (and he surely included himself in this), they personified what he saw disappearing in the current age of specialization and mechanization.

But how was the regional outlook to spread and gain root in America? Mumford's earliest studies of regionalism convinced him that wherever regionalism had appeared as a challenge to the centralized state—in Ireland, Scotland, France, or Catalonia—it was "artists" like himself who had taken the lead. These regional revivals usually arose out of the efforts of poets, novelists, historians, and philosophers to create a new vision of life, a more settled, decentralized, and tradition-conscious pattern of living. It then became the task of reformers and regional planners to translate this vision into concrete plans and programs. This, as Mumford saw it, would be the culminating task of the Regional Planning Association of America.[31]

Mumford, the moral historian and forecaster, does not leave us, then, without "any definite prophesy," as some critics charge, "all dressed up with no place to go." The prophecy—the ideal—is there in generous detail, in books like *The Golden Day* and in his essays on behalf of regionalism. Mumford never brought together this complementary work on regionalism and cultural history into a booklength synthesis; but they formed an interconnected program for the renewal of American culture, with "artists" like himself in the vanguard.[32]

In his books on American culture Mumford was writing what he considered a new kind of history, history that includes the potential and the possible as a part of any full description of the past and the present. For Mumford, an early reader of Henri Bergson, the past, present, and future are one continuous, interconnected process. Thus, his canons of historical selectivity, what he chooses to include in these books and what he chooses to leave out, are influenced at every point by his personal conception of "the good life." Mumford begins with a view of what a culture should be, ideally, and then critically assesses the past with this as his standard of judgment. This is not history for its own sake; it is history for our sake, and on every page there are lessons and portents.

While some of Mumford's critics have been put off by this audacious effort to engage history on behalf of a better future, there is in Mumford's work a faith in the power of history as a humanizing instrument that we are not apt to find in most current scholarly history. No writer of our time has done more to encourage us to be mindful of our past.

A student of Patrick Geddes, the neo-Lamarckian biologist, Mumford sees history as the record of an ongoing intercourse between the organism and its environment. At times man submits to external conditioning and loses control over his destiny; but on occasion, in rare moments of "insurgence," as in America's Golden Day, he achieves transcendence, becomes a maker of his own history—an artist, a builder, a balanced personality. It is crucially important that we have before us records of such feats of insurgence, to give us the inspiration to wage unending war in our own time with the forces of machine civilization. The most important reminder history offers us, this modern Emerson argues, is that we do have free choice, our own yes and no—if only we choose to exercise it.

Mumford's history is itself a powerful form of cultural criticism. But it is cultural criticism of a special kind. In his studies of American development Mumford gives little attention to politics or to class action, yet his viewpoint, while fashioned primarily in aesthetic terms, is nonetheless sharply social and political. With other more celebrated critics of modernist theory like Herbert Marcuse, Max Horkheimer, and the Dutch historian Johan Huizinga, Mumford rebelled against the behaviorist dismissal of all realms of experience that could not be counted, measured, or observed. To psychologists like John Watson, whose work was much in fashion when Mumford wrote *The Golden Day*, behavior, not consciousness or meaning, was what ultimately mattered. This reduction of everything to behavior, Huizinga argued against Watson when he visited the United States in 1926, opened up the dangerous "possibility of a reconciliation with a mechanized . . . society, in which productive energy is transferred from the living arm and fixed in the dead tool." In pragmatism as well as behaviorism, moreover, Huizinga found an "antimetaphysical attitude of mind," which "automatically includes an antihistorical one."³³ The exact description of the past was more important than establishing some sort of living continuity with it. Although Mumford had not yet read Huizinga when he wrote *The Golden Day*, that is exactly where his argument led.

Mumford, however, never suggested a mere ransacking of history for moral standards; nor are his historical essays exercises in nostalgia. The examples of insurgence and organic balance he found in history were to serve notice of what was missing in modern life, but he insisted that each generation confront the conditions of its time and create its own culture, making use of the best of the past, as the fifth-century Greeks had drawn on the simpler but perhaps sounder culture of Homer and Hesiod. With the ancient Athenians, Mumford held to the idea that all healthy civilizations depended upon a balance of forces, an equilibrium between tradition and innovation, and that when this was upset they inevitably decayed.

Mumford's studies of American culture can be excessively preachy, and they do contain some unintended distortions of the historical record. They are not, nor are they intended to be, works of dispassionate scholarship. But they are characterized by imaginative daring and by a rare ability to see familiar phenomena in a new way. What Mumford would write of Herman Melville can be said equally of himself: he had, by age thirty, acquired "mastery: . . . he could take a hundred dispersed [and familiar] facts and weave them into a [new] pattern."³⁴ His American studies are among the most brilliant works of historical synthesis in the English language.

Mumford, of course, was not alone in this effort to uncover America's buried cultural past. Joining him were some of his closest literary friends—Van Wyck Brooks, Paul Rosenfeld, Waldo Frank, Constance Mayfield Rourke, and the critic John Macy, author of *The Spirit of American Literature* (1913), the first book to inaugurate this revision of the American past. Waldo Frank's *The Re-Discovery of America* (1929) gave their efforts a name, but Brooks and Mumford were the leaders of this movement to reclaim our native literary heritage, a movement that included such independently conceived contributions as Matthew Josephson's *A Portrait of the Artist as an American* (1930), H. L. Mencken's *The American Language* (1919), D. H. Lawrence's *Studies in Classical American Literature* (1923), Thomas Beer's *The Mauve Decade* (1926), Mark Van Doren's *Thoreau* (1916), William Carlos Williams's *In the American Grain* (1925), Vernon Parrington's *Main Currents of American Thought* (1930), Constance Rourke's *American Humor* (1931), and Brooks's five-volume masterwork, *Makers and Finders: A History of the Writer in America*.

Of all these pioneering "usable past" projects, Lewis Mumford's have held up the best, and have exercised the widest influence. When *The Golden Day* first appeared Van Wyck Brooks immediately recognized its significance and wrote his friend to salute his contribution. "*The Golden Day* seems to me the culmination of the whole critical movement in this country during the past ten years," the best book the movement had produced thus far and one that best summed up its leading ideas. "In your glowing appreciation of the *golden* age you have done the *positive* thing which the rest of us have mostly left out."³⁵

Yet even as he wrote this, Brooks was independently coming to the same conclusions as Mumford about America's literary culture. This change in his outlook occurred in 1925 when he began reading for his biography of Emerson, who hitherto he had considered little more than "a lofty and inspired sophist."³⁶ "For four months I have been living in a dream," he wrote Mumford in September 1925, "writing a life of Emerson." Brooks describes this as "a sort of religious experience," and it kept him at his desk for up to fourteen hours a day. He had recently suffered a severe emotional break-down, but reading about Emerson and his world had helped to restore his spirits temporarily. ("Actually," as one of his biographers writes, "he had passed from depression into mania.") Everything he had written up to this point had been an exploration "of the *dark* side of our moon, and this blessed Emerson has led me right out into the midst of the sunny side." Emerson, he concluded, was part of what could be called a classic age in American literature.[37]

The thrill of discovering that they were independently engaged in similar projects brought Brooks and Mumford closer together as friends. And though they were not as directly influenced by each other's work in these years as the literary historian Robert Spiller, for one, has argued, Brooks did take an interest in his younger friend's career that went beyond mere friendship. After the prema-ture death of Randolph Bourne, Mumford became, for Brooks, the model of the kind of artist-hero he expected to lead the reconstruc-tion effort he and Bourne had called for in the pages of the old *Seven Arts*—a prophet, a "chosen man." He was to be the fourth "in the American line of Emerson, Whitman and William James." Later in his life Brooks would tell Archibald MacLeish, " 'When this period is over and people can see it in perspective, those who are capable of appraising it will find that the great man of this time was Lewis Mumford.' "[38]

It was *The Golden Day* that convinced Brooks of his friend's genius. And Brooks was not alone in his extravagant praise for that book. "This is the best book about America, if not the best American book that I have ever read," George Santayana wrote Mumford.[39]

Mumford's new book didn't make him wealthy, but it sold much better than his previous books, over 4,000 copies. These royalties, however modest, along with the by-products of the book's success—lectures and invitations to publish for better-paying magazines like *The Saturday Review, The Atlantic Monthly,* and *Scribner's Magazine*—gave him and Sophia more financial security than they had ever enjoyed before. His income climbed to around $5,000 a year; whereas in 1926, a good year by previous standards, he brought in $2,900 ($600 of which went to his mother).

More importantly to him, *The Golden Day* set the seal on his reputation as a first-rate literary and philosophic mind, an all-around man of letters. With its publication, even Sophia's old associates from *The Dial* began to look on him as a literary man; psychologically, this was terribly important to him.

But Mumford also wanted his book to make a difference in the world—to change people's minds. He thought of it as a radical, even a revolutionary book. The difference between the prewar socialists "and those of us who have survived and kept our wits," he wrote Van Wyck Brooks in 1925, "is that they, essentially, were contented with an uprising, which would transfer power from one class to another, whereas we want . . . a revolutionary social change which will displace a mean and inferior kind of life with a completely different kind. An uprising merely means a new deal; a revolution means a different kind of game."[40]

In this struggle Mumford thought he had, in Brooks, a lifelong ally. Together they might accomplish great things. "Emerson was right," Brooks wrote him, "when he said that it only needs two or three men to give a new turn to the public mind."[41] Every page of *The Golden Day* declares Mumford's equal faith in the power of an inspired few to bring important changes to the world.

Mumford was not, however, to have Brooks for long as a fellow soldier in this campaign for "revolutionary social change." As these two friends entered the 1930s their interests and ideas began to diverge sharply. For Brooks, the Emerson biography was the beginning of a lifelong preoccupation with the American past. In 1931 he miraculously pulled out of a five-year-long mental crisis that had stopped his work and brought him to the brink of suicide. That year he began reading the first of the some 5,000 books of every genre he would consult for his multivolume study of the American literary mind. Although Mumford refused to criticize in print his friend's work-in-progress, for fear that this might upset Brooks's delicate mental balance, he found these books thin and sentimental; they lacked the bite and social thrust of Brooks's earlier essays.

Beginning with *The Flowering of New England*, published in 1936, Brooks deftly described the cultural milieu of our major and minor writers, but made almost no effort to capture or criticize their leading works and ideas. These historic panoramas were, Mumford felt, the work of a gifted portrait painter, an artist no longer interested in looking beneath the surface of things. Once Brooks emerged from his psychological ordeal he refused to ever again face the darker side of experience, refused to even function as a critic.

Instead, he labored to piece together what Mumford once described as a "new kind of history, a poet's history, replete with living images of people and places and events, as brilliant as a patchwork quilt." But privately, in letters to other friends, and in his own notebooks, Mumford was more candid. There was something of immense importance missing in Brooks's picture of the past, one entire side of the human experience—the tragic side—which he knew that Brooks, in his precariously unsteady state of mind, could not confront.[42]

By 1931, Mumford, too, had reached an important juncture in his career. He had just written the last of his American studies (with the exception of a later book of essays on the architecture of the South), and he was ready to take on new themes encompassing all of Western civilization. While Brooks looked backward for the solace and stability he desperately needed in his life, Mumford was eager to move forward into unexplored territory. But before he began his four-volume Renewal of Life series, a project even more ambitious than Brooks's history of American literature, he passed through a trial that almost broke his spirit. Van Wyck Brooks had his "season in Hell." After helping to put his friend on the path to recovery, Mumford would pass through an almost as difficult "period in Purgatorio."

14

A Period in Purgatorio

In living one swims through seas strewn with wrecks,
where none go undamaged. It is as bad as going to Congress:
none comes back innocent.

—RALPH WALDO EMERSON

In *The Golden Day* Mumford called for a new American literature, stirring works of vision and imagination that would inspire a second national awakening in the arts. The very year his book appeared he was drawn into a project to promote the work of writers in whom he glimpsed the promise of such a rejuvenated America.

The American Caravan was born in the mind of Paul Rosenfeld, *The Dial's* music critic, who became Mumford's closest literary friend in these years. Mumford had met Rosenfeld in New York early in the decade, but it was not until the period from 1926 to 1936, when they worked together on *The American Caravan* and saw each other frequently in New York, that their friendship solidified.

Rosenfeld was a disciple of Alfred Stieglitz, the doyen of American photographers, whose complete commitment to the arts he took as a sacred rule for living. In the manner of his master, Rosenfeld was always looking for ways to encourage the work of young artists and writers. In the summer of 1925, while vacationing at Stieglitz's Lake George retreat, he was drawn into nightly discussions with the poet Alfred Kreymborg on the sagging state of American magazine publishing. Rosenfeld was upset that there were so few outlets for the work of up-and-coming writers; *The Seven Arts*, *The Freeman*, and *Broom*, which Kreymborg had edited in Europe, had all disappeared, and *The Little Review* was about to go under, a casualty of the overbearing expense of producing a quality magazine for a select audience. These and other "little magazines" had been almost the sole hope of young experimenters, as established organs like *The Atlantic Monthly*, *Harper's*, and *Scribner's* were generally unreceptive to the new and the untried. Even *The Dial* sometimes turned down the work of promising Americans, like Ernest Hemingway, in favor of contributions from better-known Europeans. Rosenfeld was eager to start a new literary periodical, but Kreymborg, who had some sobering experience in experimental publishing, having edited three financially unsuccessful journals, talked him instead into doing a less expensive book-length miscellany along the lines of the Russian and American yearbooks of the nineteenth century. Before they left Lake George, Rosenfeld had convinced Kreymborg to help him publish such a volume.

This would still be an expensive undertaking, but, as luck would have it, the two friends found a sponsor that summer in Lake George Village. Samuel Ornitz, the literary editor of the Macaulay Company and a close friend of Kreymborg's, happened to be vacationing near Stieglitz's place with his family, and when he heard about the yearbook project he offered to underwrite it. His company, he promised, would give them an editorial free hand, provided they made every effort to keep the venture in the black. That fall contracts were signed in New York, and the new editors were given an office of their own in the Macaulay Company's building on Fourth Avenue.

Rosenfeld and Kreymborg had asked Mumford and Van Wyck Brooks to join them as coeditors. Mumford agreed at once, but Brooks was too ill to participate. (The editors ran his name on the opening *Caravan* anyway because he had been an inspiration to all of them.) Rosenfeld chose the name *The American Caravan* and Mumford composed the manifesto, sent out under Rosenfeld's name, inviting authors, "known or unknown," to submit manuscripts for the first yearbook, which was to be published in the fall of 1927.[1]

While all three editors gave a generous portion of their time to the *Caravan*, Paul Rosenfeld was the directing force of the enterprise over the course of its brief but brilliant history. This was a project wonderfully suited to his talents and inclinations. A native New York from a prosperous German-Jewish family with a taste for classical music, he had first made his mark as a contributor to *The Seven Arts*, where his friend and fellow Yale graduate, Waldo Frank, was an associate editor. By 1921 his essays on composers and orchestras in *The Dial* had gained him a reputation in some circles as this country's finest music critic.

Rosenfeld wrote on all the major European composers, but he became best known as the strongest advocate in the critical world of the new American composers, of robust, rising talents like Leo Ornstein, Ernest Bloch, Aaron Copland, Roger Sessions, and, later, Charles Ives. In *Port of New York* (1924), he issued an Emersonian call to American painters and musicians to embrace their country and make it better by their contributions. It had a great influence on Lewis Mumford, who read it the year it was published.

Rosenfeld could be a devastatingly tough critic, but the coat he wore most comfortably was that of a sympathetic promoter of what he considered the best of the art, literature, and music of his day. It was his firm belief that "the best attack on the bad is the loving understanding and exposition of the good." As his friend Aaron Copland once said of him, "Paul Rosenfeld was a music lover first and a critic afterward."[2]

Rosenfeld lived comfortably on a generous inheritance from his family, but he spent a good amount of his fortune on his artistic friends, particularly the younger ones, giving them money for rent, for books and instruments, and in the case of Sherwood Anderson and his second wife, the sculptor Tennessee Mitchell, for a vacation to Paris, Anderson's first trip overseas. Rosenfeld thought they should go in order to widen their cultural horizons, and he offered to pay their way, provided they agreed to have him along as their *cicerone*.

Meetings of the *Caravan* triumvirate—Rosenfeld, Mumford, and Kreymborg—were held every Saturday at Rosenfeld's apartment at 77 Irving Place, near Gramercy Park. "I do not remember any room in America," Alyse Gregory described Rosenfeld's living room, "that conveyed to me in so striking a manner the feeling of having been given its atmosphere by a person of taste—a Cosmopolitan and an epicure of the art of living."[3] Mumford would come in from Sunnyside for these all-day meetings, his briefcase bulging with stories, plays, essays, and poems he had read during the previous week. He and his two fellow editors would sit on the living room floor around several piles of manuscripts and debate the merits of each and every submission before they made a decision on publication.

This would sometimes lead to hotly contested arguments, but, to their surprise, they generally found themselves agreeing on what deserved publication in their yearbook and what did not. Their Saturday sessions were made all the more amiable by their obvious fondness for one another, leading Rosenfeld to describe their earliest meetings as "veritable kaffeeklatsches among old women."4

Although Mumford never became intimate friends with Kreymborg, he respected his literary judgment, and when they were together at Rosenfeld's apartment or at their editorial office on West Fourth Street these two native New Yorkers got along famously, joking and cursing at each other in German in imitation of a Weber and Fields dialogue. Kreymborg was a physically unassuming man—small, slight of build, and withdrawn—but inside him were flame and steel. As a struggling young writer living in a garret on West Fourteenth Street, he had supported himself for eight years largely by playing chess, winning tournament after tournament and almost beating the legendary Western champion Chajes. He eventually had to give up tournament chess because it exacted too great a toll on his health, but in succeeding years he went after a literary reputation with the same determination he brought to his chess game, publishing some forty books of poetry.

Although Mumford, Kreymborg, and Rosenfeld were somewhat removed from many of the slightly younger, more disillusioned writers of the decade, they welcomed their work and published it with pride. Among the younger writers who made an appearance at one time or another in the *Caravan* were William Faulkner, Robert Penn Warren, Erskine Caldwell, Delmore Schwartz, Katherine Anne Porter, Harry Crosby, Robert Cantwell, Jean Toomer, Hart Crane, and Richard Wright. The editors also received manuscripts from older, better-established writers, including work by Eugene O'Neill and Robert Frost. However, if they didn't feel that a piece fit their intentions they were not afraid to turn it down, regardless of the author's reputation. On one occasion they had the courage to reject a contribution from Gertrude Stein; on another they decided against a poem by Ezra Pound. After learning of their decision Pound, as Mumford recalls, "hurled such screamingly dirty abuse at us by letter that, for the honor of the human race, we threw it into the fire."[5]

Sometimes, however, the editors aggressively went after the work of a big-name writer in order to add luster to their fledgling enterprise. In his own account of the *Caravan* years, Kreymborg tells of their efforts to land the elusive Robert Frost, a perfectionist who hated to rush any of his work into print. On learning that Frost was in New York, Kreymborg invited him to Christmas dinner with the editors at Luchöws. Rosenfeld reserved a table for them underneath the huge electric tree in the restaurant, "and there," as Kreymborg tells it, "sat the Yankee blinking like a lost soul." Frost was known for his gift of improvisation and for his corrosive wit, but throughout the meal—a full-course turkey dinner accompanied by tall glasses of pilsener—he didn't utter a single word. "Mumford and Rosenfeld, masters at the art of conversation, began a brilliant tour of anecdotes, without once mentioning the desired manuscripts," Kreymborg recalls. "They ranged the world of life through the world of letters with a wealth of appropriate quotations." Frost began to thaw, but the cagey old poet didn't melt, although Kreymborg could tell that he was secretly enjoying himself. When they completed their meal Frost got up stiffly, thanked Rosenfeld and Mumford for inviting him, and walked with Kreymborg to the nearest subway station. He said nothing until they reached the entrance. Then a smile crossed his craggy face, and turning to Kreymborg he muttered dryly: "Jesus, Alfred, those fellows have read a lot of books." Several weeks later the editors received in the mail the manuscript of Frost's poem "The Walker."[6]

In their *Caravan* days Rosenfeld would invite the Mumfords over to his apartment on weekends for informal dinners, which he prepared and served himself. Lewis enjoyed these dinners immensely, and although he was not a partygoer he looked forward to his friend's celebrated literary evenings, with their salon atmosphere and lustrous roster of guests. Rosenfeld worshiped artists. "To have artists about one is wonderful," he once told Mumford, "and to be loved by them almost divine." At any one of these "evenings," as Rosenfeld called them, the guests might include Alfred Stieglitz and his wife, Georgia O'Keeffe, John Marin, Sherwood Anderson, Marianne Moore, Hart Crane, Carl Sandburg, Wallace Stevens, Mark Van Doren, Ernest Hemingway, Edmund Wilson, and Walter Lippmann. There would always be entertainment, invariably provided by the guests themselves. Aaron Copland or Leo Ornstein would play the piano, and Kreymborg and e. e. cummings would read their poetry. Throughout the evening Rosenfeld, dressed in one of his expensively tailored suits that made his round body look much sleeker than it was, would glide gracefully about the parlor mixing with his friends. At his parties some of the guests must have felt that they were living in the pages of a Balzac novel. Leaving a Rosenfeld party one evening, Mumford remembers thinking that "a dozen such salons might magically transform the spiritual life of the whole city."7

The first *American Caravan* was an instant success. The Literary Guild, whose membership was nearly 30,000, adopted it, and that, along with its favorable critical reception, gave the Macaulay Company confidence to publish three more *Caravans* in the following four years (in 1928, 1929, and 1931). Then after a lapse of five years, a final *Caravan* was published by the scholarly press W. W. Norton, although it was a financial failure.

The depression was hardly a propitious time for experimental publishing of this sort, and the 1930s were not good years either for Paul Rosenfeld. He lost a good portion of his family inheritance in the crash of 1929, and was eventually forced to give up 77 Irving Place and trim back his profuse lifestyle. He also found it more difficult to get his best work published, for many of his former outlets, like *The Dial*, had expired. And, too, Paul Rosenfeld's spirit, so ideally suited to the gay twenties, was badly out of tune with the social concerns of the thirties. Though many of Rosenfeld's more liberal friends stopped seeing him, Mumford remained loyal and continued to send him his work to review. He valued Rosenfeld's literary judgment over anyone else's and eventually made him one of his literary executors. He also promoted his work whenever he had the chance, and when he gave up his position as art critic at *The New Yorker* in the mid-thirties, he persuaded the editors to take on Rosenfeld as his successor. Rosenfeld's ornate style, however, did not sit well with *The New Yorker*'s editor, Harold Ross, who refused to print Rosenfeld's first two reviews, thereby terminating their informal agreement. This was a near-lethal blow to Rosenfeld's fast-declining career, and it injured his delicate sense of propriety. "Into what brand of brigands did you introduce me?" he angrily wrote Mumford in 1937. "I have never met with rawer treachery."[8]

Toward the end of the decade Rosenfeld contracted diabetes, but it was more than his failing health that caused some of the life to go out of him. His former exuberance was not unconnected to the kind of lifestyle his money had permitted him to live—free to travel widely, to buy expensive paintings and first editions, and to entertain lavishly when he felt like it. Mumford would still get together with him in New York whenever he could, and Rosenfeld would occasionally cook dinner for him in the kitchenette of his tiny apartment on West Eleventh Street, serving it "with his old air of largess though the crockery was becoming battered, [and] the glasses no longer matched." But the Paul Rosenfeld Mumford would remember with the greatest fondness was the all-including spirit of the early *Caravan* years, the voice of a new America they both saw emerging in the arts. Rosenfeld would always exemplify for him what was sound and fine in the art and life of the 1920s. He was the living embodiment of their "Great Expectations."[9]

Editing *The American Caravan* brought Mumford to the center of the New York literary world. H. L. Mencken and other editors who became his new friends were now eager to publish his work, and after all these years he was offered his first prestigious editorial position when Walter Lippmann asked him to join the staff at *The World*. This was an offer he would have pounced on earlier in his career, but now he turned it down, fearing that the job would take too much of his time. His present routine of "grubbing hard for half a year, and writing hard the other half . . . ," he told Lippmann, "gives me much more freedom and less daily strain than a steady editorial connection would."[10]

Mumford turned down several other attractive career opportunities that came his way, including two other editorial positions and an offer to become part-time art adviser to the Du Pont de Nemours Corporation. This last offer, which came in 1928, when he had little income, stirred some debate in the Mumford household. Sophia wanted him at least to ask the Du Pont people how much they might be willing to pay for his services. But he didn't want to do this, he emphatically told her, because he suspected that they might offer him an income at least three times his current one, an offer he might find too tempting to refuse. Besides, they had a nest egg of $2,000 tucked away in a postal-savings bank, money Lewis had received the previous year for assembling a library for the Manhattan office of the J. Walter Thompson advertising company. This money helped him and Sophia pay their bills until the royalties from his next book, a study of Herman Melville, began coming in.

In the spring of 1927, John Farrar of Doubleday, Doran had asked Lewis to write a critical study of Herman Melville for a series of short biographies his firm intended to publish. Just before this Lewis had turned down offers from several publishers to undertake books on architectural themes, one of them a biography of Frank Lloyd Wright. Literature had always interested him more than architecture, and he found Melville a fascinating subject. So he accepted Farrar's offer and that summer he began reading for his book while vacationing on Martha's Vineyard with Sophia and Geddes in a beach cottage a mile from their nearest neighbors, their Sunnyside friends, Charles and Helen Ascher.

The summer was not all Herman Melville, however. Mumford read some of Melville's early novels, but most of his working hours were given over to several literary projects. One of them was a sardonic autobiographical prose-poem, "The Little Testament of Bernard Martin, Aet. 30"; the other his partially completed play "Asters and Goldenrod." He finished both in July, and then wrote the first draft of a play on the building of the Brooklyn Bridge, a theme that had possessed him since his first childhood walks across the Roeblings' East River span.

"The Little Testament" was published in *The American Caravan*, but Mumford was never able to find a producer for "The Builders of the Bridge." This epic play (he was reading *War and Peace* at the time) was too sprawling a creation for the theater. The building of the Brooklyn Bridge was a theme better suited to the movies, Harold Clurman told him, although Clurman advised him that he would have to infuse more action into the play's central scenes if he hoped to get it accepted as a stage production or the outline of a film script. But Mumford suspected that Clurman was merely being courteous.

"In its present form" the play "is bad, very bad," he wrote dejectedly in his notes.[11] And he was dead right. "The Builders of the Bridge" lacks dramatic concentration and quick, undivertible movement, essential characteristics of successful drama. As in his other plays, Mumford failed to keep a disciplined rein on the dialogue, and the characters tend to ramble on, tediously announcing their views, with almost liturgical solemnity, on politics, labor, engineering, marital and extramarital love, and the state of civilization. The clumsy love scenes are particularly revealing of Mumford's limitations as a writer of fiction, and even the climactic scenes are flat and prosaic.

Mumford has claimed that no creation of his ever came forth more easily, and it is no wonder, for "The Builders of the Bridge"—and this is its dominant problem—is not really about the building of the Brooklyn Bridge. It is a play about Lewis Mumford's state of mind at the time he wrote it, a creation more interesting, perhaps, to a biographer than to any potential theater or film producer.

Before he began working on the play Mumford wrote himself this revealing note:

> Future work. Plan play, woven around the building of the Brooklyn Bridge. Show conflict between the man, intent upon *getting his work done*, and the woman, intent upon extracting happiness and companionship out of the day's mixture. Her case as well as his. His insatiable restlessness. Hers, too, is one of the lives sacrificed in the building of the Bridge. All this against the sordid background of the seventies.[12]

Substitute Lewis and Sophia for the two main characters; change the words "Brooklyn Bridge" to "book," and the "sordid seventies" to the "sordid twenties" and you have what was really on Mumford's mind when he sat down to write this play.

The play came forth at a critical juncture in his development, just as he entered his thirties and had achieved, he thought, greater emotional maturity. He was in top health; his career was going well; he and Sophia were new parents; and their relationship seemed to be on a more even keel. Still, he continued to be plagued by inner doubts and frustrations, most of them, at base, emotional and sexual. In his late adolescence, troubled by mounting sexual and personal frustrations, he had poured out his feelings in a succession of callow but self-illuminating plays, most notably "The Invalids." Now once again, he turned to playwriting, unconsciously transposing into art feelings he found impossible to express to even those closest to him.

Years later Mumford would claim that he wrote this play under almost idyllic conditions.[13] Every morning he would rise with the sun and walk to a tiny shack near their bungalow to write, leaving the door open to hear the pounding of the ocean surf and to feel the sea breeze at his back. When he finished toward late morning, if the low-lying mist lifted and day broke clear, he would walk the half mile over the sloping moors to the golden-gray beach, where Sophia, with Geddes in tow, would join him later in the afternoon, after she had finished with the washing and other household chores.

This might have been a perfect daily routine for him, but it certainly wasn't for Sophia; and that summer she was in a sullen mood, something her husband doesn't mention in his later account. It was actually a trying time for both of them, a prelude to greater domestic difficulties. Sophia had had a miscarriage the previous winter, and just before leaving for the Vineyard they had taken possession of their new home in Sunnyside Gardens, a move that left them both exhausted and on edge. Lewis was able to catch his breath by losing himself in his work, but Sophia had to tend to Geddes, an eager-spirited two-year-old still in diapers. That was draining enough; but then early in July Geddes scalded himself severely with hot tea, and for a full month had to have his burns treated several times a day. These responsibilities fell on Sophia's shoulders, for Lewis had his work to do. She had never challenged this order of priorities, but now his extreme self-engrossment began to affect her more noticeably. She had given up her career to have a family, and she thought that her husband wasn't giving enough of himself to her and Geddes.

Another sore spot in their relationship was the presence of Helen Ascher, a small, darkly attractive woman who adored Lewis. Sophia resented Helen's brazen pursuit of other men, and when that summer Helen began to flirt openly with Lewis she began to see her as a rival for her husband's affection. Lewis, who liked to flirt himself, made matters worse by doing nothing to discourage Helen's undisguised interest in him. Still, in the back of her mind, Sophia believed that her husband would never stray from her. For Sophia, the real problem that summer was not Helen Ascher; it was the amount of time that Lewis gave to his work, to the almost complete exclusion of all else. He, too, began to see this as a festering problem in their relationship, transposing this conflict between marriage and career into the central scenes of "The Builders of the Bridge."

"My work is my play. . . . Building bridges is the nicest thing in the world!" Jefferson Baumgarten (a fictionalized Washington Roebling) announces to his dutiful but discontented wife, Margaret, in one of the play's more transparently autobiographical scenes. The bridge has become his life, and he will not let anything, not even the emotional needs of his family, stand in the way of its completion. Margaret knows she will never change him and she refuses to stand in the way of his pursuit of greatness. She simply wishes she had "a little more" of him.

But there is another looming problem in their relationship—a side of her husband's personality Margaret is not yet completely aware of. This becomes clear one evening when Jefferson takes Margaret's spirited younger sister, Lola, to the top of the pier of his unfinished bridge, and there takes her into his arms and kisses her passionately, only to pull away when she coyly encourages his advances. In this scene we are given a glimpse of another Jefferson Baumgarten. To all who know him, he is a sober bridge-builder and loyal husband, committed to a coldly exacting work routine. Yet behind his controlled exterior is a blazing furnace of emotions. He is a dreamer and artist with sexual urges he has so far managed to blunt and block. His wife, he tells Lola, is no longer as daring and bright-spirited as she was when they had climbed together in the Austrian Alps as newlyweds. Now she will not even climb to the top of his bridge to see his work. He admits he is still drawn to her sexually, but, lately, when he wants to get "really intimate" with her she is usually preoccupied with the children. Around her he feels emotionally cramped and domesticated. But alone with Lola, high on top of his bridge, he opens up—if only for a moment.

Later in his life Mumford mentions that this love scene fore-shadowed a future encounter, and although he never says so, this was probably with Josephine Strongin. Lola is as radiantly alive as he found Jo to be when they first met in Geneva in 1925, and she is the same age as Jo was in 1927, barely eighteen. Josephine Strongin was then living in Richmond Hill, Queens, and she and Lewis would often take afternoon walks together in Central Park. In the spring of 1928 they spent a day together at Shirley Center visiting Benton MacKaye, and although we will never know exactly what happened that day, their letters suggest that they almost became intimate and that she, in her shy, teasing way, urged him on. But he, like Jefferson Baumgarten, withdrew, still unprepared to act on his innermost desires. Besides, he felt like an "uncle" to her. "You've seen only one side of me," Jefferson tells Lola after the spell of the evening has been broken by his abrupt declaration that he can't go further because he is her brother-in-law, after all. "Margaret has seen that: she has seen a hundred other sides, too. . . . If you wish to know all that love is capable of you must be married; take the stormy days with the calm: July madness with November frosts." However far Lewis Mumford might stray from his marriage in the coming years, it was this attitude toward marriage and infidelity, along with his deep love for Sophia, that would always draw him back to her. In this way as well, his play is self-revealing and remarkably prophetic. [14]

If Jefferson Baumgarten represents one side of Mumford's character, Robert-Owen Benns represents the other, complementary side. Benns, the philosophic artist, is the spokesman in the play for Mumford's own views on art and social issues, and it is he who delivers the play's central message to Baumgarten in the climactic scene. The bridge has been completed, the opening ceremonies are about to commence, yet Baumgarten, gazing at his masterwork from his home on Brooklyn Heights, feels strangely empty, and he can't understand why. His problem, Benns tells him, is that this time he has reached his goal. "Next time try something you can't reach." [15]

Dare to do more. Reach ever higher. Think more heroically. When Mumford wrote these lines on Martha's Vineyard in late August 1927, he was obviously urging himself on to new challenges. Why do a modest study of Herman Melville? Why not expand this project into a full-scale account of that titan's art and vision? Mumford wanted to write a book more ambitious than any he had undertaken thus far, and Melville, he was beginning to see, was just the right subject, for in Melville's work he discovered something that he had failed to give sufficient expression to in his own work—what he called the tragic sense of life, "the sense that the highest flight is sustained over an unconquered and perhaps unconquerable abyss."[16]

Mumford was also in an autobiographical mood, anxious to review his own development and to examine his current way of living; and in approaching Melville he discovered a kindred spirit whose problems and personal concerns were similar to his own. All this enhanced his interest in the biography, and before he was finished he would put more of himself into this book than into anything else he had written. But in doing this he fell into the trap that lies waiting for every sympathetic biographer—he became one with his subject. At times it is impossible to tell whether Mumford is writing about Herman Melville or about himself, so close is the identification. Yet this is the real importance of Mumford's *Herman Melville*; it is his most self-revealing book and the clearest expression of his matured moral outlook.

Mumford wrote his Melville biography in one creative surge, completing the book just over a year after beginning the research. For the facts of Melville's life he relied on Raymond M. Weaver's *Herman Melville: Mariner and Mystic*, the first biography of Melville, which appeared in 1921, and on Melville's own novels, particularly the early sea tales, which he mistakenly took to be reliably autobiographical. Midway through the second draft he went on a two-week research trip to dig up new materials and to check his interpretations against the available facts of Melville's life. He first went to the New York Public Library to read the correspondence of Melville's literary friend, Evert Duyckinck; then to Edgartown for several days to interview Melville's granddaughter, Mrs. Eleanor Melville Metcalf, who allowed him to examine her grandfather's journals. On his return, he stayed for several days on Martha's Vineyard with the Aschers, and this time he almost became intimate with Helen, who was "brown and warm and tempting."[17]

Except for some unprinted materials that Weaver loaned him and a trip to Pittsfield, Melville's home in the Berkshires, this was roughly the extent of Mumford's firsthand research. He would like to have done more, but writing, his chief passion, was also his chief means of earning a living, and he wanted to get the book out by early 1929 because he and Sophia were expecting another baby then. "I am dependent upon my books for income," he confided to a fellow Melville scholar, "and must publish them when the wolf barks at my door, whether they are complete or incomplete, infirm or final."[18]

Considered sheerly as a feat in concentrated writing, the Melville book is a tour de force. Mumford began writing it at Sunnyside Gardens in the early winter of 1928 and had completed almost 30,000 words by the end of the first month of work. He stopped for a month or so to coedit a second *American Caravan*, write a three-part essay on regionalism, and edit and help revise Benton Mac-Kaye's *The New Exploration*, then returned to the biography in the late spring, finishing the final draft toward the end of the summer at Leedsville in another cottage he and Sophia rented from Joel Spingarn.

In the Dutchess County countryside Mumford was restored to top form, physically and mentally, and every morning he was at his desk by eight o'clock. He usually worked straight through until noon, producing from 2,000 to 4,000 words, and after lunch he would spend the afternoons swimming, hiking, reading, or lounging around with his Troutbeck neighbors, Joel Spingarn and Walter Pach. In the evenings he was back in his tiny makeshift study preparing his notes for the following day. "All the internal engines are working like a Rolls-Royce on a perfect road," he wrote Jerry Lachenbruch.[19]

By this time Mumford had a new publisher for the book, which he thought was becoming far too ambitious a biography for Doubleday, Doran's series of literary studies. Boni and Liveright, publisher of Mumford's three previous books, would have seemed the obvious next choice, but Horace Liveright wasn't that interested in the book.

Liveright was then one of the hottest publishers in New York. Since forming his firm with Albert Boni in 1917 he had published, among others, Freud, Faulkner, Hemingway, Pound, Eliot, cummings, O'Neill, Anderson, and Dreiser. But he lived recklessly and flamboyantly, and that, unfortunately, is exactly how he ran his press. In 1924 he did a business of over one million dollars and at the end of the year he didn't have a nickel in the bank. "Seven men in the organization had the authority to run in bills for 'entertainment,'" Bennett Cerf, his former partner, wrote of his association with

Liveright. "Authors in the waiting room were often outnumbered by bootleggers. One of the big executives had a bottle of whiskey in every drawer of his desk, the top of which was piled inches high with weeks-old communications of the greatest importance."[20]

On top of this, Liveright lost vast amounts of money in the stock market and on a succession of ill-fated theater productions, the stage being one of his leading passions. Mumford had earlier approached him about producing one of his plays, and for a time Liveright seemed interested; but when Mumford went to him with his Melville project he got a lukewarm reception. Liveright probably would have printed the book had Mumford pressed him, but Mumford was not sure that Liveright's preoccupation with women, drink, and the theater would provide "a safe haven" for his later books. So he hastily outlined a program for three future books, offering it, along with his Melville biography, to four other publishers who had expressed an interest in his work. He found that his stock had risen substantially; all of these publishers were willing to give him almost anything within reason that he asked for. He finally decided to go with Harcourt, Brace (Joel Spingarn's firm), then one of New York's newer, more adventurous publishers. Alfred Harcourt agreed to give him 15 percent of royalties starting from the sale of the first book, a handsome offer that sealed an association which lasted into the late 1970s.[21]

When Mumford's *Herman Melville* came out in early 1929 it was received enthusiastically by most reviewers, including some outstanding Melville scholars. The influential critic Thomas Beer found it "the best biography of a man of letters yet written by an American"; and while some reviewers protested that Mumford strained too hard to establish Melville's largeness as a writer (he insisted that *Moby Dick* was a work the equal of *Hamlet, The Divine Comedy,* and *War and Peace*), there was general, if not unanimous agreement that Mumford had come forward with the most completely satisfactory book on Melville to date.[22]

Melville scholarship was then in its infancy; it was only in the 1920s that Melville began to be recognized as a writer of world stature, and Mumford's book helped to solidify that status. It appeared almost forty years after Melville's obscure death in a red-brick house on Manhattan's East Twenty-sixth Street. In the literature textbooks of the time he was seen as a minor writer of sea tales, a "man who lived among the cannibals" and returned to write about his adventures. *Moby Dick* was widely referred to as a rousing whaling story "spoiled by a crazy bent for allegory," and hardly anyone remembered that Melville had written anything after *Moby Dick*. In his final years Melville was regarded by those few who knew of his later work as an eccentric and a misanthrope.[23]

All this had begun to change in 1917, two years before the one hundredth anniversary of Melville's birth, when Carl Van Doren published a modest four-page appreciation of his work in the new *Cambridge History of American Literature*. That same year Van Doren had persuaded young Raymond Weaver to write an article on Melville for *The Nation*, and Weaver followed this with a biography. In the next several years, Frank Jewett Mather, John Freeman, D. H. Lawrence, Van Wyck Brooks, and Percy H. Boynton aided in the work of resurrection.[24]

Mumford's biography was published at the midpoint of this Melville revival, and he could not have written it in such a short period of time without Weaver's pioneering work on the outlines of Melville's life. Mumford, however, was less interested in chronicling Melville's life than in writing a passionately personal account of Herman Melville, the writer and the man. It was Melville's personality and personal development that aroused his interest; that and his vision of life, so close to the Puritan sense of darkness and intrinsic limitation. In his biography Mumford considers Melville as a moral philosopher, like Dante, who gave forth his ideas in poetic form. Herman Melville "lives for us . . . because he grappled with certain great dilemmas in man's spiritual life, and in seeking to answer them, sounded bottom."[25]

Melville was a "diver," Mumford confided to Jo Strongin just before he began his biography, one who knifed beneath the surface of life to explore the darkest depths of the human psyche. In doing this he had paid a harrowing personal price, almost slipping into madness; but unless one becomes "a diver" at some point in one's life "one remains a superficial [person] in the sense of never being aware of anything but the surface." Clearly, Mumford was referring to himself here; he had been far too "timid and unadventurous" in his work and his emotional life.[26] Writing about Melville would give him an opportunity to deal with moral and explosively personal issues he had treated only cursorily and rather callowly in his previous writings. Only in coming closer to Herman Melville he hoped to avoid Melville's "destiny," as he called it. As it turned out, he almost didn't.

The high point of Mumford's biography is its powerful and pene-trating analysis of *Moby Dick*. Mumford undoubtedly read more into this poetic epic than Melville consciously put there, yet herein lies the significance of his analysis for the biographer. In summing up Melville's vision of life Mumford formulated for the first time his own innermost moral beliefs. In this chapter on *Moby Dick* there is a fusion of novelist and biographer which creates a tone unlike any in modern biography. It is as if Mumford has become Herman Melville, returned from the grave to explain his words and work to a modern audience. Mumford even takes the liberty of using Melville's own language to describe his subject's "experience and his state of mind," omitting quotation marks, thereby making it almost impossible to recognize whose voice we are hearing, that of Herman Melville or his empathetic interpreter.

It is in *Moby Dick*, according to Mumford, that Melville exhibits his greatest strength as a thinker: his unobscured awareness of evil and his refusal to be overwhelmed by it. Unlike his great rival, the eternally optimistic Emerson, Melville "had an eye for the dank-ness, decay and for the inscrutable malevolence of the universe: he was no sun-dial that recorded only the smiling hours of life." Yet this same writer, who knew that death and blankness awaited us all, struggled in his art to give some purpose and moral meaning to our ultimately hopeless strivings against the unconquerable forces of the universe. That, to Mumford, was Melville's true significance. He showed us why life, in the end, was worth living. More than that, he gave us a lesson in how to live it intently.

Mumford saw the white whale, not Ahab or Ishmael, as the central figure in *Moby Dick*. To every reader of that novel, of course, the whale stands for something different, something closer, per-haps, to the reader's own vision and temperament than to the author's. For Mumford, the white whale is the universe, the untamed forces of "Nature and Destiny," and the novel is primarily "a parable on the mystery of evil and the accidental malice of the universe." While the whale represents the blind overpowering forces of nature, Ahab is "the spirit of man, small and feeble, but purposive, that puts its puniness against this might, and its purpose against the blank senselessness of power." In this deadly, uneven struggle Ahab comes to a tragic end. It is not that he is beaten; that isn't tragic, it's inevitable. It is that he is consumed by the very evil he has set out to conquer. In his vengeful war with the great beast he is made over into the image of the thing he despises. His heroic self-defiance—his unwillingness to bow down and accept evil—becomes in the end utter madness. In the act of asserting his humanity, tragically, he loses it.

This happens, Mumford argues, because he battles evil "with power instead of love." The very things that Ahab throws off in his fanatical pursuit of the whale, "the love and loyalty of Pip, the memory of his wife and child, the sextant of science, the inner sense of calm, which makes all external struggle futile, are the very things that would redeem him and make him victorious." He was destined to lose this struggle with the whale, no matter what; yet in losing it he might have saved a part of himself.

The universe *is* blank and meaningless—Mumford reads his own meaning into Ahab's demise—but power is not the way to bring to it some discipline and significance. "Growth, cultivation, order, art—these are the proper means by which man displaces accident and subdues the vacant external powers of the universe: the way of growth is not to become more powerful but to become more human." Reading Melville, Mumford began to see all of history as a tale of man's unending effort to conquer the whale, "to create a purpose that will offset the empty malice of Moby-Dick." Without such purpose life seemed to Mumford neither bearable nor significant. Melville, as well as any other writer who sent his words into print, understood this; and his own method of battling the universe, of declaring his humanity—the method of art—was superior to Ahab's. Mumford took "art" to mean "all humanizing effort"—poetry, myth, science, city building, simple faith; it is the means by which man "circumvents or postpones his doom, and bravely meets his tragic destiny. Not tame and gentle bliss, but disaster, heroically encountered, is man's true happy ending." With these words Mumford summed up his underlying "faith for living" and gave a foreshadowing of the central moral theme of all of his subsequent work.

Still, Ahab remained for Mumford an essentially noble figure.

Man's physical powers will perhaps never be commensurate with his spirit, but that defiant spirit which led Ahab (and Melville) to battle against the universe is ultimately what justifies living, even though we face certain defeat. Dostoyevsky's hero says that if there is no god we may commit murder. For Mumford, God represents "the totality of human purposes and meanings," the best of what Patrick Geddes called the social heritage—a realm of ideas and excellent practices that is "independent of the hostile forces in the universe and cannot be lightly shaken by their onslaught."

But in *Moby Dick* Melville does much more than call for a more human-directed culture. Like Frank Lloyd Wright's architecture, Melville's epic, Mumford argues, points the way to a new age of organic balance. *Moby Dick* is many things in one: it is a work of mythology and of exact science, of metaphysics and of seagoing exploration, a stirring adventure tale that is also an accurate account of whaling and of the anatomy and ecology of the whale. In this respect, it is a true work of synthesis, one that "brings together the two dissevered halves of the modern world and the modern self—its positive, practical, scientific, externalized self, bent on conquest and knowledge, and its imaginative, ideal half, bent on the transposition of conflict into art, and power into humanity."[27] Reading Melville's contribution this way, Mumford turned that dark genius into a prophet of renewal, a great dreamer and inspirer not unlike Emerson, his philosophic opposite. It is doubtful, however, that Melville, or Emerson for that matter, would have appreciated the comparison.

Mumford's biography is actually two books: an audaciously speculative assessment of Melville's writing, and an astute dissection of his life. It is the first full-scale effort to examine the "hidden soul" of Herman Melville, and it stands with Van Wyck Brooks's earlier work *The Ordeal of Mark Twain* as one of the first psychological biographies in American letters. Tell me your dreams and I will tell you what kind of person you are, Emerson had said.[28] Mumford had no evidence of Melville's actual dreams, but he believed he had equally reliable clues to his interior life—his writings of a lifetime, the truest projections of his innermost feelings.

Mumford, however, relied on this kind of evidence far too heavily, using Melville's writings not simply as records of his subjective life but as clues to the actual outer events of his life. For his reconstruction of Melville's early manhood, for example, he relied upon Melville's early sea tales, *Typee, Omoo, Redburn,* and *White Jacket,* but as later Melville scholars would discover, these autobiographical books are untrustworthy sources for the facts of Melville's life. Thus when Melville describes White Jacket's fall from the mast and his near escape from flogging, Mumford assumes that he is writing autobiographically, when in fact both events have been shown to be sheerly imaginative. [29]

All this is perhaps pardonable, given the undeveloped state of Melville scholarship at the time Mumford was writing his biography. Yet even when the sources *were* available to Mumford, he sometimes failed to consult them, or failed to scrutinize them closely enough because of his haste to get his book into print. This pressure to publish, as much as his decision to use Melville's fiction as a biographical source, caused Mumford to commit some calamitous mistakes, which some reviewers spotted immediately. [30]

Still, a number of scholarly arbiters argued that this was a work of criticism "so penetrating that we can hardly doubt its accuracy as a reproduction of the mind of Herman Melville." [31] The real question we ought to ask ourselves is not how Mumford could have made so many mistakes in the book, but how he could have written so convincing an interpretation of Herman Melville, given his scanty research and the amazingly short period of time it took him to complete the book. And the answer, we already know, is that Mumford was not writing about Melville primarily, but about himself. As one of his closest friends commented to him after reading his biography: "from cover to cover it is YOU." [32]

Mumford read into Melville's early life some of the patterns of his own forming as a writer and as a man. While it would be too tedious to recount all the places in the biography where he did so, some attention must be given to the more significant intersections he discovered in their lives, for these throw light on his own view of himself just before he descended into a soul-searing emotional crisis.

Melville had not been illegitimate, but he had lost his father on the eve of adolescence, and from age thirteen he was raised by a discontented, intellectually shallow woman in what has been described as a kind of genteel poverty. His mother, like Mumford's, never gave him the kind of attention he inwardly craved; and one of his biographers observes, "it was not long before a sense of orphanhood began to grow upon him."[33]

Melville was a reserved, politely amiable boy, but inside him was a boiling emotional life; he was torn by tensions he would never completely resolve. Although strongly attracted to women, he suffered from some kind of sexual blockage and was probably, Mumford speculates, "abstinent sexually during his nonage." Melville was also torn by a conflict between freedom and duty. He wanted desperately to break away from his suffocating household, to experience the world on his own, but he felt an obligation to remain at home and help support his mother and sisters. This was the same kind of guilt-edged sense of duty that had entered Mumford's relations with his own mother and his childhood nurse.

Melville, all his biographers agree, never completely shed these early anxieties about sex and financial insecurity, but in these same troubled years his talents were being forged, arguably, by the very factors that were cramping and limiting him emotionally. This is one of the central paradoxes of Herman Melville's development, and of Lewis Mumford's as well. And we have more than a hint that Mumford was aware of this in the passage in the biography where he attributes Melville's awakening interest in writing to the "reflective turn" he acquired as a result of his narrowly confined childhood, of what Mumford calls, interestingly, Melville's period of "invalidism." "In such dull, quiet states is the beginning of a meditative life." Here again Mumford seems to have been arguing more from the facts of his own life than from Melville's. And while Mumford doesn't quite say this, the mental talents and habits Melville developed in these early years were to be that writer's instrument of liberation from the aimless kind of life his mother and the rest of her family led. In this Melville, too, we see Mumford's reflected image.

When Melville finally broke away from home to go to sea for the first time (with a long stopover in England), Mumford relates this experience in words suspiciously reminiscent of his own impressions of his days at Le Play House, *his* first extended stay away from home. "There is no better experience for a well-prepared lad than to be thrown in a strange city, not too remote in habit and culture from his original home, with long days for exploration, experience, meditation." This, Mumford insists, perhaps too didactically, is what finally made Melville a true writer: he learned of life firsthand, "in a whaling ship and in cities like Liverpool."³⁴ We know, of course, that New York had been all this to young Mumford, his Yale College and his Harvard. What he learned and what he saw there became as important to his development as a critic as Melville's adventures in the South Seas were to his development as a novelist. And so Mumford goes on, explaining nearly every critical point of Melville's forming in terms of his own life experience.

When Mumford's Melville returns from the South Seas to Boston in 1844 he is prepared, as Mumford had seen himself prepared in 1920, for the attempted leap to "greatness." Melville had once said that until he was almost twenty-five he had hardly developed at all; that from his twenty-fifth year he dated his life. That "could be said of my life too," Mumford would remark later.³⁵

Fully a third of Mumford's biography is given over to Melville's life after he completed *Moby Dick*, the forty-year period Weaver has called The Long Quietus, when Melville, after a concentrated spurt of creativity in the 1850s, ceased to be a breadwinning writer and faded into obscurity. Mumford felt that Weaver had given insufficient attention to this part of Melville's life, and that Melville was neither a misanthrope nor a man close to madness in the last part of his life, as Weaver claimed. After a near breakdown following the shattering ordeal of completing *Moby Dick* in little more than a year, Melville recovered his energies, if not all his creative powers, and produced some subtly crafted work, including *Billy Budd*, solid proof, Mumford argues, that he was not mentally unbalanced. Toward the end of his life he ceased to be a tense, bitter, harassed man, and developed a warm relationship with his wife Elizabeth and with his grandchildren.³⁶

Several reviewers found this—the dispelling of the "legend of misanthropy and even of insanity that has gathered about Melville's hidden years"—one of the main merits of Mumford's biography.³⁷ But there were a few dissenters, most prominently the influential critic Joseph Wood Krutch. "Mr. Mumford understands the harmonies of Melville, but he is distressed by those dissonances which form so conspicuous a part of his music," Krutch shrewdly pointed out. ". . . He speaks of Melville's 'demon,' but it is just this creature

which eludes him; he refers . . . to the depths of sunless ocean and
the blackness of interstellar space from which his hero brought back
the tragic sense of life, but it is from just these depths and black-
nesses that he prefers to turn away his eyes—perhaps because he is
determined to make Melville more truly a part of the Golden Day of
New England than he really was."38

This is one explanation for Mumford's sanguine view of Melville's
life and vision. But there is much more to it than this, as Mumford
himself admitted at the time his book was published to his new
friend and fellow Melville scholar, Dr. Henry A. Murray, head of
Harvard's Psychological Clinic. Murray felt that Mumford's biography was true to the spirit of Melville's life up to the time he began
Moby Dick, "but at this point Melville discovered the Unconscious
and commenced to explore it," and, in the process, "proceeded to
lose himself." It is dangerous, Murray argued in his review in *The
New England Quarterly*, to follow Melville into these " 'boundless
deeps,' " yet "such a sojourn in darkness and chaos might lead to an
awareness of Melville's dilemma which would differ somewhat from
the intellectual formulations presented by Mumford."39

Throughout his life Mumford remained exceedingly sensitive to
criticism, especially when it was delivered in print. He never forgave Krutch, whom he disliked personally, for his review, yet he
took Murray's criticism in stride. Both Krutch and Murray had
located what he realized was the central flaw of his book, but
Murray was a friend and Krutch was not; and Mumford badly
needed a close friend and confidant at this point in his life. At the
time he read Murray's review he was in the advanced stages of a
severe depression, and in Murray he had found someone to whom
he could reveal the true reasons he had not approached closer to the
darker side of Herman Melville.

With the single exception of Patrick Geddes, no person made a more
powerful first impression on Mumford than Henry Murray. Indeed,
in Murray Mumford discovered a truly Geddesian figure, brilliant
and far-ranging in his interests: a surgeon, psychologist, research
scientist in physiological chemistry, student of literature, biblical
studies, and medieval philosophy. And what is more, Mumford
found Murray, a handsome man with sparkling eyes and immense

charm, far easier to get along with than Geddes. Murray was not only a convivial conversationalist, but also a patient, sympathetic listener. Mumford never had a father confessor, but Henry Murray—Harry as his friends called him—came as close to filling that role as anyone. "Falling in friendship is a rarer thing, I think, than falling in love," Mumford wrote Murray not long after meeting him, "and while I have a handful of partial friendships, I have yet to experience a friendship that is complete, that involves all one's attitudes and interests."[40]

When Mumford first met him Murray was at a turning point in his life. He had just decided to abandon medicine and biological research for a career in psychology, and Herman Melville loomed large in that decision.

Two years older than Mumford, Murray came from a wealthy New York family and had attended Harvard, where he majored in history and was a superb athlete and notorious playboy. Although he would become one of the formative figures in modern American psychology, Murray showed no interest in psychology as an undergraduate. He attended one psychology lecture—it bored him and he walked out.

After Harvard he went on to study medicine, eventually practicing surgery for two years at Presbyterian Hospital in New York, but he soon discovered that his interest was research, in this case the chemistry of embryology, and for several years he was at the Rockefeller Institute of Medicine, where he did some path-clearing work in the field. In 1927, one year before he met Mumford, he took his Ph.D. in physiological chemistry from Cambridge University. But by this time his interests had shifted to psychology and to Herman Melville—interests not unrelated.

Earlier in the decade, as a young physician, Murray had read *Moby Dick* on board ship on one of his annual trips to England, and the novel transformed his life. Melville opened up to him the mysterious territory of the unconscious, that dark genius's "world of wondrous depths."[41] Not long after this magical immersion in Melville, Murray read Carl Jung's *Psychological Types*, and, after spending three weeks undergoing analysis with Jung in Zurich, he became permanently interested in psychology. In 1926, when his friend Dr. Morton Prince founded the Harvard Psychological Clinic for research and for the treatment of psychoneurotics, he asked

Murray to assist him, even though Murray at the time had no professional training in the field of psychology. Murray remained at Harvard for the remainder of his career, becoming director of the clinic in 1929. Almost a decade later he published *Explorations in Personality* (1938), one of the half dozen most influential books in American psychology. And with Christiana D. Morgan, his colleague and mistress, he developed the Thematic Apperception Test, a widely utilized method for the investigation of personality that employs the device of storytelling to uncover the patient's deepest assumption about himself and his world.

In the late 1920s, while still practicing surgery and doing research in embryology at the Rockefeller Institute, Murray would spend several evenings a week at the New York Public Library doing research for a biography of Melville, who, he believed, had anticipated at least a dozen or so of Freud's most penetrating discoveries. He never completed this work of a lifetime, but he later published a handful of essays that rearranged the terrain of Melville scholarship. Murray, a perfectionist, ever reluctant to publish his work, did not allow most of these essays into print until much later in his life, but already in 1928, when he met Mumford and generously shared some of his Melville materials with him, he had arrived at a far different understanding of Melville than he found in his friend's biography.

As thinkers Murray and Mumford actually had a great deal in common. Murray was a generalist, like himself, opposed to all closed intellectual systems, all attempts to explain natural phenomena through one all-governing idea or set of formulations. Although he had been influenced by Freud, Murray placed greater stress on the role of sociocultural and physiological processes in personality formation. Over the course of his lifetime he did more than anyone in the field of modern psychology to introduce a holistic method of assessing personality. "Like a frigate," Melville had written, "I am filled with a thousand souls." So our personalities, Murray argued, are formed by a thousand influences, and this process is continuous throughout life and must be approached in this way. Living beings, he claimed, must be studied as living wholes.[42]

Above all, Murray shared with his new friend a deep distrust of behaviorism, both believing, with Santayana, that "in the human being imagination is more fundamental than perception." This influenced their studies of Melville. In common, they approached him as a mythmaker, a poet who used his visionary powers to illuminate the human condition and who revealed through his work much about his inner self. Although Murray would later argue that modern psychology's great failing was its inability to devise theories for understanding the healthy, creative processes of human personality, in his Melville scholarship he was most interested in uncovering the sources of Melville's forbidding view of the human condition and of his psychoneurosis. *Moby Dick*, he agreed with Mumford, was a completely whole and healthy work; yet its deliverer was not, he disputed Mumford, a whole and healthy man when he brought this book to birth. As Mumford thought over Murray's criticism of his biography, criticism less veiled in his letters than in his printed comments, he began to suspect that he himself had not been the contented man he had thought he was when he wrote it, and that his unwillingness to confront that fact had kept him from "tunneling into the black inner core" of Herman Melville.[43]

Perhaps the book came out as it did, he told Murray, because he wrote it under extremely favorable conditions, when he was in a state of near "euphoria."[44] But there is more to it than this. It is likely that Mumford didn't probe deeper into Melville's troubled state because he discovered that Melville had been burdened by emotional problems similar to his own, and a closer scrutiny of these problems could easily have turned into a dangerous process of self-examination that might have broken his mood of "euphoria" and prevented him from finishing the book.

Throughout the writing of *Herman Melville* Mumford was indeed in high spirits, his sails stretched full, confident he was writing his best book so far. But on completing the final draft he was thrown into a state of mental exhaustion and depression, the same sort of gray despair that had come over Melville after he finished *Moby Dick*. "I felt myself being sucked down helplessly into [a] whirlpool, unable to overcome the unconscious forces that were threatening to drag me to the bottom. This was the Cape Hatteras of the soul Melville had prophetically warned about." And at several times during this period Melville's words came back to him:

But, sailor or landsman, there is some sort of Cape Horn for all! Boys! beware of it; prepare for it in time. Graybeards! thank God it has passed.

In a verse he addressed to Melville on finishing the biography
Mumford prophetically described his relation to him as that of a
nurse to a sick man in danger of dying. Toward the end of his long
bedside vigil "the weakened nurse became the patient: I watched the
fever take possession of my bones." Yet Mumford shook this fever,
and in the midst of his Melvillian depression arrived at a truer
understanding of Melville, and of himself. Like the sage from the
book of the *Tao Te Ching* he ceased to be sick "because he saw sickness
as sickness."45

Mumford's crisis, like Melville's, was brought to a head by a wicked
succession of personal setbacks, not nearly as shattering as those
that had ruined Melville's career as a writer, but severe enough to
bring him dangerously close to a mental breakdown. After a serene
summer in the Amenia countryside, during which time he completed his *Herman Melville*, he and Sophia were forced to return to
New York earlier than they had planned when Sophia learned that
her pregnancy was in danger. Thus began what Mumford has
described as the "most desolate year of our whole lifetime until our
son's death in 1944."46

Sophia had a miscarriage in New York in October, followed
several weeks later by a painful curettage. During this period most
of the domestic duties fell on Lewis, who badly needed a rest
following his ordeal with Herman Melville. "The strain [of Sophia's
illness], on top of the Melville, was almost too much for me," he
writes in one of his Personalia notes, adding mournfully that he had
spent these weeks composing obituaries about himself as he walked
the streets of the city.47

In January, just as Sophia was regaining her strength, Geddes
became seriously ill. A severe cold settled in his ear, forming an
abscess. When Lewis cut short a lecture trip to the Western states
because of a tonsillitis attack, he returned to New York to find
Sophia ill (with tonsillitis) and Geddes bedridden and in the care of a
nurse. Geddes, they soon learned, was in real danger; his doctor had
misdiagnosed his problem. He had a double mastoid, they were told
when his condition worsened and other doctors were called in, and
he would have to be operated on immediately. As it turned out, they

got him to the hospital just in time. In a matter of six or seven hours the mastoid would have eaten through to the brain.

But that wasn't the end of it. A second infection developed and for three weeks after the operation he hung precariously between life and death, his mother keeping an around-the-clock vigil by his hospital bedside, sleeping when she could on a cot. Geddes remained in the hospital for seven weeks, and for many more weeks after his release Sophia had to bring him back to the hospital every day to have his dressings changed.

This ordeal drained Sophia and Lewis of almost all their energy, and most of their financial savings, which went for doctor and hospital bills; and Lewis, naturally, got almost no writing out. "We would have been pretty well wrecked and prostrated," he wrote Jerry Lachenbruch, "but for the fact that the Literary Guild took over an edition of Melville."[48] That brought in $6,700, which they used as a cushion for the next several years. It did nothing for their spirits, however.

They had planned to vacation together in Europe that summer. Lewis had a return invitation to lecture at Zimmern's school in Geneva and he also wanted to get to England to see Patrick Geddes. But now they both decided that he should go alone; she would take a recuperative vacation on the beach at Martha's Vineyard with Helen Ascher. He, too, was desperately exhausted and not mentally prepared to travel, but he thought that the trip might revive him and give him some idle time to himself to come up with a solid idea for his next book (he was thinking of writing a British companion to *The Golden Day*, dealing with British culture since the age of Shakespeare).

The trip, however, turned out to be a complete disaster. His tonsils, which had troubled him all winter, swelled up again on the steamer on the way over, and this triggered a bout of depression that he did not shake until he reached Geneva several days later. His throat cleared up and he was able to give his lectures, but he was still in no mood for travel. About this time he abruptly abandoned his idea for a book on British culture, leaving him with no great need to go to England. He was in no mood to be around the all-demanding Geddes, so he wrote him his apologies and took the next available boat back to America, meeting Sophia and Geddes in Leedsville, where they spent the rest of the summer in a cottage they decided to buy from Joel Spingarn with the money that had come in from the Melville biography.

Within weeks Lewis's physical strength returned, but "the inner me," he wrote in his notes, "has never been worse." He was overwhelmed by a "Melvillian feeling of despair: vast, senseless, but unaccountably desperate. [Melville's] image is bad medicine; and when I am feeling down I begin to regret that I had anything to do with him."[49]

This massive depression brought to the front emotional and sexual problems he had been struggling with since adolescence. In describing Melville's dilemma he had, in truth, described his own. Herman Melville might have seemed to others "a pale scholarly man, immersed solely in things of the mind," he had written in his biography, "but what a caricature that apparition was of the actual man!" Behind that grave, reserved manner was a fiercely passionate man "who in his marriage had kept to the letter of the pledge, and yet found himself struggling against its spirit—struggling, yet paralysed. . . . If only he could remake himself, or free himself from this disturbance . . . this feeling of disunity, this being but half of a mismatched whole."[50] For Mumford, however, this sexual blockage was part of a deeper emotional problem.

In his various writings, particularly on the writers of The Golden Day, he had argued the case for a balanced life that gives equal weight to mental work and passionate living, and in his biography he portrays the early Herman Melville as such a personality, a poet and a sailor-adventurer. Yet, at other points in his book, his psychological dissection of Melville directly contradicts this. Although he never quite says so, the Melville of his biography was suffering from a crisis of the divided self; and so, it seems, was he.

As a young sailor, while living as a wounded captive in the valley of the Typees, Melville met a Polynesian maiden, Fayaway, who served as his nurse and constant companion. Although attracted to Fayaway, Melville escaped to civilization, and after his marriage, and for the remainder of his life, attempted to bury in his subconscious the erotic feelings she had aroused in him. But these urges remained dangerously near the surface and emerged full-blown in Pierre, the crude psychological melodrama he wrote immediately after Moby Dick. In his biography Mumford found in this novel and in Melville's subsequent poetry strong evidence of his "sexual blockage," but it was not until after he finished the book that he connected this with Melville's passionate feelings for Fayaway.[51]

Mumford took Melville's encounter with Fayaway as a personal warning, resolving to give fuller release to his own sexual and emotional urges. Up to now, his outward reserve and self-control prevented him from acting on his innermost desires. He had been trying to overcome this, but even many of his closest friends continued to see him, as he had characterized himself in one of his earliest plays, as a disembodied intellectual, more head than heart. In the desolate weeks following his panicky return from Geneva, he "finally recognized how different the inner man was from the outer one" and determined to do something about it.[52]

Throughout this crisis Blake's lines rang constantly in his mind: "Sooner throttle a babe in its cradle than nurse an unacted desire."[53] But driving him in this direction he had more than the lesson of Melville's disastrous experience with self-renunciation; he had the example of his friend Van Wyck Brooks.

While Mumford was writing his *Herman Melville*, Brooks was going through the most horrifying stages of a life-threatening psychosis. When Mumford saw him briefly at Troutbeck in the summer of 1928, Brooks was a broken man, depressed and dangerously suicidal. He had already made several attempts on his own life. Despite Mumford's own multiplying personal burdens, he took a brotherly interest in Brooks's welfare, imploring his wife Eleanor, who distrusted psychology, to get him into the care of a competent therapist, which she eventually did. He also offered to raise money to pay for Brooks's medical bills; and he and Maxwell Perkins persuaded Carl Van Doren, an editor at the Literary Guild, to accept Brooks's latest, still uncompleted book, *The Life of Emerson*. Brooks's conviction that his book was a failure had badly aggravated his illness. With the tactful encouragement of Mumford and several of Brooks's other friends, Brooks was finally made to see the book's merits; and he agreed to submit it for publication in 1931, a decision that opened the way, almost miraculously, to his recovery.[54]

The causes of Brooks's malady are too complex to delve into here, but it is relevant to note that Mumford was convinced at the time that at least part of his friend's problem was sexual; and that it was like the problem Melville had encountered at a similar point in his life.55

Through Paul Rosenfeld, Mumford learned that Brooks had fallen in love with the Irish writer Mollie Colum, the high-spirited wife of his friend Padraic Colum. The Colums lived in New Canaan, twelve miles from Westport, and Mollie, who believed Van Wyck lacked emotional intensity, became intimately involved in his treatment, too intimately, it turns out. In 1926, while Eleanor was in Carmel, California, Brooks had what he later called an affair with Mollie. They never, apparently, had sex, but Brooks was so overwhelmed with guilt that he confessed everything to Eleanor. Although she forgave him, his condition grew far worse after this, and he told his doctors that he would feel forever guilty because he had kissed Mollie Colum.56

All this verified Mumford's growing suspicion that Van Wyck was a deeply repressed man, unable to give healthy release to his passionate inner feelings. Even when they got together informally with their families in the country, Brooks struck Mumford as diffident and oddly distant. He seemed capable of expressing his emotions only in their correspondence; yet even his letters were coolly controlled. Although Mumford was not nearly as indrawn as Brooks, he must have seen some part of himself in his friend; and he was determined to avoid the fate that had overtaken Brooks and Melville, "partly through their suppression of their libido."57

But Mumford's problem was not just his superego. While he was pulled toward other women—to Helen Ascher, and recently to Eva Goldbeck, a friend from his *Dial* days whom he visited in Paris on his most recent trip to Geneva—he still wanted, as did Melville, "the warmth of domesticity"—a home, a family, children. Marriage had brought additional burdens, responsibilities, and financial debts that often took him from his "real" work and threatened "to curtail," as he wrote of Melville's family responsibilities, "that inner development which he had come to prize above all things."58 Yet it gave his life an indispensable emotional center, and he remained very much in love with Sophia.

Adding to his inner misery was his guilt about his total devotion to his work, which prevented him from giving more of his time to Sophia and Geddes. "I shun father and mother and wife and brother, when my genius calls me," Emerson had proclaimed in "Self-Reliance," words that Mumford himself might have written. And like his Concord mentor, he believed, not uncavalierly, that "I must be myself. I cannot break myself any longer for you, or you. If you can love me for what I am, we shall be the happier."

Sophia could and did, and Lewis in his politely imperious way demanded it. But he knew that he owed her more, and he worried about the consequences of his extreme self-absorption. In this way as well, he took Melville's life as a portent. In his ferocious concentration on Ahab's battle with the whale, Melville, like Ahab, his creation, had cut himself off from the human contacts that would have allowed him to maintain his inner balance. He became an "isolato," and remained one for much of the burden of his life, coldly ignoring not only his wife but his four children, who "cursed him in his presence." Mumford had seen the lingering and messy evidence of this when he wrote to Melville's surviving daughter, who agreed to an interview with him on one unbridgeable condition— that he not so much as mention her father's name.59

For Mumford, then, it was not just a question of seeking greater freedom and emotional release. There were others, those he deeply loved, to consider as well.

His crisis reached a climax when he returned from Europe and noticed a change in Sophia. She seemed distant and dissatisfied with him, and he blamed this on her spending several weeks with Helen Ascher at the Vineyard. Sophia, he suspected, secretly envied Helen's sexual freedom. She had wanted this earlier in their marriage, but he had insisted that she remain faithful to him. Now, with a young child and without a career of her own, she was feeling more caged in than ever, and he felt he was being blamed for this. He should have realized that all she wanted was a little more of his time and attention. In any event, he was feeling miserable and emotionally isolated and was desperate to "recover that élan and hope and appetite for living" that had completely deserted him for the first time in his life. While claiming to feel "pity" for Sophia, his unfulfilled wife, he writes in his notes that he is "looking to breakaway."60 Not from marriage, we can only guess, but from marital fidelity.

That summer he went to bed with Helen Ascher, blaming this, in part, on Sophia's coldness toward him. Yet while he was overcome

with guilt, guilt so great he was physically unable to have intercourse with Helen, he read his decision to be unfaithful as a "genuine step toward emotional maturity: I had faced the man I was," he
confided to Jo Strongin, "and I had dared to do what Sophy had
only dreamed of."[61] Helen, with whom he fell in love, also gave him
something that for the moment had dropped out of his marriage—
sympathetic understanding and tenderness. After a short affair with
Helen, however, the "psychic strain" of his impotency was too much
for her, and they stopped seeing each other in early 1930.[62]

But the previous fall, while he was still seeing Helen, he met a
woman who forever changed his life.

He first set eyes on Catherine Bauer in the offices of Harcourt,
Brace, where she was in charge of advertising. She was twenty-four
years old, glowing-eyed and beautifully proportioned, with short
blonde hair, a high forehead, and sharply chiseled Nordic features,
and she was immediately drawn to him. He was handsome, suntanned, and muscular, with a confident, unhurried manner. He
looked like a man who knew exactly what he wanted and how to
get it.

They began to have lunch together regularly late that fall and
Lewis claims he was more charmed by her quick mind and spirited
personality than by "the curve of her breasts under her tight jersey."[63] She was a promising student of planning and architecture
and had studied art at Vassar, so they had much in common. She
also had quite a gift for flattery, telling him shortly after they met
that she had read *The Golden Day* while touring France on bicycle
and that it had influenced her to return to the States.

At the time they met Mumford was preparing his Dartmouth
lectures on the American arts, and Catherine often accompanied
him on his afternoon architectural tours of Manhattan, helping him
to appraise the buildings he would describe in *The Brown Decades*.
They had different tastes and temperaments, but in their first exciting months together these very differences "incited the free play of
our minds," Mumford recalls; "we plunged and leaped in a sea of
ideas like two dolphins . . . before our bodies were ready for any
other kind of play."[64] After a few months Lewis introduced Catherine to Clarence Stein, who brought her into the inner circle of the
Regional Planning Association.

Catherine was seeing another man that winter and Lewis was still

carrying on an affair with Helen Ascher. He was also having problems with his teeth and with his tonsils. All this prevented them
from meeting more often and from carrying the relationship to a
deeper level. In a later letter to Josephine Strongin, Lewis speculated that he might never have had sex with Catherine had his
relations with Helen Ascher been more physically complete. But
"the wrecked aviator must take to the air again; and in that mood I
[eventually] made love to Catherine."[65] At first he again experienced
problems with potency, but he and Catherine soon fell into an
intense sexual and emotional relationship that burned hot and
strong for the next five years. Although this affair, which Sophia
learned about from her husband in its earliest stages, almost
wrecked his marriage, it had, he later claimed, a liberating impact
on his work and his emotional health. The sexual exhilaration he
found with Catherine helped him to break through his emotional
blockage and released energies for his future work. Bauer also
became his most trusted intellectual associate, the only one to whom
he would ever show the first draft of anything he had written. In her
enthusiasm for his work, she urged him to write longer, more
ambitious books, and Lewis likened her liberating role in his intellectual development to that of Hilda Wangel in Ibsen's play—urging
the Master Builder to quit building modest houses and "to erect
instead an audacious tower," at any risk.[66] While it is doubtful that
Catherine had this decisive an effect on his intellectual development
(he was preparing, before meeting her, to take on larger literary
projects), around her he did begin to open up emotionally; for the
first time ever he felt close to achieving that balance of intellect and
passion he had set as the supreme aim of his life. In the excitement of
that realization, and in his physical attraction to Catherine, he
blinded himself to the hurt he was causing Sophia. And what began
as a dangerous pleasure nearly turned into a marital disaster.

At age thirty-five Dante is said to have had a vision of awakening in a
dark wood and finding his way to paradise. Mumford would turn
thirty-five—"the top of this arch of life"—in October 1930, and for
the first time in his life he felt fully mature. That conviction was
related to his recent reading of Dante's *Divine Comedy* and to his
immersion in Dante's world through Karl Vossler's magnificent

study of the poet. In the end, Dante's philosophy of good and evil, no less than Melville's, helped him to find his way out of the "rough and stubborn wood" into which he had stumbled.[67]

As a very young man Mumford had put up impossibly high moral standards for himself and society. If his search for perfection had been more effective, he now told Catherine Bauer, he would have killed himself "through an excess of virtue." He was saved, he believed, by his recent discovery that he "was neither so virtuous, so faithful, nor so inhibited as I had made myself out to be. Conclusion? Damn utopias! Life is better than utopia."[68]

Mumford pushed the point to an extreme here. He had never been an innocent believer in the perfectability of man; even his book about utopias was an avowedly anti-utopian tract. But from his Melville biography on, he did place greater emphasis in his work upon the impossibility of any final or complete resolution of social problems and of the unavoidable tragedy of the human condition. "I don't believe that if man is only left alone he is so innocent that he'll behave in an ideal way."[69]

The deteriorating state of civilization, the onset of an age marked by economic depression, fascism, total war, and nuclear annihilation, influenced him in his direction, but just as important was his confrontation with Herman Melville. "Humanity," he wrote Catherine Bauer not long after completing his *Herman Melville*, "would starve in utopia . . . ; for a good spiritual diet must contain a certain amount of phosphorus, iodine and arsenic, although they are poisonous if taken in large quantities. The problem of evil is to distribute the poison in assimilable amounts."[70]

His own experience before and during his Melville crisis— Geneva, Troutbeck, and the critical success of *The Golden Day*, followed by his descent into a hell of his own—convinced him that Dante's poetic rendering of the Inferno, the Purgatorio, and the Paradiso was "a true picture of mankind's historic experience and daily life." Truly "heaven and hell and all that lies between are, in varied measure, everyone's daily portion from cradle to grave." Having reached this point, he could at last face his problems, setbacks, and conflicting emotional loyalties as nettlesome but unavoidable aspects of all human lives. He was also able to accept his affair with Catherine Bauer, and immediately after that an affair with a friend of Catherine's, as part of "life's unexpected blessings." As he had written of Herman Melville (almost in justification of his own future decision), he had failed to realize "that the lust of the satisfied man is comparably more cleansing to the spirit than the tormented chastity of the unsatisfied one."[71]

Was all this, this new so-called tragic view of things, a complicated spiritual rationalization for what his libido and his ego had been driving him to do for some time? Nothing is so simple, but certainly these inner drives and desires brought on the crisis out of which he formed his revised view of experience and of himself. Once he had done this, there was no turning him back. "In some ways," Sophia once told him, "you are the most exasperating man—because you are so sweet—and so absolutely ruthless."[72]

15

Crisis and Opportunity

*Whilst philosophers debate, hunger and love are settling the
affairs of the world.*

—SCHILLER

Late in the winter of 1928, while Calvin Coolidge sat in the White
House presiding over the recent Republican prosperity, Lewis
Mumford wrote to Victor Branford about the prospects for reform
and revolution in America. "There are various signs that the criticisms and constructive proposals we've made during the last five
years are about to bear fruit. We are in for a period of industrial
depression in America; unemployment has already begun in the big
cities." When America's flimsy credit system teetered, "we will be
forced to think a little more furiously and effectively: men will suffer
but ideas will prosper."[1]

And that, of course, is exactly what happened. The economy
collapsed a year later, and people, many millions of them, suffered;
but social ideas flourished as they never had before. For radicals and
reformers of every kind, the stock market crash of October 1929
inaugurated a decade of feverish public activity; the nation, they
believed, had reached a crucial crossroads. All of Mumford's work of
the 1930s emerged from this widely shared perception that America, indeed the entire human community, had entered an unprecedented period of crisis and opportunity.

The Great Depression was America's gravest national crisis in the era between the Civil War and our own time, and the first years of that crisis were the most punishing of all. By the early winter of 1933, on the eve of Franklin Delano Roosevelt's inauguration, unemployment was over 13 million, and tens of thousands of rural families were struggling to hold on to their lands and their homes in the face of a massive foreclosure movement. In Detroit, Philadelphia, New York, Chicago—all over urban America—long lines of dispirited men huddled daily outside the doors of soup kitchens and rescue missions waiting shamefully for a meager handout; and everywhere ragged armies of the unemployed tramped the roads in an aimless search for opportunity. "Fifty years ago," complained one Pennsylvania miner, "we used to work six months a year and live good. . . . Even in Cleveland's administration, when Coxey made his march, I ain't seen times like these."[2]

As the depression reached its third terrible year, the *Saturday Evening Post* asked the British economist John Maynard Keynes whether there had ever been anything like it before. "Yes, it was called the Dark Ages and it lasted 400 years."[3]

Accompanying the economic decline and compounding its severity was a deep public unease about the nation's future. Three years of industrial paralysis had begun to erode the confidence of millions of Americans in the likelihood of a quick recovery. Yet while some angrily blamed capitalism itself for the crisis, the prevailing national mood was profoundly nonrevolutionary, a curious compound of fear, bewilderment, and sullen discontent. Those who experienced prolonged economic suffering for the very first time were more confused than angry.

Lewis Mumford, however, managed to weather the depression quite comfortably. In 1931 he was hired to take over *The New Yorker's* architecture column, "Sky Line," and later, he became that magazine's art critic as well. *The New Yorker* position gave him a regular income; and his next two books, *Technics and Civilization* and *The Culture of Cities*, sold reasonably well and brought him some additional income. But like everyone else who had his eyes open in these difficult years he could not escape for a single day the depression's blighting impact on the spirit of its victims. One incident stayed with him for the rest of his life. On a winter evening early in the depression, while he was walking along Madison Avenue on his way to dinner, he was approached by a respectable-looking man dressed in a black business suit. The man politely asked him for a few dimes, and Lewis, without much hesitation, handed him enough to buy his dinner. After thanking him, the unlikely beggar continued to walk beside him up the avenue. "What he wanted," Lewis recalls, "was what every human soul wants when in distress: another soul to listen to him."[4]

Men like this do not make revolution. Nonetheless, Mumford thought that the country might soon be ready for large social changes. The economic crisis would be long-term, and sooner or later there would be a slow, steady disillusionment with capitalism. When this began to occur, he wanted to be prepared to give the unformed rebellion clear direction. Along with many other radical intellectuals, Mumford welcomed the depression as a disguised social opportunity. This was the crisis that might offer them an opportunity to lead.

No radicals were more confident about socialism's future than the leaders of the Communist and Socialist parties, America's two largest Marxist organizations. After a decade of sectarian infighting, government harassment, and lagging popular influence, the entire Marxist movement was charged with new vigor. The Communists, more than any other radical organization, seemed intent on confronting the problems of the disprivileged, and this defiant activism drew scores of intellectuals to its standard.

Mumford belonged to no political party (up to now he had rarely voted), but he shared the radicals' disappointment with Roosevelt's New Deal, which he saw, from the first, as a pale substitute for the kind of thoroughgoing changes the recent emergency demanded. "Fundamentally, I have no faith in Roosevelt," he wrote to Benton MacKaye just after the new President took power, "except as a sort of political Mary Baker Eddy. As a faith healer he is all right. As a surgeon, he is useless, because he doesn't believe in operations."[5]

Early in the depression Mumford seemed prepared to commit himself to a radical movement, or at least to an effort to help create one. In 1932 he joined Waldo Frank, Edmund Wilson, and Malcolm Cowley in an attempt to frame a manifesto outlining an Americanized form of Communism (Wilson had suggested that they "take Communism away from the Communists"). Mumford saw his work of the previous decade on behalf of regional planning as an effort to lay the foundations of a new kind of radical movement, and the time had come, he now believed, "to harness up these projects with militant demands and tactics."6 The problem, however, was that he could find no existing political group or coalition of activists to align with.

As he saw it, the Communists were the only radical party in the country pressing for a total revolution, and he admired their militant dedication to social justice and their later support for the beleaguered Republican forces in Spain. Over the course of the decade he supported several of their "popular front" efforts and was briefly a member of the board of the American Artists Congress, which became heavily influenced by the party, but never was he tempted to establish an alliance with the official party, which he regarded as intellectually sterile, opportunistic, and unduly influenced by the Soviet Union.7

This country needed a radicalism, in Mumford's view, that grew out of American ideals and was committed to our democratic traditions. Moreover, he continued to insist that the Marxists were not nearly revolutionary enough in terms of their fundamental social aims. "I should be only too happy to throw my lot in with the Communists," he told Wilson and Cowley, "if I could see that their animus and habits of mind would lead toward a communist society."8

Mumford had been calling himself a "communist" since first reading, of all things, Plato's *Republic* as a very young man, and he resented the current "fashion" in America to join the communist church. "It will change," he wrote the English writer Llewelyn Powys, "and though I will still be a communist when it is over, I suspect that half the young men who have been converted will be whoring after some other gods once the wheels begin to turn again."9

Mumford's so-called communism was a creature of his own creation. Broadly and briefly stated, it envisioned an economic system that substituted social welfare for private gain as the chief aim in production, and that transferred the legal rights of ownership in land from individual property owners to the community—in effect, the original garden city principle of Ebenezer Howard. Furthermore, communism, to him, meant that the government establish a minimum guaranteed income for every citizen; that this be a right of citizenship. Once this was done, however, he urged that government move immediately to slow down the pace of industrialism and "turn society from its feverish preoccupation with money-making inventions, goods, profits, salesmanship . . . to the deliberate promotion of the more humane functions of life." This he upheld as the driving aim of what he called not the Red, but "the Green Republic."[10]

Mumford agreed with most liberal and radical writers of the time that there would have to be national planning to revive the economy, but he insisted in all his writings of the 1930s that only that part of the economy producing the basic necessities would have to be centrally planned and managed; here the capitalist market would give way to a communal distribution system based on human need rather than ability to pay. And in contrast to most Communist and technocratic planners, Mumford urged sharp limitations on the scope of the national planning effort and on the powers of the planners. Wherever possible, planning decisions should be made at the local level, by those most directly involved in the outcome of these decisions.

Mumford was not unaware of the role technology could play in reducing poverty; poverty was more dehumanizing, in his view, than any machine. Nonetheless, he continued to describe the good life in nonmaterial terms, and to advocate constraints on economic growth, even at a time when one out of five American workers was unemployed.[11]

Mumford's proposed stationary state challenged the standard American approach to social justice—an approach emphasizing expansion rather than fair division. America's usual way of meeting the economic needs of the lower and middle classes has been to increase the overall economic output, thereby raising the income of all classes, while leaving the wealth of the upper strata virtually untouched. But in the economy of "basic communism," as he called his economic system, the claims of the lower classes for a decent income would be met by diminishing the income of the upper groups. All would be forced to accept a "normalized standard of consumption," a term Mumford never adequately described. Mumford hoped that the constraints of growth would, in this way, encourage a cooperative ethic and more disciplined consumption habits. The watchword of the new age should be "stability, not expansion."[12]

Mumford disagreed as well with the Marxist prescription for

revolution, convinced that the American working class would never lead a movement for a scaled-down, less consumption-oriented civilization. Most workers, he suspected, were committed to the acquisitive ideals of bourgeois society. Even the more progressive labor unions appeared content to bargain merely for bread-and-butter benefits, and not for real power and responsibility in the factory, or for what Mumford called a new kind of life, the morally disciplined, nonacquisitive life he saw himself trying to live.

Mumford realized that the industrial working force would have to be part of any successful insurgent movement, but he seemed to prefer a "revolution" led by men of his own class and temperament—highly trained, socially concerned writers, architects, planners, economists, educators, scientists, and production managers— people, and he often named them, like John Dewey in education, Clarence Stein in housing, and Benton MacKaye in regional planning. These professionals possessed the skills needed to build and run the new regionally based society Mumford envisioned. His old teacher, Thorstein Veblen, had argued this same point in *The Engineers and the Price System*, a book that enjoyed a brief revival in the early 1930s.

American capitalism, Mumford predicted in 1931, will not be changed by a sudden storming of the banks and statehouses: "It will be changed by the continuous pressure of organized economic groups, working towards concrete ends, the control of industry, the socialization of a municipal utility, the nationalization of a resource, the planning of great public works."[13] Throughout the decade this remained his strategic advice—that radicals of all stripes cease sloganizing about "the Revolution" and begin working in their communities and in the nation at large for specific social changes, advice he himself heeded as he continued to press, in concert with his colleagues in the Regional Planning Association, for a vastly more ambitious federal housing and new town program than Congress or the Roosevelt administration seemed willing to support.

All the while he realized that even hundreds of small lobbying groups like the RPAA could not, by themselves, bring about a revolution in public policy. To carry through fundamental changes, a new progressive front of economic and political groups would have to be assembled. Could middle-class professionals be persuaded to join such an effort? Veblen had thought not; and Mumford had to agree that millions of middle-class Americans were still, early in the depression, firmly wedded to the capitalist system. On the other hand, many of them are "unwilling servants of the stupidity and greed of capitalism [and] are ready," he declared in an unpublished manifesto written fully a year before Franklin Roosevelt coined the political slogan, "for a new deal."[14]

Mumford never made explicit the role he expected the middle classes to play in the political movement he envisioned, nor did he suggest how the intellectuals, technicians, and workers could be won to the idea of revolution. Never greatly interested in politics or in matters of political strategy, he left these and other questions of policy and strategy largely unanswered; and throughout the decade, indeed to the end of his life, he maintained an almost Erasmian aloofness from all organized political movements. It was not that he thought politics unimportant; he simply continued to believe that political action by itself was insufficient, that it would have to be accompanied by "a moral and spiritual regeneration." The present responsibility of the far-seeing writer, he argued early in the depression, is to keep alive in himself the values that he seeks to encourage in others—to be a kind of twentieth-century Thoreau. Then, when the time is right, he added with almost sublime naïveté, "his ideas will march into action: there will be parties, movements, campaigns."[15]

Yet while Mumford remained virtually isolated from all progressive groups working for change in the 1930s, this was not by choice. Unable to find a reform philosophy congruent with his views, he set out in the 1930s to frame his own, urging his friend Waldo Frank to join him in creating "not a new political party, which is not our talent, but a party of ideas, which would in time lead toward political action."[16]

"We must have something better than the official Communist party in this country, even if you and I have to take off our shirts and create it," he wrote Edmund Wilson early in the depression.[17] And that is exactly what he proposed to do in the book he was then mapping out in his mind, a synthesis of human history that would point the way to a new society.

Mumford had been wanting to write such a book since reading Karl Vossler's masterly study of Dante and his times in 1929. Dante Alighieri might seem "the most distant of poets," he wrote in his review of that book, "not because we have left him behind, but because he strides on ahead of us," an inspiration to the present age. Unlike Dante's time, when a unity existed in thought and in the arts, a widely agreed-upon conception of good taste and of the good life, the current age suffered from what Mumford described as an absence of "form." No unifying philosophy had arisen to replace the liberal and radical creeds discredited by World War I. What was needed, in Mumford's view, was a philosophic synthesis as close to the day-to-day world and to the depths of the soul as Dante's *Divine Comedy*, the supreme achievement of the Middle Ages. And Mumford was bold enough to believe that he could be that poet of synthesis.[18]

Reading Vossler's study of Dante had awakened all of Mumford's smoldering ambition, and he found himself making notes for large projects of his own. In 1931, while serving as a visiting lecturer at Dartmouth College, he attended an address by Charles Beard on the need for national planning. Beard called for a "new Aristotle" to describe the goals of the planning effort, and this made Mumford feel "more keenly than ever before," he reported in his notes later that evening, "the need for 'Form' and my duty to put utmost into it."[19]

"Form" was the shortened title of the book "Form and Personality" he had begun to write in the summer of 1930, a volume bringing together his ideas on architecture, cities, regionalism, the machine, the personality—even love and marriage. After completing the first draft, however, he had abruptly begun another project, a collection of his essays of the 1920s entitled "A Preface to Action," which he submitted in preliminary form to Harcourt, Brace. While not rejecting the book outright, Alfred Harcourt urged him to make his next book "a more substantial and integrated affair."[20] Mumford would mark this as one of the most important letters he ever received. It made him realize that he had been backing away from the big book he had been intending to write for some time. He returned almost immediately to "Form and Personality," and the deeper he plunged into that work the more he realized that he had the makings of not one, but at least three or four books. Twenty years later he completed his four-volume Renewal of Life series, one of the great intellectual undertakings of our time.

Mumford was driven to write these books by an accumulating

desire for public influence, and by an inner need, which was ever there, to test his talents to the maximum. Even as an adolescent he had secretly believed that he was marked for greatness; Nietzsche's idea of the Superman, the superior human figure whose task it is to save the world by sheer force of will, is a persistent theme in his earliest unpublished writings. And by the time he reached thirty-five he possessed in full measure the soaring pride the Romans had called "superbia"—a quality, he once confessed, that is "dreadful" at a dinner table but is "marvelous in a work of art."[21]

Plagued as an adolescent by recurring sickness and disability, Mumford had ordered much of his career up to this point on the assumption that he would probably not live beyond forty, "so that every work was conceived and finished on a limited scale," he confided to Van Wyck Brooks in 1931, "with a short breath, as it were, as though it were my last!"[22] He now felt ready to give himself to the kind of synthesis of knowledge Patrick Geddes had always wanted to write.

"To produce a mighty volume," he had written of Herman Melville, "you must choose a mighty theme."[23] His would be nothing less than the making of the modern world. Mumford had in mind a book in the manner of Oswald Spengler's *The Decline of the West*, the prophecy of doom that greatly influenced a generation of war-weary European and American writers. That big and oddly brilliant book, the work of a reclusive German schoolteacher, had been on Mumford's mind since 1926, when he reviewed the English translation of the first volume for *The New Republic*, finding it, despite its numerous factual inaccuracies and lapses, its wild combination of Nietzschean mysticism and arrogant Junkerism, an "audacious, profound . . . exciting and magnificent" work, "one of the most capable attempts to order the annals of history since Auguste Comte." Not even Spengler's later support of the Nazi takeover would shake Mumford's original opinion of the book, which he chose in 1939 as his contribution to Malcolm Cowley and Bernard Smith's *Books That Changed Our Minds*.[24]

It was Spengler's style of history, his brilliantly original approach to the material, that excited Mumford's interest. Abjuring every canon of so-called objectivity, Spengler placed himself at the center of his history, observing, sympathizing, criticizing, comparing. Spengler probably came as close as anyone Mumford had yet encountered to writing the kind of history that he had set out to write in his several books on America. Spengler was less interested in recording the principal events of history than in uncovering what he called its "significances." He searched, above all, for the characteristic style of a culture, its essential inner idea, as expressed in its art, architecture, literature, philosophy, music, and statecraft.

And something even more fundamental drew Mumford to Spengler: his history was actually a form of moral prophecy. Mumford, however, had a vastly different view of the future than that mordant Prussian Platonist.

The master theme of *The Decline of the West*, the progression of societies from an organic to an inorganic way of life, from the biological to the mechanical, was the very theme that Mumford had been developing in his own work on American culture. Reading Spengler gave him some ideas about how to extend this thesis to the whole of Western culture. Spengler traced the cycle of development and the "form" of three dominant Western cultures: the classical culture of ancient Greece and Rome; the Magian culture of Jewish, Christian, and Arab societies; and the modern, or Faustian, culture of northern Europe which, in his view, arose around 900 with the development of Romanesque architecture. Each of these cultures had its own organic life cycle—its spring, summer, autumn, and winter phases—precisely the organic metaphors, coincidentally, Mumford had used in *The Golden Day*. In the spring and summer phases there were fresh departures in the arts, and there was an affinity for the earthly and the organic. Life was lived close to the soil in small regional communities or in cultural cities of modest size such as ancient Athens or medieval Florence. Eventually, however, every culture passed into its autumn and winter season, where there was a steady erosion of artistic creativity and a movement toward the abstract and the mechanical. Human beings became nomadic, urbanized, and cosmopolitan, indifferent to the vital processes of life that had meant so much to the plowman and the townsman of the "culture" phase. This devitalized, traditionless civilization became embodied in the megalopolis or world city, which grew at the expense of the old regionally based culture centers. Faustian culture prized bigness, rationality, order, bureaucracy, and physical expansion. In architecture it favored the gigantic and the imperial, the skyscraper being the modern equivalent, in Spengler's view, of the Colossus of Rhodes. Great poetry and art were no longer possible in this final stage of the culture cycle; the new world of steel and asphalt belonged to the soldier, the engineer, and the businessman.

Mumford agreed with Spengler that Faustian culture had entered the "winter" of its development; but where Spengler peered into the future and saw only spreading blackness and blight, Mumford saw a brilliant post-Faustian world, a great revival of the regional and the organic outlook. As he prepared to begin his Renewal of Life series he saw Faustian civilization at a parting of the way. If modern society moved toward the philosophy of regionalism, it might pass through a short winter and into spring.[25]

Mumford, as we have seen, rested his hopes for the future on the very class of people Spengler left no creative role for in his sprawling moral drama—the intellectuals—the makers of ideas and ideals. In his series Mumford set out to frame their manifesto and chart their course. No ivory-tower thinker, he was as urgently interested in shaping history as he was in recording it.

Written during a period of rapid social disintegration—of economic depression, spreading totalitarianism, and world war—the four volumes of the Renewal of Life series (*Technics and Civilization*, *The Culture of Cities*, *The Condition of Man*, and *The Conduct of Life*) record a profound change in Mumford's social outlook—a gathering pessimism, but not despair, about the possibilities of human renewal. The first two volumes, however, which were completed before the beginning of World War II, are expressions of Mumford's resolute social optimism, seasoned by his Melville interlude. They are also the most original and stimulating works of the series. "To me," W. H. Auden wrote Mumford in 1938, "they are the two most interesting books of our time."[26]

While a number of other writers in the 1930s emphasized the incompatibility of technology and humanism, of collectivism and individual freedom, Mumford put forward a philosophy to harmonize democracy and planning, the machine and the human spirit, a conception of change encompassing personal as well as institutional regeneration. We also find in his work an ecological perspective and an appreciation of the non-rational sources of human behavior largely absent from the social criticism of the 1930s. More than any other writer of the decade, Mumford foresaw the dangers of a careless overextension of urban and economic growth.

Technics and Civilization, the first in the series, is about the rise of the machine and the machine mentality in the Western world. Mumford had been closely interested in technology since his student days at Stuyvesant High School, but the immediate impetus for writing a book on this theme had come in the form of an invitation from Professor Robert MacIver, in 1930, to offer a course in Columbia University's extension division on the Machine Age in America, probably the first of its kind ever given in the United States. Preparing for this course led Mumford to systematically explore the entire field of technological studies, then in its infancy. Armed with this new knowledge, he changed the course's emphasis from America and the modern world to Western civilization and the technical changes that began in the twelfth century. Before he had delivered his first lecture, he realized that he had almost enough material for a book. To do it properly, however, he would have to go to Europe first, to visit the great technical museums of Vienna, Paris, London, and, above all, Munich, and to see for himself the new experiments in architecture, housing, and city planning that were going forward in Germany, France, and the Netherlands.

At the time he was being encouraged to make such a trip by two people close to him. After reading *The Golden Day* Victor Branford wrote to him urging him, in his next book, to take his readers "to the prospect half-promised in the closing passage, the vision of that 'New World' to which 'the road is open.' To write such a book you will have to come over to Europe again."[27] And it turns out Catherine Bauer had been telling him the very same thing since the moment they became intimate. Before you are forty you must take a "*wanderjahr*," she wrote him. "Tell [Sophia and me] temporarily to go to hell" and go off to Europe. "You have such an enormous and God-given genius for fresh correlation, evaluation—for imaginative seeing—that you almost owe it to yourself and society to tie up the loose threads of Western civilization."

But in what she herself called a "more feminine, more practical" mood, she suggested that both she and Sophia meet him "at different points for a while." Catherine even offered to take care of Geddes for a few months. To cover his expenses, she suggested that Lewis apply for a Guggenheim or borrow money from a friend. At all costs you must cut free and do this book, for "[you are] the person most capable of evolving a new synthesis."[28]

Several months later Lewis applied for and received a Guggenheim award, and in April 1932 he sailed for Bremen. Catherine would join him in Munich for the first part of this trip to help him research some articles on European housing he had agreed to do for *Fortune* magazine; and Sophia would meet him later in England. As Lewis boarded the *Europa* the spring morning he left for Germany, he wondered whether he had been thinking clearly when he made these travel plans. He was usually an extremely cautious man. But lately Catherine had been working a change in him.

Lewis Mumford, age ten, and his mother, Elvina.

Mumford's grandfather,
Charles Graessel, 1900.

Lewis and his Nana,
Nellie Ahearn.

Pencil drawing by Lewis
Mumford of Nellie Ahearn, 1917.

Lewis Mumford, 1904.

Euchre party at Elvina Mumford's brownstone on West Ninety-third
Street, New York, circa 1904.

Lewis Mumford's first house at 230 West Sixty-fifth Street, New York, where his mother took in boarders. Elvina Mumford is seated second from the left, and Lewis is the child.

Lewis Mumford in 1919.

Lewis Mumford as a student at Stuyvesant High School.

Beryl Morse.

Patrick Geddes, 1929.

Watercolor by Lewis Mumford, "View from my Bedroom Window," May 8, 1916.

Untitled watercolor and pencil sketch by Lewis Mumford, 1916.

Pencil sketch by Lewis Mumford of the Brooklyn Bridge, 1917.

Pencil sketch by Lewis Mumford of Victor Branford, 1920.

Sophia Wittenberg at 18.

Mumford and his son, Geddes, in Leedsville, 1926.

Sophia and Geddes at Martha's
Vineyard, 1927.

Joel Spingarn at his Troutbeck estate.

Sunnyside Gardens, Queens, which Mumford helped to plan and where he
lived with his family from 1925 to 1936.

Henry Wright.

Benton MacKaye, 1924.

Hudson Guild Farm, May 1923. Patrick Geddes (leaning against tree), Lewis Mumford, Benton MacKaye, Sophia Mumford, Clarence Stein, Aline MacMahon, and other unidentified people.

Clarence Stein, Walter Curt Behrendt, and Lydia Behrendt, 1936.

JAN. 5, 1921

Poor - but Used by Editors
of Sketches in Life.

Paul Rosenfeld.

Pencil sketch by Lewis Mumford of
Van Wyck Brooks, January 5, 1921.

Mumford (second from right) being sworn in by Mayor Fiorello La Guardia
as a member of the New York City Board of Higher Education, 1935.

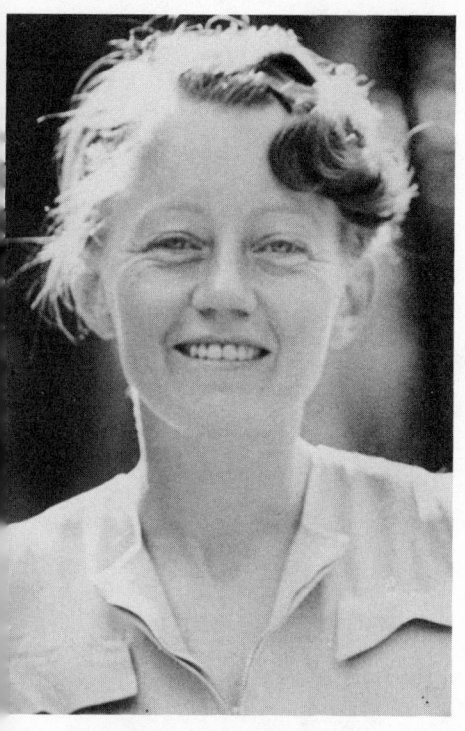

Top left. Catherine Bauer.

Top right. Alice Decker.

Josephine Strongin.

The Mumford's house in Leedsville, N.Y., 1941.

Geddes Mumford.

Alison Mumford.

Pencil sketches by Lewis Mumford of his home in Leedsville and of Troutbeck Lake.

Lewis in England just after his son
Geddes's death.

Frank Lloyd Wright.

Lewis Mumford with Van Wyck and Gladys Brooks, 1951.

Lewis and Sophia in 1957.

Lewis Mumford, 1980.

Lewis Mumford, 1987.

Lewis Mumford's study.

16

The Renewal of Life

*Every man who is settled in a house should hold the hasty
heart firm. Thou shouldst not pursue after a woman; do not
let her steal away thy heart.*

—INSTRUCTION OF ANI,
LATE EGYPTIAN EMPIRE,
11–8 B.C.

"The true artist . . . ," wrote Shaw in *Man and Superman*, a play
Mumford read and reread as a youth, "gets into intimate relations
with [women] . . . knowing that they have the power to rouse his
deepest creative energies, to rescue him from his cold reason, to
make him see visions and dream dreams. . . . [They] enable him to
act Hamlet better, to paint a finer picture, to write a deeper poem, a
greater play, a profounder philosophy! . . . In the rage of that creation he is as ruthless as the woman, as dangerous to her as she to
him, and as horribly fascinating."[1]

By the time Mumford left for Germany, Catherine Bauer had
become almost as important to him as his work.* Young, beautiful,
and radiantly outgoing, she was making him into a different man—
more open to sensual pleasures, more confident of his masculine

*A note to the reader: My reconstruction of the love affair between Lewis Mumford and Catherine
Bauer is based largely on letters, notes, and other personal materials in the restricted portion of the
Lewis Mumford Collection in Van Pelt Library, the University of Pennsylvania. In 1970, Mumford wrote that his correspondence with Catherine Bauer "can't alas! be published in my lifetime
and may . . . never be published at all!" Their letters were simply too "intimate," he thought at the
time, to be printed as long as he and his wife were still alive, although he later published carefully

powers, and more assured than he had ever been about his creative capacities. Around her he felt, for the first time, totally alive— emotionally, intellectually, sexually. She energized every part of him.

He had always looked for two things in a woman: sensuality and intellectual passion. Helen Ascher, "the daughter of the earth," possessed one of these; Josephine Strongin, "the daughter of the sky," the other. Catherine possessed both.[2]

What made Catherine especially exciting to him was that she walked into his life at a dangerously vulnerable moment in his marriage, when he and Sophia, although still in love, were not emotionally responsive to each other. Almost every married couple "has drifted at one time or another in this weedy Sargasso Sea" Mumford would write in an unpublished portion of his autobiography, "and at some point the appearance of another person on the horizon comes like the first flapping of sails on a becalmed boat, when an offshore breeze breaks through the sleepy torpor and drives it again out on the open sea. In the exhilaration of that moment one revives the promise and reopens the experience that had once brought about the marriage. With another potential lover other facets of one's personality, other potentialities, surprisingly come to the surface; before one can foresee the consequences, repressed impulses are released."[3]

When they first became intimate in April 1930, it was Catherine, playfully brash and outgoing, who had taken the lead. Mumford was just ending his affair with Helen Ascher and was feeling downcast and confused, wondering whether his new sexual freedom was not, after all, another form of "bondage," and more harmful to his work than fleeing temptation. No doubt he was also worried about his inability to perform sex with Helen. What would happen if he

---

edited selections from this correspondence in two autobiographical chronicles—*Findings and Keepings* (1975) and *My Works and Days* (1979). When he deposited his papers at Van Pelt Library in 1982, Mumford stipulated that this correspondence with Bauer, along with other letters and notes dealing with the most private parts of his life, be sealed for the foreseeable future.

In 1983, Mumford allowed me access to these letters and to all the other previously sealed portions of his papers; and, later, Sadie Super, Catherine Bauer's daughter, gave me permission to quote from her mother's letters to Mumford. I have used these materials to write the following four chapters of this biography describing Mumford's relations with Catherine Bauer and two other women who played an important part in his life: Alice Decker Sommers and Josephine Strongin.

went to bed with Catherine, who had such a carefree and breezy attitude toward sex?

So when they first started seeing each other regularly on winter afternoons in Manhattan he was self-consciously tentative and extremely preoccupied. All he talked about were his lingering problems with Helen and his continuing difficulties with Sophia. He had always had a large capacity for self-pity, and Catherine spotted this almost immediately and soon decided she had had enough. She could tell by the way that he looked at her that he wanted to go to bed with her, despite his insistence that he was more attracted to her mind than her body, and she couldn't quite believe him when he told her that he was too ill from a carbuncle to make love to her. "All I can say is this," she brashly wrote him after one of their emotionally tense afternoons together, "if you *would* like to go to bed with me, I wish you would some time, because I'd rather go to bed with you than anyone else I know at the moment. . . . And if you wouldn't, you'd better keep away from me, for I feel perfectly irresistible and very lusty."4

The note had its intended effect; the following week they became lovers, although he did have some embarrassing physical difficulties at first. On the first afternoon together in bed in her apartment he was unable to perform sex. She told him not to worry; it often happened to a man the first time he went to bed with a woman. "How well I know that," he remembers thinking.

"It would be funny," she told him at dinner later that day, "if I did get a case on you: it might hurt." If she wanted to "save" herself, he replied, she had "better pray that [he] continue impotent."5 He did have problems performing sex for the next month or so, but it didn't seem to bother either of them. They were even able to joke about it. "Only some lingering shred of faith can make you think of the Dionysiac Lewis as anything but a vain imposter," he wrote her that June. After losing her job at Harcourt she had gone to Germany for the summer to study housing and architecture, and he was now desperately in love with her, and desperately disconsolate.6

"Catherine satisfies every part of me," he confided in his notes, "spirit, mind, body, in a way that no one else . . . has ever done: she is Sophia's first real rival and if I were to choose between them the odds—dare I say it?—would be against Sophia despite her greater physical beauty."7

At this time his long developing problems with Sophia came to a head. It began when he told her about Catherine. If he was going to stray from his marriage he felt honor-bound to be honest about it with his wife, but he took his honesty—or was it his guilt?—too far. Around the house his conversation began to be filled with Catherine, and whenever it came time to meet her he made no effort to disguise where he was going. In doing this, of course, he wounded Sophia far more than he would ever admit. If he was not consciously trying to hurt her, his "honesty" had that effect. In his relations with his wife, this socially sympathetic man could be ruthlessly self-willed, always ready, however, to defend his behavior with spacious moral justifications. As a writer he had a remarkable ability to experience empathy with his subjects, but as a husband he was too often lacking in sympathy.

His relationship with Catherine had not hurt Sophia all that much, he wrote Jo Strongin that spring. There were many ways of being unfaithful in marriage; being interested in another person was only one of them. "I am much more of a brute when I am writing a book; and the hurt to Sophie's ego is quite as great, too: because no person has ever held me as firmly as my own thoughts, at least over a long period." Until recently he had avoided having affairs with a number of women he had been attracted to because he feared that his marriage would not be able to absorb the strain. "Adolescent . . . cowardice," not loyalty to Sophia, he confessed to Jo, was behind his decision to remain faithful. He had hurt Sophia "far more with this fear," he justified his recent infidelity, than he had "by living it down," for it had made him childishly jealous and unreasonable, and had narrowed Sophia's circle of friendships. But this, to be sure, remained *his* interpretation of the effects of his infidelity on Sophia—not hers.[8]

Yet something sound did emerge from his decision to tell Sophia about Catherine: it helped to open her up, as she finally raised the resolve to confront him with what had been troubling her about their marriage for the past several years.

It was actually his dishonesty, or evasiveness, about his fast-progressing relationship with Catherine that swung Sophia to the offensive. When he had first told Sophia he was seeing Catherine he asked her to give him several weeks to see where the affair was heading; until then, no decisions would be made. Sophia grudgingly agreed to this, but then saw what was really happening. "It just occurred to me," she wrote him in May, feeling that she could best put her thoughts in the form of a letter, "that when you asked me" to bear with you for a while, you really meant until Catherine leaves for Europe. It wasn't that he expected that he and Catherine would be through with each other by that time, but that Catherine would be removed from the scene; and then "you will return to me. It seems to me, my dear, that I should be kept in complete ignorance, or else that I should know how things stand. This in between state is ghastly."

Then she struck straight to the heart of the matter, spilling out all her hurt and frustration. He took the organization of her life as being completely dependent upon his. As a couple they always seemed to be doing what *he* wanted to do. Every family decision was made with his life, his career, the uppermost consideration. "Until very recently I thought that a virtue. I'm beginning to doubt it."

What angered her most of all was the way that she had been betrayed. In the first years of their marriage it was *she* who had wanted some freedom to experiment, but he had insisted that she give herself completely to the marriage. And she had, up to now. At first this had not bothered her, for she wanted to be a full-time wife and mother. It began to annoy her only when, with the increasing success of Lewis's work, he started to spend more time away from home; and when she began to see that he had an eye for other women.

Lately, Sophia had been experiencing a crisis of her own, and she didn't think that he was being understanding enough. She was approaching her thirties, without any career of her own and few close friends to turn to. He was growing, but she was not. She also feared that she was losing her beauty, something she feared she had relied on too strongly "to carry me through up to now."9

At this vulnerable moment she learned of her husband's affairs with two women, one of them her friend and neighbor, the other a younger, more vivid woman with whom she felt hard-pressed to compete. "Both the people you needed this year to supplement me are free lances," she confronted Lewis. "Helen has a freedom from her children that would horrify you in your own household, and Catherine [has] superior mental equipment to mine, [and] can keep it up with all the contacts she has—contacts arising out of the work she is doing. You cut . . . that end of my life off and I am left with no proper place of my own. I'm a hanger-on to you." She had few friends of her own because all the people she enjoyed spending time with liked to go out together; Lewis was bored in their company and made no effort to disguise it. The only time in the past several years he had agreed to stay out until well after midnight with Sophia was when they went to a party at which Catherine was a guest.

Sophia wanted Lewis to know that men still flirted with her, but when they became serious she politely but firmly turned them down. "You see, my darling, I've kept your 1922 morality, and you left it behind."

They couldn't count on sex alone to hold their marriage together, she told him. He had progressed as a lover, but Sophia found it distressing that their deepest enjoyment of each other was in bed. "That should supplement life," she admonished him in words he might have chosen for one of his own moral tracts, "not be it." She was beginning to feel, she said, like "a kept woman."

Sophia had been desperately trying to get him to see just how perplexed she was, but "I've always been met either with uncomprehension, or else an airy and witty and ever so charming casting aside of the problem." She didn't want to be put off like this anymore; nor did she want him to see her as "an understanding person or a good sport" in this marital crisis. "If you can't see that I am a human being in distress I am lost."[10]

Throughout this entire ordeal Sophia had a Damoclean feeling that she was on trial; that if her conduct wasn't "up to the mark" she'd be replaced. She was also afflicted by self-doubt, which occasionally turned into self-censure. Her husband obviously wanted a more intellectually stimulating, sexually aggressive woman. She was losing him, she feared, because she had become too withdrawn and domesticated. She didn't go out much, or read the latest books, or keep up with current affairs. But she wanted Lewis to know that he had helped to make her that way by his jealousy and his insistence that she give her entire self to husband and family.[11]

A long time afterwards, when Sophia was able to look back with a level eye at this stormy interval in their marriage, she admitted that several other things were working away at her. She wanted to have more children, a family at least as large as the immigrant household she had grown up in, but Lewis, eager to get on with his career, was reluctant to expand their household. She also resented being known as "merely" the wife of Lewis Mumford. Yet at the same time she doubted whether she had the "ambition or talent enough to warrant . . . being known as anything but Lewis's wife." What bothered her most of all, however, was that her husband was not "sufficiently adult" to help her through this crisis; "his answer was to fall in love elsewhere."[12]

Why did she stay with him even after he refused to stop seeing Catherine? First of all, there was Geddes to think of—she didn't want to break up the family. In some matters Sophia was a thoroughly traditional woman. Divorce was never an active choice for her; no one in her family had ever gone through a divorce. But these were not her deepest reasons for staying with Lewis. What mattered to her was her belief that Lewis had never fallen out of love with her, even when he was most passionately involved with Catherine. The fact that they continued to have satisfying sex together throughout his affair with Catherine further convinced her of this.

If he had asked her for a divorce so that he could marry Catherine, she probably would have given him his freedom. But he never did. For the sake, perhaps, of her own self-esteem, Sophia continued to believe throughout her life that Lewis had fallen in love with Catherine "not because he had sought to, but because it had happened to him. So that there was no course open to me except to wait it out."[13]

The most difficult days of all were the middle months of 1930, when they examined all the "crumbling piers and rotten beams" that underlay even the most solid-seeming marriages. They had just moved into the summer home of their modest dreams, a spacious wooden house that fronted the maple-canopied Leedsville Road, its rear rooms facing south, toward patches of trees, wildflowers, and sloping farm fields. But when they took possession of this deserted, musty-smelling house, it was in terrible repair, and the land surrounding the house and its companion barn, which they eventually set up as a playhouse for Geddes, was overgrown with thick grass and weeds. Like two eager sparrows repairing their nest after a storm, Lewis and Sophia set out to bring some order to their new Troutbeck hideaway—plastering, painting, patching, building bookcases, trimming the lilac bushes, and planting a small garden. "Every fresh patch of order was a personal triumph: we were gods dawning on chaos."[14]

The house helped to save their marriage, but equally important was a monthlong holiday from each other. Sophia decided she needed time to herself to come to terms with Lewis's interest in Catherine and with her own "innermost needs." She would take a walking tour of Germany and Austria, setting out alone, to be joined later by a younger German girl who ran the Sunnyside nursery. As Lewis helped her pack her bags he wasn't sure—and neither was she—if she would want to continue the marriage when she returned.[15]

"I feel like the lonely prisoner in his cell," he wrote Catherine from Leedsville just after Sophia's departure, his only companions the cockroaches and little Geddes. He gave his mornings to his writing, and in the spacious Leedsville afternoons, too lonely even to read, he wrote letters, little pieces of conversation—sometimes two a day—to Catherine, and waited for the postman to bring him her letters from Heidelberg, Stuttgart, and Frankfurt, letters he likened to "a sudden burst of oak and maple in the landscape: I am drunk with the color of them."[16]

These and later letters to Catherine are among the most revealing records of Lewis Mumford's inner life. "What a marvelous correspondence you and I are cooking up for posterity!" he wrote her in the first summer of their relationship. Her letters, ranging in subject matter from "teleology to toilets," gave him his first true glimpse of the power and range of her mind, and convinced him that she was a born writer. Never had he received letters "so perceptive, so exciting, so keen in expression of that combination of intellectual stimulus and frank erotic pleasure" that made up their relationship.[17] He would forever treasure these letters—his as well as hers—and at low moments in his life he would pull them out of a perfectly arranged manila folder and read them well into the night, bittersweet reminders of how it had been to live life at full pitch. "Our life together," he scribbled on a scrap of notepaper long after they parted, "still means a great deal to me: sometimes I find a smile in my face when some aspect of that life crosses my vision, as I am walking perhaps . . . one of those streets down which we walked together so often."[18]

When Catherine was away in Europe he fell even more deeply in love with her. She aroused feelings in him he thought he had lost forever. He even began to write poetry again. "It's good to feel these storms again," he wrote her, "and to know that, after all, one is still young and ginger is hot in the mouth."[19]

Part of Catherine's attraction for him was that she was the antithesis of Sophia. "Every man, in his middle thirties, falls in love with his wife's opposite," as he himself said years later.[20] Sophia had black hair, dark skin, and brown eyes, while Catherine was fair, with sharp, upturned Alpine features and blazing green eyes. Sophia was patient and steady-going, but a little unsure of herself intellectually; Catherine was hard-driving, high-strung, and self-confident. Sophia had deep reservoirs of passion, and so did Catherine; but Catherine wore her emotions on the surface. And while his sex with Sophia had improved, he found her much harder to arouse than Catherine. He and Sophia were not "physiologically matched," he confessed to Henry Murray, who was his closest confidant in these matters. (Murray also had a mistress and was going through some marital difficulties.) When they were first married he used to think Sophia was slow to reach orgasm because he was "an inexperienced duffer at sex." But now he was convinced that it was either physiological or a sign that she desired "another kind of partner."[21]

Lewis, who never felt he had truly experienced anything until he had written it down, recorded in his notes these temperamental and anatomical differences between Catherine and Sophia, precisely describing, and even making pencil sketches of, the most intimate parts of their bodies. He also gave detailed descriptions of his lovemaking with both of them.

Some of these notes form a kind of sexual ledger, as he balanced Catherine's attributes as a lover against Sophia's deficiencies, and vice versa. Though it looked as if he was trying to make a choice between them, he actually wanted both of them: they satisfied different parts of him. Catherine was killing off the last remnants of his youthful priggishness. He was becoming, finally, a confident lover and a fully robust man. "I am almost a free spirit now, aren't I, darling?" he announced to her with almost embarrassing innocence in the first year of their affair. "But oh! the pain of getting there."[22]

No person had a greater immediate impact on his emotional development or his work, not his mother nor his wife, nor even Patrick Geddes. He always considered himself the sort of writer who, by tremendous concentration and effort, brings his talents (which he thought fell short of genius) to the highest pitch. He was further convinced that he was not likely to achieve his full potential as a writer on the basis of hard work and concentration alone: he would need some sort of outside stimulation. Catherine Bauer provided this. A woman of furious vitality, she expanded that part of him he considered most deficient—what he called his poetic and imaginative side. This young woman released the demons in him.

He found himself declaring to Catherine what he had declared to Sophia when he was hotly pursuing her earlier—that their union would energize his work. Up to now he had produced only a "few pamphlets," but he felt a big book growing inside him. He couldn't wait for her to return, he wrote her in the summer of 1930, for she alone was capable of inspiring him to bring it to birth, large and healthy and soundly formed. At the moment he considered himself only a modestly successful writer; with "a really ingenious and handy partner, I might . . . become another Leonardo."[23] He could easily have written this book without Catherine, but he was trying to convince himself that he couldn't; that would give him greater justification for continuing the affair.

Yet as much as he desired and thought he needed Catherine, he did not want to lose Sophia. His life was his work, and in order to work well he had to seal himself off from the world. When he was writing a book he lived a life of regularity, order, and impeccable domesticity. Sophia had more than accommodated herself to this routine; she had made it into a positive life purpose. She absolutely believed in his work and sacrificed to see that he got it done without the usual interruptions the world puts in the way of creative effort. She answered the phone for him and kept Geddes quiet or out of the house when he was writing, and she did scores of other little things, such as typing his books and preparing the indexes, to keep him free for his work. Catherine, he knew, would never be that kind of woman. Nor did he want her to be. One Sophia—one wife—was enough for him; he needed Catherine, free-spirited and irresponsible, as a counterbalance. This left him, he described his plight to Henry Murray, like the jackass in the medieval scholastic dilemma, immobilized equidistant between two bales of hay.[24]

So while he wrote ardent letters to Catherine in Germany in the first summer of their affair, he admitted to her that he still loved

Sophia. And after finishing a letter to Catherine, he would write a long letter to Sophia telling her how much he missed her. His problem, he confessed to Catherine, was that he happened to be that "curious psychological anomaly: a one-girl man; and you are so damned lovely, so attractive, so spiritually exhilarating that . . . [leaving Sophia] becomes, for the first time in ten years, thinkable: indeed I have scarcely thought about anything since last March." But he was not just a one-girl man, he might have added; he was a marrying kind of man. "Permanence and solidarity are my particular game: but why should a one-girl man turn Catherine into a one-man girl and divert all her talent into a biological career?" A "heroic" solution to his problem might turn out to be a "disaster" for her, with her passionately independent ways. This, he added tellingly, might be our "real incompatibility."[25]

His decision might have been made for him that summer had Sophia returned from Europe in a different mood. She had left for Germany feeling "middle-aged and mediocre," Lewis reported to Catherine. "She returns feeling confident and young, having found her youth and charm in other people's eyes." Last spring she was a "distracted, bitter and panicky girl. . . . In that mood it would have been impossible to have gone on living with her, and equally impossible, without horrible reproach, to have parted. Now she has a firm grasp on herself, and a dash: even her face is more finely chiseled."[26]

Not long after her return Sophia and he arrived at an unspoken truce about Catherine. Sophia would allow him to continue his affair with Catherine, confident, or at least she told herself, that he would return to her when he and Catherine were through with each other. Catherine would have his afternoons; she would have the rest of his days. For now, she realized that was all she could hope for. It was a desperate attempt on her part to salvage the marriage, and it took some unusual twists. Once, when Lewis was bedridden for several days, Sophia invited Catherine to the house to cheer him up; and the following summer, without even consulting her husband, Sophia gave Catherine the use of their Sunnyside home while they were in the country. By then she and Catherine had actually come to like each other. "Drat your friend Catherine," Sophia blurted out after seeing her at a party at Clarence Stein's, "I hate her—because I really like her so much and I can understand why you do too."[27]

And Lewis himself settled something in his own mind that summer of 1930. This resolutely "one-girl" man now reconciled himself to the fact that it was "painful, but possible, to love two girls at one time."[28]

Lewis believed that his relationship with Catherine actually improved his sex with Sophia and helped to bind her more tightly to him. In an odd way it had helped, he thought, to salvage his marriage. Once the first strain of his affair with Catherine was over his relations with Sophia reached "a new depth," he wrote to Jo Strongin several years after he and Catherine had parted. "She received something from her 'unfaithful' Lewis she had never known in the arms of her more prudent and repressed mate."[29]

But Sophia, too, was changing; there was a new "dash" and "abandon" in her sexual play. At Leedsville they sometimes had sex in the out-of-doors, on a hillside by the Webutuck River or on the lawn behind the house. "The orgasms still come too infrequently," Lewis reported in his Personalia, "but this no longer spoils matters."[30]

So Sophia still had a strong hold on him, even as he was telling Catherine that he was considering marrying her. What finally began to drive that idea, that option, from his mind was Catherine's "unfaithfulness."

That September Catherine wrote him a letter that forever changed their relationship. She felt he had a right to know that she had recently gone to bed with another man, an architect she met in Germany. Amazingly, given his enormous capacity for jealousy, he wrote back calmly reassuring her that he would rather she had done this than go on in a "desperately chaste and faithful way," at odds with her inner feelings. This would have caused her to resent him, he felt sure. He had seen it happen in his relations with Sophia earlier in their marriage. "How nice it will be to sin with you," he added, almost reassuringly, "now that I won't have as a burden on my conscience and a deterrent to my natural erotic reactions, the memory of an unmitigated period of chastity on your part: how very nice."[31]

But as one of Lewis's friends once said to him, the first unfaithfulness changes everything. She had cut him deeply, and this incident would ever so slowly poison their relations. Lewis could be magnanimously forgiving, but he was a man who rarely forgot. If she had been "faithful" to him, he told Catherine at the end of their relationship, he probably would have left Sophia for her. Catherine refused to believe this, however, and with good reason. Though she had really wanted to marry him, she had never believed for a minute that he was ready to leave Sophia. They seemed too settled a pair, and he was not the kind of man who made rash and reckless decisions. Thinking about leaving Sophia was one thing; actually walking out quite another. In this respect Catherine knew him better than he knew himself, for his pride and ego often opened him up to self-delusion.[32]

When Catherine returned from Germany in November they quarreled on their first evening together and for weeks afterwards, for he found it impossible to mask his hurt and anger. But within a month they resumed their affair on an even higher pitch. Catherine fell totally in love with him, and he allowed her into parts of his life no one else had ever entered. He began to share his work with her, giving her the manuscript of "Form and Personality" to read and comment on, and, what's more, he actually heeded her advice.

With her, he let down his emotional as well as his intellectual barriers. He even told her his "Meredithian" secret—that since he was a boy not yet ten years old he had suspected that he was the illegitimate son of a "mysterious Jewish gentleman" who sent him handsome presents and occasionally visited their home. He wanted to open his whole life to her in a way he had not done with anyone else. And as he slowly regained his sexual confidence, overcoming his occasional impotency, they became eager, impassioned lovers. Sex, not the greatest part of their early attraction, became central to their whole relationship, far more important, although he would never admit it in print, than the intellectual bond.[33]

In his autobiography Mumford claims that at this point in their affair, with Catherine just back from Europe, it was she, not Sophia, who was "on probation"; that Sophia and he "were now closer than ever."[34] But this gives a false picture of his feelings for Catherine. When he met Catherine he told her that he had "no need for erotic compensation in another woman." Sophia satisfied his sexual needs. Later in the year all this changed. Their sexual relations became "so complete and deep that they tended to displace Sophia from one place in my life where . . . her position had seemed impregnable," he wrote Catherine in the second summer of their affair.[35]

Catherine was finding this high-minded, somewhat aloof man a surprisingly passionate lover; he was teaching her as much about love as he was about life. "If you really wanted to perform a public duty," she wrote him not long after her return from Germany, "you ought to give lessons to modern men on how to make love," which is exactly, of course, what he wanted to hear, being so unsure about his abilities as a lover. If she hadn't met him she might have gone through the rest of her life thinking she was "a frigid girl, incapable of getting much out of going to bed with a man. I did it very easily because it didn't matter: it was part of our convention not to be excited by sex or pay much attention to it. I never used to agree with you when you said it was central and important." But now she did.[36]

Their letters began to register the exhilaration they found in sex together. These letters, full of explicit references to their lovemaking, show a different side of him, the passionate, even bawdy Lewis Mumford. And the fact that he preserved them and placed them in his papers (with tight restrictions on their use) shows that he was as proud of his triumphs as a lover as he was of his successes as an author. "As to your orgasms," he wrote Catherine, "I count them along with *The Golden Day* as the only two really successful works of art I have produced so far."[37] Catherine said she had never had an orgasm before meeting him; now, in their lovemaking, she claimed she rarely failed to. If he wanted to preserve "even the semblance of a fine respectable intellectual friendship" he would have to find some way to keep her from having orgasms, she wrote him.[38]

When he was living at Sunnyside Gardens they would usually meet several times a week in Manhattan for part of the afternoon, with Lewis always leaving punctually by five o'clock to return home for supper with Sophia. (Even in matters of the heart, this writer who railed in his books against the clocklike regularity of modern life was an exasperatingly regular man.) In the summer, when he and Sophia were in Leedsville, he would come down to New York on the train for several days every few weeks and he and Catherine would stay at the Hotel Lexington, their nights and days, as Lewis described them, "concentrated almost vehemently upon our bodies."[39] However, even with Catherine his work came first, and sometimes this caused considerable tension, as in the summer of 1932, when he refused to break away from his writing to spend a few days with her on the New England coast.

In the midst of this disagreement he happened to be reading Carl Jung, and some of Jung's revelations, he wrote Catherine, were causing him "to think clearly about us and our little difficulties."

Jung had written that a man who writes "does not want to tell of the secret alliances, the *faux pas* of his mind. . . . Just as a woman erects her stronghold of power in sexuality, and will not give away any of the secrets of its weak side, so a man centers his power in his thinking and proposes to hold it as a solid front against the public, particularly against other men." A man was more likely to let down his intellectual guard with a woman, Jung argued, especially a so-called "hetaira" type, who feels that his thinking is "something embryonic which she helps to develop. Paradoxical as it may seem, even a cocotte may sometimes know more about the spiritual growth of a man than his own wife."

This "[gives me] a very sharp image of you and me," Lewis explained to Catherine, ". . . I had seized you and appropriated you in just this relation: and you had accepted the seizure and appropriation because it fitted the person you had been and wanted to be; for it was not entirely as a jest—was it?—that you have accepted the label of the 'Mistress type' from that girl at college."[40]

But lately this had been changing. Catherine, the casual mistress, was becoming the wife; and Lewis saw danger in this, for though a wife may tolerate a mistress, she cannot possibly tolerate another wife. Catherine wanted him for herself, not to share. Last summer he had thought about marrying her, but now he admitted to her that he was more awake to the problems this would bring, aside from those of breaking up "very close and real ties" and the almost insoluble "economic problems [of] divorce."

Catherine's behavior in Germany and his growing doubts that she would ever be willing to give up her independence, as Sophia had, had caused him to stop thinking about leaving Sophia. He would demand this of any woman he married; that and complete fidelity. On both counts he wasn't sure he could trust Catherine to surrender to his demands.

He also worried about Catherine's possible impact on his future work.[41] At the moment their sex together was energizing his writing, but he feared that if they became permanent partners this, too, would change. Catherine would try to pull him away from his work to be with her. Deserting Sophia to be with her would be "easier" than deserting his work, he told Catherine, "for my work is the foundation for my self-confidence and self-respect." Every now and then, just to prove this to himself, he broke an engagement with Catherine with the excuse that he had pressing work to do. There is a terror at the bottom of every writer's heart, he once remarked to Catherine, "that he may get so involved in his feelings as to forget that very precious part of his life which is the source of his manliness, not his sexual organs, but his mind."

Still, running against all these currents of withdrawal was his love for her, his desire to be with her constantly. These were the paradoxes of their relationship. "How can I preserve our marvelous hetaira relation without making you a wife; and how [can] you become a wife without destroying the hetaira relation?"[42] He must have secretly suspected that their failure to resolve this dilemma would eventually kill their relationship.

Like any long love affair, theirs ebbed and flowed, and each time they argued Lewis, ever the pessimist, suspected that the end was in sight. His notes and letters are filled with panicky false alarms. Underneath his outward poise and self-confidence was a layer of insecurity, a lurking fear that he would do something to lose her. Neither of them, apparently, was careful about birth control, and in early 1932, a time when they were not getting along together very well, Catherine became pregnant. Lewis was teaching at Dartmouth, so she went for an abortion by herself. He knew that she had had two previous abortions, which had ended two earlier relationships, so he feared for the worst. But when he returned from Hanover, New Hampshire, just after her recovery, they found themselves once again "feverishly, deliciously" in love. "Life seems so complete Catherine no longer wants to marry me," he wrote in his notes.[43]

This is how things stood when Lewis prepared to leave for Germany in the spring of 1932. Sophia knew that Catherine would join him in Germany; and Catherine was aware that Sophia would meet him in England as soon as she returned to the States. Neither woman was pleased with this arrangement, but both were determined to make the best of it.

Lewis would later describe these several months abroad as one of "the best and worst" periods of his life; the four-month trip turned out to be a turning point in both his intellectual and emotional life. Inspired by his discoveries at Munich's Deutsches Museum and by what he saw in Europe of the new order in urban planning and architecture, he outlined the first volume of his Renewal of Life series on the long sea journey back to New York. "That was a decisive moment in my life," he wrote years later. "I saw the whole series take form before me."[44] And in Europe that summer his relationship with Catherine Bauer also took a decisive turn.

17

Love and Work

When I die probably no one will realize that the old man in the coffin was once a great lover.

—CARL GUSTAV JUNG

That summer Mumford's best days were spent alone in quiet study in the spacious library of Munich's Deutsches Museum. There, with the help of its director, Oskar von Miller, he discovered studies on technology written in German and French that no American scholars had consulted. He also visited lovely old cities like Lübeck, a place he lost his heart to. But he had gone in search of the new Europe, not the old, the exciting experiments in architecture, housing, and city planning that he had followed with fascination in the pages of Walter Curt Behrendt's journal *Die Form*. The splendidly designed factories, schools, and housing developments he visited in Berlin, Frankfurt, and Zurich convinced him that in Europe "a new world was dawning" where the machine would be applied "to the relief of man's estate." In technology, architecture, and urban planning Europe was far in advance of his own country. Even the European automobiles seemed to him more soundly designed than America's, while the very kiosks and telephone booths on the streets "spoke a fresh language that was unknown in America." After a devastating war Germany had remade itself into a nation "clean and strong and powerful."[1]

In his travels that summer Mumford met scores of influential architects, writers, and city planners, including Le Corbusier, Erich Mendelsohn, Martin Wagner, Ernst May, and Siegfried Giedion, the French art historian who was preparing a major work on the history of technology; but it was a visit with Karl Vossler, the biographer of Dante, that left the strongest impression on him. At one point in their leisurely afternoon conversation in Munich, Vossler asked his American guest if he had met Thomas Mann. When Lewis said he had not but that he had read *The Magic Mountain* three times, Vossler rose slowly from his chair, picked up the phone, and arranged an appointment. "No author," he raised his forefinger for emphasis, "could resist such a reader!"[2]

These Munich days crowned Mumford's stay in Germany. It is a measure of just how engrossed he was in his work that he failed to give more attention in his travel notes to the fascist movement that was about to storm to power. In Lübeck, where he spent considerable time, the Brownshirts were everywhere, marching in twos and threes. Yet while Lewis feared for the worst, he was shocked when the Nazis overturned the republic without great resistance less than a year later. The dawn that he had seen breaking in Europe "turned out to be a false dawn; and the sense of a new civilization was a mirage," he wrote later.[3]

In Paris, Lewis rejoined Catherine Bauer, who had met him earlier in Munich but had gone off on her own to research the articles on European housing Lewis had arranged to write for *Fortune* magazine. Just after Lewis sailed for Europe, Sophia had sent him an anxious note asking him to remember when he was with his "companion" that "Sophy has her points too."[4] As it turned out she needn't have worried. His days with Catherine convinced him that, as much as he loved her, he would never leave Sophia for her. There was "something finer and more noble in [Sophia]," we find him writing in his notebook just before meeting her in London, "something unselfish that brought out a greater devotion." Marriage to Catherine would be "suicidal for me, probably for both of us, just because of our intellectual stimulation and sympathy." When they were together for long stretches of time he and Catherine found that they tended to wear each other out sexually and intellectually.[5]

When they first met in Munich, Lewis had wanted to work, but she had wanted to make love, to spend all of her hours with him.[6] In Paris, when he was ready for lovemaking she had a great urge to work; all she talked about their first night together in a Paris hotel was housing reform.[7] So they quarreled for the next few days, and he began to see Catherine's coming to Europe with him as a colossal mistake. The intervals he was alone were periods of relief and "recovered wholeness." He also resented the tedious fact-gathering he had to do on the housing situation, work he had taken on so that Catherine could be with him. By the time they prepared to leave for London they were both tense and irritable.[8]

He was certain now that he would never leave Sophia for Catherine; and Catherine, of course, sensed this too. From this time on, there was an ever-present tension in their relationship. For Lewis, at least, it was the "possibility of permanence" that made the crucial difference in a sexual relationship.[9] That was henceforth missing in his relations with Catherine.

Still, the entire trip was an unlocking experience for him, a "magnificent procession of days," as he described it in a letter to Henry Murray. "I never studied to such purpose or lived quite so intensely before."[10]

On his return to New York, after completing the *Fortune* articles and doing some "hack work" to pay expenses for another ear operation for Geddes, Lewis gave himself completely to his new book. While he continued to see Catherine regularly, she took second place to this large project she had inspired him to take on. She was understanding about this, assuring him that she cared more about his work than she did "about you personally-and-me." A man with his kind of passion and ambition could not satisfy these drives "and be *first* a helpful husband and a kind and considerate lover," she told him. "If those things follow along, then you and the ladies are just lucky, but it's not really so very important. . . . Ladies don't fall in love with men like you for primary purposes of kindness and consideration."[11]

He had the capability to produce a great book, she wrote him just after their return from Europe, and that must be his first responsibility. But with Catherine it was never all business. "Books aside, it would be rather a good [time] for one of our . . . sensual, exhausting, [and] delicious afternoons. What's that? We must work? We must write housing articles so that we can have money so that we can work some more so that we can write books? Bunk! Take your clothes off."[12] That was Catherine. Just as he got superserious about something, often with her encouragement, she would bring him back to earth—and to her. Very few people in his life ever had that kind of power over him.

That fall Lewis felt more at ease emotionally than he had since 1926, the most satisfying year of his life up to then. He had arrived at an understanding with Catherine, or so he thought, and with Sophia, who seemed so much better poised, and hence had more to give him. By December he was in a state of mind near-perfect for work. "The worldly life does not mean anything to me and does not satisfy me," he declared in his notebook in January 1933, more a New Year's resolution than a completely candid declaration of his outlook. He had learned a lot in the last four years; it was time to go back to work, to "the real life."[13]

Once he began the writing he worked in virtual seclusion, living a strict and regular life, refusing telephone calls and asking even his closest friends to confine their contacts to correspondence. With his usual penchant for self-dramatization, he began to feel that his entire life had been a preparation for this new book, which was forcing him to draw more demandingly upon his creative powers than he had ever before. His earlier books were interpretations of writers and facts most of his readers were generally familiar with, but in this new book he had "to supply the materials, as yet ungathered and uncoordinated, as well as the interpretation," he explained to his friend John Gould Fletcher. This was presenting enormous problems of physical organization as well as of style, for the book incorporated a tremendous amount of material, and parts of the argument would be difficult to follow without close concentration.[14] Yet though he had never worked so hard on a book, the writing had never gone more easily. The book was driving him "like the voice of Jehovah"; it would make everything he had written up to then seem thin and amateurish by comparison. It would be a book, he boasted to Van Wyck Brooks, "to out-Bentham the Benthamites, to out-Marx the Marxians, and in general, to put almost anybody and everybody who has written about the machine or modern industrialization or the promise of the future into his or her place." Its scheduled publication date was April 19, 1934, exactly one year after he had begun writing: "an auspicious day! It is the battle of Lexington for *my revolution*."[15]

Mumford's heavy program of reading for his new book reinforced his conviction that the commanding problem of the current age was Western society's unquestioning commitment to material progress, a strongly planted faith that involved an almost complete abdication to the machine and machine processes. In *Technics and Civilization* he traces the rise and triumph of this cult of the machine in the Western world, recording its often debasing impact upon imagination, free choice, and creative living. (Mumford borrowed the word "technics" from Oswald Spengler, and used it to designate the industrial arts themselves, as distinguished from their systematic study, technology.)

Mumford divides the modern machine age into three overlapping phases, each characterized by a particular mode of energy and technology: the eotechnic, the paleotechnic, and the neotechnic. He borrowed the latter two terms from Patrick Geddes, who had used them to designate the age of coal and steam, and the succeeding age of clean-burning electricity and new metals, such as aluminum and steel. But he believed that his Scottish master had ignored the critical "period of preparation," when all the key modern machines necessary to universalize technology were either invented or foreseen. He called this period the eotechnic age, and it became for him the European equivalent of America's Golden Day.*

Mumford's eotechnic era stretched from the Middle Ages to the dawn of the Industrial Revolution in the eighteenth century. In this period, often mischaracterized as technologically backward, a series of inventions and discoveries opened the way for the industrial and scientific revolutions, chief among them the mechanical clock, the telescope, the printing press, the magnetic compass, and the blast furnace. It was an era of rich cultural diversity and technological achievement, an age that joined its accomplishments in the mechani-

---

*In 1959, Mumford rejected this three-part division—eotechnic, paleotechnic, and neotechnic—calling it "the most original and yet in some ways the most dubious part of the whole book." See LM, "An Appraisal of Lewis Mumford's *Technics and Civilization* (1934)," *Daedalus*, LXXXVIII (Summer 1959), pp. 527–36.

cal and practical arts with a cultivation of the sensual and the spiritual, with magic, myth, and ceremony. Society's standard of value was not power and economic success alone "but a greater intensification of life: color, perfume, images, music, sexual ecstasy." In the rounded culture of the late Middle Ages, machine technics were used directly "in the service of life," to build cities and cathedrals, for example, that were outstanding works of art and utility.

This balanced civilization, however, gave way eventually, in Mumford's sweeping moral drama, to the paleotechnic era, an age dominated by science, technology, and capitalism. Eotechnic man had been vitally interested in science and technics, but paleotechnic man transformed this estimable concern into a determined effort to bring the whole of human experience under the direction of science and the machine. Capitalism further contributed to this process of cultural debasement by subordinating all values to profit and productivity, and like the new science, it glorified power as well as "abstraction, measurement and quantification."[16] As Mumford would comment elsewhere: "It was not by accident that Newton, the physicist, became master of the mint."[17]

The entire age was characterized by an absence of a sense of limits—growth was its supreme imperative. The merchant could not be too rich; the state could not possess too much territory; the city could not become too big. Progress came to be reckoned by the amount of goods produced, and work, once considered merely "a necessary part of living," became "an all-important end."

This Faustian age, however, was not the beginning of the end of civilization, as Oswald Spengler had predicted. Mumford saw himself living in the dawning decades of an age that promised to redirect science and the machine in the interests of freedom and social community. At this point in his book hard analysis often gives way to wishful thinking, as he cites all the new advances in architecture, engineering, city building, transportation, industry, and science that promise to bring into being the kind of regional, or "neotechnic," civilization he had been promoting for over a decade. Recalling the words of Matthew Arnold, he describes America as a nation "living . . . between two worlds, one dead, the other powerless to be born." America has at its disposal the skill and knowledge to shape a new world, he argues; yet the persistence of outdated paleotechnic habits, and of capitalism in particular, prevents the full utilization of these technics for human enrichment.[18]

Technics and Civilization is a pioneering work in the history of technology, a book that would begin to establish Mumford as this century's leading critic of the machine age. Along with Siegfried Giedion's later work *Mechanization Takes Command*, published in America in 1948, and Abbott Payson Usher's more narrowly focused study *A History of Mechanical Inventions* (1929), it created the new field of the history of technology.[19] It is both the first full-scale study in the English language of the rise of the machine in the modern world and one of the first scholarly studies in any language to emphasize the interplay of technology and the surrounding culture. Mumford describes not simply the work of inventors and scientists but also the cultural sources and moral consequences of the breakthroughs in technology and science. He places technology squarely within the context of what he calls the social ecology.

Drawing on the latest German scholarship, Mumford analyzes the process of ideological preparation for full mechanization. Before his book appeared most English-speaking scholars placed the beginnings of the Industrial Revolution in the eighteenth century, when Watt introduced his steam engine and when machine power was applied to the production of textiles. In Munich, however, Mumford discovered a challenging new literature on the history of technology that caused him to locate the origins of the machine age as far back as the Middle Ages, when a number of cultural transformations occurred that prepared the ground for the larger technical revolution that altered all of Western culture. "Men became mechanical," in Mumford's words, "before they perfected complicated machines to express their new bent and interest." The passion for order, regularity, and regimentation appeared first in the routinized world of the medieval monastery, then spread to the army and the counting-house before it finally entered the factory. In this mental transformation the clock played a crucial role. It, not the steam engine, was the most important machine of the industrial age, an interpretation now widely accepted by historians of science and technology. The mechanical clock brought a new regularity to life, for it was not merely a means of keeping track of the hours but of synchronizing human behavior. The first primitive clocks were used in monasteries to regulate the ringing of the bells, which in turn regulated the daily movements of the monks; later, to become "as regular as clockwork" became "the bourgeois ideal." Timekeeping also became essential to an efficiently run system of production and transportation.[20]

With the new conception of time came a closely related concern with exact measurement; together these developments led to the emergence of what Mumford calls a new scientific picture of the world. In its urge to comprehend and control the physical world, the new science, he argues, defined as "real" only those aspects of experience that were external and repeatable, that could be studied and verified by careful experimentation. Existence was separated into units that could be "weighed, measured or counted"; all else was judged "unreal." This denial of the organic, in Mumford's view, allowed the West to surrender to the machine, to turn inventions and mechanical contrivances that other cultures, such as the Chinese, possessed in abundance, into what he calls "the machine." By this term he meant not only mechanical devices but a mode of life geared to the pace of high-speed technology, and committed to the technological ideals of specialization, automation, and rationality.

For Mumford, then, the emergence of the machine was fundamentally a mental revolution, a movement from organic to mechanical thinking; this is in direct contradiction with Karl Marx, who saw technology shaping values and ideas, and not the reverse. Mumford's refusal to see the machine as a force independent of human will and purpose explains the underlying optimism of *Technics and Civilization*. Rejecting all forms of technological or economic determinism, he insists that human desires, decisions, and dreams influenced the course of modern invention fully as much as invention influenced the modern sensibility. Our modern machine world was a creation of human effort and will, and any thoroughgoing change would first involve a change in values and social priorities. Mumford had said this before, but from this point forward this theme became *the* theme of his life and art.[21]

"The great book arrived yesterday noon," Van Wyck Brooks wrote Mumford in early 1934, "and I sat me down and read it for seven hours straight. . . . It is . . . an absolute triumph. . . . You may have written the great book of the epoch."[22] The reviews were all that an author could ask for, and the book sold reasonably well, about 5,000 copies in the first year. Its success surprised even Alfred Harcourt, who had not had great faith in it as a commercial venture. Lewis should have been riding high, but all that spring and summer he was absolutely miserable; just as his book went to press he and Catherine ended their affair. Now that he was free finally for "lovemaking and adventure and needed it most," he had apparently lost her for good.[23]

The break had been coming for some time—since Germany something vital had gone out of their relationship—yet it was a shattering experience for both of them, for Lewis especially. It was not just that he still loved her. It was the way they parted. She had taken another lover, whom she had been seeing on and off over the past year, and he was a recent friend of Lewis's. What he had done to Sophia several years earlier Catherine had now done to him.

Clarence Stein had introduced Lewis to Oskar Stonorov, a young German architect and sculptor, in New York in 1929, shortly after Stonorov emigrated to the United States. In the spring of 1932, Lewis ran into him again on board the *Europa*, and the dashing Stonorov, then only twenty-seven years old, treated him like "a long-lost brother," taking him to Lübeck and introducing him to his circle of friends.[24]

Back in the states, while Lewis was writing the first draft of *Technics and Civilization*, Catherine, who knew Stonorov through his friendship with Clarence Stein, took a job with him on a labor-sponsored public housing effort in Philadelphia. They were physically attracted to one another, and sometime early in 1933 they went to bed together. Catherine didn't tell Lewis this at the time, but she did admit (probably because she felt he would find out anyway) that she had flirted with Stonorov, and that she was attracted to him and to at least one other man.

Lewis was convinced that she had become interested in other men because he had been totally absorbed in his book. When a writer really gets down to his work "nothing outside really matters," he told her, "nothing can break in; and no matter how satisfactorily one may fuck and dally, one's lover cannot help knowing this." This Catherine-inspired creation had actually distanced him from her. Yet while he was certain that it was "the book" that was destroying his relationship with Catherine, he was unable to convince her of this. He pressed her incessantly on the matter, trying to dig out "the truth" so stubbornly, so overbearingly insistent that he feared she was beginning to see him as "some horrible combination of a psychoanalyst and a district attorney." Catherine kept assuring him that there was nothing to the Stonorov thing; that she loved him more now than she ever had before. But he wasn't convinced. He saw her attraction to Stonorov as a sure sign of her diminished interest in him, and behind this, he suspected, was her rising resentment over his concentration on his work. He demanded that she admit that this was the problem so that they could "face it and face it down." He wanted the truth. But when she finally came out with it, it wasn't what he expected, or wanted, to hear.[25]

In what is probably the most revealing letter she ever wrote him, Catherine calmly explained that it wasn't his commitment to work, but his commitment to Sophia that had been bothering her. Their problem, she told him, in an ingenious twist of his own theory of the interconnection of past, present, and future, "[is that] we have to live in the Present. We have no Future." At the very beginning of the affair they both thought they had a future, but after their trip together in Germany she finally saw that they didn't. It was at this point that she began to be more "conscious of other men." She couldn't tie herself exclusively to him any longer because she couldn't have him; he was Sophia's man. "And don't be an idiot! This has nothing whatever to do with your *work*. Your work is part of my life and our love, whether you want it to be or not."

She wasn't going to apologize for her behavior with Stonorov, or even promise that it would not happen again. There were times when she would want to have "temporary relationships—situations which I dominate, which I start and stop and [can] make anything I please of, and in which I call the tempo. . . ." He would have to learn to live with that. They both knew, however, that he would find that impossible. Nor could Catherine ever get him to admit that it was his commitment to his marriage that was causing their problems. He even protested that it was unfair for her to bring up a limitation in their relationship that he could do nothing about, not seeing, or at least not admitting, that that was just it: she *did* want him to do something about it. She still loved him as much as before, but to protect herself she couldn't give him as much of herself as she once had, knowing he would never leave Sophia.

She pleaded with him not to break off their relationship, but if he did, she wanted him to know that she would not be bitter. He had done so much for her—had opened up "a whole new world of possibility . . . of large desire and of hopeful delight in my capacities. . . . You transformed an insufferable smart-y dilettante into a good semblance of a serious and responsible worker." He had even started her thinking about marriage—her a resolutely independent woman who had once thought she was destined to lead a life of "bachelordom." She knew now she couldn't have him for a husband, but she still wanted him as a "lover and master."[26]

They both knew, however, that he never intended to leave her, and they were soon back together. But after this it was never as good as it had been before. He detected a coolness in her attitude toward him, and though they became more technically proficient as lovers, their lovemaking was not as satisfying to him as it had once been.[27]

When they had started seeing each other, Catherine was not even remotely interested in social issues. She didn't much like "reformers," she had told him, and talk about politics or city planning bored her.[28] Yet this somehow had made her all the more attractive to him. She had been a challenge for him, a woman to be conquered and converted.

But once Catherine was drawn into Lewis's life, her own life had taken a different direction. She began to read more widely on politics, labor, and city planning, and became increasingly involved in the Regional Planning Association, becoming executive secretary of the organization in 1932. Clarence Stein also gave her a job as his research assistant, work that further advanced her burgeoning interest in community architecture and low-income housing.[29]

Catherine was a fast learner. By 1932, after her European trip with Lewis, she felt she knew enough about new housing departures to write a book of her own. "Rereading [your] *Golden Day*," she wrote Lewis, "makes me feel that perhaps *I* can write a good little book."[30] That year she began work on it with a contract from Houghton Mifflin.

It was at this time that she was drawn into the New Deal's public housing effort, and into an affair with Oskar Stonorov. With Lewis's encouragement, she took a position in Philadelphia as principal adviser and executive secretary of the Housing Labor Conference, which was then working with the American Federation of Full-Fashioned Hosiery Workers on the Carl Mackley Houses, one of the first housing projects of the New Deal. Stonorov was the chief designer, and John Edelman, later an important labor leader, was the Hosiery Workers' man on the project. Together with "Casy," as her friends called Catherine, they became a formidable brain trust and lobbying team, at one point leading a labor march on city hall. Catherine loved working with the kind of committed, practical-minded people she met in the union movement, and she threw herself into her new job, putting in regular sixteen-hour working days. When she wasn't immersed in labor projects she was writing her book, and the strain took its toll on her relations with Lewis. She returned to New York only infrequently, and her letters to him began to be dominated by talk of housing and the labor struggle. Even when they met occasionally for an afternoon in a New York hotel room, she often was too tired or preoccupied for the kind of intensely passionate sex they had once enjoyed.

In becoming more like her lover, she had less time for him, and Lewis could blame only himself for this. He admired her new passion for reform, but he missed the old bawdy, irresponsible Catherine, the carefree girl with "no social conscience" he had fallen in love with. "I reach for you [now] and what do I touch?" he wrote her in Philadelphia. "A housing expert. I call for you in the stillness of the night and what do I hear? The percentage of vacancies in *Laubengang* apartment houses in Germany as compared with cottages."[31]

Nor did he like the direction her career was taking. He had always believed that her true talent was writing, that she had the ability to be another Virginia Woolf, one of his favorite authors. But now she was veering toward social activism. She was finding that she preferred the immediate excitement of public activism to the reflective life. He saw this as a rejection of him.

It was actually, however, more an assertion of her independence than anything else. Lewis had helped to drive her interests in a new direction, but now she began to question his approach to the social changes they both envisioned. It started with her questioning the strategy of some of the leaders of the Regional Planning Association. Architects like Clarence Stein and Henry Wright believe that changing society is largely a matter of training "experts" who would build better communities *"for* people," she wrote to him from Philadelphia while involved in the Carl Mackley project. But working with Stonorov was convincing her that workers and common people must take the lead in any movement toward a better world, and that once intelligently planned communities were built, the residents must have an active part in their governance. Most of the RPAA types, she added, "would rather see 'perfect' housing developments issuing solely from a sort of supertechnical machine than less perfect (possible) ones which represented a real gain in understanding, power and responsibility for the people who live in them."³²

She also began to aim some arrows directly at him. "There isn't a society in which the isolated intellectual, an intellectual, as an *individual* writing and talking to the general public, can expect to provide *direct* leadership, straight-line influence on policy and action." Leaders must "win their spurs thru [sic] organizational activity of one sort or another." She didn't deny that, in the long run, "indirect influences may be more important," or that organizational activism "can be wasteful of time and energy, blunting of purpose and philosophy, corrupting even." But she wanted him to know that there was another and, to her mind, more effective way, to introduce change.³³

He tried to take a high-minded view of all this, telling her that he had watched her development with an almost motherly pride. But her drive toward independence would not be complete, he feared, until she had left him. The instrument of her release, he had predicted early in their affair, would almost surely be another man. No matter what the extent of Catherine's involvement with him, the affair would probably kill their relationship.³⁴

He couldn't have foreseen their future more accurately. When he met Catherine on one of her trips to New York in April 1934, just after he finished *Technics and Civilization*, she talked of nothing else but her involvement in the Philadelphia housing struggle, an involvement that he suspected meant an involvement with Oskar Stonorov as well. He asked her if she was sleeping with him. She said she wasn't, but he saw that her mind was on him. She talked about their work together even as she undressed to go to bed with him that afternoon. That was too much for his pride, and he refused to have sex with her. They quarreled, and she returned to Philadelphia that evening. It was the last time they were together as lovers.

Later that month *Technics and Civilization* appeared. He sent Catherine an advance copy, but she was too preoccupied with her own work to read even a part of it. This finally convinced him that their relationship was over, for he could not disassociate Catherine from his new book. It was the *"leit-motiv"* of their entire intellectual and sexual relationship.[35] He had begun the book when they first fell in love; it was interrupted for two years by his absorption with her; they began to drift apart after their summer together in Europe, when he compiled the essential research for the book; and she had her first flirtation with Stonorov just as he began writing it. Now he suspected that she had returned to Stonorov just as he was putting the final touches on the manuscript. He learned that he was right about this several weeks later, when she wrote him a letter confessing that she had recently gone to bed with Stonorov and might be in love with him, even though she still claimed to love Lewis as much as she ever had.[36]

She couldn't have hurt him more. Why, he wrote her, did she have to end the affair like this, when several weeks earlier he had "gracefully" arranged for his own "exit" so that they could remain friends? He accused her of treachery and unfaithfulness. She had never stopped being unfaithful to him.[37]

What made all this doubly difficult for him to accept was his growing realization, after his break with Catherine, that the happiness he and Sophia had experienced together over the past four years was "bound up," as he confided to Henry Murray, "with the continued presence of Catherine, as a balancing factor" in his intellectual and sexual life. With Catherine gone, "the deep physiological weakness" of his marriage was exposed again.[38] Secretly, he had long suspected that the greatest problem in his marriage was that he and Sophia were physically "mismatched . . . for the purposes of sexual intercourse": that she would have been happier with someone with "a larger and more insistent penis," and that he would have been happier with a woman he could arouse more easily. He and Catherine had such a "perfect" physical match.[39]

In losing Catherine he would also be losing his closest confidante. The real value of psychology, as he once told a friend, is that it gives a troubled person an intelligent, sympathetic listener. One's notebooks were not enough. "I know, I use them."[40]

Catherine probably would have continued her relationship with him had he agreed to let her go on with Stonorov, but he couldn't share her with anyone else. When that became clear to her, she completed her retreat from him. He didn't make this easy, however. In letter after insistent letter he told her that he wanted at least to keep up their "intellectual friendship." If he couldn't have "the Catherine of the Flesh" he would settle for "the Catherine of the Spirit." But on this matter he was not being completely honest, even with himself. He wanted both Catherines, and he undoubtedly hoped to use a renewed intellectual relationship to win her back as his lover. He knew that they could not have an entirely intellectual relationship; their lovemaking and their "thinking" had always been intimately connected.[41]

The demands he made on her for the resumption of their "friendship" indicate that he was thinking this way. Before they met again they must have the whole thing out, he wrote her. There would have to be some sort of purgation. This had always been his way of dealing with an unsettling emotional problem—to face it and to face it down, as he liked to say. But Catherine wasn't up to it. She thought it would only make matters worse between them. In a transparent effort to bait her, he informed her that summer that he had made her coexecutor of his literary papers (with Paul Rosenfeld), but this didn't work either.[42] She began to write less frequently and made no effort to see him.

He took the break harder than she did, and smoldered about it for far longer. He formed the habit of waking every morning at four-thirty, and while he lay in his bed, unable to return to sleep, he would have stormy arguments in his mind with Catherine. Again and again, in his random notes and his occasional letters to her, he reviewed their entire relationship—all the hurt and joy they had known together—and he continued to plead with her to get together with him to go over the "real" reasons for their separation.[43]

He was never able to accept her explanation for the break, which she reiterated to him one final time not long after they parted. He had been blind not to see "the jealousy and frustration" that had accumulated in her because he was "living perfectly happily and without serious disturbance" with his wife and family. "That's my worst grudge against you."[44] She had complained for over two years that they met only when he arranged it, when it conveniently fit his schedule. But he had ignored her protests and, further, had demanded from her complete fidelity. And when he had been unable to make her stop seeing Stonorov he had to make her feel guilty about him. This was the one side of him she had never liked: "You who used to get mixed up in [my] nightmares with my mother."[45]

All this, she told him, wasn't something they could " 'have out.' Going over and over it only . . . leaves us sorer than ever. Can't we just leave it behind?" After reading this letter Lewis knew in his heart that he had lost her forever.[46]

Catherine had good reasons for not resuming their intellectual friendship. She knew it might lead to something more, and she didn't want that to happen. She might have in the first weeks after their break, but not after Sophia became pregnant later that summer. "Sophie's being pregnant is somehow the final *finality*," she wrote Lewis in September 1934.[47]

Throughout his affair with Catherine, Lewis had resisted Sophia's desires to have another child because he feared that Catherine would leave him if Sophia became pregnant. Now he felt miserably guilty for what he had done to Sophia. In spite of this, however, he wanted Catherine, even after he knew she was lost to him forever. In this case, his heart couldn't march in step with his conscience.

He and Catherine continued to correspond and would see each other occasionally in New York. Even after he gave up hope of resuming their affair, he continued to try to influence her thinking and to control her life. Catherine had found a career better suited to her natural bent and talents than writing, but he couldn't agree, as he constantly reminded her, especially after she was drawn to the center of the government housing movement following the publication of her nationally acclaimed book *Modern Housing* (1934). Catherine Bauer went on to become one of the principal moving forces for a federal program of public housing, as a policy adviser to a succession of presidents, from Franklin D. Roosevelt to Lyndon B. Johnson, and as a professor of city and regional planning and associate dean of the College of Environmental Design at the University of California at Berkeley. But even her rapid rise to national influence failed to impress Mumford. She had been unfaithful to him as a lover; now she was being unfaithful to herself by accepting "a smaller mould" than she was capable of filling. If she could no longer be his lover, couldn't she at least be a loyal pupil, loyal to the spirit of his example? "You have far too good a mind to let itself be wasted on routine. [Alter the] future of [your career]," he warned her in the solemnest tones, "before the shades of the prison house close about the growing girl."⁴⁸ It was exactly the wrong track to take, however, for she had always disliked this self-righteous side of him. And in any event she had set her course.

They were never again close friends, although Lewis kept trying to bridge the breach between them, even after Catherine married the architect William W. Wurster in 1940. Keeping her in his life was desperately important to him. "We sailors know," he wrote her, "that even . . . a casual halloo can diminish the immense loneliness of the ocean."⁴⁹ But their correspondence only drove them further apart, for inevitably the conversation turned to their diverging ways of pursuing social change. On this issue they both had too much at stake to give in, even a little.

After reading *The City in History* in 1961, Catherine wrote to him hailing the book as an "unbelievably rich and challenging experience," but something continued to bother her about the tone of his writing. He was far too pessimistic about the future of cities, far too "apocalyptic" in his judgments of the world situation, and, finally, far too contemptuous of urban policymakers. There had been some important advances in housing over the past several decades, and these changes were largely the work of activists, not philosophers, she sharply reminded him. Her work was as important, if not more important, than his; and she resented him for continually taking her to task for not broadening her sights. She was her own person, with her own ideas and ideals. She was not a "thin carbon" of Lewis Mumford.⁵⁰

Three years later Catherine Bauer Wurster died in a hiking accident in the hills near her California beach home. She had wanted to be alone that day, and while walking down a steep mountain trail she apparently hit her head and lost consciousness. She was found thirty-six hours later by a group of friends and students who had been searching for her night and day. They discovered her lying against a tree, a look of repose, almost a smile, on her face. She had died of exposure, never having regained consciousness.

Lewis took her death hard, but in the letters he wrote to friends about Catherine in the months following her death there is an undertone of resentment that stemmed from what had happened between them the year before she died.

In 1962, Lewis had returned to the autobiography he had begun a number of years earlier, sketching out two chapters on his relationship with Catherine Bauer. He wanted the story of his life to be unsparingly revealing, but a detailed account of his affair with Catherine might, he realized, hurt her and her family. So he invented a fictional character, a perfect counterpart of Catherine, but with a different career, thinking that only those who knew them would guess that it was she. Catherine, he was certain, wouldn't object to what he had written. "She would be pleased to encounter her earlier self" as seen through his "appreciative and grateful self." Nevertheless, her husband and her daughter had to be considered. When he finished the first draft of the chapters in 1963 he arranged to meet Catherine on one of her trips to New York to give them to her, assuring her that she need only say no, without explanation, and he would cut them from the book.

He didn't hear from her for many weeks. Then he received a letter informing him that she did not want him to publish the chapters. Her husband didn't object, although he naturally hoped the chapters wouldn't be published in such detailed form; it was their nineteen-year-old daughter whom they were concerned about. She might be hurt, for the fictional disguise was too transparent. Catherine's decision, Lewis claimed, "was easy to take"; her justifying letter was not.[51]

She told him that she had her own personal objections to what he had written. She had never cared for the "self-analysis side" of his work, even when it had nothing to do with her. "There always seems to me something more behind it than just the desire to prevent a truthful picture of the whole man: a touch of self-pity or self-punishment, even of confessional exhibitionism."

What she said next hurt him even more. Theirs had been "essentially a master-pupil [relationship] rather than an enduring husband-wife emotional unity." That was probably, she said, why she and Sophia had never hated each other. She admitted that she did try to "get possession" of him at several points in their relationship, "but I think I more than half-realized at the time that this was mainly the kind of low female chemistry which is almost certain to operate sooner or later in any such liaison."[52]

All this was ego-damaging enough, but even more devastating to Lewis were the notes that accompanied the chapter drafts she returned to him several months later. She had written these notes in longhand on her flight back to California, and though she now warned him that they were not meant for his eyes, how could he resist reading them? Here was the "raw uncensored version" of the explanatory letter. Here she claimed she had never really been in love with him, and that his influence on her had not been as great as he thought.[53]

The contents of these notes were so searing that he was not able to look at them again for many years. That summer he developed heart symptoms that he was sure were caused by his shock over Catherine's response to his chapters. He was devastated by her forgetfulness, he wrote Henry Murray; it brought to mind something Alfred Stieglitz had once said to him: "the cunt has no memory."[54]*

Catherine destroyed what had become almost as important to him as their original relationship—his affectionate recollection of that relationship. He had the longest memory in the world, he liked to say, longer than the oldest living elephant, and even into old age he relived in his mind the times they had "skipped from revelation to revelation, . . . orgasm to orgasm, and crisis to crisis." Her letters had helped keep those memories alive; he had often turned to them in order to replenish his energy and spirits. Now all this was gone, he wrote dolefully in his notes, "not merely gone, but torn to pieces, willfully destroyed."[55]

After he received the manuscript from Catherine he made no mention to her of the notes that accompanied it. He merely apologized for not realizing that his chapters might hurt her. No further words passed between them. "There was nothing left to say."[56]

---

*Mumford later destroyed his fictional account of his affair with Catherine, although he did include a briefer account of their relationship in his autobiography.

18

One More Love

The grave is dug, you the earth, you the digger.
There I will lie, asphyxiate, while you heap
The dust, the rubble, the torn sod. . . .

—LEWIS MUMFORD

In the summer of 1934, just after Lewis and Catherine parted, he and Sophia spent a pleasant few days with Van Wyck and Eleanor Brooks at their country cottage in Westport, Connecticut. Brooks was deeply into the first volume of his history of American literature, and he wanted to have his friend's impression of what he had written so far. While Brooks worked in the mornings in his tiny study at the back of the house, Mumford read his manuscript in the front sitting room. Later in the day the two writers would join their wives for a swim in Long Island Sound and a walk along Westport's country roads. After dinner they would all sit at a table outdoors under a wide-spreading apple tree, sipping wine and talking. It was a relaxing succession of days and it put Lewis, once again, in a mood for work.

He had another big book on his mind, a history of the city, and he was determined not to allow his breakup with Catherine to destroy his urge to work. "The chapters of your book gave me a new appetite to go on with mine," he wrote Brooks just after returning to Leedsville, but something else had happened at Westport to redirect his attention to this new literary project.[1]

Late one evening Eleanor Brooks had taken Lewis aside and asked him to show her his hand. Looking at his right palm, which is supposed to indicate a person's original endowment, she said: "It is the hand of a man with modest talents who, if he followed the lines here indicated, would have had a smooth and happy life." But "here are lines," she added, taking his left hand, "that show that you have sacrificed your happiness by erecting a series of purposes and goals, which will give you a more interesting life, but a more difficult one. In early middle age there is a serious break: maybe . . . a woman enters, I can't say: but after a period you go beyond it. This line indicates the affections: there are various women in your life; but although they mean something to you, they do not mean enough to deflect you from your purpose."[2]

Lewis was stunned, for neither Eleanor nor Van Wyck, he was quite certain, knew anything about his affair. "Of course it is all 'superstition!' " he wrote Catherine Bauer two days later. "But how remarkably correct as biography and character analysis." He *was* that kind of man: work had always come first for him. "If my sexual life is narrower," he wrote Catherine at another point that summer, ". . . my intellectual life will be that much more concentrated and intense." Recalling the words of Goethe, he would confront his future with "ironic cheerfulness. 'We must work, my friends: in work lies our salvation.' "[3]

Yet although the will was there the work did not come that easily. For the remainder of that year he found it impossible to give the best of himself to his book. In October he turned forty, but he felt much older than that, and he was becoming more self-conscious about his physical appearance. He had begun to put on weight and he was balding rapidly. His face was losing its lean look, he felt sluggish and irritable, and he had recurring bouts of indigestion. Always sensitive to the psychological origins of his physical maladies, he attributed some of these symptoms to the "ultra-abstemious sexual life" he had been living since his separation from Catherine.[4] Even his conversation was not as sharp without Catherine's "sharp mind to whet it"; and "since I've been living too continent a life," he reported to her, "the old confident masculine flair is gone, drooping like a pennant on a windless day."[5]

Catherine was one reason he was unable to give his full attention to his work; Alice Decker was another. Alice was married, and was Catherine Bauer's closest friend, and although Lewis knew that she was the wrong woman to fall in love with, and with Sophia due to deliver a baby in the spring, that this was absolutely the worst time to have another affair, he found it impossible to stop himself. "Well does the drowning man know his danger; willingly would he avoid it; and yet the unfortunate wretch will drown." This warning from Herman Melville kept running through his mind all that winter.[6]

Alice Decker is the hidden love of Lewis Mumford's life. He has entirely eliminated her from the written story of his life: she does not appear in any of his autobiographical writings, and there are only a few oblique references to her in his published correspondence; never is she mentioned by name. Although Mumford kept almost all his records, even his earliest adolescent love letters, there is only one thin brown envelope of letters to and from Alice Decker in his private files. A year or so before they parted, he and Alice burned the letters they had exchanged in the most passionate phase of their relationship. Neither wanted their spouses to come upon these letters; reading them, even after an interval of many years, would be too wounding, the contents, they thought, too searing. When Lewis wrote his fictionalized account of his relationship with Catherine Bauer he did not even mention his affair with Alice, and this was one of the things that had most annoyed Catherine when he gave her these chapters to review, with the explanation that he had written in such detail about their emotional and sexual relationship because he did not want to write the "half-true kind of autobiography" Henry Adams had, concealing important truths about his marriage and personal life. But "leaving out Alice," Catherine had rightly objected, "means that it isn't really a complete emotional history."[7]

"Each life," Lewis confided to an old friend while he was struggling with this part of his autobiography, "has [a] . . . story hidden away in it, which sometimes is 'told' only in neurotic breakdowns or psychotic outbreaks. I find myself wondering what on earth to do about a few wonderful but terrible, and even tragic years of my own life, which involve . . . the sin of . . . adultery. I could tell the story myself, were it not so painful to Sophia, and would be even more so, I suspect, to [my daughter] Alison. . . . Henry James's solution, to burn all the evidence and to discourage any biographic probing, may be the only answer, and even that is no final one, as Leon Edel's volumes prove."[8]

He began his affair with Alice Decker while Sophia was carrying the child she had desperately wanted to have for eight years (she had had two miscarriages), and he continued to see Alice, on and off, for two years after Alison's birth. Neither Sophia nor Alison, he feared, would ever forgive him completely for this.[9] There were other aspects of his relationship with Alice he wished to bury forever. He had come close to leaving Sophia for her, and when he didn't Alice became extremely distraught and suffered a series of psychological setbacks for which he felt partly to blame. Their parting was messy, with Alice bearing a grudge against him for several years. Later, when he began to put together his autobiography, he found it impossible to relive these experiences. And for him—a writer whose sense of the past was as keen as his sense of moment—that is what writing about them would have entailed.

He never had the kind of high-charged intellectual and sexual relationship with Alice Decker that he had with Catherine Bauer, but he would later claim that his short, stormy relationship with Alice was the "deepest union in a spiritual sense" he had had with anyone up to this point in his life. This affair, like that with Catherine, accompanied the writing of one of his most significant books, although Alice did not influence his thinking in the way that Catherine had. He began seeing Alice in late 1934, just as he started on the first draft of *The Culture of Cities*, and they parted when that vast work, perhaps his finest book, was completed. "Three months of high tragedy: three moments of joy: three years of misery. . . . The pall of those three years will long lay across my life," he wrote Jo Strongin when it was over.[10]

Lewis had known Alice for several years through Catherine Bauer. She and her husband, Duncan Ferguson, lived in New York and occasionally would run into the Mumfords at literary parties or on weekend afternoons at Alfred Stieglitz's combination studio, gallery, and salon, An American Place. Alice, then in her early thirties, was a promising sculptor who supported her art by doing occasional social work in the city. She was bright and attractive, with short brown hair and a slim-hipped, boyish figure. Although not as alluring or as obviously intelligent as Catherine Bauer, she had a captivating personality, and Lewis found her a compassionate, deeply sensitive woman. She was also something of a romantic, who came at life expecting miracles.

Alice was dissatisfied in her marriage—the passion had gone out of it—and she wanted to have a child but couldn't. She turned to Lewis primarily because Catherine had told her that he was an excellent lover, sensitive to a woman's needs. Her husband considered her cold because he could no longer rouse her, and she wanted someone to help her recover her poise and self-confidence. She had no intention of breaking up Lewis's marriage or her own; perhaps she thought that an involvement with him would somehow rekindle her marital relationship, or at least make it more tolerable. Lewis might have reinforced this idea in her mind, for, as we know, he was convinced that his "domestic balance" depended upon his maintaining an "amorous friendship, always close to love if not actively sexual, with one or more other women."[11]

When Lewis began seeing Alice he was still in love with Catherine Bauer, and it was Alice who helped him to get over her. Within a few months after they started meeting secretly he described himself as being "romantically in love" with Alice, while only "intellectually in love with Catherine." All the while he remained "domestically in love with Sophia."[12]

One reason Sophia tolerated Alice's entrance into her husband's life is that she felt sure that Alice had forced her way in. Alice had come uninvited to a small New Year's Day open house party at the Mumfords' Sunnyside Gardens home, and from then on "took possession. . . . I realize that I've put it all on Alice's shoulders. . . ," Sophia recalled. "I know she could not have succeeded in getting Lewis to be her lover without some acquiescence on his part, but I am certain that he would not at that time [with Sophia pregnant] have been the one to make advances."[13]

Sophia even came to appreciate Alice in a grudging kind of way, seeing her as a meritable rival for her husband's affections. "Lewis always used his talents on worthy subjects, which undoubtedly made it easier for me to accept," she wrote in her diary in 1972; "I would have resented being rivalled by lightweights."[14] For her part, Alice liked Sophia very much and never tried to hide her feelings for

Lewis from her. She and Catherine both considered Sophia "a fine sport" for allowing them to share Lewis "without getting a bad conscience over it"; and like many women who must share a man, they felt a strange sort of emotional alliance with the other woman in his life. When Sophia was in the hospital after Alison's birth, Catherine and Alice jointly visited her and presented her with a bouquet of flowers, inviting her to become a co-member of their newly formed "League Against War, Fascism and Lewis Mumford." Sophia later sent them a note accepting charter membership, adding in a postscript, "He's a nice man anyway."[15]

Because Alice was married, with a possessive husband, it wasn't easy for her to meet Lewis, so they were unable to have the kind of regular sexual relationship he had enjoyed with Catherine. They met when they could, for lunch or at a friend's apartment, always a little nervous that they would be discovered. Then, in April, the month Sophia delivered Alison, Alice's husband found out about their relationship and angrily demanded that Alice stop seeing Lewis. Under pressure, she agreed.

For a brief moment after Alison's birth, Lewis felt a sense of fulfillment in his relations with both Sophia and Alice. He loved Sophia; he loved their new daughter; but he also loved Alice—and he felt he could have her and Sophia, too. He and Alice had parted two weeks before, but on the night before Sophia's delivery Alice had appeared at a meeting he was expected to attend. She was overwrought about their separation and had to talk to him. He took her aside, and instead of attending the meeting, wandered with her for several hours in Central Park with both of them feeling "tragic, and desperate and ecstatic." They both sensed, at that moment, that they would go on seeing each other, no matter what the obstacles. "So here I am," he wrote Henry Murray, "with the bounty of life running over me, feeding as it were on the pain and blood of two women, with nothing lacking except the sober even rhythm of work." He was leaving for Leedsville at the end of May, "to wander and ponder and wonder and write."[16]

But that was not how it was to be. The tension between him and Sophia mounted steadily in May, and the skies broke open shortly after he saw Alice in New York in early June. Alice's husband had discovered that she had resumed her affair with Lewis and, again, he forced her to call it off. This time it looked to Lewis as if it might be for good, for Alice announced that she was moving with Duncan to Baton Rouge, Louisiana, later in the summer. She loved him more than she loved Duncan, she told Lewis tearfully, but she didn't want to break up her marriage. Not, at least, until he was ready to leave Sophia.

Lewis returned to Leedsville in a black mood, expecting to find " 'staunch old Sophy' " waiting for him, "ready to bind the wounds and restore all the missing portions of my aching Ego." He found instead his marriage in a state of near ruin. It was the worst crisis of his marital life, and neither he nor Sophia recovered from it unscarred. [17]

Sophia had not known, until after the birth of Alison, how much Alice Decker meant to her husband. When Lewis told her in the spring that he wanted to be "friends" with Alice, she had deceived herself into taking him literally. He had let out other hints she had failed to pick up—for one, trying to persuade her to name the baby Eunice instead of Alison. "Now I find it bitter," she wrote in her diary, "to face his feeling for Alice when my own baby's name is a constant reminder of her." She regretted having the baby, she told him, and she had been having suicidal thoughts since coming to the realization that Alice, or a succession of Alices, might be a permanent part of their marital landscape. [18]

Once again Sophia was hurt by her husband's excessive candor, the overflow of his self-punishing guilt. In early June, just before he had gone down to New York to see Alice, he confessed to her how much Alice meant to him, how he felt so akin to her emotionally that he could predict her responses. Sophia didn't resent him for telling her he loved Alice—if he was involved with another woman she wanted to know—but she did not want to know all the details. "The poor dumb-squitch. Does he think it makes me feel happier to know that some other woman is in such close harmony with him?" [19]

She could understand his attraction to Alice, even his going to bed with her; but she found it impossible to forgive him for the timing of the affair. He had always claimed that he respected her more than anyone else in his life, and now he had done this! Was there any depth to his sincerity? Was he all charm and no substance? She wasn't sure. She also began to wonder how many more women like Catherine and Alice there would be in his life. "If . . . he is always going to want another female on the horizon . . . then I don't know that I want to go on with him," she wrote in her diary. But by this she did not mean a divorce, for there were now two children to consider. She would stay married to him, but it would not be a full-souled commitment. She would have to "train" her feelings differently. For the moment she would swallow her pride and anger and learn to live with his being in love with Alice. All she could do was bide her time "and hope." She could be a "good sport" about something that had already happened, but not if it meant "a lifelong callousness to Lewis's shifting heart." She would "adjust" to this infidelity, but not to any more, she emphatically told Lewis, and he knew that she meant it. [20]

It was at this time that Sophia decided that she would never have another child. "I'm not young, and every successive baby will be an even greater strain, and if I can't *know* that Lewis is there, waiting for me, it just won't go. And I no longer believe he would." [21]

Their marriage healed slowly after this crisis-torn summer, and they had a good winter together. Lewis got back to his book, and Sophia, who wanted to talk further about this whole matter, did not bring it up again because she feared it would disrupt his writing. "The best thing is to be silent." [22]

Alice's move to Baton Rouge helped to ease some of the tension in Lewis and Sophia's marriage, although Lewis continued to write to her "in friendship," even though he knew that her husband was reading his letters (the condition Duncan Ferguson placed on his grudging permission for her to continue the correspondence). Then, in October, Alice returned to New York unexpectedly on business, throwing Lewis into a "perfect tumult of indecision and cross-desires." They saw each other, but he made sure that it was always in a public place. If they were alone he would want to make love to her, and that, he feared, would ruin her resolve to repair her marriage—she might not return to Duncan. On the one hand, he selfishly wanted that to happen; on the other, he knew it would have dire consequences for his own marriage and his work. Seeing Alice in New York had been "a terrible mistake," he wrote Henry Murray; both of them were devastated when she went back to Baton Rouge. Confused and deeply distraught, Alice told him that she was thinking of suicide. She wanted to know if he would ever leave

Sophia for her: she had to know! But he couldn't give her an answer.[23]

Two months later Alice and her husband were injured in an automobile accident. He came through with only cuts and bruises, but Alice suffered a severe concussion, compounded by hemorrhaging. When Lewis learned of the accident from Catherine Bauer, who rushed immediately to Baton Rouge and telegraphed him about Alice's condition, he impulsively sent a bouquet of flowers, signing his name to the card, even though he knew that Alice was unconscious. His fear was that, after temporarily regaining consciousness, she might die "without even having the consolation of a symbol" from him.[24] This gesture infuriated her husband, who wrote Lewis a note accusing him of rank thoughtlessness and "romantic childish gesturing." This was his affair and he wanted Lewis to "stay out of it." When Lewis showed the note to Sophia she told him that she agreed with Duncan, for whom she must have felt some vicarious sympathy. "Your sending the flowers was a piece of unthinking egotism. Alice was unconscious. To whom would the flowers mean anything?" What Sophia didn't know was that Lewis, in a panic, had almost gone to Baton Rouge when he learned of the accident.[25]

For the next several months, throughout Alice's long period of recovery, made more difficult by the recurrence of the psychological symptoms she had suffered before the accident (depression, massive guilt, and thoughts of suicide), Lewis closely followed her progress through correspondence with Catherine Bauer. He even offered advice on doctors through Catherine, advice he was getting from Henry Murray; and at one point he wrote to Alice's New York psychiatrist to let him know that she had been having emotional problems well before the accident, and that these were undoubtedly complicating her recovery.

Lewis learned from Catherine that Duncan Ferguson was working patiently and honorably to help bring Alice and their marriage back to full health. "When I am honest with myself I pray for Duncan's reunion with Alice," he confided to Henry Murray, whom he now leaned upon for advice more than ever before, "not because I love her less, but because I know no way of managing a life attached to two loves of such equal valence." (It was Alice's perception of this, he thought, that made her decide to make one last try with Duncan.) All the while he doubted, and perhaps secretly hoped, that Duncan would not be able to repair their marriage. He thought that Duncan was too possessive and narcissistic to recover her love.[26]

It was at this point that Alice burned Lewis's letters to her in a ritual of eradication, probably on the advice of her doctor, who, after learning of her affair with Lewis, pleaded with her to forget the past and live for the present. She was getting along better with Duncan, and Lewis had become, in her mind, the obstacle to her complete reunion with him. She wanted to "remove the objective evidence that would recall, for anyone, the true state of our relations and my actual attitude toward her and her marriage," Lewis told Henry Murray when he learned she had destroyed his letters. Now she undoubtedly felt, with Duncan's encouragement, that "I was the evil irresponsible force seeking for purely selfish indulgence to break up her marriage! . . . For the moment I am buried; and what happened before the accident belongs to the 'dark ages.' . . ."[27]

He wrote a verse about his feeling on this matter, but he couldn't publish it or send it to her, as much as he wanted it someday to reach her. It was called "Resurrection," and it went, in part:

> *The grave is dug, you the earth, you the digger*
> *There I will lie, asphyxiate, while you heap*
> *The dust, the rubble, the torn sod . . .*
> *I will be deep below: the surface will not tell*
> *Your feet when you lead his feet across,*
> *Your double heels upon my face . . .*
> *I will remain inviolate, unvisited,*
> *Within the grave you dug,*
> *You tamped in haste*
> *Lest my expired breath should ruffle chaos*
> *On your brow.*[28]

"To complete the holocaust in fair romantic fashion," he burned most of Alice's letters to him the following week. He did this, he told Catherine Bauer, to protect Sophia. The letters "would have had the power of doing real damage" should she have come upon them after his death. But his deeper reason was to try to forget Alice.[29]

He could not push her out of his mind. Although he didn't dare write to her, he continued to keep in touch with her personal life through Catherine Bauer, and in late May he learned that she was definitely "out of love" with her husband and would probably leave him and return to New York in the fall.[30] When he met her that October for lunch at one of their favorite Manhattan restaurants he saw immediately that she was in a desperate state, depressed and dangerously suicidal. Seeing her in this vulnerable state brought back all his original feelings for her. She told him that they couldn't possibly resume their old relationship, but that perhaps they could build a new one, an intimate friendship, not an affair of the heart. Even while she spoke he knew she didn't believe what she was saying. Yet as much as he wanted to pick up where they had left off the previous year, he saw that his first responsibility was to bring her back to health, to reawaken her will to live.

She asked him to suggest a New York analyst, but he recommended that she first see Henry Murray on his next trip to New York. "Alice is a love—an enchanted reflection of the soul," Murray wrote him after meeting with her several weeks later. Murray advised against analysis for the present; a gradual recuperative healing would take place over the next few months, he thought, if she saw Lewis once a week and got back to her work. "You're the only man in America who can save her from drowning." But he warned Lewis not to get passionately involved with her again, for Alice's sake and his own. "I think your life's routine should remain undisturbed this winter. Keep your relationship with wonderful Sophy *solid* and give Alice an oasis in her week." She was overcome with guilt about leaving her husband; "let her weep in your arms, but keep your aplomb and don't modify the shape of your life."[31]

It was good advice, but Lewis couldn't heed it, as much as he knew that, with a book in progress and his relationship with Sophia on a more even keel, it was the only sane and sensible thing to do.

That winter Alice went back to her work with new spirit, arranged to take an apartment with Catherine Bauer (with Lewis agreeing to pay part of her rent), and resumed an active social life. "The bleak look of pain [is] gone from her face," a relieved Lewis wrote Henry Murray, convinced that his friend had helped to work a miracle. "Never before have things been more real between me and Alice. Our coming together again has released a block in my own work." He now decided to drop his regular *New Yorker* column on the art world (although continuing his "Sky Line" segment) and complete his book over the course of the next year.[32]

Though work on the book went well after this, his relations with

Alice steadily deteriorated. It was the same problem he had had with Catherine—she demanded more of him than he was prepared to give. She would not settle for only a part of him; she wanted "all or nothing." Although Alice loved him one part of her, he suspected, was filled with angry reproach against him—"against the scholar and the prudent man who would not dare anything and who relinquished her to Duncan a year ago when she begged me silently to have her stay." He could understand her anger, yet he knew that his unwillingness to leave Sophia for Alice was not based primarily on a fear of taking risks and beginning life afresh, as Alice suspected. He simply didn't want to lose Sophia. When pressed, he always saw that she meant more to him than any other women he might also be in love with.[33] So he and Alice argued constantly, even as their sexual relationship became more regular and intense. "Our meetings," Lewis wrote her in frustration, "make us feel further apart than our partings. . . . I am not like you . . . I don't believe . . . in ultimatums or 'total renunciations.' "[34]

With Alice, as he recalled to a friend some months later, "there was never the possibility of our having together such easy amorous relations as I had had with Catherine: even after the worst effects of Alice's accident had been lived down, that was not possible: on the contrary, her torture increased in proportion to our very success as lovers: it was after reaching the highest point of ecstasy that she was thrown into an abyss of despair."[35]

Finally, he could no longer take her constant criticism of him for not having the "courage" to leave Sophia. He started seeing her less, and she soon fell in love with another man. They ended their affair in December 1937 (just as he finished *The Culture of Cities*).[36]

But she did not leave his life entirely. She divorced Duncan, remarried, and moved to an old farm near Sharon, Connecticut, only fifteen miles from Leedsville. While she and her new husband worked to fix up their run-down farmhouse, Lewis and Sophia, on Sophia's initiative, supplied them with fresh vegetables and honey and lots of advice on the charms and hardships of living in the country. "It is all very cosy," Lewis wrote Catherine Bauer, "just like Paolo and Francesca in Hell."[37]

A part of him would always feel tied to Alice; he couldn't deny that. But now that he was free from her, he felt as if he had "escaped the embraces of a boa constrictor, something fascinating, magnificent, and ruinous. At least I am alive."[38]

The month he and Alice parted and he completed *The Culture of Cities*, he had fallen into a state of extreme exhaustion and depression. This time, however, he broke free of Melville's ghost in a matter of days, and returned to health and work, putting the finishing touches on the captions for the book's illustrations. In early January he delivered the manuscript to the Manhattan offices of Harcourt, Brace and Company.

Two months later the book was published to sensational reviews, and his picture appeared on the cover of *Time* magazine. This was the crowning moment of his life as a writer.

19

The Culture of Cities

The city is built
To music, therefore never built at all
And therefore built forever.

—ALFRED LORD TENNYSON

Lewis Mumford began writing *The Culture of Cities* in September 1935, and for the next two years he worked at it with almost unbroken concentration, refusing to allow his problems with Sophia and Alice to divert him from this consuming project, his only anchor in these difficult times. When he completed the book he felt that he had written his finest work, although, to Catherine Bauer, he did confess a concern about its length: "The middle-aged vice of completeness and overcomprehensiveness has taken the place of my youthful vice of sketchiness and superficiality. . . . I am afraid I will have to be content with one of those classic treatises which no one ever has the courage to read from cover to cover, but which, like *Das Kapital*, makes its impression decisive through the impact of one or two great chapters."[1]

In early March he sent Van Wyck Brooks an advance copy of the book, and several weeks later his good friend wrote him the letter he had been hoping to get, hailing *The Culture of Cities* as an "extraordinary" achievement, "so packed with ideas that a whole generation might live on the crumbs from your feast."[2] Over the next several months the reviews were almost universally favorable. The book was seen by several critics as a landmark in urban literature, perhaps the finest book written about the city.[3]

This book had been building inside him since his first encounter with the world and work of Patrick Geddes. More than any of his previous works, it showed his great debt to his Scottish master and, less obviously, to Oswald Spengler, whose interpretation of culture cycles continued to influence his thinking. Like his writing on architecture, *The Culture of Cities* draws extensively on Mumford's firsthand knowledge of cities, on the enormous body of notes he made in two decades of urban observation in America and Europe. The book, in fact, is like a great city in itself, packed with all the vitality, imagery, and energy of the urban spectacle it describes. It is a work of history, certainly, but it is history with an unmistakable didactic thrust. The entire book is shaped into an intricately woven argument for the kind of city Mumford had been advocating in his work for the Regional Planning Association of America. In this sprawling, richly illustrated book, Mumford sees all of urban history through the prism of his regionalist faith. He describes the cities of the past and present as a basis for building the cities of tomorrow.

The book's unifying theme is consistent with everything of importance Mumford had written up to this point: it is a study of the erosion of a balanced, decentralized civilization and its replacement by one with an oppressive metropolitan centralization of power, people, and culture. The story begins in the medieval town, here depicted as an earlier version of the garden city—compactly designed, limited in size, and surrounded by open countryside—and proceeds to describe subsequent urban history as a fall from grace, a long plunge into chaos and moral confusion. Yet Mumford concludes the book on a hopeful note, calling for a new City of Man even more closely tailored to human needs than the great cities of the age of Abelard. The creation of such cities, he argues, requires the creation of a new image of the city, and this cannot be formed without a clear understanding of the soundest features of historic cities, as well as the mistakes of past urban planners.

Mumford's history of cities is really a history of civilization itself, for it is in the city, he contends, that the power and culture of a civilization are concentrated. It is here that we find the social heritage best preserved, embodied, and transmitted. The city's architecture and physical layout, its domes and spires, its wide avenues and enclosed courts, tell the story of "different conceptions of man's destiny."[4] Yet while Mumford brilliantly uses architecture and art forms to illuminate the record of urban development (there are over 150 captioned photographs in the book), his overriding concern is with the city as a human community, as a stage or physical setting for the great drama of living. He puts social, not aesthetic, questions first, as he does in his architectural criticism. Is this city worthy of man? Is it compatible with basic human needs? Does its design foster pedestrian movement and face-to-face communication? These are the questions that interest him most.

The reader, however, will search in vain in this book for a detailed blueprint of the city of Mumford's dreams. A moralist, not a professional planner, his concern is to lay down the social principles that are to guide the planning process. For Mumford, planning questions are primarily value questions; only when these questions are directly addressed, he cautions, should the builders and technicians be called in.

Mumford found his near-perfect embodiment of an organic community in the medieval city, in the "eotechnic" age he had described in *Technics and Civilization*. These ground-hugging cities, with their occasional lofty spires and towers, conformed to the irregular contours of the land and were held to pedestrian scale, with every building within walking distance and with plenty of green space and open areas for public worship, spectacle, meeting, trading, and politicking. The enclosing walls gave the towns a tight urban form and clear outer boundaries, while the balance of the horizontal and the vertical, the bounding wall and low-slung houses set against the soaring cathedral towers, was one of their myriad visual delights.

In the main market, located close by the church or cathedral, processions and plays were held, with townspeople joining in as active participants. The streets that connected this focal public place—part amphitheater, part acropolis—with the various quarters of the city were essentially footways, narrow, twisting corridors that visually offset the amplitude of the wide public squares, as in Siena, and protected the shopfronts from the wind and the rain. Freestanding houses, wasteful of land and exposed to the elements, were rare, Mumford writes, with the recent examples of Radburn and Sunnyside Gardens in mind; houses, most of them small and crudely constructed, were usually built in rows around the perimeter of their rear gardens.

Such tightness of design encouraged associational life and a lively, gossipy street life. But the medieval towns provided as well for withdrawal and retreat, for sanctuary and solitude, in hidden gardens behind homes, in cloisters, and in interior courtyards. In opening our modern houses and buildings to sunlight and the outdoors, in the manner of Frank Lloyd Wright, we must not forget our need for quiet, privacy, and retreat, Mumford reminds us. Today the only place in the home "sacred from interruption is the private toilet."[5]

But perhaps the most important lesson the medieval town held for present-day planners was its restraint on physical growth. No medieval town extended for more than a mile from its center. Between the eleventh and fourteenth centuries surplus population was cared for by providing new cities, spaced in France a half a day's walk from one another. "The medieval city did not break through its walls and stretch over the countryside in an amorphous blob." Still, they were, like the new garden cities, set close to the open countryside, which lay just beyond the walls. Mumford emphasized, perhaps excessively, the rural character of the medieval cities to offset the then prevalent notion that they were dangerously overcrowded and unsanitary. He argued, in fact, that most of them, like England's Stow-on-the-Wold, were closer to what we would call a small country town than a city. But even in the larger cities, usually no bigger than 40,000, the size of fourteenth-century medieval London, the flavor of the country was brought to the city in numerous rear gardens and orchards, and in the colorfully arranged foods in the public markets.[6]

The physical layout of the medieval town mirrored its principal secular and spiritual concerns; its outward unity of structure reflected an inward unity of tradition. Mumford was especially drawn to the medieval city's apparent unity and order, best exemplified for him in the church and the guild, the pillars of town life. Men in communities, he believed, ought to share certain common values that invest their lives with significance. In the medieval city this universal bond was the pursuit of virtue or salvation, that age's understanding of the good life.

Medieval life was, above all, corporate or communal, and that, too, attracted Mumford, a communitarian in the style of Ruskin and William Morris, and a passionate critic of bourgeois individualism. "To exist, one had to belong to an association: a household, a manor, a monastery, a guild. There was no security except in association, and no freedom that did not recognize the obligations of corporate life." With caprice held in check by church and guild, these were towns, as Mumford portrays them, that truly met Aristotle's definition of a community as "the common interest in justice and the common aim, that of the good life."[7]

While Mumford's depiction of the medieval city is wonderfully evocative, if too idyllic, the most arresting chapters of *The Culture of Cities* are those describing the baroque or imperial city, a city of discipline, order, and class privilege. Mumford uses the term "baroque" to express the two contradictory elements of the age: its concern for mathematical order, expressed in rigorous street plans, formal city layouts, and geometrically ordered landscape designs; and its embracement, in its painting, sculpture, costume, sexual life, and statecraft, of emotion, passion, and irregularity. For him it was the first cluster of traits that best defined the age. Drawing on the work of Oswald Spengler, Mumford detects between the fifteenth and eighteenth centuries a movement from universality to uniformity, from localism to centralization, from the absolutism of God to that of the temporal sovereign and the new nation-state, a change best exemplified by Versailles, "a spoiled child's toy."[8]

Mumford's powerfully suggestive, if somewhat unbalanced critique of the baroque city deserves close examination, for in the culture that produced it he found the sources of many of the problems afflicting twentieth-century cities and civilization.

In the baroque period the modern state emerged as strong kings began to centralize authority and create a permanent bureaucracy, courts of justice, treasury, and standing army. This centralization of authority demanded a capital city, and these princely capitals— London, Rome, Naples, Milan, Moscow, Berlin—stripped power from the local centers and sent them on a path toward stagnation. The design of the baroque city expressed the new powers of the princes and the values the new age prized. The avenue was the commanding symbol of the new urban order. Long, straight, and wide, cutting through the old medieval courts and triangles, it was designed to move wheeled traffic and military troops. On this grand parade ground, the armies of the despot were put on constant display to awe and intimidate the common citizenry, who became mere spectators in the urban pageantry, always a sign, for Mumford, that a city was on the decline. The symmetrical building style of the late-baroque period, the long uniform rows of bourgeois homes and shops, accentuated the aura of order and class rule. "The buildings stand on each side [of the avenue], stiff and uniform, like soldiers at attention: the uniformed soldiers march down the avenue, erect, formalized, repetitive: a classic building in motion. The spectator remains fixed: life marches before him." This urban design was not accidental. To rule by coercion one had to have "the appropriate urban background."9

But Mumford also had the example of America's own Imperial City in mind when he wrote this chapter. In Washington, D.C., a city he often visited, he saw the errors of baroque-style planning tediously repeated, with a concern for show and spectacle, and for the convenient movement of wheeled traffic, overriding neighborhood needs and human scale. "The framework [is] excellent," he remarked after one of his first visits to Washington, "if cities [can] live by government alone."10

In describing the transition from medieval to baroque civilization Mumford skipped across the contributions of the Renaissance to city design, a deficiency he corrected twenty-five years later in *The City in History*. In this later work he approved of the efforts of fifteenth- and sixteenth-century planners to open up the cluttered late-medieval city and give it sorely needed breathing space through the introduction of elegant squares and wide straight streets. These improvements, however, were carried to excess by some baroque planners, who substituted emptiness for openness. But in *The Culture of Cities* the only complete examples of good urban form he found in the entire period between the Middle Ages and our own time were Amsterdam, which he had visited for the first time in 1932, and the Puritan villages he had extolled in *Sticks and Stones*. Amsterdam, with its unified block fronts and its web of canals connecting the city with the countryside, kept alive in the age of merchant adventurers the civic spirit and sense of human proportion that had characterized the medieval city. Lovely Amsterdam was capitalism's only "outstanding urban achievement."[11]

In the age of industry, most large cities took on the sordid characteristics of Dickens's "Coketown." But it was the greed not the grime of Coketown that most disturbed Mumford, who was, after all, writing a book he hoped would point the way toward a more cooperative society. In the age of "carboniferous capitalism" all was subordinated to economic gain. Cities grew fantastically, with no common plan or controlling purpose other than to enhance the profits of wealth-seeking capitalists. Coketown was their town: they built what they pleased and where they pleased, with no public restraints on their activities. Their factories claimed the best physical sites, and there, almost abutting the plant, often on piles of coal or slag, they built hovels in the name of housing for their workers. Focusing less on how these cities evolved than on what they came to look like in full growth, Mumford sketched an urban profile of unrelieved ugliness. His is one of the most withering indictments of the industrial city ever written.

Coketown capitalism centralized production in the steam-driven factory; the financial city that grew up toward the end of the nineteenth century centralized nearly every other aspect of economic life—banks, brokerage houses, and all the attendant agencies of advertising, marketing, and publicity. All roads now led to Megalopolis, where in towers of concrete, steel, and glass bankers and brokers plotted the future. "There is a special name for power when it is concentrated on such a scale: it is called impotence."[12]

As Mumford completed *The Culture of Cities* in 1937 the world crisis was ever on his mind. Left to its present course, Megalopolis, he speculates, would devolve, first, into Tyrannopolis, with gangster-dictators arising to impose order on a fast-disintegrating civilization, with the consent, if not cooperation, of the middle classes; and finally into Nekropolis, a city turned into a tomb by war, disease, and famine. Yet though the signs pointed to an approaching age of totalitarianism, Mumford continued to hold out hope for a rebirth of regionalism. There is no need to review here his arguments for a new neotechnic civilization, which occupy the final chapters of the book, as he had been putting forward these ideas for over a decade. In this long, digressive section of the book, written during a period of great personal stress and fatigue, he urges a complete reorganization of society around garden city nuclei, setting this as the commanding task of politics for the upcoming generation.[13]

This book, then, is as much a political manifesto as a history of the city. But its weakness is the great weakness of all of Mumford's previous writings about the good society—his failure to offer a political strategy for the achievement of his regionalist republic. In *The Culture of Cities* Mumford describes an agenda for radical change—inner conversion leading eventually to a total societal reorganization—yet he fails to specify how this great cultural and social revolution is to be accomplished. Even if, say, an Emersonian vanguard were to achieve some public influence, how were they to bring around the rest of the population to their way of thinking and then proceed to reorganize the entire society? This curious avoidance of practical questions of power and class action can be explained as much by Mumford's reliance upon the organic method of social analysis he derived from Patrick Geddes as by his great debt to the equally evasive Emerson.

Instead of analyzing society from a class angle, as a structure organized in terms of productive relations and economic interests, Mumford compares society to a biological organism whose health depends upon the smooth cooperation and unity of purpose of its component parts. Harmony, balance, and internal cooperation—the keys to bodily health—are deemed essential to community health as well. This kind of inner harmony and common purpose existed in the late Middle Ages, in Mumford's roseate view of that period, when all classes and social groups joined in the pursuit of universally agreed-upon values.[14]

Actually, Mumford's organic interpretation is less an analysis of change than an attitude toward it. While he brilliantly describes the course of urban technological changes in the Western world, he fails to identify the dynamics, or causative factors, of such changes. Economic classes and powerful interests do not induce change; change just seems to happen. This is not surprising, for the organic view leads naturally to an emphasis on gradual assimilation and integration rather than on class or mass action. Large changes, when they occur, occur over the long term, in an evolutionary manner.

This commitment to an organic perspective allowed Mumford to call himself a revolutionary while he patiently preached orderly, peaceful change.

Mumford's organic interpretation also tends to mask the class character of society. This is most immediately apparent in his rapturous view of the late Middle Ages, a view that fits too neatly his pleadings for a rebirth of organic regionalism. What social cohesion and consensus he found in the Middle Ages was probably attributable less to the age's universal cultivation of a balanced way of life than to a religiously sanctioned, hierarchical class structure that kept the lid on social mobility and class tension. Mumford's organic approach is thus inadequate as a political strategy not only because it conceals important kinds of class exploitation but, just as critically, because it offers little clue as to how certain classes come to social dominance. In both *Technics and Civilization* and *The Culture of Cities*, one civilization seems to yield to another through the workings of a mysterious cosmic determinism. Falling back on a formless and diffuse theory of change, a kind of shallow eschatology, Mumford's work, like that of the pre–World War I reformers he had attacked in *The Story of Utopias*, fails "to lead out of the muddle."[15]

"The belligerent talk in this book is mere bluster," as the Marxist critic Meyer Shapiro put it, perhaps too harshly, "in view of its neglect of the cold fact of class power." Other critics argued further that Mumford's program for social change—with its insistence that reform begin in the hearts of individual men—is based on a too simple belief in the power of faith and miracles.[16] But while Mumford might not have paid sufficient attention to politics and to class issues, he did not stand behind a pulpit, arms outstretched, and call for miracles. In his writings, particularly for the Regional Planning Association, he offered scores of specific workable suggestions for reconstructing modern society; and he not only called for new communities, he helped to plan two of them, imperfect examples of his ideal regional city. He remained an urban activist into the 1930s, even though he never got the call to Washington, as some of his friends in the RPAA did. When the City Housing Corporation, the financial arm of the RPAA, went bankrupt early in the depression, and some RPAA members went to work for the Roosevelt administration, Mumford, along with Henry Wright, Henry Churchill, Albert Mayer, and Carol Aronovici, formed the Housing Study

Guild to train architects to take part in the new public housing efforts begun by the federal government. They also lobbied for a more ambitious federal housing and new town program that President Roosevelt and most of his advisers envisioned. Mumford did not expect the New Deal to usher in the New Society, but unlike most orthodox communists, he was willing to work to move it in a more progressive direction.

Eleanor Roosevelt had been a board member of the RPAA, and Franklin Roosevelt, as governor of New York, had seemed in sympathy with the idea of regional resettlement. He had attended a conference of the RPAA at the University of Virginia in 1931, and in his off-the-record comments indicated his support for a regional hydroelectric power project similar to the soon-to-be-created Tennessee Valley Authority. As president Roosevelt appointed several RPAA members, including Catherine Bauer and Robert Kohn, to positions in his administration; and Henry Wright and Clarence Stein were called in as consultants on the Resettlement Administration's greenbelt housing program. But no one in the RPAA was named to a top policymaking post. And Roosevelt proved unwilling to extend or continue for very long his most promising initiatives in federal housing, regional planning, and new town development for fear of alienating conservative members of his own party, who complained that these programs were dangerously socialistic.[17]

Mumford had great hopes for the Tennessee Valley Authority program, but to his disappointment the TVA did not engage in large-scale regional planning and new town development. It remained mainly a quasi-government corporation to make and sell electric power and fertilizer. And while Rexford Tugwell's Resettlement Administration originally announced plans to build fifty experimental communities, only three were actually constructed. For these failures Mumford blamed the man in the White House. By not providing strong executive support, Roosevelt had blundered a magnificent opportunity for large-scale regional planning.[18]

Throughout the 1930s Mumford kept exerting pressure on his friends in the Roosevelt administration to raise their voices for bolder action, particularly on the housing issue. In a succession of hard-hitting articles, public statements, and letters directly to administration officials, he and his associates in the Housing Study Guild urged "a gigantic program of urban reconstruction and community planning and building" for the economic emergency and beyond.[19]

There would be no fundamental change in housing policy or urban resettlement, he was convinced, so long as capitalism in its present form existed. The experience of building Sunnyside Gardens and Radburn demonstrated to him the limitations of a private-market approach to the housing problem. Without substantial government intervention in the housing area, in the form of direct subsidies to home buyers, federally guaranteed low-interest loans, and a guaranteed income policy, the great mass of lower-income Americans would never be able to own a house in a decent community. Finance, not planning or design, was the keystone of a successful housing program, and into the 1930s the RPAA continued to urge that low-income housing be made a nonspeculative industry. But where many of his friends in the RPAA were willing to settle for vigorous government intervention in the housing field short of socialism, Mumford was not.

In the end President Roosevelt's housing program did exactly what Mumford feared it would. It made government the shield of private building speculators by protecting their investments through federally guaranteed mortgages, "the powder for the post-war suburban explosion."[20] The very aim of these programs was to save the country's construction industry (in 1933, 30 percent of the jobless were in the building trades), and to open the possibility of home ownership to the middle classes—not to provide soundly built, affordable housing for the neediest. Under Roosevelt and succeeding presidents, furthermore, almost all public housing was constructed on high-priced urban land, not on less expensive land in the countryside, as the RPAA suggested. This policy of urban concentration diverted already scarce funds from actual housing construction to land purchase. The result, more often than not, was barracks-style housing that was badly out of character with the building stock of the surrounding neighborhood. In the meantime, suburbs were allowed to develop in a hopelessly haphazard fashion.

The RPAA was powerless to stop these trends, although for the remainder of his life Mumford clung to the belief that if the group had stuck together in the 1930s and "gotten Roosevelt's ear the whole history of housing and planning in this country would have been different—and far better."[21] The RPAA might have been more influential, he later speculated, if some of its brightest members, like Catherine Bauer, had stayed out of government and helped make the organization a forceful independent lobbying group.[22] But this is extremely unlikely. While it is true that one of the reasons the RPAA had been able to exert some influence on the New Deal's new town program is that it had built, on its own, two experimental garden communities which became prototypes for several government-built greenbelt towns, during the depression there was no private money available for such departures. The RPAA thus had to depend on Roosevelt, and the only way to "get his ear" was to get into the administration. But as Catherine Bauer and other RPAA staffers learned when they entered government service, Roosevelt was not committed to the broad-reaching changes they had in mind. Neither, for that matter, was the country, and that was crucial, for Roosevelt never moved too far ahead of public opinion.

The Regional Planning Association did not survive the Great Depression. In 1934, Henry Wright and Clarence Stein had a personal falling out over questions of housing design, and they never resumed close relations. Two years after his break with Stein, Henry Wright died of arteriosclerosis at the age of fifty-eight, and at roughly the same time Stein began to suffer recurring physical and nervous breakdowns that prevented him from doing sustained work for the remainder of his life. When he temporarily regained his strength and energy in 1947, he tried, with the help of Mumford, Catherine Bauer, Benton MacKaye, and Albert Mayer, to revive the old RPAA as the Regional Redevelopment Council of America, but as Mumford remarked to a friend after one of their first meetings in New York, "something of the dynamism we used to have in the twenties has vanished with old age." Nor were they able to find a committed group of younger architects and planners willing to carry on their work. "We just have to recognize that the old magic circle has busted up," Mumford wrote MacKaye in the summer of 1947, "and what is left is only a ghost."[23] In the early 1950s the Regional Development Council quietly disbanded.

Mumford continued to work for regional reforms after the RPAA broke up, but from this point on he worked alone, and that made an enormous difference. Without the stimulating regular company of his former colleagues, he gradually lost touch with some of the newest thinking on city design and became less concerned with transforming big ideas into small concrete programs, and more concerned with working in the long term for vast changes in values and social objectives. That some of his practical proposals for urban design still remain relevant to current needs is a testimony to their original brilliance, not the result of any great change in his thinking. "The fact is," he once sadly admitted, "none of us were as good after [the Regional Planning Association broke up] as we were together."[24]

But this is to anticipate. In 1938, just after the publication of *The Culture of Cities*, Mumford was at the peak of his influence as an urban thinker. In greenbelt towns near Cincinnati, Milwaukee, and Washington, D.C., planners were experimenting with his ideas for urban resettlement, and he was asked by the American Institute of Planners to write the screenplay for a film, *The City*, which became one of the most popular attractions at the World's Fair in New York City in 1939.* (A critic called it "one of the most brilliant jobs of film making ever accomplished.")[25] At this time Mumford was flooded with requests to give advice to city and regional planning groups. In the summer of 1938 he accepted two offers because they presented opportunities to apply his ideas to areas of America possessing unusual potential for regional planning: Hawaii and the Pacific Northwest. Never before had he been called in as a planning consultant. This was a long-desired opportunity to directly shape urban policy, as Patrick Geddes had in India and Palestine at approximately this same point in his career.

Mumford's plan for the city of Honolulu, prepared for the city's Park Commission, can be considered almost an appendix to *The Culture of Cities*, an application of that book's ideas to an actual city. Although his ambitious but solidly practical proposals were largely ignored by Honolulu officials, his report gives as true an indication of his organic approach to city planning as anything he ever wrote. In his Honolulu report we see Lewis Mumford at his pragmatic

*The film was made by American Documentary Films under the auspices of the American Institute of Planners as a propaganda piece for the improvement of housing in the United States. Aaron Copland did the score.

best, hewing closely to Geddes's advice that planners should seek to make "the most and best of each and every place," instead of "imagining an impossible no-place where all is well."[26]

Mumford had first gone to Honolulu early in the summer of 1938 to speak at a conference of the International Fellowship for Education. Worn down by his work on *The Culture of Cities* and his breakup with Alice Decker, he looked forward to the trip as a chance to relax and unwind. He was a little skeptical about Hawaii itself; from afar it seemed like "a romantic movie set. But the first nine days I spent there proved to be the most intense, the most esthetically vivid, the most intellectually rewarding I have perhaps ever spent anywhere."[27]

"If we ever have another reincarnation together," he wrote Sophia on the evening of his arrival in Honolulu, "[this] is the place where you and I will go to on our honeymoon." He was staying in a bungalow a stone's throw from Waikiki Beach, and from his many-windowed bedroom he could hear the pounding of the waves and the voices of hula dancers, who were singing on the spreading lawn of a nearby hotel. His day had been "one long delirium of beautiful sights, magnificent vistas, fragrant odors, friendly gestures." He had spent the afternoon touring Honolulu with the head of the city's Park Commission, Lester McCoy, a hardy, white-haired fellow who took him "everywhere," from the lowest slums to the palatial homes and private beaches of the island's planter elite. Mumford found the island beautiful beyond compare. Orchids grew in the open, and poinciana trees, with brilliant orange and scarlet flowers, lined the streets. Looking out over the city from the surrounding hills he felt as if he had been treated to a glimpse of paradise. He now saw why Melville had been entranced by the place.[28]

McCoy and his architectural collaborator Harry Sims Bent had read *The Culture of Cities*, and when they learned that Mumford would be in Honolulu at a conference, they had written asking if they could talk with him about doing some planning work for the city. After introducing Mumford to the leading businessmen and city officials, they asked him to return in August to advise the city about park planning and slum clearance, offering him $2,000 for three weeks' work. This generous fee allowed Mumford to bring Sophia and the children in what was to be their first extended vacation as a family. Little Alison was so excited when her mother agreed to the trip that she marched around the house for days chanting "Glory, glory Honolulu."²⁹

For Geddes Mumford, who had just turned thirteen, Hawaii turned out to be a dream come true. Geddes's natural element was the wide outdoors. A graceful athlete and a crack fisherman, he took to Hawaii like a native. By the time he left Honolulu he could climb to the top of a curving coconut tree with his bare feet as fast as any of his island friends, and had learned to surf with skill in the waters near the spacious beach house his parents were given rent-free. In the evenings he would go spearfishing on the rugged coral reefs between Diamond Head and Waikiki, using a hand-held torch for light and wearing rubber-soled shoes to protect his feet.

This stay in Honolulu brought Geddes as close to his father as he would ever be, though adversity provided the bind. One week after they arrived in Honolulu, Sophia came down with a serious case of viral pneumonia and had to be hospitalized for three weeks; at one point she was thought to be close to death. This family crisis forced father and son to rely on each other for some of the things that Sophia had done for both of them. Every morning they would arise at six-thirty, slip into their bathing trunks, and climb over the seawall for a swim in the warm surf, returning a little later for a breakfast of fresh island fruit served on the lanai by their Japanese "man-of-all-work." After breakfast Lewis would begin his workday of urban surveying and writing, counting on Geddes to take care of himself at the beach (Alison was in the care of a nurse). In the evenings, when Lewis returned to the hospital for his third visit of the day, he had to count on Geddes to get Alison to bed. After Geddes had gone to sleep Lewis would sit alone in the study adjoining the living room and write letters to friends, a regular nocturnal ritual.

In many ways it was a trying five weeks for the entire family, but when it came time to leave Hawaii they were all sad to go, no one more than Geddes. He felt this was his "proper home" and he begged his parents to let him stay. A notoriously indifferent student, he even promised to study hard if they granted him his wish. As their ship pulled out of Honolulu harbor he hung over the rail, throwing lei after lei into the water, hoping, as he had been told, that these fragrant floral streamers would bind their ship to the pier.³⁰

All throughout his five weeks in Hawaii, Lewis had worked

steadily on his survey of Honolulu, touring the city by automobile and by foot, meeting with city planners, politicians, and labor people, and occasionally with "the fabulous monsters who . . . govern the pineapple and sugar plantations." His guide was Lester McCoy, whom he grew to like enormously. Lewis knew that McCoy, a straightbacked Tory, was uncomfortable with some of his ideas, so before writing the final draft of his report he had asked him what topics he ought to cover, knowing that after he left Honolulu McCoy would be responsible for putting the plan into actual practice. "When I ask a professional man for advice," McCoy bluntly told him, "I don't want him to tell me what is in my mind; I want to find out what is in his." McCoy proved to be a man of his word, backing the entire proposal and eventually resigning his chairmanship when the conservative members of the park board would not act on its recommendations.[31]

Mumford began his beautifully written report on Honolulu with a survey of the city's principal resources: its landscape and people. Honolulu then had a population of only 180,000 and had not yet succumbed to high-rise hotel development. Although it had some of the most wretched slums anywhere, and its beachfronts had been "stripped to almost nothing," the city had not completely lost its contact with the sea, sky, and sheltering hills. It was a city that had only to learn how to conserve and properly utilize its splendid natural advantages—its wide stretch of ocean beach, mild climate, and regular tropical rainfall—to remain one of the most lovely spots on earth.

The current city plan, Mumford pointed out, made absolutely no effort to conserve and accentuate these great God-given advantages. Pedestrians, for example, scarcely realized that they were on an island. Only a few midtown streets led to the waterfront, and there were hardly any roads or walkways that afforded even partial views of the harbor or the open Pacific. Mumford considered this "visual neglect of the water" the principal defect of the city's street plan.

Away from the harbor front, the city's streets were arranged in a bewilderingly haphazard fashion and the houses were built too closely together. This snug street plan might have been appropriate for a medieval city in cold, damp northern Europe, but Mumford thought it ill-appropriate for this tropical city. The entire layout of streets and buildings failed to take advantage of the invigorating ocean breezes that swept in from the northeast, a cost-free air-cooling system. To maximize the advantages of the sea and the trade winds and to relieve downtown congestion aggravated by a "higgledy-piggledy" street design, Mumford recommended an open type of planning in accord with Hawaii's open-air life, urging, among other things, the building of a pedestrian promenade and several well-shaded boulevards leading directly to the water.

But Honolulu could not remain a life-promoting city through mere cosmetic changes in its commercial core. The belt of slums that encircled the city center would have to be cleared out like so much cancerous tissue and replaced by well-designed low-cost housing, built on the superblock principle to take full advantage of sunlight, breezes, and the natural-growing tropical foliage. While superblock planning would protect new residential neighborhoods from the intrusion of the automobile, Mumford's plan recognized the passenger car as an unavoidable part of urban life. Honolulu badly needed a main traffic artery to relieve downtown congestion, and he proposed the construction of two tree-lined arterial parkways on the rim of the city: one running along the ocean, the other along the base of the hills. Such highway planning was far preferable, in his view, to cutting wide roadways directly through the heart of the city, tearing down existing buildings and piling up traffic at the center.

The parkways would have the additional advantage of connecting the city with the sea and countryside, but the real aim of Mumford's plan was to introduce the countryside and the sea into the city. Here he surely had Amsterdam in mind. Honolulu already had a system of drainage canals to take off the excess of water from the tropical downpours. Mumford proposed that the city expand this canal network and undertake an ambitious landscaping and park building program along these winding waterways. This would create a continuous ribbon of water, green space, and garden, spreading the existing park system, which, like New York City's Central Park, was extensive but too spatially concentrated, to every area of the city. Mumford urged that this be coordinated with a plan to place greenbelts and "park girdles" around residential areas. Along with the canals, these bordering parks would give the city's neighborhoods order and coherence, and provide protection against speculative development and sprawl.

To formulate and carry through a plan along these lines, Mumford recommended the creation of a new office of city planning. The person heading this office, he argued, should be "a dominant personality of marked administrative or designing talent," a man such as New York's Robert Moses, who was then head of New York's park system. "Wherever one encounters the highest type of planning work, one discovers such a personality, such a mind at the head of it." But Mumford went on to recommend that Honolulu's citizenry be given an active voice in planning decisions through an advisory city planning council made up of the principal interest groups of the community.[32] These recommendations, it should be noted, were advanced before Robert Moses acquired great influence and power. Several years later Mumford would dramatically revise his opinion of planning czars in general and of Moses in particular.[33]

Mumford's master plan, "Whither Honolulu?," was published in December 1938, and received front-page coverage and a favorable editorial in the Honolulu *Advertiser*. It was largely ignored, however, by city officials, one of whom called it "sixty-seven pages of Mr. Mumford's mumbling."[34] Even so, some planners familiar with Honolulu continue to see it as relevant to the city's needs. "The problems he saw are still here," one planning expert wrote in 1980 of Mumford's report; "many of his proposals would have made the problems more manageable."[35]

"Your [book] *The Culture of Cities* . . . is causing young men to see visions and old men to dream dreams all over the United States," Ben H. Kizer, a Spokane planning official, had written Mumford just before he had left for his first trip to Hawaii. Kizer invited him to come to the "lands of the Douglas fir and the bull pine" for several weeks in July to offer advice on regional development to the area's chief planning agency, the Pacific Northwest Regional Planning Commission. The commission would pay him $500 for several weeks work. For Mumford, this was an ideally timed opportunity, for he could do the work while Sophia and the children prepared to join him on the West Coast for the trip to Honolulu.[36]

In late July, after visiting Jerry Lachenbruch in Los Angeles, Mumford took a train up the coast to Spokane to join Kizer for a whirlwind automobile tour of the old Oregon Country. Kizer shuttled him from Portland and the Willamette Valley to Seattle, to Boise and the Snake River basin, to the Island Empire, and back to

Spokane. They traveled an average of 250 miles a day, exploring the area's cities and forests and its stupendous power projects in the Columbia River gorge. In between surveying and touring Mumford met with the area's leading regional planners, and spoke at luncheons and dinners to businessmen, bankers, and city officials. He would have preferred a slower-paced tour, with time to take in this astonishingly beautiful part of the country, but he submitted grudgingly to Kizer's hectic, tight-paced itinerary. At the end of two weeks, however, when he was scheduled to be driven the following day some four hundred miles to visit Grand Coulee Dam and, on the way, to deliver a luncheon address in Kizer's hometown, he finally balked. He would not go one step further, he firmly informed Kizer. "I am traveled out." Kizer begged him to reconsider, as three hundred or so invited guests would be waiting for him at the luncheon. But Lewis stood his ground, and in a letter to Jo Strongin he wondered what Kizer's "sexual life was like . . . to give him this intense drive and yet make him so ridiculously incompetent in planning out this gruelling, inhumane, tour for me."37 The truth was, he had never been much of a traveler. "The queer thing about traveling around is that my eye and my mind are tremendously stimulated; but my heart is just not in it." He was like one of "those rare wines," he once remarked, "that lose their bouquet when they are transported."38

For Mumford, this entire trip to the West—to Washington, California, and Honolulu—was tremendously exhilarating. He got a taste of what it was like to be an "honored authority," and he had needed to get away for a while from his writing. But the feeling of release did not last long, and he found his new fame a "tonic, almost a medicine," but not his "daily food." He was eager to get back to Amenia, where he could get down to some "real" work and back to some "real" living.39

That following fall in Amenia he wrote a brief memorandum on the planning possibilities of the Pacific Northwest. In order to preserve the area's attractions as a place for good living "[you must] resist the dream of indefinite urban expansion." Seattle and Portland were already growing overcrowded, and Mumford urged the regional planners to move at once to curb further growth and to redistribute increases in population to new cities spaced throughout the area. The region's new hydroelectric power grid offered possibilities for such an orderly distribution of population and industry; and to preserve the unspoiled beauty of the Columbia River gorge from reckless industrial growth, Mumford proposed a TVA-like authority for the entire river basin. This authority, he advised, should be vested with powers to zone, to buy and dispose of land, and to plan new towns.[40]

Kizer invited Mumford back the following year to do a more exhaustive survey and to prepare a fuller report, but the mounting world crisis turned Mumford's attention away from city and regional planning to the task of preparing his countrymen to meet the spreading menace of fascism. Two books had recently brought him international fame; now he was about to enter a period of trial and testing, and of shattering personal tragedy.

From Lover to Monk

When we were young, we could ask ourselves: what can we conquer? Now we can only ask: what can we save? That shrinkage of ambition is not due to age but to the times we live in.

—LEWIS MUMFORD,
LETTER TO VAN WYCK BROOKS,
JULY 24, 1936

"A man dwells in his native valley like a corolla in its calyx, like an acorn in its cup. *Here*, of course, is all that you love, all that you expect, all that you are."[1] With these words, Henry David Thoreau described all that Lewis Mumford's own native realm, the Oblong valley that forms the southern gateway to the Berkshires, came to mean to him. His decision in the summer of 1936 to move year-round to this green and sheltered valley was one of the great turning points of his life. Country living, along with the succession of public and personal crises he confronted in the decade after 1936, changed his entire outlook on life. It is impossible to understand the Lewis Mumford of the later years without understanding what happened to him in this period, a time of his life he would leave out of his autobiography because it was too painful for him to relive. Only family and work, and the simple pleasures of rural living, allowed him to maintain his balance throughout this difficult period.

Mumford's first winter in Leedsville was not nearly as relaxing as he had thought it would be. He had been recently appointed to the New York City Board of Higher Education, and every week he had to go to the city for three or four days to take care of board business and to write his art and architecture columns for *The New Yorker.* This "disrupts everything," he complained to Van Wyck Brooks. "It ruins domesticity, health, equanimity, and work. . . . The alternative is to quit *The New Yorker* or to quit Amenia; and that leaves only one answer: chuck *The New Yorker.*"

But it was not nearly as easy as that, for, in truth, he enjoyed both of these "devilish" responsibilities; he also enjoyed being in the city for at least part of the week.[2] His appointment to the Board of Higher Education gave him a chance to get together occasionally with some of his former professors at City College, and it brought him closer to his old college friend John T. Flynn, another board member, a blunt-spoken radical who dressed like a bank president and drank whiskey like an Irish ward heeler. At board meetings Mumford enjoyed pitting his wits against slick Republican lawyers and street-smart "Tammany-hacks," who called him Professor, he guessed, "because the thought of such a lowly beast makes them less uncomfortable than the notion that they harbor a writer in their midst." He even discovered he had a talent for committee work. "I'm getting so good at this," he told Sophia that winter, "and I find it so fascinating, that if I don't resign soon I'll probably be running for Governor of New York."[3]

But New York took its toll on him. When he wasn't attending to board business or sitting in committee meetings that often dragged on into the early-morning hours, he was immersed in his work for *The New Yorker,* writing a bimonthly column on the art scene and a monthly "Sky Line" piece on architecture. He was paid well for his work, $150 an essay, and he liked exploring the galleries and museums and walking the streets of Manhattan, as he had in his younger days, taking notes for his reviews, writing that put him in touch with a far wider audience than he was able to reach through his books. He was also treated regally by *The New Yorker's* editors, Harold Ross and Katherine White. They allowed him to write on whatever interested him, and they published his pieces almost exactly as he submitted them. As much as he loved this kind of work, however, Mumford found that it cut too deeply into the time he set aside for his more "serious" writing. Every Monday morning he would take an early train from Amenia to New York, check into a center-city hotel, work several days on his columns, and return home late in the week, too tired to do any concentrated work for at least another day.

When he was in New York he also spent a good deal of time with Alice Decker, who he feared was close to suicide and needed his steadying presence. The year before, his friend Eva Goldbeck, wife of the young composer Marc Blitzstein, had committed suicide; he had visited Eva often and had brought in Henry Murray to help him in his desperate efforts to prevent her from ending her life by slow starvation. Now he was fighting, also with Murray's help, to save Alice.

That spring, when Alice seemed out of danger and on the way to full recovery, Mumford resigned from the Board of Higher Education and informed Harold Ross, not an easy man to confront with bad news, that he intended to leave *The New Yorker*. Ross, a gruff, hard-dealing editor, was determined to make his magazine the best in the country. He considered Mumford one of his top writers and was not about to lose him. After considerable discussion he managed to persuade Mumford to continue to write his "Sky Line" column on his own, not on a regular monthly schedule, but he was unable to talk him into staying on as the magazine's art critic. He offered to pay Mumford more for his work, but with Mumford money was rarely an issue of deciding importance. At age forty-one he felt an urge to return to the unhurried existence he had known as an apprentice writer; and in the back of his mind there was still the idea that he had a talent for creative writing, a talent that might blossom now that he felt he had achieved greater sexual and emotional maturity. He wanted to complete *Victor*, his unfinished novel, write a play or two, and spend more time sketching and painting. He also had a marriage to repair. For all this, he would need a long succession of uninterrupted days. Now, thanks to the money he had already earned at *The New Yorker*, he had reached the point in his life when this sort of "retirement" was financially possible. He would be a "coward and a fool," he thought, not to cut loose from New York.4

When he and Sophia had moved up to Leedsville the previous summer, they had no intention of leaving the city for good. They would stay in the country for only a couple of years, they assured their friends; both had New York too strongly in their blood to think of giving it up entirely. But they had made a clean break by selling their house at Sunnyside Gardens, which had become too small for a family of four. Had Sophia had her way they probably would have stayed in New York, using their cottage in Leedsville only as a summer retreat, but Lewis, like Walt Whitman, found ever-active New York a "good market for the harvest" but "a bad place for literary farming."[5] He hated the incessant demands the city made on his time and energy, especially now that he was a widely recognized writer. "I look back at my slow breathed adolescence with regret," he wrote Waldo Frank, "and wonder how I can recover something of the same rhythm without becoming altogether a hermit." Living year-round in Leedsville was his answer: he could have his coveted solitude and jump on a train to New York, only two hours away, whenever he worked up a "deep man's size thirst for the big city."[6]

But country living worked a slow change in him, making him, in time, more a villager than city man in temperament and outlook, more like Hesiod, the rural philosopher, than Plato, the consummate Athenian. In the country he led a life in line with his innermost temperament: orderly, slow-paced, balanced. While he would sometimes write of his occasional hunger for the unplanned and the unexpected, he preferred to lead a rigorously regular existence. "If you were as prudent as I am in chess and I were as careful as you are in life," his son Geddes once told him, "we'd make a good pair."[7]

Mumford lived with his family in Leedsville for the next six years, broken only by two winters in New York. Over the course of their lives he and Sophia often resided elsewhere for parts of the year, or for a whole year at a time, but they always returned to this "Great Good Place," as they called their old farmhouse and its surrounding acres. In the very act of living in this house and making it over it became like a person to them; and like a good friend, they grew more fond of it with closer and deeper acquaintance. Every patch garden and lawn, every vista and view, carried the imprint of some of the best hours of their lives.[8]

Whatever comeliness the house and the land came to acquire he and Sophia gave it by sheer hard work. Yet despite their hundred and some improvements, it remained always a simple, some would say spare, home. They always kept a generous stock of good wine, the walls of their beamed-ceiling living room came to be lined with first editions, and over Lewis's reading chair they hung paintings by Marin and O'Keeffe, gifts from Alfred Stieglitz; but the furnishings remained modest and a little worn, and they would never have many modern appliances or conveniences. When they first moved into the house they owned a small radio, and soon they purchased a phonograph and installed a telephone, but that was about it. At Sophia's urging they did buy a secondhand car in 1936, but Lewis refused to learn to drive, leaving yet one more household responsibility to Sophia.

He had one experience with "Betsy," their 1932 Chevrolet, that cured him forever of any will or desire to drive. One afternoon just after they had bought the car, he decided, with some persuasion from Sophia, to give it a try. He got into the car and cautiously started up the engine, but he let out the clutch too fast and the car lurched forward, almost slamming into one of the stately maples in front of their house. Lewis jumped out of the car and swore never again to take the wheel of an automobile.⁹

Amenia and its encircling hamlets was an indrawn community of farmers, storekeepers, and rural laborers, dominated socially by old Republican families who kept to themselves. Although Lewis and Sophia didn't mix regularly with their neighbors, preferring to get together with the Spingarns and their frequent guests, they always kept on friendly terms with them, especially the Duffys, a large Irish family who informally adopted both Geddes and Alison. It was the Duffys and their other neighbors up and down the Leedsville Road who helped them to adjust to rural living, lending them tools and garden equipment, giving them helpful hints on home repairs, and taking care of their house and garden when they were away. Living in Leedsville reinforced Mumford's conviction that "something of the village must be reproduced in the most sophisticated urban neighborhood[s]" if a city was to be truly livable.¹⁰

Like almost all of his fellow villagers, Lewis took up gardening, which became for him a rejuvenating release from mental work. Though he had grown plants and flowers as a boy of nine or ten in his backyard in New York, his first real experience with gardening was at Sunnyside, where he experimented with bushes and turnips and irises. After they took possession of their Leedsville home as a summer retreat, and planted their first garden in 1931, his appetite for this kind of work grew slowly, until he began to live in the countryside year-round and keep orderly records of his plantings. From then on gardening captured more and more of his energy and imagination and soon became an integral part of his life. Later, when they were regularly away from Amenia for part of the year, coming back in the spring to put in the garden became "an essential matter" for him.

He and Sophia grew all their vegetables on their one-acre plot, which they cultivated as intensively as a Japanese garden. Every phase of the process, from comparing notes with Spingarn and other gardeners in the village, to picking the seeds from the spring catalogue, to spading the soil, to the final act of picking the crop, delighted him, absorbed him. Gardening put him in touch with the world of living organisms and processes, reinforcing by experience what he had learned from his reading of Samuel Butler and Patrick Geddes—that only if one meets nature halfway, instead of trying to dominate and conquer it by sheer force, can one build a truly habitable world. But what he found most immediately satisfying in gardening was that he could follow "this whole process through, as only a mother can follow it through insemination, gestation, and birth in the growth of her child; and this," he observes in one of his innumerable notes on the pleasures of gardening, "gives a sense of wholeness and completion that hardly any other part of one's life gives today." As a writer he found that much that went into the production of a book escaped his supervision or notice, and that is why the final picking of the vegetables became for him "a precious part of the whole process: one I . . . eagerly seek to do, day after day," even, he might have added, into old age, when as a bent man in his eighties he would limp out into the garden just beyond their back door to do some light planting on clear spring days.[11]

Gardening gave him what he described as a "religious sense of harmony" with the forces governing the world, so much so that the words he chose for the central act of his life, his Renewal of Life series, came not only from Christian associations but also from his own activities in the garden. And gardening, like the countryside itself, had a restorative influence for him. Whenever he was harried or troubled, his favorite "prescription" was to get outdoors and get his hands into the soil. Gardening, he soon found, went hand in hand with his writing. It both put him in a mood for writing and was a way of escaping from it; and it actually improved what he wrote. This short run of manual work after a morning at the typewriter cleared away the cramps and cobwebs and left his mind and body fresh for the rest of the day. Gardening was another of those activities, he liked to tell his friends, which kept him from being a "mere intellectual."[12]

Living in the countryside enhanced his powers of observation and enlivened his prose, now—more than ever before—filled with imagery and metaphor drawn from nature. He became, in time, not only a passionate nature lover, but a first-rank nature writer as well. His best-written book, *Green Memories*, his memoir of his son Geddes, is also a beautiful account of the joys of outdoor living; and some of his finest essays are on keen observers of the natural world, such as John James Audubon, whose life and work he fell in love with all over again after moving to Amenia. Sometimes he would take notes for these essays as he tramped the fields and wooded paths around Troutbeck. He also loved to sketch and paint in the outdoors, on the banks of the Webutuck, with Geddes nearby fishing for trout with his bamboo pole, or alone, on the side of a hill carpeted with goldenrod and wild strawberries. Some of his most striking watercolors and oils are sensitive renderings of what still remained primeval in his Amenia scene.

In his notes and in his numerous letters to friends (as many as ten a day), he described changes in every part of his country environment, from week to week, from month to month—the budding and flowering of plants, the variety and movements of wildlife—salamanders, peepers, woodchucks, and deer—the changes in the sky, the weather and the landscape, the moon and the stars. Hardly anything escaped his notice; all of his senses were open to the living world around him, even when he was indoors. He had long been a sharp-eyed observer of the urban scene, but in many ways the country excited his senses even more than multifarious New York. In the city one lost consciousness of the weather, except as a newspaper or radio weather report, he wrote after one of his regular walks in the woods. "But in the open country the sky is visible and every part of the day . . . has something to tell me." Like Alfred Stieglitz, he loved to watch the clouds "at every moment of the day, and in every mood." On days when the cloud formations were especially striking he would call the whole family outside to observe them, and sometimes, like an ancient Roman, he'd search for signs and portents. One afternoon he was sitting outdoors looking at the clouds when he saw a formation of them forming a profile of his head. He excitedly called to Sophia to look and tell him what she saw. Pointing to the right part of the sky, she exclaimed, with a smile, "Why it's your head!" "That's a good augury," he told her confidently. [13]

Of all of them, young Geddes took most strongly to the outdoors. When he was a child his parents named him "the mushroom hound"; they would shout ahead to him and point with their arms, as they cut through the pastures south of their farmhouse, and he'd gallop off to retrieve a big mushroom. At age seven he had his own garden and was fascinated, like his namesake, by the world of plants, animals, and insects. But by the time he was nine years old he was ready for more "manly" pursuits: fishing, hunting, and trapping. "The butterfly hunter of six," his father writes of him, "was trapping woodchucks at nine, and finishing them off in swift proper fashion, somewhat to his parents' queasy aversion." Geddes would get up at 5 A.M. on bitterly cold winter mornings to go down to the river to check his traplines, bringing back his prey for Sophia to prepare.

Hunting, however, was his passion, and in an effort to get closer to his son, Lewis took up the sport. Lewis had been taught how to handle a gun on his boyhood vacations in Vermont. But he had never hunted before he began to go out in the woods with Geddes after he bought him a .22 single-shot Winchester not long after they moved to Leedsville. Outside hunting season they would have target practice together on weekday afternoons in a field by their house. On the range Lewis remained Geddes's equal, but in the field Geddes was his superior; and that told something about both of them.

When Geddes reached adolescence, however, he preferred, like most boys of that age, to be away from his parents and with his friends, in his case the Duffy boys, his favorite companions for roaming and hunting. Geddes had the instincts of an Indian scout; he knew the ponds and woods and meadows around their home more intimately than his father knew the books in his library. Like old Leatherstocking, "alone in the woods with his gun he was at peace with himself." [14]

Moving up to the country gave Lewis more time to spend with his

children. In winter he and Sophia often took the children toboggan-
ing on a hill beside the Farley house, or skiing in the Taconics, or
skating on Troutbeck Lake. In fall there was pheasant and squirrel
hunting with Geddes, father and son returning toward evening to a
warm country kitchen, their family's common room, where Sophia
was usually waiting for them with homemade doughnuts and sweet
cider fresh from the cider mill.

On summer evenings, when Geddes was very young, he and his
parents would go out in the yard after supper, form a triangle, and
pass a ball around; or Lewis would roughhouse with Geddes and
some of the neighborhood boys. In these games, as in most things he
did with his son, Lewis felt it important to establish his masculinity,
fearing, perhaps, that Geddes would see him merely as an intellectual. "Mollycoddle though his father often seemed to him, I have no
doubt he still kept a certain respect for my physical prowess," Lewis
writes revealingly of their relationship—and of himself. "At Chinese
wrestling, I remained a match for him till the end: the look in his
eyes when we gripped hands is my most private and sustaining
memory of our relations as father and son."[15]

Often, after dinner the family would linger at the table and listen
to Lewis read from *The Oxford Book of Poetry*. "Geddes truly loved it,"
his mother remembers, "and sat quietly, even when he was very
young. It became ritual finally and continued on into Alison's childhood. She, too, would sit relaxed while Lewis read." When Sophia
was preparing dinner Alison, at age six or seven, would sit on a small
stool beside her father's lounge chair, and they would "read"
together, he out of *The Oxford Book of Poetry* and she out of a collection
of children's verses. She knew them by heart, of course, but wanted
her father to believe she was reading them. "It was always," Sophia
says, "a lovely half hour."[16]

Occasionally, in the afternoons, when Geddes was older and off
by himself, Lewis would go up on the hill in back of their barn and
play house with Alison. Yet though he loved both of his children
equally, he probably spent less time with little Alison than he had
with Geddes when he was a child. Alison, a demanding child,
sometimes found it hard to get his full attention; and she would
often become sullenly angry when he went off to his study after
breakfast, closed the door, and lost himself in his writing for the
entire morning. But sometimes she thought he wasn't paying atten-

tion to her when he really was—in his own way. On one occasion when she was twelve years old, Alison rushed home from school with an exciting discovery she had made in her art class. When she stopped her father at the door of the kitchen and blurted out her idea, he just stood there, frozen, looking off into the distance. Then, seconds later, he turned around, and, without uttering a word, retreated to his study. Alison was crushed; her father wasn't interested in anything she did. She learned a few days later, however, that her father had been so excited by her discovery that he wanted to get to his desk to write it down while it was still fresh in his mind. He wanted to record as well his daughter's excitement in her find, and his pride as a parent.[17]

"All the village children loved Lewis," Sophia wrote in her own notes just before her husband's eighty-third birthday; "to this day children and animals will go to him first, ignoring other adults in the room. He pays just enough attention to make them feel noticed and wanted, but never concentrates on them in a sticky fashion. He respects them and they him." She could just as well have been describing her husband's earlier relations with his own children.[18]

Country living, with its regular round of family activities, also helped Lewis and Sophia pull together their marriage after Lewis stopped seeing Alice Decker. The terrible strain of that affair on him, and, most devastatingly, on Sophia, convinced him that neither his life nor his marriage could survive another experiment in "bi-polar" love. Sophia was adamant about this; she had been hurt enough. Lewis realized what this meant for him. He could not so much as be tempted by another woman, for it seemed that whenever he began a relationship he was not satisfied until he had gotten the woman to fall in love with him to the point of wanting to marry him. If he was to keep Sophia he would have to adhere strictly to the letter of his marital pledge; and in the first months after he and Alice parted he appeared prepared to do just that, to turn from "lover to monk." "My marriage is a rock, once a rock of refuge behind which a weak man cowered; but now a solid foundation upon which a firm man continues to build, knowing that the structure and its foundation, no matter what their original weaknesses, have become one."[19]

He sent these words as a gentle reproach to Josephine Strongin, who was married now and living in Richmond, Virginia, and who was making a dead-ahead assault on the "rock" of his marriage—just as he had decided to change his ways.

Although he and Jo had remained in touch by letter since first meeting in Geneva in 1925, they hadn't seen each other for some years when Lewis arrived in Richmond on business in late 1937. Still fresh-faced and girlish-looking, Jo was in a dangerously vulnerable mood. She was having sexual problems with her husband, whom she still loved, but who failed, she blushingly told Lewis, to fulfill her completely. When Lewis talked freely about Catherine and Alice and mentioned that his affair with Alice was about to end, she undoubtedly saw her chance, confessing to him what he had long suspected—that she had been secretly in love with him since Geneva, but had been too immature to pursue him, and, later, too concerned about breaking up both their marriages. Now she was ready to risk an affair with him. He, apparently, was capable of loving other women without leaving his wife, and her husband, she had learned recently, was seeing another woman. She didn't want to break up Lewis's marriage or her own, she assured Lewis at a later point. She was content to share him with Sophia, whom she considered a dear friend. She did not think that she would hurt Sophia greatly, since Sophia had put up with his affairs with other women.[20]

Later, when she confessed to her husband that she was in love with Lewis Mumford and wanted to consummate her love, he flew into a fit of jealous rage, demanding that she stop writing him and not see him again under any circumstances. But there was no stopping her. To Alice Decker, who had by now found another man she planned to marry, Lewis described Jo's love for him as a "madness. My image torments her and dominates her." She begged him to ask Sophia to let her have him, even if for one night. And when he would not, she impulsively wrote to Sophia revealing her feelings for Lewis and asking her to understand, even if she couldn't forgive, her behavior.[21]

Josephine chose absolutely the wrong time to go after her man. He was in no mood for passion; he needed a loving friend—what she had long been to him—not another lover. He realized even better than Josephine what she really wanted from him—all of his love, not a small portion of it. But his marriage had been shaken too badly by his experience with Alice, he told her, to stand "another earthquake," another period of having to choose between Sophia and a lover. As he explained to her over and over again, he was not the kind of man who was capable of having a passing affair with a woman he cared for. "My touch isn't light enough: life becomes a matter of all or nothing; and when all is impossible, nothing leaves behind colossal wreckage."[22]

But here he was not being completely honest with her, leading her to believe (perhaps in order not to hurt her) that he didn't want to begin anything with her for fear that he would fall in love with her. The truth is, however, he was not physically attracted to her. He *did* see her love for him as a possible threat to his new marital stability, and he *was* feeling emotionally inert in the months after they met in Richmond. But what would have happened if Jo had been a different kind of woman? On this point, one of his Personalia notes is revealing: "I will not pretend that I would be immune . . . to such [a] challenge if it came in a different form: if she were not a frail slip of a woman, scarcely even adolescent in body: if instead of this she were a lusty, full bosommed wench, healthy and inexhaustible, offering passion rather than love, a few months of interest rather than a life time of devotion, if in short she were a second Catherine . . . I doubt if I could escape her at the present moment."[23]

As it was, though, he found it difficult to resist her, for he was in love with her mind and found it exciting to be in her company. While Jo was shy and almost childlike in some of her ways, she had a mischievous streak and was determined to live life to the limit. Lewis had been warning her that he could not return her passion, but when they met in New York in the spring of 1938 they went to bed together, Lewis nervous, guilt-ridden and hesitant, Josephine relaxed and at ease. Lewis, however, was physically incapable of making love, and his impotence was probably his body's way of telling him that he must not stray from Sophia. "My present life . . . is a unity: my work, my household, my marriage—all are one," he wrote Jo the following year, after a near-exact recurrence of what had happened in their Manhattan hotel room the first time they had tried to come together. He and Sophia had mended many of the tears in their relationship and were getting along better than ever before. This is why he could never tell Sophia what had gone on between him and Josephine, why he never even hinted of it to a single friend, not even Henry Murray. He feared that such an act of honesty might ruin both her life and his. Besides, there was nothing to confess, he reasoned; "nothing had happened."[24]

Josephine, however, took his resistance as a challenge; her love for him seemed to rise most strongly when he denied her. She was trying to create love by showing it, by demanding it; and there was, of course, no worse way. So although he continued to write to her, he tried not to see her after their second attempt at sex, even when she visited New York. All this perhaps explains why the strongest sections in *The Condition of Man*, the book he was writing at the time, are on the "satisfactions of the monastery. The need of peace and certainty: the love of God which supplants the love of women and men."[25] At this point in his life he seemed to be looking for the monastery gate.

He was reluctant, however, to break off contact with Jo. It was not just his affection for her; at the time she was the only "other woman" in his life, and he had always found it difficult to focus all his passional energies on his marriage. He wanted, but knew he couldn't risk having, the excitement and pleasure of a mistress. So Jo became a kind of distant, untouchable lover. In his letters to her he alternated between reminding her that his "time of roving" was over and telling her how much he wanted to make love to her, if only he could. He found it most paradoxical, he told her, that his "properest part" remained limp when he held her in his arms and began "to start and quiver" at the very thought of her, in the act of writing to her, "prudent when I should be passionate, and passionate only when I am safe!"[26]

There is something of a pattern to these sexually teasing letters. He wrote them most often when he was hard at work on his writing. "The work has been good on my book," he wrote her while completing *The Condition of Man*. His paunch was gone and his face was lean again. But there was another predictable "physiological reflex . . . a compensating tendency to become lecherous, in thought, if not in action; so only the memory of past humiliations would keep me from making flirtatious passes at you."[27]

Yet when he made love to her by letter he made her want him

more in the flesh. And whenever she pressed the issue he backed off, claiming, at one point, that it was not possible for him to work with unfaltering concentration as long as his "erotic life was split between a domestic and an outside love."[28] This is a long way from his earlier claims that his love for Catherine Bauer strengthened his marital relations and enlivened his work, but he was a different man, and Jo, after all, was not Catherine.

Jo, who worshipfully watched his every move and tried to read his every mood, noticed a change coming over him. There was a new seriousness in his face, she told him after seeing him on one of her visits to New York, a new determination in his piercing copper eyes. He didn't want to tease her and flirt with her; he talked only of his work and his marriage and family. He seemed like a mysterious stranger to her.[29]

It was only then, apparently, that Jo finally realized that she could never have him. She had only one consolation. Perhaps her very exclusion from his love would assure that she remained forever in his life. They could never part, as Lewis had once told her; they were like the figures on Keats's Grecian urn: "caught and immobilized."[30] After 1944, when Jo met the Richmond surgeon who became, eventually, her second husband, she and Lewis stopped writing to each other as regularly or as intimately as they once had, but they remained close until Josephine's death in 1969.

Even before Josephine met her future husband she had written Mumford a letter that might have served as a farewell; it was a warning, too, for she feared that Lewis had begun a retreat from youth, and from the world itself, that was both premature and unhealthy. He had been telling her in his letters that at this point in his life, after his affairs with Catherine and Alice, he needed most of all peace and stability "in order to give my undiffused energies to that which may quicken the mood of creation in the world again— without which we all die." But he was too young, she admonished him, for that kind of monkish withdrawal; his fullest years, as a man and a writer, were still ahead of him.[31] This was 1943, after he had struggled for five hard years, at great risk to his health and his work, trying, first, to mobilize a strong American challenge to fascist expansion and, then, to get his country's leaders to fight for something more ennobling than the unconditional surrender of the enemy. In these passionate personal causes, he developed a more sober outlook on the human condition; and this deepening pessimism was accompanied by a feeling of diminished power in his ability to change the world. In this fight to defend and advance democratic values, Lewis Mumford became a different man.

21

The Barbarian Eruption

*I could smile when I hear the hopeful exultation of many, at
the new reach of worldly science and vigor of worldly effort;
as if we were again at the beginning of new days. There is
thunder on the horizon, as well as dawn.*

—JOHN RUSKIN

War and fascism are the insistent themes of Mumford's writings of
the late 1930s. While many Americans were convinced as late as
1939 that Hitler could be appeased and war avoided, Mumford held
to the view that the very existence of fascism was a declaration of war
on democracy. A policy of neutrality would be a betrayal and a
sacrifice of our friends in Europe and of America's own interests as
well, for when these democracies succumbed to fascism we would
be truly isolated. Then we would have not peace but panic, and
perhaps the final surrender. This is the message Mumford tried
to hammer home to his countrymen as he campaigned with passionate determination to commit America to a war against Germany, turning himself into a one-man "national propaganda
department."[1]

Mumford, though, did not actively enter the struggle for American military intervention in Europe until March 1938, when Hitler
was threatening to annex the Sudetenland, and for the remainder of
his life this would be a source of embarrassment and shame for him.
Like most of his countrymen, he had not acted soon enough; in fact,
the white hot rancor and desperate urgency of his antifascist writ-

ings can be attributed, at least indirectly, to the slowness of his response to the challenge of Nazism.

When Mumford was in Germany in 1932 doing research for *Technics and Civilization* he had seen signs of the danger ahead, but had failed to take them seriously. He remained convinced, like so many other foreign observers, that the great majority of Germans would never support "a screaming psychotic like Hitler." By the time he reached Munich to interview Karl Vossler he had seen displays of *Mein Kampf* in the bookstores and had read reports in the democratic press of the gathering power of Hitler's Nazis, but when he asked Professor Vossler if Hitlerism posed an immediate threat to the republic, that esteemed classicist dismissed the question with a smile, and these reassuring words: "Nazism? It's just a disease of childhood, like the measles. We had it very badly here in Bavaria, and we got over it: now it has infected the North. But in another year, my dear Mumford, we shall have recovered. No leader who speaks such bad German could possibly rule such a well-educated people as the Germans."[2]

Mumford, however, was not completely convinced by this. When he returned with Sophia that next week for a second visit to Lübeck, the seaport city of Thomas Mann's *Buddenbrooks*, a temporary ban on the wearing of Nazi uniforms had been lifted, and the Brownshirts had taken over the streets. At receptions and dinner parties he and Sophia encountered cultivated Germans who expressed support for Hitler's program against the Jews, not knowing that Sophia was Jewish. Despite all this Mumford was so impressed by the progressive Germany he saw represented in the works of architects and town planners like Walter Gropius, Ludwig Mies van der Rohe, and Ernst May, and so absorbed in the work that had brought him to Europe that summer, that he failed to complete the article he began on his impressions of the political situation. And although he later claimed otherwise, he seems to have been surprised, if not shocked, when Hitler took power in January 1933.

At this point he realized that the democratic nations might eventually have to go to war to save themselves from fascism. Although he would not say this in print for several years, in his conversations with Sophia, who was still a pacifist, he began to insist that the time was coming when those who believed in peace would have to be prepared to fight for justice. In 1935, on two occasions, he announced his change of mind publicly.

In the spring of that year he was asked by a group of Dartmouth students who assumed him to be in sympathy with their views to address a pacifist rally against American military preparedness. Toward the end of a long round of antiwar speeches, Mumford took the podium and told these young men that the day was fast approaching when they would have to prove their allegiance to freedom by putting their lives on the line for it. In a world of Hitlers and Himmlers an unqualified commitment to peace was a certain surrender to barbarism. It was a short, fiery address, but when he finished the audience remained completely silent; not a single person applauded.[3]

Later in 1935, in a symposium in V. F. Calverton's *Modern Monthly*, Mumford was the only American writer in the issue to advocate hard measures against Hitler, calling on his government to declare its intention to go to the assistance of any democracy attacked by fascism and to invoke immediately a blockade of all war materials to Germany.[4] Throughout that year, however, he was deeply absorbed in *The Culture of Cities* and was not yet prepared to give his working hours to anything else. For a time he salved his conscience by signing manifestos and joining antifascist organizations like the American Writers Congress and the League of American Writers, but after Hitler's designs on Germany's neighbors became apparent to him, he realized that this kind of response was not enough. So after reading proofs for *The Culture of Cities* in early 1938, several months before Neville Chamberlain's appeasement at Munich, he wrote an article for *The New Republic* urging Roosevelt and the Congress to impose a policy of complete nonintercourse with the fascist states, refusing their goods and prohibiting tourist travel in these countries, and to begin building a huge two-ocean navy for the unavoidable global struggle with fascism. "Strike first against fascism; and strike hard," he exhorted his countrymen, "but strike." After the war Mumford would proudly call this essay, widely attacked by liberals as the work of an alarmist and a war monger, "his card of identity" to the men who had spilled blood in the struggle against fascism. His only regret was that he had not written it three years earlier.[5]

When Mumford wrote "Call to Arms" he realized that he was staking his reputation as a responsible man of letters upon the accuracy of his predictions that Hitler would seek to rule Europe by levying tribute, and that Hitler would be stopped only by strength of arms. He did not realize he was also destroying his credit with most of his contemporaries, and with some of his closest friends as well. Like the most ardent antebellum abolitionists, Mumford became a declared witness not only against a corrupt system but also against those who refused to take an unqualified stance against it. In this struggle he pitted himself against some of his closest friends— Van Wyck Brooks, Frank Lloyd Wright, Stuart Chase, John T. Flynn, Charles Beard—and his country neighbors, Malcolm Cowley and Matthew Josephson, and his friendship with several of these men did not survive the decade.

When Mussolini stormed into Ethiopia in October 1935, inaugurating a decade of fascist plunder, diplomatic crisis, and world war, most American progressives were holding to a policy of strict neutrality in foreign affairs, convinced, as a result of World War I, that America should steer clear of foreign entanglements and concentrate on the battle for social justice at home. Even General Francisco Franco's Nazi-supported attack on the democratic government of Spain in July 1936 failed to convince many of these liberals that America should get directly involved in Europe's problems. By 1938, however, this tight noninterventionist consensus had been split beyond repair, and the American Left stood divided into two hostile camps, irrevocably at odds over the question of a proper American response to the spread of fascism. One group of independent progressives, among them Mumford, Waldo Frank, the theologian Reinhold Niebuhr and the poet Archibald MacLeish, along with the American Communist Party and its fellow travelers, demanded strong collective security measures against Germany, Italy, and Japan. While they were urging the United States to form an antifascist alliance with France, Great Britain, and the Soviet Union, noninterventionists like Flynn, Chase, Beard, and Alfred Bingham and Selden Rodman, editors of *Common Sense* magazine, were insisting that the war that might result from the creation of such a coalition would not be a clear-cut struggle between freedom and totalitarianism, for the partners to that proposed alliance shared in the sins of fascism. Stalin's Soviet state, they argued, was as brutal a regime as Hitler's, and both France and Great Britain ruled over colonial empires maintained by racist exploitation. If there were a European war France and England would be fighting to preserve their imperial possessions, not democracy or freedom. The principal menace to American democracy, these noninterventionists claimed, was not Nazism but war itself. War would bring in its wake a colossal home-front mobilization, sweeping abridgments of democratic freedoms, and a dangerous expansion of the national bureaucracy. It would also kill a promising movement for social justice at home. Here the legacy of World War I remained strongly compelling.

Mumford, too, feared the possible home-front consequences of a major war, but he was certain that Hitler could not be stopped by diplomatic appeasement. This was his major point of difference with Flynn, Beard, and other liberal noninterventionists. Fascist aggression, in their view, was fueled by economic urgency, by a driving need for natural resources essential for autarchy, or self-sufficiency. Once Germany and Italy had carved out spheres of economic influence in the Mediterranean and central Europe, their appetite for conquest would be sated. Even after Spain fell to Franco, and Hitler forced the Anschluss and seized the Sudeten territory from Czechoslovakia in September 1938, Flynn, Beard, Bingham, and other prominent noninterventionists continued to insist on a policy of appeasement that guaranteed the Axis powers territories and economic materials essential to their survival. This, in their view, was the only way to prevent war.[6]

Mumford was completely baffled by the conduct of his progressive friends. How could men of goodwill and conscience argue this way? What explained their weak-willed response to fascism? His efforts to understand their behavior drove him toward an analysis of the entire liberal tradition, which took the form of an all-out attack on what he considered soft and morally deficient in the tradition of "pragmatic liberalism."

In May 1940, with France about to fall to Hitler's invading armies, Archibald MacLeish unleashed in *The Nation* what stands as perhaps the most famous broadside against the noninterventionist liberals. In "The Irresponsibles," MacLeish attacked his fellow liberals for advising neutrality in the face of a monstrous threat to "the common culture of the West." Mumford and Waldo Frank, however, took the arguments of "The Irresponsibles" one step further, marshaling a blistering indictment of what they called pragmatic liberalism, a philosophy they held responsible for the liberals' failure to react decisively to fascism.[7]

Mumford and Frank had been contributing editors to *The New Republic* since the late 1920s, and good friends well before that. In the winter of 1939–40 they began meeting regularly in New York City with Reinhold Niebuhr, a close friend of Frank's, to discuss the deteriorating international crisis. Now that the war was on, they became increasingly disturbed by the refusal of *The New Republic* senior editors, Bruce Bliven, George Soule and Malcolm Cowley, to support a policy of immediate aid to the Allies. At editorial meetings these disagreements turned into heated exchanges, with Mumford and Frank accusing the editors of political naïveté and moral cowardice, and the editors accusing them of succumbing to irrational fears about fascism's capacity for conquest. It soon became apparent to Mumford and Frank that they could no longer associate themselves with the magazine. Accordingly, after writing their respective challenges to *The New Republic*'s foreign policy views—Mumford's "The Corruption of Liberalism" and Frank's "Our Guilt in Fascism"— they resigned from the editorial staff.[8] (The following year Mumford, Frank, and Niebuhr made plans to launch their own magazine, *The Western World*, to be dedicated "to staying the forces of barbarism and laying the foundations for an organic . . . human culture," but they never found financial backing for their venture.)[9]

"The Corruption of Liberalism" comes from the pen of an aroused man, and a conversation Mumford had with a liberal friend who supported American neutrality goes a long way toward explaining its tone and fervor. This man told Mumford that he found it morally impossible to support a policy that might lead to war and to the death of other human beings. When Mumford objected that the failure to make such a decision in the present international situation would "lead to the less fruitful death of these same human beings six months or six years hence," the man confessed that for him "any extra time spared for the private enjoyment of life seemed that much gained." This man, Mumford remembers thinking as he walked away from him, had "ceased to live in a meaningful world. For a meaningful world is one that holds a future that extends beyond the incomplete personal life of the individual; so that a life sacrificed at the right moment is a life well spent, while a life too carefully hoarded . . . is a life utterly wasted." This, for Mumford, was the central problem with the liberal arguments for appeasement: they rested on the belief that life was worth living at any cost. Mumford traced this "survival mentality," as Christopher Lasch has called it in his criticism of some factions of the antinuclear movement, to deficiencies in the philosophic foundations of "pragmatic liberalism," a creed he had been attacking, only never so vehemently, since the early 1920s.[10]

In "The Corruption of Liberalism" and its book-length sequel, *Faith for Living*, Mumford describes two types of liberalism: "ideal liberalism," a body of universal values intimately associated with the Judeo-Christian and Western humanist tradition; and "pragmatic liberalism," a philosophy arising from the scientific and economic revolutions of the seventeenth and eighteenth centuries. Pragmatic liberalism shared certain core values of "ideal liberalism"—its commitment, for example, to democracy, racial tolerance, and to the ideals of "justice" and "objective reason." Unfortunately, however, it wedded these values and ideals to a naïve faith in the essential goodness of man and to a related idea that most human problems, including war and fascism, could be attributed primarily to malignancies and malfunctionings in the socioeconomic order. Whereas liberals like Bingham and Beard considered evil as the mere absence of good, Mumford saw it as an active and awful force, a destroyer and corrupter, always at work in the world. His reading of Herman Melville, more than anything else, had convinced him that there were traces of evil and irrationality in man that no amount of social engineering could subdue, a viewpoint he found support for in Reinhold Niebuhr's writings. Certain human beings, he believed, were so filled with evil, so pathologically malicious, as to be beyond reform; mere economic adjustment or a diplomacy of appeasement would not halt their destructive advance. Such policies rested on the erroneous conviction that fascism emerged from a flawed economic and international order, from economic depression and revengeful memories of an unjust settlement at Versailles. The real sources of fascism, however, were not to be found in the Treaty of Versailles or in the economic blundering of Weimar politicians, but in a perverse strain in the German character extending at least as far back as Martin Luther. "The raucous hatred that shouts on every page of *Mein Kampf* received its first classic utterance in Luther's denunciation of the Peasant's Rebellion; and the direct line of connection between Luther and Hitler, through Fichte, Nietzsche, and Wagner, is familiar to all those who know the history of German culture." An economic or class analysis could not explain a movement whose springs were moral and psychological. It was not to Ricardo, Marx, or Lenin, but to Dante, Shakespeare, and Dostoyevsky that one had to go for an understanding of the true sources of fascism. [11]

This analysis of fascism led Mumford straight to an argument for war. Since fascism was unresponsive to rational treatment, only a war of extinction—forced conversion, Mumford called it—could save the democracies from its lawless fury. "One might as honorably keep out of Europe today," he wrote Van Wyck Brooks in 1940, "as a doctor out of a stricken home." [12] War, Mumford admitted, was a dangerous method of conversion—in battle, men often become the image of what they hate—but there were times when forceful resistance was the sole safeguard "against the conduct of men who mean ill against society, and without doubt," Mumford concluded *Faith for Living*, "this is one of those times."

Yet while the current crisis called for unhesitant action and unyielding force, American liberals urged caution and compromise. Mumford attributed this to two further defects in pragmatic liberalism: its pallid value relativity and its underregard of the passional sources of behavior. Lacking a clear standard of values and countenancing an ex post facto logic, pragmatic liberals withheld judgment from repressive movements like Soviet Communism and National Socialism until these so-called experiments were given a chance to demonstrate their "success" or failure; and too often the sole pragmatic criterion of success was mere economic progress. This dubious standard of judgment explained the pragmatic liberal's "tenderness" for fascism, a movement that had demonstrated some capacity for economic growth. Pragmatic liberalism's slippery value relativity made it incapable even of distinguishing between barbarism and civilization. Those who were unable to discern the moral difference between the atrocities of the fascists and the lesser evils of the French and British colonial regimes were color-blind, Mumford angrily charged, to "moral values."

Mumford claimed not to be surprised by the pragmatic liberals' inability to make resolute ethical judgments; for in pragmatic thinking, as he had argued before, emotions and feelings were subordinated to rational calculation. This was the pragmatist's mark of good judgment—a decision divorced from the heated claims of passion. This effort to separate intellectual judgment from its emotional referent was not only impossible to accomplish, but in some instances it was dangerous to attempt. If we encounter a poisonous snake, Mumford argued in "The Corruption of Liberalism," "it is important, for a *rational* reaction, to have a prompt emotion of fear"; for fear releases the adrenaline that puts us on the alert and gives us "the extra strength either to run or to attack. Merely to look at the snake abstractedly . . . may lead to the highly irrational step of permitting the snake to draw near without being on guard against the reptile's bite." This was the pragmatists' problem. Distrusting the emotions, lacking, in truth, a developed "sense of danger," they were incapable of fathoming the destructive potential of fascism.[13]

Mumford was aware of the possible consequences of a war with fascism; he was convinced, for one thing, that such a war could not be won without a temporary suspension of civil liberties. Well before the United States joined the war he was calling for legal restrictions on those suspected of sympathizing with the fascists. At the very least, he demanded that these "poisonous" elements be denied the right of free speech and assemblage and the use of the federal mails; and for those *known* to be in league with the fascists, he recommended jail or exile under a new statute making their beliefs treasonous. "Neither our Constitution nor our Bill of Rights nor our American traditions would survive," he argued in an excess of emotion, "if the nation itself went under: democracy must at least have the resolution to ensure its own survival."[14]

When Albert Guérard, in his review of *Faith for Living*, accused Mumford of going too far on this question of censoring opinion—"If Mumford had his way he would jail me and ultimately shoot me for daring to challenge his view"—Mumford wrote to him explaining that "it is not you or any other American citizen I would suppress but the Fascist agents who would utilize our freedom and tolerance in order to overthrow freedom and tolerance." Why should we allow fascist "saboteurs" to use the American press and radio to spread their lies and confusion?[15]

War, Mumford darkly predicted, would impose other and perhaps even more painful sacrifices on the citizenry. To defeat Hitler, all of the nation's productive energies would have to be harnessed to war-related aims. This would mean a sharp curtailment of luxuries and extravagances, the transition, in sum, from a consumption economy to the kind of "life-centered" economy he had argued for in *Technics and Civilization*.

To nurture and sustain this faith of hardship and collective responsibility, Mumford called for a return to the region and the land, and for a "new joy" in family life and "fecundity." In order to win the war America would have to become "a nation of villagers." In the village and the region the emotional satisfaction of life lived close to the soil and enhanced by the pleasures of family and communal life would more than compensate for the Spartan austerity of the national mobilization. In this way, the region, the village, and the family would form the core of a life-forwarding culture that would see the nation through the war crisis toward a larger "regeneration" effort in the years beyond the democratic victory. [16]

But America's first business was war, not reform. With fascism on the loose it was futile to even dream of a better world, and on the question of America's responsibilities to the Allies Mumford would abide no debate or discussion. His break with his friend Frank Lloyd Wright, a staunch isolationist, reveals the depth of his concern for the survival of democracy. [17]

In the spring of 1941, as Mumford was reading the proofs of an article he had written on Wright's architecture, he found in his afternoon mail an isolationist broadside with Wright's name on it. He was so incensed by this that he sent Wright a note that evening. "I have read and re-read . . . [your pamphlet] with growing astonishment . . . over its crassness, with incredulity over its blindness, with anger over its shameless defeatism, and with indignation over its callous lack of moral perception. Did *you* write that broadside—or your worst enemy?" At a time when the free world looked to great men for inspiration, Wright had become a spineless appeaser, willing to "abandon to their terrible fate the conquered, the helpless, the humiliated, the suffering. . . . In short: you have become a living corpse: a spreader of active corruption. You dishonor all the generous impulses you once ennobled. Be silent! or die in the flesh, before you bring upon yourself some greater shame."[18]

"Listen, my young friend," Wright replied immediately. "I liked to call you and talk to you occasionally when I got to the great city but I see that you, too, are yellow with this strange ancient sickness of the soul: the malady that has thrown down civilization after civilization by meeting force with force. Is meeting force with force the only way you see? Then I am sorry for you—you amateur essayist on culture."[19]

Wright, too, knew how to use words as weapons, and this stormy exchange ended a close friendship. The following month Mumford broke with another of his old friends, John T. Flynn. In urging America to stay out of the war isolationists like "you . . . [are] cooperat[ing] with the Gestapo and the concentration camp," he angrily wrote Flynn. "Stand up for America in your own way: that is your duty. . . . Do not, in the name of isolationism and 'peace' become a mouthpiece for the barbarians in Berlin." Flynn was rightfully incensed by Mumford's inflamed denunciation of what, for him, were opinions based on conscience and principle. He never spoke to Mumford again; nor did Mumford try to reestablish their friendship.[20]

Mumford's unyielding commitment to American military intervention caused him to split, too, with the historian Charles A. Beard, one of the earliest promoters of his work; and years later, when Van Wyck Brooks defended Beard's right to take the position he did in the 1930s, Mumford came perilously close to ending that treasured friendship as well. In 1947 the National Institute of Arts and Letters, of which Brooks was chairman, awarded Beard its gold medal of distinction for his contributions to history. The day Mumford learned of the award he shot off an enraged letter to Brooks claiming that Beard, in his work, had "served the purpose of traitors and fascists. . . . He is no longer my friend; nor should he remain the friend of any other self-respecting man."[21] That same week Mumford resigned in protest from the institute, the first to do so in the institute's fifty-year history. Brooks stood his ground and personally presented the award to Beard, an old friend, but Brooks refused to allow this disagreement with Mumford to kill their friendship, which had somehow survived their foreign policy disagreements of the late 1930s; and neither would Mumford. "Perhaps

only time will heal the wounds we've both, alas! inflicted," he wrote
Brooks, "but to speed that process I offer you my hand, in old
friendship and love."²² It was the least he could have done for
putting such pressure on the ailing Brooks to break his friendship
with Beard.

Before Mumford entered the debate over American intervention in
Europe he was known as a man of strong opinions, but as a writer
not given to rash and reckless criticism. Now he found himself being
attacked in the liberal and radical press, and in private, by some of
his friends, like Malcolm Cowley, as a "madman," and, even worse,
a fascist—the "Führer of anti-fascism." "In a kind of sickness of
soul, in an anguish of fear and passion, you have taken the tone and
the methods of the enemy," his Connecticut neighbor Matthew
Josephson wrote him in 1940. In a slashing editorial, "Lewis Mumford's 'Mein Kampf,' " *The New Masses* denounced *Faith for Living* as
"the most flagrant statement of the 'liberal case' for Fascism which
the war has so far produced." To insist that "uninhibited . . . emotional reaction is the road to health and safety" was to engage in
behavior characteristic of Nazism, *The New Republic* agreed in its
official reply to "The Corruption of Liberalism." Was it not, after
all, the mark of the fascist to set "primitive emotional impulses
against reason . . . glorifying the former by contrast." Mumford's
case against "empiricism," the novelist James T. Farrell argued in
The Southern Review, was "stated on the worst possible level, that of
mere name-calling and abuse." In fact, Mumford was not even
capable of describing his own "faith for living." His ideal liberalism
was nothing more than a philosophic catch basin for all he considered valuable in the human heritage. Incapable of framing an intellectually defensible argument for war, Mumford offered "no real
ideas to refute. He has only muddled assertions and abuse left in his
arsenal."²³

In this bruising debate both sides reverted too frequently to "mere
name-calling and abuse," but in attacking Mumford in an article in
Common Sense the poet A. Fleming MacLiesh managed to get close to
one of the reasons Mumford pursued his case for intervention with
such ardor. In "The Corruption of Liberalism," Mumford had
assailed pragmatic liberals for refusing to speak out earlier in the

decade against the repressions in Stalin's Russia, citing this record of "passivism" and "retreat" as evidence of liberalism's moral bankruptcy. But the majority of liberals opposed to intervention had not, MacLiesh observed, supported a pro-Stalin line, "though Mr. Mumford himself surprisingly did!"[24]

MacLiesh was not entirely correct about this. Mumford had never openly endorsed Stalin's Russia, yet he had kept silent about the fate of freedom in Russia at a time when Bingham, Dewey, Beard, and other pragmatic liberals were inveighing against the dictatorship. This makes his distinction between "pragmatic" and "ideal" liberalism difficult to consider seriously. This crude distinction served as little more than a device for separating those who agreed with him on intervention from those who did not. In fact, Mumford himself admitted privately to Van Wyck Brooks what he never admitted in print: that it was *he* who had refused to speak out against Stalin, and that the guilt and shame generated by that silence fueled the ferocity of his opposition to Hitler and all who now refused to wage war against him. "Maybe I am vehement on the subject [of intervention] now, all out of reason," he wrote Brooks in 1940, "because I feel deeply my own guilt during the past twenty years, when, despite my extreme skepticism of the totalitarian tyranny that was being built up in Russia, I said nothing and did nothing to counteract it, . . . thinking that Russia could work out its own salvation, and must therefore be protected from hostile criticism."[25]

Our aim, Mumford told Brooks in this revealing letter, must be to move at once to extinguish fascism and to erect a "universal society moved by a common set of human ideals." We cannot question the sincerity of Mumford's commitment to such ideals, but in the heat of an undeniably just cause, he indulged in a manner of thinking that often contravened those ideals. Even Henry Murray, his closest friend, accused him of arguing his case in an "autocratic" manner. "You can[not] forcefully impel people by machine-gun phrases to agree with you."[26]

In arguing their case for a kind of holy war against fascism, writers like Mumford, Niebuhr, and Frank advanced arguments that would set a dangerous precedent for the postwar years. Where Niebuhr, for example, would insist upon the superiority of force over reason as an instrument of international deterrence, cold war "neorealists" would use similar arguments in support of another, yet

different campaign of ideological containment; and where understandable outrage against Hitler would provoke Mumford to
demand a suspension of the Bill of Rights for those suspected of
trafficking in fascism, later democratic zealots (although not Mumford himself) would treat lightly of the Constitution in prosecuting
an equally fervid campaign against Communist sympathizers in the
1950s. The call for repression in the name of freedom was not
unique to the later era of Communist containment.

Yet this does not invalidate Mumford's central argument of the
late 1930s—that Hitler could be stopped only by military force.
And after the fall of France in June 1940, Mumford had considerably more support for his position. That winter he joined William
Allen White's Committee to Defend America by Aiding the Allies,
and in early 1941, when White's committee refused to urge an
immediate American declaration of war, he joined Herbert Agar's
militantly interventionist Fight for Freedom Committee. In these
battles Sophia was his strongest ally. She headed the local Amenia
chapter of the Committee to Defend America by Aiding the Allies,
writing hundreds of letters to friends and neighbors in Dutchess
County asking for commitments of money and organizational help.
In the winter of 1939–40, with the world situation rapidly deteriorating, the Mumfords moved back to New York so that Geddes, a
sluggish student, could get a better education at the Bronx High
School of Science, and so that Lewis could take a more active part in
the fight against fascism. That winter, at parties and dinners they
attended or hosted, the conversation invariably became strained
when the subject turned to the war in Europe, for most of their New
York friends still hoped that America could stay out of the conflict.
Gradually the Mumfords stopped seeing these friends and turned to
those in sympathy with their views, like Waldo Frank, Reinhold and
Ursula Niebuhr, Paul Rosenfeld, Lee Simonson, the writer Thomas
Beer, and when she was in New York, Constance Rourke.

As a married couple they had never felt so isolated. They eventually stopped entertaining, and every evening, as a family, they
would gather in the living room of their Bleecker Street apartment
to listen to the reports from Europe of Edward R. Morrow, William
L. Shirer, and other CBS reporters, the first regular transatlantic
coverage of a major European story. They listened intently, nervously, as Morrow, from Vienna, described the German armies

goose-stepping down that city's broad baroque avenues and the gangs of fascist thugs racing through the streets shouting *"Ein Reich, ein Volk, ein Führer!"* It was on their tiny radio set that they first heard the screaming, screeching voice of Adolf Hitler. The night the Führer addressed a huge Nazi rally in Nuremberg they could clearly hear him hammering the speaker's platform with his fist and could pick up in the background the thunderous accompanying cheers of *"Heil Hitler, Sieg Heil."* While some of Mumford's friends felt he was painting the devil on the wall, the devil, in fact, was "at work in the world." About this time Mumford bought a new .30-.30 rifle, feeling that he might have to use it some day soon to fight, perhaps as a member of the American underground, an invading fascist army.[27]

His and Sophia's involvement with the cause of antifascism took up time they would have ordinarily given to their children. "Children and the world crisis don't mix!" Sophia confided to a friend. "I never dreamed I would find myself almost resenting the time I must give listening to Geddes's confidences or assuring Alison her dolly is beautiful." There was less time for gardening, or for picnics and Sunday walks, and sometimes when the children needed them most "we would not be there." It was a difficult household to grow up in, especially for Geddes, a high-strung teenager, and a difficult time for any young man to grow up, with the threat of war and the possibility of death hovering in the background. If America were to go to war—and Geddes kept hearing his parents insisting that America *must* join the fight—he knew he would be called to serve.[28]

But Geddes supported his parents' position on the world issue, and he was in the audience, pulling for his father, when Lewis debated Congressman Hamilton Fish, a German sympathizer, in the crowded auditorium of Amenia High School in 1941, with Eleanor Roosevelt and Mrs. Henry Morgenthau in attendance. Some five hundred persons jammed the auditorium of the high school, while three hundred or four hundred others assembled outside, listening to the debate through loudspeakers. Hundreds of others sat in their cars nearby with their windows open. Throughout the entire debate Geddes sat on the edge of his chair, elbows on his knees, his chin cupped in his hands, with "tears of excitement in his eyes, hanging on every word," fearing at one point that Fish, a large man, was going to attack his father with his fists when Lewis called him a Nazi accomplice. "Get out of the Congress," Lewis told Fish, his eyes blazing with anger, "get out of the army, get out—before we throw you out."[29]

These political struggles did bring Lewis and Sophia closer together spiritually, but they took their inevitable toll on another part of their relationship. "Our intimacy," Lewis confessed in one of his diary entries, "has not been as rich: our souls are closer though our bodies have enjoyed each other less. At night we are emotionally exhausted."[30] And in the spring of 1940, Sophia began to grow concerned about Lewis's deteriorating health: during the day he seemed anxious and overwrought, and at night he had trouble sleeping. He had recurring nightmares of being captured or "pinned down"; of desperately trying to return to America and being unable to; of a German invasion of England; and of face-to-face confrontations with Hitler. His blood pressure shot up and his heart began to beat too rapidly. Finally his doctor advised him to retire to Leedsville for a week or two and to wall himself off from the outside world.

He and Sophia went to the country on May 10, not knowing that Germany had invaded Holland that day, and while resting in Leedsville, Lewis did not read a newspaper or listen to the radio. He did little but read and garden and walk in the spring-green woods behind their farmhouse, and he quickly rebounded back to health. On one of their last days in the country he and Sophia took a drive into Amenia, and although Lewis never got out of the car he could tell by the look on people's faces that something terrible had happened. When he and Sophia returned to New York that Sunday they learned that the German armies had stormed into the Netherlands and that Winston Churchill had been named Prime Minister of England. That June, after the fall of France, Mumford wrote the first draft of *Faith for Living*, a 333-page book, in ten days, handing in the completed manuscript on June 24, the day Nellie Ahearn, his childhood nurse and second mother, died in a Staten Island rest home.[31]

Mumford completed his revisions of the book in three weeks, driven by anger and grief, working from eight in the morning to seven at night. The book, his largest commercial success to date, sold 20,000 copies the first year, and it was even more successful and influential in England, though one entire edition was destroyed when a German bomb hit the building it was being printed in.

During the dark days of that summer Mumford worked on the script for a huge exhibit to be shown at the Museum of Modern Art depicting what the world would look like if the fascists gained control. (The museum directors withdrew support for the exhibit later in the summer.) He also met a number of times with Niebuhr, Herbert Agar, and other prominent interventionists to draft a "Declaration on World Democracy," denouncing pragmatism and fascism and calling for war on Germany. The group's leading spirit was G. A. Borgese, an old-fashioned man of letters who had been exiled from Italy for refusing to take the fascist oath. Borgese was a close friend of Joel Spingarn's, and he and his wife Elizabeth, the daughter of the novelist Thomas Mann, who had recently fled to America and who met occasionally with Borgese's group, settled near Amenia and worked with the Mumfords to convince Roosevelt and the Congress to go to the aid of beleaguered Britain. "The Country looks to you for positive leadership. . . ," Mumford cabled the President that June. "Upon your ability and willingness to exercise this leadership during the next few weeks will depend whether you will go down to history as the Buchanan or the Lincoln of the present world civil war."[32]

But though Roosevelt moved to aid England, he did not move decisively enough for Mumford. By this time, most of the former noninterventionist liberals, including the editors of *Common Sense* and *The New Republic*, were urging American aid to the Allies "short of war." The noninterventionists had insisted that England and France could defeat Germany without American aid, and that, in any event, the Western Hemisphere was invulnerable to military attack. The frightening success of the Nazi blitzkrieg undercut both these assumptions, and destroyed once and for all the illusion of a fortress America; while Hitler's redoubled persecution of the Jews made it impossible to argue that there were no great moral issues at stake in Europe. Germany had shown itself to be considerably more than a "have-not" nation struggling for the economic materials essential to autarchy. Its ambitions appeared limitless, its military might awesome and increasing. Americans now began to fear that if England fell their country would be Hitler's next target. While a

Fortune poll of October 1937 had found 62 percent of Americans neutral toward Germany and unprepared to risk war for England's sake, by January 1941 a Gallup poll indicated 68 percent of Americans supporting all-out aid of England, even at the risk of war. And while not yet prepared to declare war, the American Congress, pressed and pushed by a determined Roosevelt, made it plain in the summer of 1940 that this country was ready to transform itself into "the great arsenal of democracy."33

With the Nazis in Paris, many of Mumford's friends approached him to apologize for attacking his "hysterical" predictions of fascist military expansion. Yet while these liberals began urging aid to threatened England, and to Russia, which Hitler attacked in June 1941, Mumford had only to up the plea to a demand for war to have these same sympathetic friends raise objections or retreat into embarrassed silence. Actually, Mumford was even more pessimistic about the world situation in the summer of 1941, after the Battle of Britain and Russia's entry into the war, than he had been in the summer of 1940, when England had seemed about to fall; "for then," he wrote despairingly in his notes, "I at least hoped that the presence of danger would immediately rouse us."34

Mumford was at Dartmouth College the Sunday evening he learned of the Japanese attack on Pearl Harbor. That afternoon Geddes had hitchhiked down to Hanover from Goddard College, where he was a student in a special program, to have lunch with his father at the Hanover Inn. After lunch one of Lewis's Dartmouth colleagues drove Geddes part of the way back to Goddard, and Lewis rode along. When Lewis returned to his room at the Hanover Inn the phone was ringing. As he brought the receiver to his ear the voice at the other end blurted out: "What do you think about what those Japs did to us?" We were finally at war. He should have been relieved, but the thought of this immediately brought to his mind what he had been trying to suppress for the last two years. It would be a long war, and his son, then sixteen, would be called into the fight. Lewis Mumford also thought of himself that evening: what would be his role in this enormous global struggle?35

22

The Primacy of the Person

*When a society is hopelessly corrupt and incapable of reform-
ing its institutions, it is the individual who must first be
saved; saved by escaping the meshes of his society and
becoming part of a new one.*

—LEWIS MUMFORD

Mumford was quick to decide where he could make his strongest
contribution to the war effort. Too old to serve in the armed forces,
and lacking the training and experience to assume a large role in the
home-front mobilization, he thought that he could be of greatest use
as a voice of conscience, clarifying the goals for which the
democracies ought to be fighting. America's slow response to fascism convinced him that the majority of his countrymen had lost
sight of the founding ideals of their cultural heritage. There was a
need for a restatement of these values, for if the democratic world
was to be saved, it would be saved "not by machines and guns, but
by a capacity to produce a higher type of human being." Big
machines are of little use, he liked to say, if they are run by little
men. [1]

The war reaffirmed Mumford's conviction that social renewal
must begin with the "rebirth of the person." This became the
central argument of the book he had already begun when America
entered the war, *The Condition of Man*, the third volume of his

Renewal of Life series, and this is one of the major reasons he agreed in 1942 to head Stanford University's newly established School of Humanities. At Stanford his mission, he told Van Wyck Brooks before leaving for California, would be to give "the young the vision and discipline they will need to lift themselves out of the muck and chaos that their easy-going elders have created."[2]

Mumford was invited to teach at Stanford after giving a passionately eloquent address at the fiftieth anniversary celebration of the founding of the university in the summer of 1941. In this speech he argued that the strengthening of the humanities must be the first item on America's educational agenda. By not responding early enough to a fascist movement that threatened to overthrow not just this or that democratic government, but the very ideas and principles upon which Western culture had been founded, his generation had failed to meet their responsibilities to the wider human community.[3] It was his hope that a reinvigoration of humanities education at Stanford and other colleges would produce young men and women capable of responding to the equal challenges of the postwar years. In the renewed cultivation of the humanities, Mumford rested his hopes for the very future of humanity.

This was a theme in near-perfect accord with the sentiments of a group of Stanford faculty who were reshaping the university's humanities program, and less than a year later they were able to offer Mumford an appointment as full professor and head of the new humanities school, at a salary of $7,500 a year. Up to this time the humanities at Stanford had been a mere assemblage of fragmented disciplines, many of them unimaginatively taught. The founders of the School of Humanities wanted to bring them to life and connect them to the sciences and social sciences; and Mumford's appointment gave impetus to their efforts. He would be their "man on the white horse," they informed him when he arrived on campus.[4]

Mumford looked forward to this Stanford appointment as an opportunity to put into practice an educational idea "I have had for many years," he told a reporter from *Time* before he left for California, "which is that the humanities and sciences are not in inherent conflict but have become separated in the twentieth century," an idea C. P. Snow would later popularize in his influential book *The Two Cultures and the Scientific Revolution*.[5] Yet while Mumford was excited about the prospect of molding a new approach to the humanities, he never quite adjusted to the Stanford scene, and part of this had to do with the circumstances of his arrival.

The summer before he set out for California he tried unsuccessfully to complete his book in progress—already over four hundred pages long. This left him little time to prepare for his fall semester courses, and when he arrived in California he was physically run-down and anxious about his new teaching responsibilities, as he had never liked to lecture. Stanford officials went out of their way to make him and Sophia comfortable, providing them with a spacious house on campus with a lovely garden of roses, heather, and Hawaiian ginger, but Lewis found the house, and Palo Alto in general, too suburban for his tastes. Being without a car also left him and Sophia housebound, unable to escape on weekends to the beaches or into the spacious California backcountry.

Their first few weeks in California were harried and exhausting. Sophia was ill with a tumor on her uterus which caused hemorrhaging and left her weak and anemic (eventually she had to have an operation), and they were unable to find household help. So for a time Lewis became "Professor of Cooking, Dishwashing and Carpetsweeping," and this took him away from his course preparations.[6] Even so, his first classes went well. After the opening lecture in his course on ancient Greek culture he received a long round of applause from the students and the twenty or so faculty who had turned out to hear him. Although he was never completely at ease in the classroom, he became one of the more popular professors in the humanities program, a powerful lecturer who also worked well with the students in the more informal discussion sessions. And he went out of his way to make the humanities relevant to the everyday concerns of his students.

Mumford drew on lessons from his own life to enrich his lectures on great thinkers. In the final class in his course on The Nature of Personality he spoke movingly and with great candor of his own struggle to live in accord with the Athenian ideal of balance. When he finished speaking the students broke into spontaneous applause, bringing tears to his eyes. "I was touched by it," he wrote in his journal the following day, "for I think that maybe twenty out of the class of ninety-five or so who have listened to me actually have gotten something from the course: moral strengthening as well as intellectual insight."[7]

He was old-fashioned enough to consider such moral strengthening an indispensable part of teaching. The humanities, he
believed, should give ordinary men and women an understanding of
their world and lessons on how to live purposively in it. This was
especially important during wartime. Properly taught, the humanities would give a "fighting generation" an appreciation of "all the
things that are worth while living for, struggling for, fighting for,
and if need be, dying for."[8]

At the end of Mumford's first term at Stanford, one of his students, a young married woman expecting a child, came to his office
to talk to him about what she had learned. Before she entered
Stanford, she told him, she was a "disheartened" woman. She could
find no meaning in the war or in life itself. She even resented her
pregnancy, for her husband, a lieutenant in the navy, was going to
sea in a few months and might never see her or the child again.
"Now . . . I don't feel that way any more. This course has made me
understand what we are fighting for. At last, life has some meaning
for me, and you ought to hear me argue with the officers and wives
back at the station, trying to make them understand some of the
things the humanities have made me see so clearly. But I haven't told
you the best thing I got out of the course," she added with a smile as
she was about to leave his office. "I am *glad* I am going to have my
baby, whether my husband comes back from the war or not. I have
something to give the child now, and if my man dies he won't die in
vain."[9]

Had Mumford been able to reach all his students in this way he
might have stayed longer at Stanford, but such moments of supreme
satisfaction in teaching were rare for him. He found most of his
students uninteresting, and, worse than that, uninterested in their
own education, "spoonfed middle class children" concerned most of
all with getting a good grade. To his surprise, he wasn't even
physically attracted to his young female students. "Plainly I am
getting old," he confessed playfully to Jo Strongin. "I never dreamed
fifteen years ago that there would come a time when I would look on
a girl of 18 or 20 and find her . . . flatly uninteresting." Now, as they
sat in his office and discussed their problems with him, he listened
to them with "fatherly aloofness."[10]

The one "student" he *was* completely interested in was his son
Geddes, who had spent the previous summer on a ranch in Wash-

ington State and was waiting for his parents when they first arrived at their new house on Alvarado Row. Geddes, his parents discovered, had a new maturity, a new sense of purpose, and, to their amazement, had become interested in his studies, probably because his new girlfriend back east was a bright, involved student, and he wanted her to consider him as her equal. Geddes had been a hottempered, rebellious teenager, and there was more than a little tension in his relationship with his father, as they were near opposites in temperament and outlook. Now father and son found themselves locked in dinnertime conversations on a range of subjects, from biological evolution to the current state of the world. In these spirited exchanges, which would sometimes carry on into the late evening, they gained a new respect for one another. "If I don't know more about Civilization than his Humanity [sic] students by the end of this year," Geddes wrote his girlfriend Martha, "I shall be very surprised. . . . Where the guy picks it all up is beyond me, but it's there for the asking, which is just what I have been doing"—for the first time, he might have added.[11]

Living in California brought the Mumford family closer together, but this in itself wasn't enough to keep Lewis there. He was not at Stanford two months before he began talking about returning to Amenia for the duration of the war to give his time to his writing. "Without the regular practice of this art I am not, and never have been, a healthy man," he wrote his Troutbeck neighbor Amy Spingarn.[12] He also found it difficult to be on the sidelines, without any influence, while the war raged on; and he thought his book would be his largest contribution to the war effort. This talk of leaving Stanford became an obsession with him when he learned in late 1942 that the military was going to take over a large part of the university for army training, which would make possible only a severely curtailed program in the humanities. Almost all of his students would be women, and that did not fit with one of the principal reasons he had agreed to come to Stanford—to help train young men about to enter wartime service. In order not to lose Mumford entirely, the university gave him a leave of absence from June 1943 to the following January; when he returned he would be expected to give half of his time to the School of Humanities and the other half to assisting the new president, Donald Tresidder, in reorganizing the entire university, possibly adding, at Mumford's suggestion, a school in regional and urban planning. It was this new challenge, and his personal fondness for Tresidder, that persuaded Mumford to agree to return to Stanford for at least another year.

That summer in Leedsville he fell back into his healing routines. Old friends dropped by to visit—Catherine Bauer and her husband William Wurster, Henry Murray, and others—but as much as Lewis enjoyed seeing them, he usually couldn't wait until they left so that he could get back to his book. In these months in the country, with Sophia fielding his telephone calls and keeping visitors to an absolute minimum, he put the finishing touches on *The Condition of Man*, and then returned immediately to Stanford with the family.

But even with his book behind him, he was in no mood to take on his new responsibilities. The faculty was resistant to Tresidder's plans for curricular change, and when Mumford threw himself into committee work in support of these reforms and met some stiff opposition his heart began to act up again. He was ordered to bed by his doctor, who could find nothing wrong with his heart. Mumford knew, however, that the trouble was not with that organ but with the entire organism—exhaustion and a desperate need to be released from these new pressures. He had seen his friends Van Wyck Brooks and Clarence Stein give way under similar pressures, and he was determined not to let this happen to him. He would leave the university at the end of the semester, he told Tresidder. Nor did he intend to return, although he didn't tell Tresidder this at the time. He had come to Stanford not just to become a professor—affecting a few students—but to transform the "aims and methods of the modern university, using the School of Humanities as a central fulcrum." He had quickly discovered, however, that such changes would take many years to carry through, and he was simply not prepared to give himself, in the fifth decade of his life, to this long-term effort. He was beginning to see "that the university [is] the last place in which to expect renewal."[13]*

Mumford looked to the May 1944 publication date of *The Condition of Man* with a mixture of confidence and uncertainty; this would be, he

---

*The School of Humanities disappeared in 1948 and became the School of Humanities and Sciences, a program Mumford's efforts helped to get going.

thought, his *Moby Dick*, his masterwork, but he learned that its importance and impact would not be immediately felt, for its theme and message were at odds with the prevailing mood of the times. And he, the author, was fast becoming a forgotten man.[14]

At Stanford, and later in Leedsville, observing the war from the sidelines, Mumford felt isolated and ineffectual. He had some friends in high government positions, but not one of them offered him a job or approached him for advice, even in matters well within his expertise, like public housing. He was being ignored, he suspected, because of his earlier attacks on President Roosevelt for not moving quickly enough against Germany, although he had no direct evidence to support his hunch. His battles on behalf of intervention had convinced him, moreover, that his kind of thinking, with its call for passion, sacrifice, and hard struggle, was currently out of favor, that he was considered too extreme in his views, too moralistic, and worst of all, in a country never without hope, too pessimistic, with his somber warnings of chaos and ruin. But this was a complete misreading of his point of view, he complained to his friends. If he held out no hope for humanity he would not be writing at all.[15]

Earlier in the war Mumford had read Fichte's addresses to the German people, and although he was annoyed by their shrill cultural chauvinism, he came away profoundly impressed by Fichte's diagnosis of Germany's ailments and by his cure for overcoming them—through a "renewal of the entire concept of education." To Mumford this meant a fresh restatement of human ideals, the ideals, that is, that he prized most. In the manner of most apocalyptic thinkers, he looked for some sort of crisis or catastrophe to hasten the changes he called for; if the recent economic depression had not moved his countrymen to alter their priorities, perhaps the war would. But there would have to be inspired spiritual leadership. "I would like to be the Fichte, not of my country alone, but of the entire democratic world," Mumford wrote Walter Curt Behrendt as he put the finishing touches on *The Condition of Man*.[16]

Mumford's work during this period of his life moves simultaneously in two directions—forward, into the postwar world he hoped to influence, and backwards, into the distant past, further back into human history than he had ever journeyed in his published writing, as he continued to hold to the notion that by reshaping the map of the past he could rearrange the terrain of the future. Like a number of other wide-scoped thinkers who were his contemporaries, he returned to history for a sharper perspective on the events of his day and as a guide to present conduct. He had begun the two previous books in his Renewal of Life series with the Middle Ages, a natural starting point for histories of the machine and the modern city. But when he moved from a consideration of man as a tool-using, city-building creature to the development of the human personality itself, to the evolution of man as a symbol-making creature, he had to go back to classical Greece and Rome, when modern Western man first emerged. But while *The Condition of Man* opens in the Greece of Socrates and Sophocles, its focal chapters deal with the decline of the classical age and the spread of Christianity. In primitive Christianity's slow but near-complete triumph over the Roman world, Mumford locates lessons for his own age.

In this far-ranging book Mumford set out to describe the origins, evolution, and present condition of the Western world, exploring mankind's major breakthroughs in the arts, philosophy, science, and religion. *The Condition of Man* is a summation of all Mumford had learned about man and his history. It is a crowded, deeply learned book, but it is also ponderously argued, repetitious, and sharply judgmental; too often solemn pronouncements substitute for judicious analysis. Mumford draws on the advice and ideas of an amazingly diverse range of thinkers, from Plato to Alfred North Whitehead, in an effort to bring together these scattered insights into a new philosophic synthesis, which he called organic humanism. Yet while he earnestly argues for such a synthesis, he fails in this book to fashion it.

The Condition of Man also surveys considerably less ground than it claims to cover. It is, in the main, a profoundly personal, that is, scrupulously selective interpretation of humankind's spiritual development. Mumford had already written several confessions of his faith, but this is the first of his books to deal in depth with the religious factor in history. The book takes its direction from the time in which it is written, a period of war and totalitarianism, of institutional and moral collapse. Mumford, with Reinhold Niebuhr and Arnold J. Toynbee, saw this world crisis as essentially spiritual in nature, "a schism of the soul," Toynbee called it, or in Mumford's words, a complete "breakdown in stable behavior." Mumford brought to the analysis of this crisis an expressly psychoanalytical point of view. In our search for recovery and stability we would have to confront our past "as fully as a neurotic patient must unbury his personal life." For him, this is the importance of the early Christian example. "To understand our present selves, we must understand the central core which formed the primitive Christian; not because we can live again within that archaic mold, but because we can then see into the nature of our own plight and direct our efforts towards an even more positive renewal."[17]

Mumford began his research on early Christianity while he was living in New York City in the winter of 1939–40, at the time of his most intense involvement in the fight for American intervention in Europe. This struggle, and two of his closest allies in it, greatly influenced *The Condition of Man*. In his conversations with Waldo Frank and Reinhold Niebuhr, he gained a fuller awareness of the importance of religion and religious values in history. Around this time he read several of Frank's and almost all of Niebuhr's books, and with Niebuhr's guidance he began to read the church fathers, from Cyprian and Tertullian to Augustine and Jerome. Every weekday morning around nine o'clock he would leave his Bleecker Street apartment and walk up Fifth Avenue to the library at Forty-second Street, spending five or six hours, often without a lunch break, reliving in his mind the great moral debates that shook the Western world over a thousand years ago, and it was not long before he began to see that world as an earlier incarnation of his own. "Nobody has better expressed than Seneca the soul of man under despotism" he told a friend that winter, with Nazi Germany on his mind. And in the late Roman rulers, who refused to believe that their empire was falling apart, who insisted that there would always be a Rome, he saw the image of his isolationist friends who kept assuring him during the Battle of Britain that there would always be an England. Mumford read almost all of Seneca and much of Marcus Aurelius, but it was the Christian thinkers who truly excited his interest. They had confronted the kinds of problems that he was presently concerned with—problems having to do with sin and evil, death and rebirth, and with the need for withdrawal, repentance, and conversion.[18]

After reading Samuel Dill's sprawling studies of the late empire Mumford became convinced that none of the common historical explanations of Rome's decline had reached the real truth. Rome fell not because of political or economic ineptitude or even because of the barbarian invasions; it collapsed through "a leaching away of meaning and a loss of faith." At the time Mumford was doing his research on Rome, he was still under the spell of Arnold J. Toynbee's *A Study of History*, and from Toynbee he took the idea that civilizations are held together by an organizing idea or principle, never precisely stated verbally, but continually at work in every important institution. At first this idea was incarnated in a single person, a Jesus, a Buddha, a Confucius. Then, through a process Toynbee called "mimesis," the idea took hold in many persons and institutions, becoming a new pattern of living, a new way of organizing the world. When this original idea became exhausted, when those who lived under its sway failed to recover and replenish it—as the church, for example, had failed to take St. Francis of Assisi's advice to return to the simple moral teachings of Jesus Christ—the whole civilization slowly gave way, and a new idea began its unstoppable rise to dominance.[19]

All this suddenly became clear to Mumford as he read one of the more fascinating works of Christian apologetics, "The Octavius of Minucius Felix," a third-century debate between a pagan defending the Roman way of life and his militantly pious Christian companion. In this spirited disputation, which takes place in the book as the two men are walking from Rome to the seaport of Ostia, Mumford saw the key to Christianity's triumph over the Roman order. Intellectually, the worldly Roman wins the argument hands down. He has greater literary and philosophic reach, and he is a practiced and polished rhetorician, while Octavius's Christian arguments are shrilly anti-intellectual—he calls Socrates a fool and is contemptuous of all worldly philosophers. "We do not speak great things but we live them." In the end, however, it is Octavius's unyielding faith, not Caecilius's level-eyed logic, that wins through. By the time they reach Ostia the Roman is ready to convert to Christianity, and his flight from reason to faith, of course, foretold an actual historical transformation.[20] The Roman preached a sounder line, but the Christian practiced a sounder form of living. "I am going to try to understand, by way of Rome, what is happening to us," Mumford wrote excitedly to Jo Strongin the week he finished reading "Minucius Felix," "before I try to show . . . what alternative unknown to Christian or Roman, we may possess."[21]

To Mumford, it was the Romans' unwillingness to reexamine and reconstruct their whole scheme of living—a way of life founded upon "pillage and pilfer"—that made them vulnerable to Christianity, a simple faith based, as the earlier Roman way of life had been, upon rigorous purposeful living. Rome fell, then, because of a "barbarization from within," an unleashing of the forces of the id best evidenced by the sadism and brutality of the Colosseum spectacles. The Christians realized that they could save themselves only by withdrawing from this society and becoming part of a community in which their values were respected. It was, in the end, the Christians' superego—their capacity for sacrifice and withdrawal—that gave them, in Mumford's view, a clear edge over the Romans.[22]

In *The Condition of Man*, however, Mumford did not call for a return to the faith of the first Christians, as Toynbee had. To fanatical Christians like Jerome and Benedict of Nursia, salvation was to be gained by a retreat from life that Mumford considered morally irresponsible. Then again, this simple faith became over time rigidly institutionalized in the doctrines of the official church. Christianity's supple insights were transformed into an inflexible orthodoxy. When this happened the original Christian synthesis was superseded by a faith more encompassing than Protestantism, a mere reformist variant, in Mumford's view, of primitive Christianity. This was the new religion of science and material expansion, and it became the dominant faith in the Western world, Mumford argued, from the waning of the Middle Ages to our own time.

From this point forward, *The Condition of Man* is an elaborate reiteration of Mumford's familiar indictment of the modern scientific world picture, which undervalues the emotional or subjective life, with one important difference. In *The Condition of Man* Mumford turns this argument into his most sharply effective attack on the modern notion of reason as the sole guide to correct conduct, and relates the rise of fascism to this Cartesian suppression of imagination and emotion.

* * *

"Pure intelligence," Mumford writes in *The Condition of Man*, "ceases to be a useful guide to life as soon as it attempts the role of absolute ruler." Put in psychological terms, if the superego repressed the id too ruthlessly it could create the potential for "an explosive discharge" of the id. Instead of sublimating barbarism, an excessively rational and orderly civilization sometimes produced "a more terrible variety of barbarism, for to the animal energies in which all men share it adds those powerful technical and social facilities which civilization has itself created." Here Mumford could only have been thinking of Nazi Germany.[23]

There are strong echoes of Giovanni Battista Vico, the eighteenth-century Italian philosopher, in this argument. In his studies of cultural evolution Vico, whom Mumford first read in 1937, describes two ways of seeing the world—the imaginative universal and the intelligible universal. The intelligible universal is a narrowly focused, object-oriented epistemology in which reality is apprehended by the intellect, not the imagination; and the imaginative universal is a holistic mode of understanding that relies heavily on the sensations. One view values myth, poetry, dance, song, ceremony, and magic; the other logic, reason, and precise measurement and calculation. The language of one is metaphoric; the other coldly precise, denatured. The shift from the imaginative to the intelligible universal that marked the rise of modern science opened the way for great material advances, but it also opened the way, Vico argues, to the "disease of abstraction," to a single-minded emphasis upon reason and intelligence as guides to experience.[24]

In *The Condition of Man* Mumford expands these Vichian insights into a full-scale indictment of modern science. In order to understand and manipulate the natural world, scientists such as Newton had to simplify it, breaking it down into abstractions—into formulas, laws, numbers; reality had to be quantified—first time itself, and then space and motion. In this effort to "abstract" reality, the clock, as Mumford had argued in *Technics and Civilization*, was a revolutionary breakthrough. The clock "dissociated time from human events and helped create the belief in an independent world of mathematically measurable sequences: the special world of science."[25]

All this had to occur for science to proceed, and Mumford was no enemy of science itself. But the great power over the world that science acquired by its narrow representation of reality was not accompanied by an increase in moral insight or human understanding. For Mumford, the new scientific view was best symbolized by the human skeleton: "something solid, definite, clear. Clarity at the expense of life." The physical world of Galileo and Newton was neat and orderly, but it was a world devoid of moral values or significance, memory or consciousness, a world of "rarefied abstractions," a half-world only.[26] In their narrow pursuit of "objectivity," many scientists, and their fellow travelers in the social sciences, ignored entire realms of experience that science was incapable of understanding, precisely because of its concentration upon hard, empirical knowledge. This was a part of our world that could not be measured or reduced to cold abstractions. And exactly because of their magical ambiguity, the arts and letters—the traditional humanities—were our true guides to this more expressive side of experience.

Mumford related this critique of the scientific worldview to his earlier attack on pragmatic liberalism. Those who worked in the scientific spirit of modern liberalism urged us to separate emotion from judgment, to approach all problems with cool detachment, but Mumford feared that the modern suppression of emotion was turning people into machines incapable of anger when it was morally called for.[27] He was amazed, for example, that so many millions of young soldiers fought so bravely in the war with so little emotion, and with so little attachment to ideals like justice and freedom. After the war Mumford read the memoirs of General George Patton, and an incident Patton describes struck him as symptomatic of the kind of moral indifference he had described in "The Corruption of Liberalism." Patton tells the story of a German soldier who was left behind enemy lines to blow up an American troop bridge. He executed his mission perfectly, killing several infantrymen who happened to be passing over the bridge. When the smoke cleared the Nazi soldier walked toward the surviving Americans with his arms raised high in a gesture of surrender. Instead of shooting him in his tracks the Americans took him prisoner. On this matter Mumford stood with Patton: loyalty to their fallen comrades should have moved these soldiers to gun down the German. "They were exhibiting," Mumford thought, "not Christian forgiveness of a wrong, but human indifference, a far lower quality than the impulse to kill in anger."[28]

Mumford saw the same kind of moral callousness in the protests of Herbert Matthews and other American newspaper reporters to the mob lynching of one of Mussolini's leading agents of terror several months after the liberation of Rome. "No civilized person can approve of such mob action," he wrote *The New York Times* in September 1944. But equally no civilized person can condemn these acts, for the punishment the Roman mob dealt out to these thugs "is, morally speaking, more adequate to the crimes they have committed than the cold, meticulous justice of the court of law." The "superficial sensitiveness" of Matthews and other liberal reporters covered over "a deeper indifference to moral evil." It was for those who had suffered under fascism "to express both their own judgment upon the oppressors and such restraint upon vengeance as their own conscience may in the long run dictate: for them alone."[29]

Mumford wrote *The Condition of Man* to encourage in a saving minority of his countrymen the kind of passionate moral commitment he saw lacking in the reaction of Herbert Matthews to the lynching of a fascist terrorist, and he concluded the book on a note of guarded optimism. As he looked at the world in 1944 he was unsure which way civilization was heading—toward ruin or renewal. Yet for all his uncertainty about the future, he was still unshakably sure of one thing—that *if* a renewal occurred it would occur first in many separate individuals, and then spread, as Christianity had, by a centuries-long process of "memesis." Balanced personalities like Patrick Geddes and Albert Schweitzer (and surely Mumford grouped himself with them) would be the precursors and initiators, the Bacons and the Leonardos, of the emerging organic age. What they believed and thought, millions would believe and think a generation or so in the future.

But what would the world look like once this process reached a point Toynbee called "materialization," when the new civilizational idea took hold in social institutions and in the state itself. Mumford was still as unclear about the institutional shape of his "eutopia" as he was about the means of getting there.

As Mumford half expected, the reviews of *The Condition of Man* were mixed. There was some unqualified praise—from Reinhold Niebuhr and others, yet while *The Condition of Man* sold better in its first year than either *Technics and Civilization* or *The Culture of Cities*, critics generally agreed that it fell far short of the standard of Mumford's previous work. In private, Mumford complained to his friends that most reviewers had not given the book a careful enough reading; either that, or they were not ready to accept the hard program of action and austerity it called for.[30] Yet the truth is that it was not so much what Mumford said, as the way he said it—like an angry Old Testament prophet, or rather a prophet without honor, that most annoyed the critics, and probably a good number of his most loyal readers.

Even Paul Rosenfeld, whom Mumford could always count on for support and encouragement, tried to point this out to him. And so did Catherine Bauer, whose judgment he still respected. He didn't have enough faith in the slow give-and-take of practical politics, Catherine told him. He was always looking for a messiah to set in motion some sort of spiritual transformation. Here Catherine came dangerously close to the mark, and this undoubtedly explains the vehemence of Mumford's reply. He had never put his trust in a so-called "Messiah," he wrote Catherine; the spiritual "authority" he pleaded for was accessible to everyone "in all the works of art and thought and religion." But on this point he was not altogether accurate, for he had argued, since his earliest infatuation with Nietzsche and Shaw, that the new life would first become incarnated in an inspired few. And while it is true that he saw such a transformation of values as only one part of the entire process of change, not as a substitute for political action, as Bauer implied, he had not made this clear enough in *The Condition of Man*. In that book the essential appeal is to faith, not works.

Nonetheless, he continued to blame these "misunderstandings" on his critics. Catherine, too, had misread him. When the next volume of his Renewal of Life series appeared, he would have to get her husband's permission to lock her into a room with all four volumes "till you have read them through from cover to cover all over again," he told her. In this letter he quoted, but failed to take to heart, Patrick Geddes's advice that the good angler never blames the fish for not biting. All he could think of was that he could not count on his friends to defend him when he needed them most, when he feared his reputation was sinking disastrously.[31]

When Mumford mentioned to his friend Lee Simonson that he

was planning to begin a sequel to *The Condition of Man*, Simonson warned him not to "orchestrate it too heavily." Simonson was alarmed by the number of unfavorable reactions he had been hearing to *The Condition of Man* from people who had high regard for Mumford's earlier work, "unfavorable," he reported to Mumford, "not to its contents, but to its style, and the difficulties this seemed to create for them, too Jeremiah like, . . . too gloomily prophetic, or to some pretentiously so." The book, he said, had the effect of "a vibrating organ rendition of a theme originally written for a violin"; in contrast to the "Mozartian line, grace, and clarity" of *Sticks and Stones* and *The Golden Day*.[32] Simonson and others close to Mumford, like Jo Strongin, saw—and were concerned about—what he himself only partially recognized—that over the past decade he had become a different man, a different writer, with a far more somber view of the human condition and with less tolerance for those who didn't share his outlook.

What choices were left for the person of conscience in a world gone "mad"? This man, who liked to call himself a revolutionary, had no faith in revolutions. "Revolution in the light of the constant miscarriage of every revolution from 1789 onward is nothing more than the form through which a decadent civilization commits suicide. Historically, the only constructive way out in such a situation is by withdrawal: not as a permanent condition, but as a means of relaying the human foundations of our culture."[33]

But Mumford himself could not withdraw completely from the world, although he often felt the urge to. Beginning in August 1945, with the bombing of Hiroshima, proof to him that fascism had corrupted its democratic enemies, he dedicated himself for the next twenty-five years to an all-out effort to awaken his countrymen to the gravity of the situation humankind confronted. Year by year his pessimism deepened, but he refused to give up hope. His slender yet stubborn faith in the future comes through in a letter he wrote late in his life to his Italian friend Bruno Zevi. "I have not the heart to tell [people] . . . what I actually think about our human prospects unless something approaching a miracle takes place." He then told Zevi a story he had heard about a famous palmist in Berlin in the 1920s. Writers and artists flocked to this man. He told them things about their character and lives he could have known only by intuition. He also made predictions that turned out to be frighteningly accurate. He prophesied early deaths, divorces, financial catastrophes. His predictions became so dismal that people hesitated to go back to him. Eventually he became so tortured and dispirited by his own readings that he committed suicide. "I can understand his predicament!" Mumford confided to Zevi, "though I have no intention of committing suicide. For I still believe in miracles."[34]

23

The Age of Frustration

'Tis the time's plague when madmen lead the blind.

—WILLIAM SHAKESPEARE, *KING LEAR*

The year 1944 was the most desolate and emotionally devastating of Mumford's entire life. After his physical breakdown in California, which convinced him to leave Stanford at the close of the winter term, he returned to Leedsville to the disappointing reviews of *The Condition of Man*, and that following summer he was in a tense, distracted state, unable to begin the final volume of his Renewal of Life series. But it wasn't his health or his literary reputation that he was most concerned about in these months; it was his son Geddes, who had entered the army the previous summer and was in combat in Italy, north of the Arno River. In August, Geddes's infantry company was preparing for the initial assault on the powerfully fortified Gothic line in the mountains near Monticelli. Geddes was an advanced scout for his company, and he would be among the first to face intense enemy fire. Yet, despite his thirst for front-line action (he had volunteered for the job), he had no great urge to be a hero, and "a purple heart is something I don't intend to get," he wrote his parents. "With luck I'll be home for my next birthday." He told them not to worry, but that was all they did that August and September.[1]

Geddes wrote to them one more time, from behind the lines, then the letters stopped. By the first week of October his parents knew something terrible had happened to him. Though they had not heard from him for a month, they continued to write to him almost every day, never once mentioning to each other what they both secretly feared. Two days after Sophia's birthday a telegram from the government arrived. Geddes had been missing in action since September 13. In the following days their hopes rose a little as they learned from friends of "missing" soldiers who had come back; perhaps Geddes had been taken prisoner. In anticipation of this, they prepared a Red Cross package to send to him the moment they received news of his capture, but on October 17 the final word came. They were sitting at the dinner table when Lewis, getting up to go to the kitchen, heard a knock at the door. It was Mr. Flanagan, the stationmaster, with a telegram in his hand. Lewis knew instantly what this meant. He took the telegram without saying a word, and as he closed the door and started back to the dining room he decided not to break the news to his family until he had some time alone with Sophia.

After dinner he put Alison to bed, telling her her usual bedtime story, and lingered in her room for almost an hour, for she was unable to sleep, sensing that something was wrong. Then he went downstairs and broke the news to Sophia. "Darling, we knew in our hearts all along," she whispered to him. "What happened to us both thereafter no one need know," he wrote later in his notes.[2]

The next morning Sophia called Alison to her bed and told her she had lost her brother. Alison was silent at first, but seconds later, pulling close to her mother, she said in a low, almost expressionless voice, what they all felt: "Life will never be the same again."[3]

The only way Lewis could cope with his grief was to pour out his feelings on paper, alone in his study every morning of every day. All that November and December he spent part of every day going over the records of Geddes's life—photographs, letters, whatever else he could lay his hands on. Although he did assemble some of his essays for a collection called *City Development*, it failed to absorb him; he wanted to write a book about his son's life. But he couldn't get started on it. "The emotional strain of reflecting on Geddes's life and on what might have been often becomes almost unbearable," he confessed in his notes. So he put that project aside and began a book on the issues of the war and the upcoming peace. Geddes had written to him that the war would not be truly won until the soldiers who fought it knew what they had been fighting for. This would be

Geddes's book, but after several false starts he found it impossible to proceed in his mood of empty despair.4

Although he could not work well that winter, he continued to try, and these fitful bouts, often interrupted by heart spasms and dizziness, helped to allay somewhat his grief and depression. Sophia found it even harder to pick up the threads of her life. As she told her husband: he at least had begun to face Geddes's image; she could not. Lewis, through his writing, could also help to create the kind of world that would justify their son's death. What could she do?5

Meanwhile, they both secretly dreaded the return of the young soldiers, the victory parades and speeches. Lewis had kept a tight check on his emotions, had held his tears inside him, but on the August evening of the President's announcement of Japan's surrender, as a parade of cars on Leedsville Road honked their horns in celebration, he quietly left the house in the middle of the radio broadcast and walked to the sandpit near the river where he and Geddes used to test their guns, a place that had become a symbol for him of Geddes's life and of their best days together. There, alone, he broke down and wept uncontrollably.

The winter following Geddes's death was unrelievedly bleak for Lewis and Sophia. It was the coldest winter in years in Amenia, and it snowed nearly every week from December on, with the wind piling up drifts of up to twenty feet high. Their old wooden farmhouse wasn't tightly built, and the freezing winds would whistle through the clapboards and the loose joinings of plaster and window. "The inner cold of grief," Lewis grimly reported that February, when there was hardly a day that the thermometer did not drop below zero, "has added to the outer cold of the weather."6

He would rise every morning before 7 A.M., prepare his own breakfast, have a cigarette, and then settle down to try to do some work, dressed for his drafty study as if he were going outdoors. But all he could produce, besides notes and letters, was a handful of poems in memory of Geddes. At eleven o'clock he would leave his desk, put out the mail, and shave; and in the afternoon he would write letters and read. Occasionally he and Sophia would go for a walk, but it was so unbearably cold that they usually could not stray more than a hundred yards or so from the house. After supper the family would sit in the living room and listen to Mozart, Beethoven, and Bach. Then Lewis would put Alison to bed, and within an hour he and Sophia would retire. Sometimes, before going to bed, Lewis would walk into Geddes's bedroom and wonder how an empty space could be so full of a person.

Every day was almost exactly like the others, and they had few visitors that winter to enliven the household or break into their stale routine. "We have huddled indoors," Lewis wrote one evening that winter, "more isolated, more desolate, than we have ever been over such a long period in our lives."7

Finally they could take no more. Their friends in Hanover, New Hampshire, Artemus Packard, a Dartmouth professor, and his wife Marjory invited them to come up and stay in a house left vacant by the death of Marjory's father. In mid-February they decided to move, even though it would mean a change of schools for Alison. They all needed some human companionship, and several of their dearest friends lived in Hanover. Since the 1930s, when Lewis had begun going up there regularly as a visiting professor, Hanover had been a "second home" for him. When he and Sophia moved into their new house there in early 1945, they found it spacious and comfortable, with the Baker Library just around the corner. Best of all, there "[are] friendly faces all round us," Lewis wrote Van Wyck Brooks on arriving in Hanover.8

Mumford had first set foot on the Dartmouth campus in the fall of 1929 when he gave a weeklong series of lectures on art and architecture in America's "Brown Decades." He had been invited to the college by Packard, a young professor recently appointed head of the art department by President Ernest Martin Hopkins, who had hoped this man of driving energy would enliven interest in the arts on campus. Packard was excited by Mumford's mind, and the two men liked each other immediately. With Hopkins's encouragement, Packard invited Mumford back for a series of regular visits as a kind of roving professor, without set duties or schedule, although the position carried the rank of full professor. Occasionally Mumford would lecture, but ordinarily he held informal seminars with selected groups of students on an ever-changing range of topics. When his students would ask him what his field of specialization was, he would simply reply with a smile that he was *Professor der Allerlei Wissenschaften*, professor of things in general.9

Mumford had enjoyed the atmosphere at Dartmouth in the 1930s. President Ernest Martin Hopkins was trying to transform the school "from a country club for young barbarians to a serious place of work," Mumford wrote Patrick Geddes after his first visit to Dartmouth.[10] Hopkins was an easygoing, affable man, and he was willing—in fact, eager—to take chances. As part of his efforts to improve the learning environment at the college, he made known his displeasure with what he called the Germanic "Ph.D. fetish" by hiring a number of young professors before they began to specialize in one narrow research area, and informing them that their future at the college depended upon strong teaching and campus service. He also tried to break down barriers between academic departments, and he invited to the campus a succession of distinguished outside scholars and artists, including two men who became close friends of Mumford, the poet Robert Frost and Adelbert Ames, Jr., a Harvard-trained lawyer who had changed careers twice, first to painting and sculpture and then to the fields of optics and psychology.[11] Every now and then Mumford would drop by the Dartmouth Eye Institute to watch Ames's world-famous optical experiments, and he also liked to get together with Frost in the late afternoons for tea and conversation. Though the crusty old poet had a reputation for being ruthlessly irascible, around Mumford he was the very picture of geniality. He liked Lewis's directness, his willingness to speak his mind on issues of concern to him. "You know Lewis is one of my heroes," he once whispered to Sophia when her husband was out of the room. Both men distrusted academics—viewing the Ph.D. as a "sign of mediocrity"—and they loved to trade gossip about the petty-mindedness and timidity of "the professors."[12]

It was his contacts with a small group of maverick minds like Ames, Frost, and Packard, and with Stearns Morse and Sidney Cox of the English department, that had drawn Mumford back to Dartmouth year after year. He became lifelong friends with these men, and he was instrumental in bringing to Dartmouth another of his good friends, Walter Curt Behrendt, an architect and engineer who had been in charge of the planning of Berlin under the Weimar Republic. Behrendt and his wife, Lydia, a well-known concert pianist, were forced to leave Germany after Hitler took power (Behrendt was a nonpracticing Jew; his wife a Christian), and Mumford, a man fiercely loyal to his friends, raised money to help the couple resettle in the United States. He persuaded Packard and Hopkins to find a place for Behrendt on the Dartmouth faculty, and his own publisher, Harcourt, Brace, to take Behrendt's book *Modern Building*, one of the important early statements of the modern movement in architecture. Later Dartmouth hired Lydia Hoffman-Behrendt, who became close friends with Sophia Mumford.[13]

The month the Mumfords moved to Hanover Walter Curt Behrendt lay dying of a heart condition in the bedroom of his home looking out over the Connecticut River valley. Lewis and Sophia visited him almost every day, for he dreaded being left alone when Lydia was teaching. Behrendt's lingering illness, and his death that April, further darkened the Mumfords' first season in Hanover. Every morning following Behrendt's death Lewis would head for his study in the Baker Library to try to lose himself in his work. Between bouts of reading in the library basement his attention would often shift to a painting on the wall that mirrored his view of life and of the state of the world in that black stretch of days in early 1945—the magnificent mural of the Mexican, José Clemente Orozco.

This painting had been important to him from the moment he had first set eyes on it. He had, in fact, watched its slow creation, staggered by its savage truth. "Anyone who does not look at this mural and come out a changed man is dead," he declared at a Dartmouth dinner for Orozco.[14]

Orozco had been brought to Dartmouth in the early 1930s by Artemus Packard. Shortly after he arrived he took over the basement hall of the Baker Library as his "classroom," and on a span of wall the full width of the library began to demonstrate to his students the art of mural painting through a historical depiction of the settlement of North America from pre-Columbian times to the present. It was an enormously controversial fresco; some, including Eleanor Roosevelt, thought it pure propaganda. Even Packard was offended by Orozco's grisly interpretation of the stillbirth of academic knowledge. This is symbolized by a human skeleton in labor on a dissecting table delivering a hideous-looking embryo wearing a mortarboard on its head, while a group of ghoulish corpses in academic gowns looks on. Packard told Orozco that a person could not look at this painting without having to vomit. "But I want to make that impression," Orozco stormed. "If that is what you want,"

Packard shot back, "you might as well take down your pants and shit on the floor." Orozco changed this fresco panel somewhat, but it retained all its withering power.[15]

Before and after his classes in Baker Library, Mumford had watched the tiny, bespectacled Mexican working with furious energy, his crippled left arm hanging limply at his side. Although he never got to know Orozco well because neither of them spoke the other's native language, this mural powerfully influenced the book he was writing at the time, *Technics and Civilization*.

Perhaps his best account of his first reaction to Orozco's mural is contained in a letter he wrote to Catherine Bauer as he was completing *Technics and Civilization*. "As painting and [symbol] there is really nothing like it anywhere in America: . . . The Gods of Power and the Gods of Life are at work in Mexico. Horrible brutality on one side, and the great maize culture with the stone sculptures on the other. Science dawns there, too: a man with closed eyes reaching up into the black unknown. Quetzalcoatl, representing the spiritual life, comes to the Mexicans and promises to return. . . . [And] at length [his] prophecy [is] wryly fulfilled: the Spaniard comes in his sable armor; and out of that springs—it is really an illustration for my book!—the Machine: . . . orderly and powerful, disintegrating and dehumanizing.

"At the end of the room one beholds . . . the spiritual life, represented by the vultures that have stolen the Keys of Heaven. Finally: a burst of flame . . . Christ has risen and with a terrible axe he has cut down his own cross, has shattered the temples of Zeus and Buddha and Mahomet and has obliterated all the dead creeds and moribund forms of living."[16]

The question here, of course, is whose vision Mumford is writing about. Is it not his own as well as Orozco's? And did he not sometimes see himself in this Christlike role, a searing voice of cleansing and clarification? Never more so than in 1945, when he came back to Orozco's mural, for in that year a team of scientists, working in absolute secrecy in the Western desert, put into the hands of America's military leaders a weapon of almost unthinkable power, and Mumford felt it his duty to speak out against this threat to the very existence of human life on earth.

* * *

On the evening of August 6, 1945, Mumford was sitting in his living room in Leedsville when he heard Quincy Howe announce on the radio that a single atomic bomb had been exploded over Hiroshima, annihilating the entire city. This was the first Mumford, and nearly every other person, learned that this horrifying weapon had been perfected, and his immediate reaction was one of "almost physical nausea." The power that the bomb places in the hands of human beings "is too absolute to be entrusted to them; and the very fact that we used the bomb is proof," he wrote in his notes, "that we were neither intelligent enough nor morally sound enough to be in charge of this weapon." In defending his decision to use the new bomb, President Harry S Truman claimed that it would shorten the war. "Apparently he did not stop to consider that it might also shorten the existence of the human race."[17]

Mumford did not object to the development of the bomb, given Germany's own atomic program; he objected to its use without warning, and, most deplorably, its employment a second time against Nagasaki before Japan had had sufficient time to surrender. There was no great hurry to use the bomb, in his view, as the invasion of Japan was not scheduled until the spring of 1946. Well before then, Russia's entry into the war would undoubtedly have brought about Japan's surrender.

Mumford's first public response to the opening of the nuclear age was the aroused essay, "Gentlemen: You Are Mad!" which appeared in the *Saturday Review of Literature* in early 1946. "We in America are living among madmen. Madmen govern our affairs in the name of order and security. And the fatal symptom of their madness is this: they have been carrying through a series of acts which may lead eventually to the destruction of mankind, under the solemn conviction that they are normal responsible people, living sane lives, and working for reasonable ends." Why do we allow these madmen to "go on with their game without raising our voices"? Why do we keep our calm in the face of the threat of global destruction? "There is a reason: we are madmen, too. . . . Our failure to act is the measure of our madness."[18]

Mumford was one of the first and the few to act in protest, organizing a petition movement from Hanover in early 1946 to have the government stop military testing of atomic weapons, dismantle its entire stock of atomic bombs, and declare its readiness to submit to a system of United Nations inspection and control of atomic weapons and atomic energy. With the development of this awesome weapon the only safeguard against a war of global extermination was a world government far stronger than the newly formed United Nations. The unilateral, and some might say politically naïve, action Mumford asked for in his petition to Congress and the President would be the first step, he hoped, toward this end. Since America had created the bomb "we have the duty to lead the way toward world security."[19]

Given Russia's fears and suspicions of the West, Mumford was not sure its leaders would react reasonably, even if the United States set this "good example," but he thought the experiment was "worth trying." In accompanying letters he urged those receiving the petition to call public meetings in support of the policies it outlined. He also sent a personal letter to President Truman and a later letter to General Eisenhower asking him to use his influence to dissuade the President from further experimentation with atomic weapons.[20]

For the first time in years Mumford felt he had important public work to do. He threw his energies into this new cause, feeling in his heart that unless he won on this issue the Allied victory in the war, and his own son's death, would have been in vain. But this intense public activism, going back to 1938, cut into his productivity as a writer. He wrote less, and what he did was not his best, for he felt he was reaching out for an audience that wasn't listening. Writing, as he used to say, was "like making love: one needs a response in order to awaken it further."[21] The public indifference to his ideas further deepened his feelings of frustration and isolation. He felt completely alone, he told Henry Murray, "in an unfriendly, if not actively hostile world which I respond to, I am afraid, with equally cold unfriendliness." But what continued to fuel his commitment in these years was his powerful feelings of obligation to his children. "Having helpt [sic] betray my son's generation by my indifference to politics [during the 1920s and early 1930s] I could not have the same sin on my conscience in relation to my daughter."[22]

The invention and employment of the atomic bomb had a large and lasting effect on Mumford's outlook. It showed him that "Hitler had . . . conquered the minds of the most democratic governments."[23] But in his fervent postwar essays in favor of nuclear disarmament, Mumford argued that America's slide into "moral barbarism" actually began midway in the war, when the air force adopted the policy of obliteration bombing against German cities like Dresden and Cologne, abandoning centuries-old restraints against the wanton killing of noncombatants. It was this "moral reversal" that he was most concerned about, for it vastly widened the destructive capabilities of nuclear weapons. Cosmic power and moral nihilism, Mumford agreed with Henry Adams, was truly a deadly combination.[24]

In a succession of hard-hitting articles, books, and speeches, Mumford maintained his fight for nuclear disarmament long after his Hanover-based campaign fell apart.[25] Where earlier he had called his country to war, he now sounded a retreat to sanity, urging his government to unilaterally cease production of all nuclear weapons. The desperate urgency of these pleas can be explained by his very real fears that, having such weapons, governments were likely to use them, and by his growing concern over the government's campaign to gain public support for new chemical, biological, and radiological weapons. Mumford was not, however, in favor of unilateral military disarmament. In fact, he advocated a buildup of conventional forces, claiming that America's preoccupation with nuclear weaponry had resulted in a dangerous weakening of its tactical ground and air forces. This is what prevented America from winning the war in Korea, he argued later; and it would make us vulnerable in similar types of military actions in the future.

Mumford also spoke out early and consistently against programs to develop nuclear power for peacetime uses, on the ground that we had not yet discovered safe methods of disposing of the fissionable by-products of atomic energy. Humankind, he warned, was playing with a new kind of fire, a fire it did not know how to put out.[26]

When his direct pleas to government and military leaders failed to alter official policy, Mumford turned to the scientific community. In the late 1940s he called for a world congress of scientists, under the sponsorship of the United Nations, for the purpose of issuing a factual report on the likely human and ecological consequences of an atomic war. "Let them gauge the prospective results in terms of millions of lives exterminated, of slow-dying cripples and embry-ological monsters in various species, of vegetation wiped out, eco-logical partnerships ruined, water supplies contaminated, soil and atmosphere permanently poisoned," he told his colleagues in a speech before the American Philosophic Society. Such a "full dress rehearsal in the mind" might drive the American people to demand an end of the arms race with Russia. "Let the truth now be told, as perhaps the one means left to keep the heavens from falling."

Conscience-driven scientists like Linus Pauling, Leo Szilard, and Harold Urey had spoken out publicly against the further develop-ment of atomic weapons, but most of the scientific community had remained silent. Mumford tried to wake them from their "sleep-walker's" trance. They had a responsibility, he admonished them, to evaluate the human results of their work and to anticipate its possi-ble applications, a responsibility they had so far in history largely ignored.[27]

Mumford waged his antinuclear campaign most intensely at a time in this country's history when such ideas were being labeled as treasonous, but he spoke out as passionately against McCarthyism as he did against the atomic bomb. In an Open Letter to the American People he issued in 1950, he pleaded with his country-men "to cast off these panicky fears, and to cease regarding those who differ from them as if they were agents of a foreign power. . . . Nothing that the worst traitor in our midst has accomplished has been so damaging to America's security and sound judgement as the current habit of suspecting those whose lives are above suspi-cion. . . ." Two of those falsely charged with treasonous activities happened to be friends of his, J. Robert Oppenheimer and Henry Murray, both the object of FBI attention; and in 1952, Mumford himself came under suspicion when a Michigan congressman accused him of having been a Communist organizer in the 1930s.[28]

Looking back at the past half century, Mumford could think of only one group of creative minds who had accurately predicted the coming violence and irrationality—daringly inventive painters and sculptors like Orozco, Picasso, Dali, and Miró. Their work, which some critics considered dangerously demented, gave Mumford a better understanding of contemporary civilization than he had gained from anything he read. "It would be absurd to dismiss Surrealism as crazy," he had written in 1936. "Maybe it is our civilization that is crazy," as the surrealists have prepared us to see.[29]

In the spring of 1946, Mumford tried for a second time to put together a book about his son's life, but he found himself in too aroused a state as a result of the political situation and still too burdened by grief to write the kind of book he had in mind—a tribute to Geddes's surging spirit and stoic courage. So he put that project aside once more, and, at Sophia's urging, went on his own to England for the summer. This trip turned out to be the beginning of his coming to terms with his son's death. He needed to write his book on Geddes in order to go on living with intensity; his summer in England finally put him in a mood to write it.

He was invited to England to consult with government authorities on the postwar rebuilding of Greater London, and to receive the Ebenezer Howard Memorial Medal from the Town and Country Planning Association for his contributions to British town planning. The British government was moving ahead with an ambitious garden city program, and his book *The Culture of Cities*, perhaps the most influential planning statement of this century, had helped to swing support for this idea. Frederic J. Osborn, the successor to Ebenezer Howard as leader of the garden city movement, had read *The Culture of Cities* in 1938 and brought the book to the attention of a number of key figures in the British planning community. Where previously the garden city movement had been made up mostly of laymen and social workers, Mumford's book, and several pamphlets he wrote on postwar building at Osborn's invitation, helped to bring in scores of influential economists, sociologists, architects, and planners.[30]

These two crowded months in Britain had a restorative effect on Mumford's spirits. After meeting with most of the big names in British architecture and urban planning at a dinner in his honor at the House of Commons, Mumford made a tour of England and Scotland, consulting with ministers, mayors, and planners in Oxford, Birmingham, Manchester, and finally Edinburgh, his favorite city. "Imagine anyone in similar circles in the United States begging for the opportunity of consulting me," he wrote proudly to

Sophia after a meeting with several important Cabinet ministers. Mumford also used his time in London to get together with old friends like Raymond Unwin, William Holford, and Frederic Warburg, his British publisher, at whose house overlooking Regent's Square he met Rebecca West for the first time. And he went to Welwyn Garden City to spend a few days with Osborn, a red-faced, cordial man in his early sixties whom he had met once before, briefly, in 1932 when he was in England with Catherine Bauer. After corresponding for almost ten years these two men, the major voices in their respective countries for the garden city idea, had a chance for a leisurely exchange of ideas, the beginnings of a friendship that would last a lifetime. As for Welwyn itself, Mumford found it "not a perfect place as far as town planning goes"—its ground plan was too open, making it look more like a suburb than a real city—"but very close to perfect in its gardens."[31]

Mumford had been most anxious to come to Britain, he told audiences, because it was "on the verge of the most important change that has taken place since the Industrial Revolution. You are getting ready to transform the Black towns of nineteenth century industrialism . . . into Greenbelt Towns." Plans to create these towns were already on the drawing board, and Mumford urged the planners he met not to build them according to a single formula (advice that was not heeded). He also recommended that these new towns not be built "too finished and complete." This, as he saw it, was the genius of historic cities like Oxford and Lincoln—they had grown organically over the centuries in response to changing circumstances, and they supported a rich mix of architectural styles and urban plans. Why not build several of the new towns neighborhood by neighborhood, as Stein and Wright had tried to do at Radburn? In this way mistakes originally made could be corrected, and unanticipated needs incorporated in later plans. This would also allow the residents themselves to have a hand in the development of their communities.[32]

Mumford's tour of Britain reawakened his interest in planning, and on his return to Amenia he mapped out plans for a major revision of *The Culture of Cities*, with an eye to strengthening his chapters on the contemporary city. He wanted to write a final section that would "really ring the bell," but when he sat down to the task he found another project crowding his mind, his biography of Geddes.[33]

The year before this Mumford had dedicated a collection of his wartime essays, *Values for Survival*, to Geddes. In this vehemently argued book he placed part of the blame for the war that had taken his son on his own countrymen, but he saved most of his fire for the German people. Mumford's ancestors and some of his closest friends were German, but he believed that there were inherent defects in the German character, a strain of pugnacity and authoritarianism, and a servile loyalty to leaders, that had made fascism almost inevitable. And now that fascism was defeated, he urged the Allies not to be too easy on Germany. The Nazi leaders, then on trial at Nuremberg, did not even deserve the decency of a legal hearing, Mumford insisted on another occasion in 1946. Orders should have gone out toward the end of the war to "shoot them on sight, as an act of war," thereby denying them the chance they were being afforded to justify publicly their atrocities. At these trials the Allied nations were also making the enormous mistake of placing the entire blame for Nazism on the Nazi leaders, when in fact Hitler and his henchmen could not have remained in power without the "consent and connivance of the German people. . . . Nothing could better serve the ultimate purposes of the Nazis than to lift from the German people themselves the great burden of their guilt." Mumford had admitted his own errors, his own failure to act against fascism as quickly as he might have, and he expected the German people to admit theirs, too. There could be no true regeneration, this modern St. Paul believed, without an honest unbaring of the soul. He was not, he cautioned, calling for blood revenge against Germany, "but premature absolution of the German people should . . . be out of the question." Accordingly, he urged that Germany be placed in "confinement" for an indeterminate number of years, "with an abatement of punishment for good conduct," a policy that even Reinhold Niebuhr found too extreme.[34]

Having unleashed his anger, Mumford felt he could now write the kind of book about Geddes he had wanted to write all along, a book more about his son than about himself, and when he finished *Green*

Memories in 1947 he thought he had done just this. It was Geddes's book, not his. But Lewis Mumford was incapable of writing anything without bringing himself into it, and in this case he was paying tribute to a son to whom he felt he had not been enough of a father.

While writing this passionately self-revealing book, his sternest challenge as a writer, Mumford continually searched for the reasons he was finding it so difficult to go back over Geddes's life. It was more, he knew, than grief alone. For one thing, he was overcome by the terrible luck that stalked Geddes throughout his life, his many illnesses and accidents, his persistent problems in school, his stormy relations with his teachers and parents. But the larger reason, he had to admit, was that he felt that he had been "but half a father to him: I did not make up by love and sympathetic understanding what life deprived him of." He and Geddes had had many good moments together, but "I never changed my own plans and purposes so as to embrace his more fully." The cause of so many of his problems with Sophia (and arguably, of his success as a writer)—his extreme self-absorption—was the cause as well of his problems with his son. In *Green Memories* Mumford comes close to admitting this, but the full extent of his shattering pain and guilt can be seen only in the notes he kept for his own eyes.[35]

A Rorschach test Mumford took at this time uncovered an almost suicidal depression. The physician who administered the test urged immediate therapy, but for Mumford there was only one anodyne— he would fashion an account of his relationship with Geddes that allowed him to say to Geddes's memory what he had found it impossible to say to him directly. Furthermore, in writing this book he would give Geddes the days and months he had not given him when he was alive. "One visits the dead for only one reason," Mumford wrote in his diary, "to bring them back to life."[36]

No book Mumford wrote placed such demands on him; no book took more out of him; no book was more important to him. Geddes's death changed his life. This book gave his new life a new direction.

When Mumford first informed Henry Murray of his plans to write an unsparing account of Geddes's life, Murray strongly urged him not to. It would place too great a strain on him; and beyond that, the reader would get the impression "that you have imposed a kind of crucifixion on yourself as an atonement for something which

. . . bears down upon your spirit." All parents go through a period of self-criticism after the death of one of their children, "but a public confession . . . does not seem proper, since the world can learn nothing from it. It is a matter between you and your conscience."37 Perhaps Murray was right, but then again, this is not the kind of book that Mumford eventually produced. In *Green Memories* the emphasis is on what the title suggests—the sunlit days in Geddes's life, and in their relationship as father and son. Though left unsaid, it is also about the kind of relationship they might have had if Geddes had survived the war, for by all accounts their last days together were among their best. Home on furlough, Private Geddes, still as invincibly uncompromising as Melville's Ahab, had shown a new self-confidence and poise; to his passionate energy, he had added the ballasting virtue of maturity. It had been a happy reunion, and when it came time for Geddes to leave, his father, mindful of Geddes's insistence that partings should be made with no fuss or tears, shook his hand, looked into his eyes, and said simply, "Good luck, soldier!" But Lewis had not been quick enough, he recalls in a somber note taken down after Geddes's death, "to meet his own first impulse, quickly inhibited, to embrace and kiss." Putting down these words must have been difficult for Mumford; writing *Green Memories* unbearably so.38

The equal tragedy is that Geddes had not been able to communicate to his father exactly how he felt about him. To others, Geddes used to brag about his "old man's" books, his "old man's" muscles, his "old man's" courage, but he had shown his love shyly, undemonstrably, and rarely with words.39 His father *did* show his love with words—the faithful records he kept of his son's storm-swept life, notes remarkable for their tender and prescient understanding of the boy he loved so overwhelmingly—but Geddes never saw these notes.

Just before Geddes had left for the army, his father had tried to make one last effort to tell him how much he loved and admired him. "I have hovered around him, hoping for some moment of renewed intimacy," he wrote that week, "wishing to say a million things that will forever be left unsaid, plagued by my conscious muteness."40 But riding with Sophia and Geddes in the front seat of the car to the railroad station at Rhinecliff, his arms around Sophia and on his son's shoulder, Lewis felt more completely in touch with him than he ever had before, and he sensed that Geddes felt that way, too. "That hour," he wrote Walter Curt Behrendt on his return to Leedsville, "will forever be for me one of those high moments of pause and fulfillment which sum up and justify a whole lifetime."[41]

While *Green Memories* is a book about the man Geddes promised to be, Mumford did reveal the darker side of his son—his unruliness, his inarticulate moodiness, his hot temper and sullen behavior. Sophia, in fact, thought the book presented too negative a portrait of Geddes and of their life together as a family; and when Henry Murray read sections of the book in manuscript he wrote Mumford questioning the wisdom of "a parent (who is privileged to witness the secret life and humiliations of the child, before the child can control or perfect itself . . .) publishing anything at all that would bring the slightest discredit to the child. I believe in the Rousseau model—expose yourself; and even, if necessary, in the *Pierre* model—expose your parents—but not in the Expose your Child idea."[42] But Mumford was undeterred. He didn't see his book in this way; and, anyway, he had not tried to absolve himself of any blame for Geddes's behavior. While this is true, the emphasis in the book on the manner of Geddes's upbringing is curiously misplaced, and most revealing about Mumford's own self-image.

In *Green Memories* Mumford questions whether he and Sophia raised Geddes correctly. Perhaps they gave him too loose a rein, in the interests of allowing him his independence? But Mumford's own private notes suggest that his great concern was that he and Sophia had been *too strict* with Geddes. Geddes was irrepressibly independent; he refused to be controlled. And perhaps this streak of almost reckless rebelliousness was exacerbated by his parents' efforts to set too many restrictions on his behavior—to hold him too long to a regular and early bedtime, to put early curfews on his evenings as a teenager, and to impose tight restrictions on him in the house when his father was working—no listening to the radio, no loud talking, no friends in the house. Perhaps also, as Mumford himself suggests in his notes, he and Sophia had been too anxiously oversolicitous about Geddes's health and welfare, depriving him of "the kind of indulgent understanding and human sympathy that only love can give."[43] Geddes rebelled against these controls, this hovering concern. Even his dreams, as Mumford related them to Murray, seemed to Murray to show aggressive resentment of parental control, with the father as the main target (although Murray never explained them this way to Mumford).44 This might be normal in an adolescent male, especially of Geddes's temperament, and who would want to place after-the-fact judgments on such affectionate parents? Who is to say how Geddes should have been raised? What is germane here is why Mumford did not give *this* account of Geddes's upbringing in *Green Memories*. Was it perhaps that this account was less in line with his basic philosophy of life, with its emphasis upon the open expression of the emotions? Then, too, it would have revealed a side of himself he was not proud of—his excessive solicitude about his *own* health, his obsessive regularity and sometimes inflexible professional discipline, his self-absorption, and worst of all, as far as he was concerned, his difficulty in expressing his emotions in face-to-face relations, of showing great anger or great love, as he could do so easily in his writing, *Green Memories* most movingly of all.

Toward the end of *Green Memories* Mumford hints at this, when he argues that Geddes was in many ways a better man than he—more adventurous, more giving, more emotionally mature at age eighteen than he was at age thirty. He had led a sheltered, ingrown adolescence; Geddes had lived with the abandon of a young stallion. And Geddes was just learning to discipline his great energies before he was killed. He had turned into a first-rate soldier, ready to die for what he believed in; and he had met a hero's end, leading his patrol into the teeth of the German defenses, dying in the style that he lived: "So, long before his work was done/ He was the father, I the son."45

This is what made Mumford proud. Unlike Patrick Geddes's son, his had not tried to justify himself by carrying on his father's work. He thought Geddes had hidden talent as a writer, but he never tried to force him to take the path he had chosen; nor did he or Sophia pressure him to go to college, although they wanted him to. He understood that Geddes had to make his own way, and that he had to challenge his father's attitudes and ideas. If Geddes hadn't done this he would have lost entirely his sense of identity. Lewis's friend Ben Kizer, whose family Geddes stayed with for part of the summer of 1942, showed a sensitive understanding of this: "[Geddes] has an excellent mind," he wrote Lewis in 1942, "but he seems to disdain to use it. It is as if, standing in affectionate awe of his father's culture and personality, he said to himself, 'Since I can't ever be so expressive as my father, I will seek other fields, so far removed from his that I will not be compared with him to my disadvantage.' "⁴⁶ But neither of Geddes's parents needed to be told this. Geddes should have been born in the Maine woods, the son of a fur trapper, Sophia would often say to Lewis. If this had been his lot, she felt, he might have turned out to be a first-rate writer. Writers' sons, as Geddes himself had confided to a friend, should always be anonymous.⁴⁷

Geddes was never pressured, then, to be anything but what he set out to be. In this important sense he had had his freedom. In the mere act of living, moreover, he fulfilled an attitude toward life his father celebrated in all his books, though Geddes had read only one of them, *Herman Melville*, when he was fourteen. Just after completing *Green Memories* Mumford had a vivid dream about his son. "It was," as he reports it, "like a long visit." He decided to show Geddes a copy of the book so that he would understand the depth of his feeling for him, but even before he did, he was able to express to him his "overwhelming love; and [Geddes] reciprocated it with the same degree of feeling. We planned a climb together; we spent a day or more in each other's company; and it was such an overwhelming relief to have him back with us once more!"⁴⁸ In the future Lewis and Sophia were to make many changes in their old farmhouse, but the one room they left completely untouched was Geddes's bedroom, for they could feel his presence where he no longer was.

It had been desperately important for Mumford to write *Green Memories*, but the book took its toll. Several times in the course of the writing he suffered heart spasms that sent him to his bed for several days; and when the book came out he was crushed when it was largely ignored by reviewers, though the reviews it did get were strongly favorable.⁴⁹ For many years after the book appeared, Mumford received letters from people, fathers of sons mostly, telling him how much this book had meant to them, but its disheartening public reception—none of his books was so completely ignored or sold so few copies—saddened and angered Mumford, who saw this as a "last indecent blow to Geddes."⁵⁰

The book cost him in other ways. He never forgave Henry Murray, his closest friend, for urging him not to write it. Though they continued to correspond and to see each other frequently, there was an unstated tension in their relationship. (Mumford never told Murray the real reasons for his disaffection, leading Murray to believe the problem stemmed principally from their differences concerning the tone and style of Mumford's work after *The Culture of Cities*.)[51] Worse still, writing *Green Memories* rekindled old problems with Sophia. In many ways this had been a collaborative work. In writing it Lewis drew extensively upon Sophia's memories of their son, for she had a closer relationship with him, and was closer to him in temperament and outlook—passionate and expressive, quick to anger and just as quick to clear the air with a smile and a hearty laugh. In going back over Geddes's life they were forced to retrace their own lives together, and problems in their marriage that had been buried for years suddenly surfaced. Sophia had been going through a difficult period following her hysterectomy in 1943, and, once more, she felt Lewis was not giving her enough sympathy, the kind of attention, she sharply reminded him, he had given to Alice Decker when *she* had needed help. And their troubles were compounded by the presence in their household of Lewis's mother, who spent the summers of 1944 and 1945 with them in Leedsville. Elvina was feeble and needed constant nursing care, and had also lost most of her memory. Sophia took good care of her and loved her like her own mother, for she had been a devoted grandmother to Alison and Geddes, but in her last years Elvina was not herself, and Sophia could not help being bothered by her irritating habits of interference and her alternating moods of bossiness and childlike helplessness. Just as Lewis was preparing to return from England in 1946 the situation became impossible for Sophia when Elvina became utterly helpless and incoherent (she probably suffered a cerebral hemorrhage), and he knew that he had to act. He had thought of asking his mother to live with them year-round, but he now saw that this would be impossible. Not long afterwards he decided, with extreme reluctance, to put her in a small family-run nursing home in Hanover, where she spent her final days.[52]

By the summer of 1947, with *Green Memories* behind him, Lewis was in better health and spirits than he had been in the previous ten years. Feeling at full strength again, he prepared to begin the final volume of his Renewal of Life series, a book for which he had been reading, on and off, for the past six or seven years. "He who knows not gloom or grief," Melville had written, "knows aught that an heroic soul must learn." Before Geddes's death Mumford thought he had tasted both gloom and grief, but that loss dropped him into "a hell so deep that above it our usual hell would serve for heaven." Mumford considered this knowledge the final step in his own "spiritual growth." Out of it he hoped his further work would grow.[53]

His new book turned out to be the most difficult in the series to write. For one thing, he found himself tied to a number of other responsibilities. In 1947 he had resumed writing his "Sky Line" column for *The New Yorker*, and in the following year he began a visiting professorship at North Carolina State College's newly formed School of Architecture and Landscape Design, which took him to Raleigh for three ten-day stretches over the course of the academic year. He liked teaching there, finding the students spirited and responsive, and he had many friends on the faculty, including the Dutch architect Henrik Wijdeveld, the Russian sculptor Naum Gabo, and Matthew Nowicki, the brilliant young Polish architect Mumford helped to bring to Raleigh to head the School of Architecture. Mumford also renewed acquaintances with Howard Odum of the University of North Carolina, one of the country's outstanding regionalists, who arranged for him to give regular lectures at Chapel Hill in the department of city and regional planning. Mumford's visits to the School of Design brought him in touch with new developments in architecture and planning, yet as much as he enjoyed his work in North Carolina he had taken the job—and stayed on several years—primarily for the money ($6,000 a year), funds he needed to support his family in New York City, where they moved in the fall of 1948.[54]

He had decided to move back to New York, to an Upper West Side duplex, to give Alison, who was showing talent in painting, an opportunity to attend the High School of Music and Art. And however much he had enjoyed living in Hanover, he found it too small and intellectually enclosed to make it his permanent home. Being in New York would also put them closer to Amenia. His days in the city were naturally busier than they had been in sleepy Hanover. He had his "Sky Line" column, and there was a steady procession of guests, people from all over the world, many of them visiting European architects and planners seeking his advice, or just wanting to meet the man who had written *The Culture of Cities*. This book was read during the war by a coming generation of urban

visionaries, including Matthew Nowicki, who had told Mumford
when he first called on him that it had been his "Bible." Whenever
Matthew and his friends talked of rebuilding Warsaw, Nowicki's
wife Siassia remarked to Mumford at the end of their visit, they
would ask: "How would Mumford do this?"[55]

Mumford also had a chance to see such dignitaries as Field Marshal Montgomery and Prime Minister Nehru of India, and he himself was much in the news after attacking Rober Moses's Stuyvesant
Town project in *The New Yorker*. He was back at the center of things,
and for a while he found it exhilarating—and financially rewarding.
His income was higher than it had ever been before, over $13,000 a
year, with Harold Ross at *The New Yorker* paying him twice as much
as he had when he quit. "There is no one else," Ross had written
him, offering him back his job. "The new generation is a collapse. It
has produced no talent of any kind to speak." If he didn't take the
job, *The New Yorker* would drop its "Sky Line" feature.[56] But the
money, the excitement, even the recognition, were not enough to
make him completely happy. His real work—his book—wasn't
going well. His days were too crowded, and at night he had to sleep
with ear stoppers because of the noise from the traffic and the
drunks in his run-down neighborhood of redbrick apartment buildings and ill-kept brownstones.

But even in the Amenia summers he found the writing difficult.
For a while he suspected it might be his health, though he felt in top
form. He had been drinking a little more than usual lately—
although never to immoderation—so he decided to cut back from
two glasses of wine, a glass of vermouth, and whiskey nightcap to a
single glass of wine and a single jigger of whiskey a day. This seemed
to work for several months. His writing picked up, but soon he
found himself becalmed again. He had been worrying about
Sophia's health, which had not been good for several years, and
about his mother, who was growing more helpless and incoherent,
and he felt guilty about leaving her in Hanover in the care of
strangers. All this surely affected his writing, but then again, he had
written all three previous books of his Renewal of Life series during
periods of even greater personal anxiety. Had the spring run dry at
age fifty-three? Or was it just the normal frustration of a writer in
the midst of a large task? He wondered; and worried.[57]

The problem, he finally realized, was that he was not writing the book he really wanted to write. He was working from notes he had taken as he was completing *The Condition of Man*, his most pessimistic book, and although he found the world situation far blacker than it was when he began *The Condition of Man*, he felt that this demanded a different kind of book. "Today, I must plan my book in the way that a wise man will direct his conversation on a life raft" a thousand miles from land, he wrote Catherine Bauer, "not letting himself deal with the discouraging *facts* of the situation, but conjuring up for himself and his companions the life images that will give them hope and courage to endure the ordeal." If the life raft was to reach shore, he would have to give its sagging crew a sustaining faith to drive them on. His book, accordingly, must deal with "not what is, but what may be and must be"—the ideal personality, the ideal community.[58]

He now felt he had a definite sense of direction, yet the writing never went completely well. When he finished *The Conduct of Life* he tried to convince himself that he had written a "great book," but he realized that he had not.[59] He had cut the book down, eliminating large sections on love and marriage, on education and politics. It now focused on ethics, philosophy, and religion, and the prose was leaner, the argument more sharply directed, but it was not, by any means, one of his better books. He handed it over to Harcourt, Brace in December 1950, a month after his mother died. He had been a devoted son, but when he buried his mother his great regret was that he had not given her enough attention in her last years, the same "sin" of self-absorption that had prevented him from being a better husband and father. "Geddes's premature death, my mother's belated death, each weigh upon me in a different fashion," he wrote in his Personalia notes some weeks later, "bringing to the surface my own weaknesses and inadequacies as father, son, husband. And in a sense that load will never be lifted."[60]

What manner of book is *The Conduct of Life*? In a letter Mumford wrote to a Stanford colleague back in 1944 he gave a foreshadowing of its message and intention. "The main theme of my next book will be the stripping down of our life to its essentials. . . . It will be, in effect, a modern re-statement of the New Testament; . . . such a restatement implies a making over of our whole culture as drastic as

that which transformed classic civilization into Christian civilization."⁶¹ "The main task of our time," he announced in *The Conduct of
Life*, "is to turn man himself, now a helpless mechanical puppet, into
a wakeful and willing creator." The reassertion of the self remained
for him the first step in the process of social renewal. Nothing is new
here, but in *The Conduct of Life* Mumford offered as clear a prescription for inner change as we are apt to find in his writing. An
intensely personal book, a book packed with advice for survival and
salvation, it is also Mumford's most disappointing exercise in public
philosophy.

Like *The Story of Utopias*, it is more an attack on existing social
philosophies than a fresh fashioning of a different one. In "The
Fallacy of Systems," the book's pivotal chapter, Mumford assails the
naïve notion that one encompassing ideology can do justice to the
mind-straining variety and complexity of human life. Life cannot be
reduced to a system. In place of a single system—Marxism, Freud-
ianism, capitalism—Mumford proposes a philosophy of the "open
synthesis." Those who took the open synthesis as their creed would
be identified "by the absence of labels." The "skepticism of systems"
is the central argument of the book.

Mumford saw this open-ended philosophy best expressed in men
such as Michelangelo, William Morris, Walt Whitman, Alfred
North Whitehead, and, of course, Patrick Geddes, personalities
who prefigured in their aims and actions "the collective transformations that must take place." This is Mumford's familiar theme of the
artist as hero, but nowhere in his work is it so forcefully developed.
Abjuring the Spenglerian cycle of culture and civilization, of
growth and decline, Mumford bases his interpretation of civilization
on the analogy of drama, an analogy he had used so fruitfully in his
work on the city. Only here, the hero takes on even larger significance.

"Every culture produces a drama, and *is* a drama: it interprets life
and *is* life." Man, as interpreter and symbol maker, is the "playwright, manager and scene builder," and his religions are of transcendent importance in this collective drama. Religion sets the main
themes and outlines the "plot" of any culture. But Mumford—who
practiced no religion, and who doubted that there was an afterlife—
describes religion in the loosest possible terms. It is for him what
other historians have called the spirit of the age—its dominating

idea. "That which moves men to dramatic action in roles other than their natural ones is in fact their religion, no matter by what name they may call it. Thus the active religion of the Romans was not the worship of the gods, but the construction of the Roman imperium. It was for ideas like this that men struggled and sacrificed and willingly died." The hero first formulates and embodies this unifying idea. Later, however, each member of the community is drawn into the action and assigned a role; and eventually the action shifts from the original central characters to the entire company of players; everything—set, scenery, action—is transformed in accordance with these general beliefs, now made over into a universal way of life. Such was the way of Christ and Christianity, Mohammed and Mohammedanism.

In *The Conduct of Life* Mumford describes the kind of change he envisions as an axial revolution, using that term in a double sense, meaning a change in values, "and further a change so central that all the other activities that rotate around this axis will be affected by it." This is what he had always meant when he referred to his belief in the possibility of miracles. Only in this book he puts forward a "scientific" case for believing in miracles—James Clerk Maxwell's theory of "singular points." This is a physical theory as well that takes account of the formative role of personality in historical change, a theory close to Patrick Geddes's idea of "insurgence."

Science, the physicist James Clerk Maxwell points out, is organized to study continuities and stabilities, but even in the physical world there are unpredictable moments when a small force may produce a large, unexpected result—"the little spark which kindles the great forest, the little word which sets the whole world a-fighting." Similarly, at rare moments in human history, in crisis perhaps, a few individuals, through timely intervention and the correct interpretation of the nature of the moment, may produce an effect out of proportion to their physical powers, Mumford argues. Decisive personalities or small groups of purposeful men had changed history at such singular points before, and they might do so again. Such a singular point "may actually be at hand"; if it occurred we had to be ready, like the early Christians, to take bold action—"to be the spark that kindles the great forest."

Most persons, when they sense the need for great changes, join a party or sign a pledge; Mumford enjoins his readers to hide themselves and to undergo a ruthless process of self-denial and self-criticism. He had gone through such a purgation after his son's death, and in *The Conduct of Life* he turns his therapy into a social program. "The new person is . . . one who has honestly confronted his own life, has digested its failures, and been re-activated by his awareness of his sins, and has re-oriented his purposes." As an aid to achieving this self-understanding, he recommends that each person set aside, as he usually did, at least one half hour a day for uninterrupted meditation and reflection. As he was writing *The Conduct of Life* he was reading *The Brothers Karamazov* for the fourth time, and Father Zossima's advice becomes his advice to his readers. "Every day and every hour, every minute, walk around yourself, and see that your image is a seemly one." Escape the "time cage," slow down your life, avoid the purposeless routine of television, radio, "cocktails," "motor trips," and spectator sports, live frugally and simply, eliminating "every element of purposeless materialism," Mumford preaches. Such is his prescription for the recovery of "inner autonomy."

But this inner change had to lead outward. The purpose of withdrawal is "to re-awaken our appetite for life," just what writing *Green Memories* had done for him. "Once we have taken the preparatory steps, we must return to the group and re-unite ourselves with those who have undergone a like regeneration." Mumford did not predict how long this transformation would take, although surely he was thinking in terms of many centuries. It was not the purpose of social philosophy, he had always argued, to set the timetable for human change; the living drama must be left to the actors themselves.[62]

The Conduct of Life is hardly Mumford's most original work. Heavily, almost solemnly moralistic, it is a richer elaboration of the principal themes of *The Condition of Man*. But the book has all the faults of *The Condition of Man* and few of its compensating strengths. Unlike the first two volumes of the Renewal of Life series, it lacks the salt and substance of real-life experience; and too many of its arguments are based not on logic but on visceral conviction. Nor is it as inspirational a book as Mumford intended it to be. It calls for movement into fresh territory, but gives no guide to the new terrain, and only the haziest description of the ultimate destination. It is more a manifesto for personal renewal than for collective action,

Mumford's fullest description and defense of his own way of life. Yet here, in embryonic form, are ideas he would later build into original and important critical arguments. None of his more substantial books could have been written without this examination of the nature of man and role of religion as a shaping force in human culture.

Mumford sent a draft of *The Conduct of Life* to Catherine Bauer, and she uncovered its weaknesses better than any subsequent reviewer. Our American society, she wrote him, "is probably at its best at the 'common sense' level, and would either be untouchable or sent berserk by a great emotional religious appeal. . . . The best developed values of our culture are rationalistic." She herself was "*afraid*" of religious movements: after all, Nazism itself was an appeal to the 'subjective and the intuitive.' " In fact, what made Bauer doubly distrustful of Mumford's appeal to faith was his own analysis of humankind's underlying irrationality.[63]

No book of Mumford's received as hostile a reception as this one, and only *Green Memories* received less coverage. It was one thing to be attacked, another to be ignored. Mumford felt as if he had been "buried alive."[64] Surely the book's reception must, in part, be attributable to the political climate of the country—it appeared when Senator Joseph McCarthy was reaching the peak of his damaging influence, and America was entering a period of unprecedented economic prosperity—and Mumford tried to convince himself that this was the real reason for his lagging public influence. His ideas challenged what most Americans saw as a comfortable way of life. But Henry Murray, always a perceptive reader of his work, suspected that it might also be a matter of "tact and strategy." Mumford's proposals might, indeed, be too far-reaching for the majority of middle-of-the-road Americans, but he could never hope to convert an audience he spoke to in such autocratic tones. "What disturb[s] me [is] a too pronounced moral contempt for your audience, a people whose conception of democracy is 'I am as good as you are.' "[65]

If Mumford's tone was not quite that of an Ezekiel or an Isaiah it was certainly close to that of the democratic oracle he most admired, Ralph Waldo Emerson. But these were not Emerson's times, and Mumford's moral passion was greater than Emerson's. He took sides and never wavered. Yet that very certainty that his was the only way is perhaps one of the reasons, as Murray told him after reading *The Conduct of Life*, that though "you have said the best things during these critical years . . . you haven't got a hundred thousand followers."[66]

As was his practice Mumford sat down at his desk in the first days of 1952 and reviewed the previous year of his life, "a year that began with illness and anguished toil and ended in frustration." He had had repeated bouts of influenza throughout the winter, and though he recovered in the spring he failed to bound back to full strength. This, he suspected, had to do with the indifferent reception of *The Conduct of Life*. Even Harcourt, Brace seemed unhappy with the book and failed to promote it aggressively, leading him to threaten to sever relations with them.[67] As he was in the middle of this battle with his publishers, he learned of Harold Ross's death, and though Ross was not a close friend it made him feel older and more isolated. "Year by year the leaves of my generation are falling from the tree; and since I am a poor hand at making new friends I find myself facing the usual blight of old age, which I watched in the case of my mother: loneliness and desolation. All but two of the closest friends of my youth are now gone." So, too, was Matthew Nowicki, killed the previous year in an airplane crash in the Sahara on his return from a city planning job in India. Mumford considered this glowing young man "the most beautiful spirit" he had ever met and the finest architect of his generation. He had lost a friend he had come to love like a son.[68]

At this low moment of his life all of Mumford's earlier work seemed inconsequential to him. Aside from *Green Memories* he had written nothing that was likely to be read by anyone, he feared, but a Ph.D. "and to be read by Ph.D.'s is nothing short of a second burial." As he looked back at his life over the past decade, and forward into an uncertain future, he was reminded of H. G. Wells's description of this epoch in history, which all too accurately described his life at the present moment. This was, for him, the Age of Frustration.[69]

24

Cities of Men

He saw many cities of men, and learnt their mind.

—HOMER, *THE ODYSSEY*

On a golden summer morning in 1960, at sea on the S.S. *Queen Elizabeth*, Lewis Mumford sat down at the desk in his cramped cabin and began a review of his life over the past decade and a half. It had been nearly forty years since his first passage home from Europe, from his five-month stay at Patrick Geddes's Le Play House in London. His return to America in 1920 had marked the real beginning of his career as a writer, and now as he steamed back to New York for the ninth time, he saw himself again at a crucial crossroads. "The last fifteen years of my life have been *meager* ones in actual achievement," he wrote in his notebook. "Except perhaps for my memoir of Geddes I've produced nothing that will live, or that deserves to live." He had allowed too much of his time, he thought, to be taken up with teaching, having spent part of nearly every year as a visiting professor at one or another university. Instead of teaching, he should have tried his hand at a novel or play. At age sixty-five he was still haunted by the image of the writer he might have been, had originally set out to be, even though he had stopped writing plays when he was thirty-five and had never returned to *Victor*, the unfinished novel in verse he wrote in 1939. Was a fresh start possible at his age? Whatever the answer, it seemed "now or never" for him. As he wrote this, he promised himself one thing: as soon as he put the finishing touches on his new book on the history of the city he would give the next six months "to solitude and to exploring those inner sources out of which an imaginative work . . . might spring forth."[1]

He never wrote this work of fiction; he never returned to "literature." Yet in one important sense he did. The three landmark books on the history of technology and the city he published in the next decade, his most richly productive period as a writer, have the concentrated power and profound comprehension of truly great literature. They are history and cultural commentary of Tolstoyan scale. The year 1960 did mark a decisive change in the direction of his creative life, as he had foreseen on his return from Europe. The next ten years were ones of apogee and influence for him; but the 1950s had not been a period of squandered opportunity, as he suggested in his report from the S.S. *Queen Elizabeth*. It was a time of gestation and preparation and of considerable achievement. In the 1950s he wrote the great part of his greatest work as a writer, *The City in History*, and made original discoveries that led to his two-volume study *The Myth of the Machine*, his culminating statement on technology and the human condition. Teaching may have taken up time he might have given to creative literature, but his successive appointments as a visiting professor at the University of Pennsylvania, Brandeis University, and MIT had a far greater influence on his intellectual development than he would ever admit, given his lifelong aversion to academic specialization and professorial timidity. He was paid well for these guest professorships, and the money and a light teaching load gave him the time he needed for research and writing. In a sense, university teaching, which he considered a job, not a career, allowed him to remain an independent intellectual, a masterless man, in an age when it was becoming almost impossible to survive as a self-supporting writer. Teaching also brought him into contact with minds that helped to set his own moving in fascinating new directions.

In 1952, Mumford was prepared to give up teaching completely. That September he had begun his second year as visiting professor at the School of Fine Arts of the University of Pennsylvania, teaching courses on city design, a subject he found himself rapidly losing interest in. He had arrived in Philadelphia for the fall term still physically weak after an operation the previous month for the removal of his prostate, his first experience with major surgery. He recovered quickly from the operation, which, at Henry Murray's suggestion, he had prepared for by learning yoga, and he looked ruddy and healthy when he showed up for his first class. Yet he noticed that he tired easily, and he felt lethargic most of the time. He also began to have problems again with his teeth; this time it was a painful gum infection. And he didn't care at all for Philadelphia. If he was going to live in a big city, he preferred a more stimulating place. To make matters worse, he and Sophia were staying in a two-room apartment in the Hotel Drake, a living arrangement he found uncongenial to creativity. So it was a time of low productivity, "one of the worst years I've been through since the year following Geddes's death," he wrote in his notes on New Year's Day 1953.[2]

But the ensuing year turned out to be one of the best of his life, a new beginning for him. His course on the city gave him the impetus to begin the revision of *The Culture of Cities* he had been planning for some time, though he went about revising that book in a different way than he had initially planned. Originally he had wanted to add a stronger concluding section on the contemporary city, but his spirited discussions on ancient history with his brilliant young colleague Martin Meyerson, an urban planner who later became the president of the University of Pennsylvania, and his own persistent interest in uncovering the deeper sources of the problems of modern civilization, provoked him to trace the history of the city to its earliest beginnings. In the era before the rise of classical Greece, he hoped to uncover the origins of modern warfare and of the kind of debased behavior that had led eventually to fascism and obliteration bombing. The book he envisioned would be a history not just of the city, but of the entire sweep of civilization, and as he began writing it he realized that he had tackled a subject that would take him more than one book to cover adequately.[3] Unknowingly, he had set for himself an agenda for the remainder of his productive life as a writer.

"I have just come to the end of the happiest six months of my life," we find him writing in August 1954. Sophia had just emerged from a difficult midlife period, Alison was enrolled at Radcliffe and enjoying her studies, and he had settled into a consuming writing project. All this helped to bring him and Sophia closer together. It was the beginning of an Indian summer of their sex life, "more lovely in its colors," Mumford describes it in his notes, "than any spring I can remember." In these years Sophia had a recurring dream, always exactly the same, which she took great delight in. In the dream she found in their house new rooms whose existence she had been completely unaware of. "Yes, in the good old house there are new rooms," Lewis writes after one of their nights of lovemaking, "at the end of passages one thought one had thoroughly explored long ago."4

That summer of 1954 he began work on a short book for a series called World Perspectives. This was to be a preparation for the larger work he had in mind on the city and civilization. Originally, the book was to be about religion and democracy, but it soon became a *Discours sur l'histoire universelle*. He wrote a complete first draft of *The Transformations of Man* in three weeks, working with ease and excitement. The book came so easily it seemed to him like a gift of his unconscious. He had been reading the final volumes of Toynbee's history of the world, and he thought of his own brief book as a "pocket-sized alternative" to Toynbee. It is "one of the most lucid, perhaps even the most brilliant statements that I—or anyone else—has made in summarizing human.history," he wrote to Frederic J. Osborn just before beginning the final draft.5 But he soon realized that it needed a lot more work. The major arguments, which questioned some well-established assumptions about biological and cultural evolution, had to be more solidly supported by anthropological and historical evidence. In their present form they were no more than brilliant guesses. "Now it seems to me a terrible botch," he complained to Benton MacKaye on finishing the book in July 1955. "With the slightest encouragement I'd consign the whole ms. to the wastebasket."6

The book was neither one nor the other. It was certainly not the masterly historical synthesis he originally thought it was, nor was it a total "botch." *The Transformations of Man* is actually two books: a tight, often too turgid summation of Mumford's previous work, and a fascinating foreshadowing of all that he would write afterwards. The arguments he developed in brief compass in this book caused him to revise his views of the history of technology and the city, and led him eventually to rewrite the entire Renewal of Life series. The book is most significant, then, not for what it is, but for what it led to—three larger works of lasting importance: *The City in History* and

the two-volume study *The Myth of the Machine*. These works are a
world removed in temper and tone from the early volumes of the
Renewal series. In *Technics and Civilization* Mumford had predicted
that the human and ecological devastation of the paleotechnic, or
industrial, era would soon give way to "neotechnic improvements
promised by hydroelectric power, scientific planning, industrial
decentralization, and the regional city."[7] Twenty years later he
found this interpretation far too sanguine. War and fascism had
brought to the surface all the irrational forces of modernization and
mechanization. It was Mumford's efforts to understand these
changes that drew him back to the shadowy origins of human
culture. Starting there, with man's first halting efforts to know
himself, he spun a boldly original interpretation of human development, one of those radically challenging hypotheses that change our
very image of ourselves.

While the seeds of this new theory of human development can be
found in *The Transformations of Man* (and even earlier in *The Conduct of
Life*) it is best to describe these ideas in their maturest expression. At
this point it is necessary to suggest only the central set of insights in
The Transformations of Man that opened the way for this more richly
textured interpretation of cultural evolution.

Mumford's theory of human origins underscores the importance
of dream, language, and religion. Man, he argues, is not primarily
homo faber—a toolmaking creature. Rather, he is a symbol-creating,
"ritual enacting . . . god-seeking figure," a dreamer and an artist,
whose supreme achievement was the reshaping of his own organism
and the creation of a personality vastly different from his original
biological self. Man fashioned himself before he fashioned his first
sophisticated tools.[8]

Language—the miracle of speech—is, for Mumford, the greatest
of all human inventions. Speech and dream, the chief symbol-
making activities of man, infinitely enlarged the domain of human
potentialities, allowing man to escape the constraints of the animal
world and shape a brilliantly unique culture. These subjective activities played a more significant part in human development than
man's technical mastery of the natural environment through tools
and weapons.

For a long part of man's time on earth, the two sides of his nature,
the technical and the artistic, had been in relative balance. It was

only since the decline of the Middle Ages, an argument Mumford had made many times before, that Western man had abdicated to the machine, overdeveloping technics at the expense of his own emotions and subjective promptings. To right the balance, Mumford urges the cultivation of a new myth. In place of the myth of Prometheus, which begins with the assumption that the gift of fire, stolen by Prometheus from the gods, is the original source of man's development, Mumford offers the myth of Orpheus, the player of the lyre, who symbolizes a part of man's nature that Prometheus, "for all his love of man, never could bring to its full development." It was Orpheus, not Prometheus, Mumford argued in a series of lectures he gave at Columbia in 1951, and published one year later as *Art and Technics*, who "was man's first teacher and benefactor. Man became human, not because he made fire his servant, but because he found it possible, by means of his symbols, to express fellowship and love, to enrich his present life with vivid memories of the past and formative impulses toward the future, to expand and intensify those moments of life that had value and significance for him."

The promise of man, then, resides within himself. This is the real meaning, for Mumford, of the myth of Orpheus, and he would spend much of the remainder of his life searching for substantiating evidence for this "saving" intuition.9 Man as interpreter and symbol-maker, as maker of meanings and values, is the image on which Mumford erects his philosophy of history—a theory of human development in perfect accord with his own chosen role as writer and vision-maker. In Mumford's highly personalized reading of history, the word and the symbol, the writer and the artist, truly matter, and the arts take a central place in life. On this theme he had already said a good deal in his writings of the 1920s, and he would have more to say in work to come.

Mumford hoped that *The Transformations of Man*, the briefest, most accessible of his recent books, would reach a large audience of readers. The sales and critical reception, however, turned out to be as disappointing as they had been for his last several books. "The failure is complete: the rejection absolute," he wrote disconsolately after the first reviews and sales figures came in.10

This time, however, he refused to allow an indifferent public reception to his work to bring him down for a long period of time. After completing a first draft of his autobiography in the winter of 1955–56, he returned to his revision of *The Culture of Cities*, certain that he had original things to say that no specialist in history, anthropology, or sociology would dare say without risk to his reputation. With his public influence at its nadir, feeling like a forgotten man, he moved ahead purposefully, but not without occasional bouts of doubt and despair, with the major work that would restore him to influence.

Ironically, with his readership down to its lowest point, at least as far as his books were concerned, he never received more invitations or higher fees for lectures, personal appearances, and teaching appointments, and this helped to bolster his self-confidence. "Face to face with me a lecture audience will greet my words with great enthusiasm," he wrote with some puzzlement to an old friend; "left to read the same words in a book they turn aside, with positive antipathy."[11] But this should not have been that difficult for him to understand. His most recent books were long, thickly detailed, and complexly argued. Even some of his most brilliant friends found them tough going. Mumford's colleague at the University of Pennsylvania, Ian McHarg, tells the story of the first time he tried to read *The City in History*, which runs to over 650 pages. He had borrowed the book from a friend, and it took him many months to finish it. When he finally turned to the last page with a surge of relief and accomplishment, he laughed out loud when he saw what his friend had written in bold letters at the bottom of the page: "Thank God!"[12]

Mumford was in demand on college campuses because he was a riveting speaker and an accomplished classroom teacher. As a lecturer he exuded strength and power, and an almost Olympian certainty. The supremely self-assured tone that left so many of his readers flat could be impressive on the podium. He was, as his teaching colleagues testified, "a force," "a presence." He took hold of a class or a public audience and established complete control.[13]

At the University of Pennsylvania he gave courses to overflowing classes in religion and American literature, as well as civic design. He also headed a successful effort to establish a new humanities curriculum based on original texts in philosophy, religion, literature, and the social sciences, and he helped to redesign the curriculum in the School of Architecture. He found it difficult, however, to keep up his interest in teaching when he was immersed in a big literary project, so in 1957 he accepted an offer to become a Bemis Professor at MIT, an appointment for one semester a year with almost no teaching duties. This freed him to complete the initial draft of *The City in History*, which he began writing in 1958, following his return from a trip to Europe the year before, a trip as important to his intellectual development as the European study tour he had made in 1932, just before beginning his Renewal of Life series.

It was a summer crowded with memorable days: on some it was the landscapes and cities he was seeing for the first time; on others it was the people he met. In all, Europe opened to him "as it had never done before." In Belgium and the Netherlands, on the first leg of his journey, he met his friends Naum Gabo, the constructionist sculptor, and Henrik Wijdeveld, the Dutch architect, and Gabo took him to see his imposing sculpture in Rotterdam's rebuilt shipyard, which had been battered by the Nazi Blitz. At Bruges he gave a seminar on the nuclear age at the Collège d'Europe; then it was on to Paris, where Sophia joined him, and south to Avignon and Marseilles on their way to Italy, after an afternoon pilgrimage to Chartres. While staying in Florence they went to see Bernard Berenson at his villa, I Tatti, and made a trip into the hills of Tuscany to visit their son's grave. Then they headed south to Rome, by way of Venice, for the triumphal part of their tour. In Rome their enthusiastic host was the architect Bruno Zevi, who told Mumford that his life had been changed by *The Culture of Cities*. Zevi, a courtly, handsome man whose wife was a member of the Olivetti family, gave Lewis and Sophia a lavish Roman reception. At a garden party he hosted at his remodeled villa, two hundred people—writers, architects, painters, planners, city officials, and friends—were there to meet the Mumfords. Several times during the evening the festivities were stopped as one guest after the other stepped forward to give a salute to Lewis Mumford.[14]

Lewis and Sophia stayed at the Hotel de Ville at the top of the Spanish steps, and the Olivetti family put a car and a chauffeur at their disposal to take them anywhere they wanted to go outside the city. They first chose Ostia, where they had a splendid day walking among the ruins and dining at a small fish restaurant on the road

back to Rome. Several days later they went out along the Appian
Way to a starkly impressive war monument to three hundred
Romans slain by the Nazis. It was a moving experience for both of
them, and Lewis wrote an account of it for *The New Yorker*.[15]

Their final stop in Italy was Turin, to visit Adriano Olivetti, the
family patriarch, who had expressed a desire to meet Mumford.
They then spent much of the final three weeks of their European
trip in London, staying in a top-floor apartment of the home of one
of Lewis's closest English friends, the architect William Holford. At
a large gathering at Livingstone Hall, Westminster, with Holford as
first sponsor, Mumford was presented the gold medal of the Town
Planning Institute, the first time the institute awarded its gold medal
to a non-British subject. Afterwards there was a formal dinner at the
House of Lords in Mumford's honor. The entire trip, Lewis told
Sophia, reminded him of a great actor's farewell tour, only for him
this was actually a fresh start.[16]

Mumford began work on his history of the city in Cambridge,
Massachusetts, where he had access to Harvard's Widener Library,
which possesses a splendid collection in ancient archaeology, a new
interest of his. This was the first time he was able to write a book
with no economic pressures or outside responsibilities, and he was
in a bright mood and excellent health throughout most of the writing. He had felt much older at age fifty than he did now at sixty-
three, although he did notice one telling sign of advancing age: he
was slower at performing intellectual tasks he used to take in stride.
But slow by his standards was astonishingly fast by those of most
others, as he produced as many as 4,000 to 5,000 words a morning.[17] A course he had given on ancient religion at the University of
Pennsylvania in 1955, using original Egyptian and Mesopotamian
texts, had opened up new vistas for him on the role of containers—
pots, vases, cisterns, and barns—in early urban civilization, and he
pursued these new leads with blazing energy. In 1958 he tried out
some of his new ideas on the most challenging audience of all, giving
the opening and closing remarks at the Oriental Institute's symposium at the University of Chicago on Urbanization and Cultural
Development in the Ancient East. The enthusiastic reception he
received from prominent archaeologists, philologists, and classical
scholars gave him the confidence he needed to carry his work to
completion.[18]

Mumford's new book took command of him. His research pushed him into new intellectual territories and raised questions about the origins and nature of cities and civilization he had deftly sidestepped in his youth. He was concentrating almost all of his energies on the four opening chapters on the emergence of civilization and the first cities, having decided definitely not to write a concluding section on the contemporary city. In the summer of 1960, before finishing his chapters on ancient Greece and Rome, he went with Sophia to Paestum, Pompeii, Athens, and Delphi, his first visit to these historic places. In Athens, where he and Sophia were guests of the urban planner and futurologist Constantinos Doxiades, Lewis went back to the Acropolis every day for a week, seeing it at sunset, in the early morning, in the searing afternoon sun, and in evening by full moonlight. When he had seen what he wanted to see, he decided to leave a week earlier than planned, even though Sophia, much more the tourist, was hungry for more. "He has what he came for. . . . He has breathed the air and smelt the perfumes and has seen the sites and he is content to leave," Sophia wrote in her travel notes.[19] That September, in Leedsville, her husband finished his book.

The time between his submission of a book to his publisher and the appearance of the first reviews was always a time of great anxiety for him, and, predictably, his mood oscillated from the loftiest confidence to the deepest foreboding. He felt he had produced a book almost revolutionary in its importance, but he feared that it was too densely argued, too overladen with the "details of scholarship."[20] "When I was young," he wrote a friend, in a revealing analysis of his work, "I could magnificently condense and, what was better, I was never bothered by any deficiency of knowledge: I either jumped over the open spaces or filled them up with fabrications of the imagination. Those who knew better might be indignant but they could hardly be bored. Now I find myself writing as if I were the very creature I had sworn all my life not to be: a specialist, writing with the circumspectness of one courting the good opinion of rival specialists, and nothing could be more fatal to literary felicity." He also worried that this, his most original work, would be greeted by the "same dull 'So what?' " that all his recent books had encountered.[21]

But to Mumford's surprise, he found his editors at Harcourt, Brace talking about his new book with almost the same superlatives he was using. In confidence, Mumford had boasted to Henry Murray that there were only three other American books he would put on the same shelf with *The City in History* for richness of scholarship and insight: William James's *Psychology,* Henry Adams's *Mont-Saint-Michel and Chartres* and George Perkins Marsh's *Man and Nature.*²² Though that is quite a claim, this book *is* a classic, perhaps *the* classic in its field. William H. Whyte has called it the greatest book ever written on the city.²³

The reviews were the best Mumford ever received, and honors began to pour in. *The City in History* was awarded the National Book Award for nonfiction and it sold over 15,000 copies in the first eight months after publication, 55,000 in the first three years. Mumford was flooded with offers for university appointments and honorary degrees, and the Canadian Film Board made his book into a six-part film, *Lewis Mumford on the City.* After years of dreary, dispiriting neglect, he was being resurrected as "The Grand Old Man," the Old Man Eloquent of Milton's sonnet, and he enjoyed every minute of it.²⁴

That summer he and Sophia sailed for England, where he was to receive the gold medal for architecture of the Royal Institute of British Architects. On a trip to North Wales the week before the ceremonies in London they stayed with their old friends Clough Williams-Ellis, the architect, and his wife Anabel, in their rebuilt sixteenth-century manor house in the blue-black hills near Portmeirion, a fanciful Italianate village Williams-Ellis had built on a secluded peninsula on Cardigan Bay. Here Lewis had his first opportunity to relax since finishing his book. After tea one afternoon, he and Sophia called on Clough Williams-Ellis's friend Bertrand Russell, who lived nearby in Plas Penrhyn with his American wife. Russell, then ninety-two years old, was to have given one of the speeches preceding Mumford's receiving the gold medal, but an attack of shingles prevented him from traveling. This was the first time Mumford met Russell, and he flattered him by telling him that his *Problems of Philosophy,* published in 1913, was one of the first books on the subject he had read; although he failed to add, in the interests of politeness, that he had not been in the least impressed by anything Russell had said and had never liked his philosophy in either its "stoic or its later epicurian phases."²⁵

The following day he and Sophia boarded a train for Edinburgh, where they stayed for a week at the University before going to London for the presentation of the gold medal and several days of meetings, lectures, and television appearances.[26] The week ended with a reception for two hundred guests at the Guildhall in London, with the Lord Mayor in full regalia, surrounded by a company of pikemen in red dress with armor plate. Mumford, sitting at the dais with fifty honored guests, wore his gold medal on his chest, and for once drank too much champagne. He and Sophia danced as they hadn't since Harold Ross's *New Yorker* parties in the 1940s, "entranced by the people, by the whole scene, by each other, and not least by the orchestra leader, a perfect Cockney with the face of an old-fashioned London comedian."[27]

In all, he had never had a more eventful and stimulating trip.[28] He was exhausted, however, and the seven boring, rainy days on board the S.S. *Mauretania* were a heaven-sent relief. His book had taken him three years to write and he was feeling bone-weary. He had already committed himself to teach that fall at the University of California at Berkeley, but as he sailed back to New York he looked forward most of all to his return to Amenia in January, where he planned to begin a long period of rest and detachment, going over his life and work in preparation for completing the autobiography he had begun in the 1950's.

The book he had just put behind him is his masterwork, and it deserves a long look, for there is so much of Lewis Mumford, the mind as well as the man, in it. *The City in History* is the distillation and summation of a lifetime of urban observation and a book that touches close to the living core of Mumford's mature moral philosophy.

"Before the city, there was the hamlet and the shrine and the village." Here, in the twilight of prehistory, Mumford begins his epic drama of urban evolution; in the Paleolithic shrines and burial places, homes of the gods and the ancestral spirits, he locates the first traces of active civic life. "The city of the dead is the forerunner, almost core, of every living city." These sanctuaries, cemeteries, and ritual centers served as magnets, drawing nomadic peoples together, like so many pilgrims, in a spirit of awe and reverence.

All of these life-enhancing elements—ritual, spiritual communion, family nurture—were carried over into the Neolithic village, the first real unit of settled associational life. In the Neolithic village women as planters and food providers were dominant, and some of the critical technology assumed female forms. "The bones and muscles of the male dominate his technical contributions"—spears, hammers, axes, and knives—but "in women the soft internal organs are the center of her life: her arms and legs serve less significant for movement than for holding and enclosing, whether it be a lover or a child; and it is in the orifices and sacs, in mouth, vulva, vagina, breast, womb, that her sexually individualized activities take place." Neolithic culture was made possible by the domestication of animals and seed plants, and its principal innovations, Mumford claims, revising a considerable body of anthropological theory, were in the realm of containers for food and water—vats, pots, jars, bins, barns, cisterns, granaries, houses, and of "great collective containers, like irrigation ditches and villages." With the ability to store things came continuity of life, and, through the years, the villages, containers of men, grew in stability and security.

For Mumford, this is an almost idyllic age of security, communal cooperation, and face-to-face intimacy. Work was punctuated by regular rounds of play, conversation, religious ritual, and sexual activity; and a rough social equality prevailed.[29] The cities Mumford has always favored are those that retain these village values, well-proportioned cities with compact civic centers and a vivid neighborhood life. The village in the city is his ideal community. Nowhere is this more apparent than in *The City in History*, a book he began in Cambridge, Massachusetts, a place with the "intimate charm of the village," as he described it to a friend after he and Sophia moved there for the first time in 1956, "and with the sophisticated dash of a metropolis."[30]

The actual emergence of the city, Mumford agrees with then-accepted archaeological theory, came roughly 5,000 years ago with the introduction of plow culture and large-scale irrigation projects. During the agricultural revolution the diverse elements of civic life scattered over the great valley systems of East Asia and North Africa were fused together—in what Mumford called an urban implosion—behind the cyclopean walls of the city. At this moment the masculine contribution reasserted itself in the form of a driving desire to dominate and control nature and to exercise "a predatory power over other human groups." The Neolithic village, whose strength lay in reproduction, nurturing, and planting, gave way to cities ruled by masculine warriors and priests who presided over the development of revolutionary innovations, among them, the draw bow, the potter's wheel, exact astronomical observation, the calendar, and writing.

It is in this movement from the female-oriented village to male-oriented city that Mumford finds the origins of warfare, the modern power state, and the first organized labor machines. It is here that he locates the source of what he calls the "trauma of civilization." These are his most original and, to some critics, unsupportable arguments.*

Most of the archaeologists Mumford consulted in his research attributed the emergence of the city and civilization to the introduction of revolutionary techniques like the plow and large-scale cultivation of cereals in open fields. While Mumford concedes the importance of such technical improvements, he sees behind them a more impelling motive, a new type of social organization that brought about vast changes in every area of social life—the institution of kingship.

The appearance of the city coincided with the elevation of the Paleolithic hunter-chieftain to deified kingship. Building on the controversial findings of the anthropologist Henri Frankfort, Mumford describes the king as the catalytic agent in the first urban implosion. In his drive for supreme power, the king was aided by a new priestly class who invested him with cosmic authority, and by a retinue of courtiers, generals, and palace bureaucrats who further broadened the scope of his imperium. The power of the deified ruler was symbolized in the monumental architecture— the pyramids, ziggurats, palaces, and temples bedecked with ferocious-looking lions, bulls, and eagles—he erected to honor his image and to strike "respectful terror" in the hearts of the citizenry. While the king's authority sometimes brightened into justice, making possible a society of uniform laws, the citizens of the first cities were voiceless spectators, not involved participants, in the drama of

---

* Mumford's failure to use footnotes to document his findings irked many scholars.

civic life—onlookers and supernumeraries, thousands of whom
were regularly conscripted into the work gangs that built the king's
showy edifices.

In a striking new interpretation of the thin evidence of urban
origins, Mumford claims that these early construction gangs and
their supervisory personnel were humankind's first complex
machines—operating with precision, discipline, and centralized
coordination. These machines were long unnoticed by archaeologists because they were composed entirely of human parts. Mumford would make this argument the central theme of his next book,
The Myth of the Machine: Technics and Human Development; in *The City
in History,* however, his concern is with the effects of this new
military-style order on urban life, a multiplication of order and
discipline he considers dangerous in the extreme. In the first
cities—control centers, not marketing or manufacturing centers—
the growing division of labor made everyday work more specialized
and routinized, and this had enfeebling psychological and physiological consequences. The repression Freud saw as an accompani-
ment of civilization was not, in Mumford's view, confined to sexual
activities. It applied to most human functions and expressions. This
is the historic alienation Karl Marx referred to, and it began, Mumford argues without having closely read Marx, when a mutualistic
village life was absorbed by power-oriented cities.[31]

Once Mumford had made this discovery in his research—that
religious and temporal power, not the transmission of culture or the
enlargement of trade, was the original motive force for the city—it
was easy for him to see that modern warfare actually began with the
emergence of the city. At this point in his work on the book, with his
genius for synthesis, he began to see a connection between mass
anxiety, human sacrifice, organized warfare, and the development of
cities. There was only one problem, however: he had no hard
evidence to support the hypothesis he was forming in his mind, for
the emergence of both warfare and the city antedated the written
record. An absence of evidence, however, had never stopped him
before, and his argument—really a brilliant piece of scholarly con-
jecture, which he covers over with prose of priestly certainty—is
one that will forever incite controversy among students of the city.

This, in brief, is his thesis. As the primitive Neolithic community
spread out and became more interrelated, it became more suscep-

tible to anxiety-producing dangers and hardships. To appease the gods, and to relieve these neurotic fears, primitive peoples sacrificed human victims, usually captives from other communities. Under the king, these raids to capture victims for religious sacrifice became organized campaigns to control or wipe out other communities. Fears of retaliation further inflamed anxieties, producing in time a veritable cult of warfare in every ancient city. It was war or be warred upon. In the first city-states, popular hatred of the ruling class was diverted into hatred of foreign enemies, and the oppressed and the oppressors, instead of fighting one another, joined in aggressive action against a common outside enemy, in this case a rival city. Warfare, in this way, became a safety valve for the oppressions of civilization.

Thus the sources of warfare, in Mumford's audaciously speculative interpretation, lay in the same "mythic constellation" that made possible cities and the first military states, and not in a biologically inherited belligerence, or in a simple demand for territory, booty, or slaves. It was personally important for Mumford to structure his argument this way, for if warfare was not connected to any innate pugnaciousness in human beings, if it had its origins in a humanly fashioned institution—the first power state—there was some hope for his own age. Despite Mumford's apocalyptic tones he reached for every reed of hope he could grasp hold of. Nor, this book shows, had he lost his faith in the morally instructive power of history. In our own day, he warns in the tones of a lay preacher, the destructive fantasies that lamed the ancient city might burst forth again and destroy the very civilization the city first nurtured and sustained. But if we act in time, he argues almost against himself, the health-giving influences of the village and the region will counter the aggressive tendencies of big cities and power complexes. And in *The City in History* he charts a course back to sanity and order, masterfully marshaling the scattered evidence of the urban past into an argument for the regional city.[32]

This is most evident in his treatment of the Greek polis, which, along with the medieval town, is his favorite form of civic life. In the Aegean area between the eighth and sixth centuries B.C. there was a "devolution of power from the citadel to the democratic, village-based community." The Greeks' village ways made them distrustful of kingly power and centralized rule; they demythologized their leaders and made them dependent upon popular support and a common constitution. Even their gods were made to appear slightly ridiculous, susceptible to the same amorous drives and jealous rivalries as those they supposedly ruled over.33

Athens, the queen city of this civilization, was not handsome architecturally, but as with any great city, "the life it contained was more significant than the container." This was a civilization presided over by gifted amateurs contemptuous of specialists and mousy administrators. It was the all-rounder whom the Greeks—and Lewis Mumford—most admired. Of all men, Mumford surely understood Aristotle's comment that a gentleman should be able to play the flute—but not too well.34

Mumford sees these achievements concentrated in the polis, and its agora, or common meeting ground, both of which drew their original sources of nourishment from the Aegean village culture that Hesiod, his favorite Greek, had described in his *Works and Days*, a title Mumford would take for one of his own collections of memoirs. The spare mountain villages of the western Aegean had practiced in Hesiod's day what Mumford describes as a rudimentary form of "basic communism." Even in the best of times they had no overflowing surplus of goods. "What they had"—and once again Mumford seems to be writing as much about himself as the ancient Greeks— "was a surplus of time, that is leisure . . . available for conversation, sexual passion, intellectual reflection and esthetic delight."35 *The City in History* is a song to the world of the *Works and Days*, against whose virtues Mumford sets all the corruptions of the metropolis.

Mumford's explanation for Athens' decline is too complex to review here, but we find him saying, in essence, that Athens began its fall when it became more a metropolis than a large country town—a crowded, wealthy city center with a wide-spreading trade and colonial empire. Every urban drama has its final act, and in the end a war brought on by Athens' unwillingness to give freedom to its tributary cities "dragged the polis back to the more aggressive pattern of the earliest king-centered cities."

The Hellenistic city that replaced the Periclean polis was more prosperous and architecturally unified, but Mumford considers it decidedly inferior in its ability to generate cultural creativity. It was in Rome, however, that Meletian-style town planning, with its preference for geometric precision and uniformity, was carried furthest, and there it was fused with town building ideas drawn from Asia and North Africa to produce what Mumford assails as the most debased form of urban civilization in recorded history. In all of literature there is perhaps no more damning an indictment of Roman urban culture than in *The City in History.*

The Romans were quintessentially a city-building people, and their cities, Mumford concedes, were often marvels of dignity and formal composure. By the Augustinian period the Romans had built hundreds of new towns, simple in layout and patterned to human dimensions, towns Mumford had recently visited, like Pavia, Verona, Turin, and Florence, all of them graced with exquisitely proportioned piazzas, campos, and arcaded streets. Rome itself shared some of this dignity of design, but under the emperors it became a city of excess and exhibitionism—loud, filthy, noisy, overbuilt, and morally rotten to the core, a city where all was for show or sale.[36]

From imperial Rome Mumford moves directly to a consideration of the medieval city, and from this point on his book follows the familiar ground of *The Culture of Cities*, tracing the process of urban development through the baroque city, Coketown, and megalopolis. The leading themes, the organizational pattern, and even most of the prose are taken directly from that earlier work. It is only in the last section of the book that Mumford fully reveals how greatly he had changed over the course of the quarter century that separates the publication of these two ground-breaking works. Here he puts forward his most forbidding anticipations about the future of civilization, sounding at times like Oswald Spengler.

Where in *The Culture of Cities* he had suggested wide-sweeping plans for urban design, the emphasis in *The City in History* is on control and discipline as "values for survival," the title of one of his postwar collections of essays. In this book Mumford reaches down into what T. S. Eliot has called the "dark embryo" of the unconscious to locate the disturbances he fears will bring the city and civilization to ruin. A more profound understanding of these aggressive compulsions, he argues, will allow us to tame and master them, "such a knowledge as is achieved by a neurotic patient in facing a long-buried infantile trauma that has stood in the way of his normal growth and integration." It is to this end that he wrote *The City in*

History, a book in which diagnosis and discovery, the Freudian's first step toward health and balance, take precedence over everything else.[37]

Mumford concludes *The City in History* with his many-times-reiterated argument for the garden city, but the sentences do not carry their former conviction, no doubt because he himself had undergone a change. Just before writing *The City in History* he had a chance to examine the new towns the British began building after the war, and what he saw fell far short of his expectations.

Mumford's original attraction, we must remember, was to Ebenezer Howard's garden city *idea*, not to any *existing* garden city. Before World War II he had briefly visited Howard's two experimental new towns—Letchworth and Welwyn Garden City—but not until the 1950s did he have a chance to closely examine Howard's idea in practice, when he toured the new towns the British government was constructing on the outskirts of London. These experimental towns disappointed him, and he revealed his disappointment most keenly in his correspondence with his two friends who were most sympathetic to the garden city concept, Clarence Stein and Frederic J. Osborn, fearing, no doubt, that any all-out public criticism from him might discredit the garden city idea itself, which he continued to see as promising, despite its bleak representation by British planners. Yet even in his published accounts of these garden cities he found it impossible to hide his disappointment. What these accounts reveal, in fact, is his preference for historic cities, for the new towns lacked, in his estimation, the cultural variety, liveliness, and handsome architectural form of cities like Venice, Siena, and Amsterdam. Worse still, they did not even look like real cities. With their wide streets, lined on either side by well-kept houses with trim front gardens and lawns, they reminded him of the neatly manicured dormitory suburbs of New York and New Jersey. Even their density patterns were suburban—twelve to fourteen houses to the acre. In their understandable reaction against the overcrowded British industrial centers, the planners—many of them, ironically, disciples of Mumford—had sacrificed the urban virtues of sociability and community closeness for privacy and open space. In the garden city the garden had replaced the city.[38]

Considered by many an uncritical apologist of the garden city, Mumford was one of the first and most astute critics of the British new towns. Critics of his work, like Jane Jacobs, author of one of the most influential books on the modern city, *The Death and Life of Great American Cities*, have accused him of favoring so-called garden city ideas he was actually one of the first to speak out against. So we find as perceptive an urban observer as Paul Goodman taking Mumford to task, in a review of *The City in History*, for favoring a sharp separation—through zoning—of work, residences, and commercial areas; whereas Mumford, in the very book Goodman was reviewing, condemns such rigid zoning as inimical to urban life, arguing that each superblock, each distinct district of the city, should be, as much as possible, a city in miniature.[39]

The architecture of the garden cities is barracks-like and boring, it has an institutional look and feel, others have argued.[40] But so did Mumford, and well in advance of most of these critics. In congruence with the thinking of his friend Ian McHarg, the influential landscape planner, Mumford urged that the new towns be built to the terrain—designed with nature—as one of the later new towns, Cumbernauld, was, with its houses and apartments set on a steep Scottish hillside, like a cliffside Mediterranean village. Cumbernauld also has densities far higher than any of the earlier new towns. Later in his life Mumford would see in the designs for Tapiola, near Helsinki, a new town of architectural variety, liveliness, and human warmth. Living in a new town did not have to be like living in a grimly gray housing estate; Heikki von Hertzen, Tapiola's creator, had made that stunningly clear.[41]

Mumford had other objections to British new town planning far too numerous to concern us here. The point to be emphasized, however, is that he never completely lost faith in the garden city idea itself—a constellation of medium-sized communities set in publicly protected open spaces given over to agriculture and recreation. Sweden, France, Finland, and other industrial countries have experimented with variations of this scheme, but Mumford would never find an existing urban pattern that met his exacting social and aesthetic expectations; and he had nothing but criticism for the scores of privately built new towns that went up all over the United States in the 1960s, when for several years the Department of Housing and Urban Development gave the new town idea lukewarm support. He regarded even the best of these communities—Reston, Virginia, and Columbia, Maryland—as little more than attractively sited dormitory suburbs dressed up to look like urban centers. Reston, he wrote Frederic Osborn after reviewing its plans, is "a purely upper-class New Town . . . a sort of suburban Bath, twentieth century model." Its builder, the enlightened businessman Robert E. Simon, had invited Mumford to discuss the town plan with him, but Mumford had politely declined the offer, feeling that Simon had come to him "too late to get the sort of advice he really needed." Besides, Mumford told Simon he did not believe that sound communities of this scale could be built with private money, an amazing statement, given that Radburn and Sunnyside Gardens, Queens, had been built entirely with such funds. What is more likely is that Mumford had no faith in a community he, or someone close to his thinking, had no part in shaping.[42]

By the 1960s, Mumford was too old, he thought, to lead the fight in America for a garden city program, as he had in the 1920s and 30s. But he continued to advance the ideas of his RPAA days as one set of solutions to the urban problem, even though these ideas ran directly against the American preference for single-family detached houses and for a market approach to housing construction and community design. When his friends in the federal housing program would gently remind him that he was overlooking the thick tangle of political and administrative difficulties his regional program would surely run into, his reply was always the same: his responsibility was not to suggest what was practical and possible at any given moment, but what was humanely desirable.[43] And he did have a point here, after all: he was a dreamer, and his are the kind of dreams that often have opened the way to great changes, just, it occasionally happens, when the most hardened realists are crying "impossible."

An intellectual would just as soon meet a bear in the woods as live in a garden city, Paul and Percival Goodman remark in their influential book *Communitas*.[44] And it is doubtful that Mumford himself would have been entirely content in a new town, even one of his own making. For most of his life he was a man at home in two worlds—the city and the countryside. He loved these opposite environments almost equally, living part of the year in some big city and the other part in tiny Leedsville. But most people, he realized, could not afford to live this way. The garden city—combining the city's energy and diversity with close contact to nature—seemed to him a sensible compromise. That is, the garden city of his dreams, for few garden cities have been able to function as true cities, and the reason for this is because their housing densities are simply too low.

Though Mumford supported higher housing densities for new towns, he never supported densities high enough to satisfy critics of garden city thinking like William H. Whyte and Jane Jacobs. For garden cities, indeed for almost all cities, Mumford favors medium densities of between 100 and 125 persons per acre, densities Jacobs and Whyte consider incompatible with urbanity and the economies of encouraging diversity.

Jacobs and Whyte represent an important reaction against Mumford's ideas on the city—a reaction that began to build, ironically, in the early 1960s, when he was at the peak of his influence. Jacobs and Whyte prefer the standard grid-style street design to the enclosed superblock, arguing that a city needs streets, lots of streets teeming with people and activity, if it is to be a safe and lively place. Crowded streets tend to be safer, Jacobs argues, because so many eyes are watching, whereas the secluded culs-de-sac and superblocks are open invitations to the criminal. The most dangerous areas in most cities, Jacobs and Whyte claim, are those neighborhoods with the lowest densities, blighted areas like New York's East Bronx; whereas the neighborhoods with the highest densities, almost impossibly high densities by Mumford's standards, are often the healthiest areas, places like Brooklyn Heights or Philadelphia's Rittenhouse Square. But it is the garden city idea that Jacobs, Whyte, and other influential proponents of high densities single out for scorn, picturing it as the brainchild of village minds. Mumford's and Howard's prescription for saving the city, Jacobs charges, is "to do the city in."[45]

Whyte's criticism is more measured than Jacobs's; still, he argues in his equally important book *The Last Landscape* (1968) that as a means of saving the city the movement to the garden city is like taking a mistress to improve one's marriage. You cannot move away from the metropolis and reconstitute its successful elements in tidy new cities on the fringe. Urbanity is not something that can be "lacquered on; it is the quality produced by the great concentration of diverse functions and a huge market to support the diversity." To be great, a city has to be a central place, and it has to be big and, yes, crowded. The music, theater, galleries, sporting events, and other entertainments that draw people to places like New York are supported by high population densities, and so, too, are successful mass transit systems. On this point Whyte agrees entirely with Jane Jacobs.[46]

It was Jane Jacobs who received most of the attention in the 1960s, and unfortunately for Mumford, her book was published in the same year that *The City in History* appeared. Unfortunate, because many critics unfavorably compared his ideas with Jacobs's, the ideas of a dusty old urban warrior with those of a fast-advancing young challenger. This irked Mumford, even though his book was chosen over Jacobs's book, another nominee, for the National Book Award. But what turned Mumford's rancor into boiling rage was Jacobs's crude portrayal of his and Howard's ideas, an analysis of garden city thinking he considered almost "comical" in its inaccuracy. Mumford used his considerable influence at *The New Yorker* to get the editors to publish the full-out attack on Jane Jacobs he began composing in his mind the very afternoon he finished reading her book.[47]

"I held my fire on [Jane Jacobs's] book for a whole year," he wrote to an old friend on finishing his *New Yorker* essay, "but when I got down to write I discovered that the paper burned, in spite of the long cooling period."[48] He originally wrote three long articles, but the editors asked him to reduce his argument to a single essay, and to tone it down a bit. He did, but still the essay blistered and boiled, for Jacobs, he believed, in one of his stormy fits of overreaction, had gone at him with hate in her heart. They had been allies in earlier battles against Robert Moses's urban renewal projects, and on that subject, and on highway development within the city, they were in complete concord. But when two people are so close together in their thinking, and so eager for influence, they often magnify their differences to the point of outright caricature. The Mumford-Jacobs debate is immensely interesting because the level of thinking is so high, and so pertinent to current urban concerns; and also, we might add, because they were both so wonderfully adept at pouring scorn on the opposition—Jacobs with her cracking, straight-from-the-shoulder urban style, and Mumford with his Olympian thunder flashes. When the dust finally cleared, and they exchanged cordial letters, they admitted that they had great respect for each other.

Jacobs told Mumford that she was flattered by much of what he had said about her book, which he privately told friends he found both "stimulating and awful."[49]

These are perhaps our two most influential modern writers on the city, and their differences go well beyond their disagreements on matters of density and neighborhood design. It is a question of order versus disorder, of well-planned urban development versus a more haphazard, hit-or-miss approach. Jacobs argues, often with uncommon good sense, that we should allow cities to grow naturally, and that a city's streets, not its parks and pedestrian promenades, ought to be the focus of social life. She is also interested in introducing greater vitality into urban life, the kind of lively street and neighborhood life she finds in her own section of Greenwich Village; whereas the emphasis in Mumford's later work, we have seen, is on village-like stability and order. For both Jacobs and Mumford, sound planning is first of all neighborhood planning. Only Jacobs's "urban villages," one supposes, would be far more active places than Mumford's, filled with people and noise, and lit through the early hours of the morning; and many of them would be lined with stores and seedy bars that no planner could hope, or perhaps should even want, to shut down.

In *The Death and Life of Great American Cities* Jane Jacobs presents her ideas in a way that makes her seem more "urban," and more streetwise, than Mumford, and this infuriated Mumford, who wore his city background proudly like a chestful of combat ribbons. Here was a woman from Scranton, Pennsylvania, telling him, who had lived for over half a century in New York, that he had a small-town outlook! He had lived in a two-room apartment on Clinton Street in Brooklyn Heights with "a tailor, a laundry, a florist, grocery stores, and restaurants—Mrs. Jacobs' favorite constellation for 'urban liveliness'—immediately at hand," he wrote in his *New Yorker* essay, but he still preferred the quiet flat he had occupied on tree-shaded Hicks Street, with its fine rear garden overlooking an old stone church, to "all the dingy 'liveliness' of Clinton Street as it was back in the twenties." What was behind Jacobs's insistence that the street carry all the multiple functions of a well-balanced neighborhood? The answer seemed evident to Mumford. "Her ideal city is mainly a new organization for the prevention of crime." But Mumford went on to question Jacobs's very assumption that lively streets deterred crime.

If pedestrian-filled streets are a preventive to criminal behavior, why, he asked, is crowded, ever-active Harlem so unsafe? Or why, for that matter, was eighteenth-century London—which also met Jacobs's prescriptions for good planning—such a hoary haven of violence and delinquency?

Then Mumford cut straight to his main point, a conclusion he had come to reluctantly over the past several decades. As a boy he had walked all over Central Park—the kind of vacuous park that Jacobs saw as a collector of crime—at all times of the day and night. Now he would not dare do so. It was not, then, the "form" of New York—the way it was architected and designed—that made it so unsafe, it was "the increasing pathology of the whole mode of life in the great metropolis . . . a pathology connected to its vast size, materialism, congestion, and disorder," the very conditions Jacobs held up as signs of urban vitality. On this point Mumford would have more to say later.

His final objection to Jacobs's plans for the city was that they had no place for beauty. "A city," Jacobs flatly declared, "cannot be a work of art." This collided with Mumford's basic beliefs about urban design. Good buildings were not everything for him, but everything he wrote about architecture said that they did make a difference. It was the peerless beauty of the cathedrals, palaces, and parks of Europe that had preserved the urban cores of the great historic cities for centuries; and contrariwise, bad design, as in sterile tower blocks for the poor, often encouraged pathological patterns.[50]

Though Jacobs and Mumford continued to disagree on questions of residential congestion, there was one type of urban congestion they spoke out against as one voice—that caused by the automobile. The private motorcar, they agreed, was the single greatest menace to the health of the modern city, and the man who had done more to open the city, New York City especially, to the automobile was Robert Moses.

When Mumford completed *The City in History* he planned to write a sequel on the contemporary city, its problems and prospects. He never got around to this book, as other projects absorbed his remaining energy, yet his essays from the 1940s through the early 1960s on the modern city, and on the kind of urban policies being put forward by Robert Moses, the federal government, and the big real-estate developers, in concert with some of the country's leading architects, form that important sequel he never wrote. The dispute between Robert Moses and Lewis Mumford—a large part of that unbound book—is one of the most important urban policy debates of the twentieth century.

25

The Endangered City

A city exists, not for the constant passage of motorcars, but for the care and culture of men.

—LEWIS MUMFORD

Robert Moses had a comprehensive plan for New York and unprecedented power to carry it out; Lewis Mumford was one of those critics most responsible for preventing him from driving that plan to completion. For nearly two decades beginning in the 1940s, Mumford fought almost every one of Moses's major highway and urban renewal projects. Though he lost nearly all of these battles, in the process he helped to bring about a change in our thinking about highways, mass transportation, and urban renewal. In these years, when we did so much to destroy our cities, Lewis Mumford was America's urban conscience.

They called Robert Moses the Master Builder. Neither an architect, nor a professional planner, nor a politician, Moses shaped modern New York City, wielding czarlike control over public works for more than four decades through his domination of a succession of city and state commissions and powerful public authorities. America's greatest road builder, perhaps the greatest road builder ever, he built nearly every one of New York City's major roads; and, from 1931, all of its bridges, including the longest suspension bridge in the world, the magnificent arching span over the Verrazano Narrows. His was the largest road- and bridge-building program since the Roman Empire, and like the emperors of old, Robert

Moses built great parks and public places: Lincoln Center, the New York Coliseum, the United Nations headquarters, Shea Stadium, Jones Beach State Park. He renovated Central Park, badly rundown after decades of neglect, and built hundreds of smaller parks, playgrounds, and pools everywhere in the city—everywhere, that is, except in black and Hispanic neighborhoods. And he built the nation's first modern parkways, over four hundred miles of them, beautiful roads, shaped to the landscape and closed to trucks and commercial traffic. As the head of the mayor's slum clearance program in the 1950s, Moses was also responsible for the largest urban renewal effort in the country.

But the Master Builder's influence extended far beyond the city's borders. He had immense statewide and national influence, especially over highway construction. In 1956, when Congress passed the Interstate Highway Act, a bill he helped to shape, most of the engineers who were hired to construct the new national highway network were men who had worked for or been strongly influenced by Robert Moses, who, except for a few driving lessons he took in 1926, never drove a car in his life.[1]

These engineers came to Moses to learn more than how to build highways. They wanted to know how to build highways that cut straight through the heart of the city, for Moses was the first highway builder to bring the expressway directly into the center of the city. Even the impressive roadways of two previous imperial builders, Benito Mussolini and Adolf Hitler, skirted the city. Moses drove his multilaned expressways—six of them by the late 1950s— right into the congested core of New York City.

Robert Moses was not just a builder; he was an "un-builder," in Lewis Mumford's opinion. To construct his mammoth expressways he had to remove 250,000 people from their homes and level scores of neighborhoods, many of them lively, close-knit places like East Tremont. When you build highways in an overbuilt metropolis "you have to hack your way with a meat ax," Moses declared.[2] And while he did build housing for the poor, and for some of the families he evicted to make room for his roads, he built dispiriting concrete slabs, hundreds of them, one long wall of prison-like towers extending for miles up the East Side of Manhattan.

"In the twentieth century, the influence of Robert Moses on the cities of America was greater than that of any other person," Lewis

Mumford told Moses's biographer, Robert Caro. But that influence, he thought, was a massively destructive one.[3]

Mumford had supported many of Moses's earliest projects, particularly his parks and parkways, built with the best design talent available. Moses's parkways are the closest practicing examples we have in this country of Benton MacKaye's proposal for townless highways, and whenever he was in Leedsville Mumford would tell friends from New York City who were coming by car to visit him to take Moses's Taconic State Parkway, a winding ribbon of road through the beautiful Hudson River valley.

In the 1930s the nation badly needed roads to move its increasing volume of automobile traffic, and Moses's parkways seemed to Mumford an ideal way to meet this part of the transportation problem. But in the 1940s, when it became clear that Moses envisioned highways as the sole solution to the transportation problem, and when he began to build highways within the city itself, Mumford attacked him with full fire. He was the first of Robert Moses's major critics, the most persistent, and, in the end, the most effective.

No amount of highway building will alleviate congestion; the more highways you build the more automobiles, buses, and trucks you will lure to them. This was Mumford's simple, insistent point. And no sooner had Moses completed a highway to relieve congestion on an older highway than that new highway was hopelessly clogged, making New Yorkers' daily travel a daily travail. Motorists noticed this—commuters on Moses's Long Island Expressway continue to refer to it as "the Big LIE"—yet these commuters clamored for more expressways. Few people in public power were prepared to oppose Moses's policies; "highways," Mumford explained in 1946, "are an impressive, flashy thing to build. No one is against highways."[4] The new American religion is the religion of the automobile; the new aim of regional planning is to open every area of the metropolis to the motorcar, giving it a "sacred right to go anywhere, halt anywhere, and remain anywhere as long as its owner chooses." In our fascination with the automobile, we were remaking the city, Mumford feared, to fit the outsized imaginations of Detroit.[5]

But Mumford did not see this problem confined to the United States. Amsterdam is becoming so crowded with cars that it is impossible in some places to see the canals through the solid walls of parked cars lining their banks, he told his *New Yorker* readers; and when he visited Florence and Rome, Mumford had trouble sleeping at night because of the deafening noise of automobiles and motor scooters. But for some people this was the unavoidable price of "progress." Whenever Mumford met with mayors and other city officials in Europe, they would invariably show him new plans for many-acred midtown garages, arterial highways, overpasses, and underpasses. "We are not far behind you Americans," an Italian politician told him proudly. "We know of your Robert Moses."[6]

In 1955, as construction was about to begin on the Long Island Expressway, Robert Moses's greatest road, Mumford wrote a series of articles for *The New Yorker*, "The Roaring Traffic's Boom," summing up his case against the Master Builder's master plan. Here he asked his readers to ponder one question before they threw their support to yet another massive road-building project: consider what has already been done to New York by Robert Moses. Under Moses, New York "has become steadily more frustrating and tedious to move around in, more expensive to do business in, more unsatisfactory to raise children in, and more difficult to escape from for a holiday in the country." Moses's roads, bridges, and tunnels, designed to carry people to further and further destinations, were not curbing congestion; they were widening chaos.[7]

Mumford, however, did not confine his fire to Robert Moses; he attacked the entire federal highway program that Congress approved in 1957 as a national defense measure. "The most charitable thing to assume about this action," he wrote just after that $26 billion program was signed into law, "is that they hadn't the faintest notion of what they were doing." Within the next fifteen years they would find out, but by then it would be too late to correct the damage done to the cities and the countryside.[8]

Mumford, like Moses, did not drive a car, but he was not obdurately anti-automobile, as Moses claimed. Although he preferred to travel by train, he liked to tour the Amenia countryside with Sophia at the wheel, and he considered the automobile an indispensable part of modern life. But in its overenthusiasm for the private car, the nation was sacrificing every other means of transportation to it, offering the airplane as the only other long-distance alternative. He prophetically saw New York as an illustration of what was happening all over the country. The city's failure to keep existing rail lines in decent repair and to build lines into newly developed areas was forcing more and more commuters to use their cars. The long-term consequences for the city would be calamitous. The point will soon be reached, he darkly predicted in the 1950s, when the very businesses and industries that gave rise to the congestion will abandon the city because of it, leaving behind "a tomb of concrete roads and ramps covering the dead corpse of a city."[9]

In the 1940s and 50s, Mumford offered scores of specific suggestions for creating a more balanced urban transportation system in New York and elsewhere; he understood that without a good mass transit system the regional decentralization he favored would further increase people's dependence on automobiles. While it is impossible to gauge the impact of his ideas on public policy, he helped to shape the thinking of a new generation of urban writers and planners. "No other writer," says the influential urbanist Kevin Lynch, "has had such a deep and enduring influence on the field of planning." Portland's former mayor Neil Goldschmidt, who served as secretary of transportation in President Jimmy Carter's administration, has said that, as a great admirer of Mumford, he initiated a number of his proposals in his city. "Portland is a better city . . . thanks in large part to the wisdom and foresight of Lewis Mumford."[10] Portland today is a pedestrian city, one of the first cities in the country to stop the encroachment of cars and concrete at the center, and this, Mumford has long argued, must be the aim of all sound transportation policy. "No city can solve its transportation problems if it neglects the greatest self-propelling vehicle of all: the pedestrian."[11]

But weren't Americans supposed to hate walking? "Where walking is exciting and visually stimulating," this longtime city walker declared in 1958, "whether it is in a Detroit shopping center or along Fifth Avenue, Americans are perfectly ready to walk." But to make cities attractive to walk in we would have to do more than plant trees and build parks and outdoor cafes. Planners would have to repattern the entire city, scrapping the rigid zoning procedures that turn huge areas, too spread-out for pedestrian use, into bleakly monotonous single-district zones—for shopping, for industry, for commerce.[12]

Mumford was no mere sitting sage, however, as Robert Moses suggested. He took part in several efforts to save the city from the dangerous flood of automobile traffic, and in two major instances these citizen-led campaigns were successful. One of them helped to turn the tide of public opinion against Robert Moses; the other helped to kill a road proposal that would have done irreparable harm to one of the world's most magnificent city centers.

In 1958, Robert Moses threatened to build a four-lane highway through Washington Square, in the heart of Greenwich Village, and Mumford led the fight against him. He considered this plan an act of civil vandalism, and in a succession of public petitions and pronouncements, urged that the square be closed entirely to automobile traffic. "Washington Square," Mumford commented in a press release put out by the Committee to Close Washington Square to Traffic, "was originally used as a Potter's Field for paupers; it might now prove to be a good place to bury Mr. Moses' poverty-stricken and moribund ideas on city planning." That did not happen for some time, but the square and this vital area of the Village were saved; and Mayor Edward Koch, who was then a young city politician living in the Village and a member of the neighborhood action group that was fighting Moses and city hall, recalls that Mumford's contribution to this victory was decisive. "Today, community input into such decisions by city government is an inviolable fact of American life," Koch has said. ". . . For that, a generation of urban planners, activists—and Mayors—owe a large debt to the fight Lewis Mumford led to save Washington Square Park."[13]

New York may have listened to Lewis Mumford on occasion, but the only city in which his advice on a specific planning issue was solicited was Oxford, England. There one of Oxford University's oldest and most prestigious colleges, Christ Church, "the House" as it was called, came to him for help. The issue was a city and national government proposal to drive a "relief road" through Christ Church Meadow, a lovely stretch of pastureland between the college's rear gardens and the Isis River, a place where cattle graze even today.

Since World War II a number of proposals had been made for a road through the Meadow, and for what looked to be a good reason—to relieve the congestion on the High Street, one of the most splendid thoroughfares in Europe. Into the 1960s each of these plans had been beaten back by college pressure, but in 1964 Christ

Church feared it might lose. This time the government's road plan was being supported by some of the biggest names at the university, in a desperate effort to protect their own colleges, whose impressive Gothic facades flanked the High Street. In the midst of this intensely fought struggle, the Treasurer of Christ Church, Sir F. Anthony Gray, had "an inspiration" that came to him, he says, in his bath.[14] The college had already hired Professor C. D. Buchanan, Britain's leading expert on urban traffic problems, to represent its case to the government, but Gray felt he needed an even bigger name on his side, one that would influence both the government planners and the college dons. In his youth Gray had read Mumford's early books and considered him the greatest living authority on the city. Why not invite Mumford to give testimony against the road plan? He knew from talking with several of Mumford's friends at Oxford that he would be a hard man to get because he was writing another book, but Gray, an enormously charming man, with years of experience in the foreign service, knew exactly what to do. He appealed to Mumford's vanity. The college, he wrote him, needs a "voice of over-powering authority and unimpeachable detachment—such as yours."[15] So Mumford found it impossible to turn him down, busy as he was.

Yet more than Gray's persuasive powers were at work here. Oxford was, in many ways, Mumford's ideal city—compact, architecturally harmonious and pulsating with life, a city ringed by a wreath of parklands, pastures, and riverside pleasances. He had first visited Oxford in 1920, and every time he returned to England he returned to Oxford. On one of these visits he and Sophia had spent a delightful afternoon punting on the River Cherwell and picnicking on the banks of Isis, just by Christ Church Meadow. Later he recorded that scene with a watercolor, in the style of Monet. How could he turn down Gray's plea to stop this, "the first radical incision in the body of historic Oxford"?[16]

Mumford refused to testify in person, however, even though Gray offered to pay him a sizable fee for his services. He could not now leave his writing table, he explained to Gray; he would draft a short report instead, which could be entered as testimony. He did not tell Gray, however, his other reason for not appearing in person at the government inquiry. On a recent visit to London he had seen a British barrister mercilessly turn an expert witness into a "stuttering jackass," leaving him "entirely stript of his pelt," he confided to David Liebovitz just after he received Gray's first letter. "No thank you to that!"[17]

The "short report" he began writing, with some help from Gray, who came to Leedsville for several days, turned into a full-dress proposal for the replanning of the city of Oxford. It made what Gray called an "unanswerable" case not only against invading Christ Church Meadow, but against the current misuse of the automobile in the city. The relief offered by the road, Mumford insisted, would be temporary; the damage done to Oxford's central glory permanent. Instead of a relief road, he recommended that the city take strong measures to expand public transportation and discourage private automobiles from entering the city center during business hours. When he finished the report he was pleased; he had been flattered to be asked to do it, and it had been fun to write. But why, he wondered, was he doing this for Oxford, and not for twenty or so American cities he knew far better?[18]

Mumford's memorandum was unveiled by Gray at a crucial moment in the college's battle against the road, and it received wide notice in the British press. Mumford had recently been awarded the Queen's Royal Gold Medal for contributions to architectural thought, and his books were required reading for city planners in England. As the London *Financial Times* remarked: "To ask [Mumford's] views on a planning issue is like calling down Moses to advise the president of Israel. . . . The grand old man is not only movingly eloquent but cunning; as he makes Oxford a test case for all cities of the world."[19]

Shortly after Mumford's report was presented as evidence, the Meadows road plan was turned down by the Ministry of Housing and Local Government. The Minister of the Environment, Richard Crossman, later told F. Anthony Gray that Mumford's report had an influence on the decision; it had been the "ace of trumps." Never had he read a more persuasive argument against a planning proposal.[20]

In his fight to save the city Mumford's main battleground, however, remained New York. As he grew older he insistently referred to himself in interviews and public appearances as a "big city man," a

New Yorker to the core, even though he made his home in Leedsville. This became a matter of supreme importance for him, and one incident in particular speaks volumes. In 1973, when he was about to be interviewed in his Leedsville living room by Bill Moyers for Moyers's television show, he refused to wear the red plaid shirt the director thought was perfect for the program. Mumford was adamant about this. He would not give his reasons to the TV crew, but they were clear enough. He felt that some people had written him off as a writer who had retreated to the country, and the red flannel shirt fit that image. He wanted to look like a city man, he told Sophia privately, so he would wear a jacket and tie. At this point, when there was no persuading him otherwise, Bill Moyers, who was wearing a turtleneck sweater, took it off, put on a coat and tie, and began the interview.[21]

By 1960, however, this "big city man" was going into New York only for business, and almost never for more than a day at a time. He occasionally visited his daughter Alison, who in 1959 had married a young theater director, Chester Morss, and was living in Brooklyn Heights, but he made it known to her that he preferred that she and Chet come to Amenia. He no longer felt comfortable in crowded, crime-ridden New York, a city that in his youth had for him, as for young F. Scott Fitzgerald, "all the iridescence of the beginning of the world."[22]

New York had been ruined, in his view, not just by the automobile and the rising level of criminal violence, but by the skyscraper, which he considered not just a building form, but a "common method of congesting population and ground rents."[23] In the pages of *The New Yorker*, he continued to wage the war he had begun in the early 1920s against the high-rise tower, "New York's greatest enemy," in the words of his friend Clarence Stein.[24]

In these years Mumford produced a body of architecture criticism of unrivaled quality and prescience, even though architecture had ceased to be an absorbing subject for him, or so at least he claimed. He had become bored with architecture, he began to tell people. And, anyway, architecture was not going to change the world; it reflected the dominant social values, and it was these values that had to change if we were to have a better world, and for that matter, better architecture. But Mumford's "Sky Line" reviews helped to pay his bills and finance his trips to Europe, and there is much evidence that he enjoyed writing them even if he didn't care to be known as an architecture critic. His essays on architecture bristle with energy and insight; they are not the kind of writing one produces in a state of boredom and eroded interest. Well before he stopped writing his "Sky Line" column in 1963, he was generally recognized as this century's greatest architecture critic.

Mumford's ideas on architecture remained remarkably consistent throughout his life. Into the 1960s he continued to judge architecture according to social and moral canons he had laid down in his earliest work on the subject, though there is a subtle shift of emphasis in his later architecture essays. They show him even less concerned than he had been in the twenties and thirties with individual buildings, and more concerned with the impact of building trends on the overall urban environment. This later work, moreover, reveals his deep disappointment with the direction that modern architecture took after World War II.

Modern architecture, the movement toward functional clarity and austerity begun in Europe in the 1920s by Walter Gropius, Adolf Loos, Jacobus Oud, Ludwig Mies van der Rohe, Le Corbusier, and other avant-garde architects and designers, swept the globe after the Second World War. What were almost universally judged to be good buildings had smooth surfaces, flat roofs, lots of windows, and clear white walls. They were severely symmetrical, stressing volume, not mass, and they went to engineering, not nature, for inspiration. One of the first American critics to welcome the International Style, Mumford had organized the housing section of the International Style exhibition at New York's Museum of Modern Art in 1932. Years later, one of the pioneers of the new movement, the expressionist architect Erich Mendelsohn, paid him the supreme compliment of asking him to write his biography, and Philip Johnson, co-organizer of the International Style exhibit, and another name synonymous with modern architecture, has said, only half humorously, that if it wasn't for Mumford's early influence on his life he would have turned out to be "a shoe clerk."[25]

Mumford had liked the look of the new minimalist buildings he saw for the first time in 1932, in visits to Stuttgart, Rotterdam, Zurich, and Dessau, home of the Bauhaus. They were stylishly simple buildings that met clear social needs—light and airy schools, factories, apartments, and civic centers. But in one of his early

essays on the new style, he argued that while the absence of ornament and the clear expression of form-in-function "is what consti-
tutes the modern feeling, . . . there must be more." That
"something more" included "feeling," decoration, and, most crucial
of all, a more complex appreciation of human needs.[26] At times we
might want to have plenty of air and sunlight, but we also need
privacy. We might want to have a perfectly engineered kitchen in
which everything is exactly where it is supposed to be, but in our
living areas we might prefer a touch of the lyric and the unexpected.
A concern for Euclidean simplicity did not have to inform the entire
structure.

Mumford was one of the first critics on either side of the Atlantic
to detect in modernism what would become all too apparent in its
more mature manifestations: an almost fanatical fascination with
purity of form. This superficial aesthetic, as he called it, tried to
make the new buildings look as if they respected the machine, no
matter how they were constructed. Le Corbusier proclaimed that
we live in a machine age, so our buildings must be machines to live
in. But it was only a short step from buildings as *machines à habiter*,
Mumford had prophetically warned, to buildings as characterless
air-conditioned boxes. This fatal step was taken by architecture in
the years after the war, and the architect Mumford blamed most for
this was Mies van der Rohe, the disciple of Gropius, who emigrated
to America in the 1930s, and whose ideas captured the leading
schools of design in the years after the war.[27] The elegantly proportioned glass towers he built in New York and Chicago epitomized
the modern style and won the approval of some of the toughest
critics of skyscraper design. "The Miesian skyscraper is the basis of
a superb vernacular," Ada Louise Huxtable has observed, "probably
the handsomest and most useful set of architectural conventions
since the Georgian row house."[28]

But the kind of aesthetic considerations crucial to Huxtable and
most other architecture critics are simply not that important to
Mumford. He certainly considers architecture an art form, but,
unlike painting or poetry, one that must be shaped to useful human
purposes. This is the difference between architecture and most of
the other arts, and this is what he felt Mies had forgotten. Mies's
soaring glass shells have a "crystalline purity of form," Mumford
observed in his famous essay "The Case Against 'Modern Architec-

ture' "; however, "they existed alone in the Platonic world of his imagination and had no relation to site, climate, insulation, function or internal activity."29

But Mumford thought that the best of Mies's transparent towers, like his bronze and glass Seagram Building, were at least lovely to look at, unlike the sterile imitations of them that began to appear in midtown Manhattan in the 1950s. This was a purely corporate architecture, and it had become ubiquitous by the 1960s. "Architecture," Mumford had written in his notes in the early 1930s, "is either the prophecy of an unformed society or the tomb of a finished one."30 We do not have to guess where he placed the new skyscraper architecture.

Even if we must have skyscrapers, they do not have to look the same; and Mumford offered Lever House, on Park Avenue, as telling testimony. An expressive "house of glass" set on a horizontal podium well off the street, this creation of Gordon Bunshaft is Mumford's favorite postwar skyscraper, and it is easy to see why. It is a tall building, but not swaggeringly so; and it is light and spacious inside and outside, as handsome as it is utilitarian. Unlike most office towers it is "designed," Mumford wrote after studying the building when it opened its doors in 1952, "not for maximum rentability but for maximum efficiency in the dispatch of business." At Lever House the modernists' preoccupation with surface is allied to a concern for what goes on inside the building. Unlike the General Assembly building of United Nations headquarters, where the outer offices are reserved for the higher officials, on many floors in Lever House there is no differentiation between secretaries and managers. They have equally good working spaces, with the same amount of light. For years Mumford had watched businessmen trying to outdo one another in putting up the tallest tower in Manhattan. Perhaps the Lever building would begin a new competition, he wrote in *The New Yorker*, "a competition to provide open spaces and a return to human scale."31 Secretly, however, he feared that buildings like Lever House would soon become obsolete. They were simply not high enough to satisfy their corporate backers, or even the leading architects, for that matter, who wanted to go higher and higher. And why not? Tall buildings meant tall commissions.

Mumford's comments on the Lever building indicate that he had no abstract objection to tall buildings. For certain types of uses, the

high-rise might be ideal. "If you have a tall building it must justify
itself by serving some particular use that can only be served by a
vertical organization," he told Graeme Shankland in a 1961 interview in London. The problem with the skyscraper in America is
that it is a means of increasing land values, of making an enormous
profit at the cost of the city itself.[32]

Mumford warned Londoners that summer that their city was
rapidly going the way of New York, just as he had predicted it
would back in the early 1950s, when he urged that London remain a
city of low buildings and ancient boroughs. When a city is built low
to the ground its most notable spires, towers, and domes stand out
and give the cityscape a look of elegance and historic significance, he
observed in a "Sky Line" column on London. But when one high-
rise is surrounded by many others, "height loses its special distinction: esthetically, the buildings cancel each other out and produce a
heaving mediocre mass that flattens out visually any better structures that may remain below."[33] When one tall building is built on
top of another one, architecture itself, in other words, ceases to
matter.

Mumford saw the social errors of modern architecture perfectly
exemplified in one of its most celebrated achievements, Unity
House (*Unité d'habitation*), Le Corbusier's daringly designed housing
development on the outskirts of Marseilles. Mumford first came
upon this building in 1957, five years after its completion, on his
way from Paris to Rome. Always attracted to seaport cities, he found
it difficult to pull himself away from Marseilles' teeming harbor
area, but he felt he had to see the building that was being hailed as
the answer to high-rise housing. As he left the Old Port by cab, past
the docks where fishermen were selling their catch from open stalls,
and out the shaded Boulevard Michelet, the terrain flattened, and he
passed through a wooded area just on the edge of the city. Then
suddenly it loomed up in front of him, a "man-made mountain," a
massive rectangular block of coarse concrete, seventeen stories high,
perched on exposed pillars (*pilotis*). There it stood—alone—in a
spreading expanse of parkland and orchard, a building "liberated,"
as Le Corbusier had boasted, from the ground. It was a striking
structure, darker and heavier than any of the earlier "paper-box"
creations of Le Corbusier that Mumford had seen. It seemed to
Mumford even more striking as he drew away from it and viewed it

against the background of gray jagged mountains in the distance. It was only then that he realized Le Corbusier had meant it to be a piece of outdoor sculpture in high relief. As a visual experience, the building is a clear success, Mumford thought to himself as he walked around it, taking notes. But when the architect who was showing him Unity House took him inside his worst fears were borne out.

Unity House was designed to be a city district in small: it housed 1,600 people and had ample facilities for recreation and shopping. It was the apartments, however, Mumford asked to see first; they would be the true test of the building. As he looked at several of the one- and two-bedroom flats he saw that the very devices Le Corbusier had used to make the building work as a piece of monumental sculpture spoiled the living space within. With the exception of the living room, the ceilings of the rooms were "oppressively low," and fully one-third of the interior space lacked access to daylight, vistas, and open air. The apartments felt closed and cramped, and in the larger apartments the master bedroom was set on a mezzanine overlooking the living room, open to the noises and smells from below, privacy being for Le Corbusier a bourgeois obsession. Even the external success of the building was a partial one, it occurred to Mumford as he went for a second look at the outside. By putting the building on stilts, Le Corbusier had made the open parking lot more conspicuous, but more importantly, he had established no clear relationship between the building and its environment. "Like the Great Pyramid, it might as well be in the midst of a desert, for all the positive use it makes of the natural environment," Mumford penciled in his travel notes that night in his Marseilles hotel. Having seen Unity House, Mumford made it a point to go back to Neubühl, a beautifully designed low-rise housing development near Zurich that he had visited in 1932, and, even on a gray drizzly afternoon it "dazzled" him once again. The buildings were set in parallel rows on a hillside close by the shores of Lake Zurich and were flanked on one side by attractive gardens and terraces. The interiors of the houses were open to the wide expanse of lake and mountain and garden, and the rooms protected privacy as well; there were no false partitions or open mezzanines. Neubühl made Mumford appreciate even more the folly of Unity House, whose outstanding failure he saw as the outstanding failure of modern architecture, a Procrustean habit of fitting the people to the building. Unity House verified Mumford's impressions not simply about modern architecture, but about modern architecture criticism, whose "feebleness" he saw recorded in the lavish praise the critics showered on this "extravagant piece of stage decoration."[34]

It was Le Corbusier, the city planner, however, who drew Mumford's heaviest fire. Although Le Corbusier discarded some of his more doctrinaire notions about city design later in his career, Mumford's mind remained fixed on the earlier Le Corbusier, seeing him, often erroneously, as the source of many of the worst excesses of modernism. In his widely influential Voisin Plan (1922–25), Le Corbusier proposed to raze the run-down historic Right Bank of Paris, preserving only the central monuments, and replace it with a gleaming city of tall office buildings and apartments, spaced far apart so that each glass-enshrouded tower would be surrounded by green space and have a wide and fine view. These freestanding towers were to be linked to one another by a rapid-speed underground and elevated transportation system.

In its pure form this design was applied to only one city, Brasília, the futuristic capital of Brazil; but in the 1950s it became the model for urban rehabilitation in the United States, in part because of Le Corbusier's influence in the top architecture and planning schools, but mostly because his plan, in its various hybrid and grossly distorted versions, fitted the needs of real-estate speculators and corporate clients. It became in time the architecture of the Organization Man.[35]

A city of tall towers, spacious parks, and high-speed motorways, this was Le Corbusier's Radiant City, but it seemed to Mumford to be Robert Moses's grand vision for New York as well. When, in 1962, Mumford wrote that Le Corbusier's "imagination worked like a bulldozer on an urban renewal project" in its eagerness to tear down well-rooted neighborhoods to build his "City in a Parking Lot," he was surely thinking of Robert Moses as well.[36]

When Moses began his enthusiastically acclaimed urban renewal effort in New York City, Mumford was one of the first to question what this massively funded program would do for the people it was supposed to be benefiting. Under the Urban Renewal Act of 1949, old slums were to be razed and their residents relocated in government-subsidized housing. Mumford, however, had an early inkling

of how these displaced slum dwellers were going to be "re-housed."
Two years before urban renewal began in New York he went to the
East Side to see Stuyvesant Town, a housing complex for 24,000
tenants being built by the Metropolitan Life Insurance Company,
with Robert Moses's generous backing. This was to be democracy's
answer to the housing problem; it looked to Mumford like "the
architecture of the Police State." A vast high-rise complex, grimly
and uniformly designed, and patrolled by its own private police
force, it had the word "control" written into its design. Yet Stuyvesant Town was being built not for the poor, but for the younger
middle-class army veterans. Mumford did not have to guess what
Moses's new housing for the poor was going to look like.

There was another problem with this Moses-backed development
that Mumford feared might cast an even darker shadow on the
future of housing in the city. A neighborhood had been leveled to
build Stuyvesant Town, and neither the city nor the Metropolitan
Life Insurance Company had made provisions to rehouse the people
driven from their homes, people either too poor or not "desirable"
enough to become tenants in the new towers. "Only in the Looking-
Glass world of Lewis Carroll," Mumford wrote in *The New Yorker*,
"does any of this make sense."[37]

In the following decade Moses supervised the construction of
hundreds of tower blocks for the poor. These housing projects were
undeniably a step up in the world for tens of thousands of New
Yorkers, from filthy, rat-infested tenements to clean, well-lighted
quarters, but Mumford saw no reason they had to be so unrelievedly
bleak and dull, and planned, as they were, without concern for the
needs of family and neighborhood life. "There is nothing wrong
with these buildings," he wrote after inspecting several of the city's
new public housing projects, "except that, humanly speaking, they
stink."[38] They were based, moreover, on a dubious architectural
proposition: that a tall tower can be a substitute for a neighborhood.
In constructing these projects, most of them without any community facilities, the city was merely "exchanging slums for superslums." These buildings are not as bad as the slums they replaced,
Mumford told a reporter, "but they will be in 50 years."[39]

What is more, these superslums promised to be more dangerous
places to live in than the two- and three-story walk-ups they had
replaced, Mumford predicted; the architecture made sure of that.

The residents of the new elevator apartments were cut off from the protection of neighbors and passersby, while the elevators, long corridors, and wide concrete enclosures of these buildings were sure to become breeding areas for crime. But bad designing aside, the truly tragic thing about this entire urban renewal program, Mumford wrote Frederic J. Osborn in 1958, is that people were making big money on it. The power of eminent domain was placed in the hands of real-estate operators, allowing them to build luxury apartments on property cleared with federal assistance. "Socialization for the sake of the rich accompanied by expropriation and expulsion of the poor!" This had made urban renewal, a term Mumford thought he might have invented, "a filthy word."[40]

What was Mumford's alternative to urban renewal, Moses-style? What kind of city would he have built, had he had Moses's power? The answer to this is contained in the scores of specific suggestions for change he advanced in a lifetime of writing on the problems and possibilities of the modern metropolis. Those who look for an image of the ideal city, his own version of The Radiant City, in Mumford's work, look in vain. "Is there a metropolitan region anywhere in the world that matches your prescriptions for a richer city life?" Graeme Shankland asked Mumford in 1961. "It does not yet exist," was Mumford's immediate reply. Nor can we ever hope to build a perfect city, he added. And, anyway, why should we want to? "Who would want to live in utopia?"[41] The architect Harry M. Weese has perhaps shown the most sensitive understanding of Mumford's way of influencing the future of the city. "[Mumford] speaks of values and of living with nature in a reasonable habitat, of family life, and of self-discipline. Unlike the planners of utopias, he does this without offering solutions but by illuminating the virtues of the good life in humane cities."[42]

Mumford calls the type of planning he favors organic planning. The term, admittedly, is a slippery one, but it is as precise as he can make it; what he has in mind is almost undefinable, since organic planning leaves so much to the future.

In building new cities and in rebuilding old ones, he argues, we must take into consideration the one factor architectural despots and slide-rule planners tend to ignore—time itself. Great historic cities are collective works of art, products of a centuries-long succession of small changes. No truly stimulating city, architecturally expressive and culturally varied, can be brought into being in a single generation or by a single architect or architectural conception. In a city, beauty and diversity are introduced, as often as not, by time, and not by the planner.[43]

Still, Mumford argues that city planning must be guided by carefully thought-out social, biological, and aesthetic principles, and his articulation of these principles remains his outstanding contribution to the art of urban design. Mumford reminds us, however, that city plans must be flexible and open-ended, leaving a wide area of freedom for future changes and improvements. Good planning does not begin with a detailed, preconceived image of the ideal city; "it moves," in Mumford's words, "from need to need, from opportunity to opportunity, in a series of adaptations that themselves become increasingly coherent and purposeful, so that they generate a complex design, hardly less unified than a pre-formed geometric pattern."[44]

Venice's Piazzo San Marco, a square Mumford loved to sit in, is perhaps as fine an example as there is of what he means by organic planning. The buildings of this great public place conform to the styles and needs of the periods they were built in, yet today they merge almost miraculously into a harmonious unity. Variety in unity is the distinguishing mark of Venetian urbanism. A twentieth-century equivalent of such inspired planning would require a close understanding of urban culture, a constant reappraisal of social needs, and a sensitive regard for the integrity of older buildings and neighborhoods.[45]

Mumford's long-standing concern for the architectural heritage of the city has led some present-day preservationists to claim him as the spiritual founder of their movement. Yet though Mumford led the fight to save treasured buildings like New York's Pennsylvania Station, he disliked being lumped with the preservationists. Too often preservation meant "gentrification," where the well-to-do remove the well-settled poor, and in any case, there were many old buildings, in his opinion, that did not deserve to be saved. If Mumford had been an urban planner, one suspects that he would have worked in the spirit of Robert Morris's remark about interior decoration: "Have nothing in your home you do not believe to be beautiful or know to be useful."[46] Indeed, a memorandum he sent to Arturo Tofanelli, who asked his advice in 1954 on the replanning of Venice, is a masterpiece of common sense for planners and preservationists. By all means, he advised Tofanelli, tear down decaying buildings that have no value as works of art or history and replace them with modern buildings adapted to modern needs. This will not ruin the character of Venice; it will preserve it. Above all, do not, like the Victorians, make the new buildings imitations of older ones. This would be "false piety. . . . True piety means respecting the spirit of the old and creating something that does justice to our own needs and our own aspirations, in our own style, for it is in the nature of a living tradition to produce fresh forms." The city that is merely a museum "has already become a cemetery."[47]

This is what Patrick Geddes called conservative surgery—removing decay and encouraging healthy growth without damaging working organs. Mumford proposed an updated form of conservative surgery as an alternative to the ideas of the two prevailing groups of civic renewers: the "touch-me-nots," who would wait until gangrene sets in before consenting to an operation, and those, like Melville's Mr. Surgeon Cuticle, who are so eager to operate that they remove both healthy and diseased tissues, and thereby kill the patient.[48]

Mumford perfectly described what he thought should be the motivating concern of historic preservation in a comment he made about Boston's Faneuil Hall. He was happy, he said, to see old Faneuil Hall and the buildings around it restored to life. He liked the new Boston marketplace, however, "not primarily because of the restored buildings but because a city center, a kind of modern agora, has been created where people of all classes can meet and find interesting things to do."[49]

Imaginative projects like this one, and the Baltimore Harbor Reclamation, gave Mumford some encouragement in his later years. But they would not be enough, he insisted. No urban policy that focused on the city alone could solve the city's problems. Urban rehabilitation efforts would have to be coordinated with related national programs for energy conservation, pollution control, industrial decentralization, and even local agricultural production; and these initiatives would have to be funded by money that presently goes into the overinflated military budget. All this, moreover, would be impossible without a complete overhauling of our present way of life. Toward the end of his career Mumford was still arguing, in Emersonian fashion, that a change in social direction hinged on prior change in morals and values. Relying on planning and architecture, or even money, as solutions to our urban problem is like "applying a homemade poultice for the cure of a cancer."[50]

Mumford made this point most emphatically in his testimony in Washington, D.C., before Senator Abraham Ribicoff's Subcommittee on Executive Reorganization in April 1967. This, and the two essays he wrote as a postscript to his testimony, might serve as his summation on the urban prospect.[51]

The Ribicoff hearings had been called to look into the Model Cities legislation then before the Senate. The morning of Mumford's appearance, the committee room was jammed with spectators, and there was a full array of newspaper and television reporters and cameramen. Mumford began his testimony with Ribicoff alone on the rostrum before him, but as he talked other senators began to drift in, Robert Kennedy greeting him with a smile of recognition. Mumford was nervous, and the glare of television lights bothered him, but he looked poised and self-assured. He had agreed to appear before the subcommittee with reluctance, he began his deliberately delivered testimony, because he knew that his views on the urban problem would not be popular in Washington. He had no easy answers or pat recommendations, and his conclusions, he warned, called for large and long-term changes.

Most of the urban problems America is facing today were evident in the 1920s, he told the committee, when his own concern about the plight of the city had drawn him to the Regional Planning Association of America. He was proud of that organization's efforts to bring these problems to the attention of the nation and of its farsighted proposals for change. Unfortunately, however, every major suggestion the RPAA had put forward was either ignored by government or adopted in partial form and "caricatured or permanently disfigured by forces—technological, bureaucratic, financial, above all financial—that we had failed sufficiently to reckon with." Yet even if the RPAA had succeeded in all it had set out to do, it would not have prevailed against the forces currently threatening the city, he added, pausing briefly for emphasis. Garden cities were built in England, but today that country's urban problems are far worse than they were immediately after the war. Urban planning had not been able to counterbalance the problem of poverty. Yet poverty, he emphasized, in what was surely the most controversial part of his testimony, was not the sole cause of urban decay and disorder. Our most pressing urban problems were traceable to what Mumford described as a massive breakdown in civilized behavior, a breakdown in communal discipline, family closeness, and neighborhood solidarity. Poverty and racism certainly contributed to this problem, but even some of the most destitute and racially persecuted immigrant families in the New York of his youth, he pointed out, had held firm to these stabilizing values. The disintegration of our cities, Mumford warned in Spenglerian tones, is a sign of a disintegrating society.

At the time Mumford was appearing before the Ribicoff committee, the federal government was considering spending $50 billion over a ten-year period on the cities. He must have shocked the senators when he cautioned them to think twice before they voted through such a massive appropriation. With this money as attractive "bait," the powerful, profit-hungry housing industry, with its systems experts and computers "[will] design housing units even more prison-like in character than those we now have." It would be better to "experiment with small measures and small units, until you have the time to prepare better plans and to organize new public agencies to carry out those plans." For the moment, "go slow," advice that must have cheered the hearts of the conservative senators who misunderstood the radical drift and intent of his advice.[52]

This was the spring of 1967. American cities had been torn apart by racial rioting the previous summer ("A vomit of criminal disorder and imbecile destruction," Mumford called it in a letter to Jerry Lachenbruch), and more rioting and arson were predicted for the coming summer.[53] In this crisis atmosphere it was certainly not Mumford's intention to stand in the way of any immediate federal efforts to address the problems that had set off these riots, and he made this clear to the senators in the questioning that followed his statement. But the success of these much-needed short-term measures to provide jobs and better housing, he later explained in a published elaboration of his testimony, hinged upon a change in the motivating aims of our current urban renewal efforts.

He had meant to say "start slow," not "go slow," and it is clear that he had in mind an urban initiative of greater audacity, reach, and cost than anyone in Washington envisioned, a program aimed at restoring the stabilizing values of family and neighborhood that present federal welfare and housing policies were helping to undermine. He had seen enough of what Robert Moses had done for the poor in New York to make him distrustful of any instant cash program coming out of Washington. While many urban experts looked to Washington for solutions to the urban problem, Mumford saw Washington itself as part of the problem.

What few people who heard or read Mumford's testimony realized is that he was proposing a program not just for minorities or for the city. He saw the deterioration of human values as a pervasive national problem whose roots lay far too deep to be affected by any well-meaning urban legislation. In this sense, as he said, there is no black problem, no Puerto Rican problem; there is "a human problem." "The time for action," he concluded his testimony, "has not yet come. But the time for fresh thinking on this whole subject is long overdue"—the kind of fresh thinking he himself was giving to the problems at the very time he appeared before the committee.

Just after completing *The City in History*, Mumford had begun what would become a decade-long effort to answer the question he raised in rhetorical form in his statement to the Congress. Why had he failed to influence his age? Why had most of his urban proposals either been ignored or transformed into policy in a bastardized form? His search for an explanation took him back 5,000 years, following a clue he had uncovered while researching the origins of the ancient city. The explanation he arrived at took him two massive books to elaborate, and the criticism and counsel he offered in these wide-sweeping studies he considered his "passport to the future."[54]

26

Harvest Time

They are white already to harvest.

—ST. JOHN, NEW TESTAMENT

After completing *The City in History* Mumford looked forward to a period of solitude and reflection, to what he saw as "a harvest time." Instead of reseeding the ground, he would gather and sort the late crop on the land "long ago planted," completing a number of projects he had begun earlier in his life. He was now nearly sixty-six years old, and though he felt hale and healthy he began to fear that he was working against time and might leave unfinished the autobiography he thought would be his final book. So as he sailed home in the summer of 1961 from his memorable tour of Great Britain he wrote an outline of his life, a decade each day, in the bold and beautifully flowing Italian chancery script he had recently taught himself. "This is the time," he wrote, "to tidy up the edges of my life."[1]

But first he was obliged to spend a semester at the University of California at Berkeley, an appointment he now regretted having accepted. That September he and Sophia moved into a sprawling redwood house on a pine-wooded hillside a mile above the university campus. Their neighbors were William and Catherine Bauer Wurster, who had found the house for them, and just around the corner were other old friends, Alexander and Helen Meiklejohn. The house had wide windows on every side that looked out into the tall trees, and Sophia fell in love with it. She also enjoyed having neighbors "busy enough with their own lives so that we don't get in one another's hair, but with leisure and friendliness enough for short, rewarding visits," she wrote in her diary after settling in. "Just the kind of life I've always yearned for." Lewis came to like their living situation almost as much as she did, but that year his life was so full that he didn't have the same need for good neighbors she did.[2]

Mumford made his presence felt as soon as he arrived on campus. At the University Meeting that officially opens the Berkeley academic year, he delivered an empassioned speech against the nuclear arms buildup and the fallout shelter campaign—the "save me first movement," he called it—then gathering momentum in California, taking his theme from Shakespeare's *King Lear:*

> *The weight of these sad times we must obey*
> *Say what we feel, not what we ought to say.*[3]

The overflow audience gave him a standing ovation, and so many people requested copies of the speech that it was mimeographed for campus distribution, and a local political action group printed over 5,000 copies. This speech, and a later one he gave at a university convocation attacking the collusion between university-based scientists and the government defense establishment, made him something of a hero to campus radicals. His convocation address, "An Apology to Henry Adams," was taped for television and shown on educational stations across the country, and afterwards he was swamped with invitations to speak to college and civic groups. His Berkeley students and colleagues urged him to stay on for another semester, and Sophia, who had dreams of settling permanently in California, would have welcomed this. By December, however, he was eager to get back to Amenia. He had no desire to be a leader of student radicals, he wrote Stearns Morse from Berkeley; their "beatnik-existential" response to the world left him cold. Besides, speechmaking and political activity sapped his strength and put strains on his health.[4]

Nonetheless, this was a surprisingly fulfilling interlude for him, and as he left California in January he had only one real regret—that he and Catherine Bauer had not been able to come closer together, not as lovers but as friends. They had been alone together on only one occasion, when Catherine drove him to a planning conference at another campus. On their way back to Berkeley they stopped at a restaurant for dinner, and not a personal word was spoken between them. There was not even a light-spirited allusion to their old affair, and Catherine seemed uneasy in his company. "We no longer sparked each other," he later commented in his journal, "and this was simply not due to the fact that we had grown old."5

When Lewis returned to Amenia he decided, at Sophia's urging, to declare a "moratorium" on political writing for at least a year. He lacked the temperament and constitution for sustained public activism, and Sophia was becoming concerned about his health. On several occasions in recent months he had become aroused almost to the point of physical illness because of something he had read in the newspaper. He had voted for John F. Kennedy in 1960 only because he loathed Richard Nixon, and he felt that in his first year in office Kennedy had brought the country dangerously close to war with the Soviet Union over the issue of Cuba.6 He knew that he would be in no mood to work on his autobiography if he continued to speak and write on public issues, so he promised to avoid mentioning politics even in his correspondence. But this was a vow he knew he could not keep. Even his most casual letters to old friends on occasions of celebration—birthdays, Thanksgiving, Christmas—are filled with astringent commentary on Kennedy's "appalling" foreign policy. "No one can tell me," he wrote at the tail end of an otherwise gossipy Sunday morning letter to Stearns Morse, "that these murderous raids . . . [on Cuba] are not the works of Central Unintelligence. . . . Did I say I wasn't going to say a word [about politics]?" he added half-apologetically. "See how hard it is. We are living among madmen. . . . Stop the world: I want to get off."7

Still, his self-imposed restriction on political writing did help him to relax, as did his familiar Amenia surroundings, where his entire household was arranged to support his work. Sophia would have enjoyed the occasional company of houseguests, but Lewis preferred that they invite no overnight visitors, not even her family. The older he became the more he seemed to need complete solitude in order to concentrate properly. For this reason they stopped having household help, except for an occasional cleaning woman. The mere presence of one extra person in the house is "disturbing" for Lewis, Sophia wrote her niece Evelyn on one occasion, gently explaining to her that they could not have her as a houseguest, as much as they both loved her company.[8]

That winter and spring Lewis occupied himself with several of his "harvest time" projects—a series of lectures on technology and culture he had agreed to give at his alma mater, the City College of New York, several introductions to books written by friends, and a preface to a new paperback edition of his Melville biography. After writing in the morning and reading in the afternoon, his usual disciplined routine, he and Sophia would go for a short walk, and then broil steaks or chops in the fireplace of their old-fashioned country kitchen. After dinner they would sometimes linger at the kitchen table and play chess, or Lewis would read aloud to her from Emerson's *Journals*. "I used to live with Emerson," Sophia once remarked; "Emerson, Lewis, and me."[9]

When spring arrived Lewis began working in the garden every afternoon. His big project for that year was to carve a path through the thick growth behind their house so that they would have a walk for their advanced age, when they were confined to their home acres. That July, after finishing the walk and putting his old notes and correspondence in order, he returned to his autobiography, beginning with a chapter titled, appropriately, "Roots in the Countryside."

This was to be a different kind of autobiography than the one he had begun writing in 1956. He had deposited that manuscript in the safe of his publisher, Harcourt, Brace, and when his new editor, Jeannette Hopkins, read it in early 1961 she urged him to bring in more information about his personal life. She thought it a warm and beautiful book, but she wanted him to give a fuller picture of Sophia and of their life together, and she hoped he would have something to say about his father and mother. He had not mentioned his parentage or his earliest upbringing, portraying himself instead as "a child of the city." "New York," he wrote in an opening chapter, "exerted a greater and more constant influence on me than did my family." That might have been so, but Jeannette Hopkins did not think it sufficient reason to leave his family out of the book altogether. Mumford, however, needed no prodding on this point. He had already made up his mind to give a full and frank account of his personal life, far more self-revealing, he began telling friends, than the famous confessions of St. Augustine and Rousseau.[10]

He had deep secrets he had kept from even his closest friends and members of his own family, and now he decided to divulge them, although he doubted that a book of such complete candor could be published in his lifetime, or perhaps for some years afterwards. The two women he was passionately involved with in the 1930s were still alive and had families with whom he and Sophia were friendly. But he was worried most of all about his daughter Alison's possible reaction to the book—and he was not thinking merely about his sexual indiscretions. He had not yet told Alison about the facts of his birth, despite her and Sophia's persistent efforts to get him to do so. This was especially upsetting for Alison, who kept waiting for him to tell her about the "grandfather" she knew nothing about. On one occasion, shortly after Alison's eighteenth birthday, Lewis had come close to telling her about his parentage. He asked her to walk with him to Troutbeck Lake, and not far from the house he stopped suddenly, turned toward her, and said that he had something very personal and, for him, painful to tell her. "At last," Alison remembers thinking at the time, "he is going to tell me about his parentage." "Long ago I had an affair with Catherine Bauer" were his next words, and then he continued walking, his features frozen, and said no more.[11]

Mumford kept for posterity a complete record of his life—massive files of correspondence and notes, descriptions—year by year, or often day by day—of the changing state of his soul. Yet up to this point he had revealed almost nothing about his personal life in print. What he had published showed little of the searching honesty he applied to his conduct and motivation in his private notes, and in his day-to-day life he had let few people into his confidence. He was not the kind of man who sits around with friends over drinks and bares his soul. Even to those who knew him best, Lewis Mumford was something of a mystery.

But now he was determined to unburden himself, and was somewhat relieved, as well—or so he claimed. Like Havelock Ellis, whose autobiography he read just before resuming work on his own, he worried that he would ruin by his honesty the very image that he was trying to create in his book—of a man who had lived in accord with his deepest ideals. On the other hand, he had been reading a book about Paul Tillich's life which exposed Tillich's sexual transgressions, and he confided to a friend that, unlike Tillich, he would not want to leave it to someone else to discredit his philosophy "by digging up a dark side of my life."[12]

This was not an easy book for him to write, all the more so because he needed Sophia's help to do so. Together, they had to go over the most difficult periods of their marriage, for he wanted to get everything exactly right. He allowed Sophia to read "the most scarifyingly candid" parts of the manuscript, and to go through his old love letters.[13] On one occasion, when she was reading his letters to Catherine Bauer he asked Sophia if this was too painful for her, and her reply surprised him. This "sort of thing I can face," she said quite casually. She had put it behind her. Then she smiled and assured him that a blameless life was not her idea of a good life.[14]

But there was something else at work here. Sophia had always wanted to take a stronger part in his work. An experienced editor and a fluent writer, she typed and proofread his manuscripts, and he usually read to her his work-in-progress to get her reaction, but now she was being drawn into the creative process itself, and she and Lewis found that they worked together beautifully.[15]

Although Lewis brushed up on his past by reading old notes and correspondence, he did the actual writing without his notes in front of him, in order to produce a book that had the feel and form of a novel. As he worked on the book he remembered Patrick Geddes's words that a good life "is a dream of youth, fulfilled in old age," and by that standard he thought he had led a full and authentic life. Old friends he wrote to for help in piecing together his life story provided warming reinforcement. "I believe you are the *only* man I know who has answered his own high calling, and kept his own true course, through the jungle of problems . . . that crowd in upon us all," Geroid Robinson wrote him. And from the Abbey of Gethsemane, in Kentucky, came a letter from Thomas Merton telling him that his books had helped Father Merton to tighten his "spiritual purposes" and clarify his "motives for not being too closely a part of 'the world.' "[16] Supportive letters like these were immensely important to him at this point in his life, for he had lost many of his closest friends in recent years and was about to lose another. As he was working on his autobiography in Amenia, with the autumn sumac turning from scarlet to crimson, Van Wyck

Brooks lay dying in his home in nearby Bridgewater, Connecticut, too enfeebled to recover from a succession of emergency operations to prolong his life.

What made Brooks's impending death especially difficult for Mumford to bear was that he and Brooks—through a forty-two-year-old friendship—had not come to know each other more intimately. While they loved and respected one another, on Mumford's side it was the love and respect a son feels for a father he admires from afar but cannot get close to, and Brooks at times seems to have considered Mumford less as a flesh-and-blood person than as some sort of spirit or force at work in history, the prophet, as he once hailed him, of the coming "Age of Reconstruction."[17] A walled-in, remote man, Brooks was never able to interact easily with Mumford as a friend, and Mumford could never bring himself to discuss his private life and personal problems with Brooks, as he did with Henry Murray. He also continued to withhold criticism of Brooks's multivolume history of American literature, which he found shallow and far too sanguine, lest that criticism shatter the ever-so-fragile psychological balance Brooks had reachieved after his breakdown in the late 1920s. So even when they confined their serious discussions to literature—as they did late in their friendship—they were rarely candid and searching exchanges. "At the end I felt sadly that, despite our love and admiration for each other, we had never met," Mumford wrote Stearns Morse after Brooks's death in May 1963, "and that if we had really met freely, we would have disagreed as often as we would have found ourselves of the same opinion."[18] True enough, only Mumford put the wrong meaning on his own remark. Such disagreements in close conversation might have broken down the barriers and transformed their friendship into the kind of relationship they both wanted it to be. So when Mumford grieved for Brooks, he grieved as well for the kind of friendship they might have had.

Brooks's terminal illness also brought Mumford to ponder his own end. He did not want to die as Brooks was dying, held for months in a helpless limbo between life and death by the so-called miracles of modern medicine. When Lewis and Sophia went to visit Brooks just before he died, what they saw, to their common horror, was "the mere wraith of a man, enfeebled, shattered, dismantled, as if he had just emerged from prolonged torture in a concentration camp."

Brooks was living on goat's milk and honey, although he somehow managed to struggle to his study every morning to do an hour's work. "His spirit," Mumford wrote after that visit, "was withdrawing like a wounded animal to the deepest cavern of his being," and he was too hurt to cry out. There was no reason, Mumford thought, to prolong life like this. Brooks's medical bills were over $500 a week, a terrible drain on his family—all this "only to die a dog's death." He and Sophia were so horrified by Brooks's last days that they eventually consulted a lawyer and drafted a statement about their views on dying, to be given, at the proper moment, to their doctors if either of them became terminally ill. Under no circumstances did they want to be subjected to life-sustaining interference.[19]

Brooks's illness provoked another strong subterranean reaction in Mumford: it made him feel guilty that he had discouraged Brooks from writing a biography of him. Despite Mumford's protestations Brooks had pushed ahead with this project just before he became seriously ill, determined to raise to sainthood the contemporary thinker to whom he felt in closest sympathy. In his own autobiography Mumford confesses to having had grave misgivings about this project, yet he does not say what was behind his apprehension. It is clear from his letters to other friends, however, that he felt Brooks did not know enough about his life to do an accurate or inspired portrait, and what he was really implying is that only he could execute such a portrait. He didn't need Brooks to "serve as a sort [of] John the Baptist" for his book.[20]

Though Brooks never finished his biography of Mumford, neither was Mumford able to finish his own autobiography that year, as he had planned. Brooks was ever on his mind as he tried to complete his work, but other factors entered more strongly in his decision to put the book aside once more. That spring he fell into a deep depression as he struggled to tell the story of his life in the years between his affair with Alice Decker and the death of his son Geddes. He had no wish to relive this period in his mind, but his editor, Jeannette Hopkins, wanted a full autobiography. So he pushed ahead into this emotional minefield, and then he stopped and could go no further. The strain and tension became "almost unbearable."[21]

The painful events of his life did not disturb him so greatly when he was younger, he confided to Waldo Frank, because they were canceled out by new hopes and plans; even the worst sins and errors were "retrievable in the mere flow of life." But now what he faced in his past could no longer be outlived, and hence remedied or merely left behind. His past had become, as it were, a kind of death.[22]

He did manage, as has been mentioned, to write an account of his affair with Catherine Bauer, for he still had pleasant memories of their relationship, and it was just after he went to see Brooks for the last time that he showed these chapters to Catherine. Her refusal to allow them to be published, and her claim that she had never really been in love with him, brought him near to physical collapse. This would not be, could not ever be, the unsparingly honest autobiography he claimed he wanted to write, and at this point he decided that even if he were to finish the book and to publish it in his lifetime, he would also leave out the chapter dealing with the "secrets" of his birth. Complete candor was not worth the emotional havoc it might provoke, and here, undoubtedly, he was thinking about himself as well as Alison. "My apologies to St. Augustine and Rousseau!" he wrote in his notes. "I [now] understand their difficulties and condone their evasions!"[23]

That spring he retreated into himself, convinced that he did not have even Sophia's full sympathy. She had told him she could understand Catherine Bauer's reaction to his chapters on their affair, for in reading what he had written about their marital relations in his autobiography she saw that his view was not always that of the other person about whom he was writing.[24]

All this was made worse by a sudden realization that he had crossed over into old age. He was a grandfather now, Alison having given birth to a girl in October 1962, and while he took to his new role as a grandparent with enthusiasm, he was bothered by the mounting signs of physical decay. His last few front teeth had to be extracted; he noticed a swelling in his knee; he began to have pains in his back; and, worst of all, he began to lose vision in his left eye. At first he thought he simply needed glasses, but after a while he realized that the core of his vision was gone, and this affected not just his reading but his motor coordination in typing. He went to an eye doctor, who told him that he had a small cyst, and prescribed medication, but it had no apparent effect, and he thought he would lose his sight completely. He kept this from Sophia, but he could not keep it from himself. "Loss of teeth, loss of hair, loss of mobility, loss of vision: this is old age; and though one has watched it in others and in a sense steeled oneself to it in advance, the actual facing of it is a shock."[25] As he wrote this in his notes he must have been thinking that his creative days would soon be coming to an end.

That spring, however, the condition in his eye disappeared and his sight returned. This was an enormous relief to him, but it was work on a new book that finally pulled him out of his despair, a book on technology and culture he had begun in the summer of 1962 as one of his "harvest time" projects. He had been working on it, on and off, while he was writing his autobiography, and now he gave it his full attention. By July he was well into it, writing steadily and reading furiously, and feeling as if he had been restored to life.

His original theme for the book was one that had been claiming him for some time. When he finished *Technics and Civilization* in the mid-1930s he realized that he had sidestepped an immensely important question. He had described the modern age's overvaluation of technology, but he had not sought to locate the origins of this "myth of the machine," the widely held view that technological progress and the expansion of power in its various forms—military, financial, and political—were the chief goals of the human endeavor. He had, however, addressed this question in the chapters in *The City in History* dealing with the appearance of the first power systems in the ancient cities of Egypt and Mesopotamia, and this new book, like so many of his previous ones, developed more as a restatement of his answers to an important question than as a reconsideration of his questions. In the first centuries of urban life he had discovered what he believed to be the driving assumptions and aims of all large-scale technology for the past 5,000 years, arguing that some of the greatest, if not the most benign, advances in technology have been made by centralized organizations that seek to expand power tremendously in order to achieve control over both human communities and the natural environment. This was his theory of the megamachine, and in an essay he published in 1963, "Authoritarian and Democratic Technics," he emphasized the fundamental antagonism between such big political-military systems and older and smaller systems, based mostly on human skill and animal energy, which were less powerful but more resourceful and resilient. The great megamachines of the United States and the Soviet Union were, in this view, monstrously magnified reincarnations of older, less sophisticated bureaucratic-military models. But where the center of authority in the old system was an actual person, the absolute ruler, in the modern megamachine the center of authority was the system itself. "Unlike Job's God, the new deities cannot be confronted, still less deified."[26]

These were the spinal ideas of the new book Mumford was planning. He had his conclusions; he merely had to find a way of substantiating them. But for this very reason he had a difficult time proceeding. The kind of book he initially had in mind, a swiftly written elaboration of older arguments, did not really challenge him. Almost as soon as he began concentrated research in the summer of 1963, reading the multivolume history of technology edited by Charles J. Singer, E. J. Holmyard, A. R. Hall, and Trevor I. Williams, and rereading old Egyptian texts, new questions and themes began to fill his head. His mind started working in its familiar way, making fresh connections and seeing new combinations, and before he knew it he was off—committed to the kind of big book he had sworn he would never undertake again.[27]

He had a hundred new ideas, but the organizing concept that seized him was a theory he had only sketchily suggested in previous books: that the development of the mind and its greatest creations, language and ritual, were more important to human evolution than the introduction and utilization of the first primitive tools, that "minding," as he put it, was more important than "making." In his speculative rereading of history, he would try to shift the emphasis from physical survival to cultural and mental development, and he had a strong personal reason for doing this, which he revealed in a letter to Benton MacKaye. If his theory was correct, he told Mac-Kaye, then man still has sufficient resources to alter the direction of modern technology, and is not, as Jacques Ellul argues, a passive victim of technological society. We might call this hypothesis "the primacy of the mind," and to prove it Mumford had to reinterpret the history of human origins. By the time he was finished with this book "the corpses of a lot of dead ideas will be strewn all over the stage," he predicted to MacKaye, "as in the last scene of Hamlet," and a clearer picture of humankind's development will emerge.[28]

That fall he continued to work on the book as a fellow at Wesleyan University's Center for Advanced Studies in Middletown, Connecticut, where he and Sophia lived in a large house provided by the university. They both needed a break from the winter's solitude in Amenia, and Lewis's responsibilities were minimal: one informal seminar a week. He had secretarial help, a private study, and they had a chauffeured car when they needed it. The campus was lovely—it had the most beautiful beech trees Mumford had seen anywhere—and it seemed an ideal place for him to work. But away from his desk in Amenia he found it difficult to write, so he spent his working hours in the university library, exploring the new subjects of anthropology and linguistics his book had opened up for him. By December he was eager to get back home, and he decided not to return for the second year of his appointment. He wanted to spend uninterrupted months on the book that had suddenly taken over his life.

The following year was one of the most productive of his life, as he completed the greater part of what was probably his most intellectually demanding book, working in fields far from his former interests. Indeed, he wrote so well that year, felt so strong and spry, that he was surprised, sometimes, when he looked in the mirror and saw the old man staring out at him. The inner man and the outer man no longer corresponded. When he looked into shop windows and saw his reflection, he would feel as if some sinister character out of a Poe story was shadowing him. He had been "watching that fellow for a long time," he wrote one of his friends, "and sometime I'll turn around and take him by the throat, if that's the only way to get rid of him."[29] What made old age doubly difficult for him to bear was the disappearance of familiar outer landmarks that had always given him a sense of inner direction. New aluminum-sided ranch-style houses were going up on the Leedsville Road, and huge cement trucks came roaring past his house at all hours of the day. Even nature itself seemed to be conspiring against him. A thick growth of cedar trees had covered the pastures he used to walk, closing off the finest distant views. The familiar sights of his youth were disappearing, and Mumford counted the loved ones he had lost among these disappearing landmarks.

In September 1964, Sophia's father, "Father William" as the fam-

ily affectionately called him, died at the age of ninety-four. He had
been coming to Amenia regularly to spend part of the summer and
had developed a close relationship with his son-in-law, who enjoyed
his colorful stories about life back in Russia or in turn-of-the-
century New York. When they went to see him on his deathbed,
Lewis showed Father William the Medal of Freedom he had recently
received from President Lyndon Johnson, the highest medal
awarded to an American citizen, and William was deeply touched.
Too weak to move, he motioned his son-in-law to come closer and
said: "Lewis, don't be discouraged. Your work is for the future." He
died the next day, and Lewis buried his ashes in Leedsville under
the bench where he loved to sit and watch the sky and dream.[30]

Two months later Catherine Bauer died. We know Lewis's reaction; Sophia's was less complex. "I am very sad," she wrote in her
diary, "for Catherine was my true friend."[31]

That winter in Leedsville Mumford worked on *The Myth of the
Machine* with furious energy, refusing all the usual invitations to give
lectures and speeches. He seemed a driven man and was determined
to stay out of the public eye until his book was completed. As he
grew older he complained of feeling like an automatic toaster, ticking
ever more rapidly, and it was this sense of a speeding-up process that
kept him from traveling to the places he wanted to visit—Japan,
China, Israel, Mexico. In January he even refused a personal invitation from Lyndon Johnson to appear at the inaugural proceedings.
When the White House called him back, asking him to reconsider,
he again politely declined, though Sophia urged him to go, feeling
that it was time that he "emerge and play the part of the 'wise man'
he so aptly can." He would not even break away from his work that
January to take part in a memorial service for his old friend Alexander Meiklejohn, asking Sophia to call Meiklejohn's wife, Helen,
to tell her that, as much as he loved her husband, his book, at this
time, had to take precedence.[32]

But the next month he did stop writing, and well before *The Myth of
the Machine* was completed. President Johnson had just announced
another massive increase in American involvement in Vietnam, and
as a recent recipient of the Presidential Medal of Freedom, Mum-

ford felt he had to speak out publicly against the government's Vietnam policy. He even considered returning his medal, but Sophia persuaded him otherwise. "This is the Bay of Pigs disaster all over again," he wrote Stearns Morse that February, "and it can only terminate in another Dien-Bien-Phu." He had now lived to see three kinds of Democratic presidents: "A New Dealer, a Fair Dealer, and a Double Dealer."33

Mumford was one of the first American intellectuals to speak out publicly against the war, at a time when only three United States senators were opposing the President. Although he would later write disapprovingly of the street violence of young radicals, his thundering attacks on Johnson's Vietnam policy express the aroused moral outrage that fueled those demonstrations of defiance.

After much debate with Sophia about what to do, he sent telegrams of protest to Senators Robert Kennedy and Jacob Javits, and to the President himself; then he addressed a scorching three-page letter to Johnson, copies of which he mailed to a dozen or so newspapers. Sophia had urged him not to send an earlier letter he had written to Johnson—it was too angry, she thought, to be effective— but it is difficult to imagine how he could have written an angrier letter than the one he did send, attacking the President for risking this country's future on a war we could not win. It was Johnson's "hypocrisy" that really made him burn, his insistence that the war was being fought for democracy and freedom. "Your professed aims are emptied of meaning by your totalitarian tactics and your nihilistic strategy. We are ashamed by your actions, and revolted by your dishonest excuses and pretexts." Bill Moyers, Johnson's aide, later told Mumford that the President received two letters from public figures immediately after his announcement that he would begin bombing Hanoi: one from Senator George McGovern, the other from Mumford. Johnson answered McGovern's letter but ignored Mumford's.34

Only two newspapers printed Mumford's letter—the *St. Louis Post-Dispatch* and the *San Francisco Chronicle*—although he did receive a flood of supportive letters and some invitations to lead "teach-ins" at colleges and universities. He refused these offers, feeling he would be exhausting himself to no purpose. If he attended it would look as if he had incited those demonstrations, whose

effectiveness, he felt, depended on their spontaneity and local backing. He continued to stubbornly insist, moreover, that "the single
unaided voice, if not used too often, carries a longer way and does its
job more effectively—with a little luck." For these reasons he would
remain "aloof," he told friends who were urging him to take further
action.35

But like Melville's Billy Budd, he felt the need to make some kind
of dramatic gesture of protest. That May he had his opportunity.
Early in the month he was awarded the Emerson-Thoreau Medal of
the American Academy of Arts and Sciences. The awards dinner
was in Boston, and, for Mumford, this should have been a festive
occasion. Many of his Cambridge friends were in attendance, and of
all the honors and awards he had received thus far this one meant the
most to him, for it was for his contributions to literature. Mumford,
however, broke into the evening's mood of celebration by fiercely
attacking Lyndon Johnson's Vietnam policy. Two weeks later he
went to New York, tired and bothered by a severe cold, to chair the
annual awards meeting of the American Academy of Arts and
Letters. As president of the academy, a select group of fifty members chosen from the wider membership of the American Institute
of Arts and Letters, he knew full well that it is academy policy to
avoid any mention of political issues at its spring ceremonial, but he
also knew that there would be nearly a thousand influential people
in the audience and scores of newspaper reporters.

At a luncheon preceding the meeting he chatted amicably with
old friends Walter Lippmann and Reinhold Niebuhr, giving no hint
of what was to come; he had told no one except Sophia what he
intended to do. When he took the podium to call the meeting to
order his face was pale and his features were tense, but there was not
a quiver of nervousness or indecision in his voice. He realized full
well, he began his prepared remarks, that this was ordinarily a
joyous occasion, but "I cannot artificially manufacture an atmosphere of joy for this meeting, when under the surface of our ritual a
rising tide of public shame and private anger speaks louder than my
words, as we contemplate the moral outrages to which our government . . . has committed our country." What he had to say, he
emphasized, was his own opinion; he was speaking not as president
of the academy, but as "a private citizen." Some would say that this
was not the time and place for these remarks, but if he did not speak

out at just such a public occasion, he said, he would be false to his vocation as a writer.[36]

At this point there was applause and some scattered boos from the audience, and then, just off to his right, Mumford heard someone calling out in a shrill, angry voice. It was the painter Thomas Hart Benton, who was on the stage to receive an award. He was shouting for Mumford to stop—"I'm not going to listen to this tripe"—and after people tried to quiet him down he shot up out of his seat and stormed out of the hall. Mumford continued with his speech, and when he finished he turned the meeting over to George Kennan, president of the institute, left the auditorium, and went directly by train to Amenia with a fever of 101 degrees.[37]

He and Sophia had agreed beforehand that she would stay for the reception that followed the meeting "to witness the repercussions of his blast." A few people came up to her to congratulate her for Lewis, but an angered John Hersey told her that Lewis had used the platform as an act of self-indulgence. Later Mumford learned that George Kennan and some other members of the academy felt that he had misused his office and violated the spirit of the occasion and the procedures of the academy by airing his personal political views.[38]

The following day Thomas Hart Benton, a friend of Mumford's for over forty years, resigned from the academy, charging that "there are some people in that organization . . . who have entirely too much sympathy to Communist views."[39]

Later, Mumford wrote to George Kennan, explaining that, while he was sorry for the distress he had caused the academy and the institute, he would not apologize for his "breach of etiquette." He respected the academy's conventions against such actions in ordinary circumstances, but these were not ordinary circumstances. "To go on with our usual routines and rituals . . . is to behave like the crowds who thronged into the arena to witness the games, when the Vandals were hammering on the gates of Augustine's Hippo."[40] However extreme the analogy and the language, this letter honestly expressed Mumford's intentions and outrage. He had anguished over giving this speech; his conscience had moved him to act. Furthermore, as he later reminded John Hersey, his academy speech was perfectly consistent with what he had been doing for the past thirty years, breaking into the accepted routines of his "sleep-walking contemporaries by reminding them of the kind of world they are actually living in." Mumford's public demeanor might have been that of an Oxford don, but beneath his outer reserve was a soul of fire; he was a man whose court was always in session.⁴¹*

After his speech before the academy Mumford was eager to withdraw again from public life until he had finished his book. He had been a lonely figure in February 1965 when he penned his first indictment of Johnson's war policy; now the protest had broadened to the point where it was becoming a full-scale movement. He had played a part in triggering this reaction; his aim now was to complete his book. Still, he could not wall himself off from the world, much as he might have liked to. He anxiously followed the course of the war in the newspapers (he still had no television), and Vietnam kept popping up in his writing in the most unlikely places, as, for example, in one of the final drafts of *The Myth of the Machine* when he remarks that one of Ashurbanipal's more outrageous boasts of power "sounds uncomfortably like a Pentagon publicity handout."⁴² Mumford knew many people would be troubled by these recurring allusions to Vietnam in a book about ancient history—his British publisher, Frederic Warburg, even warned him that it would hurt sales in the United States—but he couldn't keep Vietnam out of anything he wrote at this time. "A book that is meant to last," he told a friend, "must be nourished partly by the ordure its own period produces."⁴³ Even Mumford's Christmas letters to his closest friends opened with solemn reports on the progress of the war: "Who, in his right mind, could say [Merry Christmas] this year, after reading in detail what the Air Force has been doing in Vietnam, firing on villages in the open, for safe, easy practice before the young pilots push their buttons on military targets—if any."⁴⁴

Mumford took part in several meetings of independent intellectuals that Erich Fromm convened in New York in 1968, and he gave early and enthusiastic support to Senator Eugene McCarthy's bid to unseat Lyndon Johnson as the Democratic presidential candidate, and to the candidacy of an antiwar candidate for Congress in his home district, but this was the extent of his organizational efforts.⁴⁵ He was put off by the raucous anti-establishment style of the youth

---

* In 1968, Mumford resigned in protest from the academy when he learned that Thomas Hart Benton had been received back into membership without informing him first or asking Benton to apologize to him for insinuating that he was in sympathy with the Communists. He remained a member of the institute.

movement, and ill at ease in the company of these shaggy, irreverent insurgents. Although he claimed he did not dislike long hair, on more than one occasion he was heard to say, when referring to ill-kempt radicals, that the habit of mutual grooming was one of the first signs of man's mammalian ancestors beginning their upward climb. But it was the retaliatory violence of the young that bothered him the most. In the pursuit of civil rights for black people and an end of the war in Vietnam, he preferred the tactics and approach of Martin Luther King. Mumford participated in several peaceful street marches against the war in Cambridge, but he vigorously opposed the forceful tactics of campus radicals against the university. He found himself in strong opposition as well, as he wrote to an academic friend, "to those sympathetic liberals who are trying to atone for past errors and negligences by making the even greater blunder of surrendering to force or to the threat of force." He saw the "shilly-shallying" tactics of college administrators in the face of SDS threats as a more recent example of "the corruption of liberalism" he had described in the 1930s, when liberals showed a "willingness to submit to the Nazis rather than risk the need for using force in opposing them."[46]

A determined minority of the young had, he believed, performed a moral service their elders had shirked. They had helped to restore civil rights, democratize the university, and challenge an immoral war, often at great personal risk. "You have awakened our country," Mumford declared in a statement he sent to be read at a student protest meeting at the University of California at Berkeley, where police had used strong-arm tactics against peaceful demonstrators, ". . . but I am concerned with . . . your reaction to violence." Although his words were not read at the rally, for reasons that will become apparent, this is Mumford's most revealing statement on the youth movement. It is a plea for moral conversion and self-discipline, a call to the young to change their ways and alter their purposes, to begin a process of moral self-examination. "No angry shouts: no ugly threats: no childish obscenities: . . . no mutilation of your minds by drugs."[47] No words Mumford ever uttered better explain why he never became a cult leader of the young, like Herbert Marcuse. Much of what he said was perfectly reasonable, but the problem with this kind of advice is that self-examination must lead eventually to outward action, as Mumford himself often argued, and his advice was to the first order of business only. What were the remoralized young supposed to do when they reached the new state of consciousness and self-discipline Mumford called for? What form should their protest take? On issues of tactics and strategy Mumford continued to be infuriatingly vague, probably because he himself did not know the answers to these questions.

In the summer of 1965, just after his academy address, Lewis and Sophia left for a short vacation in England and Scotland. He was to receive an Honorary Doctor of Laws degree from the University of Edinburgh, a ceremony he eagerly looked forward to. He had turned down eight or nine such honorary degrees, but this offer he accepted almost immediately: Edinburgh was Geddes's old city, the city Mumford associated with the beginning of his own lifelong interest in urban culture. But aside from two glorious days in Edinburgh it was a disastrous trip. The weather in England was horrid, and Sophia took ill and was bedridden for several days. When Lewis also caught a cold he told her he wanted to call off the rest of the trip, but Sophia insisted that they stay; there were so many places she thought they should see. He reluctantly agreed, but for the rest of their stay was in a terrible mood, which he did not snap out of until well after their return from England.[48]

That October he turned seventy. Two years before Sherman Paul, a professor of American literature with whom he had been in correspondence for several years, had proposed to put out a *Festschrift* in honor of his seventieth birthday, a collection of personal testimonies from Mumford's friends. Although Mumford eventually called off the project, deciding that his own autobiography must precede any book dealing with his personal life, as his seventieth birthday approached he began to wonder how many of the people Paul had contacted two years before would remember the day he was to turn seventy and be moved to write to him. Except for Martin Meyerson, however, who phoned him from Berkeley, only a handful of friends sent birthday greetings, a great blow to an old man who carried over from childhood a delight in birthdays.[49]

Later that same day he was moved to write a note about old age. He was still, at seventy, a fit and well-set-up man, clear-eyed and full of energy, but this willful, powerful man had not been able to stop age from taking at least part of its toll. His fantasies about sex and his responsiveness to women other than Sophia had almost completely disappeared; even his nightdreams were "barren of sex." He had begun to forget familiar names and events. He was making more errors in his typing and handwriting. He was sleeping five or six hours now, not his usual eight, and he needed glasses for reading and for target shooting. But he found that the worst feature of aging, is "the knowledge that, if one lives longer, things will get worse, not better. . . ." Only now did he completely understand what Sophocles meant when he said: "Count no man happy until he is dead."[50]

He was driven to write this doleful note by the difficulty he was having that morning, and all that week, writing *The Myth of the Machine*. This was not, he thought, the "normal frustration of all writing, but something extra, due to inadequacy . . . and I feel that this is probably the last time I shall be able, if indeed I *am* actually able, to tackle such a large, complex, energy-exhausting theme."[51]

He wrote this from Cambridge, Massachusetts, where he was a visiting scholar at Harvard University. The following day he spoke on the Vietnam War to an audience of Harvard students and faculty. The hall was jammed to the doors, and though it was a bitterly cold evening people were standing outside, straining to hear. As Mumford approached the podium he realized that he had forgotten the lecture notes he had been working on for the past two days. It did not matter; he was never more in command of his material or his audience. No one stirred or spoke during the lecture, which continued for an hour and a half. It was a masterly performance by an old man who feared that he was losing his touch. The next year in Cambridge he finished his book.

27

The Myth of the Machine

*If mankind is to escape its programmed self-extinction the
God who saves us will not descend from the machine: he will
rise up again in the human soul.*

—LEWIS MUMFORD

The Myth of the Machine: Technics and Human Development arose from
Mumford's sobered view of the age in which he had lived.* It is a
search for an answer to what he considered the central question of
the century: Why had technological progress brought with it such
catastrophic ruin? This is the same question Oswald Spengler had
raised in *The Decline of the West*, a title that exactly describes Mumford's reading of recent history. Mumford was a witness to what he
thought were the worst twenty years of humankind's history, the age
of Hitler and Hiroshima, and he wanted an explanation of what had
gone wrong. Was the modern association of power and productivity
with mass violence and destructiveness merely coincidental?[1]

In this book Mumford puts the problem of the misuse of technology into the widest possible historical context: the modern "religion" of technology, he argues, is based upon a gross misconception
of human origins and human nature. Furthermore, our modern
doctrine of progress, with its association of technological advance
with human advance, is merely a "scientifically dressed up justifica-

---

* Mumford in 1970 published a second volume, *The Myth of the Machine: The Pentagon of Power*,
hereafter referred to as *The Pentagon of Power*.

tion" for practices the ruling classes had used since the time of the pharaohs to gain and hold power.[2]

This last insight led Mumford's analysis of technology in a new direction. Up to this point he had been principally concerned with the impact of technology upon culture, but in *The Myth of the Machine* he moved to an analysis of the anatomy of technological complexes—of their origins and inner workings as well as their historic consequences. This gave his writing greater weight, breadth, and explanatory power, but often at the expense of the prose.

Having already described Mumford's theory of the megamachine, we might inquire here as to how he sought to substantiate it. As ever, he worked more like an artist than a historian, and was less concerned with writing so-called objective history than with writing usable history, history that serves as a guide to life.

In canvassing the history of early technology for a seminar he gave at MIT in the mid-1950s, Mumford had been impressed by the ability of the ancient Egyptians to turn out perfect machine work without the aid of complex machines. The colossal stones of the pyramid of Gaza are cut to an optician's standard of precision and they were hauled across the blazing desert and placed into position without the aid of a wheeled wagon, pulley, or windlass. This is machine work, yet the Egyptians had no machines. But it struck Mumford that the pyramids *had* been built by a machine, one hitherto unrecognized by archaeologists because it was composed entirely of human parts, a highly centralized and coordinated labor system whose chief assembling agent and prime mover was the deified king. An understanding of the origins, inner workings, and line of descent of this megamachine and the power myth that grew up around it would open the way, Mumford felt sure, to a fresh understanding of the origins of our overmechanized culture and of the fate of modern man. Since the historic record disclosed so little about the megamachine, he would be forced to piece together an argument for its existence from the most fragmentary evidence. To prove this, his boldest and perhaps most original historical hypothesis, he would have to cut into territory even the most radically speculative archaeology had avoided. What he eventually uncovered led to still further questions and to even more challenging conclusions. In observing the building of this book, using as evidence

Mumford's own notes and correspondence, we have a wonderful opportunity to watch the way his mind worked, as he leads us back through the centuries in search of the earliest evidence of human behavior.[3]

In reconstructing ancient history Mumford relied heavily on the brilliant archaeological work of V. Gordon Childe. But where Childe emphasizes the part played by inventions like the plow and the military chariot in the emergence of civilization and the first military states, Mumford argues that the critical tools that led to the assembly of the megamachine were inventions of the mind: mathematics and astronomical observation, writing and the written record, and, finally, the religious idea of a universal order derived from observation of the heavens, an idea that gave divine authority to the king. The megamachine emerged when the idea of an absolute cosmic regularity and authority was fused by the king's astronomer-priests with the notion of a human order whose rulers shared in its godlike attributes. By associating the king with the supernatural order of the heavens, the king's priests greatly augmented his political authority. At this juncture the sky gods, particularly Ra, the sun god, became preeminent. By the end of the first month of his research, Mumford was convinced that the megamachine was born of this first union of sun worship and political absolutism. He now had an idea, he realized, that would take him two books, not one, to develop, for this idea gave hint of a later relationship between modern science (another form of sky gazing) and political absolutism.[4]

The Myth of the Machine: Technics and Human Development is a brilliant but erratically organized book, filled with both flashing genius and repetitious moralizing. Mumford's learning is staggering, and he develops a number of new ideas, but in large sections of the book he is merely pouring new water over old tea leaves. His central argument is often difficult to follow, as he cuts back and forth across immense spans of historic time, drawing risky, sometimes far-fetched analogies between earlier ages and our own. Readers and reviewers found one argument particularly arresting—and controversial: Mumford's claim that the modern power state is an updated version of the first megamachine. Two devices, he insists, were essential to make both megamachines work: expert scientific knowledge and an elaborate bureaucracy for carrying out orders. In both systems, moreover, scientific knowledge had to remain secret—a priestly monopoly—secret knowledge being the key to all systems of total control. In the ancient city, the king's word was transmitted by a loyal corps of scribes, messengers, stewards, superintendents, and gang bosses—the first primitive bureaucracy. With the priests and the army, they formed a level of interlocking power just below the king; they were the brains and nervous system of a power complex that organized scattered populations and put them to work on a scale without previous precedent.

Mumford sees this "invisible machine" as the archetype for all later complex forms of mechanical organization, though later the emphasis shifted from human operatives to more reliable mechanical parts. The megamachine anticipated the central features of modern production: the interchangeability of parts, the external direction of work, the centralization of scientific and technical knowledge, and the regimentation of the work force. Our modern machine age had its origins, then, not in the Industrial Revolution of the eighteenth century, nor even in the Middle Ages, as Mumford had argued in *Technics and Civilization*, but at the very outset of recorded history, in the organization of a machine composed of men made to endure forced labor at mind-dulling, repetitive tasks in order to ensure the power, glory, and material well-being of a small audacious elite.[5]

The belief that this machine was "absolutely irresistible—and yet ultimately beneficial," provided one did not oppose it—Mumford calls the myth of the machine. "That magical spell still enthralls both the controllers and the mass victims of the megamachine today." But the great lesson (and this book is packed with admonitory advice) Mumford hoped to drive home to his readers was the role of religion, in this case king-worship, in holding together the first power complex. Once the polarizing force of kingship was weakened, the original megamachine collapsed. This revolt against the grim impositions of kingship occurred, Mumford had first argued in *The Transformations of Man*, between 900 and 600 B.C., "when new voices arose, those of an Amos, a Hesiod, a Lao-tzu deriding the cult of power" and proclaiming values antithetical to those of the power systems. These teachers of righteousness thundered against "gigantic images, imposing buildings, gluttonous feasts, promiscuous sexuality, human sacrifices," and preached withdrawal, fasting, and meditation. The values they, and later prophets like Jesus, Buddha, and Mohammed, fostered eventually broke the magico-religious spell of the megamachine. Their words had the force of a thousand armies. Thus, just as the megamachine had been built on a stronghold of human belief, so, when that belief was withheld, it buckled and fell. Such, at least, was Mumford's reading of a long and complex span of human history, an interpretation that surely reveals as much about his mind and moral outlook as it does about the ages he describes.

For many centuries after the revolt of the axial religions, the megamachine was confined almost solely to the military, but toward the end of the Middle Ages it began to be reassembled along modern lines. Capitalism, with its emphasis on calculation and record-keeping, the rise of political absolutism, and the introduction of the clock, prepared the way for a new megamachine on a scale that not even Cheops could have thought possible. Only one further thing was needed to polarize the new components of the megamachine: the reappearance of the sun god. In the sixteenth and seventeenth centuries, with Copernicus and Kepler acting as accoucheurs, a new sun god was born. And it is at this breaking point of history that Mumford concludes volume one of *The Myth of the Machine*. Volume two, *The Pentagon of Power*, picks up the story here, describing the rise of the modern megamachine.[6]

When Mumford submitted volume one of *The Myth of the Machine* for publication he had already written a good part of what would become *The Pentagon of Power*, his most passionate and polemical work. It is an all-out assault on perverted science and the technological state, an indictment so massively unrelenting, however, that it draws attention away from Mumford's governing purpose: to prove that human nature is biased toward autonomy and against submission to technology in any of its forms. While most reviewers found *The Pentagon of Power* the better of the two books, perhaps because it is a less difficult work and deals with history and events familiar to most readers, *The Myth of the Machine: Technics and Human Development* is a more original and important book. It is largely, of course, about the evolution of the megamachine; but there is a subtler and more significant argument in this book, one crucial to understanding everything Mumford ever wrote about technology.

In *The Myth of the Machine* Mumford attempts to undercut the idea of *homo faber*, of man as primarily a toolmaking creature, a myth, he contends, that is behind the modern age's total commitment to technology. In overweighting the role of tools and weapons in early human culture, social theorists from Thomas Carlyle to Karl Marx to Thorstein Veblen had distorted the actual course of evolution and played directly into the hands of the apologists of the modern megamachine, Mumford asserts. The word "asserts" seems perfectly appropriate here because, like a priest's assertion of the existence of the Holy Trinity, Mumford's hypothesis is impossible to verify from material evidence. In challenging the myth of the machine he constructs a myth of his own, one closer, he insists, to the facts of human development than modern anthropology has provided thus far.

Reaching back to the argument of *The Conduct of Life*, Mumford emphasizes the role of language in human development. "But even before language could be invented," he wrote Henry Murray early in his research, sharing with him some of the new discoveries he planned to bring into the book, "man had to lay a basis for it in the expressive use of his entire body: so if man was anything fundamentally he was a dancing, acting, mimicking, ritual-making animal."[7] Play, not work, had first made us human, an idea Mumford found verification for in Johan Huizinga's *Homo Ludens*. In this part of man's development, his dreams and playful fantasies, his magic, rituals, totems, and taboos contributed fully as much to his creativity as his primitive tools. From the beginning man was a dream-haunted animal, and the richness of his dreams enabled him to escape from the restrictions of a purely animal existence. The dream, along with the sexual drive, was responsible for our creativity, but it was likewise responsible for much of our destructive behavior.

Primitive man, Mumford argues in the most difficult but intellectually engaging chapter of *The Myth of the Machine*, was a dreaming animal, but a deeply disturbed one; and the source of his most irrational fears was his own hyperactive brain. Building on the views of Alfred Russel Wallace, Mumford points out that man's overgrown brain, stimulated by his liberated sexual activities, put him at the mercy of unconscious promptings, some of them destructive and suicidal. Before he could advance, man had to find a way to tame the demons of the psyche. In this task ritual was crucially important. The performance of ritual—the constant repeating of movements and gestures in the company of others—laid down a pattern of order eventually carried over into language and other expressions of human culture. Where Thorstein Veblen regarded ritual as mere waste, a practice that slowed down productivity, Mumford sees it as the key to our humanness.[8]

In the early 1930s, Henry Murray had written to Mumford suggesting a clue to the role of ritual in human development. "I have always been puzzled by the widespread and spontaneous appearance of regular repetitive acts—touching things a certain number of times, counting steps, repeating words, etc.—in children, usually boys. In adults, it appears as a symptom associated with an unconscious sense of guilt. It is related to magic and religious ritual but is more fundamental than any of them. You find it in the infant who wants a story repeated with exactly the same words—it is the most elementary form of mechanization and is in contrast to the whimsies of impulse."[9] In *The Myth of the Machine* Mumford builds on this idea, suggesting that the mechanical order of ritual may have kept early man, literally, from going insane.

Ritual created order and meaning where none had existed, and, later, restored them when they were lost. It allowed man some control over nature and his own irrational promptings. Even some of man's later mechanical proclivities seemed to derive, Mumford wrote Murray while working on *The Myth of the Machine*, from his early fondness for repeating the same gestures, and "uttering the same cries long enough to attach some meaning to them."[10] This led Mumford to the argument that mechanization itself had its origin in ritual, ritual being based upon repetition, order, and predictability, an argument that suggests no original separation between art and technics.

Primal satisfaction in repetition thus laid the basis for language as well as ritual. Knowing that he lacked the linguistic qualifications for the job, Mumford nonetheless attempted a hypothetical reconstruction of the birth and development of language, agreeing with Leslie White that the ability to symbolize was the most formidable human achievement, the basis and substance of all human behavior, every advance in human culture, even toolmaking, depending upon advances in language and the symbolic arts.*

So while the making of fire and weapons contributed immensely to human development, even more important, from Mumford's perspective, was the slow evolution of the social heritage expressed in ritual, religion, social organization, art, and, above all, language. From the time he dwelled in primitive caves, man possessed an all-purpose tool more important than any other—his overdeveloped brain; and he used this excess mental energy to make himself human and to humanize his world. Man, with his great gift of self-transcendence, had been a controlling figure in cultural evolution, and this leaves the future wide open. Even the megamachine, after all, was largely a product of the mind.[11]

But in Mumford's view, man, the controller, is both a superrational and a deeply irrational being. (It was probably Nazism that demonstrated to him that these traits could exist side by side in the same person, the same nation.) With Freud, Mumford sees the soul as the sphere of an eternal conflict between two forces, one constructive and life-promoting, the other destructive and life-denying. Since his biography of Melville, Mumford considered the handling of these ambivalent gifts the supreme human problem. Before man can tame his technology he has to tame himself, and the first step toward control is the defeat of the demons.

History, humankind's collective memory, can help us to do so, Mumford insists in *The Myth of the Machine.* The cultural historian can serve as a kind of midwife to the soul, drawing out the deeper sources of humankind's demonic behavior, knowledge of a problem being essential to its solution. To break free of the myth of the machine, we would first have to bring it clearly into view and unmask its principal fallacies. But in *The Myth of the Machine* Mum-

---

* Noam Chomsky provides scholarly verification for this idea that language developed independently of toolmaking and was probably more important. In his eagerness to overthrow the so-called Marxist idea of man as a toolmaker, Mumford relied too much on the disciples and popularizers of Marx and Engels, instead of going directly to writings of Marx and Engels. In *The Origin of the Family, Private Property and the State* Engels, for example, argues that the appearance of speech was the most important event of prehistory. And as Erich Fromm pointed out to Mumford after he read *The Myth of the Machine,* Marx was influenced by Vico; and for Marx the concept of work, not the concept of toolmaking—which he called the Yankee idea of Benjamin Franklin— was essential.

ford attempts to do much more than this. He suggests a therapeutic routine to set the patient—civilization—on the path to recovery. He apparently hoped to be minister, as well as midwife, to the soul.

What had kept humankind from going mad in the past? Ritual, along with other stabilizing influences like family, land, and fulfilling work, the so-called village virtues Mumford had been emphasizing in his work since his first confrontation with fascism in the 1930s. As the world became more disordered and irrational, the old stabilizing props and points of support assumed even greater importance. And so did history itself. Escape from the past, escape into an unknown future in the name of progress, is "an excellent prescription," Mumford once remarked, "for sending mankind to the looney bin."[12]

All this helps to explain why Mumford was attracted in old age to Carl Gustav Jung, Freud's disciple and leading rival. In Jung's life and ideas, he found corroboration for his own ideas on the eternal importance of ritual and tradition. While researching *The Myth of the Machine* Mumford read at least twice Jung's autobiographical *Memories, Dreams, Reflections,* and at the same time he read Ernest Jones's biography of Freud. Freud and Jung had located the territory where the demons lurked, but Jung, in Mumford's estimation, offered sounder advice for controlling them.[13]

Mumford had seen Jung only once, at a lecture Jung gave on a visit to the United States in the 1930s, but the image he left endured. "He gave a quite commonplace lecture, yet he redeemed it by his presence, which seemed that of a shrewd old peasant, his own archetypal Wise Old Man, a man whom one would go to for advice in the barn if not in the clinic." Yet in reading Jung's autobiography Mumford discovered another, more vulnerable man, afflicted in midlife by a severe neurosis. What particularly struck Mumford, however, was not so much Jung's revelation about his illness, but the "ancient therapy" that saved him, a therapy different from the psychoanalytic method he and Freud had been using with their patients. Jung's description of that crisis and cure bears emphasis, for it reveals as much about Lewis Mumford as it does about Carl Jung.[14]

Jung writes that at the time he was working on the history of fantasy and dreams he "needed a point of support in 'this world,' I may say that my family and my professional work were that to me.

It was most essential for me to have a normal life in the real world as a counterpose to that strange inner world. My family and my profession remained the base to which I could always return, assuring me that I was an actually existing, ordinary person. The unconscious content could have driven me out of my wits. But my family, and the knowledge: I have a medical diploma from a Swiss university, I must help my patients, I have a wife and five children, I live at 228 Seestrasse in Küsnacht—these were actualities which made demands upon me and proved to me again and again that I really existed, that I was not a blank page whirling about in the winds of the spirit."[15]

Family and work had performed the same function in Freud's life, as Mumford pointed out in a self-revealing essay on Freud and Jung that he wrote while working on *The Myth of the Machine*. Both physicians were family men, and work was the blood and bones of their lives; Freud maintained this driving discipline through a sixteen-year battle with a horribly painful cancer of the palate, until his death at the age of eighty-three. "As with primitive man, work for them was at once a personal function, an economic necessity, and a compulsive ritual whose daily repetition served, like the prayers of the faithful, to alleviate anxiety: above all, this life-nurturing routine was a means of keeping in check . . . the inordinate, crazily destructive impulses that they might have found it impossible to control had they been 'free'; that is open to the demonic incursions of the unconscious."[16] Put more simply, family and work gave them a solid hold on reality; and Mumford might have gone on to say that they had done the same for him, a villager and family man who took to heart the timeless admonition of Hesiod: "Whatever be your lot, work is best for you."[17] Mumford must have found Jung's advice on the importance of family and marriage especially reassuring, for Jung, too, had freely experimented in erotic relationships, although in *Memories, Dreams, Reflections* Jung did not disclose much about his long-standing affair with Antonia Wolff, a psychiatrist and former patient, at the request, reportedly, of surviving family members. Mumford was disappointed by this omission. After his relationship with Catherine Bauer he was intrigued by Jung's remark to Freud that "the prerequisite for a good marriage . . . is the license to be unfaithful."[18]

Mumford's reading of Jung's life is a lesson on the perils of fast-paced change. All the points of support that had helped Jung to keep his balance—clear and agreed-upon values, recognizable faces and landmarks, steady vocational duties—Mumford saw threatened in our growth-driven age. But how were we to hold on to these traditional values? Here is where Mumford found Jung more helpful than Freud. Jung saw the unconscious as not merely the "hiding place of the demons but the province of angels and ministers of grace."[19] These archetypes, as Jung called them, were forces of health, unity, and ethical direction, ideas and social practices thousands of years in the making. To try to escape from our past, to ignore these values and experiences, is to mistake forward movement for retreat and rout. Thus, the final task Mumford leaves us in *The Myth of the Machine* is to recover the autonomous functions, orderly processes, and stabilizing associations we were surrendering to the machine.*

In the spring of 1964, a week before *The Myth of the Machine* was published, the Mumfords sailed for Italy, where Lewis was to receive an honorary degree in architecture from the University of Rome. "You will not need this honor," the architect Bruno Zevi had written him, "but Italy does."[20] He would also be lecturing at the Jung Institute in Zurich. He had shown such uncanny insight into Jung, Jung's former colleague Dr. Jolande Jacobi informed him in the invitation, that many members of the institute wondered if he had undergone a Jungian analysis.[21] Just before he and Sophia boarded the S.S. *Michelangelo* in New York, Lewis confided to Sophia that he desperately wanted his new book to be a smashing critical success. He was physically and mentally exhausted and needed the injection of energy this would give him in order to finish *The Pentagon of Power*. Indeed, he was so anxious about the book's reception that he planned to disregard his old rule about not reading the reviews of a book of his until at least a year after its publication.[22]

When he and Sophia returned from Europe the news on his book was not good. Advance sales had topped 10,000, but by midsummer they had dropped dramatically. The book actually received some

---

* Jung, like Mumford, was also interested in the role of religion in helping us to master our anxieties, whereas Freud equated religion with rank superstition, and argued that the religious impulse was based on fear and guilt.

superlative praise; in a letter to Mumford, Erich Fromm called it "the most important analysis of human development" he had ever read.[23] But Mumford, rarely satisfied with anything but complete approval, fixed his attention on reviews like the one that appeared in *Time* characterizing his critique of technology as "slightly hysterical," and calling him up for urging a reversion to Neolithic culture: "Mumford would perfect man with weaving, pottery and thatched-village anarchy."[24]

Too proud and sensitive to ignore this kind of facile criticism, Mumford worked himself into a cold rage. The reviewers were "spiteful" and "hostile" because they were not intelligent enough to understand his ideas. People hated all he stood for since the alternative was to hate themselves! Mumford did manage to muster the energy to return almost immediately to *The Pentagon of Power*, but he would go on with his work, he wrote in his notes, because he enjoyed the effort of writing, not because he thought his ideas would change the shape of things. In this spirit, he scanned the board and made his next move.[25]

That fall and winter, while he worked on *The Pentagon of Power*, he was glum and withdrawn, and began, again, to refer to himself as the Invisible Man. When his birthday arrived, and he received only a handful of congratulatory letters and telephone calls, he took it as a further sign of his lack of influence. News of the Vietnam War continued to haunt his days and nights, lowering his vitality and making it doubly difficult for him to work. "I feel today the way decent Germans must have felt under Hitler," he wrote Frederic J. Osborn, ". . . but I am just as helpless as they were to do anything about it." When he looked at the contemporary cultural scene he became even more depressed. There were concerts where no recognizable music was played, movies without meaning, and verse whose words bore utterly no resemblance to language.[26] Earlier in the century the twisted images of Dadaism had, "like a loud fart in a polite salon," called attention to the inrushing madness. But the seismographic sensitivity of Dadaism had given way to the "vacuous imbecility" of pop art, or "madhouse art," as Mumford called it. "What prospect has any book of mine of surviving in this insane world?" All his efforts of the past fifty years had proved powerless to prevent this "tide of madness from sweeping over every nation."[27]

Mumford took the current state of the world as a pathetic indication of his own ineffectiveness as an exponent of renewal, but the world *had* proved him right as a prophet, though this is not how he wanted to be remembered.[28]

A psychiatrist who knew Mumford only casually once remarked to Sophia at a party that he had never met a man so little ridden by anxiety about himself, "his inner man." Now that inner certainty began to crack a little, and it was not a pleasant sight for Sophia to witness, particularly the growing embitterment and the agonizing rationalizations that accompanied it, as when he began to insist that he had helped to bring on "this neglect" because he was "playing a little game of my own, to find out if it was possible to survive on one's merits alone, without any effort at publicity and self-promotion." If this was the game he had been playing he had actually won it, for the irony is that he complained of being forgotten at a time when his work was in greatest favor, when he was being showered with awards for his contributions to architecture, planning, literature, and technology. But for every accolade he received he would point to an area where his influence had been ignored, seeing the whole world, in the year or so after the publication of *The Myth of the Machine*, in various shades of black and gray. Instead of feeling honored that *The Myth of the Machine* had been nominated for a National Book Award, for example, he became bitterly dejected when he learned that the award had gone to another book.[29]

It is a measure of his concern about his "invisibility" that he finally decided to do something about it. He had more important things to say than "charlatan[s]" like Buckminster Fuller and Marshall McLuhan, and he would start to say them "in the limelight."[30] He would go public and see how well he fared.

That September he had prepared for publication a collection of his essays on the modern city, and directly before the book went to press he agreed to make almost a dozen television appearances, including spots on the *Today* show and the Mike Wallace program. He also made detailed suggestions to Harcourt Brace on how to advertise *The Urban Prospect*, and helped to write the jacket copy and some of the publicity flyers. If the book didn't sell 20,000 copies in the first six months after it was published, he told William Jovanovich, he would regard this effort to seek publicity as a complete failure.[31]

The book did sell reasonably well, around 8,000 copies in the first few months, but not nearly as well as Mumford thought it would, and he found the reviews lukewarm. He also thought that he projected the wrong image on television. Others said he looked at ease and in complete command; he felt he looked like an ancient and pompous sage. "All this has caused me to review carefully my whole position," he wrote disconsolately in his journal. The results of this monthlong self-review were to have a profound effect on the tone and spirit of *The Pentagon of Power*.[32]

After seeing what had happened to two very different books, *The Myth of the Machine* and *The Urban Prospect*, he thought he knew at last what the trouble was: he was living in a culture that rejected completely the values and ideals he stood for. Those who favored "senseless order and willful chaos" were in command of the intellectual scene, he wrote Stearns Morse that June.[33] Here, of course, he was referring to writers and artists on the Left, not to those in favor of the status quo. Later that summer he resumed work on his book, which, not surprisingly, turned into an all-out attack on the culture that he considered responsible for his failure to gain wider influence as a writer. *The Pentagon of Power* is belligerent in tone and piercingly polemical. Analysis turns too often to assertion, considered criticism to sweeping condemnation. The enemy is misapplied science and technology—nothing new here; but it is the culture that Mumford believes they have brought about, whose corruptions run from television to LSD, that comes under the heaviest fire, the culture of "pop art, junk sculpture, organized sadism, pornography" and the theatrical Marxism of the young radicals. These self-styled Marxists, Mumford remarks in *The Pentagon of Power*, reject the so-called power complex at the same time that they are becoming hooked on its products and services—driving to rock concerts in fast cars, swelling their egos by appearances on television, obliterating their minds with drugs and "druglike music electrically amplified." It was, Mumford had convinced himself, this ideological breach between himself and the millions of Americans tied, directly or indirectly, to the megamachine, not any avoidance of publicity on his part, that had made him an invisible man.[34]

In February 1970, Mumford delivered the manuscript of *The Pentagon of Power* to his publisher, just two months after receiving the

Leonardo Da Vinci Medal of the Society for the History of Technology. No book of his had been written under worse conditions. Even after he overcame his brief crisis of confidence, he had painful problems with his infected teeth; he suffered a bad fall, tumbling headfirst down a flight of library stairs; and he had a recurrence of his eye problem, which left him able to read and type only with great effort. It is no wonder that he considered it a "miracle" that he had been able to complete the book, but after he finished it he had some doubts about its merits. For fully two months after he turned in the corrected galleys he would get up every day at dawn and read through his copy, searching for mistakes that could be corrected in the page proofs. He was undoubtedly searching as well for evidence to assure him that this was a fine and solid book. When he finished rereading it he concluded that it was the best book he had ever written.[35]

Just before it was published he received some confirming support for his opinion. The editors of the Book-of-the-Month Club accepted it as a main selection, guaranteeing big initial sales, and William Shawn, the editor of *The New Yorker,* called Mumford in Amenia to say that his magazine wanted to publish more than half the book in four installments, for which he suggested the sum of $40,000. "It is a majestic and awesome work and will, I know, endure," Shawn told him.[36] Mumford also learned that Gerald Holton, the Harvard physicist and historian of science, would review the book on the front page of *The New York Times Book Review* section. Holton and his wife Nina were among his and Sophia's closest friends in Cambridge, and Holton was a thoughtful critic of socially irresponsible science. Mumford couldn't think of a better person to review the book.

Several weeks before his review was published Holton saw Mumford on the Harvard campus and handed him an envelope containing a draft of his review and a letter explaining why he had written it. It was a strongly critical essay, and Mumford was devastated by it, feeling that Holton had betrayed him and had tried to sabotage his book. If the review had been unsigned, he later told Sophia, with hurt in his eyes, he would have assumed it to have been from the hand of a personal enemy.[37]

Holton had apparently agreed to review *The Pentagon of Power* thinking that he would find himself in general sympathy with Mumford's ideas, but in reading the book he discovered, to his "horror," he explained to Mumford, that he had fundamental disagreements with large parts of the argument. He was particularly concerned that this book, which was sure to reach a large readership, would "be used (and abused) by many who have been looking for any weapon they can find against the rational (and its close relative, the scientific) side of man's imagination." In the youth movement Holton saw such a revolt—a turn from the rational to the emotional—already well in the making. "The current of the time had caught up with [Mumford]," he argued in his review, "[and] he will now find himself at the head of a popular parade that may adopt his new book as a battle flag."[38]

Holton told Mumford that he realized this review could put their friendship in jeopardy, but he decided to go ahead because he thought that Mumford would understand that he had to say what he believed.[39]

But Mumford did not see it that way, and he thought that Holton's review grossly misrepresented the book's central thesis. "The book [Holton] has castigated exists only in his own mind," he wrote in a furious letter to *The New York Times*, breaking, for only the second time in his life, his practice of never answering reviews of his work. *The Pentagon of Power* was not an attack on science and scientists, as Holton argued, "but an attack upon the Power Complex's threat to undermine all human values and purposes, including those of science itself." Mumford's conversations with a number of scientists at Harvard and MIT convinced him that Holton's criticism was provoked by his and a Nobel Prize–winning colleague's fear that the current popular reaction against science, given support by this book from a world-renowned scholar, would result in large cuts in funding for scientific research. This animus against his work by some scientists was made clear to Mumford when a physicist seated next to Sophia at a dinner of the American Philosophical Society in Philadelphia told her that her husband should be thrown out of the society for his vicious attacks on science and scientists.[40]

The morning Holton handed Mumford his letter, Sophia Mumford had called Nina Holton to invite her and her husband to dinner. Needless to say, on mutual consent, without ever mentioning the

letter or the review, they agreed to "postpone" the dinner. Nina
Holton did invite the Mumfords to celebrate Christmas with them,
"but neither of us," Sophia remarked in her diary, "believed in it."[41]

Mumford felt vindicated, however, when he learned from his
editor that his book was receiving extravagant praise and selling
enormously well. "I am fortified against poverty, rejection and dis-
paragement," he wrote jubilantly to William Jovanovich, "but I have
no armor to protect me against success. Some sleepy sentry seems to
have permitted me to get inside The Pentagon of Power without
showing my suspicious credentials."[42]

The Pentagon of Power is a work of energy, invention, and vast
erudition, a masterly summation of ideas Mumford had been developing for decades. For those broadly familiar with his work it is,
however, a disappointing book—repetitive, loosely organized, and,
too often, ponderously moralistic—but for readers approaching
Mumford for the first time, it is *the* essential book for understanding
his mature outlook on science, technology, and the modern political
state.

The book opens with a brilliant portrait of the Age of Exploration,
that unrivaled burst of scientific creativity and terrestrial discovery
that occurred between the fifteenth and nineteenth centuries. One
mode of exploration focused on the starry heavens, the other on
untracked regions of the earth, but very early in the book it becomes
clear that Mumford's main interest is in the former—an exploration
concerned with the orderly motions of the planets, with timekeeping, and with repetitive physical events and physical laws. Here
Mumford summarizes everything he has written about man's relation to science and technology, providing impressive buttressing for
his ideas from the intellectual history of science. It is true that he
does not attack science itself, his heroes being scientists such as
Charles Darwin, Claude Bernard, Clerk Maxwell, Lawrence J.
Henderson, Walter Cannon, Niels Bohr, and Michael Polanyi.
Nonetheless, this is one of the most devastating attacks on the
fundamental methods and operations of physical science in the
English language. Its spirit and temper is that of Rabelais's famous
remark: "science without conscience is the ruin of the soul."

A new world opened to man in the sixteenth century, Mumford argues, and the transforming event was a religious phenomenon—the return of the ancient sky gods, most prominently Atum-Re, the self-created sun god. Copernicus made the sun supreme once more, the center of the universe, and science, which made this shattering discovery, became the only trustworthy source of authentic knowledge. The machine-like order and regularity scientists found in the heavens, in the regular revolution of planets around the sun, became a new earthly ideal. Unwittingly, innocently to be sure, astronomy and celestial mechanics set the foundation for a political absolutism and an industrial discipline similar to that which existed in the pyramid age. It would be four centuries, however, before the master invention of the pyramid age, the megamachine, could be fully assembled again, and the remainder of Mumford's book is concerned with tracing that slow process of reconstruction. In describing the reassembly of the megamachine, Mumford attacks more directly than he ever had before the founding spirits and historic heroes of modern science—Copernicus, Kepler, Galileo, and Newton—along with allied "mechanistic" thinkers like Descartes, Locke, and Leibniz.[43] (This surely is what made *The Pentagon of Power* such a deeply distressful book to Gerald Holton.)

Scientists like Galileo and Kepler were humanistic in the fullest sense of the word, Mumford concedes. They were anxious to bring a clarifying order to a world beset by superstition, theological controversy, and rampaging religious persecution, and they were unaware that their work would point to a devaluation of the human personality and to a separation of the artist and the scientist. Their "great crime" was one of omission, not commission. Away from their work they were fully balanced individuals, but in their pursuit of so-called scientific truth they traded the totality of human experience for that small portion which could be observed and described mathematically. Mumford completely rejected Galileo's distinction between primary and secondary qualities, between verifiable reality and mere sensory illusion. In dismissing subjectivity, and surrounding their work with a halo of objectivity, Galileo, and those who worked in his wake, dismissed man himself. It was the depersonalized worldview that emerged from that one-sided point of view, not mechanical inventions alone that led to the development of the second megamachine, and to many of the miscarriages of modern science.[44]

Mumford did not put forward this argument without some inner hesitation and qualifying doubt. Among his closest friends in Cambridge were Nobel Laureate scientists like George Wald and Carl Cori, men with broad interests—cultured, widely read, and deeply human. But the problem they faced, Mumford once remarked in a television interview, was that they were often prevented from bringing these qualities into their scientific work. "They have to do less scientific work and live a life in which the various parts of their existence play into each other."[45] What was needed, Mumford believed, was an ethical doctrine of science that recognized science's own subjectivity.

In describing the evolution of science, and the second megamachine, Mumford reveals his deep, almost anarchistic fears of the overorganization of modern life. Confined initially to the armies of absolute rulers like Peter the Great and Louis XIV, megamachine values have edged their way into almost every area of human activity over the course of the last two centuries, he argues. First to succumb was work itself, as the ideas of the power system systematically captured the workshop after 1750. The essence of industrialization, Mumford perceptively points out, is not the introduction of machinery on a large scale but the monopolization of technical knowledge by an elite of scientists and experts, and the appearance of a more regimented way of organizing work and life. These developments, in turn, coincided with the maturation of capitalism and the spread of a new personality type, Max Weber's Organization Man, the supinely loyal bureaucrat willing to surrender his soul to the system he served.[46] Here is where Mumford's uncanny ability to see the larger cultural picture is most impressively in evidence. Unlike so many historians of technology, he emphasizes the interplay between technological change and related changes in values and social relations, recognizing that the latter are often the precondition, not the consequence, of large-scale mechanization.

Although most of the components of the megamachine were in existence by the early twentieth century, two things, he argues, were lacking: a "symbolic figure of absolute power, incarnated in a living ruler, a corporate group, or a super-machine; and a crisis sufficiently portentous and pressing to bring about an implosion of all the necessary components." Before this fusion took place older, cruder models of the megamachine appeared, the most menacing in Nazi Germany. It was in response to Hitler's brutal military machine that the United States and Russia produced modern mega-machines, with their inefficient human parts replaced by mechanical and electronic substitutes, and with their well-drilled armies backed, as Henry Adams had predicted, by "bombs of cosmic violence." The invention of the atomic bomb gave science and scientists a sacred niche in the new power complex. They became permanently allied with the military elite, who "fortified themselves in an inner citadel [a Pentagon] . . . cut off from inspection or control by the rest of the community." In these command centers, sealed off from democratic give-and-take, the Organization Man becomes a menace to global survival; surely, Mumford notes elsewhere, there are Eichmanns in every missile center, ready to obey orders, no matter how horrific.[47]

By manufacturing new emergencies and enemies, by instituting a state of permanent war, naïvely called a cold war, the megamachines of the superpowers became permanent institutions, headed by a new class of decision-makers who wielded world destructive powers. This, then, was the latest megamachine, or what Mumford calls, alternatively, the Pentagon of Power, since it was based on five P's: Power, that is energy; Productivity for the sake of Profit; Political control; and Publicity. But Mumford anticipates something even more frightening than the expansion of this war-oriented technocracy in the not-too-distant future. Given present trends, it is not unlikely, he predicts, that the technocentric elites will soon be replaced by a supreme ruler without human parts or attributes, the ultimate decision-maker—the central computer, the true earthly representative of the sun god.

In his earliest writing Mumford had seen electricity as a potential force for social improvement, opening the way for a decentralization of industry and population, and the revival of small industries. In *The Pentagon of Power*, however, he emphasizes the electronic computer's insidious impact on personal privacy and autonomy. To him the computer is merely another overrated tool, vastly inferior to the human brain; in the wrong hands, however, an extraordinarily dangerous one. The computer, he argues, is the eye of the reborn sun god Re; it serves as a private eye for the megamachine elite, who expect complete conformity to their commands because nothing can be hidden from them. In the future no action, no thought, perhaps even no dream will escape this all-scrutinizing eye. And perhaps this will eventually lead to the elimination of autonomy itself: "indeed the dissolution of the human soul."

Mumford makes other dark and extravagant historical parallels in this book. He sees the manned space capsule of America's Apollo program, for example, corresponding exactly "to the innermost chamber of the great pyramids, where the mummified body of the Pharaoh, surrounded by the miniaturized equipment necessary for magical travel to Heaven, was placed."[48] Close readers of his work should not have been surprised by this, for in June 1969, when *Newsweek* asked Mumford for his reaction to man's landing on the moon, his reply was quick and curt: all that money, $30 billion, for a handful of uninteresting rocks.[49]

Yet, for all his premonitions of chaos and catastrophe, Mumford ends *The Pentagon of Power* with the reminder that the megamachine, at least in the United States, is based on little more than an enticing "bribe"—if the individual gives the system his unquestioning allegiance he will have a chance to enjoy the privileges and pleasures of "megatechnic" affluence—and that this bribe, in turn, is based upon the myth that power and economic growth are the main aims of life. Once we reject this bribe and cast off this myth, the modern megamachine will, like its historic predecessor, crumble and collapse, the ironic victim of those it claimed to serve. "For those of us who have thrown off the myth of the machine, the next move is ours: for the gates of the technocratic prison will open automatically, despite their rusty, ancient hinges, as soon as we choose to walk out."

At the conclusion of this, his final statement on the human condition, Mumford comes back to withdrawal and conversion—the long-favored methods of priests and prophets. Historically, the revolutionary movements that have been most successful, he argues, were those started by individuals and small groups who nibbled at the edges of the power system "by breaking routines and defying regulations." Such a line of attack seeks not to capture the power center but to withdraw from it and thereby paralyze it. In this view Thoreau, not Marx, is the most dangerous revolutionary, for Thoreau recognized that disobedience is the first step toward autonomy.[50]

It is not, then, as a prophet of doom but as a rising voice of renewal, an Isaiah for his age, that Mumford hopes to be remembered. The optimism of *The Pentagon of Power*, however, is not altogether convincing, coming as it does after a grimly gray portrayal of the "megatechnical wasteland"; it is like something Mumford layered on at the end, almost as an afterthought. He might have been an optimist about possibilities, but he was most certainly a pessimist about probabilities, hence his often repeated assertion that humankind can be saved—but only by a miracle. While Mumford might have believed in miracles he knew enough history to realize that they do not occur very often.

His slender yet stubborn faith in miracles is a clue, however, to his evasiveness as a political thinker, for historically those who have looked to awakenings and preached of regeneration have not been very good about advising the faithful on how they are to get to the New Jerusalem. In his old age Mumford told a friend who had written a book about the impossibility of controlling technology that "detached [computerized] intelligence" will never triumph over life. "I admit that as a possibility. But I suspect man will kick over the traces before this happens." But in his own mind he had no idea how this might happen, and hence no program for challenging the technocracy. All he was able to offer was faith and hope; these, and the not unuseful example of his own life and the lives of other principled resisters, "saints and prophets of the new age."[51]

So what was Mumford's view of the future in his last years as a writer? Caution is called for here, for he was subject to extreme mood swings, by turns exuberant and despairing, speaking one moment about the apocalypse, the next about Eutopia. He is the kind of thinker who sees crisis as opportunity, who in the blackest hour of the night looks to the dawn. And like most prophets of gloom, he must have felt almost driven to be pessimistic in the hope that those who heeded him would move to prove him wrong. Realizing all this, Mumford gave, I believe, his truest inner feelings about the future in a letter he wrote to his friend and fellow social critic Roderick Seidenberg in 1969: "I think, in view of all that has happened the last half century, that it is likely the ship will sink."[52]

Still, we must remember that on the sinking whaler in Melville's *Moby Dick* the last touch is Tashtego's arm nailing a flag to the mast. That is Lewis Mumford at seventy-five. The optimism of his old age is almost a cry of defiance: I will not give in! Humankind will not give in—no matter how bad the odds! Only in this spirit, he is saying, will we be able to retain our humanity, and, perhaps like Ishmael, live to tell the story.

28

The Amenia Years

The old ship is not in a state to make many voyages. But the flag is still at the mast and I am still at the wheel.

—WALT WHITMAN

The Pentagon of Power brought Mumford the attention and critical acclaim he thought he had been denied. Yet just when his star was at its apex he again pulled back from the world, turning down almost every offer to appear in public. He taught part of the year at MIT from 1973 to 1975—mostly because Sophia dreaded the lonely winters in Amenia—but he poured all the creative energies he still possessed into his final autobiographical writings, like a weary mountaineer summoning every remaining ounce of his strength for a final dash for the summit.

In addition to his autobiography he hoped to publish an anthology of his essential writings over the past half century, and what he called a Mumford Miscellany—a collection of his notes, letters, and other assorted unpublished work. When he presented his plan for these projects to his publisher, Harcourt Brace Jovanovich, in 1971, he expected their complete support. William Jovanovich was eager to issue Mumford's autobiography, but he made it clear that he was less than excited about publishing his other retrospective offerings. This drew Mumford into a bruising personal struggle with Jovanovich that eventually caused him to leave the firm he had been associated with since 1928 and to publish his autobiography with another press. Mumford's decade-long battle with William Jovanovich, along with his near-complete absorption in his autobiographical work, put great strains on his health and marriage, and made his last creative years less satisfying than they might have been.

His problems with Sophia arose from their contrasting ideas about how they ought to spend their days together. With Lewis's final big book behind him, Sophia thought it was time that they both started enjoying life more. Although she had a painful arthritic condition she wanted to travel to places they had not yet seen— Israel, China, and perhaps even the wild game preserves of Africa— and she wanted a fuller social life, the kind of life she had briefly in Berkeley. Lewis, however, did not enjoy traveling as much as he had before, and the conversations with friends he seemed to enjoy most were those he conducted by correspondence. He had always been drawn to life as it was lived in the medieval monastery, with its regularity, order, and salutary combination of spiritual discipline and manual work. Yet although he stayed close to Amenia in his final years, away from "all the noisy crowding up of things," intellectually he continued to be a fabulous voyager.[1]

The summer after the publication of *The Pentagon of Power* he and Sophia did go to England and Ireland for several weeks, and he had his first ride in an airplane, taking a flight from London to Dublin. To his great surprise he found flying exhilarating, but the trip itself was a disappointment. It rained the entire time they were in England, and they found it difficult to cope with the small inconveniences of travel. They also found that they no longer had as many close friends in England as they used to. When they were young and in a foreign city and had nothing to do, they would walk back to their hotel room and make love, but now even walking "has become a problem for Sophia. . . ," Lewis wrote Henry Murray, "and I need hardly tell you about my problem."[2]

Work had always come first for him. In his later years, however, he seemed genuinely interested in little else. Aside from gardening he had no hobbies; thinking and reading were his ways of relaxing. "I can see it in his eyes as we sit opposite each other . . . reading," Sophia observed in her diary. "When he comes on a passage he wants to share with me, his whole face is aglow . . . you feel his whole being responding to the thought." He took an almost sensual delight in ideas; for him great adventures were adventures of the mind. Sophia, however, needed "the personal, the immediate, the communal. . . . It must have a human touch or I cannot function with it." That, of course, did not mix well with her husband's desire to withdraw, although it did meet his own Athenian prescription for a full and engaged life.[3]

She knew of no one, she once told him, who needed people less than he; she, who knew him best, called him "the cat who walks by himself." So while Sophia tried in her patient way to get him to change after he completed *The Pentagon of Power*, he remained steadfastly himself. "I find it hard to give up the hope I cherished that . . . we would live a more relaxed, social, traveling life," she remarked in her diary in 1973, when, in fact, she already *had* given up hope by this time. She claimed she bore no grudges, "realizing Lewis's is a more compelling necessity than mine," yet surely she was wounded by his inability to give her a greater taste of the kind of life she now wanted for both of them. It also pained her to see him, at this late point in his life, caught up in an emotionally draining struggle with the publisher of almost all of his books.[4]

Over the years Mumford had had a close and cordial working relationship with the firm of Harcourt Brace Jovanovich.* Joel Spingarn, a former vice president at Harcourt, had brought him to the firm in 1928, and within ten years he was one of the top authors on a list that included Sinclair Lewis, Carl Sandburg, T. S. Eliot, Virginia Woolf, and John Maynard Keynes. He got along well with both partners, Alfred Harcourt and Donald C. Brace, and enjoyed the informality that prevailed at the firm's modest offices at 383 Madison Avenue. Several times a month he would stop in unannounced to chat with his editor, Charles A. "Cap" Pearce, who later became poetry editor at *The New Yorker*, or with Alfred Harcourt or Donald Brace, whose office doors were always open. Business meetings with authors in the 1930s were usually over lunch at Longchamps, or in the downstairs restaurant of the Ritz. Mumford, who had no literary agent or lawyer, negotiated the terms of his contracts in face-to-face meetings with either Harcourt or Brace, and it was not unusual for a deal to be worked out verbally over lunch and sealed with a handshake. The firm always published whatever he

* Formerly Harcourt, Brace & Company, hereafter referred to as Harcourt.

submitted, and he was brought into almost every facet of a book's production, including the design of the book and its dust jacket. His books, moreover, went to press with only the barest of editing. Mumford insisted that he did not want anyone, not even the most seasoned and sympathetic editor, tampering with his prose.

Relations between him and Alfred Harcourt did cool somewhat in the late 1930s, when Harcourt, a friend of Charles Lindbergh, disapproved of Mumford's strong stand in favor of American military intervention in Europe, and at one point apparently considered dropping him as an author, although Mumford did not find out about this until many years later. But by that time power in the company was swinging to Donald Brace, a more easygoing if less dynamic personality, and Brace's relationship with Mumford remained rooted in mutual respect.

There were, of course, the usual problems between author and publisher, the most often being Mumford's complaints that the firm did not believe strongly enough in the sales potential of one or another of his larger, more difficult books. And, on occasion, Mumford became irritated over the firm's notorious tightness when it came to advertising expenditures. But as a compensating factor, there was absolutely no pressure to follow up one successful book with another, and no demand, as Mumford later remarked, that the author "waste time" signing books in bookstores or appearing on radio programs and "exploiting" his personality. When Donald Brace retired and William Jovanovich, a self-made man from a Colorado mining town, took over as president in 1954, at age thirty-four, the firm expanded its list of books, went aggressively into the textbook market, and moved into larger, more modern offices on Third Avenue. Jovanovich then launched a diversification effort that made his firm a true corporate giant, with investments in television, magazines, restaurants, insurance, school supplies, and three marine theme parks.

Mumford regretted this shift in emphasis, as he saw it, from concern with literary quality to concern with sales and profits; and at one point in 1964 he thought that Jovanovich had taken advantage of his "innocence" in negotiating contracts by getting him to accede to a cut in his share of royalties, from 15 percent on the first 10,000 copies sold to 10 percent, which in the new world of corporate publishing was becoming the standard rate. When Mumford learned that other prominent authors at Harcourt were still getting the old 15 percent because they had demanded it, he asked for a retroactive revision of his contract that would restore the 15 percent rate and Jovanovich grudgingly agreed.[5]

Mumford's problems with Jovanovich escalated in 1970. Despite the brisk sales of *The Pentagon of Power* Mumford complained to his new editor, William Goodman, that Jovanovich was not giving the book enough publicity, and at one point hinted that he might take his next book to another publisher. This does not seem to have been a serious threat, but the following year he had a dispute with Jovanovich that forever destroyed their relationship as author and publisher.

In the summer of 1971, Mumford gave Goodman the manuscript for a collection of his writings over the past half century on literature, history, and technology, "a one-volume Mumford" to mark his fifty years of publishing books. He already had a contract for the book, but this was a much longer work—over 250,000 words—than Harcourt had agreed to publish. Concerned about this, Goodman asked Mumford to come to New York to discuss the project with Jovanovich. In their conversation Jovanovich explained to Mumford that its great length would require they price the book too high for Harcourt to expect a sale of more than 2,000 copies. Jovanovich then abruptly shifted the subject and, as if to soften the blow, offered Mumford a contract for the Miscellany he had already begun putting together. Mumford was too stunned by Jovanovich's decision to turn down his book to say anything in reply, but by the time he returned to Amenia later that day he was in a boiling rage. After forty years with Harcourt he thought he had reached a position where a book of his would not be treated sheerly on the basis of its immediate prospects of profit and loss, and he felt certain, moreover, that his new collection of essays would sell at least 10,000 copies.[6]

After composing several angry letters to Jovanovich which Sophia persuaded him not to send, he wrote to Sophia's brother Philip Wittenberg, a New York lawyer, to ask him how he could break his ties with Harcourt without doing irreparable damage to his books that were still under contract with them. He then sent a long letter to Jovanovich, spilling out all his hurt and outrage, and threatening to leave the firm unless he received the kind of treatment he thought he manifestly deserved. "When a writer has been loyal to a single publisher for more than 40 years, there is an implied moral obligation of a similar loyalty on the part of the publisher." After meeting with Philip Wittenberg, Jovanovich reconsidered his decision and sent Mumford a contract for the book, to be called *Interpretations and Forecasts, 1922–1972*. Mumford, however, sent back the contract and made Jovanovich a counteroffer. If Jovanovich would lower the book's price and treat it on the basis that it would sell 10,000 hardcover copies the first eighteen months, he would forgo all royalties until that figure had been reached; but if at the end of eighteen months 10,000 copies had been sold he would expect 15 percent royalties on the entire sale. To Mumford's surprise, Jovanovich accepted his offer; and to his relief as well, it is fair to say, for breaking away from Harcourt would have been, for Mumford, like breaking up a long marriage that had produced a large and flourishing family.7

Interpretations and Forecasts did sell just over 10,000 copies, and the Franklin Library adopted it for its series of Great Masterpieces of American Literature. Mumford won his battle with Jovanovich, but it took a toll on his health and well-being. All that winter he was in a tense and terrible mood: he was unusually irritable; he had problems sleeping; and in the afternoons, after completing his writing for the day, he needed several glasses of whiskey to relax. One morning he awoke at five o'clock, feeling dizzy and with his heart racing wildly. He tried to stagger to the bathroom, but, reaching for the end of the bed to brace himself, tumbled forward and hit the floor hard. Later in the morning, without telling Sophia what had happened, he made it downstairs, shakily, but did not dare take a shower for fear of falling in the bathtub.8

Worse still, as far as he was concerned, he found it almost impossible to write. All he could think about was William Jovanovich, who was deliberately trying to suppress his work, he was convinced, because in *The Pentagon of Power* he had attacked writers Jovanovich respected, like Marshall McLuhan and Arthur Clarke. From this point on it became a matter of pride for Mumford to try to force Jovanovich to agree to every one of his terms for the next several books he planned to publish with the firm. Sophia agreed with her husband that Jovanovich had acted deplorably, but she disliked the person Lewis had become in his determined battle with Jovanovich. "It is fine to . . . demand your place . . . but what good is your place if in the act of claiming it you lose yourself," she told him quite bluntly.[9]

When Mumford completed his Miscellany, which he called *Findings and Keepings: Analects for an Autobiography*, he turned in the manuscript to Harcourt in plenty of time for them to publish it just before his eightieth birthday, which fell in October 1975. There were, however, several delays in preparing the book for publication, and when it did appear late in the fall publishing season Harcourt gave it only a minimal promotional effort. Suspecting Jovanovich's every move, Mumford accused the publisher of trying to diminish the book's sales in order to get back at him for being correct about *Interpretations and Forecasts*. Again Mumford threatened to leave Harcourt, again he was entirely serious, and again Jovanovich compromised at the final moment.[10]

This time he worked through Julian Muller, a vice president at Harcourt, a courtly, engaging man who had a strong personal interest in Mumford's work. Muller got along beautifully with Mumford, and before long the two men worked out an agreement to cancel the three contracts Mumford had signed for future work, including his autobiography, and to treat each forthcoming book separately, giving Harcourt first refusal. Muller also promised to give Mumford full participation in every detail of the publishing and promotion of his books. At this point Jovanovich sent Mumford a long personal letter apologizing for any mistakes his firm might have made with his most recent books, and offering to publish another, and even larger Miscellany, which he promised to promote aggressively. Finally, he offered to serve himself as Mumford's editor, claiming that their disagreements arose because they had to conduct their affairs through intermediaries. A week later Mumford wrote back, coldly refusing Jovanovich's offer.[11]

This time Mumford suspected that Jovanovich feared what he might say about their publishing relationship in his forthcoming autobiography. If Jovanovich established better relations with his author he might be able to convince Mumford to delete this damaging material. Mumford, however, had no real evidence for his suspicion, and actually had no intention of writing anything about Jovanovich in his autobiography. Although he accused Jovanovich of conspiratorial and vindictive behavior, Jovanovich seems to have been merely acting in the increasingly accepted fashion of big-time publishers, who, when they considered books, considered sales value as real value. Mumford's recent books had been modest commercial successes, but in corporate publishing this counted for little, as Mumford knew all too well; a good book, Mumford had heard one publisher say, is a book that sells good.[12] Jovanovich actually admired Mumford's work, and as a young man had been much influenced by *The Culture of Cities,* which he once referred to as his first investment in learning. He was proud to publish Lewis Mumford and did not want to lose him as an author, but in the current economics of publishing, Mumford's influence and authority were far less now than they had been in the "Golden Age" of publishing that Mumford would recall so fondly in his autobiography.[13]

By this time Mumford had made up his mind to leave Harcourt Brace Jovanovich. When they failed to give his second miscellany, *My Works and Days: A Personal Chronicle,* the kind of all-out promotional effort he had expected, he began looking for another publisher for his autobiography with the help of his friend Hilda Lindley, formerly with Harcourt, who became his literary agent for this one book only. She was forming her own firm, and Mumford, out of friendship, agreed to let her handle his book, which might help to get her established.[14]

While Mumford was assembling these "invitations" to his autobiography he was hard at work on the book itself. "There are moments when [these] books bear down on my bosom like an incubus, threatening to smother my real life!" he described the terrible strain of this effort to Julian Muller.[15] It has been said that when people reach advanced age they tend to become more attached to their possessions, treasured links to their past and to their former selves. When their passions and hopes begin to desert them, they desperately cling to what is left in their lives. For Mumford, this was his immense body of published and unpublished writing; nothing except his family meant more to him. "To live is to feel, to experience powerful emotions," Stendhal had written. Mumford had lived in this fashion, and his accumulated work, including his letters and notes, was his proof of this, the record of the way he wanted to be remembered—as a writer of almost Leonardan range, not just an architecture critic or an "urbanologist," and as a man who had lived a life of passion and profound significance. Each of the several autobiographical works he produced after 1970 is scrupulously organized to call attention to these claims. This, ultimately, is why he gave so much of himself to them and pressed his publisher so relentlessly to give them enthusiastic backing.

Mumford devoted so much effort to these autobiographical exercises for another, and related, reason: he had absolutely no trust in his future biographer. Accordingly, *My Works and Days* is thick with clues and suggestions for his prospective biographer, some of them useful and revealing, others playfully, almost purposefully elusive. In the introductions to the various sections of the book Mumford watchfully stands guard over the record of his past, instructing his future biographer as to what is important and what is not, what to consider seriously and what to ignore. It is a superbly orchestrated performance, one that speaks to his claim that only he could write the authoritative biography of Lewis Mumford. As he assembled this book he began to suspect that he might not be able to marshal either the energy or the will to write a complete autobiography, and for this reason *My Works and Days* is a more revealing personal testimony than his autobiography. Unlike that later book, moreover, it covers the entire span of his life.

Mumford organized his miscellanies to give a rich sampling of the range of his interests and erudition. We see him as philosopher and biographer, historian and literary critic, poet and dramatist; in sum, the complete man of letters. Interestingly, however, we do not see him as observer of cities and architecture; and this is unfortunate, for, like most writers, Mumford wrote best about what he knew best—cities, buildings, and, of course, himself. His essays and books on these themes, and most especially his evocative autobiography, will stand forever as his strongest claims to a reputation as a writer.

But if *My Works and Days* is not the best guide to Lewis Mumford as a pure writer, it does give a revealing glimpse of his private life: his friendships, his family life, and his life-changing relationship with Catherine Bauer. Only a glimpse, however. We do not have, for example, Catherine Bauer's side of their relationship; nor do we have Sophia's reaction to it; and Mumford says hardly anything at all about his other love affairs. There is a section in the book on Josephine Strongin, but Mumford strongly hints that their relationship was entirely platonic. Yet although there is mention of fuller revelations to come in the autobiography, we get a much better, if still limited, sense of the range and intensity of Mumford's erotic interests in this book than in his autobiography.

But Mumford does give a fascinating account of his intellectual and emotional maturation, of a mind and a man in the making. This is surely the most interesting part of this book and of the autobiography that followed. In these works we witness the slow coming to form of what is surely Lewis Mumford's most impressive work of creation—himself.

These autobiographical works, as dear to him as his life, nearly cost him his life. In 1972, while working on *Findings and Keepings*, he noticed blood in his urine, and it was later found that he had a growth on his kidney. His doctors recommended immediate exploratory surgery, but he decided against it because it would interrupt his ongoing plans to put his literary affairs in order. Seven years later, just after reading the proofs of *My Works and Days*, he had a recurrence of these symptoms, and crushing pain in his midsection, and had to be rushed to the hospital for emergency surgery on his kidney and prostate. He recovered from the operation with amazing speed, but had he died, he would have been satisfied to leave *My Works and Days* as his personal summation. It is true that in his autobiography he often writes with an old man's candor about his life, but if we are searching for the inner Mumford, the man behind all those big books, the place to go first is *My Works and Days*. Yet in reading it we must keep in mind what Emerson said of other writers, and by implication, himself: "You may have all that they have published: I will take what they have suppressed!" In his more private moments Mumford himself was heard to second that sentiment.[16]

These autobiographical books placed unusually heavy demands on Mumford's marriage. Once again, he and Sophia had to reconstruct, and hence relive, the most trying moments of their relationship, and in the process they found themselves hurting each other all over again. Several times they called a halt to this endless analysis of their lives, agreeing that it was futile to go over past grievances at a time when they found themselves growing closer to each other, but always a new circumstance, sometimes a book, or a movie they saw, or a casual reference to another person, "brought us back," Sophia recalls, "to the dissection of our own lives, . . . No psycho-analysis, I believe, could have dug deeper or more honestly than our probings." When Mumford finally wrote the last word on this part of their lives, and Sophia finished reading the section in his autobiography on Catherine Bauer, which was not nearly as revealing as the semifictionalized account he had written earlier, they both felt enormously relieved. "Now I can cry. Look! We have come through!" Sophia wrote with joy.[17] They had, they both agreed, a good marriage; what it lacked in tranquility it more than made up for in intensity. Better still, this entire process of re-creation brought him and Sophia closer together than they had ever been before. In old age they stood as one.

What made this time of their lives especially gratifying for Sophia was that she had become a partner in her husband's work, as she was briefly ten years before when she helped him with the second draft of his autobiography. He still wrote every word of every one of his published books, but she helped him to assemble his miscellanies and to reconstruct the story of his life, for by this time she had a far keener memory than he did, and considerably more energy. If Lewis, earlier in his life, "had tried to bring me along with him," Sophia wrote in her diary, "if he had tried, instead of . . . turning to other women for stimulation, he might have brought forth from me some of the qualities he now so welcomes. For the last few years have been quite wonderful in the common responses we have discovered in one another. And it saddens me to think we might much earlier have had at least some measure of it if we *both* had tried. But truly the sadness pales before the delight of these years." They had known life in both its heights and its depths, but it was from the heights that they now beheld it, as Lewis observed in *My Works and Days*, a book he dedicated to Sophia.[18]

After spending the spring semester of 1975 at MIT as a visiting professor, Mumford took no further teaching positions, and he and Sophia began living all year round in Amenia. They missed the stimulus of Cambridge, where Lewis had many close friends, and the harsh Amenia winters were still difficult for them, yet he and Sophia were not nearly as lonely as they had been other previous winters in the country, for Alison and her family lived just down the

Leedsville Road in the old Maples cottage, which she and her husband had bought from Amy Spingarn in 1973. Sophia purchased a television set so that their two grandchildren would have something to occupy themselves with when they visited, and every Friday around the dinner hour Alison would drop the children off for an evening with their grandparents. The poet and lawyer Melville Cane, an old friend of Mumford's from Harcourt, lived nearby and would have dinner with them once a week, and occasionally some friends from Cambridge would drive over for the afternoon. Lewis and Sophia also became close friends with Santha Rama Rau, the writer, and her husband, Gurden Wattles, who lived a few hundred yards away on the Leedsville Road, and periodically the sculptor Naum Gabo, Mumford's closest male friend in old age, would drive over with his wife from Middlebury, Connecticut. Gabo was a boisterous Russian with a booming voice and vigorous opinions on art, politics, and literature, and despite their contrasting temperaments Mumford loved his company and shared his steaming outrage at the way modern art had evolved. "If this is modern art," Gabo once thundered, pointing to an Andy Warhol representation of a Campbell's soup can, "I never was a modern artist."[19] When Gabo died in 1977 while writing his memoirs, Mumford delivered a eulogy, ranking him with Picasso as the two greatest artists of the twentieth century. That same year, after recently losing two other close friends, Clarence Stein and Benton MacKaye, Mumford had a reconciliation with Malcolm Cowley, whom he had feuded with in the 1930s over the question of American neutrality, feeling that old age was no time to carry old grudges.

These years were the quietest of Mumford's life; he left Amenia only occasionally, usually to accept some award he valued particularly. In 1976 he flew to Paris to accept the Prix Mondial del Duca for his lifetime contribution to letters, and earlier, in November 1975, he was made an honorary Knight Commander of the British Empire at a ceremony at the British Embassy in Washington, D.C. That year, on his birthday, congratulatory telegrams came pouring in from all over the world, and in the afternoon Martin Filler, a young editor at Architectural Record Books, arrived unexpectedly with flowers and gifts, and the first copy of a book of Mumford's architecture essays he had arranged to be published in honor of Lewis's eightieth birthday. By evening Lewis was completely exhausted. Just as he was about to go to bed the phone rang again. "This is Albany Western Union. I have a message for Mr. Lewis Mumford. Are you Mr. Mumford?" "Yes I am," Mumford replied. "Are you famous? I never heard of you!" It was the perfect end, Lewis thought, to a perfect day.[20]

Mumford's last years as a writer were given over almost completely to his autobiography, which he completed in 1981. Now that he had excised the fuller account of his relationship with Catherine Bauer, the only "secret" this book disclosed was the story of his parentage. For some reason he was never able to explain, even to himself, he continued to withhold the facts of his paternity from his daughter Alison, but when Alison finally learned the truth from Sophia's oldest sister, Miriam, and confronted her father with what she knew a number of years later, in 1967, he saw that there was no reason not to publish his autobiography in his own lifetime. There was nothing more to keep from Alison, for earlier that year he had told her about his love letters to Catherine Bauer, Alice Decker, and Josephine Strongin because he expected her to be his literary executor.

As he was completing his autobiography Mumford stumbled upon a surprising piece of information about his family background which even his mother had been unaware of. He learned of it from Amy Spingarn, a frail and sick woman in her nineties who still spent part of the year in Leedsville in the Century Cottage, unable to keep up the sprawling Troutbeck estate. In Amy's last years Lewis and Sophia dropped in on her at least once a week, and Lewis occasionally read to her from the manuscript of his autobiography. She was interested in Lewis's past, and her conversations with Alison had also awakened in her a keen curiosity about Lewis's paternity. One Sunday afternoon while Lewis was reading to her from the chapter on his mother's life, Amy interrupted him to ask him the name of his father. He paused, but then succumbed reluctantly and said, "Mack." "Why, I had an uncle named Mack," she replied with enthusiasm, who had married her father's sister, Therese Einstein, and later managed her father's textile mill in Summit, New Jersey. He had two sons, Alec Wolfgang and, she said slowly, almost stopping herself, Lewis Charles. "That was my father," Lewis said matter-of-factly.

By a fantastic coincidence he and Amy, who had been friends and neighbors for almost fifty years, now discovered that they were kin as well. Mumford could only wonder what Joel Spingarn would have thought of all this. As for himself and Sophia, they were actually disappointed to have the "lovely anonymity destroyed. . . . Lewis has always been his own man," Sophia described their feelings in a private note for the family papers. "He has stood on his own feet, . . . beholden to no one but himself for what he has become." It seemed sadly ironic that he was tied to a family, the Einsteins, with considerable wealth and entrepreneurial reputation.[21]

After 1979 old age came in hard on Mumford: his memory began to fail; he developed a slight paralysis in the fingers of his left hand; he began to lose his sense of balance; and he suffered a series of debilitating illnesses, including a horribly painful case of the shingles. Only by a supreme feat of courage and persistence was he able to finish the book in the shortened form it took. But Hilda Lindley had sold the autobiography to Harper & Row, promising a manuscript covering Lewis's entire life, even though he had warned her that the book would probably deal only with his formative years. At her urging—for he liked her immensely and wanted her to succeed in her career as a literary agent—he made an effort to write several chapters taking the story of his life beyond the mid-thirties, but like most older persons, he found the middle years of his life the most difficult to recapture, and he finally gave up after completing the drafts of two chapters on the war years. He was not well enough, nor did he have a strong enough desire, to go any further with the book that he would call, appropriately, *Sketches from Life*. Besides, there were other unfinished projects that he considered more important, including a collection of his essays on architecture and urbanism, and a volume of his correspondence. This literary legacy became so important to him that he even suggested to Ann Harris, his editor at Harper & Row, that she might want to postpone the publication of his "unfinished" autobiography until after his death, and move at once to publish these other—and, to him, more significant—books.[22]

Harris, however, was insistent: she wanted the full autobiography she had been promised. At this point, in September 1980, Hilda

Lindley, realizing she could never get Lewis to complete the auto-biography she thought he had promised to write, negotiated a cancellation of the contract with Harper & Row, and returned the part of the advance of $88,ooo that had been sent to Lewis. Later that year she sold the book to the Dial Press, where the editor, Juris Jurjevics, was a great admirer of Lewis's work. Lewis received a handsome advance, which was important to him at this late date in his life. "Old age is impossible to bear in extreme poverty," he quoted Cicero to a friend, "even if one is a philosopher."²³

Mumford completed his autobiography in 1981, and he could not have done so without Sophia's editorial and secretarial assistance. She helped him to get the manuscript into final form, while his mind was on another literary project, and she fought for him several lengthy battles with the editors at the Dial Press over what to some people might seem minor matters of literary style and syntax, but to Lewis were very nearly matters of life and death. "Conformity," Sophia told the editors at one point, "is anathema to Lewis. [He] firmly believes that a book should express the author's personality and style, even if it is contrary to immediate usage. . . . He *knows* why he uses a word—as a rule," and the press ought to trust in his judgment. "After all, he has a long established reputation as a writer of beautiful prose."²⁴ In the end, Lewis—as willful and stubbornly proud as ever—won this, his final battle with a publisher. This would be *his* book, just as all his others had been.

Sketches from Life might very well be titled "The Education of Lewis Mumford," for it is about "the ways and methods and goals . . . and rewards of a life-time education." Mumford proudly portrays him-self as a man who hewed closely to Patrick Geddes's advice—to learn by living—and in this ongoing process of living and learning, the decisive influence on his development, he proclaims in the book's opening sentence, was the city of New York, "my Walden Pond." The most vividly written chapters in the book deal with the New York of Mumford's boyhood. In evoking an older New York Mum-ford is like an archaeologist describing a fascinating faraway city, lost to us forever. Through prose rich with feeling, color, and detail, and through a succession of his own beautiful pencil sketches and watercolors, he brings to life this long-ago New York; there it is, just in front of us, just the way he would have us believe it was—his city as he saw it one day from the wooden walkway of the Brooklyn Bridge, "immensely overpowering, flooded with energy and light. . . . The wonder of it was the wonder of an orgasm in the body of one's beloved."[25]

In this surging, but still to him friendly New York, young Mumford not only gained an education but marked out a place for himself amid the swirl of careers, ideologies, and political movements. If at the end of his life he was proud of one thing, it was that he had made his own way in the world, writing his first six books without outside financial support and remaining independent of the university world, with its departmental specialization and scholarly caution.

All his life Mumford was obsessively self-scrutinizing and amazingly honest about his own inadequacies, yet he never doubted the importance of his own thoughts or the power of his mind. *Sketches from Life*, better than any of his other books, reveals how that mind worked. Mumford absorbed everything around him and made it over in his mind to fit his unique vision, his own way of seeing things. So it is not New York that is portrayed here, but Lewis Mumford's New York, and it is that way with everything else of great importance in his life: his wife, his children, his friends, his lovers become what they meant to him. They move in orbit around the sun and center that is Lewis Mumford.

Sketches from Life is Lewis Mumford's last and most warmly received book, and it was nominated for the prestigious American Book Award. But even before he completed it he was well into yet another project, a "heretical interpretation" of the entire history of human evolution.[26] Every morning he would hobble into his study, his vision diminished, his entire body shaking, and there he would write for at least one hour. His unifying theme was human purpose—humankind's defiant refusal to surrender to nature. And somehow that is fitting, for that is what brought him to and kept him at his work as he approached the age of ninety.

"If I were beginning life all over again," he wrote Henry Murray in the midst of his research, "I think I'd dedicate myself wholly to biology" in order to restate the problems of chance, purpose, and causality better "than anyone has yet done."[27] As much as he admired Charles Darwin, Mumford could not accept the idea of chance, or natural selection, as the key to the progressive sequence of life. There had to be some ultimate purpose or design in nature, just as Bergson, Geddes, Samuel Butler, and others had suggested, and he would have liked to try to find it.

When Mumford spoke of purpose or design, he did not mean some clearly defined end, implicit from the beginning, toward which all organic transformations are directed; he flatly rejected this old theological idea. There could be design, he believed, without the aid of an all-knowing designer, and purpose, even though its operating laws are hidden from science, remaining perhaps forever a mystery. The purpose that surely exists in nature, Mumford wrote his friend Roderick Seidenberg, is directional and cumulative and becomes clearer in its intentions with each step toward its partial fulfillment.[28]

Mumford saw the appearance of language as the clearest evidence of the existence of design in the universe, and he planned to focus on the emergence of language and the symbolic arts in the book he continued writing in his mind when he became too old and ill to work with his pen. As he explained his thesis to Seidenberg, the creatures who uttered the first meaningful sound did not have the slightest notion that they were helping to create language. The sounds were purposeful, and little by little became functional, but at no point did the primitive users and makers of language realize that they were creating a "complex articulated structure which looking backward might seem impossible to have achieved except by a masterfully conscious design." How could these archaic creatures have guessed that they were preparing the way, by their fumbling and ceaseless strivings, for Shakespeare and Shelley?[29]

Organic species certainly are not programmed like computers, but each species has a certain purpose of its own, a life pattern that it stubbornly sticks to, a theory that Mumford found congenial, no doubt, because it was in concord with his own pattern of personal development, as he described it in his autobiography.

In this Aristotelian notion, furthermore, we find the basis for Mumford's diminished but enduring hope for the future of human society. In Mumford's teleology, the future is always uncertain and unpredictable since the sources of those qualities he calls purpose and potentiality are often invisible until they produce actual changes in the behavior of the organism or in the outward form of the species. So perhaps in the not-too-distant future, an unexpected organic transformation will occur that will restore the human personality "to the very center of the cosmos."³⁰

Mumford's belief in this theory of purpose and progress is surely the reason he was still quoting, into his tenth decade, his favorite line in poetry, from Tennyson's *Ulysses:* "Come my friends,/'Tis not too late to seek a newer world."

While he was at work on his final project Lewis Mumford prepared for his final days. He and Sophia moved their bedroom downstairs and turned the first floor of their old farmhouse into a snug but comfortable five-room apartment. Lewis sold many of his less valuable books, and sent his massive file of papers and correspondence to the Van Pelt Library of the University of Pennsylvania, which already housed the papers of his old friends Van Wyck Brooks and Waldo Frank. In 1981, as he prepared *Sketches from Life* for publication, he was still thinking with a clarity and intensity few people his age achieve, but in the following years his mental and physical powers fell off sharply, and he found that he was no longer able to write. Next to his son's death this was the greatest disaster of his life. Unable to write, he no longer wanted to live.

But he carried on—and with dignity. He and Sophia continued to entertain guests, mostly family and old friends, and dozens upon dozens of scholars, writers, filmmakers, and artists who wanted to do projects on some part of Lewis's life, or who simply wanted to meet him. Lewis entertained his guests with charm, warmth, and wit, serving the wine even though he was barely able to walk, proposing toasts, and telling wonderful stories about his New York days. But an hour or so of this exhausted him, and when his guests departed he would sit in his chair in the living room and look out of the front windows at the trees and the sky, as if locked in a trance. Sitting there, waiting for the night, he must have felt like an old soldier who had not had the good fortune to die on the battlefield.

The only parts of his work that seemed to really interest him were his old drawings and watercolors, which his friend, the artist Vincent DiMattio, framed for him. He especially liked to look at his watercolors of the Amenia countryside he had explored as a more vigorous man. He had come to know the land in this beautiful valley in all its variety and seasonal moods, and he had found "nothing to equal this intimate experience except a long and close marriage."[31] He also liked to look at his earliest self-portraits. Sophia would set them out in front of him in the living room and he would search them closely, often for hours at a time, for signs of the man he eventually became. These paintings and drawings were put on exhibit by DiMattio in galleries near New York and Boston, and at ninety Lewis Mumford was discovered as an artist: one critic compared his work to William Turner's river scenes, Childe Hassam's streetscapes, and Toulouse-Lautrec's pencil sketches. Mumford himself was more modest in his appraisal. He was glad he had "formed the habit of making pictures, almost at random." When he looked at them now they reminded him that as a very young man he had thought briefly of becoming either an artist or a poet, but he was happy that he had realized in his youth that "there was no sense in becoming a mediocre example of one or the other."[32]

He was, however, immensely proud to be recognized as an artist, and when he learned in 1986 that he would receive the National Medal of Arts for his writing on cities and urban design he had to fight back tears. Yet none of these small pleasures compensated for his inability to write or made him any more philosophical about old age. When he glanced at himself in a mirror now he was reminded of what Alfred North Whitehead had told him just before he died. "People say, Mr. Mumford, that when you get older you get wiser. Don't believe them! You are beginning to break up." He had been feeling these dreaded signs for some time, and had been trying, like Emerson, to accept them gracefully. Yet he was frustrated, sometimes to the point of anger, that he would no longer be able to do any good in the world. "Resignation would be easier," he wrote a friend, "if the world at large was in a more hopeful state."[33]

He had never belonged to an organized religion, but in his last years, when he would retire to his bedroom in the evening well before Sophia, she would occasionally overhear his whispered prayers. He did not believe in God as an actual spirit or being; "God" was his own expression for his unshakable belief that there is a hidden purpose in nature, and that "whatever mankind has achieved in the way of knowledge and love and kindness . . . is capable of being pushed further and higher." When Lewis Mumford prayed as an old man it was to remind himself to hold to his faith "in the ultimate reasonableness of life."[34]

He had tried to live a life of deep moral purpose, realizing that the greatest teachers leave not books, but their own living example. He realized that his lifelong effort to make over himself and his world was far from complete, but there arrived a time when one had to reach a certain kind of resignation summed up by those words from the Christian prayer: "Thy will be done." "After one has done one's best and made one's own decisions as well as he knows," he had written his son Geddes just before he was killed in battle, " 'Thy will be done' is the last word."

As death came nearer it seemed far less frightening to him. Nor did he fear what lay beyond. His only concern was what would become of Sophia.

Did he believe in a life after death? he was asked in his old age. "I don't look forward to an afterlife, but I wouldn't say that it wasn't possible. I wouldn't be so sure of anything."[35]

Notes

Abbreviations in the Notes

Books by Mumford referred to in Notes:

AAS   *America and Alfred Stieglitz: A Collective Portrait.* Edited by Waldo Frank, Lewis Mumford, Dorothy Norman, Paul Rosenfeld, and Harold Rugg. Garden City, N.Y.: Doubleday, Doran, 1934.

AT   *Art and Technics.* New York: Columbia University Press, 1952.

BD   *The Brown Decades: A Study of the Arts in America, 1865–1895.* New York: Harcourt, Brace, 1931.

BD-D   *The Brown Decades: A Study of the Arts in America, 1865–1895.* New York: Dover, 1955.

CC   *The Culture of Cities.* New York, Harcourt, Brace, 1938.

CD   *City Development: Studies in Urban Disintegration and Renewal.* New York: Harcourt, Brace, 1945.

CH   *The City in History: Its Origins, Its Transformations, and Its Prospects.* New York: Harcourt, Brace and World, 1961.

CL   *The Conduct of Life.* New York: Harcourt, Brace, 1951.

CM   *The Condition of Man.* New York: Harcourt, Brace, 1944.

FFL   *Faith for Living.* New York: Harcourt, Brace, 1940.

FK   *Findings and Keepings: Analects for an Autobiography.* New York: Harcourt Brace Jovanovich, 1975.

GD   *The Golden Day: A Study in American Experience and Culture.* New York: Boni and Liveright, 1926.

GD-D   *The Golden Day: A Study in American Literature and Culture.* New York: Dover, 1968.

GM   *Green Memories: The Story of Geddes Mumford.* New York: Harcourt, Brace, 1947.

HMel   *Herman Melville.* New York: Harcourt, Brace, 1929.

MM-I   *The Myth of the Machine: I. Technics and Human Development.* New York: Harcourt, Brace and World, 1967.

MM-II   *The Myth of the Machine: II. The Pentagon of Power.* New York: Harcourt Brace Jovanovich, 1970.

PLC   *The Plan of London County.* Rebuilding Britain Series, No. 12. London: Faber and Faber, 1945.

RP   *Regional Planning in the Pacific Northwest: A Memorandum.* Portland, Oreg.: Northwest Regional Council, 1939.

S   *Sketches from Life: The Autobiography of Lewis Mumford.* New York: Dial, 1982.

SF   *The Social Foundations of Post-War Building.* Rebuilding Britain Series, No. 9. London: Faber and Faber, 1943.

SS   *Sticks and Stones: A Study of American Architecture and Civilization.* New York: Boni and Liveright, 1924.

SS-D   *Sticks and Stones: A Study of American Architecture and Civilization.* New York: Dover, 1955.

SU   *The Story of Utopias.* New York: Boni and Liveright, 1922.

SU-D   *The Story of Utopias.* New York: Viking, 1962.

TC   *Technics and Civilization.* New York: Harcourt, Brace, 1934.

TOM   *The Transformations of Man.* New York: Harper & Brothers, 1956.

TOM-H   *The Transformations of Man.* New York: Harper & Row, Torchbook edition, 1972.

UP   *The Urban Prospect.* New York: Harcourt, Brace and World, 1968.

VFS   *Values for Survival: Essays, Addresses, and Letters on Politics and Education.* New York: Harcourt, Brace, 1946.

WD   *My Works and Days: A Personal Chronicle.* New York: Harcourt Brace Jovanovich, 1979.

WH   *Whither Honolulu? A Memorandum Report on Park and City Planning.* Prepared by Lewis Mumford for City and County of Honolulu Park Board. Honolulu, T.H.: The Author, 1938.

Manuscript Collections:

AGP   Albert Leon Guérard Papers, Manuscript Division, Cecil H. Green Library, Stanford University, Stanford, California.

AJNP   Albert Jay Nock Papers, Yale University Library, Manuscripts and Archives, New Haven, Connecticut.

CCCA	Christ Church College Archives, Christ Church College, Oxford University, Oxford, England.
CSP	Clarence Stein Papers, Cornell University Libraries, Department of Manuscripts and University Archives, Ithaca, New York.
FJOC	Frederic J. Osborn Correspondence, Mid-Hertfordshire Division Library, Welwyn Garden City, England.
GRP	Geroid T. Robinson Papers, Columbia University, Butler Library, Rare Book and Manuscript Library, New York City.
HMC	Henry A. Murray Collection, Harvard University Archives, Cambridge, Massachusetts.
JGFP	John Gould Fletcher Papers, University of Arkansas Library, Fayetteville, Arkansas.
JSP	Joel Elias Spingarn Papers, Columbia University, Butler Library, Rare Book and Manuscript Library, New York City.
LMC	Lewis Mumford Collection, University of Pennsylvania, Charles Patterson Van Pelt Library, Department of Special Collections, Philadelphia.
LMC-C	Lewis Mumford Collection (the confidential portion of the Mumford Collection), University of Pennsylvania, Charles Patterson Van Pelt Library, Department of Special Collections, Philadelphia.
MCP	Malcolm Cowley Papers, Newberry Library, Chicago.
MFP	Mumford Family Papers, in the possession of Lewis and Sophia Mumford, Leedsville, New York.
MJP	Matthew Josephson Papers, in the possession of Eric Josephson, Sherman, Connecticut.
MKFP	MacKaye Family Papers, Dartmouth College Library, Hanover, New Hampshire (contains the papers of Benton MacKaye).
MLP	Max Lerner Papers, Yale University Library, Manuscripts and Archives, New Haven, Connecticut.
NAP	Newton Arvin Papers, Smith College Library, Rare Book Room, Northampton, Massachusetts.
PGC	Patrick Geddes Correspondence, National Library of Scotland, Edinburgh.
SMP	Stearns Morse Papers, Dartmouth College Library, Hanover, New Hampshire.
VWBP	Van Wyck Brooks Papers, University of Pennsylvania, Charles Patterson Van Pelt Library, Department of Special Collections, Philadelphia.
WFP	Waldo Frank Papers, University of Pennsylvania, Charles Patterson Van Pelt Library, Department of Special Collections, Philadelphia.

WLP   Walter Lippmann Papers, Yale University Library, Manuscripts and Archives Division, New Haven, Connecticut.

WOCP   William Van O'Connor Papers, Syracuse University, George Arendts Research Library, Syracuse, New York.

Mumford's Notes:

P   Personalia. Mumford kept several distinct species of notes, one of which he labeled Personalia. These are intensely personal notes. In the Lewis Mumford Collection, University of Pennsylvania, Charles Patterson Van Pelt Library, Department of Special Collections, Philadelphia.

P-C   Personalia, in the confidential portion of the Lewis Mumford Collection.

RN   Random Notes. A species of notes, the most common in the Mumford Collection. In the Lewis Mumford Collection, University of Pennsylvania, Charles Patterson Van Pelt Library, Department of Special Collections, Philadelphia.

RN-C   Random Notes, in the confidential portion of the Lewis Mumford Collection.

Names:

BMK   Benton MacKaye

CB   Catherine Bauer (Wurster)

CS   Clarence Stein

DCL   Dorothy Cecilia Loch

FJO   Frederic J. Osborn

HM   Henry A. Murray

JL   Jerome Lachenbruch

JS   Josephine Strongin

LM   Lewis Mumford

PG   Patrick Geddes

SM   Sophia Mumford (Wittenberg)

VB   Victor Branford

VWB   Van Wyck Brooks

Interviews:

IAMM	Interview with Alison Mumford Morss, in Leedsville, New York.
IHM	Interview with Henry A. Murray, in Cambridge, Massachusetts.
ILM	Interview with Lewis Mumford, in Leedsville, New York.
ISM	Interview with Sophia Mumford, in Leedsville, New York.

Preface

1. Van Doren quote in Harcourt Brace Jovanovich publicity pamphlet, no date, LMC.
2. Mumford, "Call Me Jonah!" address delivered December 13, 1972, and published in Mumford, WD, pp. 527–31; Ralph Waldo Emerson, "War," *The Works of Ralph Waldo Emerson*, vol. II (Boston, MA: The Jefferson Press, 1883), p. 550.
3. Malcolm Cowley to Julian Muller, October 1978, LMC.
4. ILM, May 6, 1986; Emerson, "The American Scholar," August 31, 1937, in Ralph Waldo Emerson, *Essays and Lectures* (New York: The Library of America, 1983), pp. 70–71.

I

1. S, pp. 3, 25.
2. RN, 1919.
3. ISM, May 6, 1986, May 22, 1985; ILM, July 6, 1983.
4. S, p. 57.
5. LM, "Inscription for a Gravestone" (autobiographical fragment), March 28, 1952, p. 5, MFP; ILM, July 6, 1983.
6. S, p. 57.
7. LM, "Radcliffe Commencement Address," June 3, 1956, LMC.
8. Ibid.
9. Ibid.; S, pp. 42–43.
10. LM, "Inscription for a Gravestone," p. 6.
11. Ibid., pp. 7–10; S, pp. 68–70; ISM, May 6, 1986; ILM, July 8, 1984.
12. S, pp. 25–26; SM, statement, January 1, 1968, MFP.
13. Elvina Mumford, "Autograph Album," February 1891, MFP; S, p. 28.
14. S, pp. 28–29; LM, "Inscription for a Gravestone," pp. 10–18.
15. Quoted in S, p. 30; SM, statement, December 3, 1967, MFP.
16. S, pp. 30–34; ILM, July 8, 1984, May 22, 1985.
17. S, pp. 30–35; ISM, May 6, 1986.
18. ILM, May 6, 1986; LM, "Inscription for a Gravestone," pp. 10–19; LM–Alison Mumford Morss, April 14, 1967, LMC-C.
19. S, p. 32; LM–CB, August 20, 1930, LMC-C; JL–LM, February 16, 1963, LMC.
20. S, pp. 32–33; ILM, July 8, 1984.
21. LM, "The Little Testament of Bernard Martin, Aet. 30," LMC, pp. 1–10; ILM, July 8, 1984; S, pp. 3–4.
22. LM, "Memorandum," 1962, LMC.

23. S, p. 43; ISM, April 2, 1988.
24. LM, "Inscription for a Gravestone," p. 26; S, pp. 40–49; ILM, July 6, 1983.
25. S, p. 41.
26. ILM, July 8, 1984.
27. Elvina Mumford–LM, 1921, MFP; ISM, May 6, 1986.
28. LM, "Inscription for a Gravestone," p. 1.
29. Ibid., pp. 34–35.
30. S, p. 44.
31. Ibid., p. 45.
32. William Manchester, *The Last Lion: Winston Spencer Churchill; Visions of Glory, 1874–1932* (Boston: Little, Brown, 1983), p. 118.
33. S, p. 47.
34. LM, "Inscription for a Gravestone," p. 23.
35. RN, 1915.
36. LM–Stearns Morse, November 15, 1950, SMC (copy in LMC); JL–LM, February 16, 1913, LMC.
37. LM–Alison Mumford Morss, April 14, 1967, LMC-C.
38. LM, "My Boyhood Fiction" (unpublished chapter fragment of LM's autobiography), April 17, 1968, LMC.
39. S, p. 44.
40. LM–Stearns Morse, November 15, 1950, SMC (copy in LMC).
41. LM, untitled fragment of his autobiography, written aboard the S.S. *Mauretania* in July 1961, p. 7, LMC (hereafter referred to as "S.S. Mauretania").
42. RN, November 28, 1963.
43. S, pp. 49–53; ILM, June 28, 1977.
44. ILM, June 28, 1977.
45. S, pp. 50–52.
46. Ibid., p. 55.

2

1. S, pp. 13, 61.
2. Ibid., pp. 14–17; LM, "A New York Childhood: Ta-Ra-Ra-Boom-De-Ay," *The New Yorker*, December 22, 1934, p. 21.
3. ILM, July 8, 1984; S, pp. 16–17; LM, "The Metropolitan Milieu," AAS, pp. 33–38.
4. ILM, July 8, 1984; S, p. 18.
5. S, pp. 6–7.
6. Ibid.
7. Quoted in Gunther Barth, *City People: The Rise of Modern City Culture in Nineteenth-Century America* (New York: Oxford University Press, 1980), p. 210.
8. LM, July 8, 1984; S, pp. 121–22.
9. S, p. 8.
10. RN, 1915.
11. S, p. 89.
12. Ibid., p. 86.
13. Ibid., pp. 87–89.
14. Quoted in S, pp. 18–19; ILM, June 28, 1977.

15. S, p. 64; LM, "New York Childhood," pp. 18–23.
16. S, p. 66.
17. James Schleicher–LM, October 26, 1916, MFP.
18. S, pp. 76–77; ILM, June 28, 1977.
19. S, p. 85; LM, "A New York Adolescence: Tennis, Quadratic Equations, and Love," *The New Yorker*, December 4, 1937, pp. 86–89; LM did not start school until he was seven years old.
20. Quoted in S, p. 98.
21. MM-II, p. 304.
22. LM, "My Technical Background" (autobiographical fragment), February 8, 1979, LMC.
23. LM, "New York Adolescence," pp. 86–89.
24. S, p. 84.
25. LM, "New York Adolescence," pp. 86–89; S, p. 21.
26. Thomas S. Bates–LM, October 23, 1912, LMC.
27. LM–FJO, December 25, 1948, FJOC.
28. LM–David Liebovitz, November 16, 1963, LMC.
29. Mumford's school records and his writings for the *Caliper* are in the LMC.
30. S, p. 177; LM, "S.S. Mauretania," p. 7, LMC.
31. LM, "The History of a Prodigy," *Smart Set*, August 1921, pp. 49–52; "S.S. Mauretania," pp. 7–10, LMC.
32. LM, "New York Adolescence," pp. 86–94; LM, "New York Childhood" (manuscript, no date), LMC.
33. Mumford's correspondence with Beryl Morse is in the LMC.
34. S, p. 104.
35. LM, "The Growing Age" (manuscript, no date), LMC.
36. LM–CB, April 30, 1931, LMC-C; S, p. 104.
37. RN, June 20, 1915.
38. S, p. 108.
39. LM, "Prodigy," p. 50.
40. Beryl Morse–LM, no date, LMC; S, pp. 97, 107.
41. S, pp. 105, 109; LM, untitled verse, September 5, 1914, LMC.
42. LM, "None But the Brave," 1916, LMC.
43. LM, untitled manuscript, no date, LMC; ILM, June 28, 1977.
44. S, p. 114.
45. Ibid., p. 115.
46. LM, "Eros in Central Park" (manuscript, no date), LMC.
47. Quoted in S, p. 113; ILM, June 28, 1977; LM, "Eros in Central Park," LMC.

3

1. S, pp. 34–35.
2. LM, "A New York Adolescence: Tennis, Quadratic Equations, and Love," *The New Yorker*, December 4, 1937, pp. 86–94.
3. S, pp. 160–61.
4. Ibid., pp. 131–32.
5. S. Willis Rudy, *The College of the City of New York: A History, 1847–1947* (New York: The City College Press, 1949), pp. 266, 304.

6. S, p. 132.
7. Ibid., p. 133; LM, "Fruit: A Story," *The Forum*, December 1914, pp. 889–92.
8. WD, p. 51.
9. LM, autobiographical fragment, July 15, 1961, LMC.
10. JL–Sherman Paul, February 23, 1964, Sherman Paul's Lewis Mumford Collection, in the possession of Sherman Paul, University of Iowa, Iowa City.
11. FK, pp. 38–39.
12. RN, 1915.
13. Quoted in S, p. 101.
14. S, pp. 135–36; LM, "My Literary and Intellectual Lineage," August 20, 1963, LMC.
15. LM, in George Schreiber, *Portraits and Self-Portraits* (Boston: Houghton Mifflin, 1936), p. 119.
16. Quoted in LM, "Patrick Geddes, Insurgent," *The New Republic*, October 30, 1929, p. 295; PG, "Huxley as Teacher," *Nature*, May 9, 1925, pp. 740–43.
17. See, especially, PG, *Cities in Evolution: An Introduction to the Town Planning Movement and to the Study of Civics* (London: Williams and Norgate, 1915). There are four collections of Geddes's papers, each of which contains materials from, by, or pertaining to Mumford: Sir Patrick Geddes Publications, Cornell University Libraries, Department of Manuscripts and University Archives, Ithaca, New York; Patrick Geddes Correspondence, National Library of Scotland, Edinburgh (this contains his correspondence with Mumford); Patrick Geddes Papers, University of Strathclyde, University Archives, Glasgow, Scotland; and Patrick Geddes Papers and Miscellaneous Materials, Patrick Geddes Centre for Planning Studies, Outlook Tower, Edinburgh, Scotland.
    Philip Boardman has the complete bibliography of Geddes's publications in *The Worlds of Patrick Geddes: Biologist, Town Planner, Re-educator, Peace-Warrior* (London: Rutledge and Kegan Paul, 1978); see also Boardman's *Patrick Geddes, Maker of the Future* (Chapel Hill: University of North Carolina Press, 1944).
18. Quoted in Park Dixon Goist, "Patrick Geddes and the City," *American Institute of Planners, Journal*, January 1974, p. 34. Some of Geddes's ideas on Le Play are described in the notes he made for a sociology course he gave in 1891. They are in the Geddes papers at the University of Strathclyde.
19. PG, *Cities in Evolution* (New York: Harper Torchbooks, 1971), pp. 13–15. Mumford wrote an interesting unpublished essay in 1974 on Geddes called "The Geddesian Gambit," LMC.
20. See, especially, PG, *City Development: A Study of Parks, Gardens, and Culture-Institutes: A Report to the Carnegie Dunfermline Trust* (Edinburgh: Geddes and Colleagues, 1904).
21. Quoted in Marshall Stalley, ed., *Patrick Geddes: Spokesman for Man and the Environment* (New Brunswick, NJ: Rutgers University Press, 1972), p. 75.
22. S, p. 152.
23. For a recent study of Geddes's work at the Outlook Tower, see Michael Cuthbert, "The Concept of the Outlook Tower in the Work of Patrick Geddes," Thesis, Department of Scottish History, University of St. Andrews, 1987.
24. Paddy Kitchen, *A Most Unsettling Person: The Life and Ideas of Patrick Geddes, Founding*

Father of City Planning and Environmentalism (New York: Saturday Review Press, 1975), p. 131.

25. PG, "The Third Talk: The Valley Plan of Civilization," in "Talks from the Outlook Tower" in Stalley, *Geddes*, pp. 321–33.

26. PG, *The Masque of Learning and Its Many Meanings: A Pageant of Education Through the Ages* (Edinburgh: Geddes and Colleagues, 1912); Philip Mairet discusses Geddes as a sociologist in *Pioneers of Sociology: The Life and Letters of Patrick Geddes* (London: Lund Humphries, 1957).

27. LM, "Bernard Martin," republished in FK, p. 117.

28. At this age, Mumford fits, rather well, the psychological profile of alienated college students of the early 1960s that Kenneth Keniston draws in his book *The Uncommitted;* see Kenneth Keniston, *The Uncommitted: Alienated Youth in American Society* (New York: Dell, paperback ed., 1965), pp. 78, 80–89.

29. RN, January 9, 1916.

30. Ibid.

31. LM, "The Invalids," LMC.

32. CC, p. 3.

4

1. LM, "A Disciple's Rebellion: A Memoir of Patrick Geddes," *Encounter*, September 1966, pp. 11–21.

2. RN, 1916.

3. S, pp. 183–84.

4. S, pp. 140–41.

5. Ibid., p. 141.

6. LM–Stearns Morse, November 3, 1968, SMP.

7. S, pp. 123–24.

8. All quotes on Johnson and Dickens from John Wain, *Samuel Johnson* (New York: Viking, 1975), p. 58.

9. In his studies of alienated youth, Kenneth Keniston observed this same habit of walking as therapy. See Kenneth Keniston, *The Uncommitted: Alienated Youth in American Society* (New York: Dell, paperback ed., 1965), pp. 80–81.

10. RN, June 20, 1915; LM, "Who is Regius Storm?" 1917, LMC.

11. LM, "Memorandum for LM," 1962, LMC.

12. SU, p. 38.

13. Quoted in S, p. 143.

14. RN, 1915.

15. Ibid., 1914.

16. Ibid., 1918.

17. See Samuel Butler, *Notebooks*, edited by Geoffrey Keynes and Brian Hill (New York: Dutton, 1951), p. 5 for Butler's advice to a writer to keep a small notebook in his waistcoat.

18. RN, no date.

19. LM, autobiographical note, August 29, 1980, LMC; LM, "The Marriage of Museums," *Scientific Monthly*, 7 (September 1918), pp. 252–60.

20. LM, "Reflections: Prologue to Our Time," *The New Yorker*, March 10, 1975, pp. 56–57.

21. PG and J. Arthur Thomson, *The Evolution of Sex* (New York: Humboldt, 1890), pp. 246, 251–52; PG and Thomson later collaborated on a more extensive volume, *Life: Outlines of General Biology* (London: Williams and Norgate, 1931).

22. LM, review of *Life: Outlines of General Biology*, 2 vols., by PG and J. Arthur Thomson, *The New Republic*, September 16, 1931, pp. 130–31; LM, "Geddes, Insurgent," *The New Republic*, October 30, 1929, pp. 295–96.

23. LM, "Patrick Geddes, Victor Branford and Applied Sociology in England: The Urban Survey, Regionalism, and Urban Planning," in *An Introduction to the History of Sociology*, edited by Harry Elmer Barnes (Chicago: University of Chicago Press, 1948), pp. 689–90.

24. Butler, *Notebooks*, pp. 194, 2, 4.

25. Ibid., pp. 115, 116, 73.

26. LM, "The Gorgon's Head," 1917, LMC.

27. LM, autobiographical fragment, July 28, 1980, LMC.

28. LM, "My Literary and Intellectual Lineage," August 20, 1963, LMC.

29. RN, 1915.

30. PG, *Cities in Evolution: An Introduction to the Town Planning Movement and to the Study of Civics* (London: Williams and Norgate, 1915), p. 210.

31. RN, 1919.

5

1. Quoted in Joseph Jay Rubin and Charles H. Brown, *Walt Whitman of the New York Aurora* (State College, PA: Bald Eagle Press, 1950), p. 18.

2. Michael Gold, *Jews Without Money* (New York: Liveright, 1930), pp. 13–14.

3. RN, January 1916.

4. HMel, p. 194.

5. RN, January 1916, August 21, 1916.

6. LM, "Architecture as a Home for Man," *Architectural Record*, February 1968, p. 113.

7. RN, August 21, 1916.

8. Ibid., 1917.

9. Ibid.

10. Quoted in Justin Kaplan, *Walt Whitman: A Life* (New York: Simon & Schuster, 1980), pp. 109–10.

11. S, pp. 125–26.

12. RN, no date.

13. Ibid., 1916.

14. LM, "Garden Civilizations," 1917, MFP; later published as "Garden Civilizations: Preparing for a New Epoch," *Town and Country Planning*, March 1955, pp. 138–42.

15. RN, 1916.

16. LM, "The Geographic Distribution of the Garment Industry," 1916, LMC.

17. LM, "Counter-Tendencies: An Outline of a Regional Policy for Manhattan," 1916, LMC.

18. ILM, July 7, 1983.

19. LM, "Geography as a Basis for Social Reform," no date, LMC; LM, "Regionalism: A Bibliographic Note," no date, LMC.

20. S, p. 169.

21. "Nineteen-Seventeen," LMC.
22. LM, "The Pittsburgh District," August 1917, LMC; LM, "Methods of Civic Research: A Hint from Pittsburgh Experience," 1917, LMC.
23. S, p. 176.
24. LM, "Memorandum: Plan for a Civic Background Series," no date, LMC.
25. Ebenezer Howard, *Garden Cities of Tomorrow*, edited by Frederic J. Osborn (Cambridge, MA: MIT Press, 1965), p. 48; originally titled *To-Morrow: A Peaceful Path to Real Reform*. For more on Howard and his ideas, see Stanley Buder, "Ebenezer Howard: The Genesis of a Town Planning Movement," *American Institute of Planners, Journal*, November 1969, pp. 380–98; and Walter R. Creese, *The Search for Environment* (New Haven, CT: Yale University Press, 1966). Howard's papers are in the Hertfordshire County Archive, Hertfordshire, England.
26. LM, "Garden Civilizations," p. 139.
27. S, pp. 167–68.
28. LM, "Nineteen-Seventeen," LMC.
29. Emory Holloway, ed., *The Uncollected Poetry and Prose of Walt Whitman*, 2 vols. (Garden City, NY: Doubleday, Page, 1921), pp. 66–76.
30. Quoted in LM, "The Metropolitan Milieu," AAS, p. 43; Holloway, *Uncollected Poetry and Prose*.
31. LM, "Nineteen-Seventeen," LMC.
32. LM, "Cities in Evolution," 1916, LMC.
33. LM, "Autobiographical Essay," no date, pp. 11–22, LMC.
34. Samuel Butler, *Notebooks*, edited by Geoffrey Keynes and Brian Hill (New York: Dutton, 1951), p. 93.
35. RN, no date.
36. LM, "The Brownstone Front," 1917, LMC; LM later changed the title of the play to "Asters and Goldenrod."
37. Quoted in Erik H. Erikson, *Identity: Youth and Crisis* (New York: Norton, paperback ed., 1968), p. 19.
38. LM, "Thoughts: Pleasant and Unpleasant," 1915, LMC.
39. S, pp. 128–30.
40. Walt Whitman, "City of Ships," in *Leaves of Grass: Comprehensive Reader's Edition*, edited by Harold W. Blodgett and Sculley Bradley (New York: New York University Press, 1965), p. 294.

6

1. LM, "A New York Apprenticeship," p. 1, LMC.
2. See Edward Shils, "Lewis Mumford: On the Way to the New Jerusalem," *The New Criterion*, May 1983, p. 38.
3. S, p. 180; LM's first three published essays were "Jones and I," *Metropolitan: the Liveliest Magazine in America*, February 1914, p. 13; "Community Cooking," *The Forum*, July 1914, pp. 95–99; and "Fruit," *The Forum*, December 1914, pp. 889–91.
4. S, p. 181.
5. JL–Sherman Paul, February 23, 1964, Sherman Paul's Lewis Mumford Collection, in the possession of Sherman Paul, University of Iowa, Iowa City.
6. S, pp. 182–83.
7. RN, August 29, 1916.

8. LM, "New York Apprenticeship," pp. 8–9; LM, autobiographical fragment, 1956, p. 46, MFP.
9. S, pp. 179–80.
10. LM–Daniel Aaron, January 17, 1959, LMC.
11. Quoted in Allen Churchill, *The Improper Bohemians: A Re-creation of Greenwich Village in Its Heyday* (New York: Dutton, 1959), pp. 34–35.
12. Quoted in Ibid., p. 11.
13. Daniel Aaron, *Writers on the Left: Episodes in American Literary Communism* (New York: Harcourt, Brace and World, 1961), pp. 85–87.
14. Michael Gold–LM, September 2, 1954, LMC.
15. RN, 1918.
16. LM, "A Study in Success," 1923, LMC.
17. LM, "S.S. Mauretania," p. 19B.
18. Michael Gold–LM, September 2, 1954, LMC.
19. LM–Daniel Aaron, January 17, 1959, LMC.
20. S, p. 71.
21. LM, "Nineteen-Seventeen," LMC.
22. Quoted in S, p. 195.
23. John Reed, "One Solid Month of Liberty," *The Masses*, September 1917, pp. 5–6.
24. LM–Michael Gold, no date, LMC.
25. RN, 1917.
26. S, p. 195.
27. LM, "1918," LMC; S, pp. 196–97.
28. David Liebovitz, "Lewis Mumford: A Memoir," in *The Lewis Mumford–David Liebovitz Letters, 1923–1968*, edited by Bettina Liebovitz Knapp (Troy, NY: Whitston, 1983), pp. 237–38.
29. Ibid., pp. 241–42.
30. JL–LM, February 2, 1918, LMC.
31. S, p. 199.
32. BD, p. 51.
33. S, pp. 201–10.
34. LM, "1919," LMC.
35. S, p. 209.
36. Ibid., p. 199.
37. Robert Morss Lovett, *All Our Years* (New York: Viking, 1948), pp. 153–56; RN, August 16, 1919.
38. Nicholas Joost, *Scofield Thayer and The Dial: An Illustrated History* (Carbondale, IL: Southern Illinois University Press, 1964), pp. 3–6; see also Joost, *Years of Transition: The Dial, 1912–1920* (Barre, MA: Barre Publishers, 1967).
39. S, p. 184.
40. Ibid., pp. 214–16.
41. LM, "My Literary and Intellectual Lineage," August 20, 1963, LMC, p. 8.
42. S, p. 220.
43. LM, "My Literary and Intellectual Lineage," p. 9; S, pp. 220–21.
44. Quoted in Sidney Lens, *Radicalism in America* (New York: Crowell, 1969 ed.), p. 257.

45. S, p. 219.
46. LM, review of *The World War and Its Consequences* by William H. Hobbs, *The Dial*, April 19, 1919, pp. 406–407.
47. S, p. 251.
48. Joost, *Years*, pp. 238–42.
49. Quoted in William Wasserstrom, ed., *A Dial Miscellany* (Syracuse, NY: Syracuse University Press, 1963), p. xv.
50. P, November 11, 1919.
51. LM–Michael Gold, October 2, 1919, LMC.
52. S, p. 253.

7

1. "Bernard Martin," in FK, p. 125; P, February 4, 1920; LM–VB, July 9, 1919, September 20, 1919, LMC.
2. LM–VB, July 9, 1919, November 29, 1919, LMC.
3. VB–LM, December 10, 1919, LMC.
4. LM–VB, January 11, 1920, LMC.
5. LM–VB, February 13, March 19, 1920; P, February 4, 1920, LMC.
6. P, June 1, 1921.
7. S, p. 224.
8. Ibid., pp. 227–28.
9. GM, pp. 192–93.
10. ISM, July 6, 1983; P, February 4, 1920.
11. SM, account of her family background, November 20, 1952, MFP.
12. SM, "A Few Remembered Anecdotes about Grandfather William, 1869–1964," no date, MFP.
13. RN, June 16, 1947; GM, pp. 10–11.
14. S, p. 228.
15. Ibid., p. 230.
16. P, February 4, February 22, April 3, May 21, 1920.
17. Ibid., December 23, 1919.
18. LM–Elvina Mumford, October 4, 1918, LMC.
19. P, April 3, 1920.
20. WD, pp. 69–70.
21. S, pp. 254–55; Loch was Branford's private secretary when Mumford first met her. In 1921 she was made secretary of the Sociological Society, serving in that position through 1923.
22. S, p. 260.
23. LM–PG, PGC; S, pp. 261–63.
24. LM, "Victor Branford," *The New Republic*, August 27, 1930, p. 43; S, p. 259.
25. LM, "Branford," p. 43.
26. S, p. 262.
27. LM, "Branford," p. 44.
28. Ibid.
29. S, p. 255.

30. LM–PG, July 31, 1921.
31. P, June 7, 1920.
32. LM, "S.S. Mauretania," p. 7.
33. S, p. 235.
34. LM–SM, September 10, 1920, LMC.
35. LM–DCL, May 1921, LMC.
36. LM–JL, August 5, 1920, LMC.
37. LM–SM, no date, LMC.
38. S, p. 280.
39. Ibid., pp. 257–58.
40. LM, "The Year 1920: Retrospect," LMC.
41. LM–PG, May 12, 1921, PGC.
42. LM–DCL, January 29, 1921, LMC.
43. LM–Sarita Lifschitz, July 18, 1920, LMC.
44. S, p. 283.
45. LM–SM, July 4, 1920, LMC.
46. Quoted in LM–SM, August 18, 1920, LMC.
47. S, p. 277.
48. LM–SM, August 18, 1920, LMC.

8

1. P, October 25, November 3, November 8, 1920.
2. Nicholas Joost, *Years of Transition: The Dial, 1912–1920* (Barre, MA: Barre Publishers, 1967), pp. 157, 182; Alyse Gregory, *The Day Is Gone* (New York: Dutton, 1948), pp. 136, 175–76.
3. Gregory, *The Day Is Gone*, pp. 136, 175–79, 209; Llewelyn Powys, *The Verdict of Bridelgoose* (London: Jonathan Cape, 1927), p. 115.
4. Gregory, *The Day Is Gone*, pp. 210–11.
5. Quoted in Joost, *Scofield Thayer and The Dial: An Illustrated History* (Carbondale, IL: Southern Illinois University Press, 1964), p. 81.
6. ILM, July 6, 1983; P, November 3, 1920, LMC.
7. S, p. 288.
8. LM, "Nineteen-Twenty," LMC.
9. P, January 27, 1921.
10. Ibid., February 26, 1921.
11. ILM, July 6, 1983.
12. LM–Beryl Morse, November 15, 1949, LMC.
13. LM–DCL, July 9, 1921, LMC; S, p. 289.
14. S, p. 291; LM–SM, July 5, 1921, LMC.
15. S, p. 290; P, June 6, 1921.
16. LM–SM, July 25, 1921, LMC; S, p. 293.
17. Quoted in S, pp. 292–93; SM–LM, August 20, 1921, LMC-C.
18. P, July 31, 1921.
19. LM–SM, August 18, 1921, LMC-C.
20. P, June 2, 1921.
21. JL–LM, July 7, 1921, LMC; see also JL–LM, August 17, 1920, LMC.
22. LM–JL, June 27, 1920, LMC.

23. P, February 26, 1921.
24. LM–Stearns Morse, November 15, 1949, SMP.
25. Ibid.
26. ISM, July 6, 1983.
27. LM–DCL, September 23, 1921, LMC.
28. SM–LM, July 26, 1921, LMC-C.
29. SM–LM, July 20, 1921, LMC-C.
30. Quoted in S, p. 294.
31. P, October 27, 1921.
32. ISM, July 6, 1983; S, p. 296.
33. LM–Stearns Morse, November 15, 1947, SMP; S, pp. 300–301.
34. LM–PG, January 15, 1922, PGC.
35. S, p. 298.
36. P, January 23, 1922.
37. LM, autobiographical fragment, April 8, 1979, LMC.
38. SM, Personalia, November 1, 1955, LMC-C.
39. SM–JS, June 11, 1938, LMC-C.
40. SM–LM, August 20, 1921, LMC-C.
41. P, January 23, 1922.
42. SM–JS, June 11, 1938, LMC-C.
43. ISM, July 6, 1983.
44. LM–Stearns Morse, November 15, 1949, SMP.

9

1. Frederick J. Hoffman, *The Twenties: American Writing in the Postwar Decade* (New York: Free Press, rev. ed., 1962), p. 33.
2. RN, 1963–1973, LMC.
3. LM–DCL, September 23, 1921, LMC.
4. LM, "The Beginnings of a Literary Friendship," in *The Van Wyck Brooks–Lewis Mumford Letters: The Record of a Literary Friendship, 1921–1963*, edited by Robert E. Spiller (New York: Dutton, 1970), p. 1.
5. VWB–LM, July 12, 1922, VWBP; LM–JL, August 5, 1920, LMC.
6. Susan J. Turner, *A History of The Freeman: Literary Landmark of the Early Twenties* (New York: Columbia University Press, 1963), pp. 2, 8, 19–22, 27–29, 45–47; Franz Oppenheimer, *The State*, translated by John M. Gitterman (New York: Vanguard, 1926).
7. Turner, *Freeman*, pp. 12–13; VWB, *Days of the Phoenix* (New York: Dutton, 1957), pp. 52–65; LM–Robert Crunden, July 20, 1961, AJNP.
8. VWB, *Phoenix*, p. 57; Raymond Nelson, *Van Wyck Brooks: A Writer's Life* (New York: Dutton, 1981), p. 153.
9. Quoted in VWB, *Phoenix*, p. 56.
10. Quoted in Turner, *Freeman*, p. 28.
11. S, p. 362; James Hoopes, *Van Wyck Brooks: In Search of American Culture* (Amherst, MA: University of Massachusetts Press, 1977), p. 152.
12. LM–VWB, February 14, 1959, VWBP.
13. VWB, "A Reviewer's Notebook," *The Freeman*, May 5, 1920, p. 191.

14. S, pp. 366–67; Harold Stearns, ed., *Civilization in the United States: An Inquiry by Thirty Americans* (New York: Harcourt, Brace, 1922).

15. Quoted in Allen Churchill, *The Improper Bohemians: A Re-Creation of Greenwich Village in Its Heyday* (New York: Dutton, 1959), pp. 240–41.

16. Churchill, p. 243; VWB, *Phoenix*, pp. 159–69.

17. S, p. 368; LM–DCL, September 23, 1921, LMC.

18. P, March 23, April 1, 1921.

19. RN, December 19, 1921.

20. JL–LM, July 15, 1921, LMC; see also letter of JL to LM reprinted in letter from LM to Ruth Lachenbruch, 1971, LMC.

21. LM, autobiographical fragment, October 1971, LMC.

22. Geroid Robinson–LM, February 26, 1921, LMC.

23. LM–DCL, March 11, 1922, LMC; LM–Horace Liveright, February 20, 1922, LMC.

24. LM–Joel Spingarn, February 5, March 1, 1923, JSP.

25. S, pp. 368–69; LM–DCL, 1922, LMC.

26. LM–DCL, 1922, LMC; LM–VWB, August 1, 1922, VWBP.

27. S, pp. 303–304.

28. LM, "S.S. Mauretania," LMC.

29. Quoted in S, p. 306.

30. LM, "Bernard Martin," in FK, p. 137.

31. S, p. 314.

32. Ibid., pp. 310–14.

33. RN, June 1923, LMC.

34. LM–JL, December 19, 1922, LMC.

35. S, p. 316.

36. See, for example, Alfred Zimmern, "Post-War Utopianism," *The Literary Review*, January 20, 1923, p. 387.

37. VWB, *Phoenix*, p. 154.

38. Quoted in Justin Kaplan, *Walt Whitman: A Life* (New York: Simon & Schuster, 1980), pp. 168–69.

39. LM, "Abandoned Roads," *The Freeman*, April 12, 1922, pp. 101–102.

40. LM, "The Collapse of Tomorrow," *The Freeman*, July 13, 1921, pp. 414–15.

41. LM, "Contemporary Disillusion; A Dialogue," *The Nation*, December 10, 1924, pp. 636–37.

42. LM, "The Adolescence of Reform," *The Freeman*, December 1, 1920, pp. 272–73.

43. SU, pp. 164–67.

44. LM, "Toward a Humanist Synthesis," *The Freeman*, March 2, 1921, pp. 583–85; SU, p. 247; LM, "A Modern Synthesis," *The Saturday Review of Literature*, April 12, 1930, pp. 920–21; May 10, 1930, pp. 1028–29.

45. LM–PG, July 31, 1921, PGC; SU, p. 281.

46. SU, pp. 290, 302–303.

47. Ibid, p. 307.

10

1. SS-D, p. vi.

2. Frank Lloyd Wright–LM, January 7, 1929, in *Letters to Architects: Frank Lloyd*

Wright, edited by Bruce Brooks Pfeiffer (Fresno, CA: The Press at California State University, 1984), p. 143.

3. S, p. 426.
4. LM, "Houses, Machines, Cities," June 9, 1931, LMC.
5. S, p. 333.
6. LM–PG, November 26, 1929, PGC.
7. HMel, p. 71; LM, *Architecture: Reading with a Purpose*, no. 23 (Chicago: American Library Association, 1926), p. 34.
8. LM, "The Modern City," in Talbot Hamlin, ed., *Forms and Functions of Twentieth-Century Architecture*, vol. 4, *Building Types* (New York: Columbia University Press, 1952), p. 802.
9. LM, *Architecture*, pp. 1–18.
10. LM, "Architecture and History," *Journal of the American Institute of Architects*, April 1924, p. 192.
11. LM, *Architecture*, pp. 12–13; LM, "American Architecture Today: Part I," *Architecture*, April 1928, pp. 181–88.
12. Quoted in Christopher Tunnard and Henry Hope Reed, *Skyline: The Growth and Form of Our American Cities and Towns* (New York: New American Library, Mentor ed., 1956), p. 155.
13. LM, "The Metropolitan Milieu," AAS, p. 40.
14. LM, "Our Modern Style," *Journal of the American Institute of Architects*, January 1924, pp. 26–27.
15. Col. W. A. Starratt, "The Mountains of Manhattan," *Saturday Evening Post*, May 12, 1928, pp. 24–25, 72.
16. Quoted in Bayard Still, *Mirror for Gotham: New York as Seen by Contemporaries from Dutch Days to the Present* (New York: New York University Press, 1956), pp. 261–62; for an excellent recent study of the skyscraper, see Paul Goldberger, *The Skyscraper* (New York: Knopf, 1981).
17. S, pp. 428–29.
18. See, especially, LM, "New York vs. Chicago in Architecture," *Architecture*, November 1927, pp. 241–44.
19. LM, "The Arts," in *Whither Mankind?: A Panorama of Modern Civilization*, edited by Charles A. Beard (New York: Longman's, Green, 1928), pp. 296–98.
20. LM, BD-D, pp. 49–82.
21. LM, *Architecture*, p. 27.
22. BD-D, pp. 59–75.
23. Robert Fishman, *Urban Utopias in the Twentieth Century: Ebenezer Howard, Frank Lloyd Wright and Le Corbusier* (New York: Basic Books, 1977); Siegfried Giedion, *Space, Time and Architecture: The Growth of a New Tradition* (Cambridge, MA: Harvard University Press, 1941); Le Corbusier, *Vers une architecture* (Paris, 1923).
24. S, pp. 11–12.
25. LM, "Function and Expression in Architecture," *Architectural Record*, November 1951, pp. 106–17.
26. Philip Johnson–LM, January 3, 1931, LMC.
27. Quoted in Pfeiffer, ed., *Letters to Architects*, p. 145.
28. Frank Lloyd Wright–LM, 1930, in Pfeiffer, ibid.

29. LM, "The Sky Line: A Phoenix Too Infrequent-I," *The New Yorker*, November 28, 1953, pp. 133–39.
30. Frank Lloyd Wright–LM, January 1952, in Pfeiffer, p. 149.
31. S, pp. 431–33.
32. Frank Lloyd Wright, *An Autobiography* (New York: Longman's, Green, 1932), pp. 168–70; for Wright's life and ideas, see Robert C. Twombly, *Frank Lloyd Wright: His Life and His Architecture* (New York: Wiley, 1979); and a more recent biography by Brendan Gill, *Many Masks: A Life of Frank Lloyd Wright* (New York: G. P. Putnam's Sons, 1987).
33. S, p. 433.
34. Frank Lloyd Wright–LM, January 1952, in Pfeiffer, p. 149.
35. Louis Sullivan, "An Unaffected School of Modern Architecture," in Louis Sullivan, *Kindergarten Chats and Other Writings*, edited by Isabella Athey (New York: Wittenborn, Schultz, 1947), p. 30.
36. Henry-Russell Hitchcock, Jr., *In the Nature of Materials* (New York: Duell, Sloan, Pearce, 1942), p. 6.
37. BD-D, p. 76.
38. Henry-Russell Hitchcock, Jr., and Philip Johnson, *The International Style: Architecture Since 1922* (New York: Museum of Modern Art, 1932).
39. S, p. 346.
40. LM, "Phoenix-I"; LM, "A Phoenix Too Infrequent-II," *The New Yorker*, December 12, 1953, pp. 116–20.
41. S, p. 438.
42. Ibid.
43. First part of quote in Frank Lloyd Wright–LM, June 4, 1958; second part in Wright–LM, May 22, 1958; both in Pfeiffer, pp. 151–52.
44. Frank Lloyd Wright–LM, June 4, 1958, in Pfeiffer, p. 152.
45. LM, "Phoenix-I," pp. 133–39; LM, "Phoenix-II," pp. 116–20.
46. BD-D, p. 79.
47. Quoted in Edgar Kaufmann and Ben Raeburn, *Frank Lloyd Wright: Writings and Buildings* (Cleveland: World, 1960), pp. 92–93.
48. LM, "Our Modern Style," *Journal of the American Institute of Architects*, January 1924, p. 27.

II

1. For a history of the RPAA, see Roy Lubove, *Community Planning in the 1920s: The Contributions of the Regional Planning Association of America* (Pittsburgh: University of Pittsburgh Press, 1963). For an excellent assessment of the RPAA's contributions to regional planning, see Carl Sussman, ed., *Planning the Fourth Migration: The Neglected Vision of the Regional Planning Association of America* (Cambridge, MA: MIT Press, 1976); the minutes of the RPAA meetings are in the LMC.
2. LM, introduction to CS, *Toward New Towns for America* (Cambridge, MA: MIT Press, 1966 ed.), p. 13.
3. LM, "A Modest Man's Enduring Contributions to Urban and Regional Planning," *Journal of the American Institute of Architects*, December 1976, pp. 19–29.

4. Lubove, *Community Planning*, pp. 31–48.
5. Quoted in CS, "Henry Wright: 1878–1936," *American Architect and Architecture*, August 1936, pp. 22–24.
6. LM, autobiographical fragment, August 5, 1975, LMC.
7. LM, "The Theory and Practice of Regionalism," *Sociological Review*, XX, January 1928, pp. 18–19; LM, CC, p. 342. For a superb essay on this theme, see Thomas P. Hughes, "The Industrial Revolution That Never Came," *American Heritage of Invention and Technology*, Winter 1988, pp. 59–64.
8. PG, *The Masque of Learning and Its Many Meanings* (Edinburgh: Patrick Geddes and Colleagues, 1912).
9. LM, "The Culture of the City," *Journal of the American Institute of Architects*, June 1961, pp. 54–60.
10. LM, "The Intolerable City: Must It Keep Growing?" *Harper's Magazine*, February 1926, pp. 286–87.
11. LM, "Theory and Practice," p. 24; see also CS, "Dinosaur Cities," *The Survey Graphic*, May 1925, pp. 134–38.
12. LM, CC, pp. 397–99, 484–89.
13. Ibid.; LM, "The Social Function of Open Spaces," *Landscape*, Winter 1960–61, pp. 1–6.
14. Jane Jacobs, *The Death and Life of Great American Cities* (New York: Random House, 1961), p. 19.
15. E. B. White, "You Can't Resettle Me!" *Saturday Evening Post*, October 10, 1936, pp. 8–9, 91–92.
16. Quoted in Robert A. M. Stern, Gregory Gilmartin, and Thomas Mellins, *New York 1930* (New York: Rizzoli, 1987), p. 38. This is the most complete account of New York's architecture in the interwar years, a splendid study.
17. LM, "Regional Planning and the Small Town," *Journal of the American Institute of Architects*, August 1950, p. 84.
18. LM, "Regionalism and Irregionalism," *Sociological Review*, XIX, October 1927, pp. 277–88; LM, "Cities Fit to Live In," *The Nation*, May 15, 1948, pp. 530–33. LM, "The Social Functions of Open Space," in *Space for Living*, (ed) Sylvia Crowe (Amsterdam: Djambatan, 1961), pp. 22–40.
19. LM, "Cities Fit to Live In," pp. 530–33.
20. Quoted in Mel Scott, *American City Planning Since 1890* (Berkeley, CA: University of California Press, 1971 ed.), pp. 250–51.
21. Scott, *City Planning*, pp. 248–52.
22. CS, *New Towns*, p. 24.
23. GM, p. 13.
24. For a history of the Radburn experiment, see Daniel Schaffer, *Garden Cities for America: The Radburn Experience* (Philadelphia: Temple University Press, 1982).
25. CH, plate 51.
26. CS, *New Towns*, pp. 37–73.
27. LM and BMK, "Townless Highways for the Motorist," *Harper's Magazine*, August 1931, pp. 347–56.
28. ILM, July 12, 1982.
29. LM, "Social Function," pp. 1–6.

30. LM, "The Neighborhood and the Neighborhood Unit," *Town Planning Review,* January 1954, pp. 256–70.
31. LM, "The Fate of Garden Cities," *Journal of the American Institute of Architects,* February 1927, pp. 37–39.
32. LM–PG, December 4, 1924, PGC.
33. LM review of Harold J. Laski, *Authority in the Modern State, The Dial,* July 26, 1919, pp. 59–61; LM, "What I Believe," *The Forum,* November 1930, pp. 263–68.
34. S, p. 340; LM, introduction to BMK, *The New Exploration: A Philosophy of Regional Planning* (Urbana, IL: University of Illinois Press, 1962), p. xvi. This was first published in 1928.
35. LM, "Benton MacKaye as Regional Planner," *The Living Wilderness,* January 1976, p. 14.
36. LM–BMK, March 1, 1971, MKFP; for MacKaye's ideas on regional planning and conservation, see also BMK, *From Geography to Geotechnics* (Urbana, IL: University of Illinois Press, 1968); BMK, "The Geotechnics of North America," 1969, MKFP; and Paul T. Bryant, "The Quality of the Day: The Achievements of Benton MacKaye" (Ann Arbor, MI: University Microfilms International, 1965).
37. BMK, "An Appalachian Trail: A Project in Regional Planning," *Journal of the American Institute of Architects,* October 1921, pp. 3–8.
38. LM introduction to BMK, *New Exploration,* 1962 ed., p. viii.
39. "Report of the Commission of Housing and Regional Planning to Governor Alfred E. Smith" (Albany: J. B. Lyon, May 7, 1926).
40. LM, "Regions—To Live In," *The Survey Graphic,* May 1, 1925, pp. 151–52; LM, "The Fourth Migration," *The Survey Graphic,* May 1, 1925, pp. 130–33.
41. LM–PG, October 17, 1925, PGC.

12

1. LM–DCL, February 14, 1925, LMC.
2. LM–CB, August 3, 1930, LMC-C; LM–FJO, October 17, 1963, FJOC.
3. LM–PG, July 6, 1923, PGC.
4. VWB, *Days of the Phoenix* (New York: Dutton, 1957), p. 67.
5. JL–LM, July 20, 1924, May 26, 1924, LMC.
6. ISM, May 22, 1985.
7. LM–JL, December 19, 1922, LMC.
8. LM–DCL, March 11, 1922, LMC.
9. S, pp. 383–85.
10. Quoted in Alan Trachtenberg, *Brooklyn Bridge: Fact and Symbol* (Chicago: University of Chicago Press, Phoenix ed., 1979), p. 144.
11. S, p. 386.
12. LM–JL, December 13, 1924, LMC.
13. RN, December 31, 1923; Albert Jay Nock–LM, December 18, 1923, LMC; LM–VWB, June 17, 1922, VWBP; VWB–LM, July 12, 1922, LMC.
14. LM, "The Disciple's Rebellion: A Memoir of Patrick Geddes," *Encounter,* September 1966, pp. 11–22.
15. LM–DCL, May 12, 1923, LMC.
16. Quoted in S, p. 319.
17. Quoted in Paddy Kitchen, *A Most Unsettling Person: The Life and Ideas of Patrick*

Geddes, Founding Father of City Planning and Environmentalism (New York: Saturday Review Press, 1975), p. 247.

18. S, pp. 322–25.
19. LM–PG, January 7, February 5, 1923, PGC.
20. RN, July 7, 1923.
21. Ibid., 1963.
22. LM–PG, July 6, 1923, PGC.
23. Ibid.
24. ILM, June 12, 1978; LM, "Disciple's Rebellion," pp. 11–21.
25. RN, September 11, 1925.
26. For a description of Geddes's Edinburgh, see Kitchen, *Unsettling Person*, pp. 112–42.
27. PG, "What to Do," reprinted in Kitchen, *Unsettling Person*, p. 331; LM, "Geddesian Gambit," LMC; for Geddes as an urban sociologist, see, especially, Philip Mairet, *Pioneer of Sociology: The Life and Letters of Patrick Geddes* (London: Lund Humphries, 1957); and H. E. Meller, "Patrick Geddes: An Analysis of His Theory of Civics, 1880–1904," *Victorian Studies*, no. 3, XVI (March 1973), pp. 291–313.
28. S, pp. 399–400; RN, September 11, 1925.
29. S, pp. 400–401.
30. RN, September 11, 1925.
31. PG–LM, August 26, 1926, LMC.
32. LM–PG, May 3, 1931, PGC; S, p. 404.
33. Kitchen, *Unsettling Person*, p. 319.
34. LM–HM, September 10, 1959, HMC.
35. LM, autobiographical fragment, 1956, LMC.
36. RN, March 24, 1935.
37. LM–DCL, December 8, 1925, LMC.
38. LM–PG, December 5, 1920, PGC.
39. LM–Albert Leon Guérard, November 19, 1929, AGP.
40. LM, SU-V, p. 6.
41. Caesar Finn–LM, September 21, 1947, LMC; LM–FJO, October 17, 1963, FJOC; Evangeline Adams–LM, July 16, 1930, LMC.
42. LM–DCL, December 8, 1925, LMC.
43. Ibid.

13

1. LM–PG, May 5, 1924, PGC.
2. LM–Joel Spingarn, February 5, 1923, JSP.
3. P, June 9, 1925.
4. Quoted in S, pp. 348–51.
5. P, June 9, 1925.
6. S, pp. 387–89.
7. LM–DCL, July 8, 1925, LMC.
8. S, p. 390; GM, pp. 5–6.
9. SM–LM, August 23, 1925, LMC-C.
10. WD, p. 96; S, pp. 381–83.

11. WD, p. 320.
12. LM, GD-D, pp. 1–38.
13. LM–SM, August 15, 1925, LMC.
14. ILM, July 13, 1982.
15. Quoted in Justin Kaplan, *Walt Whitman: A Life* (New York: Simon & Schuster, 1980), pp. 165–69.
16. LM–DCL, February 14, 1925, LMC; ILM, June 28, 1977.
17. WD, p. 510.
18. Joel Elias Spingarn, *Poems* (New York: Harcourt, Brace, 1924), pp. 39–40.
19. For a review of Spingarn's life and ideas, see Marshall Van Deusen, *J. E. Spingarn* (New York: Twayne, 1971).
20. LM, untitled manuscript, no date, LMC.
21. LM–Joel Spingarn, June 7, 1926, JSP; LM, GD-D, p. xvi.
22. Whitman quoted in Kaplan, *Whitman*, p. 318; LM–Joel Spingarn, December 22, 1926, JSP.
23. Sinclair Lewis quoted in LM, "The Story of Troutbeck," February 1953, LMC.
24. LM–JS, June 1, 1941, LMC.
25. GD-D, pp. 1–3, 140; LM, review of VWB, *The Ordeal of Mark Twain*, *The Saturday Review of Literature*, May 6, 1933, pp. 473–75.
26. SS-D, pp. 1–2; LM, "Life by Rule of Thumb," *The Freeman*, April 12, 1922, pp. 102–103.
27. GD-D, pp. 78–79, 83, 100–17, 124–25; SU-D, p. 243; BD-D, pp. 27–29.
28. BD-D, pp. 2–3.
29. Ibid., pp. vi, 4–8.
30. VWB, "On Creating a Usable Past," *The Dial*, April 11, 1918, p. 338.
31. LM, "Regionalism and Irregionalism," *Sociological Review*, XIX, October 1927, p. 135.
32. Norman Foerster, "The Literary Prophets," *The Bookman*, September 1930, pp. 35–44; on this theme, see Alan Trachtenberg, "Mumford in the Twenties: The Historian as Artist," *Salmagundi: A Quarterly of the Humanities and Social Sciences*, Summer 1980, pp. 29–42; Frank G. Novak, Jr., "Lewis Mumford and the Reclamation of Human History," *CLIO*, February 1987, pp. 159–81; John L. Thomas, "Lewis Mumford: Regionalist Historian," *Reviews in American History*, March 1988, pp. 158–72.
33. Quoted in Trachtenberg, "Mumford in the Twenties," pp. 29–42.
34. HMel, p. 155.
35. VWB–LM, July 26, 1926, LMC; on this theme of American rediscovery, see especially Richard Ruland, *The Rediscovery of American Literature* (Cambridge, MA: Harvard University Press, 1967); and F. O. Matthiessen's *American Renaissance: Art and Expression in the Age of Emerson and Whitman* (New York, Oxford University Press, 1941). *The Golden Day* had a strong influence on Matthiessen's classic work.
36. VWB, *The Wine of Puritans: A Study of Present-Day America* (London: Sisley, 1908), pp. 14–18.
37. VWB–LM, September 13, 1925, LMC; James Hoopes, *Van Wyck Brooks: In Search of American Culture* (Amherst, MA: University of Massachusetts Press, 1977), p. 173.

38. Brooks quote in Hoopes, *Brooks*, p. 277; MacLeish quote in RN, October 7, 1948, LMC.
39. George Santayana–LM, December 16, 1926, LMC; for other assessments of *The Golden Day*, see John Macy–LM, December 30, 1926, LMC; Sherwood Anderson–LM, no date, LMC; C.H.S., *The Cambridge Review*, March 2, 1928, p. 305; Gilbert Seldes, "The Golden Day," *The Dial*, June 27, 1927, pp. 519–21; Waldo Frank, "A Golden Dusk," *The New Republic*, December 8, 1926, p. 72; John Dewey, whom Mumford attacked rather unfairly in *The Golden Day*, replied in "The Pragmatic Acquiescence," *The New Republic*, January 5, 1927, pp. 186–89; for LM's reply to Dewey, see "The Pragmatic Acquiescence: A Reply," *The New Republic*, January 19, 1927, pp. 250–51.
40. LM–VWB, November 1925, VWBP.
41. VWB–LM, September 13, 1925, LMC.
42. LM, "Myrtle and Forget-me-nots," May 31, 1977, LMC.

14

1. Rosenfeld signed the announcement, dated July 1, 1926, LMC; Alfred Kreymborg, "The *Caravan* Adventure," in Jerome Mellquist and Lucie Weise, eds., *Paul Rosenfeld: Voyager in the Arts* (New York: Creative Age Press, 1948), pp. 26–29; LM, "Lyric Wisdom," in Mellquist and Weise, ibid., pp. 56–57.
2. Alan Tate, "Anomaly in Literary New York," in ibid., p. 141; Copland quoted in Kreymborg, "*Caravan*," ibid., p. 35.
3. Alyse Gregory, "Dial Days," in ibid., p. 20.
4. S, p. 373.
5. Ibid., p. 371.
6. Kreymborg, "*Caravan*," pp. 31–32.
7. Rosenfeld quoted in LM, "Lyric Wisdom," p. 63; Gregory, "Dial," p. 21; LM quoted in "Lyric Wisdom," p. 64; for LM on Rosenfeld, see also "Paul Rosenfeld," February 12, 1929, LMC.
8. Paul Rosenfeld–LM, October 18, May 8, 1937, LMC.
9. LM, "Lyric Wisdom," pp. 72–73; S, p. 381.
10. LM–Walter Lippmann, January 1, 1928, WLP.
11. P-C, July 1929.
12. S, p. 454.
13. Ibid., p. 453.
14. LM, "The Builders of the Bridge," in FK, pp. 222, 283–86; LM–JS, October 30, 1938, April 19, 1942, LMC-C; S, p. 128.
15. LM, "Builders of the Bridge," p. 312.
16. HMel, p. 5.
17. P-C, July 1929.
18. LM–HM, August 14, 1928, HMC.
19. LM–JL, August 19, 1928, LMC.
20. Quoted in *Publishers Weekly*, October 7, 1933, pp. 1229–30; see also Wallace Gilmer, *Horace Liveright: Publishers of the Twenties* (New York: David Lewis, 1970).
21. S, pp. 191–92; LM, "Projected Books," 1928, LMC.

22. Thomas Beer, "Good Friday Spell," *New York Herald Tribune Books*, March 10, 1929, pp. 1–2; Raymond Weaver, "Mumford Sees New Cultural Synthesis," New York *Evening Post*, March 9, 1929; see also Archibald MacLeish, "A New Life of Melville," *The Bookman*, April 1929, pp. 183–85; William Plomer, "Herman Melville," *The Nation & Athenaeum*, July 27, 1929, p. 570.

23. Frank Jewett Mather, Jr., "Herman Melville," *The Saturday Review of Literature*, April 27, 1929, p. 946.

24. For reviews of Melville criticism, see Hershell Parker, ed., *The Recognition of Herman Melville: Selected Criticism Since 1946* (Ann Arbor, MI: University of Michigan Press, 1967); and Watson C. Branch, ed., *Melville: The Critical Heritage* (London: Routledge & Kegan Paul, 1974); see also Mather, "Herman Melville," *Review*, August 1919, pp. 276–301; John Freeman, *Herman Melville* (New York: Macmillan, 1926); a good study of the Melville revival in the 1920s is Michael P. Zimmerman, "Herman Melville in the 1920s: A Study in the Origins of the Melville Revival," Ph.D. thesis, Columbia University, 1963.

25. HMel, p. 5.

26. LM–JS, January 29, 1928, LMC.

27. HMel, pp. vi, 141, 184–87, 193.

28. WD, p. 276.

29. See, for example, Leon Howard, *Herman Melville: A Biography* (Berkeley: University of California Press, 1951), p. ix; Charles R. Anderson, *Melville in the South Seas* (New York: Columbia University Press, 1939), pp. 409–17; William H. Gilman, *Melville's Early Life and Radburn* (New York: New York University Press, 1951).

30. Mumford removed most of these errors from the revised edition, *Herman Melville: A Study of His Life and Vision* (New York: Harcourt, Brace and World, 1962); for critical reviews of Mumford's *Melville*, see R. S. Forsythe, "Mr. Lewis Mumford and Melville's *Pierre*," *American Literature*, vol. 2, November 1930, pp. 286–89; A. H. Starke, "A Note on Lewis Mumford's *Life of Herman Melville*," *American Literature*, vol. 1, November 1929, pp. 304–305.

31. Stanley T. Williams, "Victorian Americans," *The Yale Review*, vol. 19, September 1929, pp. 191–93.

32. Eva Goldbeck–LM, June 11, 1929, LMC.

33. Newton Arvin, *Herman Melville: A Critical Biography* (New York: Viking, Compass Books, 1957), p. 29.

34. HMel, pp. 37, 19, 35.

35. ILM, June 28, 1977.

36. HMel, p. 351.

37. Mather, "Herman Melville," p. 946.

38. Joseph Wood Krutch, "Taming Leviathan," *The Nation*, May 8, 1929, p. 561.

39. Henry A. Murray, review of HMel, in *The New England Quarterly*, vol. 2, July 1929, pp. 523–27.

40. LM–HM, May 16, 1929, HMC.

41. HM, "In Nomine Diaboli," in Edwin S. Shneidman, ed., *Endeavors in Psychology: Selections from the Personology of Henry A. Murray* (New York: Harper & Row, 1981), pp. 83, 85.

42. Melville quote in Shneidman, *Endeavors*, p. 3; Robert W. White, ed., *The Study of*

Lives: Essays on Personality in Honor of Henry A. Murray (New York: Atherton, 1963), p. xiii.

43. HM, "In Nomine Diaboli," pp. 84–85; HM, "Vicissitudes of Creativity," in H. H. Anderson, ed., *Creativity and Its Cultivation* (New York: Harper & Brothers, 1959), pp. 96–118; WD, p. 300; interview with Henry A. Murray, July 16, 1979, Cambridge, MA; I am grateful to Dr. Murray for allowing me to read his correspondence with Mumford.

44. LM–HM, July 7, 1929, HMC; WD, pp. 300–302.

45. WD, pp. 300–302; HMel, p. 196.

46. S, p. 457.

47. P, July 19, 1929.

48. LM–JL, April 5, 1929, LMC; P, July 19, 1929; GM, pp. 35–36.

49. P, 1927–1929; LM–PG, August 26, 1929, PGC.

50. HMel, pp. 225–76.

51. Ibid., pp. 275–76.

52. LM–HM, September 9, 1973, HMC.

53. Quoted in WD, p. 301.

54. LM–Eleanor Brooks, July 21, 1928, VWBP; LM–JS, July 30, 1928, JSP; LM–Robert Spiller, September 21, 1968, LMC.

55. P, July 1929.

56. Raymond Nelson, *Van Wyck Brooks: A Writer's Life* (New York: Dutton, 1981), pp. 174–95; James Hoopes, *Van Wyck Brooks: In Search of American Culture* (Amherst, MA: University of Massachusetts Press, 1977), pp. 170–93; LM-Robert Spiller, September 21, 1968, LMC.

57. P, July 1929.

58. HMel, pp. 219–20.

59. Ibid., pp. 288, 90; RN, May 30, 1980; S, p. 456; Emerson quoted in John Updike, "Books: Emersonianism," *The New Yorker,* June 4, 1984, pp. 120–21.

60. P, July 1929.

61. LM–JS, December 19, 1937, LMC-C; LM–CB, August 14, 1931, LMC-C.

62. LM–SM, May 5, 1930, LMC-C.

63. S, p. 459.

64. Ibid., p. 460.

65. LM–JS, no date, LMC-C.

66. WD, pp. 302–303.

67. Dante quoted in Justin Kaplan, *Walt Whitman: A Life* (New York: Simon & Schuster, 1980), p. 186; WD, pp. 298–99.

68. LM–CB, July 1930, LMC.

69. "Lewis Mumford, Amenia," *Hudson Valley Sunday Courier,* September 14, 1941, p. 13.

70. LM–CB, July 1930, LMC.

71. WD, p. 299; HMel, p. 279.

72. ISM, July 13, 1982.

15

1. LM–VB, February 22, 1928, LMC.
2. Quoted in Selden Rodman, "Two Cities of Fortune," in Alfred M. Bingham and Selden Rodman, eds., *Challenges to the New Deal* (New York: Falcon, 1934), p. 27.
3. Quoted in William Manchester, *The Glory and the Dream* (Boston: Little, Brown, 1974), p. 31.
4. S, pp. 476–77.
5. LM–BMK, September 1933, MKFP.
6. LM–Malcolm Cowley and Edmund Wilson, August 17, 1932, MCP.
7. LM, autobiographical fragment, 1956, LMC.
8. LM–Malcolm Cowley and Edmund Wilson, August 17, 1932, MCP.
9. LM–Llewelyn Powys, August 18, 1932, copy in LMC.
10. LM, "If I Were a Dictator," *The Nation*, December 9, 1931, p. 631; LM, "Manifesto," March 21, 1932, LMC.
11. TC, pp. 280–83, 364–435.
12. CM, pp. 391–423; TC, pp. 364–433.
13. LM, "A Challenge to American Intellectuals: A Controversy. The Evolutionary Approach," *Modern Quarterly*, Winter 1930–31, pp. 407–408.
14. LM, "Preface to Action," 1931, LMC.
15. LM, "Evolutionary Approach," pp. 409–10.
16. LM–Waldo Frank, March 8, 1934, WFP.
17. LM–Malcolm Cowley and Edmund Wilson, August 17, 1932, MCP.
18. LM, review of *Medieval Culture: An Introduction to Dante and His Times*, 2 vols., by Karl Vossler, translated by William Cranston Lawton, *New York Herald Tribune Books*, April 7, 1929, p. 1 ff.
19. RN, November 21, 1931.
20. Alfred Harcourt–LM, March 22, 1932, LMC; LM, "Form and Personality," 1930, LMC.
21. LM–JS, March 27, 1929, LMC; RN, March 22, 1930.
22. LM–VWB, October 30, 1931, VWBP.
23. HMel, p. 151.
24. LM, review of Oswald Spengler's *The Decline of the West; Volume I: Form and Actuality*, *The New Republic*, May 12, 1926, pp. 367–69; LM, "Spengler's 'The Decline of the West,' " in *Books That Changed Our Minds*, edited by Malcolm Cowley and Bernard Smith (New York: Doubleday, Doran, 1939), pp. 217–35.
25. LM, "The Decline," *The New Republic*, pp. 167–69; LM, "Spengler's 'The Decline,' " in Cowley and Smith, pp. 217–35; LM, "Cities Old and New—The Culture Cycle and City Planning," *Journal of the American Institute of Architects*, June 1926, pp. 291–93.
26. W. H. Auden–LM, 1938, LMC.
27. RN, 1975.
28. CB–LM, no date, LMC-C.

16

1. George Bernard Shaw, *Man and Superman: A Comedy and a Philosophy* (New York: Brentano's, 1903).

2. LM–JS, no date, LMC-C.
3. LM, May 12, 1976.
4. CB–LM, March 31, 1930, LMC-C; P, April 6, 1930.
5. P-C, April 6, 1930; LM–CB, June 27, 1930, LMC-C.
6. LM–CB, June 27, 1930, LMC-C.
7. P-C, April 6, 1930.
8. LM–JS, April 30, 1930, LMC-C; LM–HM, February 10, 1930, HMC.
9. SM, note, March 5, 1930, LMC-C.
10. SM–LM, May 1930, LMC-C.
11. SM–LM, September 4, 1945, LMC-C.
12. SM, Personalia, November 1, 1955, LMC-C.
13. Ibid.; ISM, September 21, 1984.
14. GM, pp. 42–47.
15. S, p. 461.
16. LM–CB, July 23, June 23, 27, August 13, 1930, LMC-C.
17. LM–CB, June 9, 1930, LMC-C.
18. P-C, May 6, 1940.
19. LM–CB, June 11, 1930, LMC-C.
20. LM–JS, September 1, 1942, LMC.
21. LM–HM, June 26, 1932, HMC.
22. LM–CB, August 3, 1930, LMC-C; RN-C, June 10, 24, 1933.
23. LM–CB, July 23, August 3, 13, 1930, LMC-C.
24. LM–HM, May 9, 1931, HMC.
25. LM–CB, August 9, 1930, LMC-C.
26. Ibid.
27. LM–CB, November 25, 1933, LMC-C.
28. RN-C, July 1930; LM–CB, July 27, 1930, LMC-C.
29. LM–JS, no date, LMC-C.
30. P-C, September 9, 1933.
31. LM–CB, September 11, 1930, LMC-C.
32. P-C, January 24, 1932; LM–JS, no date, LMC-C.
33. LM–CB, no date, LMC-C.
34. S, p. 463.
35. LM–CB, August 9, 1930, July 25, 1931, LMC-C.
36. RN-C, December 28, 1930.
37. LM–CB, August 29, 1930, August 31, 1931, LMC-C.
38. CB–LM, no date, LMC-C; LM–CB, August 31, 1931, LMC-C.
39. P-C, January 24, 1932.
40. LM–CB, July 25, 1931, LMC-C.
41. LM–CB, March 9, 1935, LMC-C.
42. LM–CB, July 25, 1931, LMC-C.
43. P, January 24, 1932.
44. RN-C, August 2, 1965.

17

1. LM, autobiographical fragment, 1956, LMC.
2. S, pp. 467–68.

3. LM, autobiographical fragment, 1956, LMC; ILM, September 30, October 20, 1984.
4. SM–LM, June 22, 1932, LMC-C.
5. RN-C, July 2, 1932.
6. CB–LM, 1932, LMC-C.
7. CB–LM, July 22, 1934, LMC-C; LM–CB, July 19, 1934, LMC-C.
8. S, p. 465; LM–CB, July 19, 1934, LMC-C.
9. LM–HM, April 23, 1933, HMC.
10. LM–HM, June 26, 1932, HMC.
11. CB–LM, November 6, 1932, LMC-C; P-C, 1932.
12. CB–LM, September 1, 1932, LMC-C.
13. P-C, 1933; LM–HM, December 10, 1932, HMC.
14. LM–John Gould Fletcher, February 14, 1935, JGFP.
15. LM–Waldo Frank, February 25, 1934, WFP; LM–VWB, March 3, 1934, VWBP.
16. TC, pp. 3–5, 107–12, 139, 142–50.
17. CC, p. 91.
18. TC, pp. 23–28, 151–215, 265–67.
19. Arthur P. Molella, "Inventing the History of Invention," *American Heritage of Science and Technology*, Spring/Summer 1988, pp. 22–30; LM, "An Appraisal of Lewis Mumford's *Technics and Civilization* (1934)," *Daedalus*, vol. 88, Summer 1959, pp. 527–36; LM, "The Drama of Machines," *Scribner's Magazine*, August 1930, pp. 150–61; for a list of the books Mumford consulted in writing *Technics and Civilization*, see the vast bibliography he prepared for its first edition; throughout the writing of *Technics and Civilization* Mumford conducted an interesting correspondence with his friend James Henderson, whom he had met in 1920 on his way to England. This correspondence has been analyzed by Rosalind Williams in her perceptive paper "Lewis Mumford as an Historian of Technology," which she presented at the International Symposium on Lewis Mumford at the University of Pennsylvania, November 5–7, 1987.
20. TC, pp. 3, 12–16.
21. Ibid., pp. 3–7, 435.
22. VWB–LM, March 1934, VWBP.
23. RN-C, June 7, 1934.
24. LM–SM, May 2, 1932, LMC-C.
25. LM–CB, March 11, 1933, LMC-C; a pastiche of letters from LM to CB in 1933, LMC-C.
26. CB–LM, 1933, LMC-C.
27. P-C, May 20, 1933.
28. CB–LM, June 7, 1933, LMC-C; ILM, September 30, 1984.
29. ILM, September 30, 1984.
30. CB–LM, September 1, 1932, LMC-C.
31. LM–CB, June 7, 1933; LM, pastiche of letters written between 1931 and 1934, September 2, 1976, LMC-C.
32. CB–LM, September 2, 1934, LMC-C.
33. CB, "Note for LM," no date, LMC-C.
34. RN-C, July 28, 1931.
35. LM–CB, June 19, 1934, LMC-C.

36. RN-C, July 3, 1936; CB–LM, May 28, 1934, LMC-C.
37. LM–CB, May 29, 1934, LMC-C; RN-C, June 7, July 3, 1934.
38. LM–HM, July 20, 1934, HMC.
39. LM–SM, September 18, 1945, LMC-C.
40. LM–JS, March 3, 1939, LMC-C.
41. RN-C, July 9, June 11, 1934.
42. LM–CB, July 25, 1934, LMC-C.
43. Ibid., September 26, 1934, March 9, 1935.
44. CB–LM, March 7, 1935, LMC-C.
45. CB–LM, September 29, 1934, LMC-C.
46. CB–LM, March 7, 1935, LMC-C; RN-C, February 9, 1935.
47. CB–LM, September 29, 1934, LMC-C.
48. LM–CB, March 9, 1935, January 29, March 18, 1936, LMC-C.
49. CB–LM, April 22, 1937, LMC-C.
50. CB–LM, October 29, 1961, LMC-C.
51. RN-C, July 31, 1963.
52. CB–LM, April 27, 1963, LMC-C.
53. RN-C, July 31, 1963.
54. LM-HM, January 31, 1965, HMC.
55. LM–CB, March 20, 1938, LMC-C; RN-C, July 31, 1965.
56. LM–CB, May 1, 1963, LMC-C.

18

1. LM–VWB, July 30, 1934, VWBP.
2. LM–CB, July 25, 1934, LMC-C.
3. Ibid.; LM–CB, July 19, 1934, LMC-C.
4. LM–HM, February 2, 1935, HMC.
5. LM–CB, February 8, March 8, 1935, LMC-C.
6. LM–HM, February 2, 1935, HMP.
7. CB–LM, April 27, 1963, LMC-C; LM–Babette Deutsch, September 16, 1962, LMC-C.
8. LM–Stearns Morse, March 27, 1967, SMP.
9. LM–SM, September 18, 1945, LMC-C.
10. LM–JS, February 13, 1938, LMC-C.
11. LM–JS, December 11, 1938, LMC-C.
12. LM–HM, July 8, 1935, HMC.
13. LM–Donald L. Miller, November 29, 1982, in Miller's possession.
14. SM, Personalia, August 8, 1972, MFP.
15. LM–HM, July 8, 1935, HMC; SM–Donald L. Miller, November 29, 1982, in Miller's possession.
16. LM–HM, May 3, 1935, HMC; LM–SM, May 17, 1935, LMC-C; P-C, April 2, 1935.
17. LM–CB, June 25, 1935, LMC-C; LM–HM, June 23, 25, 1935, HMC.
18. SM, RN, June 23, 1935, MFP; LM–HM, June 23, 1935, HMC.
19. SM, RN, August 19, 1935, MFP.
20. Ibid., August 1945.
21. Ibid., January 8, 1936.

22. Ibid.
23. LM–HM, November 9, 1935, HMC; LM–JS, August 17, 1939, LMC-C.
24. LM–HM, January 10, 1936, HMC.
25. SM, RN, January 8, 1936, MFP.
26. LM–HM, January 10, March 5, 1936, HMC.
27. LM–HM, March 5, 1936, HMC.
28. LM, "Resurrection," LMC-C.
29. LM–CB, March 18, 1936, LMC-C.
30. RN-C, May 24, 1936.
31. HM–LM, December 15, 1936, LMC-C.
32. LM–HM, December 11, 1936, HMC; LM–CB, July 22, 1937, LMC-C.
33. LM–Alice Decker, December 28, 1936, LMC-C; LM–JS, December 11, 1938, LMC-C.
34. LM–Alice Decker, March 5, 1937, LMC-C.
35. LM–JS, December 11, 1938, LMC-C.
36. LM–JS, February 13, 1938, LMC-C.
37. LM–CB, August 3, 1939, LMC-C.
38. LM–JS, August 12, 1939, LMC-C.

19

1. LM–CB, July 22, 1937, LMC; LM–VWB, October 5, 1937, VWBP.
2. VWB–LM, March 30, 1938, LMC.
3. C. E. Ayres, *Southern Review*, vol. 4, no. 2, 1938–1939, pp. 227–29; William Holford, "A Philosophy of Planning," *Journal of the Royal Institute of British Architects*, vol. 46, November 21, 1938, p. 92; *Time*, April 18, 1938, pp. 40–43; to Mumford's disappointment, the book sold only 7,500 copies in the first year of publication.
4. CC, pp. 5–31.
5. Ibid., p. 29.
6. Ibid., pp. 58–59, 42–44, 50–51.
7. Ibid., pp. 29, 17.
8. Ibid., pp. 22, 142; CH, pp. 247, 345.
9. CC, pp. 94–97.
10. SS-D, p. 67.
11. CH, p. 439; CC, pp. 139–47.
12. CC, pp. 223–29, 192–95, 163.
13. Ibid., pp. 300–493.
14. See James T. Farrell, "The Faith of Lewis Mumford," *Southern Review*, vol 6, Winter 1941, pp. 417–38.
15. GD-D, p. 125.
16. Meyer Shapiro, "Looking Forward to Looking Backward," *Partisan Review*, July 1938, pp. 14–24; see J. B. Coates, "Inspiration Is Not Enough," *The Fortnightly Review*, February 1953, pp. 112–18.
17. S, p. 478; LM–John Gallery, February 8, 1980, LMC.
18. LM–Carl Sussman, December 14, 1974, quoted in Carl Sussman, ed., *Planning the Fourth Migration: The Neglected Vision of the Regional Planning Association of America* (Cambridge, MA: MIT Press, 1926), p. 43; CC, pp. 400–401.

19. LM, Henry Wright, Sr., and Albert Mayer, "New Homes for a New Deal: A Concrete Program," *The New Republic*, March 7, 1934, pp. 91–94.
20. Daniel Schaffer, *Garden Cities for America: The Radburn Experience* (Philadelphia: Temple University Press, 1982), p. 224.
21. LM–CS, July 5, 1949, CSP.
22. ILM, September 30, 1984.
23. LM–FJO, June 12, 1951, FJOC; LM–BMK, July 27, 1947, MKFP.
24. LM–Carl Sussman, December 14, 1974, quoted in Sussman, *Fourth Migration*, p. 43.
25. Archer Winsten, "Movie Talk," New York *Post*, June 23, 1939.
26. CD, pp. 84, 1; PG, *City Development: A Study of Parks, Gardens, and Culture-Institutes: A Report to the Carnegie Dumfermline Trust* (Edinburgh: Geddes and Colleagues, 1904), pp. 1–10.
27. CD, p. 84.
28. LM–SM, June 15, 25, 1938, LMC.
29. GM, pp. 147–48.
30. Ibid., pp. 147–55.
31. CD, p. 85; LM–JS, August 8, 1938, LMC.
32. WH, pp. 1–67.
33. CD, pp. 139–40, 147.
34. "Portrait from the Period," no date, LMC.
35. Gerald Hodge, "Lewis Mumford's Unfinished Vision of Honolulu," *Honolulu*, December 1980, pp. 90–94.
36. Ben H. Kizer–LM, May 17, 1938, LMC; CD, p. 86; the Pacific Northwest Regional Planning Commission had been set up four years earlier by the National Resources Committee to develop natural resource planning and conservation.
37. LM–JS, July 27, 1938, LMC.
38. LM–SM, July 3, 1938, LMC-C.
39. LM–JS, July 3, 1938, and no date, LMC.
40. RP, pp. 1–20; see also Carl Abbot, "Oregon Came Around to Mumford's Ideas, but 40 Years Late," *The Oregon Forum*, February 1, 1979, copy in LMC.

20

1. Bradford Torry, ed., *The Writings of Henry David Thoreau*, 20 vols. (Boston: Houghton Mifflin, 1906), 17:275, 2:34.
2. LM–VWB, January 8, 1937, VWBP.
3. RN, 1936; LM–FJO, March 23, 1936, FJOC.
4. LM–HM, September 12, 1935, April 18, 19, May 27, 1936, HMC; LM–Waldo Frank, December 12, 1936, WFP; LM–VWB, January 8, 1937, VWBP; P, November 27, 1936; Harold Ross–LM, March 26, 1936, LMC.
5. Quoted in VWB, *The Times of Melville and Whitman* (New York: Dutton, 1947), p. 324.
6. LM–Waldo Frank, March 13, 1927, WFP; LM–CB, August 6, 1945, LMC.
7. Quoted in GM, p. 106.
8. RN, December 22, 1953; LM–JS, April 30, 1942, LMC-C.
9. ISM, September 30, 1984; LM–CB, May 20, 1937, LMC-C.
10. LM–BMK, September 21, 1955, MKFP.

11. RN, August 21, 1958.
12. LM, "Countryside," August 24, 1963, LMC; RN, September 6, 1973; LM–Tsutomu Ikuta, April 18, 1950, LMC.
13. RN, August 1, 1933, June 26, 1967, August 24, 1963.
14. GM, pp. 42–98.
15. Ibid., pp. 52, 105, 112.
16. SM, RN, no date, MFP; SM, RN, October 3, 1978, LMC.
17. IAMM, March 15, 1985.
18. SM, RN, October 3, 1978, LMC-C.
19. LM–JS, July 15, 1939, LMC-C; RN, June 12, 1938.
20. ILM, July 6, 1983.
21. LM–Alice Decker, no date, LMC-C; LM–JS, December 14, 1935, LMC-C; ILM, July 6, 1983.
22. LM–JS, March 23, December 13, January 3, 1938, LMC-C.
23. P-C, December 1, 1941.
24. LM–JS, March 24, December 11, 1939, LMC-C.
25. P-C, April 28, 1940; LM–Alice Decker, no date, LMC-C.
26. LM–JS, August 25, March 6, April 9, May 13, November 8, 1942, LMC-C.
27. LM–JS, June 8, 1942, LMC-C.
28. LM–JS, April 9, 1942, LMC-C.
29. ILM, July 6, 1983.
30. LM–JS, 1938, LMC-C.
31. LM–JS, March 24, 1939, LMC-C; ILM, July 6, 1983.

21

1. LM–VWB, July 14, 1940, VWBP.
2. LM, "The Barbarian Eruption," 1957, pp. 251–67, LMC.
3. Ibid., pp. 269–73.
4. LM, "When America Goes to War," *Modern Monthly*, June 1935, pp. 203–204.
5. LM, "Call to Arms," *The New Republic*, May 18, 1938, pp. 39–42; LM, "Preface," September 1945, LMC; LM, "Barbarian," p. 274, LMC.
6. Alfred M. Bingham, "War Mongering on the Left (II)," *Common Sense*, June 1937, pp. 15–18; Bingham, "War Mongering on the Left (III)," *Common Sense*, July 1937, pp. 11–14; Bingham, "Why Commit Suicide?" *Common Sense*, May 1938, pp. 3–5; see Donald L. Miller, *The New American Radicalism: Alfred Bingham and Non-Marxian Radicalism in the New Deal Era* (Port Washington, NY: Kennikat, 1979), pp. 161–89.
7. Archibald MacLeish, "The Irresponsibles," *The Nation*, May 18, 1940, pp. 618–23; Waldo Frank, "Our Guilt in Fascism," *The New Republic*, May 6, 1940, p. 603; LM, "The Corruption of Liberalism," *The New Republic*, April 29, 1940, pp. 568–73.
8. George Soule–LM, April 1, 1938, LMC; LM–Bruce Bliven, May 27, 1940, LMC.
9. LM, Waldo Frank, and Reinhold Niebuhr, "The Western World," LMC; see also Richard Wrightman Fox, *Reinhold Niebuhr: A Biography* (New York: Pantheon, 1985).
10. LM, "Corruption," pp. 568–73; Christopher Lasch, *The Minimal Self: Self-Psychic Survival in Troubled Times* (New York: Norton, 1984), pp. 73–81.

11. LM, "Corruption," pp. 568–73; FFL, pp. 90–93.
12. LM–VWB, February 1, 1940, VWBP.
13. LM, "Corruption," pp. 568–73; FFL, pp. 88–89, 104–105, 116–17.
14. FFL, pp. 106–107, 194, 310–21.
15. LM–Albert Guérard, October 25, 1940, AGP.
16. FFL, pp. 185–217, 283–84, 312–20; LM, "A Long-Term View of the War," *Progressive Education*, November 1942, pp. 358–60; LM, "Corruption," p. 573.
17. LM–VWB, July 14, 1940, VWBP.
18. LM–Frank Lloyd Wright, May 20, 1941, LMC.
19. Frank Lloyd Wright–LM, June 3, 1941, in Bruce Brooks Pfeiffer, ed., *Letters to Architects: Frank Lloyd Wright* (Fresno, CA: The Press at California State University, 1984), pp. 147–48.
20. LM–John Flynn, June 8, 1941, LMC.
21. LM–VWB, November 26, December 3, 1947, VWBP.
22. LM–VWB, December 22, 1947, VWBP.
23. Letter to the editors, signed by Selden Rodman, Michael Bodkin, and Nathan Alexander, *The New Republic*, May 13, 1940, pp. 643–44; Matthew Josephson–LM, September 17, 1940, MJP; "Lewis Mumford's 'Mein Kampf,' " *The New Masses*, October 15, 1940, pp. 8–19; "Mr. Mumford and the Liberals," *The New Republic*, April 29, 1940, vol. 102 pp. 562–64; Farrell, "The Faith," pp. 417–38.
24. A. Fleming MacLiesh, "The Assault on Liberalism," *Common Sense*, June 9, 1940, pp. 10–13.
25. LM–VWB, February 10, 1940, VWBP; see also LM–VWB, November 3, 1939, VWBP.
26. LM–VWB, February 10, 1940, VWBP; HM–LM, 1939, HMC.
27. LM, "Preface," September 1945, LMC; GM, p. 256.
28. GM, pp. 256–57.
29. Ibid., pp. 256–70; LM–Stearns Morse, September 9, 1941, SMP.
30. P-C, December 17, 1940.
31. LM, "Barbarian," p. 284.
32. LM–President Franklin Delano Roosevelt, June 1940, LMC; Herbert Agar et al., *The City of Man: A Declaration on World Democracy* (New York: Viking, 1940), pp. 14–19; LM, "Barbarian," p. 287.
33. Miller, *American Radicalism*, pp. 196–97.
34. RN, July 15, 1941.
35. LM–JS, December 10, 1941, LMC-C; GM, pp. 257–58; LM, "Barbarian," p. 294.

22

1. LM, "The School of Humanities at Stanford," in *The School of Humanities: A Description* (Stanford, CA: Stanford University), pp. 1–2.
2. LM–VWB, July 12, 1942, VWBP.
3. VFS, pp. 187–88.
4. John Dodds–LM, August 15, 1979, LMC; RN, June 9, 1943; P, no date.
5. *Time*, June 8, 1942, pp. 61–62.
6. LM–Walter Curt Behrendt, October 4, 1942, LMC.
7. RN, December 11, 1942.
8. VFS, pp. 217–39.

9. Ibid., pp. 232–33.
10. LM–JS, February 19, 1943, October 25, 1942, LMC; RN, 1942.
11. Quoted in GM, p. 230.
12. LM–Amy Spingarn, April 11, 1943, LMC.
13. RN, June 21, July 5, 1943.
14. RN, March 12, 1944; LM–Lee Simonson, September 11, 1945, LMC.
15. LM–William Wurster and CB, August 6, 1945, LMC; LM–FJO, June 12, 1951, FJOC.
16. LM–Walter Curt Behrendt, August 10, 1941, LMC.
17. CM, pp. 1–17.
18. LM–JS, February 28, 1940, LMC.
19. LM, "The Barbarian Eruption," 1957, p. 301, LMC; CM, p. 72.
20. CM, pp. 77–79; LM, "Barbarian," pp. 301–303.
21. LM–JS, February 10, 1940, LMC.
22. CM, p. 40; LM, "Barbarian," p. 3.
23. CM, pp. 365–66.
24. Giovanni Battista Vico, *Oeuvres choisies de Vico–précédés d'une introduction sur sa vie et ses ouvrages par M. Michelet*, 2 vols. (Paris, 1935).
25. TC, p. 15.
26. CM, p. 260.
27. For an updated and brilliant elaboration of this argument, see Joseph Weizenbaum, *Computer Power and Human Reason: From Judgement to Calculation* (New York: W. H. Freeman, 1926), p. 14. Weizenbaum and Mumford became friends at MIT in the 1970s, and Mumford's work influenced Weizenbaum's thinking.
28. LM, "Barbarian," pp. 307–308.
29. LM to the Editor of *The New York Times*, September 28, 1944, in LMC.
30. RN, May 17, 1944; for reviews of *The Condition of Man*, see Howard Becker, *American Sociological Review*, vol. 9, October 1944, pp. 595–96; Phillips Russell, *Social Forces*, vol. 23, October 1944, pp. 100–101; David Cushman Coyle, *The New Statesman and Nation*, vol. 28, December 23, 1944, pp. 423–24; Daniel Bell, *The Atlantic Monthly*, July 1944, p. 131; Abram Kardiner, *The Nation*, July 29, 1944, pp. 132–34; Niebuhr's comments are on the cover of the paperback edition of *The Condition of Man*.
31. LM–CB, August 6, 1945, LMC; CB–LM, October 11, 1943, LMC; Paul Rosenfeld–LM, October 1, 1944, LMC.
32. Lee Simonson–LM, 1945, LMC; LM–Lee Simonson, September 11, 1945, LMC.
33. LM–Bruno Zevi, October 12, 1973, LMC.
34. Ibid.

23

1. Quoted in GM, pp. 326–29.
2. P-C, October 18, 1944; GM, pp. 332–37.
3. GM, pp. 335–36; IAMM, April 6, 1985.
4. RN, December 15, 1944.
5. SM–LM, May 8, 1945, LMC-C.
6. RN, February 13, 1945; P, January 1, 1945; GM, pp. 91–92.

7. RN, February 13, 1945.
8. LM–VWB, March 4, 1945, VWBP.
9. Artemus Packard–LM, September 21, 1933, LMC; LM, "Professor of Things in General," 1981, LMC.
10. LM–PG, January 27, 1930, PGC.
11. RN, February 7, 1945, LMC; S, pp. 323–24.
12. RN, May 6, 1948; LM–David Liebovitz, October 26, 1964, LMC; WD, p. 107.
13. Walter Curt Behrendt–LM, March 18, 1934; LM–Walter Curt Behrendt, October 23, 1936, LMC.
14. ILM, July 12, 1978.
15. Quoted in LM, "Professor of Things in General."
16. LM–CB, February 17, 1934, LMC.
17. RN, August 8, 1945.
18. LM, "Gentlemen: You Are Mad!" *The Saturday Review of Literature*, March 2, 1946, pp. 5–6.
19. LM, "Petition to the President and the Congress of the United States of America," 1946, LMC.
20. LM–FJO, April 5, 1946, FJOC; LM–BMK, March 17, 1946, MKFP; LM–Max Lerner, no date, MLP; LM–President Harry S Truman, 1946, no date; LM–General Dwight D. Eisenhower, 1946, LMC.
21. LM–SM, June 22, 1946, LMC-C.
22. LM–HM, no date, HMC; RN, July 2, 1960.
23. LM–Bruno Zevi, October 12, 1973, LMC.
24. LM, "The Morals of Extermination," *The Atlantic Monthly*, October 1959, pp. 38–44; LM–Sherely Ewing, April 19, 1959, LMC; LM, "Anticipations and Social Consequences of Atomic Energy," American Philosophic Society, *Proceedings* (1954), no. 2, pp. 149–52.
25. See, especially, LM, "Apology to Henry Adams," *Virginia Quarterly Review*, vol. 38, Spring 1962, pp. 196–217.
26. LM, "Morals of Extermination," pp. 38–44; ILM, July 12, 1978; LM, "Alternatives to Catastrophe," *Air Affairs*, Spring 1950, pp. 350–63; RN, September 16, 1947.
27. LM, "Anticipations," pp. 149–52.
28. LM, "Open Letter to the American People," December 29, 1950, LMC; LM–Congressman George A. Dondero, July 16, 1952, LMC.
29. LM, "The Art Galleries: Surrealism and Civilization," *The New Yorker*, December 19, 1936, pp. 76–79; CM, p. 375; S, pp. 443–46.
30. "Presentation of Howard Memorial Medal, 27th June 1946; Notes for remarks by F. J. Osborn," LMC.
31. LM–SM, June 22, 1946, LMC.
32. LM, "Britain and Her Planning Schemes," *The Listener*, August 15, 1946, pp. 201–202; SF, pp. 1–40; PLC, pp. 10–34.
33. RN, January 21, 1948; LM–SM, June 4, 1946, LMC.
34. LM, review of *The Case Against the Nazi War Criminals*. Opening statement for the United States by Robert H. Jackson and other documents, *The Saturday Review of Literature*, March 16, 1946, pp. 13–14; VFS; Reinhold Niebuhr–LM, no date, LMC.

35. RN, December 21, 1945; GM, p. 85.
36. P-C, March 15, December 29, 1947.
37. HM–LM, no date, HMC.
38. LM–SM, September 10, 1946, LMC; RN-C, no date.
39. Desmond Powell–LM, April 29, 1945, LMC.
40. LM–JS, July 12, 1943, LMC-C.
41. LM–Walter Curt Behrendt, July 30, 1943, LMC.
42. LM–HM, November 25, 1946, HMC.
43. RN, August 1, 1942; GM, p. 37.
44. IHM, July 16, 1979.
45. LM, "At Parting," *The Saturday Review of Literature*, March 10, 1945, p. 18; GM, p. 294.
46. Ben Kizer–LM, September 15, 1942, LMC.
47. SM–LM, January 19, 1941, LMC; GM, p. 184.
48. P-C, February 2, 1948.
49. Emerson Hynes, review of *Green Memories*, *The Commonweal*, December 12, 1947, pp. 235–36.
50. P, January 1, 1947.
51. IHM, July 16, 1979.
52. P-C, September 3, 1945.
53. All quotes from LM–William Van O'Connor, January 1, 1945, WOCP.
54. LM–FJO, March 1, 1949, FJOC; Henry L. Kamphoefner–LM, February 19, 1948, LMC; RN, July 28, 1948; LM, "A Thought for the Growing South," *Southern Packet*, April 1949, pp. 1–5; Mumford also lectured at the Women's College of the State University at Greensboro, North Carolina.
55. Quoted in RN, February 1968.
56. Harold Ross–LM, January 13, 1947, LMC; P, January 22, 1948.
57. LM–Stearns Morse, August 26, 1949, LMC; P, January 1, September 5, 1959.
58. LM–CB, no date, LMC; P, August 20, 1947.
59. LM–JS, September 5, 1951, LMC-C.
60. P-C, January 1, 1949; RN, February 2, 1950.
61. LM–John Dodds, December 26, 1955, LMC.
62. CL, pp. 5, 175–80, 205, 219, 226–28, 257, 268–74, 292.
63. CB–LM, January 15, 1950, LMC-C; see also Waldo Frank, "Views on Human Nature," *The Saturday Review of Literature*, September 22, 1951, pp. 11–12.
64. LM–HM, July 9, 1950, HMC.
65. HM–LM, March 16, 1948, LMC.
66. HM–LM, January 31, 1952, LMC.
67. P, January 2, 1952.
68. LM–FJO, December 8, 1951, FJOC; LM–Stearns Morse, September 3, 1950, SMP; LM–CS, September 5, 1950, CSP.
69. LM–FJO, May 6, 1948, FJOC; P, January 22, 1948.

24

1. RN, July 2, 1960.
2. Ibid., January 1, 1953.

3. Interview with Martin Meyerson, April 8, 1988, Albany, New York; ILM, May 4, 1980.
4. RN, August 15, 1956.
5. LM–FJO, February 20, 1955, FJOC; LM–HM, August 25, 1954, HMC; LM–CB, November 28, 1956, LMC.
6. LM–BMK, July 22, 1955, MKFP.
7. WD, p. 474.
8. Ibid., p. 469–471; TOM-H, p. 2.
9. AT, pp. 57, 35; TOM-H, p. 25.
10. RN, August 9, 1956.
11. LM–FJO, July 27, 1956, FJOC.
12. Interview with Ian McHarg, April 12, 1985, Philadelphia, Pennsylvania.
13. Telephone interview with Martin Meyerson, February 18, 1987.
14. RN, June 2, 1957.
15. SM, "Day Book," 1957, MFP; LM, "The Sky Line: The Cave, the City, and the Flower," *The New Yorker*, November 2, 1957, pp. 93–94.
16. SM, "Day Book," 1957, MFP; RN, June 29, 1960.
17. RN, August 30, 1958; P, October 19, 1958.
18. P, December 10, 1958.
19. SM, "Day Book," 1960, MFP; LM–FJO, August 10, 1958, FJOC.
20. LM–HM, November 21, 1959, HMC; LM–FJO, August 10, 1958, FJOC.
21. LM–FJO, September 2, 1959, August 10, 1958, FJOC.
22. LM–HM, December 3, 1960, HMC.
23. *A Tribute to Lewis Mumford* (Cambridge, MA: Lincoln Institute of Land Policy, 1982), p. 31.
24. LM–Stearns Morse, April 16, 1961, SMP; for reviews of *The City in History*, see, especially, John Friedman, "The City in History," *The Town Planning Review*, April 1962, p. 73; Gideon Sjöberg, *Annals of the American Academy*, vol. 337, September 1961, pp. 214–15; and Paul Goodman, "The Pragmatism of His Boyhood," *Hudson Review*, vol. 14, Autumn 1961, pp. 444–47.
25. SM, "Day Book," 1961, MFP; LM, "The Sky Line: From Crotchet Castle to Arthur's Seat," *The New Yorker*, January 13, 1962, pp. 82 ff; LM–Stearns Morse, August 13, 1961, SMP.
26. SM, "Day Book," 1961, MFP.
27. LM–Stearns Morse, August 3, 1961, SMP.
28. Ibid.
29. CH, pp. 1–16.
30. LM–Stearns Morse, February 26, 1956, SMP.
31. CH, pp. 21, 33–34, 65; TOM-H, p. 46.
32. CH, pp. 37–46; MM-I, pp. 185, 226.
33. CH, pp. 124, 129.
34. Ibid., p. 158; H. D. Kitto, *The Greeks* (Middlesex, England: Penguin, 1985 ed.).
35. CH, pp. 150–51.
36. Ibid., pp. 205–42.
37. Ibid., pp. 525–75; T. S. Eliot, *The Use of Poetry and the Use of Criticism* (London: Faber and Faber, 1933).

38. LM–CS, July 8, 1954, CSP; LM–FJO, April 6, 1964, August 25, 1957, FJOC.

39. Goodman, "Pragmatism," pp. 444–47; Jane Jacobs, *The Death and Life of Great American Cities* (New York: Random House, 1961).

40. See William H. Whyte, *The Last Landscape* (New York: Doubleday, 1968), p. 249.

41. ILM, July 6, 1984; LM, "Opinions of the New Towns," *Town and Country Planning*, March 1956, pp. 161–64; LM, "The Sky Line: Old Forms for New Towns," *The New Yorker*, October 17, 1953, pp. 138–46.

42. LM–FJO, August 6, 1964, September 24, 1968, FJOC; ILM, July 6, 1984.

43. LM–CS, April 3, 1964, CSP.

44. Paul and Percival Goodman, *Communitas: Means of Livelihood and Ways of Life* (New York: Random House, rev. ed., 1960), p. 35.

45. Jacobs, *Death and Life*, pp. 17–20, 540.

46. Whyte, *Last Landscape*, pp. 234, 227–43.

47. LM–FJO, August 11, 1967, FJOC.

48. LM–David Liebovitz, October 10, 1962, LMC.

49. LM–FJO, October 19, 1962, February 28, 1963, FJOC.

50. LM, "The Sky Line: Mother Jacobs' Home Remedies," *The New Yorker*, December 1, 1962, pp. 148 ff.

25

1. Robert Caro, *The Power Broker: Robert Moses and the Fall of New York* (New York: Random House, 1974), pp. 1–21; Caro's brilliant biography has been my chief source of information on Robert Moses.

2. Quoted in ibid., p. 849; ILM, July 12, 1978.

3. Quoted in Caro, *The Power Broker*, pp. 12, 20.

4. Quoted in Betty Moorstein, "City Can Be Beautiful: Ask Lewis Mumford," *PM*, May 12, 1946, p. 11; LM, "The Sky Line: The Roaring Traffic's Boom—III," *The New Yorker*, April 16, 1955, p. 78.

5. LM, "The Highway and the City," *Architectural Record*, April 1958, pp. 179–86.

6. ILM, January 6, 1984.

7. LM, "The Sky Line: The Roaring Traffic's Boom—II," *The New Yorker*, April 2, 1955, pp. 97, 103; for Robert Moses's reaction to LM's criticism, see Robert Moses to Editor of *The New Yorker*, October 30, 1948, LMC; see also "Mr. Moses Dissects the 'Long-Haired Planners,' " *New York Times Magazine*, June 25, 1944.

8. LM, "Highway and City," pp. 180–86.

9. Ibid.

10. Lynch and Goldschmidt quoted in *A Tribute to Lewis Mumford* (Cambridge, MA: Lincoln Institute of Land Policy, 1982), pp. 16, 21; interview with Perry L. Norton, February 26, 1988.

11. Mumford, "The Sky Line: London and the Laocoön," *The New Yorker*, November 4, 1961, pp. 193–94 ff.

12. LM, "Highway and City," p. 186.

13. Press Release of Joint Emergency Committee to Close Washington Square to Traffic, March 10, 1958, LMC; Mayor Edward Koch quoted in *A Tribute to Lewis Mumford*, p. 20.

14. Interview with Sir F. Anthony Gray, December 26, 1985, Warminster, England.

15. Quoted in LM–Stearns Morse, October 22, 1964, SMP.

16. LM, "A Memorandum on the City of Oxford Development Plan," January 1, 1964, CCCA; see also Roland Newman, "The Road and Christ Church Meadow," Oxford Polytechnic, Headington, Oxford, 1980.

17. LM–David Liebovitz, October 26, 1964, LMC.

18. Interview with Sir F. Anthony Gray, December 27, 1985, Warminster, England; LM–David Liebovitz, October 26, 1964, LMC; another inquiry was made in 1970, but a final rejection of the plan for a Meadows road came from the Department of the Environment in 1971.

19. London *Financial Times*, February 4, 1965.

20. Interview with Sir F. Anthony Gray, July 24, 1985, Warminster, England; London *Financial Times*, February 24, 1965.

21. SM, "Day Book," January 11, 1973, MFP.

22. F. Scott Fitzgerald, "My Lost City," in Edmund Wilson, ed., *The Crack-Up* (New York: New Directions, 1945), p. 25.

23. LM, "Is the Skyscraper Tolerable?" *Architecture*, February 1927, pp. 67–69.

24. Quoted in Robert A. M. Stern, et al., *New York 1930* (New York: Rizzoli, 1987), p. 35.

25. Erich Mendelsohn–LM, April 21, 1952, LMC; Philip Johnson quoted in *A Tribute to Lewis Mumford*, p. 19.

26. LM, "American Architecture Today," *Architecture*, April 1928, pp. 181–88.

27. LM, "The Case Against 'Modern Architecture,'" *Architectural Record*, April 1962, pp. 155–62.

28. Ada Louise Huxtable, *The Tall Building Artistically Reconsidered: The Search for a Skyscraper Style* (New York: Pantheon, 1984), pp. 52, 56.

29. LM, "Case Against 'Modern Architecture,'" pp. 155–62.

30. RN, 1934; LM–Stearns Morse, December 13, 1964, SMP.

31. LM, "The Sky Line: House of Glass," *The New Yorker*, August 9, 1952, pp. 48–54; in the 1980s there was pressure to tear down the Lever building for exactly the reasons Mumford predicted.

32. "The City as Both Heaven and Hell; A Conversation between Graeme Shankland and Lewis Mumford," *Listener*, vol. 66, September 28, 1961, pp. 463–65.

33. LM, "London and the Laocoön," pp. 193–94.

34. LM, "The Sky Line: The Marseilles 'Folly,'" *The New Yorker*, October 5, 1957, pp. 76 ff.

35. For the most recent thinking on Le Corbusier's work, see Martin Filler, "Thoroughly Modern Master," *The New York Review of Books*, December 17, 1987, pp. 49–58.

36. LM, "The Future of the City: Part II: Yesterday's City of Tomorrow," *Architectural Record*, November 1962, pp. 139–44; LM, "On Guard! The City Is in Danger!" *University, A Princeton Quarterly*, no. 24, Spring 1965, pp. 10–13.

37. LM, "The Sky Line: Prefabricated Blight," *The New Yorker*, October 30, 1948, pp. 49–50 ff; "The Sky Line: Stuyvesant Town Revisited," *The New Yorker*, November 27, 1948, pp. 65–71.

38. LM, "The Sky Line: Mother Jacobs' Home Remedies," *The New Yorker*, December 1, 1962, p. 148 ff.

39. LM, "The Sky Line: The Gentle Art of Overcrowding," *The New Yorker*, May 20, 1950, pp. 79–83; Moorstein, "City Can Be Beautiful," p. 11.

40. LM–FJO, August 10, 1958, FJOC.
41. "The City as Both Heaven and Hell," p. 465; ILM, July 12, 1978.
42. Harry M. Weese, *A Tribute to Lewis Mumford*, p. 31.
43. LM, "The Life, the Teaching and the Architecture of Matthew Nowicki: Part IV: Nowicki's Work in India," *Architectural Record*, September 1954, pp. 153–59; LM, "Social Complexity and Urban Design," *Architectural Record*, February 1963, pp. 119–26.
44. CH, p. 302.
45. LM, untitled note, no date, LMC.
46. LM, "The Sky Line: Historic Philadelphia—III," *The New Yorker*, April 6, 1957, pp. 132–41.
47. LM, "Reflections on Venice," Memorandum to Arturo Tofanelli, March 22, 1954, LMC.
48. LM, "The Sky Line: From Crotchet Castle to Arthur's Seat," *The New Yorker*, January 13, 1962, pp. 82 ff; LM, "The Sky Line: Historic Philadelphia—IV," *The New Yorker*, April 13, 1957, pp. 155–62.
49. ILM, July 12, 1978.
50. LM, "Mother Jacobs' Home Remedies," pp. 148 ff.
51. UP, p. x.; U.S. Congress, Senate Committee on Government Operations, "Federal Role in Urban Affairs," Hearing before a Subcommittee on Practical Reorganization, 90th Congress, 1st Session, April 20–21, 1967, part 17, pp. 3595–3625.
52. Ibid., pp. 208–26; RN, April 26, 1967.
53. LM–JL, October 5, 1967, LMC.
54. UP, pp. x, 226, 242.

26

1. RN, July 30, 1965; LM, "S.S. Mauretania"; RN, March 9, 1961, July 11, 1963; LM–Stearns Morse, June 6, 1962, SMP.
2. SM, "Day Book," December 14, 1961, MFP.
3. LM, "The Human Way Out," address given on September 28, 1961, LMC; LM–Stearns Morse, November 24, 1961, SMP.
4. LM–Stearns Morse, December 15, 1961, SMP.
5. RN-C, July 31, 1965.
6. LM–FJO, November 13, 1964, FJOC; LM–David Liebovitz, February 9, 1961, LMC.
7. LM–Stearns Morse, October 14, 1962, LMC.
8. SM–Evelyn Huber, August 10, 1959, LMC-C.
9. ISM, February 9, 1988; SM, "Day Book," January 5, 1965, MFP.
10. Jeannette Hopkins–LM, March 8, 1961, LMC; S, pp. 3, 25.
11. IAMM, April 17, 1985; LM–Stearns Morse, August 29, 1962, SMP.
12. LM–Grover Foley, December 22, 1973, LMC; LM–Stearns Morse, August 3, 1961, SMP.
13. SM–Author, November 10, 1985; P, January 8, 1965; LM–Babette Deutsch, September 16, 1962, LMC.
14. P-C, August 31, 1963.
15. SM–Author, November 10, 1985.
16. RN, no date; Geroid Robinson–LM, February 8, 1963, LMC; Thomas Merton–

LM, February 17, 1962, LMC; LM–Stearns Morse, November 24, 1961, SMP.

17. VWB–LM, March 2, 1946, VWBP.

18. LM–Stearns Morse, December 29, 1963, SMC. For a somewhat idealized picture of the Mumford-Brooks friendship, see Robert Spiller, *The Van Wyck Brooks–Lewis Mumford Letters: The Record of a Literary Friendship, 1921–1963* (New York: Dutton, 1970).

19. LM–Stearns Morse, December 29, 1962, SMC; LM–HM, January 17, 1963, HMC; SM–Author, June 29, 1988.

20. LM–Stearns Morse, October 14, 1962, SMP; S, pp. 363–64. Brooks's uncompleted biography of Mumford is in the Van Wyck Brooks papers at Van Pelt Library, the University of Pennsylvania. It is an unreliable account of Mumford's early life, filled with factual mistakes.

21. LM–Waldo Frank, December 29, 1963, LMC; RN, July 31, 1965.

22. LM–Waldo Frank, December 29, 1963, LMC.

23. RN, July 31, 1965.

24. SM, "Day Book," 1963, MFP.

25. RN, January 30, 1963.

26. LM, "Authoritarian and Democratic Technics," *Technology and Culture*, Winter 1964, pp. 1–8; this paper was Mumford's speech at the Fund for the Republic Tenth Anniversary Convocation, held in New York in January 1963.

27. SM, "Day Book," July 28, 1963, MFP; LM–BMK, October 25, 1963, MKFP; RN, September 11, 1963.

28. LM–BMK, May 31, 1964, MKFP.

29. LM–David Liebovitz, August 21, 1966, LMC.

30. SM, notes, September 28, 1964, LMC-C.

31. SM, "Day Book," November 23, 1964, MFP.

32. Ibid., January 10, 1965; LM–DCL, December 21, 1958, LMC.

33. LM–Stearns Morse, February 21, 1965, February 10, 1966, SMP.

34. LM–The President of the United States, February 28, 1965, LMC; SM, "Day Book," January 11, 1973, MFP.

35. LM–Stearns Morse, August 24, 1965, SMP.

36. LM, Speech before American Academy of Arts and Letters, May 19, 1965, LMC.

37. ILM, July 6, 1983.

38. SM, "Day Book," May 19, 1965, MFP.

39. *Kansas City Times*, May 20, 1965, pp. 1a, 2a.

40. LM–George Kennan, May 22, 1965, copy in LMC.

41. LM–John Hersey, June 8, 1965, copy in LMC.

42. LM, Draft of *The Myth of the Machine*, vol. 1, LMC.

43. LM–FJO, August 10, 1967, FJOC.

44. LM–Stearns Morse, December 22, 1967, SMP.

45. LM–Erich Fromm, March 26, 1968, LMC; the candidate was Eric Lindbloom.

46. LM–Stearns Morse, November 5, 1967, June 3, 1969, SMP.

47. LM, untitled statement, May 26, 1969, LMC.

48. RN, July 24, 1965.

49. Ibid., December 7, 1965.

50. Ibid.; LM–David Liebovitz, August 21, 1966, LMC.

51. RN, December 7, 1965, July 11, 1967.

27

1. LM interview with Edwin Newman on *Speaking Freely*, WNBC, January 10, 1971, transcript in LMC; WD, p. 475.
2. LM, "Prologue to Our Time," *The New Yorker*, March 10, 1975, p. 45.
3. MM-I, pp. 189, 234.
4. LM, notes for MM-I, LMC; WD, p. 476.
5. MM-I, pp. 188, 199, 211; WD, p. 476; MM-II, p. 12.
6. MM-I, pp. 189, 224, 230, 258–60, 263, 293–94.
7. LM–HM, no date, HMC.
8. MM-I, pp. 49–52, 368–69.
9. Quoted in MM-I, p. 61.
10. LM–HM, August 4, 1963, HMC.
11. MM-I, p. 125; MM-II, pp. 9–10, 430.
12. LM, review of Carl G. Jung's *Memories, Dreams, Reflections*, in *The New Yorker*, May 23, 1964, p. 185.
13. RN, June 26, 1963.
14. LM, review of Jung's *Memories*, pp. 176–77.
15. Quoted in ibid., pp. 177–78.
16. Ibid., p. 178.
17. Quoted in MM-I, p. 242.
18. William McGuire, ed., *The Freud/Jung Letters: The Correspondence Between Sigmund Freud and C. G. Jung* (Princeton, NJ: Princeton University Press, 1974), pp. 207, 289.
19. LM, review of Jung's *Memories*, p. 184.
20. Quoted in SM, "Day Book," March 16, 1967, MFP.
21. Jolande Jacobi–LM, July 4, 1964, LMC.
22. SM, "Day Book," February 1967, MFP.
23. Erich Fromm–LM, March 16, 1968, LMC.
24. "Back to the Luddites?" *Time*, June 9, 1967, pp. 62–63; for other views, see Theodore Roszak, "Mumford and the Megamachine," *Peace News*, December 29, 1967, pp. 4–6; and Edward T. Chase, "Man, Machines and Mumford," *Commonweal*, March 8, 1968, pp. 694–95.
25. RN, November 27, 1967.
26. LM–FJO, February 5, 1968, FJOC; RN, October 5, 20, 1967; P-C, February 3, 1969.
27. MM-II, pp. 364–65; RN, October 5, 1967.
28. WD, p. 528.
29. SM, "Day Book," April 1, 1962, MFP; P-C, February 27, 1967; RN, February 16, March 9, 1968.
30. LM–David Liebovitz, March 21, 1967, LMC.
31. LM–William Jovanovich, April 27, 1968, LMC.
32. P-C, June 1, 1968; LM–FJO, May 10, 1968, FJOC.
33. LM–Stearns Morse, June 2, 1968, SMP.
34. P, February 27, 1967; MM-II, p. 367.
35. SM, "Day Book," October 1966; RN, September 16, 1970.
36. William Shawn–LM, October 5, 1970, LMC.

37. ILM, July 6, 1983.
38. Gerald Holton–LM, December 1, 1970, LMC; Gerald Holton, "The Pentagon of Power," *New York Times Book Review,* December 13, 1970, p. 1.
39. Gerald Holton–LM, December 1, 1970, LMC.
40. LM–*New York Times,* December 5, 1970, LMC; ILM, July 6, 1983; LM–Grover Foley, February 1, 1979, LMC; the colleague was Victor Weiskopf, who later became friends with Mumford.
41. SM, "Day Book," December 5, 1970, MFP.
42. Quoted in RN, September 16, 1970; René Dubos, "When Man Can Choose, Trend Is Not Destiny," *Business Week,* November 14, 1970, p. 6; for a thoughtful critical review of *The Pentagon of Power,* see Victor C. Ferkis, "The Megamachine Reconsidered," *Commonweal,* February 1971, pp. 499–500.
43. MM-II, pp. 4–34, 51.
44. Ibid., pp. 56–57.
45. LM, interview with Newman.
46. MM-II, p. 142.
47. Ibid., 243, 250–53; WD, p. 15.
48. MM-II, pp. 274–75, 306.
49. LM statement for *Newsweek,* June 8, 1969, LMC.
50. MM-II, pp. 330–34, 408–409, 430–35.
51. LM–Roderick Seidenberg, February 18, 1969, LMC; LM–FJO, July 31, 1951, FJOC.
52. LM–Roderick Seidenberg, February 18, 1969, LMC.

28

1. CM, pp. 94–95; SM, "Day Book," January 27, 1971, MFP.
2. LM–HM, October 30, 1971, HMC.
3. SM, RN, April 1, 1962, January 27, 1971, MFP.
4. Ibid., January 27, 1971, August 6, 1973; LM–Catherine Roberts, January 23, 1965, LMC.
5. LM, Recollections of Harcourt, Brace & Co., for Oral History Research Office, Columbia University, 1962, copy in LMC.
6. ILM, July 6, 1983.
7. LM–William Jovanovich, January 17, 1972, LMC; LM–Philip Wittenberg, November 28, 1971, LMC; LM–Stearns Morse, October 18, 1975, SMP.
8. P, December 10, 1971.
9. SM–LM, December 1971, LMC-C; ILM, July 6, 1983.
10. LM–Julian Muller, December 10, July 6, 1975, LMC.
11. William Jovanovich–LM, January 24, 1976, LMC; LM–William Jovanovich, January 1, 30, 1976, LMC; SM, "Day Book," August 1975, MFP.
12. LM–Martin Filler, November 20, 1975, in the possession of Martin Filler; William Goodman–LM, March 21, 1976, LMC.
13. William Jovanovich–LM, January 24, 1976, LMC; S, p. 191.
14. LM–Julian Muller, May 17, 1977, LMC; ILM, July 6, 1983.
15. LM–Julian Muller, May 12, 1977, LMC.
16. SM, "Day Book," May 21, 1973, MFP; LM–Ann Harris, August 7, 1980, LMC; LM–Hilda Lindley, May 20, 1979, LMC.

17. SM, "Day Book," March 21, 1978, MFP.

18. SM, RN, May 16, 1978, LMC-C; ISM, April 16, 1985; WD, p. 82.

19. Quoted in LM, "Gabo Tribute," November 22, 1977, LMC.

20. LM–Stearns Morse, November 29, 1975, SMP.

21. SM, "Day Book," September 17, 1974, MFP; S, pp. 489–90; ILM, July 6, 1983.

22. Ann Harris–LM, July 16, 1980, LMC; LM–Hilda Lindley, May 20, 1979, LMC; LM–Ann Harris, August 7, 1980, LMC.

23. Ann Harris–Hilda Lindley, September 3, 1980, LMC; ILM, July 6, 1983.

24. SM–Carol Ryan, March 18, 1981, LMC; my thanks to Rick Kott for allowing me to examine the Mumford file at the Dial Press, and for talking with me about his editorial relationship with Mumford.

25. S, pp. 1–5, 130.

26. LM–Grover Foley, August 5, 1979, LMC.

27. LM–HM, December 15, 1979, HMC; LM's notes for this uncompleted project are in the LMC.

28. LM–Roderick Seidenberg, September 16, 1951, LMC; LM, notes, no date, LMC.

29. LM–Roderick Seidenberg, September 26, 1968, LMC.

30. RN, January 5, 1947, October 5, 1965; notes for uncompleted project on evolution, 1977–82, LMC.

31. RN, October 7, 1965.

32. Martin Filler, "Journal," *House and Garden*, April 1985, p. 214; LM–Grover Foley, February 1, 1979, LMC; Mumford sent most of his drawings and watercolors to Monmouth College in West Long Branch, New Jersey, where Vincent DiMattio is a professor of art. They are part of a permanent collection, open to scholars.

33. Whitehead quoted in LM–Grover Foley, November 30, 1976, LMC; LM–Grover Foley, September 22, 1978, LMC.

34. LM–Geddes Mumford, September 9, 1944, MFP.

35. Quoted in Cary Winfrey, "Even at 81, Lewis Mumford 'Wouldn't Be So Sure,' " *Washington Post*, July 8, 1977, F 2, from the New York Times News Service.

Index

About the Author

Donald L. Miller is chairman of the American Civilization Program and professor of history at Lafayette College (Easton, Pennsylvania). He is the author of *The New American Radicalism*, coauthor of *The Kingdom of Coal*, and editor of *The Lewis Mumford Reader*.